A Companion to 19th-Century America

Blackwell Companions to American History

This new series provides essential and authoritative overviews of the scholarship that has shaped our present understanding of the American past. Edited by eminent historians, each volume tackles one of the major periods or themes of American history, with individual topics authored by key scholars who have spent considerable time in research on the questions and controversies that have sparked debate in their field of interest. The volumes are accessible for the non-specialist, while also engaging scholars seeking a reference to the historiography or future concerns.

A Companion to the American Revolution edited by Jack P. Greene and J. R. Pole
A Companion to 19th-Century America edited by William L. Barney

In preparation:
A Companion to Colonial America edited by Daniel Vickers
A Companion to the Civil War and Reconstruction edited by Lacy K. Ford, Jr
A Companion to 20th-Century America edited by Stephen J. Whitfield
A Companion to the Vietnam War edited by Marilyn Young and Robert Buzzanco
A Companion to Native American History edited by Neal Salisbury and Philip J. Deloria
A Companion to the American South edited by John Boles
A Companion to the American West edited by William Deverell
A Companion to Women's History edited by Nancy Hewitt

A COMPANION TO
19th-CENTURY AMERICA

Edited by

William L. Barney

Copyright © Blackwell Publishers Ltd 2001
editorial introduction and organization copyright © William L. Barney 2001

First published 2001

2 4 6 8 10 9 7 5 3 1

Blackwell Publishers Inc.
350 Main Street
Malden, Massachusetts 02148
USA

Blackwell Publishers Ltd
108 Cowley Road
Oxford OX4 1JF
UK

Library of Congress Cataloging-in-Publication Data

A companion to 19th-century America / edited by William L. Barney.
  p. cm.—(Blackwell companions to American history)
  Includes bibliographical references and index.
  ISBN 0–631–20985–9 (hb. : alk. paper)
  1. United States—History–1783–1865. 2. United States—History—1783–1865—Historiography. 3. United States—History—1865–1898. 4. United States—History—1865–1898—Historiography. I. Barney, William L. II. Title: A companion to nineteenth-century America. III. Series.
  E338. C85 2001
  973—dc21   99–39780
                                                                              CIP

British Library Cataloguing in Publication Data
A CIP catalogue record for this book is available from the British Library.

Typeset in 10/12 Galliard
by Kolam Information Services Pvt. Ltd, Pondicherry, India
Printed in Great Britain by T.J. International, Padstow, Cornwall

This book is printed on acid-free paper.

Contents

Contributors

Cindy S. Aron is associate professor of history at the University of Virginia. She is the author of *Ladies and Gentlemen of the Civil Service: Middle-class Workers in Victorian America* (Oxford University Press, 1987) and *Working at Play: a History of Vacations in the United States* (Oxford University Press, 1999).

John Ashworth is professor of American studies at the University of Hull in England. He is the author of several books on American history, the most recent of which is the first of a two-volume work entitled *Slavery, Capitalism and Politics in the Antebellum Republic*, vol. 1. *Commerce and Compromise, 1820–1850* (Cambridge University Press, 1995). He is currently working on the second volume, to be entitled *Towards a Bourgeois Revolution, 1850–1861*.

Jonathan Atkins is associate professor of history at Berry College, Georgia. A specialist in antebellum US politics, he is the author of *Parties, Politics and the Sectional Conflict in Tennessee, 1832–1861* (1997).

William L. Barney, professor of history at the University of North Carolina at Chapel Hill, has authored many works in nineteenth-century US history. Most recently, he contributed several chapters to a multi-authored survey text entitled *The American Journey* (2 vols, Prentice Hall, 1997).

John M. Belohlavek is chair and professor of history at the University of South Florida with research interests in nineteenth-century politics and diplomacy. In addition to a number of articles and book chapters in print, he is the author of *George Mifflin Dallas: Jacksonian Patrician* (1997) and *Let the Eagle Soar: the*

Foreign Policy of Andrew Jackson (1985). He is currently working on a biography of Caleb Cushing of Massachusetts.

Stephen W. Berry is a doctoral candidate in US history at the University of North Carolina at Chapel Hill where he is completing a dissertation entitled "Love and the Civil War: Men, Women, Imagination, and Empire in the Old South, 1850–1865." His research has appeared in the *Georgia Historical Quarterly* and *Southern Cultures*. He is also the webmaster for the Center for the Study of the American South at the University of North Carolina.

Catherine A. Brekus is assistant professor of religious studies at the University of Chicago Divinity School. Her research interests are in the religious culture of the nineteenth-century United States, and she is the author of *Strangers and Pilgrims: Female Preaching in America, 1740–1845* (University of North Carolina Press, 1998).

Vernon Burton is professor of history and sociology at the University of Illinois at Urbana-Champaign and a senior research scientist at the National Center for Supercomputing Applications. Among his many publications are *In my Father's House are Many Mansions: Family and Community in Edgefield, South Carolina* (1985) and (with Judith N. McArthur) *"A Gentleman and an Officer": a Social and Military History of James B. Griffin's Civil War* (1997).

Andrew R. L. Cayton is professor of history at Miami University in Oxford, Ohio. He is the author of *Frontier Indiana* (1996) and *The Frontier Republic: Ideology and Politics in the Ohio Country, 1780–1826* (1986);

co-author (with Peter S. Onuf) of *The Midwest and the Nation: Rethinking the History of an American Region* (1990); and co-editor (with Fredricka J. Teute) of *Contact Points: American Frontiers from the Mohawk Valley to the Mississippi* (1998) and (with Susan E. Gray) *Imaging the Midwest: Essays on the Origins of Regionality* (forthcoming).

Robert W. Cherny is professor of history at San Francisco State University. His publications include: *American Politics in the Gilded Age, 1868–1900* (Harlan Davidson, 1998); (with William Issel) *San Francisco, 1865–1932: Politics, Power, and Urban Development* (University of California Press, 1986); *A Righteous Cause: the Life of William Jennings Bryan* (repr. edn, University of Oklahoma Press, 1994); and *Populism, Progressivism, and the Transformation of Nebraska Politics, 1886–1915* (University of Nebraska Press, 1981).

Laura F. Edwards is assistant professor of history at the University of California at Los Angeles. She is the author of *Gendered Strife and Confusion: the Political Culture of Reconstruction* (University of Illinois Press, 1997) and *Scarlett Doesn't Live Here Anymore: Women and Southern Society in the Nineteenth Century* (University of Illinois Press, forthcoming).

Stanley L. Engerman is John H. Munro Professor of Economics and professor of history at the University of Rochester, where he has taught since 1963. In addition to numerous articles, he is co-author (with Robert W. Fogel) of *Time on the Cross: the Economics of American Negro Slavery* (1974) and co-editor (with Seymour Drescher) of *A Historical Guide to World Slavery* (1998). With Robert E. Gallman he is co-editor of the three-volume *Cambridge Economic History of the United States* (1996).

Nora Faires is associate professor of history at Western Michigan University and currently holds the Fulbright Chair in North American Studies at the University of Calgary. She has published on African-, German-, Lebanese-, and Polish-Americans. She received the American Historical Association's inaugural Wil-

liam Gilbert Award for her co-authored article, "The American Family and the Little Red Schoolhouse: Historians, Class, and the Problem of Curricular Diversity." Her current work focuses on migration in the Canada/US borderlands.

Robert E. Gallman was Kenan Professor of Economics and History at the University of North Carolina at Chapel Hill, where he taught from 1962 until his death in 1998. A past president of the Economic History Association and the Southern Economic Association, he was the co-author (with Lance E. Davis and Karen Jo Gleiter) of *In Pursuit of Leviathan: the Economic History of New Bedford Whaling in the Nineteenth Century* (1997) and (with Lance E. Davis) of *International Capital Flows, Domestic Capital Markets, and Economic Growth in Argentina, Australia, Canada, and the United States, 1970–1914* (forthcoming). With Stanley L. Engerman, he was co-editor of the three-volume Cambridge Economic History of the United States (1996).

Timothy J. Gilfoyle is professor of history at Loyola University, Chicago, and associate editor of the *Journal of Urban History*. He is the author of *City of Eros: New York City, Prostitution, and the Commercialization of Sex, 1790–1920* (Norton, 1992), which received the Allan Nevins Prize of the Society of American Historians and the New York State Historical Association Manuscript Prize. He also writes a regular feature, "Making History," for *Chicago History* based on oral histories. He is currently completing a book on urban crime in the late nineteenth-century American city.

Michael D. Green is professor of American studies and history at the University of North Carolina at Chapel Hill. He is the author of *The Creeks: a Critical Bibliography* (1979), *The Politics of Indian Removal* (1985), *The Creeks* (1990), and *The Cherokee Removal* (1995).

Barbara Groseclose is professor of art history at Ohio State University. She is the author of *British Sculpture and the Company Raj: Church Monuments and Public Statuary in Madras, Calcutta, and Bombay* (1995) and

Nineteenth-century American Art (Oxford University Press, forthcoming).

David Hochfelder is a postdoctoral fellow at the IEEE History Center at Rutgers University. Before earning his doctorate in history from Case Western Reserve University, he obtained a BS and MS in electrical engineering from Northwestern University. He is currently working on a history of the telegraph in America up to 1920.

Kevin Kenny is associate professor of history at Boston College. A graduate of Edinburgh University (BA, MA modern history, 1989) and Columbia University (PhD American history, 1994), he previously taught at the University of Texas at Austin. He is the author of *Making Sense of the Molly Maguires* (Oxford University Press, 1998) and is currently writing a general history of the American Irish since 1700.

Robert M. S. McDonald is assistant professor of history at the United States Military Academy. His articles have appeared in *Southern Cultures*, *The Historian*, and the *Journal of the Early Republic*. He is currently revising his dissertation for publication as a book entitled *Confounding Father: Thomas Jefferson and the Politics of Personality, 1776–1826*.

Alan I. Marcus is director of the Center for Historical Studies of Technology and Science and Distinguished Humanities Scholar and professor of history, Iowa State University. He is the author or co-author of six books, including *Technology in America: a Brief History* (1989), now in its second edition, and co-editor of three others, including *Health Care Policy in Contemporary America* (1997). He is presently working on the history of total quality management.

Theda Perdue is professor of history at the University of North Carolina at Chapel Hill. Her publications include *Slavery and the Evolution of Cherokee Society, 1540–1865* (1979), *Nations Remembered: an Oral History of the Five Civilized Tribes* (1980), *Cherokee Editor* (1983), *Native Carolinians* (1985), *The Cherokee* (1988), *The Cherokee Removal* (1995), and, most recently, *Cherokee Women: Gender and Culture Change, 1780–1835* (1998).

Eric Rauchway is university lecturer of US history in the Modern History Faculty of the University of Oxford. He previously taught at the University of Nevada at Reno. A specialist in the foreign policy of the post-Civil War US, he is currently revising his dissertation for publication.

Molly P. Rozum, a native of South Dakota, received her MA in folklore and is a PhD candidate in history at the University of North Carolina at Chapel Hill. She has presented papers at the Oral History Association and the Western History Association's annual meetings, among others. Her dissertation is entitled "Grasslands Grown: a Twentieth Century Sense of Place on North America's Northern Prairies and Plains."

John E. Semonche is professor of history at the University of North Carolina at Chapel Hill and a member of the bar of the US Supreme Court. His most recent book, *Keeping the Faith: a Cultural History of the US Supreme Court* (1998), analyzes the role of the justices in maintaining unity in a pluralistic society. Among his current projects are a historical play centered on a nineteenth-century federal district judge, an edited volume of the legal papers of James Iredell, and a study tentatively titled *Speak No Evil: Sin, Sex and Censorship from Comstock to Helms*.

David B. Sicilia is assistant professor of history at the University of Maryland, College Park. A specialist in American business, economic, and technology history, he is associate editor of *Enterprise and Society: the International Journal of the Business History Conference*. He has authored numerous academic and popular articles and co-authored four books, the most recent of which is *The Greenspan Effect* (McGraw-Hill, 1999).

Donald R. Wright is Distinguished Teaching Professor of History at the State University of New York at Cortland. His publications include *African Americans in the Colonial Era* (1989), *African Americans in the Early Republic* (1993), and, reflecting his interests in African and world history, *The World and a Very Small Place in Africa* (1997).

Introduction

WILLIAM L. BARNEY

THIS volume invites a general audience, as well as scholars and students, to share in recent and continuing historical debates that have deepened and complicated our understanding of the nineteenth-century United States. This was the century that marked the transition of the United States from its roots in the struggling, over-whelmingly agrarian, and Atlantic-centered republic of the revolutionary era to its emergence as a major industrial and world power by 1900.

During the course of the century, localized economics increasingly became integrated into a national market, and a political and religious order anchored in deference to local elites gave way to mass-based political parties organized across the nation and religious movements that responded to popular demands for spiritual equality. Divided by race, ethnicity, and gender, new classes of wage laborers and salaried employees replaced independent white farmers and enslaved black laborers as the dominant elements in a workforce reshaped by emancipation and immigration and the rise of factories and cities.

Dealing with different phases in America's transformation in the nineteenth century, the twenty-four chapters focus on recent scholarship. Written in accessible, non-technical language, they share a common purpose in introducing readers to the ways in which historians constantly rethink the questions they ask of the past and the methods they use to arrive at some tentative conclusions. Central to the discussion also is the special attention placed on the way in which the dominant trends in recent American historiography have recast what we know or can know of the process of change in the nineteenth-century United States.

One of these trends dates back to the social activism of the 1960s. Often called the "new social history" or "history from the bottom up," this trend shifted historical enquiry away from its traditional concern with the public policies and thoughts of male political elites and redirected it toward the lives and actions of women, blacks, workers, immigrants, Native Americans, and other groups who left few written records. Conflict, not consensus, emerged as a dominant theme as historians studied the struggles of the disadvantaged and disempowered for a better life through their own "agency." Political history lost its once privileged status for academic scholars, but significant new studies continued to appear. The best of this work recognized, as Robert M. S. McDonald notes in chapter 1 on the early national period, the need to examine "a broader topography of power" shaped by a popular impulse from below in order to explain fundamental political changes.

A second major trend relates to the interdisciplinary borrowings of historians from social psychology, literary theory, and especially cultural anthropology. The emphasis here is on the subjective meaning that individuals place on their actions, on language as an encoded system of knowledge and power, and on cultures as belief systems. Drawing upon this interdisciplinary approach, historians devised new analytical concepts, most notably racism as a social construction that can be understood only in historical terms and gender as the cultural meaning imparted to sexual differences. As Donald R. Wright (chapter 14) and Laura F. Edwards (chapter 16) make clear, these concepts have undergirded much of the reformulated history of blacks and women in nineteenth-century America. Another fresh insight, and one that informs the chapters in Part I on politics and public life, has been the recasting of politics as the story of competing political cultures that reflect different visions over whose values and interests should shape the meaning and purpose of public power. As Barbara Groseclose shows in chapter 24, the very way in which America was visually depicted in art represented a continuing debate over how America was to be defined and what groups should be included in the polity. And the chapters on the regions of the South, Midwest, and Far West in Part V reveal the combination of material and symbolic forces that fashioned these parts of the nation into "imagined communities."

The third dominant trend has seen a movement away from exceptionalism, the belief that the United States was uniquely destined to escape the historical forces of class conflict and self-serving aggrandizement that corrupt and convulse other nations. Even before the end of the Cold War, when the United States proclaimed itself as the only power capable of assuming the mantle of moral leadership against Soviet communism, the growing importance of international trade and transnational affiliations – what the 1990s touted as globalization – had undermined the assumptions of exceptionalist history. By the 1980s, the central issue in American labor history was no longer the attempt to explain why Americans were alone in the industrial Western world in not developing a labor party based on socialist principles. Labor historians now recognized, in the words of Kevin Kenny (chapter 12), that "any pure form of radical class consciousness" was not to be found anywhere for it did not exist. Just as labor history became freer to examine just what American workers actually did and thought, so also did approaches to Native Americans and the West change once historians abandoned the exceptionalist notion of the American frontier as a unique source of democratic rebirth and cultural renewal. Instead, the frontier is now seen as a zone of competing peoples, cultures, and material interests, a conflicted area that replicates global patterns of expanding metropolitan power.

Each generation reads the past through the lens of its own interests and values. As a guide to multiple readings of the nineteenth-century United States, the chapters in this volume inform, challenge, and provoke. They provide not so much fixed answers as lines of enquiry opened up by the imaginative scholarship of a modern generation of historians. They move from the unfolding of public power, whether domestically or abroad, to overviews of a spreading market economy, the intersecting paths by which class, race, gender, and ethnicity shaped social history broadly conceived, the creation of regional self-consciousness, and conclude with themes in cultural and intellectual development. Scholarly apparatus has been kept to a minimum, but the key works discussed and drawn upon are given in a short reference list at the end of each chapter. A more complete bibliography follows chapter 24.

PART I

Politics and Public Life

CHAPTER ONE

Early National Politics and Power, 1800–1824

ROBERT M. S. MCDONALD

T HOMAS Jefferson choreographed his 1801 inauguration as a simple, chaste, and purely republican affair. Unlike his predecessors, whose liveried coaches had whisked them to the ceremony, this "friend of the people" walked behind a small band of local militia. George Washington and John Adams had worn swords, but he donned a plain suit. Inside the Senate chamber, Jefferson delivered a speech in hushed tones that many of the few hundred listeners described as inaudible. Afterwards, according to one report, he returned to his boarding-house and, as was his habit, seated himself for dinner at the low end of the table.

Twenty-eight years later the scene was different. Like Jefferson, Andrew Jackson was a popular figure who walked to the Capitol, dressed simply, and whispered his inaugural address. But Jackson took the presidential oath outside, where, at the ceremony's conclusion, the jubilant crowd of 20,000 well-wishers rushed forward, forcing the former military leader to retreat on horseback. The mob pursued him to the White House, where it crashed through doors, soiled carpets, damaged furniture, and shattered china. Only after barrels of punch had been placed on the lawns did people – some of whom had been injured in the fracas – begin to recede from the mansion. More than a few observers sniffed that democracy had gone awry, that America's experiment with participatory government had lowered high politics to lamentable depths.

Perhaps no one better recognized the differences between Jefferson and Jackson than Jefferson himself. Daniel Webster, who visited the third president during his long retirement at Monticello, recorded Jefferson's disdain for the hero of the Battle of New Orleans: Jackson was a "dangerous man," Jefferson thought, unfit for office and lacking restraint. Jackson, however, linked himself with his predecessor. So did the twentieth-century's New Deal Democrats, who raised glasses to both leaders at annual Jefferson–Jackson Day banquets. The connection is tenuous, but it cannot be dismissed. Although Jefferson and Jackson possessed different temperaments and agendas, many of the Jeffersonian Republicans still alive in 1828 voted as Jacksonian Democrats.

What caused the massive shift in American political culture between the inaugurations of Jefferson and Jackson? How did Jeffersonians evolve into Jacksonians? Over the past few decades, historians have broadened their efforts to answer these questions, focusing less on the actions of political leaders and the narrowly defined politics of legislation and more on a broader topography of power. The result is a dizzying array of books and articles, each one with its own nuanced interpretation. The studies discussed below, all of which contribute to our understanding of the changing natures of polity and identity in the early republic, represent a mere sampling of recent work on these overlapping themes. Nearly every one, however, considers the causes and effects of the growing number of choices available to America's free citizens. Are we now ready for a more integrated, synthetic depiction of politics in the new nation? A bold and impressive study by Gordon Wood, *The Radicalism of the American Revolution* (1992), suggests that the answer is "yes."

Wood frames his discussion of radical changes in three chronological sections. In the first, "Monarchy," he describes colonial society as a well-ordered hierarchy, enthusiastically monarchical, "in which everyone, even the lowliest servant, counted for something" (Wood, 1992: 19). Society and the state were symbiotic. Authoritarian parents raised children as members of patriarchal families modeled after the royal household; as adults, individuals achieved social status and a political voice through government grants of land or titles.

During the second phase of Wood's chronology, "Republicanism," advocates of virtue and disinterestedness co-opted and challenged monarchical society. Classical notions of civic responsibility helped America's gentry to define itself at the same time as geographical mobility, population growth, new commercial opportunities, and a breakdown in traditional family order transformed its world. Wood contends that many Americans, including members of the landed elite, cheered these developments and the possibilities that they presented for the future. But such rapid change also bred paranoia. Anxiety about political corruption and social decay which characterized republicanism caused colonists to question British policies of patronage and to fear a qualitative loss within their own communities. The War of American Independence was the result, by Wood's account, of "differing interpretations of who in America were the proper social leaders who ought naturally to accede to positions of public authority" (1992: 87). The new nation's founders established a republic that they hoped would turn British subjects into American citizens wise enough to embrace the leadership of a public-spirited aristocracy. "They hoped to destroy the bonds holding together the older monarchical society – kinship, patriarchy, and patronage – and to put in their place new social bonds of love, respect, and consent." But this ambitious project, "the greatest utopian movement in American history," faltered from the start (1992: 229).

Wood's third section, "Democracy," recounts the failure of the founders' vision. Americans put less stock in love and sociability than in material advancement and individualism. Like Vermonter James Guild, who recounted how his "sole object was to make money" (Wood, 1992: 353), many rebelled against traditional roles as simple farmers, opting instead to move from place to place in search of fortune. For ordinary citizens like Guild, equality meant that "no one in a basic down-to-earth and day-in-and-day-out manner was really better than anyone else," a belief that Wood describes as "the single most powerful and radical ideological force in all of American history" (1992: 234).

The power of this revolutionary realization became especially apparent during the first decades of the nineteenth century, according to Wood. The rise of interest-based democracy, the popularization of the image of Benjamin Franklin as the prototypical self-made man, the mocking of the notion that any sort of natural aristocracy might possibly exist – all attested to the growing strength of equality not only as a principle but also as an ideology through which Americans interpreted their world. But were the members of this new breed of citizens equally good or equally bad? By Wood's account, at least, they viewed "vulgarity...materialism ...rootlessness [and] anti-intellectualism" as virtues to be flaunted (1992: 369). No wonder that more than a few founders took with them to the grave not only hopes but also misgivings about the future. Despite their efforts, much remained unresolved about both the American nation-state and the American state of mind.

Polity

Ironically, Wood's first book, *The Creation of the American Republic* (1970), emphasized the prevalence of republicanism in early America. Together with a host of other studies that highlighted the importance of virtue, disinterestedness, and agrarian self-sufficiency, his book helped to constitute a "republican synthesis" that for a while replaced Lockean liberalism as the revolutionary era's dominant interpretative framework. In addition to the rediscovery of a once-vibrant mode of political thought, the chief contribution of subscribers to the republican paradigm was to reinvigorate early American intellectual history. Not surprisingly, proponents of a liberal synthesis responded to the new scholarly paradigm with sophisticated studies of their own.

One of the many virtues of Wood's *Radicalism of the American Revolution* is that it provides a framework for synthesizing the recent scholarship on the new nation's political ideology. While much has been made of the historiographical debate between those who view the United States as a fundamentally liberal, forward-looking nation, and those who trace its origins to a more classical, republican, and paranoid past, during the early national period, it seems, these intellectual traditions coexisted. According to Wood, however, the republicanism of the founders gradually gave way as a rising generation of ambitious and acquisitive men and women sought to expand the economic, social, and political freedoms that their elders had institutionalized. Although he calls this trend "democratization," the term "liberalization" fits equally well. But when, precisely, did the American mind-set change? As Wood hints, and as some recent studies bear out, the answer depends on which constituency is taken to represent the American mind.

Drew McCoy's *The Elusive Republic* (1980), for example, finds evidence of the continuing vitality of classical republicanism through the first decade of the nineteenth century. Like Lance Banning's study *The Jeffersonian Persuasion* (1978), which demonstrates the influence of the republican "English Commonwealth" tradition on the political thought of Jefferson, James Madison, and other opponents of Alexander Hamilton's centralized system of finance and economic development, McCoy's volume focuses on the beliefs of an elite group of well-heeled, well-read statesmen. Bad enough, they thought, that Hamilton's affinity for debt, paper money, and a national bank concentrated power; worse yet, it cultivated vice, decadence, and a pernicious dependence on corrupt office-holders who, like members of the hated British "court party," exploited the mass of common people for the benefit of a favored few.

In the tradition of Britain's "country party" opposition, Jeffersonians sought to reverse Hamilton's policies in order to stave off societal decay. They did not, however, oppose all forms of commerce. According to McCoy (1980), they sought a middle ground between the tyranny of Federalist mercantilism and the poverty of subsistence agriculture. Farming should remain the mainstay of America's economy, they reasoned, but the economy could only grow if government reduced barriers to international trade. Americans who fed Europe would retain their industriousness and virtue at the same time as they reaped profits; this extra cash, in turn, would create a market for small-scale domestic manufactures, reducing the nation's dependence on Europe for finished goods. America's rapidly growing population constituted this plan's only problem: the republic of farmers might one day run out of arable land, forcing people to retreat to vice-ridden cities where, as wage-earners, they would lose their independence. Seeking to avoid this pattern of social development, which had already corrupted much of Europe, the Republican leadership developed a program of aggressive westward expansion. Its capstone was the 1803 purchase from France of the Louisiana Territory, which doubled America's size and, McCoy contends, "guaranteed that the American empire would be able to continue to expand across space, rather than be forced to develop through time" (McCoy, 1980: 201). The republican society of agrarian virtue would remain safe for generations to come.

Joyce Appleby (1984), however, argues that "capitalism and a new social order" emerged soon after the revolution and redefined early American politics. Although the Republicans of Banning and McCoy feared the supposed licentiousness and selfishness that they associated with unbridled commerce, Appleby's Republicans greeted burgeoning trade with optimism. Since these upwardly mobile farmers, mechanics, and merchants believed that the revolution had less to do with self-restraint than empowerment, the opportunities for advancement provided by the competitive marketplace proved tantalizing. Appleby's Republicans, who had more to gain and less to lose than the protagonists of Banning's and McCoy's studies, embraced economists such as Adam Smith, who linked theories of human nature and natural law with trade. The very human instinct of self-interest, set loose in a free market (of goods, or ideas, or political options), would quite naturally yield diverse outcomes more amenable to individuals than collective systems of choice. People, they thought, could and should choose for themselves.

In a land where deference to well-born men had marked political culture since the early days of settlement, the spread of such an attitude could only destabilize society. While this fact gave Federalists cause to fear, it stood as Republicans' fondest wish. Like Wood, Appleby contends that the "political faith" of Federalists "represented a modification, not a rejection, of traditional expectations about the role of authority in public life, about the permanence of social classes and the desirable distance between the governed and governors" (Appleby, 1984: 59). But rank-and-file Republicans yearned to sit at the same table as their erstwhile masters, and "the Jeffersonians united ordinary voters through a vision of classlessness. Its intellectual origins were as old as the social contract theories of Hobbes and Locke, but its material base owed much to the recent changes in the Atlantic economy which put a premium on the commodities reaped on American farms" (Appleby, 1984: 78). Greater involvement in commerce whetted people's appetites for greater involvement in politics.

For all their differences, Banning, McCoy, and Appleby share Wood's view of the revolution as the defining moment for the American psyche, the point at which the transformation from subject to citizen profoundly altered individuals' notions of where – and why – they fitted within an American polity. But unlike Wood, for whom the revolutionary moment lasts several decades, Steven Watts (1987) argues that America came of age somewhat more suddenly and, unlike Banning, McCoy, and Appleby, he contends that its maturation had little to do with the War of American Independence. In *The Republic Reborn*, Watts characterizes the War of 1812 as the event that sprouted the seeds of a more open, more recognizably modern America. It "played a crucial role ... by energizing and validating larger liberalizing impulses in early nineteenth-century America," he writes, serving "as a vehicle for the forces of change *and* offering an outlet for the anxieties of a changing society" in which "liberal capitalism" was the "crucial fact" of life (Watts, 1987: xvii).

Like Appleby, Watts believes that this new social order germinated in the 1790s, which witnessed "the consolidation of a market economy *and* a market society" (1987: 9). Choices abounded. While Appleby's Republicans embraced new opportunities for enterprise and greater personal freedom, the more refined, more "traditional" Republicans at the center of Watts's account detected among their neighbors increased avarice, decreased self-control, and a debilitating appetite for foreign-made luxury goods. But the War of 1812 promised something better. If earlier they had associated wars with debt, taxes, and social upheaval, many Jeffersonian Republicans by 1805 were anticipating a positive outcome from a possible second war with Great Britain. According to Watts (1987: 139), they foresaw it as a "useful therapeutic tool" for a corrupted culture. It would call on young men to discipline themselves in preparation for military service and channel "the libidinous urges of Americans" into selfless acts of heroism (1987: 140).

Meanwhile, the "Liberal Republicans," long angry at Britain for harassing American shipping and retarding the growth of the export trade, appealed to traditionalists' anxieties by portraying the war as an opportunity to promote internal commerce, which would lessen dependence on overseas manufacturers at the same time as it bolstered virtuous agricultural pursuits. Old Republicans came to accept that, instead of "merely guarding the commonweal or nurturing public and private virtue, the revitalized republic would assert itself in war to demonstrate productive prowess, social vitality, and civic strength. By this process," Watts informs his readers, "the Liberal Republicans accelerated the departure of ideology and political economy from traditional republican moorings" (1987: 269). Victory in 1815 sanctified this subtly transformed republicanism, which Watts describes as "nineteenth-century American liberalism" (1987: 298).

While Watts counts President Madison, "an older but flexible Jeffersonian theorist" (1987: 310), as among the converted, Drew McCoy's second book paints a somewhat more complicated portrait in *The Last of the Fathers* (1989). This intellectual biography, which focuses on Madison between his retirement in 1817 and his death in 1836, does not quarrel with Watts's assessment of the aging Virginian's affinity for commerce; indeed, McCoy's mature Madison seems more pragmatic and optimistic, with less interest in country-party ideology (which goes unmentioned), than the younger Madison of *The Elusive Republic* (1980). Yet the idealized republic that his Constitution aimed to create continued to elude him, and at times the doting framer displayed the disillusionment of Wood's Jefferson, who in 1825 complained to an old friend about the "new generation whom we know not, and who knows not us" (Wood, 1992: 368).

As sectionalism intensified, Madison defended national union as an enduring goal and championed republicanism as the process best suited to secure it. But he viewed "the instability that arose from popular licentiousness" as "the gravest danger" threatening both the end and means of American federalism. According to McCoy, "Balance, restraint, and the discipline of personal and public passion were Madisonian – which is to say, enlightened, eighteenth-century – imperatives that appeared ever more incongruous, hence all the more necessary, in the new, nineteenth-century world that a younger generation of Americans now busied itself in making" (McCoy, 1989: 65). The "younger generation" included Jackson, whom Madison, like Jefferson, detested as passion personified. It was bad enough that respect for the presidency had fallen so low that Jackson, as chief executive, dodged the bullets of a would-be assassin. Worse still, Old Hickory erupted with rage, blamed the attack on an innocent political enemy, and displayed so little restraint during the episode's aftermath that whatever respect Americans accorded his office surpassed what he, as an individual, deserved.

But McCoy points out that the rising generation also included Edward Coles, Nicholas Trist, and William Cabell Rives, Madison protégés who, to varying degrees, shared their mentor's insistence that adherence to the orderly process of government mattered more than any particular outcome. These men gave Madison hope. To them, long after his death, Madison's memory gave solace, for all suffered as a result of their scruples. First there was the pain of embracing a brand of republicanism that neither Jacksonian Democrats nor Whigs – nor the Republican party of Lincoln – could fully accommodate. Then came the anguish of the Civil War, a conflict that they, like Madison, feared but could not forestall. Indeed, when the account of Madison's thought turns to slavery, McCoy's tone shifts from reverence to remorse. Madison understood that slavery undermined republicanism, but his commitment to the republican process condemned him to the equivocal and unworkable prospect of gradual emancipation, with compensation for masters and colonization for slaves. Not the least among the failings of this plan was its inability to define a middle ground of sufficient gravity to attract pro-slavery thinkers and abolitionists, whose positions grew increasingly extreme.

The result, of course, would be the dissolution of the federal Union that Madison had labored to establish. But long before the Civil War, the United States Constitution, in his view, had begun to unravel. Ever the strict constructionist, he chomped at the bit as growing numbers of younger men used the "general welfare" clause to justify taxes and legislation that favored particular interests and undermined the uniform justice that the nation's government had been chartered to uphold. The Constitution was a contract, he thought, and not a flexible framework subject to opportunistic interpretation. To combat this troubling tendency, he urged anyone who would listen to let history guide them; examine the records of the state-ratifying conventions, he advised, and hold true to expressions of original intent. In the Age of Jackson, however, few bothered to listen.

The reality of interest-based politics offended the cherished vision of neutral government held not only by Madison but also by Washington, Adams, Jefferson, James Monroe, and John Quincy Adams. As Ralph Ketcham's *Presidents Above Party* (1984) points out, the first six chief executives held in common a belief that leaders should be impartial, independent, and committed to the general good. All, according to Ketcham, viewed themselves as heads of state more than as leaders of factions; the very concept of party, in fact, struck them as anathema to the operation of a virtuous republic. Profoundly conservative, this view owed more to the "patriot king" ideal of Bolingbroke and other English Tories, who believed that the wise ruler cultivated national unity and personal restraint, than to radical Whigs, who believed in curtailing executive authority itself. Even so, in America this stance retarded the growth of presidential power; Monroe's anti-party inclinations, for example, nearly rendered him irrelevant.

Ketcham cautions that "the ideal of a harmonious public interest did not die when J. Q. Adams left the White House" and that the transition to the partisan presidency "was not instantaneous" (Ketcham, 1984: 151). John Adams, after all, had his midnight judges, and Jefferson ensured that his own appointees were Republicans as well as republican. But Jackson, to a much greater extent than his predecessors, viewed himself as the leader of a permanent, institutionalized party beholden to specific constituencies. No wonder scholars such as Wood and McCoy detect despair in the writings of Jefferson, Madison, and other retired revolutionaries. With each passing year, the disjunction between their elite republican theory and popular democratic practice became more stark.

Few institutions better illustrated the pitfalls of interest-based politics in the early republic than the postal system. And as Richard John's *Spreading the News* (1996) makes clear, the mail not only served as a conduit of heated public exchanges but also caused them. Politicized from the start, this early experiment with government involvement in Americans' daily lives stirred controversies about the extent of federal power and the causes for which it should be applied. Although many businessmen wished to collect their mail on Sundays, for example, others pushed for legislation to enforce the sabbath as a day of rest. While abolitionists sought to disseminate anti-slavery literature through the post, a number of southerners opposed the practice. Backcountry congressmen, seeking to spur local development, fought to route post roads in the interior, but their coastal counterparts, also mindful of constituents' interests, wanted them to pass through shoreline communities.

Journalists won an early victory in postal politics. In 1792, Congress voted to charge only a penny to deliver a newspaper within a hundred miles of its printer and a penny and a half to send it farther. Letter-writers paid for this subsidy: it cost 75 cents – the better part of a day's wage – to mail a note to a distant friend or relative. Not surprisingly, most people relied on private couriers to carry their correspondence, and even with the newspaper subsidy, John demonstrates, the post office circulated "no more than ten percent of newspapers printed in any given year" because local delivery cost less by private means (John, 1995: 38).

In addition to national politics, according to John, the mail also nurtured a national economy. Postal patronage may have done little to develop the Northeast's relatively mature road system, but in the South and West it made a difference. Merchants from all parts used it to keep abreast of financial news, and it served as a major conduit of cash, bills of exchange, and other forms of trade between the states. As John (1995) points out, however, the commerce that united America's regions also stirred sectional resentment and factionalism.

Identity

Of all the political implications of the emerging market, however, none more permanently shaped public culture than the rise of assertive individualism. Citizens came to
view themselves as consumers, not only of political ideas and manufactured goods but
also of identity itself. Unlike their forebears, for whom faith, social standing, and
vocation existed largely as functions of birth, nineteenth-century Americans enjoyed
an unprecedented opportunity to define their own selves. Increasingly, they viewed
the power to choose less as a luxury and more as a right. For the dynamics of power
within the United States, the consequences were profound.

Nathan Hatch's *The Democratization of American Christianity* (1989) makes clear,
for example, that in the years after 1800 many individuals chose to abandon Episcopal
and Congregational churches and joined upstart denominations led by charismatic
evangelicals who aimed their appeals at specific groups. By 1845, this "Second Great
Awakening" had seen the number of preachers per capita triple, and Methodists and
Baptists, minor faiths at the start of the century, accounted for about two-thirds of all
Protestants. Hatch ascribes the success of these and other insurgent sects to their
refusal "to defer to learned theologians and traditional orthodoxies," their ability to
"empower ordinary people by taking their deepest spiritual impulses at face value,"
and their confidence that "a new age of social and religious harmony would naturally
spring out of their efforts" (Hatch, 1989: 9–10). Churches flourished when they
challenged authority, honored common people, and "offered the humble a marvelous
sense of individual potential and of collective aspiration" (1989: 5). This, for Hatch,
amounts to religious "democratization;" it is liberation theology, American style.

Maybe. But it would be more precise to describe the process that Hatch so ably
illustrates as the opening of the religious marketplace. The relative elitism of Congregational and Episcopal churches should come as no surprise, for they were beholden to elites for the subsidies that usually accompanied state establishment. And it is
hardly startling that these churches, once disestablished by Jefferson and like-minded
individuals, would find themselves ill prepared to compete with evangelicals, who had
long relied on the faithful as their sole source of support. As Hatch points out, these
market-savvy religious leaders understood how "to communicate with a variety of
persons high and low, rich and poor, urban and rural, slave and free" (1989: 68). They
grounded gospel music in folk tradition, gave sermons that addressed the concerns of
specific constituencies, appealed to emotion as well as reason and faith, and employed
advances in printing technology to reach ever-expanding numbers of people.

A "Sovereign Audience" resulted, according to Hatch (1989: 125), and each of its
members asserted "The Right to Think for Oneself" (1989: 162). Like their leaders,
they had also grown savvy – if not as marketers then as consumers of messages
regarding religion and other articles of faith. Witness the Baptists of Cheshire,
Massachusetts. As a "free-will offering" of thanks for his support for religious disestablishment, they sent to President Jefferson a 1,235 lb "Mammoth Cheese." Their
parson, who in 1802 delivered the cheese amidst much fanfare, carried with him a
note from his flock that gently cautioned Jefferson against turning his back on their
interests. The cheese itself reiterated their point, for they inscribed it with Jefferson's
personal motto: "Rebellion to tyrants is obedience to God" (1989: 96). So

empowering was the religious free market that even black Americans, whose agency had otherwise been curtailed by prejudice, as well as slavery and other forms of legal persecution, received and responded to evangelicals' attention. Most aligned themselves with Baptists and Methodists, groups that took care to emphasize their egalitarianism; other African Americans started churches of their own.

The leveling impact of the new consumer culture revealed itself not only through religion, but also, as Richard Bushman (1992) argues, in the manners, dress, furnishings, and homes of an expanding circle of citizens. During the eighteenth century, Bushman demonstrates, only the wealthiest planters and merchants engaged in "the refinement of America." "Great mansions, books, fine dress became instruments of power, a superior culture to parade before the eyes of a deferential population whose compliance was necessary for the continuation of authority" (Bushman, 1992: 404). If then the colonial gentry asserted its status by patterning its social and material environments after distant Old World models, now the proliferation of cash, credit, and affordable mass-produced goods placed badges of gentility within the reach of more ordinary men and women.

Striving for "respectability rather than eminence" (Bushman, 1992: 208), middling farmers, shopkeepers, and tradesmen built Greek Revival houses and stocked them with factory-made clocks, furniture, and carpets. Although these items, once reserved for the elite, no longer signified great wealth, they served those who possessed them by communicating an elevated taste founded, most essentially, on a largely fictive disjunction of the spheres of work and home. A farmer who toiled in his field to buy fine carpets could no longer tread through his house with muddy boots, but this small sacrifice suggested to visitors that his labor yielded significant time for the leisure, contemplation, and civic engagement enjoyed only by the most well-heeled of previous generations. In other words, his material world – and the behavioral world that it implied – asserted his arrival as an individual of importance. While Bushman describes this "spread of parlor culture" as "one of the great democratic movements of the nineteenth century" (1992: 273), he acknowledges that it drew "an indelible line between the middle and lower classes in American society" and made "rudeness a cause of shame" (1992: 279). The clumsy well-wishers at Jackson's inaugural reception sought neither to degrade the presidency nor themselves but instead clamored to affirm their status as refined participants in civil society.

Members of the growing middle class did more than attempt to mimic their social "betters," however. As Daniel Howe's *Making the American Self* (1997) contends, they extolled the "self-made man" as the model American. Self-making went beyond the mere acquisition of wealth. According to Howe (1997: 184), it involved a "preoccupation with the conscious construction of character." Like Bushman's "refinement," Howe's "self-construction" manifested itself first among the colonial elite. The ideal was a hybrid, he argues, that drew from the influential examples of Jonathan Edwards, whose Protestantism urged vigilance against the ever-present danger of personal corruption, and Franklin, whose Enlightenment optimism heralded the possibilities of personal agency. It also embraced the Scottish Enlightenment's conception of "faculty psychology," which imagined the human psyche as a collection of distinct, often competing mental functions and established a hierarchy in which the most passionate of these functions would yield to the most rational. Law-makers of the revolutionary era applied the ideal of the "balanced character" not only in their own lives but also in their government. Thus Howe employs Madison's federalism, replete with checks and balances against the passions of both majorities and special interests, as an example of faculty psychology applied to the body politic.

Yet, as deference declined and old political hierarchies eroded, the growth of evangelical Christianity and the market made the visions of Edwards and Franklin more tangible for ordinary Americans. During the nineteenth century, Howe argues, people of humble origins, such as Abraham Lincoln, Frederick Douglass, and countless others, made self-improvement through moral self-consciousness and strict self-discipline life-long quests. As a result, citizens could now read Jefferson's Declaration of Independence, which asserted the right of "self-governance," as Howe believes Jefferson intended: a claim not only for the colonies but also for all individuals. The rise of individualism, therefore, undermined political restraints at the same time as it spurred broader and more open participation in churches, charities, and the other voluntary associations that formed the foundation of America's emerging civil society.

The individualist impulse spread not only through direct experience but also by way of the imaginary world of popular literature, a point made by Bushman and Howe that Cathy Davidson's *Revolution and the Word* (1986) more fully develops. Novels, she maintains, subverted traditional hierarchies while they cultivated moral sensitivities. They were, of course, a medium new to the cultural scene, made possible (and inexpensive) by the rapid commercialization of print. In part because of their newness, but also because members of "an elite minority" viewed them as a threat to their "self-proclaimed role as the primary interpreters of American culture" (Davidson, 1986: 42), novels faced fervent opposition from religious and political leaders who feared that these unmediated texts might lead astray impressionable readers, most of whom were women. Davidson's analysis, based on a thorough examination of about a hundred novels published between 1789 and 1820, reveals that this worry was well founded. Novels served "as agents and products of social change" (1986: 13), she writes, by challenging class and gender roles, critiquing traditional notions of republicanism, and championing the power of individual self-determination. The heroes (and, more often, heroines) of novels questioned society in ways that few readers would have previously contemplated. Yet many of these books also portrayed "self-made men maintaining their newfound power by resorting to the same kinds of treachery" used by "evil aristocrats" in other fictional accounts (Davidson, 1986: 218). As a genre, therefore, the early American novel undermined all concentrations of power, whether new or old.

Not everyone, however, cheered egalitarianism and individualism. The children of Virginia's genteel revolutionaries, according to Jan Lewis's *The Pursuit of Happiness* (1983), viewed self-reliance as "neither a mandate nor a challenge," but as "an unhappy fact of life" (Lewis, 1983: 156). While their parents had dominated the Old Dominion's politics and economy, these post-colonial Virginians found that democratization and the market unsettled their lives; emotional revivalism taught them to vent their woe but offered meager inspiration. They equated happiness with independence, but falling tobacco prices and rising debts reminded them of their reliance on others. The "unhappy fact" of social upheaval meant that they must either adopt vulgar Yankee habits of thrift and industry or cling to the noble but presumably incompatible southern ideals of grace, chivalry, and hospitality. "The predicament was real," Lewis (1983: 132) contends: "men and women wanted wealth but scorned struggling for it."

Many took the easy way out, ignoring their changed world and vesting "their ideal of independence in plantation slavery." Yet this stance, which wedded identity to "a form of labor that the modern world was finding increasingly repugnant" (1983: 113), further challenged their self-esteem and seldom yielded great profit. An increasing number of people, however, began to view independence as a personal quality and not as a measure of their power over others. "A new language of individualism and self-reliance now crept more frequently into Virginians' correspondence," Lewis (1983: 155) writes, as "industry, order, perseverance, and enterprise" became buzzwords for a class that once had scorned hard work. Well-born youths who viewed indolence and intemperance as badges of social distinction had by the 1820s matured into enterprisers consumed by the desire to make money. Politics, which their fathers and grandfathers regarded as a high calling, to them seemed an unworthy distraction. For satisfaction they turned inward, focusing on loving their families and opening their hearts to "new conventions" such as "warmth" and "individuality" (Lewis, 1983: 227). Even so, Lewis cautions, the inner happiness for which this generation strived proved more elusive than the public importance that preceding ones achieved.

Consensus?

Taken together, these studies of polity and identity do much to buttress and articulate the broad outlines of Wood's book, as well as his contention that the War of American Independence sanctified ideas and established conditions that led to changes much more revolutionary than the revolution itself. Like Wood's *Radicalism of the American Revolution*, Alan Taylor's *William Cooper's Town* (1995), for example, ties together several historiographical strands and weaves them into a powerful narrative. Although Wood's account better relates to recent examinations of the American polity and Taylor's study connects more neatly with works on American identity, their similarities outweigh their differences. Lest anyone criticize Wood's macrohistorical approach as too sweeping to be trusted, Taylor's focused, biographical treatment examines some of the same themes and yields remarkably similar conclusions.

Taylor's William Cooper can be taken as representative of the class of men who led Wood's movement toward "democracy." Born into a poor Quaker family, Cooper after the revolution cashed in on the misfortune of loyalists forced to abandon their land near Otsego, New York. He and a partner acquired it from their creditors and, in 1791, established Otsego County and propped up Cooperstown as its capital. Cooper also established himself, not only as this frontier area's chief economic leader but also as a political chieftain. To other men on the make, he sold on credit large tracts which they then parceled out to ambitious New York and New England farming families. The people to whom he extended opportunities also accepted obligations. Despite his humble origins and modest education, they elected him to office.

Cooper expected such deference. Later in life, especially, he had more in common with the Republicans of Wood's account than with the Democrats. He wanted to be the people's patriarch, a father more than a friend. Like the protagonists of the works by Howe and Bushman, he was self-made and strove for respectability; through his efforts, however, he aimed to establish authority over others as well as himself. As

Taylor writes, he wanted to achieve the sort of "preeminence idealized in colonial America but at odds with the legacy of the American revolution" (Taylor, 1995: 7). Cooper's story is tragic because he expressed his high social aspirations through Federalist politics, a stance that chafed against his constituents' own aspirations and led to his political downfall after the Jeffersonian "Revolution of 1800." It is also bittersweet; in many ways the men who eventually unseated him had much in common with him. They, too, wished to establish themselves as free and independent.

"New Yorkers experienced the transfer of power from Federalists to Republicans as a profound social and political watershed," Taylor (1995: 286) writes, because "the Republicans effected two momentous transformations: the creation of a political party and the construction of a new democratic political culture." While Cooper and his fellow Federalists cobbled together uneasy alliances to promote for office men of wealth, talent, and ostensible virtue, Republicans constructed an efficient organization to elect so-called "friends of the people." Their political network marshaled resources that allowed men of modest means to compete with individuals of a higher social station, and their rhetoric glorified the common and vilified the privileged. Neither the middling class of Otsego County nor the raucous crowd that greeted the newly inaugurated Jackson reveled in rudeness; these groups did, however, embrace a new standard of civility that exalted familiarity and considered ostentation vulgar.

According to Wood's chronology, the changes that took place around Otsego remained elusive in much of America until many years later. But Taylor's account accords with Wood's conception of cause and effect. As Rosemarie Zagarri (1998) affirms, claims of rights by men with power established a vocabulary through which marginalized people would later express their own aspirations. While Zagarri focuses on women, and Wood, like Taylor, concentrates on average men, the relationship between rights and reality remains the same. An elite group's use of universalist political theory to insist on its members' prerogatives to make their own political choices inspired others to make similar assertions. New choices in the economy had the same effect. Like the political marketplace, within which citizens registered preferences through voting and other activities, in the marketplace of goods, participants expressed preferences by voting with their dollars. Analogous markets developed for culture and religion, which, together with politics and economics, allowed Americans to choose their own identities. In sum, the availability of choice facilitated the rise of individualism, an early national success story that profoundly transformed the dynamics of power in America.

Any argument can be taken too far. The radical changes described by Wood, Taylor, and nearly all of the other historians considered thus far were neither so sweeping nor so transforming, for example, that they obliterated all traces of popular deference and disinterested public service. Though ambitious young upstarts challenged William Cooper's authority in central New York, Daniel Jordan's painstaking study of *Political Leadership in Jefferson's Virginia* (1983) detects few changes in the composition of the Old Dominion's ruling elite during the first 25 years of the nineteenth century. If, as Lewis (1983) argues, a growing number of Virginia's most prominent citizens abandoned politics for domestic bliss, then, as Jordan (1983) demonstrates, plenty of their well-connected cousins scrambled to fill the void. Throughout the period, holders of high office continued to emerge from the same clique of rich, educated, and slave-holding Episcopalians. Continuity trumps change in Charles Sellers's account of *The Market Revolution* (1991), as well. Unlike Appleby (1984), who finds that Jeffersonians embraced capitalism in the 1790s, or Watts (1987), who believes that the War of 1812 wedded Republicans to commerce, Sellers portrays the political mainstream as deeply conflicted over modern enterprise until the 1840s, when finally "democracy proved safe for capitalism" (Sellers, 1991: 359).

Similarly, the maturation of American individualism during the early national era cannot be accepted as a *fait accompli*. Most recent studies maintain that during this period identity became increasingly personal, depending more on choice than birth. Not long afterwards, however, individuals would fight and die in defense of sectional interests. By recognizing this paradox, Richard John (1996) surpasses many of his peers, and his explanation of it – that the growth of inter-regional familiarity bred caution as much as trust – provides tantalizing insight. Does it go far enough, however? Does petty jealousy make sense of a Civil War that killed more Americans than any other before or since? Do far-from-petty concerns about slavery offer an explanation?

The latter two questions might be answered with a singular "yes." But a more complicated, more complete understanding of the Civil War might be gained by exploring how Howe's self-governing individuals and John's self-serving political participants were one and the same. Did nineteenth-century individualism, with all its emphasis on personal responsibility, force antebellum Americans to rationalize their own lives by blaming others for their own failings? Did nineteenth-century individuals externalize the cultural insistence on self-control by seeking to control others?

REFERENCES

Appleby, Joyce O. (1984) *Capitalism and a New Social Order: the Republican Vision of the 1790s*. New York: New York University Press.

Banning, Lance (1978) *The Jeffersonian Persuasion: Evolution of a Party Ideology*. Ithaca, NY: Cornell University Press.

Bushman, Richard L. (1992) *The Refinement of America: Persons, Houses, Cities*. New York: Alfred A. Knopf.

Davidson, Cathy N. (1986) *Revolution and the Word: the Rise of the Novel in America*. New York: Oxford University Press.

Hatch, Nathan O. (1989) *The Democratization of American Christianity*. New Haven, Conn.: Yale University Press.

Howe, Daniel Walker (1997) *Making the American Self: from Jonathan Edwards to Abraham Lincoln*. Cambridge, Mass.: Harvard University Press.

John, Richard R. (1995) *Spreading the News: the American Postal System from Franklin to Morse*. Cambridge, Mass.: Harvard University Press.

Jordan, Daniel P. (1983) *Political Leadership in Jefferson's Virginia*. Charlottesville, Va.: University Press of Virginia.

Ketcham, Ralph (1984) *Presidents above Party: the First American Presidency, 1789–1829*. Chapel Hill, NC: University of North Carolina Press.

Lewis, Jan (1983) *The Pursuit of Happiness: Family and Values in Jefferson's Virginia*. New York: Cambridge University Press.

McCoy, Drew R. (1980) *The Elusive Republic: Political Economy in Jeffersonian America*. Chapel Hill, NC: University of North Carolina Press.

McCoy, Drew R. (1989) *The Last of the Fathers: James Madison and the Republican Legacy.* New York: Cambridge University Press.

Sellers, Charles (1991) *The Market Revolution: Jacksonian America, 1815–1846.* New York: Oxford University Press.

Taylor, Alan (1995) *William Cooper's Town: Power and Persuasion on the Frontier of the Early American Republic.* New York: Alfred A. Knopf.

Watts, Steven (1987) *The Republic Reborn: War and the Making of Liberal America, 1790–1820.* Baltimore, MD: Johns Hopkins University Press.

Wood, Gordon S. (1970) *The Creation of the American Republic.* Chapel Hill, NC: University of North Carolina Press.

Wood, Gordon S. (1992) *The Radicalism of the American Revolution.* New York: Alfred A. Knopf.

Zagarri, Rosemarie (1998) "The rights of man and woman in post-revolutionary America," *William and Mary Quarterly,* 3rd ser., 55: 203–30.

CHAPTER TWO

The Jacksonian Era, 1825–1844

JONATHAN ATKINS

THE term "Jacksonian era" designates the period from the election of John Quincy Adams to the presidency in 1825 to the conclusion of the administration of James K. Polk in 1848. The era derives its name from its most prominent figure, Andrew Jackson, whose eight years in the presidency provided the fulcrum for the period's political history. Jackson's administrations marked a retreat from the nationalistic and activist policies of the federal government during the "Era of good feelings" and established the decentralized, *laissez-faire* policies that would be enacted during Polk's administration and guide the national government until the Civil War. National and state politics in these years came to be dominated by what historians now recognize as the nation's first competition between modern mass political parties. The era also coincided with the emergence of the abolitionist movement and the aggravation of sectional tensions that would culminate in the Civil War. Recent reassessments of political and social developments in these years have produced several suggestions for a new label, including the "Era of the common man," the "Age of egalitarianism," and the "Era of the market revolution." None of these suggestions has gained widespread acceptance, however, and the phrase "Jacksonian era" remains the most well-known title for the second quarter of the nineteenth century.

Since about 1970, the Jacksonian era seems to have become a field in which students and scholars of American history have largely lost interest. While its proponents continue their research passionately and engage each other in often heated debate, the growth in prominence of social and cultural history appears in many ways to have bypassed and marginalized their work. A glance through recent issues of the American Historical Association's *Directory of History Departments and Organizations* indicates relatively few specialists in Jacksonian politics on the faculties of research universities. Annual job announcements likewise show limited opportunities for graduate students writing dissertations in the field, and many smaller colleges have dropped courses on the early nineteenth century from their curricula. Political histories and biographies from the Jacksonian era have been published over the past several years, but many have been produced by older scholars or by non-academic writers. Among many historians, it would appear, the study of Jacksonian politics has either been abandoned or at least relegated to the realm of "popular history."

Of course, the banishment of the study of Jacksonian politics has not been complete. The apparent decline in interest, in fact, is not so much the result of a lack of attention from scholars as it is the product of the expansion of the number of areas now considered worthy of historical enquiry. Whereas Jacksonian politics was once considered one of the most crucial subjects in American history, the Jacksonian era now stands as one of several possible fields of study. Despite this shift in its relative importance, the politics of the 1820s through the 1840s has been a vibrant subject over the past several years. Most notably, Jacksonian specialists have broadened their focus to understand politics less in terms of election results and more in terms of the political system's relationship to the emergence of a class-based society and the construction of American culture. Recent scholarship in Jacksonian politics has thus revealed as much about the broader development of the American experience as it has about historians' traditional interest, the growth of the nation's political institutions.

To earlier generations, national politics between the Adams and Polk administrations attracted attention because it seemed to involve a dramatic story over vital issues. An Olympian confrontation between Jackson and the "great triumvirate" – Henry Clay, Daniel Webster, and John C. Calhoun – dominated proceedings in Washington. These leaders knew that the outcome of their battles over such issues as the controversial presidential election of 1824, the survival of the Bank of the United States, and the Nullification crisis would determine the success or failure of the American republic. An able but overshadowed supporting cast, including Polk and Martin Van Buren, aided Jackson by reviving Thomas Jefferson's Democratic party, while Clay and Webster led a revived Federalism in the creation of a new opposition Whig party. Mavericks like Adams and John Tyler prevented the narrative from following a predictable course. The end result of the era's struggles was the establishment of a democratic polity that lay the foundation for the economic and geographic expansion that would eventually make the United States a world power. With such towering figures competing for such high stakes, historians once reasoned, surely this was the period where one could best understand the exceptionalism that distinguished American politics and the American national character.

The central issue for historians for more than a century after the conclusion of Jackson's presidency thus involved the question of the nature of "Jacksonian democracy," a term which, while variously defined, generally refers to the expansion of white male participation in electoral politics and an assumption that "the people's will" should guide elected officials in setting public policy. Notwithstanding disagreement, scholars concurred that, on the surface at least, American politics did experience a shift toward a more democratic political culture. New state constitutions omitted property requirements for voting and office-holding; older states likewise removed these restrictions as they rewrote their own constitutions. By 1832, all states but one provided for presidential electors to be chosen by popular vote, and voter participation in national elections increased dramatically during the 1830s until it peaked in 1840 and remained high for the rest of the century. The Whig and Democratic parties developed new campaign techniques designed to appeal to the average American, while party rhetoric pledged their fidelity to the will of the people. Despite these changes, historians have questioned just how truly "democratic" Jacksonian democracy was. For historians, the issue of which "people" the movement represented produced a variety of responses that might be reduced to a simple dichotomy: did Jacksonian democracy mark an awakening of the common people against entrenched political and economic interests or was it simply the means through which political and economic elites manipulated the masses to secure their own power?

Although the nineteenth-century's pre-eminent historian, George Bancroft, was an ardent Jacksonian, the first serious statement about Jacksonian democracy's significance in American history was produced by a Whig, James Parton. His 1860 biography of Jackson denounced what he described as the mob tendencies that had brought Jackson to power. While acknowledging Jackson's courage and decisiveness, Parton contended that the general's ignorance and passionate disposition made him unfit for the presidency. Jackson's supporters were thus ambitious sycophants who sought to ride his popularity into power for themselves, Parton concluded, and he echoed Whig condemnation of the "spoils system" that rewarded unqualified party hacks while preventing intelligent, experienced, capable, and judicious men from holding their rightful place in public affairs.

Parton's biography became the standard source on the Jacksonian era until Progressive historians in the late nineteenth century produced a new framework for interpretation that lasted until World War II. Historians writing in the Progressive vein – armed with a sense of professionalism and scientific objectivity and consciously contrasting themselves with "gentleman scholars" like Parton – reinforced reformers' calls for an end to government corruption and for restrictions on irresponsible wealth, for the historians argued that party machines and big business had captured the American political system and used it for their own interests rather than the public good. The tension between the people and special interests, they found, turned out to be a longstanding one in the American experience, and for the most part they found the people's will best expressed through the Democratic party founded by Jefferson and expanded by Jackson.

Frederick Jackson Turner led the Progressive revision of the Jacksonian era when he argued that Jacksonianism was the political expression of frontier democracy. Expanding on his well-known thesis that western expansion encouraged political democracy and forged the United States' distinct individualistic and pragmatic social character, Turner saw the Old Northwest as the most democratic and egalitarian section of the young United States. The brash and iconoclastic general became for Turner the personification of the West's ideals, and under Jackson's leadership the Democratic party stood for this region's new understanding of government against the aristocratic South and the puritanical East. Not all agreed with Turner's emphasis on the sectional basis of politics. One of Turner's students, Thomas P. Abernethy, presented the most severe challenge to his mentor when he depicted Jackson in a 1932 study as a frontier nabob with little sympathy for popular reforms within his home state of Tennessee. Nevertheless, Turner's description of Jacksonianism as a truly democratic movement standing against political and economic elites won wide acceptance.

The classic statement of the Progressive reinterpretation came with the publication of Arthur M. Schlesinger Jr's *The Age of Jackson* (1945). Schlesinger differed sharply from Turner by locating the origins of Jacksonianism among workers and planters in the East and South as well as among farmers in the West. The Bank War was for Schlesinger the central event of Jackson's presidency, for it reflected the triumph of the people's chosen representatives over business's control of the government. Business remained the most powerful interest group in the nation, and by adopting popular campaign techniques, first through the Whig party and later through the Republicans, this "conservative" presence remained a constant threat to the public welfare. The necessity of the conservatives having to "assume the manner of the popular party," however, meant that "the struggle would be renewed on Jackson's terms, and not on those of Daniel Webster or Nicholas Biddle" (Schlesinger, 1945:

305). The heirs of the Jacksonian tradition continued to work to mobilize other sectors of society against the rich and powerful. "This was the tradition of Jefferson and Jackson," Schlesinger concluded, "and it has been the basic meaning of American liberalism" (1945: 505). For Schlesinger, Jacksonian democracy was not a sectionally based movement, but one that defended the producing classes against capitalist business owners and financiers in a modified free-market economy. Yet Schlesinger followed Turner in portraying Jacksonianism as the expression of a democratic people's will against entrenched economic and political elites, and like other Progressives he persisted in seeing the struggle for the nation's future in the era's political history.

Just as *The Age of Jackson* was becoming the standard source for the next generation, the social and political circumstances of the nation began to shatter the foundations of the Progressive interpretation. Schlesinger had made no effort to hide his sympathy with the New Deal policies, and critics quickly noted the parallels between Old Hickory's war against the Bank and Franklin Roosevelt's struggles with the "money changers . . . in the temple." By the time of the publication of Schlesinger's study, however, the American economy had recovered from the Great Depression and had entered the most prosperous period in American history. As the Cold War with the Soviet Union came to dominate American foreign relations, for many historians the American experience now seemed to be characterized less by a constant tension between conservative business interests and liberal popular reformers than it did by a national consensus on fundamental American principles.

At the same time, the expansion and democratization of American higher education likewise undermined the Progressive view. Student bodies became less characterized by scions of elite and upper middle-class families and more populated by the children of workers and lower middle-class families. Many of these new students came to history as a way to understand their own identities and their people's "place" in the American story. The presence of students from less privileged backgrounds, and the entry of an increased number of them into graduate programs, encouraged historians to take a wider and deeper view of what constituted historical experience. Also, advances in computer technology made more easily accessible previously cumbersome sources like census data and tax lists. By the 1960s, the "new social history," with an emphasis on "history from the bottom up," appeared the most promising area for future research. Influenced by the civil rights movement, protests against the Vietnam War, and the women's rights movement – to all of which the major political parties appeared unresponsive – professional historians turned away from the once-firm belief that the study of past politics formed the core of a historian's responsibility.

The de-emphasis on political history meant that the study of the Jacksonian era no longer seemed vital for understanding the American experience. The national politics on which Jacksonian scholars concentrated was now seen as the province of elites who had little in common with ordinary people. Major issues like the Bank War and Nullification appeared to be battles among self-serving politicians that had little impact on the daily experience of most Americans. Jacksonian democracy's celebration of egalitarianism among white males – a source of admiration for Progressives – now seemed exclusivist and restricting. Jackson's brutal removal of the Native-American population and the Democratic party's defense of slavery, moreover, ranked among the worst offenses in the nation's past as the seventh president became a figure of vituperation rather than admiration. By the late 1960s, the Jacksonian era had become for many a quaint legacy from a once simpler past, but further study of the era appeared to be peripheral to the central issues in American history.

Nevertheless, many historians persisted in the study of the era, and their efforts built on the work of consensus historians such as Richard Hofstadter and Bray Hammond who challenged the class basis of politics put forward by Schlesinger. The chapter on Jackson in Hofstadter's *The American Political Tradition and the Men who Made It* (1948) stressed that Jacksonianism was "a phase in the expansion of liberal capitalism" (1948/1973: 70) and portrayed Jackson as the representative of a rising middle class that aimed "to open every possible pathway for the creative enterprises of the people" (1948/1973: 78). Hammond, a retired federal reserve official, echoed Hofstadter in *Banks and Politics in America from the Revolution to the Civil War* (1957) when he described the Jacksonians as "a party of business enterprise ... devoted to the principle of *laissez faire*" (Hammond, 1957: 365). In Hammond's view, the destruction of the Bank of the United States was not so much a popular attack on a business class as "a blow at an older set of capitalists by a newer, more numerous set" (1957: 329). Critics like Edward Pessen (1985) agreed with the consensus view that Democrats and Whigs were united in their liberal capitalist assumptions but rejected the notion that either party rested upon a popular foundation. In several works, Pessen showed the political parties to be led by elites and concluded that the Democrats in particular often contradicted the interests of workers while denying equal justice to women and to racial and ethnic minorities. Robert V. Remini (1976), probably the most recognized Jacksonian scholar in the post-World War II era, meanwhile endorsed Schlesinger's interpretation. While continuing to portray Jackson as the champion of the people against conservative, elitist, business-oriented Whigs, Remini argued that Jackson's aggressive administrations changed the nature of the presidency from a passive executive to the "Tribune of the People." The institutionalization of the Democratic party, moreover, enshrined popular democracy as a national ideal.

The most enlightening research, however, followed a different course. In *The Concept of Jacksonian Democracy: New York as a Test Case* (1961), Lee Benson took on not only *The Age of Jackson* but the central focus of the previous century of historiography. Utilizing the quantitative and statistical techniques employed by the new social history, Benson presented a close analysis of politics in New York between 1815 and 1844 that reaffirmed Hofstadter's and Hammond's emphasis on the similarities between the Whig and Democratic parties, though he acknowledged that the parties' policies reflected "competing concepts" of "positive versus negative liberalism" (Benson, 1961: 86). Yet Benson went beyond previous scholars by asking who voted for whom? Through statistical analysis of election returns, Benson found little to support Schlesinger's assumption that voters divided between the parties along class lines. Instead, his study showed Whig support to be strongest among British immigrants, Protestant "puritan" religious sects, and "native" Americans – that is, groups in the United States before 1790. Democrats, meanwhile, proved to be the party of non-British – especially Irish – immigrants, Catholics, and non-puritanical Protestants. In New York, Benson concluded, an individual's ethnic and religious identity appeared more influential on voting behavior than did national issues or class membership. The "concept" of Jacksonian democracy, as understood by the Progressives, appeared to Benson to represent myth, not reality, and he encouraged historians to abandon the

term because it "obscured rather than illuminated" (Benson, 1961: 333) their understanding of the era. "The Age of Egalitarianism" would be a more appropriate term,
he suggested, for it would direct historians to "account for the transformation from
the aristocratic liberal republic of the early nineteenth century to the populistic
egalitarian democracy of the mid-nineteenth century" (Benson, 1961: 337).

The Concept of Jacksonian Democracy was quickly recognized as a pioneering work
in the "new political history," which came to refer to studies like Benson's that
approached past politics with a heavy reliance on social science methodology and
theory. Benson's student, Ronald P. Formisano, considerably advanced Benson's
initial findings in works that came to be regarded as hallmarks of an "ethnocultural"
school, though Formisano himself disavowed the term. In The Birth of Mass Political
Parties: Michigan, 1827–1861 (1971), Formisano presented more analysis of aggregate social data and election returns to show once again that the parties did not reflect
socio-economic class divisions. Michigan's party conflict, he argued, emerged from
the popular Antimasonic crusade of the late 1820s and early 1830s, a debate over alien
suffrage at the 1835 state constitutional convention, and an evangelical desire to
promote a moral, Christian society. Whigs, Formisano concluded, succeeded Anti-
masons as a "Christian party" and drew their support from Presbyterians, Congregationalists, Baptists, and migrants to the territory from New York, New England, and
Britain. Non-British immigrants, who in Michigan consisted of Irishmen, Germans,
Dutch, and French Canadians, joined non-evangelicals who accepted "laissez-faire
ethics" (Formisano, 1971: 102) to form the majority Democratic party. Later, in The
Transformation of Political Culture: Massachusetts Parties, 1790s–1840s, Formisano
(1983: 6) described Bay State politics as characterized by a "Core" of "culturally
or religiously dominant groups seeking to maintain or extend their values" over
"Periphery" groups considered inferior by the "Core." Although the state experienced
an expansion of its electorate and an acceptance of political parties, the core–periphery
division that had underlain the Federalist–Republican split in the 1790s also became
the foundation of the Whig–Democratic confrontation, and "habits of deference in a
highly class- and status-conscious society" (Formisano, 1983: 22) persisted longer
than historians had usually assumed.

The work of Formisano and the new political historians significantly enriched the
study of the Jacksonian era. The ethnocultural approach showed that party division at
the local level usually developed from longstanding rivalries and negative associations
among various ethnic groups. They showed that political conflict could often involve
local differences over moral and cultural issues, like temperance and sabbatarianism,
rather than national economic policy. Their studies forced scholars to take seriously
the concept of "political culture," which Formisano, quoting John Stuart Mill,
defined as "those aspects of political life that are 'obvious and universal facts which
. . . every one sees and no one is astonished at, [and] it seldom occurs to any one to
place upon record'" (1983: 4). Their emphasis on the cultural aspect of politics made
once seemingly irrational movements, like the Antimasonic party, understandable as
serious expressions of popular concerns. Likewise, their revelation of the ethnic and
religious sources of party division opened for historians the grass roots world of the
once seemingly silent voter.

By directing attention away from the legislative halls to the hustings, however, the
contributions of the new political historians threatened the subject of Jacksonian

politics itself. Voters were assumed by the ethnoculturalists to be motivated by local cultural issues, while national issues came to be considered symbolic ones at best. National issues, in fact, became largely irrelevant to the new political historians. In the ethnocultural view, voters had little concern for banks, tariffs, and sectionalism – central topics for Progressive historians – as party leaders appeared to manipulate local confrontations in their efforts to create winning coalitions. Economic policy issues, meanwhile, undoubtedly dominated the national political scene, and it became increasingly difficult to see a relationship between the voters' concerns and the actions of party leaders. As Formisano (1971: 11) contended, "Historians who believe that the Bank War, states rights, or similar issues gave rise to political parties among the masses are wrongly extending the issue-orientation of limited segments of the electorate to all of it." Just as consensus historians had shown Whigs and Democrats to be united in their acceptance of liberal capitalism, and as more historians concluded that the American story was better understood through its social rather than its political history, political historians themselves seemed to find that the confrontations among political leaders had little relevance for non-elite Americans.

The contention that a wide gap separated voters from politicians was perhaps most clearly stated in Richard P. McCormick's *The Second American Party System: Party Formation in the Jacksonian Era* (1966). In this book, McCormick directed historians to consider the parties as institutions with their own dynamics rather than as organizations based upon principles or as the expression of either popular or special interests. Using traditional sources and drawing on the work of political scientist Maurice Duverger, McCormick argued that the Whig and Democratic organizations were "above all electoral machines, engaged in nominating candidates" (1966: 4) whose goal to win elections took precedence over class or group interests. "They possessed an interest of their own; they were active – rather than neutral – factors of the political process" (1966: 15). Like the ethnoculturalists, McCormick focused upon party formation in the states and found that politicians built parties within states upon factional divisions that were already present. The state organizations aligned with national parties at different rates that were determined by the popularity of regionally based presidential candidates. Party leaders developed the popular and "dramatic" campaign style that "afforded a general emotional experience" (1966: 16). Voter turnout was more affected by "the closeness of interparty competition," because campaign managers would intensify their effort to get out the vote in doubtful areas, than by "the presumed charismatic effect of candidates or the urgency of popular issues" (1966: 16). Electoral politics, in this view, was chiefly entertainment that had little impact on government decisions.

The ethnoculturalists continued to see local issues as having some significance for voters, but their findings, joined with McCormick's, had the cumulative effect of presenting Jacksonian politics as involving few substantive issues. Politics ultimately was a game between "ins and outs" who sought power for their own ends, whether it be a capitalist economic agenda or office for its own sake. For many historians, Andrew Jackson and his Democratic party now seemed irrelevant to the true significance of an era that bore the Hero's name. Recognition of the institutional role of the political parties seemed to confirm the unrepresentative nature of American politics: the issues over which the parties differed appeared to offer nothing toward an understanding of the American experience.

Not all were willing to concede the hollowness of the Jacksonian era. Another strain in the literature took seriously the rhetoric that politicians used to attract votes. These historians argued that the parties' appeals presented neither the description of reality that Schlesinger assumed nor the "claptrap" that McCormick saw, but a window into the ideology or "worldview" of a party's adherents. Even before the publication of *The Concept of Jacksonian Democracy*, Marvin Meyers's *The Jacksonian Persuasion: Politics and Belief* (1957) looked at the Jacksonian appeal in its social context and found "a half-formulated moral perspective involving emotional commitment" (1957: 10) that reflected shared values among Democrats. Meyers argued that, unlike Schlesinger's progressive liberals, the Jacksonians were better understood as conservative guardians of "a threatened republican tradition which demanded . . . right action taken from a solid moral stance" (1957: 17). In an era of increasing commercialism and liberal individualism, Meyers contended, Jacksonian society was "caught between the elements" of opportunities for economic advancement and the ideal of a simple, agrarian, yeoman republic. "Americans were boldly liberal in economic affairs . . . But they were not inwardly prepared for the grinding uncertainties, the shocking changes, the complexity and indirection of the new economic ways" (Meyers, 1957: 11). Democratic campaigns directed these unspoken anxieties against a "money power" – that is, those who gained their wealth through "financial manipulation and special privilege" (1957: 23) – and destroyed the Bank of the United States because they blamed it for "the transgressions committed by the people of their era against the political, social, and economic value of the Old Republic" (1957: 11). While Whigs addressed the hopes produced by modernization, Meyers (1957: 13) concluded, the Jacksonian Democrats "addressed their diffuse fears and resentments."

The attractions of the new political history diverted historians from immediately following Meyers's lead, but in the late 1960s renewed interest in the political ideology of the revolutionary era, particularly the emphasis on the commonwealth and republican traditions, reminded Jacksonian scholars that political language could likewise reveal much about their era. Several new works explored the appeals of both Whigs and Democrats with a view toward recapturing the worldviews that divided the parties while binding together politicians and voters. These studies were also built upon the growing recognition that in the first half of the nineteenth century the national economy was experiencing a fundamental transformation. Historians had long known the era as one of growth identified with the early stages of the American Industrial Revolution. The influence of these conditions played a central role in Meyers's argument in *The Jacksonian Persuasion*, and Benson suggested that the "egalitarian revolution after 1815" might largely have been the product of what George R. Taylor had called the "Transportation Revolution" (Benson, 1961: 337). By the 1970s, however, economic historians were viewing the pre-Civil War years less as a period of industrialization as of increasing commercialization. As more studies provided evidence that Americans were moving away from a subsistence-oriented way of life to one centered upon production for and dependence on a market economy, social historians argued that this "market revolution" entailed a change in *mentalité* from a pre-modern, community-based ethic to the acceptance of individualistic, competitive, *laissez-faire* capitalism.

For political historians, the tension produced by the market revolution placed the economic issues separating Whigs and Democrats in a different light. For many, it confirmed that economic policy remained the central focus of the era's politics. James Roger Sharp, in *The Jacksonians versus the Banks* (1970), surveyed banking and currency debates at the state level throughout the Union and found distrust of banks to be "the crucible" of the Democratic party. The Jacksonians, Sharp concluded, were best understood as the "representatives of an agrarian society who felt that their moral values were being eroded away by the commercialization of society and the quickening tempo of industry" (1970: 6). William G. Shade's *Banks or No Banks: the Money Issue in Western Politics, 1832–1865* (1972) examined politics in the Old Northwestern states with the approach and outlook of an ethnoculturalist. Shade concluded that economic issues were indeed significant for party conflict, but he presented a compelling case for these questions to be understood not simply as reflections of a conflict between *"the haves and have-nots"* but as *"an aspect of the broader conflict between political subcultures that structured partisan controversy within the area"* (Shade, 1972: 18). For Sharp and Shade, the old economic policy questions that had once concerned Progressive historians now appeared to provide a key toward understanding the social contexts of differing ideologies. Contentious debates over banks, currency, and tariffs did seem to matter after all, and the Jacksonian political struggles once again seemed to have a significance that reached deeply into the public consciousness.

One of the most important studies revealing the political significance of the market revolution examined state politics in the South. The presence of slavery and the region's attempt to defend the institution through secession and Civil War had long encouraged historians to view the protection of slavery as the only legitimate concern in the region. Ethnocultural historians, meanwhile, had found it difficult to apply their approach to the region because of its relative ethnic homogeneity and the dominance of its evangelical religious culture. But in the first section of *Politics and Power in a Slave Society: Alabama, 1800–1860* (1978), J. Mills Thornton III presented a detailed and subtle analysis of what he called differing political "styles" in a state moving from the Old Southwestern frontier to the heart of the Confederacy. Thornton agreed that white Alabamians were united in defense of slavery, but he also found them to be deeply divided between a Whig party that sought to harness government power for the promotion of economic development and a Democratic party that considered government power's primary function to be the protection of individual citizens from the machinations of the powerful. The central difference between these styles, Thornton concluded, was their divergent conceptions of freedom in an era of economic transformation. For Democrats, particularly small upcountry farmers with limited connections to the markets, "the substance of freedom was lack of economic dependence upon other men"; for Whigs, who were strongest in the black belt plantation region and in the state's small towns and cities, the only way to achieve full manhood and self-reliance was through "the amassing of a 'competence,' of sufficient wealth for one's ordinary needs. Therefore, the road to freedom was the road to prosperity and economic development" (Thornton, 1978: 57). Thornton went on to show how the commitment to protect white freedom placed Alabama on the road to Civil War. For scholars of the Jacksonian era, however, *Politics and Power in a Slave Society* presented one of the strongest arguments to date that the economic issues of the 1820s through the 1840s involved less a conflict of material interest than a contest between competing cultural interpretations of the meaning of modernization.

Over the next decade, several works continued to focus on the social, cultural, and intellectual aspects of the political parties. Two works presented the first careful studies of the attitudes, assumptions, and beliefs of the Jacksonians' opponents, the Whigs, and found that the party presented a coherent social ethic that rivaled the worldview of the Democrats. In *The Political Culture of the American Whigs*, Daniel Walker Howe (1979: 3) described Whiggery as "a culture rather than merely as a party, because the culture was more powerful than the party." According to Howe, Whigs did champion economic development, but they too were disturbed by many of the changes brought on by modernization. While desiring economic diversity and prosperity, they considered commercialism's challenges to hierarchical social assumptions, its encouragement of individualism, and its acceptance of cultural diversity to be threats to a harmonious and morally progressive society. Howe found in party rhetoric an emphasis on a commitment to "improvement," a concern for " 'duties' rather than 'rights,' " and a belief in the organic unity of society that was concerned with muting social conflict. Through biographical studies of several leading Whigs, who often disagreed on specific policies, Howe concluded that Whiggery in general was motivated by moral absolutism, a sense of paternalism, and a desire to give direction to a society that could easily lose control of itself. Six years later, Thomas Brown's *Politics and Statesmanship: Essays on the American Whig Party* (1985) expanded on Howe's interpretation by emphasizing the Whigs' commitment to the republican ideal of statesmanship – "moderation, self-restraint, rational persuasion, and a positive passion for the public good" (Brown, 1985: 11–12) – in an era in which politics was moving toward mass organizations that placed ever-increasing premiums on party loyalty. "The history – and the failures – of the Whigs," Brown (1985: 12) argued, "may be traced, in part, through their efforts to remain true to their ideal of statesmanship while functioning within a two-party system of politics."

Others engaged in studies directly comparing the origins and appeal of the Whigs and Democrats. Harry L. Watson's *Jacksonian Politics and Community Conflict: the Emergence of the Second American Party System in Cumberland County, North Carolina* (1981) used an ethnocultural approach to explore party formation in a southern county where a large minority of Highland Scots had been Loyalists during the American Revolution. While the hostility between the Scots and the county's other residents, along with cleavages along geographic and class lines, influenced voting during the years of the first party system, Watson found these divisions surpassed during the 1820s by an increasing conflict between Fayetteville, the county seat, and the rural countryside. This newer friction reflected the growing importance of commerce in conjunction with national economic development. Particularly after the Panic of 1837 made clear the potential consequences of commercialization, "the pivotal partisan controversy arose over questions of political economy. In effect, the voters had to decide how they wanted their community to fit into the rapidly developing world of international capitalism" (Watson, 1981: 14). As local rivalries, however, became fixed in the institutionalized parties by the 1840s, a political system that had arisen from a "fundamental social conflict" then "side-stepped" that conflict (1981: 322). As Democratic leaders moved eventually to accept the positive government action advocated by their opponents, they diverted challenges to the economic development into "harmless rituals" and "strengthened the national commitment to technological improvement and commercialized production" (1981: 324). This "national consensus in favor of individual liberty and technological progress," Watson (1981: 324) concluded, became a permanent and significant legacy of the Whig and Democratic confrontation.

John Ashworth and Lawrence Frederick Kohl, meanwhile, presented close readings of the parties' ideologies as revealed through the speeches and writings of their adherents in works that further highlighted the impact of the market transformation. In *"Agrarians" and "Aristocrats": Party Political Ideology in the United States, 1837–1846* (1983), Ashworth built his argument for the intellectual gulf separating Democrats and Whigs upon the contention of the incompatibility of democracy and capitalism. According to Ashworth, Jacksonian democracy contained "a clear leveling thrust" that implied "an agrarian, pre-capitalist society" (1983: 1) and rejected the era's prevailing commercial spirit. With development driving the American economy "on a collision course with the American democratic tradition" (1983: 50), radical Democrats sought "to utilize the power that democracy gave to the individual in order to resist those social and political forces which took it away" (1983: 51). Whigs presented a conservative response to the Democrats' egalitarianism in an avowedly elitist party that aggressively promoted the capitalist expansion that Democrats feared. "Radical Democrats and conservative Whigs," Ashworth contended, "wished to alter the course which the nation was taking" (1983: 271). The moderate factions of each party, however, managed to subdue the extremists and create the parties' consensus on an apparent reconciliation of the two ideals. Kohl, in *The Politics of Individualism: Parties and the American Character in the Jacksonian Era* (1989), meanwhile saw the party debates over economic issues as an outgrowth of different responses to modernization and its breakdown of traditional social institutions. As social relations became less structured by family and community, Kohl argued, the "central concern of the Jacksonian generation was the transition ... to a society based on an ethic of individualism" (1989: 6). Adopting the language of sociologist David Riesman, Kohl concluded that those best described as "inner-directed," or "comfortable with the impersonal, self-interested relationships which characterize an individualistic society, became Whigs." Those who "still felt bound to others in more personal ways" or were "tradition-directed" (1989: 6) were usually Democrats.

By the early 1990s, research on the Jacksonian era had moved far enough away from the Progressive view for a new, over-arching interpretation to seem in order, and two historians attempted to present new syntheses – the first such attempts in more than 30 years. Watson's *Liberty and Power: the Politics of Jacksonian America* (1990) located the party conflict at the center of the period. Whigs and Democrats offered contrasting versions of a common republican ideological tradition, and these appeals were constructed upon divergent responses to the impact of the market revolution. Andrew Jackson was a visible and influential force because he "could express in his words and his life the linkages between the egalitarian ideology of his age and the near-sacred precepts of the Founding Fathers" (1990: 10). Yet while Jacksonian democracy liberated men from "many of the deferential constraints of eighteenth-century political culture," the resultant party system "tended to channel popular democratic energies in conservative directions, giving recognition to the popular feelings while blunting their potentially disruptive consequences" (1990: 13). Charles Sellers presented a more pessimistic assessment in *The Market Revolution: Jacksonian America, 1815–1846* (1991). Sellers emphasized the profound cultural differences arising from the contrasting subsistence and market modes of production as he centered his account upon capitalism's expanding influence and its creation of a bourgeois society. Still, *The Market Revolution* also recognized the political story to be crucial to the era as Sellers emphasized how political development "crystallized a politics that has ever since muffled the contradiction between capitalism and democracy in a mythology of consensual and democratic enterprise." While Whigs became "unabashed champions of enterprise and the bourgeois/middle class ethic," Sellers contended, Democrats "performed the more difficult and ethically ambiguous function ... of pacifying popular discontent at the least possible cost to business" (1991: 363).

While *Liberty and Power* and *The Market Revolution* reflected how far historians had moved away from Schlesinger's *The Age of Jackson*, Watson's and Sellers's books were presented to a historical profession that no longer considered the era as a crucial one in American history. Notwithstanding the work of scholars from the 1950s to the 1980s, for many American historians the Jacksonian period remained one dominated by elite white politicians, and the only significance of the era's politics appeared to lie in its connection with the coming of the Civil War. The rise of postmodernism in academia suggests that many new historians will approach an era named after a slave-owning, Indian-slaying military hero with little interest. Yet research in the second half of the twentieth century has shown that the study of the Jacksonian era in its own right still has a lot to offer for an understanding of the American experience. At the very least, this work has prevented the era from falling into oblivion. At its best, it has shown how developments in the era did affect the future course of the nation's economic and political systems, and how both were deeply involved in the type of society that the American republic would become.

The most promising new directions for research have been suggested by historians focusing on those groups usually considered indirectly or adversely affected by electoral politics. Women, long thought of as non-participants because of their exclusion from voting, have been shown in Elizabeth Varon's *We Mean to be Counted: White Women and Politics in Antebellum Virginia* (1998) to have taken active roles in campaigns and party activities that reflected and reinforced the middle-class and elite image of women as morally pure and selfless beings. Sean Wilentz's *Chants Democratic: New York City and the Rise of the American Working Class, 1788–1850* (1984) meanwhile has presented the most careful analysis of the party system's relationship to the development of working-class consciousness. These pioneering works should stimulate further research on how the Jacksonian political system affected the lives of women and workers and might direct scholars to consider more closely its influences on the social constructions of race and ethnicity as well.

In a similar vein, other historians have shown the potential value of broadening the definition of "political culture" to include its wider cultural implications. The ethno-culturalists first suggested a correlation between a "pietistic" religious ethic and Whig politics and between liturgical religions and the Democrats. Denominational affiliations often did not clearly align with a particular party in local studies, however, and only recently has Richard Carwardine (1993) fully explained the impact of evangelicalism on antebellum politics in the North. Simon P. Newman, Len Travers, and David Waldstreicher have broken new ground in their studies of festive culture, Independence Day observations, and public celebrations in the generation after the American Revolution. Studies of similar events and symbols in the Jacksonian era's popular culture will not only further the understanding of the "political world" in which Democrats and Whigs struggled, but will provide an intriguing point of comparison for Newman's, Travers's, and Waldstreicher's arguments for early republican political culture.

Promising avenues also remain for more traditional approaches in political history. Some scholars have turned from the issue of who won control of the government to asking simply what government in the early nineteenth century was actually doing. Studies by Daniel Feller on public land policy in the Jacksonian era and by Richard R. John on the postal system indicate that government actions both influenced the era's political and social alignments and reflected larger cultural concerns. Questions such as "Who worked for the government?" and "What effects did they have?" should provoke investigations into the careers of clerks, Indian agents, customs officials, and other public employees. At the state level, much work remains to be done in investigating the political economies of local governments and the extent to which Americans always expected minimal, *laissez-faire* government. Although Jacksonian scholars have always been conscious of sectionalism in politics, comparative studies of political practices in northern and southern communities might help clarify the degree to which the antebellum republic was united by a national culture or was dividing into distinct northern and southern civilizations.

Finally, the next generation of historians should produce re-examinations of major "events" in the Jacksonian era in light of the interpretations produced by the past 30 years of scholarship. The Bank War and the Nullification crisis have been well covered, and the Eaton Affair has begun to receive attention as a crisis over gender roles. New studies of topics such as the election of 1824, the Panic of 1837, Rhode Island's Dorr Rebellion, and the origins of "Manifest Destiny" could reveal as much about American society and culture as about elite politicians. These and other subjects should once more confirm the Jacksonian era's position as a field still worthy of historians' attention.

REFERENCES

Ashworth, John (1983) *"Agrarians" and "Aristocrats": Party Political Ideology in the United States, 1837–1846*. Cambridge. Cambridge University Press.

Benson, Lee (1961) *The Concept of Jacksonian Democracy: New York as a Test Case*. Princeton, NJ: Princeton University Press.

Brown, Thomas (1985) *Politics and Statesmanship: Essays on the American Whig Party*. New York: Columbia University Press.

Carwardine, Richard J. (1993) *Evangelicals and Politics in Antebellum America*. New Haven, Conn.: Yale University Press.

Formisano, Ronald P. (1971) *The Birth of Mass Political Parties: Michigan, 1827–1861*. Princeton, NJ: Princeton University Press.

Formisano, Ronald P. (1983) *The Transformation of Political Culture: Massachusetts Parties, 1790s–1840s*. New York: Oxford University Press.

Hammond, Bray (1957) *Banks and Politics in America from the Revolution to the Civil War*. Princeton, NJ: Princeton University Press.

Hofstadter, Richard (1948/1973) *The American Political Tradition and the Men who Made It*. New York: Vintage Books.

Howe, Daniel Walker (1979) *The Political Culture of the American Whigs.* Chicago: University of Chicago Press.

Kohl, Lawrence Frederick (1989) *The Politics of Individualism: Parties and the American Character in the Jacksonian Era.* New York: Oxford University Press.

McCormick, Richard P. (1966) *The Second American Party System: Party Formation in the Jacksonian Era.* Chapel Hill, NC: University of North Carolina Press.

Meyers, Marvin (1957) *The Jacksonian Persuasion: Politics and Belief.* Stanford, CA: Stanford University Press.

Pessen, Edward (1985) *Jacksonian America: Society, Personality, Politics.* Urbana, Ill.: University of Illinois Press.

Remini, Robert V. (1976) *The Revolutionary Age of Andrew Jackson.* New York: Harper and Row.

Schlesinger Jr, Arthur M. (1945) *The Age of Jackson.* Boston: Little, Brown and Co.

Sellers, Charles (1991) *The Market Revolution: Jacksonian America, 1815–1846.* New York: Oxford University Press.

Shade, William G. (1972) *Banks or No Banks: the Money Issue in Western Politics, 1832–1865.* Detroit: Wayne State University Press.

Sharp, James Roger (1970) *The Jacksonians versus the Banks: Politics in the States after the Panic of 1837.* New York: Columbia University Press.

Thornton III, J. Mills (1978) *Politics and Power in a Slave Society: Alabama, 1800–1860.* Baton Rouge: Louisiana State University Press.

Varon, Elizabeth (1998) *We Mean to be Counted: White Women and Politics in Antebellum Virginia.* Chapel Hill, NC: University of North Carolina Press.

Watson, Harry L. (1981) *Jacksonian Politics and Community Conflict: the Emergence of the Second American Party System in Cumberland County, North Carolina.* Baton Rouge: Louisiana State University Press.

Watson, Harry L. (1990) *Liberty and Power: the Politics of Jacksonian America.* New York: Hill and Wang.

Wilentz, Sean (1984) *Chants Democratic: New York City and the Rise of the American Working Class, 1788–1850.* New York: Oxford University Press.

CHAPTER THREE

The Sectionalization of Politics, 1845–1860

JOHN ASHWORTH

E VEN the most cursory examination of American politics in 1860–1 reveals a dramatic change of agenda from the mid-1840s. In effect an inversion had taken place. Where in the earlier decade, sectional questions had been present, but had been subordinate to the party questions which had for a dozen years divided Whig and Democrat, by the time of the election of 1860 sectional tensions had eclipsed the older party issues and were indeed about to plunge the nation into the carnage that was the American Civil War.

So the process of sectionalization is undeniable. But historians have not been able to agree on an explanation for it. Of course, the origins of the Civil War form a subject which has been hotly debated since the war itself, and recent historiography suggests that a consensus is as far away as ever. In recent decades, many divergent explanations have been offered. Some scholars have emphasized factors located deep within the American social, political, or economic system and which were, therefore, to a considerable degree, beyond the control of the politicians who took the nation into Civil War. Others have stressed factors which were to a large extent, accidental – at least in the sense that they were unrelated or incidental to the sectional controversy – or which derived from the purely personal weaknesses of the individuals involved. The first of these are in reality more profound causes, not in the sense that they are necessarily more valid or powerful, but simply because they locate the central problems at a deeper level within the structures of American society, economy, or government. They are structural or systemic causes; by contrast, those interpretations which emphasize accident or personal weakness are, in a real sense, anti-structural.

At the risk of over-simplifying, it is possible to construct a spectrum of opinion here, with the most profound causal explanations (structural) at one pole and the least profound (again using the phrase in its non-pejorative sense to denote non-structural) at the other. This partly repeats the old division, common in the historiography of the Civil War, between interpretations which see the conflict as inevitable or "irrepressible", on the one hand, and those which instead insist that the war could have been avoided and was therefore eminently "repressible."

Yet although the war is perhaps the principal event in the whole of American history, certainly since the revolution, the subject has in recent years receded in importance. In part this is because political history generally has been in retreat; it has come to be seen as the study of dead white males – and elite white males at that. As social history has triumphed, subjects like the Civil War have been at least partly neglected, despite the fact that the war itself produced social consequences on a vast, indeed an epic, scale.

Nevertheless, the enthronement of social history has helped as well as hindered our understanding of the coming of the Civil War. It is now generally accepted that a history of American politics in the late 1840s and 1850s can no longer be written simply from the vantage point of the White House, the Congress, and the Supreme Court. The social historian's rediscovery of local issues, one suspects, has forced political historians to recognize the central importance of politics at local and state levels. The emphasis on the role of ethnocultural issues, especially nativism and temperance, is almost certainly a product of this process. Moreover, some historians have insisted that an understanding of the sectional controversy requires an analysis of religious developments and affiliations, of family structure as well as of the more obvious economic implications of a slave-based labor system in the South and one based upon free labor in the North. Although none of these questions was entirely absent from the older analyses of the war and its origins, there is no doubt that they have come into much sharper focus in recent decades.

Even so, the proliferation of material has brought problems. A major difficulty is that social and economic developments necessarily operate at a different pace, and according to different rhythms, from political ones. It is therefore difficult to maintain a stress on the former while doing justice to a narrative account of the latter. Also the sheer mass of secondary material available is an ever-growing problem as well as an opportunity. What a full study of the war's origins may now require is a treatment of abolitionists and pro-slavery theorists, of the northern and southern economies, of federal politics in the crucial decades before Lincoln's election and of state politics North and South in the same period. But this in turn probably requires an understanding of the ideology of the major parties – Democrat, Whig, and Republican, as well as that of the minor parties, Know Nothings, Free Soilers, Constitutional Unionists, and the rest. And if a full-scale study needs in addition an analysis of religion, family structure, and even gender roles, north and south of the Mason–Dixon line, it is scarcely surprising that very few such studies have appeared.

As if this were not enough, there is an additional pitfall awaiting the author of such a study, though in truth one that is rarely acknowledged. The era in which the Civil War and the ending of southern slavery took place also saw the destruction of unfree labor in many countries of the world, and not merely because of the direct influence of one political movement upon another. If this is not to be reduced to a coincidence, it is necessary to find common causes. Yet the historian who seeks to synthesize existing interpretations of the Civil War will be faced with many factors – the West, immigration, the American political system, the ideology of republicanism and others – which are purely American in scope. Historians generally strain to offer multi-causal explanations, yet causal pluralism here, as elsewhere, poses its own problems.

Revisionists and the Beardian Approach

The most venerable of the non-structural interpretations of the war is the so-called "revisionist" view. Revisionist historians, with Avery Craven and James G. Randall at their head, argued strongly that the failures of individual politicians and agitators were critical. Northern abolitionists and radical Republicans, along with southern fire-eaters, were the guilty men. It followed that better statesmanship might well have averted the war (Craven, 1939; Randall, 1945). This interpretation was also present, albeit in a qualified form, in the most recent of the multi-volume surveys of the sectional crisis and the Civil War, that of Allan Nevins (1950). Since that time few historians have endorsed this view, at any rate to the extent of elevating it to the status of a major cause of the war.

Why has a fully fledged revisionism, which places the responsibility squarely upon the shoulders of blundering politicians, all but disappeared? It is partly, perhaps, because such an interpretation implies political history of the narrowest kind: federal, and elitist with little attention to social or economic factors. More important, how-ever, are revisionism's internal weaknesses. For it clearly lacked a solid logical founda-tion. Time and again, in the work of Allan Nevins for example, prominent politicians were graded according to some apparently absolute standard of statesmanship and those of the 1850s – with the notable exception of Abraham Lincoln – were generally judged inferior to those of the 1830s and 1840s. Missing here was any recognition that the problems of the 1850s, being more intractable than those of the earlier decades, were more likely to confound the statesmen who had to contend with them. In other words, revisionism prompted an obvious objection. Whereas it assumed that the failures of the statesmen produced the sectional crisis, it failed to confront the rather obvious possibility that the sectional crisis produced the failures of the statesmen. And, indeed, revisionists themselves, even with a century of hindsight, often failed to offer alternative, more viable, solutions. When they did so, they frequently advanced arguments that were highly tendentious, that raised, but did not answer, more fundamental questions. For example, it was true, as revisionists claimed, that by 1860 there was no territory yet to be settled, and that therefore the struggle for a federal slave code (to protect slavery in the territories) which split the Democratic party and helped usher in the Republicans, was of theoretical rather than immediate practical interest. But this did not justify the conclusion that a wise states-man would simply have ignored the issue. For each side knew full well that the controversy lacked immediate political significance; and each therefore argued that it was easy for the other to concede. The refusal to do so confirmed, on the one hand, a dangerous and implacable hostility or, on the other hand, a retrograde and per-nicious attachment to the institution of slavery. The revisionist claim necessitated, but was not accompanied by, a refutation of these points, and the fabric of the argument accordingly has looked increasingly threadbare.

It is possible to argue that any war – indeed any event in human history – is the product of mere accident. In fact, few historians, and none in recent decades, have made this claim for the American Civil War or the sectionalization of politics that occurred between 1845 and 1860. It is, of course, an extreme anti-structural inter-pretation and in this sense it is akin to revisionism. Yet if both these anti-structural interpretations lack formal devotees, both can be glimpsed within the interstices of other explanations. Indeed, there is, as we shall see, a tendency toward a slippage: historians in effect assign either to accident or to the purely personal deficiencies of statesmen a greater role than they themselves acknowledge or are perhaps even aware of. As a result the objections to these anti-structural factors remain unrecognized, and therefore, of course, unrefuted.

At this point it is appropriate to consider the classic interpretation of Charles A. Beard, not because he now has many disciples, but because the objections to his position are more important than is generally recognized. Beard's was a structural interpretation; he found a fundamental clash between North and South which was simply not amenable to compromise. In a sense he was reiterating the ideas expressed by William H. Seward in his "Irrepressible Conflict" speech of 1858 but with a major difference. Whereas Seward stressed the role of slavery, Beard instead argued that the sectional controversy was in fact a struggle for power between different interest groups, agrarians in the South and financiers and industrialists in the North, with slavery merely a symbol of their divergence. Indeed, Beard thought slavery of little importance in accounting for the sectionalization of American politics (Beard and Beard, 1933).

The problems with this view are well known. First, it reduced ideas and ideology to economic interests in the crudest way, denying, for example, the obvious moral commitment to African Americans that was evident in the writings of abolitionists and many Republicans. Secondly, it exaggerated the Republicans' commitment to economic policies in 1860 and underestimated their commitment to anti-slavery. Thirdly, it failed to meet the objection that dissimilar economic interests might create interdependence and therefore promote unity rather than division within the nation.

The last of these objections is the critical one. For although no historians in recent years have endorsed Beard's view, it has nevertheless been replaced by an analytical schema which is open to the same objection. The problem is that a "slavery" interpretation does not necessarily imply an "irrepressible conflict" any more than a Beardian one. Even if the South was committed to slavery, and the North equally committed to free labor, why should the two have collided? Why was compromise not possible? As we shall see, it is in answering this question that historians have fallen back, often without being aware of it, upon the role of accident or the personal weaknesses of the politicians involved.

So an impasse has been reached. The anti-structural interpretations – stressing accident or personal weakness – have been discredited and, in a formal sense, discarded, but the "structural" interpretations at present lack the solidity fully to take their place. In effect we have a synthesis but it is one which threatens to combine not the strengths, but rather the weaknesses, of each approach.

Anti-slavery, the West, and the Ethnoculturalists

In recent years, the role of slavery and of anti-slavery in the antebellum economy, society, and polity has been completely reassessed. Among the beneficiaries of this reassessment have been the previously derided and reviled "extremists" on both sides: the abolitionists and radical Republicans of the North and the fire-eaters and pro-slavery theorists of the South. The ideas of both sets of extremists have been taken far more seriously than ever before and historians have gone far toward reconstructing, with a large measure of empathic understanding, the worldview of each group.

It has, however, proved far more difficult to explain the rise of anti-slavery sentiment. The economic vitality of the slave system and the billions of dollars invested in it go far toward accounting for the growth of pro-slavery ideology, and the corresponding commitment to free labor can be attributed, in parallel fashion, to the success of the northern economy. But while a commitment to free labor necessitated a hostility to slavery in the North, this did not in itself require an anti-slavery movement for the simple reason that slavery did not, by the final antebellum decades, exist in the North. So why should northern abolitionists have waged war upon a labor system that existed hundreds or even thousands of miles away? After all, slavery had been tolerated for hundreds or even thousands of years by communities and societies in which free labor was dominant if not universal, so it is by no means obvious why it should have aroused such heated criticism from the 1780s, and especially the 1830s onwards.

This question has not, perhaps, been satisfactorily answered. While some historians have stressed the links between revivalist religion and abolitionism, not all abolitionists were converts to evangelical Christianity, still less were all evangelical Christians abolitionists. And such an interpretation in any case merely prompts a further question: why the rise of evangelical Christianity? Moreover, while an interpretation of abolitionism which sees it as a product of the increasing enlightenment of Western society, as in effect a function or manifestation of the "progress" which Western nations were now experiencing, has been jettisoned, it has been difficult to find an alternative.

The most promising alternative approach is almost certainly to seek a materialist interpretation of anti-slavery, that is to say, an interpretation which successfully locates the roots of abolitionism in the economic changes within the host society. Two such attempts have been made, though with primary reference to anti-slavery in Britain rather than the United States, by David Brion Davis and Thomas Haskell. In effect, Davis argued that abolitionism was "always related to the need to legitimate free wage labor" in that the abolitionist, whether consciously or not, diverted attention from evils close at home to those on the far-off plantation. In this sense, he concludes, the abolitionists "helped to strengthen the invisible chains being forged at home" (Davis, 1975: 287). Haskell meanwhile made some damaging criticisms of the Davis thesis, and was especially critical of its emphasis upon unconscious motivation. Instead, he proposed to associate material change with the growth of anti-slavery by stressing the role of the market and of the greater number of "recipes" which capitalist development placed at the disposal of the reformer who felt responsibility for evils such as slavery in far-away places. The greater potential for successful intervention across distances that would once have prohibited all action, in other words, allowed the reformer to apply the Golden Rule and concern himself with the well-being of slaves in distant lands (or states) (Bender, 1992).

Neither of these views has commanded widespread adherence, though both are frequently (and justly) cited. The Davis view probably underestimates the challenge posed by abolitionism to the status quo even in the North, and certainly within the nation as a whole. Abolitionists were far from being conservative defenders of everything, including the wages system, that was northern, and it is possible that overall they provoked, rather than deflected, criticism of the northern social order. But the Haskell view probably neglects the contradictory impact of the market, which led many to conclude that they must leave undisturbed distant actions and activities on which they were now newly dependent. As a result, the question of the relationship between material change and the growth of humanitarianism, or between capitalism and anti-slavery, awaits a satisfactory resolution (Bender, 1992).

Of course, abolitionism contained within it a political critique of slavery and of its aggressions, and it is therefore tempting to explain its growth as a reaction to the growth of pro-slavery and the aggressions of southern politicians. The problem, however, is that pro-slavery can, with equal plausibility, be explained as a defensive reaction to anti-slavery. If both interpretations were correct, then it would follow that the sectional crisis was the product of needless misunderstanding, simple misfortune, or poor statesmanship. In other words, one would be forced back, almost without realizing it, to the anti-structural emphases upon defective politicians or the role of chance.

The same emphasis upon chance factors appears in the work of most historians who stress either the role of the West or of the so-called ethnocultural issues in the sectionalization of American politics. Westward expansion, itself brought about, it might be claimed, by a bi-sectional agreement on the need for more territory, nevertheless provoked sectional hostilities since it opened up the question of the status of slavery in new territories and future states. Clearly this was a major political issue, perhaps *the* major issue of the 1850s and the secession crisis of 1860–1. So it is possible to claim – and historians such as David Potter and Michael A. Morrison have made this claim either explicitly or implicitly – that without the problem of the West the sectionalization of American politics would either have proceeded very differently or not at all (Potter, 1976; Morrison, 1997).

Those historians who emphasize the role of the West normally argue that it exacerbated rather than created the sectional conflict. According to Potter, whereas slavery divided northerners from southerners, it was the conflict over its status in the West that fueled the sectional crisis. But this view is highly problematic. For it risks the familiar slide into revisionism. It ought to have been possible to arrive at a compromise if the West *per se* were alone at issue. Why could the Missouri Compromise line not have been extended to the Pacific? Then both sides would have had ample territory to colonize. Was this not an abject failure of statesmanship?

Of course, the problem was not so simple: the West was believed by many northerners and southerners to hold the key to the future status of slavery across the entire nation. If northerners wanted an anti-slavery nation, with slavery merely an anomalous relic within it, this implied northern dominance of the West. But the same goal implied resistance on the part of any southerners who demanded for slavery equality of status and of political power within the nation. In other words, we are back to the (unresolved) question of the origins and function of anti-slavery sentiment.

Other objections are equally applicable. We need to ask whether the debate over the West actually propelled the struggle over slavery or was instead merely the channel along which these irresistible currents of controversy happened to flow. There is much evidence to suggest the latter. For although the West was the obvious and most conspicuous site for this struggle, it was not the only one. Had there been no West to expand into, the status of slavery in the border states – highly problematic as it was – might have become the focus of concern. Moreover, if westward expansion fueled the slavery controversy, the slavery controversy also fueled westward expansion. It has now become clear that fears over the status of slavery in Texas (which was the target of British anti-slavery zeal) in the 1840s played a major part in producing the territorial gains of the 1840s. It is now equally clear that fears over slavery in Missouri played a key role in creating the conflicts over Kansas in the 1850s (Freehling, 1990). In each case the vulnerability of slavery was crucial. Finally, it has been plausibly argued that southerners needed more territory for slavery, and were therefore impelled to favor expansion into the West (Barney, 1974). There is no doubt that these demands were frequently voiced in the final decades of the Old South, though their relative importance is still, perhaps, open to dispute. But, if any of these arguments has merit, one is entitled to wonder whether the West was more the occasion than the cause of sectional strife, and whether the structural needs and requirements of slavery did not in any case provide much of the momentum for the westward movement in the first place. In other words, the attempt to raise "the West" to the status of a major causal factor has not, as yet, been entirely successful.

The same verdict can be passed upon those accounts which have emphasized the role of another set of factors that were, in themselves, unrelated to the sectional controversy: the ethnocultural issues. Some historians have noted the effect of immigration, and of nativist hostility to immigrants, and, to a lesser extent, of the temperance movement, in bringing about the collapse of the second party system between Democrats and Whigs in the mid-1850s. Clearly this collapse played a major role in transforming the political agenda and thus facilitating the triumph of sectionalism and, equally clearly, the wave of immigration (or the move to restrict or outlaw drinking) had little to do with any sectional hostility between North and South. Although these ethnocultural historians do not, in general, seek to explain the Civil War, they are implicitly proposing another accidental factor as crucial to the sectionalizing process (Holt, 1978; Silbey, 1985).

The role of immigration, of nativism, and of temperance in the sectionalization of American politics is one that resists easy generalizations. It is now apparent that the political upheaval that occurred in the mid-1850s was not simply, as used to be believed, the product of the controversy unleashed by the Kansas–Nebraska Act. Historians who have looked at the Know Nothing movement have established the prevalence of fears of immigrants, and especially of Roman Catholic immigrants, among the native-born in these years, following the upsurge in immigration around mid-century. The temporal power of the Catholic church was clearly a subject of genuine concern for many Protestant Americans, and the economic dislocations that were partly the result of increased immigration – but also partly the result of the economic growth process itself – gave the issue an additional impetus. In many states, nativism (and temperance too) attracted more voters than anti-slavery, even after Stephen A. Douglas had introduced his famous bill to organize Kansas and Nebraska in early 1854. It has also been argued that the Republican party itself, in its earliest years, was heavily influenced by nativism and temperance, and that its supporters stressed these issues even more than anti-slavery.

What are we to make of these claims? Unquestionably, the traditional focus on high politics served to obscure the role of nativism and temperance in the upheaval of the mid-1850s. It is safe to assume that there will be no reversion to the traditional view. But it is not yet clear that immigration was a major political issue throughout the decade. Indeed, even those like William Gienapp, who have emphasized the role of ethnocultural issues in destroying the second party system and in facilitating the rise of the Republican party, acknowledge that, by the election of 1856, anti-slavery was uppermost, both in northern politics generally as a source of opposition to the Democracy and, more specifically, within the Republican party itself. And still later in the decade nativism receded further as a political force, though historians do not yet agree about the extent of the concessions Republicans had to make to win over its former adherents (Gienapp, 1987).

In other words, it has yet to be demonstrated that the ethnocultural upsurge, as it might be termed, of the mid-1850s did any more than temporarily deflect the attention of the electorate and the politicians. Even if the ethnocultural issues did destabilize the second party system and play a key role in destroying the Whig party (though this remains controversial), this is not to say that the slavery question would not have also soon acquired this potential. Indeed, slavery demonstrated that it could wreck the Know Nothing party itself a little later in the 1850s and then wreck the Democratic party, the strongest political institution in the nation, in 1860. So it clearly had tremendous disruptive power.

The Republicans and Secession

In recent years two major controversies have dominated the political history of the 1850s and early 1860s. One of these is the traditional question, unavoidable in any discussion of sectionalization and the coming of the war: why did the South secede in 1860–1? The other is much newer; indeed, it is a question largely ignored until recently: what was the essence of Republican ideology and what explains the party's appeal to voters between the mid-1850s and 1860? Clearly, a resolution of these two questions would take us far toward an understanding of the entire sectional conflict.

Older studies of the Civil War tended to ignore the ideology of the Republican party, either because it was thought to be self-evident and therefore not worthy of close attention, or because party ideology itself was believed to be unimportant. But recently a productive debate has taken place. Broadly speaking, three schools of thought have developed. The first dates from the publication of Eric Foner's work, *Free Soil, Free Labor, Free Men: the Ideology of the Republican Party before the Civil War* (1970), perhaps the most influential single volume on antebellum politics to have appeared in the past few decades. Foner argued that the Republicans were indeed an anti-slavery party, with their hostility to slavery rooted not in a moral concern for African Americans (though he insisted that this was indeed widespread among Republicans) but rather in their commitment to the economic, political, and social values entailed by free labor. The Republicans were thus pre-eminently a free-soil party, but their insistence upon a West reserved for free labor was part of a larger and entirely authentic dislike of slavery. They were hostile to slavery but, out of respect for constitutional constraints, could not directly attack slavery in the states where it already existed (Foner, 1970).

Clearly, this view has enormous implications for the coming of the war. If correct, it would mean that slavery and anti-slavery were indeed the driving forces behind the disruption and ultimately the breakdown of the political system. It would also suggest that the controversies over immigration and temperance were merely episodes in parentheses or catalysts that hastened but did not fundamentally cause the upheaval of the mid-1850s. On the other hand, a second school of thought has reversed this formulation. Joel Silbey argued not that anti-slavery was unimportant as a political issue, but rather that it was "part of the larger matter of cultural hegemony." The Republicans were thus not the party of anti-slavery so much as of Yankee cultural imperialism. They sought to impose, by law if necessary, the values of their section.

Some of these were the values of anti-slavery and of free labor but others were closely related to the ethnocultural issues – temperance, nativism, anti-Catholicism. Silbey quotes a contemporary Democratic newspaper editor whose views perfectly encapsulate his interpretation of the Republican appeal: "abolitionism is but a small part of their programme and probably the least noxious of their measures" (Silbey, 1985: 166–89). If Silbey, rather than Foner, is correct, it would imply that the war arose either because of accident – in that slavery was not as central a concern in the North as has been thought and therefore need not have generated so much strife – or because of a conflict over cultural values rather than economic interests.

Finally, a third school of thought has argued that the essence of the Republican appeal was its attack upon the "Slave Power." William Gienapp and Michael Holt have each argued, in slightly different ways, that Republicans were above all concerned with the political threat posed by southern slaveholders. Gienapp insisted that what distinguished Republicans from northern Democrats was not the commitment to free labor – which was all but universal in the North – but instead a fear of the slaveholders and their dependants who were seeking to trample on the rights and liberties of northern freemen as well as of southern slaves. Holt meanwhile argued that the hostility to the "Slave Power" was one of many examples of the tendency of ante-bellum Americans to enlist in crusades to perfect republicanism, and he claimed that the collapse of the second party system left them receptive to sectional rather than traditional partisan appeals. If this view is correct, it might imply that the Civil War was a consequence not so much of socially generated antagonisms as of the political system itself. Political action and political debate would then be of paramount importance as independent variables, influencing politics with little reference to social realities (Holt, 1978).

Which interpretation is correct? It is by no means easy to answer this question, since the evidence is as yet incomplete. The Foner view has at the minimum been damaged, since it cannot, on the face of it, discriminate Republicans from other northerners, who were presumably equally committed to "free labor." Nor is it clear why this ideology should have arisen in the 1850s, since by that time the North had been overwhelmingly a free labor society for at least 30 years. On the other hand, the Silbey view suffers from the fact that for every reference to ethnocultural issues in the late 1850s, made either by the Republicans or their enemies, there were probably ten or more to slavery and sectional questions. So why should this minority of utterances be accorded privileged status? And the "Slave Power" as an organizing principle leaves unanswered the question why some northerners should be oblivious to it, while others would risk the unity of the nation in order to resist it (Ashworth, 1996).

Of course, it could be argued that fears of a "Slave Power" were a direct and essentially unmediated response to southern aggression in the 1830s, 1840s, and 1850s. This would place the responsibility for the war, and for the sectionalization of politics, squarely on the shoulders of the South. The ideology of the Republicans, and more generally the behavior of the northern electorate as a whole, could then be explained as a defensive reaction to southern aggression. The problem with this view, however, is that virtually every analysis of southern politics written in the past few decades has confirmed the opposite view: that southerners were themselves convinced that they were on the defensive. From fire-eaters like William Lowndes Yancey to reluctant secessionists like Alexander H. Stephens, southerners concluded that they wanted nothing more than their rights as guaranteed under the Constitution. They were equally convinced that northerners were out to violate those rights and deny southern equality.

Yet while historians are generally agreed that southerners, like northerners, believed that they were engaged in a defensive struggle, there is little consensus beyond this concerning their motives. Many historians have assumed that the crucial decisions were those made in 1860–1 following Lincoln's election when all the slave states considered secession, and considerable attention has, not surprisingly, been given to the debates over secession. Some states, of course, seceded more or less immediately or at least before Lincoln even took office; others did not secede until he perpetrated what they considered to be wanton acts of aggression against the new Confederacy; while others did not secede at all but instead fought, albeit with nothing approaching unanimity, with the Union when the war came. So who were the secessionists and what were their primary motives? Here several interpretations can be discerned. First, it has been argued by Michael Johnson (1977) that secession in Georgia was in effect a conservative counter-revolution on the part of the elite designed to curtail the power of the poorer whites within the state, as well as the anti-slavery forces outside the South. The goal was the creation of a "patriarchal republic." In almost total contradiction to this view, however, is the conclusion reached by J. Mills Thornton (1978) in his highly celebrated study of antebellum Alabama. Describing in detail the maneuverings of the various groups within the state, he suggested that the debate over secession simply failed to reveal any "simple division along lines of interest, social organization, or institutional ties." Moreover, the goal of Alabamians was to create in the West "a democratic and egalitarian society, in which no [white] man need be dependent on another man for his welfare." Finally, the course of events within Alabama in the 1850s – the growth of market relations and the expanding role of government – made the state's citizens highly receptive to the secessionists' argument: "it is no wonder," Thornton wrote, "that Alabamians easily made an association between the agitation to bar 'the South' from the territories and the increasing organization of their own community" (Thornton, 1978: 343). Thus Thornton's Alabama seems entirely at odds with Johnson's Georgia.

As if this were not enough, William Barney's Alabama (and his Mississippi) appear entirely different again from Thornton's. Barney (1974) found that those eager to rise to the status of planter tended to favor secession, while those who had already attained this status tended to oppose it. Barney also emphasized – as did Eugene Genovese (1965) in his study *The Political Economy of Slavery* – the importance of additional territory, either in the West or in Latin America, for slavery to expand into. Of course, most southerners would have been pleased to see slavery expand, but it is by no means clear how high a priority this commanded throughout the South. For some southerners, it seems, only the abstract right to carry slaves into the West was important; they were not especially concerned to exercise the right. But for others this was a political necessity, given the balance of power in the federal government, or an economic one, as a result of the tendency of cotton to erode the soil, for example.

As yet no consensus is even imminent on these questions. Almost the only generalization that can be offered is that, even when these historians are studying different states, they are unlikely all to be correct. It is highly improbable that the various states of the Deep South by coincidence ended up agreeing upon immediate secession, but each for essentially different, indeed often contradictory, reasons.

Another observation on secession can be made, but it will be helpful first to look at Michael Holt's interpretation of the episode (which, it should be noted, owes much to Thornton's work on Alabama). Holt is particularly concerned to explain the timing of secession: why the lower South seceded immediately whereas the upper South delayed. His argument has to do with the lack of party competition in the Deep South, which left voters there highly responsive to the sectional agitators who urged secession. Once again the urge of antebellum voters to embark on "crusades" to destroy anti-republican monsters is central to his analysis. In the Deep South, the lack of alternatives meant that the Republicans were easily cast in this role (Holt, 1978: 219–59).

But here we have, perhaps, a general weakness of many of the studies of secession. It had, in fact, been made clear as early as 1850 that many states would secede if the Wilmot Proviso were passed. Indeed, even those pledged to defend the Union against the southern rights extremists made this threat. But Lincoln's election meant that a president was now in office who was utterly committed to the principle of free soil, at least as committed as those who had endorsed the Proviso in the 1840s. Moreover, possession of the entire executive branch, with its control over patronage as well as the more formal network of presidential powers, amounted to a far greater threat than the mere passage of a single piece of legislation would have entailed a decade earlier. So in this sense, the secession of the lower South was virtually an inevitability once Lincoln was elected. And it is unlikely that the delayed secession of the upper South was a product of the party maneuverings of the previous decade. For it was generally recognized that the upper South was more moderate on the slavery issue than the Deep South. This pattern had been evident for at least a generation and so it would have been odd if it had not persisted into the secession winter.

Nevertheless, an important question does remain. Why were the slaveholders of Virginia or North Carolina less anxious about a Republican victory than those of Georgia or Alabama? The answer surely has to do with their expectations of the North, and this in turn was perhaps determined by the extent to which they felt slavery differentiated the South from the North. In the Deep South, the feeling was that slavery was the basis for a different, and of course superior, social system, one which diverged from, and would clash with, a society based upon free labor. In the upper South, however, partly because of the lower concentration of slaves there, this view was less prominent. Hence, perhaps, the greater degree of optimism there when the initial drive for secession was launched (Ashworth, 1995).

The Debate over Political Sectionalization

So how is the sectionalization of American politics now understood? It may be appropriate to look at two of the most impressive attempts of recent years to confront this problem. They are those offered by Michael Holt and by Eric Foner, aspects of whose work we have already encountered. In effect, Holt offers what might be termed a "neo-revisionist" interpretation. For him, the question is not why there was a sectional disagreement so much as why this disagreement came to dominate politics in the 1850s and why it then took the political form that it did. His answer has to do with the failure of the second party system in the 1850s to offer voters a genuine choice. As a result of the growing consensus on the traditional issues that had once separated Whigs and Democrats, voters came to feel that the republican experiment in the United States was being jeopardized. American voters had a need to join in "crusades" to perfect republicanism by destroying threats to it; when the older threats – in the form of the Democratic or Whig enemy – disappeared, the newer threats of the "Slave Power" or of "Black Republicanism" replaced them, with ultimately catastrophic consequences.

Holt's view locates the problem in the political/ideological structures of the nation, though at the same time it implies that the division over slavery was not, of itself, sufficient to bring about a war. It thus postulates a war that might perhaps have been avoided – Holt himself makes no definitive statement on this question – had consensus not broken out between Whig and Democrat and, presumably, had there not been a need on the part of voters to embark on crusades to slay "anti-republican" monsters. We therefore have here a combination of structural and accidental factors (Holt, 1978).

This interpretation has much to commend it. The emphasis on the growing consensus between Whig and Democrat, and the explanations for it, are a major contribution to our understanding of the Civil War. Holt stresses the effect of economic growth in bringing about this consensus, since it materially diminished the Democratic hostility to business and commerce that had fueled the party conflict in the 1830s and early 1840s. But did the same process not simultaneously aggravate the differences between North and South, by reinforcing the commitment of each section to its labor system? Throughout his analysis, Holt takes a rather static view of the slavery question, often asking, for example, why slavery could not be contained within the political system in the 1850s as it had been in the 1830s, the 1840s and earlier decades. But is it not possible to answer this by suggesting that each section's attachment to its labor system deepened as its economy developed? Thus the 1850s, a decade of considerable economic expansion overall, might be expected to have produced a growing sectional polarization.

Similarly, Holt's view of the relationship between sectional extremism and party consensus is not entirely convincing. The claim that sectional extremism flourished where party conflict between Democrats and Whigs (or their successors) was weakest is doubtless true, but why not reverse the causal relationship and suggest that commitment to slavery in the South, for example, and fears of northern attacks upon it, destroyed the potential for party conflict? Finally, Holt's assumptions about the electorate, North and South, are open to question. He claims that the voters had an almost pathological need to go slaying "anti-republican monsters." But as even the language implies, this assumes an irrational tendency, virtually a paranoia, which most historians simply do not discern. Moreover, Holt argues that the political parties were, before the 1850s, able to neutralize the slavery issue by saying different things north and south of the Mason–Dixon line. He also argues that the crisis of the mid-1850s was brought about by a widespread cynicism with the political process. Yet he refuses to correlate these developments. Why did the evasion of the slavery question not contribute to the mood of cynicism? It is one thing to argue that the parties could have different policies on slavery North and South but quite another to argue that these differences actually strengthened the political system. Holt gives no reason to question what might be the traditionalist's response to his findings: the different stances on slavery could be tolerated so long as slavery was not the major question, but when it became the key issue voters wanted a platform that did not dodge or straddle. Hence the sectional polarization of the 1850s.

The work of Eric Foner, by contrast, stands in almost diametric opposition to that of Holt. Foner (1980: 35) argues that slavery was indeed the key to the divergent ideologies of North and South and that "the coming of the Civil War" was, above all, "the intrusion of sectional ideology into the political system." For Foner, these ideologies were themselves, certainly in the case of the North (but presumably of the South too), reflections of the different social and economic systems of each section, based respectively upon free and slave labor. Although Foner does not explicitly argue for an "irrepressible conflict," his argument, which derives politics from ideology and ideology from social structure, inclines strongly in that direction (Foner, 1970).

And yet, even here, there is an unrecognized slippage toward revisionism and an emphasis on accident. Foner shows that the actions of the North – and of the South too, though he has not studied it so systematically – were logical given its ideology. The ideologies therefore conflicted and were fundamentally incompatible. The ideologies, too, were based upon, though in no sense merely reducible to, the different economic interests at stake in each section. But Foner has not shown, and perhaps does not believe, that the interests themselves could not, in any fundamental sense, admit of compromise; the clash was instead one of ideological structures raised upon, as it were, or derived from these interests. In other words, it was as a consequence of the key process by which ideologies were generated that the conflict became impossible to resolve. He writes that "in each ideology was the conviction that its own social system must expand, not only to insure its own survival but to prevent the expansion of all the evils the other represented" (Foner, 1970: 312). Here perhaps the key word is "conviction;" each section believed this to be true, but Foner does not confirm that this was so in reality. Now, if the belief was accurate, historians need to know why. What were the real as opposed to perceived conflicts? As yet this question has not been answered. But if it was not true, then we have returned to the realm of misperception and, in a sense, of politicians' blunders. Moreover, since an alternative set of perceptions North and South, also growing out of the economic interests involved, might not have produced conflict, we are back in the realm of chance and accident.

Unanswered Questions

From even this brief examination of some of the major recent interpretations of the coming of the Civil War, it is apparent that a consensus on the war's origins is as elusive now as it was when the fighting broke out at Fort Sumter. It is true that narrow partisanship has all but disappeared: one does not find historians siding with North or South in the way that was once common. It is also true that the crudest interpretations of the war have now disappeared. But still many of the basic questions remain unanswered. How different were North and South? How united was each section? How important was slavery to the political crisis of the 1850s? Why did slavery generate conflict, rather than mere contrast, between North and South? Why did the South secede and why did northerners refuse to let the South secede? The relative neglect of the origins of the Civil War in recent decades is therefore ironic: historical controversies often abate when the issues are resolved or the questions no longer seem urgent. Yet in the case of the sectionalization of American politics and the origins of the Civil War, the questions seem to have lost none of their urgency. Still less have they been resolved.

REFERENCES

Ashworth, John (1995) *Slavery, Capitalism, and Politics in the Antebellum Republic*. Cambridge: Cambridge University Press.

Ashworth, John (1996) "Free labor, wage labor, and the slave power: republicanism and the Republican party in the 1850s," in Melvyn Stokes and Stephen Conway (eds), *The Market Revolution in America: Social, Political and Religious Expressions, 1800–1880*, pp. 128–46. Charlottesville: University of Virginia Press.

Barney, William L. (1974) *The Secessionist Impulse: Alabama and Mississippi in 1860*. Princeton, NJ: Princeton University Press.

Beard, Charles A. and Beard, Mary R. (1933) *The Rise of American Civilization*, 2 vols. New York: Macmillan.

Bender, Thomas A. (ed.) (1992) *The Antislavery Debate: Capitalism and Abolitionism as a Problem in Historical Materialism*. Berkely, CA: University of California Press.

Craven, Avery (1939) *The Repressible Conflict 1830–1861*. Baton Rouge: Louisiana State University Press.

Davis, David Brion (1975) *The Problem of Slavery in the Age of Revolution*. Ithaca, NY: Cornell University Press.

Foner, Eric (1970) *Free Soil, Free Labor, Free Men: the Ideology of the Republican Party before the Civil War*. New York: Oxford University Press.

Foner, Eric (1986) *Politics and Ideology in the Age of the Civil War*. New York: Oxford University Press.

Freehling, William W. (1990) *The Road to Disunion*, vol. 1: *Secessionists at Bay*. New York: Oxford University Press.

Genovese, Eugene D. (1965) *The Political Economy of Slavery: Studies in the Economy and Society of the Slave South*. New York: Pantheon.

Gienapp, William E. (1987) *The Origins of the Republican Party, 1852–1856*. New York: Oxford University Press.

Holt, Michael F. (1978) *The Political Crisis of the 1850s*. New York: Wiley.

Johnson, Michael P. (1977) *Toward a Patriarchal Republic: the Secession of Georgia*. Baton Rouge: Louisiana State University Press.

Morrison, Michael A. (1997) *Slavery and the American West: the Eclipse of Manifest Destiny and the Coming of the Civil War*. Chapel Hill, NC: North Carolina University Press.

Nevins, Allan (1950) *The Emergence of Lincoln*, 2 vols. New York: Scribner's.

Potter, David (1976) *The Impending Crisis 1848–1861*. New York: Harper and Row.

Randall, J. G. (1945) *Lincoln the President: Springfield to Gettysburg*, 2 vols. London: Eyre and Spottiswoode.

Silbey, Joel (1985) *The Partisan Imperative: the Dynamics of American Politics before the Civil War*. New York: Oxford University Press.

Thornton III, J. Mills (1978) *Politics and Power in a Slave Society: Alabama, 1800–1860*. Baton Rouge: Louisiana State University Press.

CHAPTER FOUR

Civil War and Reconstruction, 1861–1877

VERNON BURTON

T HE Civil War era includes those antebellum years of intense controversy about slavery, the actual war years, 1861–5, and the Reconstruction period. At stake during this era was the very existence of the United States. The most bloody war in the nation's history, the Civil War posed in a crucial way what became persistent themes in American history: the character of the nation and the fate of African Americans.

The Civil War is the most popular subject in American history, and scholars have been vitally interested in the conflict, searching out clues therein for the identity of America. Historians have long studied the causes of the war, and will continue to do so. Scholars still attempt to explain why the North won and the Confederacy lost. Recently, scholars have looked intently at the motivations of soldiers in the Union and Confederacy and have paid special attention to the home front. Reconstruction historiography continues to ponder whether Reconstruction was, or could have been, successful. Moreover, new historiography has been moving away from an emphasis on political reconstruction to a focus on emancipation. Renewed interest also enlivens an old debate on whether the Civil War was a second American Revolution.

Despite historians' interest in the Civil War, and despite the mountains of scholarship which have been produced, no consensus exists on the causes or consequences of the war, except that all serious historians credit slavery as its underlying root. The historical debate circles around how and why slavery finally precipitated secession and war. Some view secession as rational behavior by people determined to preserve their non-bourgeois way of life or their "republican" values as they understood them; others argue that it resulted from the irrationality of extremists who used racial fears to whip citizens into a senseless terror. All major historians agree, however, that the South left the Union to preserve slavery. Thus, slavery and its consequences dominate the literature of the Civil War era, not just on the war, but on the fate of African Americans in the post-war years.

In 1858 Republican Senator William H. Seward warned of an impending sectional "collision," the causes of which would be divided into two major categories: those which held that the war was accidental and could have been avoided, and those which held it to be an "irrepressible conflict." Seward was a better prophet than presidential candidate. Historians in the twentieth century have tended to balance their arguments between those who thought the war unavoidable and irrepressible and those who thought that the war was blundered into and that, with better leadership in the 1850s, Americans could have avoided a needless civil war.

Eugene Genovese's *The Political Economy of Slavery* (1965) shaped much of the ensuing scholarship on the Civil War era. He argues that the war was irrepressible, that secession was a rational act for class self-preservation initiated by southern slaveholders. He maintains that slavery made possible an aristocracy in the South, and this aristocracy of slaveowners dominated southern society and southern values. Slaveowners were an anti-bourgeois class who clung to a wasteful style of life that condemned the whole antebellum South to backwardness. In the face of inefficiency and soil exhaustion, southern planters needed access to western land; their need for new markets and land to exploit were rational demands. The election of Abraham Lincoln in 1860, therefore, signaled the end of southern planters' hopes for the security of their slaves in the territories. The Civil War, in Genovese's interpretation, was a conflict between two completely different social orders: the bourgeois capitalist class of acquisition, competition, and commercialism in the North, and a pre-capitalist, or neofeudal, class of planters in the South. The conflict between these two dominant sectional classes, with their conflicting worldviews, set in motion the inescapable march to secession and to Civil War.

Genovese, as a Marxist, emphasizes social divisions and a growing class consciousness in the antebellum South, although he argues that non-slaveholders willingly followed the leadership of the hegemonic slaveholders because of kinship ties and social interaction. A variety of historians, not all of whom accept Genovese's interpretative scheme or his argument of an irrepressible conflict, have reinforced the idea of divisions in southern society. Indeed, several historians have emphasized that structural contradictions in southern society were at the root of secession. They point to class and inter-regional divisions over the degree of support for the institution of slavery. Freehling (1994) sees secession growing out of the fears of planters in the lower South that whites in the upper South could not be trusted in any general crisis over slavery.

Ford (1988) and McCurry (1995) downplay class conflict as both wonder why South Carolina's yeomen were so eager to line up behind the planters in the secession movement and the Confederacy. They deal with different sections of South Carolina and, perhaps because of that, they come to conclusions which are at the same time specifically different and generally similar. They both argue that South Carolina's yeomen supported secession and went to war because they perceived it to be in their best interests to do so. Both elevate the position of the yeomen to active participants in the political culture of the state. At that point, however, they diverge, for where Ford sees a variant of "herrenvolk democracy" in which planters and plain folk were united and made equal by virtue of their common republican and racial heritage, McCurry argues for a shared politics of conditional equality based upon the common oppression of dependents, slave and free, but particularly female.

Moore (1966) supports Genovese's thesis. Using a comparative analysis of various modern nations, Moore argues that the American Civil War was a revolutionary offensive by urban, bourgeois capitalists. Slavery, despite its early assistance in American industrial growth, was an obstacle to a political and social democracy; liberal capitalism as practiced in the North could not tolerate such a hideous arrangement as slavery in the same political system. Although Moore recognizes that abolitionists were fueled in part by moral fervor, he treats abolitionism as a goal dictated primarily by economics. Foner (1970), in contrast to Moore, treats Republican ideology as an intellectual and existential commitment made by individuals. Foner's radical-liberal interpretation of Republican ideology complements Genovese's development of a distinct southern worldview. Foner centers his argument upon the concept of free labor, an anti-slavery ideology based on the belief of the superiority of the rural and small-town society of the North over the slave society of the South. Free labor became a symbol of a liberal bourgeois style of life which challenged the slave power conspiracy and the aristocratic decadent style of life in the South. Northern ideals of union and liberty demanded the fight to prevent secession. Southern planters perceived correctly that Republicans were devoted to the abolition of slavery and therefore viewed Lincoln's election in 1860 as a signal of extreme danger. Foner, and those who have followed his lead, look to politics and ideology to explain why the conflict was irrepressible.

An alternative school of historians, who also believe that the Civil War was inevitable, emphasize institutional breakdown, lack of conflict management, or southern psychology. With the breakdown of political parties, the country lost any means of accommodation or compromise. As long as the Democratic party was a strong intersectional party, it linked the North and the South. When the Democratic party failed in 1860, the United States had no national institution to manage the secession crisis or arrange a compromise. Other scholars believe that southern planters and white southerners in general were in conflict within themselves about the morality of slavery and therefore fearful of perceived outside threats to slavery. Using northern abolitionists as scapegoats, they over-reacted to the election of 1860, precipitating a secession crisis. Not making an enlightened decision based upon self or class interest, white southerners were not thinking rationally when they chose secession instead of compromise.

Another interpretation holds that the war was by no means inevitable, that it was actually needless. Identified with James G. Randall, historians of the needless war school have developed a long tradition. This group believes that the war goals were not worth the cost of the war and that the Civil War could have been prevented except for human error: not institutional or systemic error, but politicians and statesmen failed to avert the Civil War. This group blames the abolitionists, with their forcefulness, demagoguery, and extremism, as the original provocateurs. They heap less blame on southern fire-eaters, who, although still involved in hyper-emotionalism, were reacting to northern provocation. Statesmen of compromise and moderation, such as Henry Clay and Stephen Douglas, receive greater credit. The anti-compromise stand of the Republicans in the 1850s is seen as reprehensible in tipping the scales toward war. This group of scholars places less significance upon the injurious system of slavery as a fundamental cause of the war. The American Civil War was not the result of basic moral precepts or conduct, but of human error.

David Donald is the foremost proponent of the needless war theory. According to Donald, the American social process had produced by the 1850s what he calls an "excess of democracy." Democratization had produced a political system controlled by a leaderless mob, a system increasingly unable to form reasonable solutions for the problems that faced American society. In Donald's view, the abolitionists were from a declining social class and were suffering from status anxiety. Their motivation was finding some mechanism to shore up their failing social position, and they felt compelled to latch on to some moral cause. Donald has indicated that the southern fire-eaters also belonged to a declining social class and were also anxious to bolster their position. While the Yankees used abolitionism, the southern fire-eaters used pro-slavery arguments. Donald contends that in the 1850s the country was leaderless, and thus Americans fell easy prey to hysterical fears and paranoid suspicions.

Michael Holt, David Donald's student, provides a sophisticated cultural interpretation of the needless war school. Downplaying the role of slavery and emphasizing religious and ethnic cultural norms, Holt (1978) suggests that issues of temperance, immigration restriction, and anti-Catholicism united the Republican party as much as did opposition to slavery. The Democratic party, on the other hand, came to stand for local authority and resistance to New England's cultural imperialism. In the North, the two parties could still contest over issues such as the Pope, but in the South, only the Democratic party remained, and the only contest became one with the North.

Holt characterizes the political crisis of the 1850s in terms of the meaning of republicanism. Each section of the nation felt that republicanism was under attack, and their commitment to preserving republicanism set the nation at war. His thesis is that sectional conflict was a symptom of the political crisis of the 1850s, not its main cause. Sectional conflict had been part of the two-party system for 30 years; the real question, then, becomes why was this conflict no longer manageable? Holt argues that the disintegration of the national two-party system was the real cause of the Civil War. As the two parties collapsed, each section of the country viewed the other as wanting to enslave it and destroy republicanism. The fear that republicanism was in jeopardy was exploited by opportunist politicians and, understandably, brought about the rise of numerous "plots" to republican liberty: Catholic conspiracies, slavocratic conspiracies, and so on. And, in the lower South, no new political mechanism arose to absorb competition so that the only legitimate redress was to get out of the Union; only in this way would republicanism be preserved.

A wholly distinct arena of historiography involves the question of why the North won and the South lost the Civil War. Historians debate whether it was due to the North's industrial base and larger population, superior leadership in government and on the battlefield, or the lack of a real nationalism in the Confederacy. Beringer et al. (1986) favor a multi-causal explanation for southern defeat, but single out a deficient nationalism stimulated by a "cognitive dissonance" over Confederate war aims as the primary reason why the South lost. McPherson (1988) introduces the idea of contingency in arguing that there were instances when the Confederacy could have turned the tide and won.

Many scholars cite the lack of a deeply held national sentiment among southern whites for the defeat of the Confederacy. Revisionist studies, however, recognize that the Confederate government was much more of a centralizing force than had previously been thought. Starting in the crucial spring months of 1862 and continuing throughout the war, a series of executive directives and national legislation regarding conscription, suspension of habeas corpus, impressment of supplies and slaves, and tithing of agricultural production was implemented to bring about a more efficient and balanced use of resources and to foster greater unity of purpose. To a great extent it worked, and despite the North's overwhelming economic, technological, and demographic advantages, the South was able to sustain rebellion for four long years.

While acknowledging that the war's military engagements and political developments merit close persistent attention, a new generation of historians maintains that
the everyday experience of men and women on the home front, when understood in
its proper social and economic context, can help explain the war's outcome and cast
new light on the ways in which warfare transforms the lives of non-combatants. For
the North, Paludan (1988) has provided an insightful and thorough examination of
the vast social and economic changes that had an impact on the wartime experiences
of northerners. Vinovskis (1990), in an edited collection, brought attention to the
demographic ramifications of the war in the North and the resulting changes in
attitudes. Others have concentrated on how the war opened opportunities for northern women through organizations such as the Sanitary Commission, on northern
wartime intellectual development, the experiences of African Americans in the wartime North, and the varied nature of dissent against the Lincoln government and the
official reaction to it. To date, the Confederate South has not received the same
scholarly attention, and no overview matches the depth of Paludan's work on the
North.

Looking at conditions on the southern home front, recent scholars have credited
the Confederate defeat to intangible factors such as economic self-interest, loss of the
will to win, and declining morale. They emphasize that defeat rose out of a lack of
commitment to the cause on the part of many southern whites and the inability of the
Confederacy to create a unified southern society to respond to the war. Some
have argued that the centralizing activities of the Confederate government worsened
class divisions and provoked a backlash that alienated both yeomen and planters
from the government and the war effort. Disillusionment with the war effort was
not a new theme. The Fleming Lectures of Charles Ramsdell in 1937 anticipated
much of the recent scholarship of social historians, particularly the emphasis on
discontent. Ramsdell quotes extensively from letters and documents that give a feel
for the disintegration and pain of the home front, and he emphasizes the inability
of the Confederate national, state, or local governments to solve the financial hardships and economic struggles faced by common folks on the home front. His
thesis that the home front's collapse was a major cause of Confederate defeat has
been reiterated by more recent studies. Indeed, a consensus has emerged that
internal social factors cannot be ignored in any explanation of the collapse of the
Confederacy.

McMillan (1986) looks at Alabama's three wartime governors and their home-front
problems to reinforce Ramsdell's earlier argument that the imposition of sacrifices for
the war increased disaffection. The governors had to find ways to recruit soldiers,
maintain a state militia, feed soldiers' families, get salt, impress planters' slaves,
regulate alcohol distillation, control crop selection and production, and protect
citizens from outlaws and deserters. As they struggled with insurmountable problems,
none of the governors was able to secure re-election. By 1863, McMillan (1986: 135)
concludes, Alabamians had:

> lost the will to fight. They longed for the reestablishment of the old Union to save them
> from the new despotism that took their property without compensation, conscripted
> them and forced them to fight against their will – a government whose policies had
> brought about a reign of terror in half the counties in Alabama.

Faust (1996) casts new light on the ways in which warfare transformed the lives of southern white women of all classes, women who both supported and ultimately undermined southern nationalism and the war effort. She analyzes the changes wrought on the home front and provides an excellent overview of such crucial issues as survival, patriarchy and paternalism, class tensions, patriotism, and desertion. Because the war was so close to home and took so many men from their farms and plantations, women had to assume roles that had traditionally been those of the men in the patriarchal South. The men at the battlefield ultimately failed in their home-front responsibilities of sustenance and protection. Hence women became disenchanted and helped undermine the Confederate war effort, contributing to the Confederacy's defeat.

Most studies of nineteenth-century southern communities, regions, or states relate in some way to the Confederate home front. The experiences of the home front, of course, varied from community to community. If a community was near the front, or was confronted with the enemy, the experience was quite different from a region that never faced invasion. Three community studies, all for North Carolina, serve to illustrate the different experiences of the home front. Although not involved in military engagements, Orange County experienced a breakdown in the self-sufficiency of local neighborhoods. Civilians began to look more to county and state authorities for aid to cope with such problems as war relief, refugees, and economic hardship. Washington County, which was accessible to invading Union forces sweeping in from the North Carolina coast, underwent its own civil war as any semblance of class unity collapsed. Planters feared that slavery could not be protected in the Union; yeomen felt that planters were willing to wreck the nation for the sake of their own property; and white laborers hoped to gain if the other two classes fought. By early 1864, guerrilla warfare racked the home front in Washington County. In the mountains of the western end of the state in Madison County, the murder of 13 suspected Unionist prisoners at Shelton Laurel revealed how class and racial tensions belied the myth of a united Confederate South.

Although many historians have written about class to make the point that the failure to establish a unified southern society was a major factor in the Confederacy's defeat, some scholars, following the lead of Gary W. Gallagher, are again placing the emphasis on the battlefield. They point out that the Confederacy mobilized more than three-quarters of its draft-age white male population, and they insist that the bulk of ordinary southerners remained fervent Confederate patriots until the bitter end. It was the superior manpower and technology of the Union, not any defect in the southern will to win, that was primarily responsible for Union victory. Studies of the Billy Yanks and Johnny Rebs have found that both Yankee and Rebel soldiers understood what they were fighting for and believed in their causes. In fact, the structure and values of the Union and Confederate armies were quite similar. These armies were much more like each other than either was like any other country's army at the time. Mitchell (1993) provides a provocative new angle on why the North won the Civil War. By using gender as an analytical tool, he takes the ideology of family and of separate spheres for men and women and applies "domesticity" to a comparative study of the Union and Confederate armies. Yankees, argues Mitchell, simply transferred the prevailing ideology of domesticity to their army: thus a military unit became a family and home away from home in protection of actual homes and families on the home front. However, Confederate soldiers, unable to return home to plant and harvest crops, had to choose between their families, sometimes near starvation, and their army units. To make matters worse, Union soldiers were invading the Confederate soldier's real home, and fear of slave insurrection provided a dilemma of divided loyalty – at home with his family or on the front with his unit.

A gauge of how historians' interest in the Civil War has changed over the years can be found in the two superb historiographical *festschrifts* for southern history. In 1965, Link and Patrick's *Writing Southern History* had four chapters on the Civil War era: one covered "The Coming of the Civil War;" one "The Confederate States of America: The Homefront;" another covered military aspects, "The Confederate States of America at War on Land and Sea;" and another dealt with "Reconstruction." Twenty years later, after the civil rights movement and a national concern with race relations, Boles and Nolen's *Interpreting Southern History* (1987) had one chapter on the war, "The White South from Secession to Redemption," and that was evenly divided between the Civil War (including the causes) and Reconstruction, and had two separate chapters on Reconstruction, "From Emancipation to Segregation: National Policy and Southern Blacks" and "Economic Reconstruction and the Rise of the New South, 1865–1900." The 1987 *festschrift* reflected the ascendancy of social history and an increased interest in the lives of ordinary people. The neglect of the Civil War by social historians was reflected in the title of another scholar's essay, "Have Social Historians Lost the Civil War?" (Vinovskis, 1990). But then attention shifted again. Due perhaps to Ken Burns's successful public television series on the Civil War, or perhaps to James McPherson's Pulitzer prize-winning masterpiece of historical writing, *Battle Cry of Freedom* (1988), a new generation of scholarship on the Civil War began, much of it influenced by social history.

The same year, 1988, Foner provided a great synthesis of work on Reconstruction, incorporating relevant literature up to that time. Although historians still see Reconstruction as a "tragedy," they no longer accept the late nineteenth-century myth of "Black Reconstruction," whereby venal carpet-baggers, viciously ignorant former slaves, and fifth columnist low-white-trash scalawags ruled the South and made a mockery of honest government and democracy during "the tragic era." Dissenting views to this myth in the 1920s and 1930s, especially by black scholars such as Alruthesus A. Taylor and W. E. B. DuBois, were largely ignored by the historical profession. However, revisionist interpretations began to take hold after World War II. Since the civil rights movement of the 1960s, historians have emphasized the positive achievements of Reconstruction's radical Republican governments, especially constitutional reform and public education, and they balance the prevalence of corruption in the South against that in the North, the Grant administration, Boss Tweed, and the Great Barbecue of private greed at public expense. Mark Twain's sobriquet of "Gilded Age" for the last third of the nineteenth century applied more to the North than to the South.

Historians, however, have continued to view Reconstruction as a tragic chapter in American history, tragic because it failed to achieve for African Americans lasting equality. The Civil War that set the period in motion ultimately concerned race and the place of African Americans in American society. One man died in that war for every six persons emancipated. Pain, suffering, and bloodshed continued throughout Reconstruction despite the great price already paid during the war. The current consensus of revisionist historiography argues that the Republican party in Congress gave up its attempt to force on the South a new balance of political power. When it did, northern Republicans, in effect, decided that their political and economic interests were better served through cooperating with the southern traditional landowning elite, thus leaving to that native white establishment the control of race relations.

The crucial question in Reconstruction since the 1970s has been whether Reconstruction could have been successful. There have been basically four schools of thought. The first, that Reconstruction was doomed to failure, grew out of the William A. Dunning school and the "tragic era" interpretation so dear to many white southerners' hearts. This emphasizes the futility of trying to change the South or any deep-seated social attitudes such as those regarding race relations. According to this view, Reconstruction was destined to fail since military occupation and black political power only induced hostility in those whom it was intended to change. The alternative would have been gradual amelioration of racial understanding for blacks and whites through economic and educational improvement.

For the past generation, a second school of thought has held dominance. This view argues that Reconstruction failed because it did not go far enough. If Congress had persevered in compelling the white South to act equitably toward freedmen, white southerners would eventually have accepted the new values. No such compulsion continued, unfortunately, because the North was influenced by ulterior motives, political and economic, and leadership for change was robbed by the deaths of altruistic leaders such as Thaddeus Stevens and Charles Sumner. Moreover, the Panic of 1873 and the subsequent depression, which began earlier in the former Confederacy, played havoc with every reform movement.

Included in this second school – that Reconstruction did not go far enough – are those scholars who focus on the issue of land. The federal government failed to follow through on a promising wartime program to distribute land to the families of the freed slaves, and only one state during Reconstruction, South Carolina, set up an agency to help former slaves acquire land. This failure to provide land to the impoverished ex-slaves left them vulnerable to a very flawed southern capitalistic marketplace. Both black and white sharecroppers were victims of general store merchants who demanded that tenants grow cotton, charged them exorbitant interest rates for supplies, and obtained first lien on crops. Most African Americans refused to be worked as gang labor, and the tenant system resulted as a compromise whereby farming was done by family units.

Class differences in Louisiana and South Carolina between the conservative, lighter-skinned, property-owning free blacks of New Orleans and Charleston and the darker-skinned, formerly enslaved landless laboring class of African Americans in the countryside hastened the failure of the Reconstruction experiment in these two states. Distinctions of caste and class among African Americans reduced the effective exercise of black political power, undermined Republican unity, and played into the hands of whites anxious to establish a fixed color line in public life.

The above explanations all conclude that the freedmen came out of Reconstruction as they went in: landless, poverty stricken, and trapped into increasingly unfavorable arrangements of sharecropping that often amounted to debt peonage. Therefore, in a "post" or "anti" revisionist mode, a number of scholars have begun to question if Reconstruction even mattered. This school of thought argues that Reconstruction was a very mild, if not conservative, era, and that nothing fundamental changed because of the Civil War. Serfdom replaced slavery, the Jim Crow legislation replaced the slave codes, and African Americans, economically, politically, and socially power-less, were still subordinated to whites. This school paints a very grim picture and holds that even land distribution to freedmen would not have altered the course of Recon-struction's failure. Many scholars now argue that, given the existing conventions at that time, there was very little possibility that the social revolution of Reconstruction would not fail.

Among scholars who believe that Reconstruction was a failure, and that the experi-ment was doomed to failure from the beginning, is Harris (1997). His study of Lincoln's Reconstruction policies concludes that Lincoln never changed his conser-vative approach to self-Reconstruction in the South. According to Harris, Lincoln never developed more radical Reconstruction policies as a means to win the war, and this cautious approach by Lincoln constrained the possibilities for federal policy during Reconstruction. Moreover, Harris and others argue that Reconstruction did little to change southern society. Persistence in power relations and white social attitudes was more the norm than the exception in the South of Reconstruction. In Arkansas, for example, the planters maintained their economic dominance through all the disruptions unleashed by the war and Reconstruction. In South Carolina, the most studied of southern states, the widespread white terrorism and violence of Reconstruction marked a continuation of the Civil War by different means. Recon-struction did not so much fail in South Carolina as be defeated by an organized white resistance.

Perman (1984) also places race and southern whites' commitment to white supremacy as fundamental in the failure of Reconstruction, but he believes that if the North had been willing after the Civil War to station enough troops, and to punish the white South more severely, then Reconstruction could have worked. He places the blame for the failure of Reconstruction squarely on the North, arguing that the white South was willing to accept Reconstruction until the election of 1876, when the North signaled that it was no longer interested in enforcing Reconstruction laws. When African Americans began to assert themselves in the Republican party, and when Democrats in the North and South embraced racism as their political rallying cry, the South took its cue from the North and rejected Reconstruction.

The fourth school of revisionist historians allows that a revolution to incorporate African Americans into full equality occurred between 1863 and 1877, but that the revolution is yet incomplete. While agreeing with others that Reconstruction repres-ented a civil war between most southern whites and African-American Republicans with some white allies, I have argued that scholars have looked in the wrong places to judge the success or failure of Reconstruction. Whatever its failures from the perspect-ive of Congress or the state houses, Reconstruction achieved some undeniable suc-cesses at the local level as African Americans and whites experimented with inter-racial democracy and responsive government. Again, the tragedy is that too many whites preferred racial discrimination, low taxes, and meager governmental services. Unwill-ing to share citizenship, let alone political power, with African Americans, many of these whites relied on violence to regain control of their local governments. Thus, it was not the failure of Reconstruction that brought about what is paradoxically called "Redemption," but the very success of former slaves in politics, accompanied by economic gains and some social mobility, that led conservative whites to illegal, violent tactics to end the experiment in inter-racial democracy (Burton, 1985).

Foner (1988) leads this fourth school of thought. He places African Americans at center stage in his book; Reconstruction was about race relations and hence black people were the significant actors. Foner's study is a synthesis of 80 years of historiography on Reconstruction in which the African American was not always central, and in which cost (social, economic, and political upheaval) was not always adjudged worth the outcome (transitory black freedom). While conceding that the egalitarian promise of Reconstruction was ultimately unfulfilled, Foner none the less sees the era as one in which African Americans made considerable gains that were to last them through the following years of trial. In particular, he stresses education and institutional stability in religion and the family.

Within the complex story of Reconstruction, Foner outlines four broad themes: the remaking of southern society; the interactions of freedmen, antebellum free blacks, Republican Unionists, poor whites, white planters, merchants, and yeomen in the New South; the growth of agrarian commercialism even among previously self-sufficient farmers; and the interconnection of race and class, a matter especially complicated because former slaves constituted an agrarian black laboring class at the same time as a white ethnic industrial laboring class developed elsewhere. Foner places Reconstruction in a national context; he shows how the Civil War and Reconstruction affected the development of a powerful nation-state and how, in turn, a more activist federal government affected the evolution of Reconstruction. Foner carefully relates changes in the North's economy and class structure to the eventual undermining of Reconstruction, and he shows a reciprocity of Reconstructions in the North and the South. Placing Reconstruction in a comparative framework, Foner emphasizes that enfranchisement itself was a revolutionary step for the nation. While Foner is sensitive to the dynamics of race, especially in the South, class, especially in the North, becomes the driving force of his analysis. Since Foner's work, the consensus view has been his: the remarkable thing about Reconstruction was not its failure, but the very fact that any attempt was made to remake southern society along more egalitarian lines.

Among recent studies of the Civil War era, the Freedom Project directed by Ira Berlin has been incredibly influential. Of course, emancipation has always been important to the Reconstruction process, but Berlin's Freedom Project shifted the emphasis to the active role of African Americans in achieving their liberation, and emancipation and its consequences now receive more scholarly focus. Reflecting the work of Berlin, Foner begins his book with the Emancipation Proclamation of 1863. The best exploration of African Americans on the Civil War home front is Mohr's (1986) study of Civil War Georgia. Mohr traces the day-to-day changes in the way in which slaves and masters interacted as the war progressed. He shows that, as opportunities arose on the home front, slaves were able to gain more freedom and change the very nature of slavery as an institution. Recently, historians have begun to study rigorously the change from slavery to freedom over the course of the Civil War. Whether in examining communities, regions, or specific groups, these studies generally unfold backward and forward from emancipation to understand what sort of free-labor system replaced African-American slavery.

Another historiographical debate focuses around the view of the Civil War as the "second American Revolution." In 1860, nearly four million African Americans were held in slavery and the rest was held in political, social, and economic subservience. In 1870, they were all free, politically equal, with no compensation going to their former masters. In 1860, there were no elected black officials; in the 1870s, African Americans held elective office at almost every level of government. For that brief interlude the bottom rail truly was on top. This was revolution – sudden, violent, and transforming.

Several prominent, contemporary observers noted that the American Civil War represented revolutionary change. One such observer was the abolitionist Wendell Phillips. Two others were journalists who later became famous for other endeavors – George Clemenceau and Karl Marx. Revolutionary conditions lay in the emancipation of millions of southern, enslaved African Americans and their overnight elevation to political equality and citizenship. And surely the scale of confiscation of southern means of production – slaves – rivals the events of the 1917 Russian Revolution. Moreover, the duration of the Republican insurgency (until the compromised election of 1876) paralleled the length of time the French Revolution lasted (until Napoleon's coronation in 1804).

Yet, unlike the Russian and French cases, the American Civil War had no revolutionary ideology. Furthermore, it was a capitalist revolution. Moore (1966) refers to it as the "last" such revolution, but he notes that the refusal of the Republican Congress to add material wealth to political freedom – the famous 40 acres and a mule – really defined the revolutionary limits of the war. Political leveling was acceptable, but economic and social leveling was not. Freedom, which was not the policy aim of the majority of the Republican party, was adopted as a wartime necessity, beginning with confiscation and escalating from there.

That the Civil War was a Republican capitalist revolution is the foundation of the "second American Revolution" school of thought. With southerners gone from Congress at the very outset of the conflict, the federal government passed a variety of measures that transformed American government and economics. Decades after it was first proposed, the so-called "American system" came into being: protective tariffs, banks, internal improvements. To this were added planks on westward expansion, education, taxation, and immigration. These measures contributed to making a very different America, and the effects of that transformation remain today.

In addition to race relations and economic relations, another aspect of the debate on whether the Civil War era constituted a second American Revolution involves gender. Although this is more problematic, some scholars suggest that there was an incipient gender revolution, beginning with the fight to include women in the provisions of the Fourteenth Amendment and continuing through the gendered relations of postbellum North and South. There may be other revolutionary aspects worthy of consideration, but it is these three – race relations, economic relations, and gender relations – that have been the locus of scholarly concern.

Historiographically speaking, whether one sees this era as revolutionary is a classic case of a glass half-empty or half-full. McPherson (1990) follows exactly the same narrative of Reconstruction as Foner, but whereas Foner believes it ultimately failed, McPherson casts it as a successful revolution. McPherson argues that the Civil War era did more to shape and change institutions and government than did the American Revolution. Foner chooses to concentrate on the outward effects of reform; McPherson on the inner revolution in the spirit of the freedmen. Political equality, economic opportunity, and the respect of society could be, and were, taken away, but the knowledge of freedom and its potential could not be.

Foner centers his story of Reconstruction on race, but McPherson adds an "external revolution" to his "internal revolution" for the slaves. This externality was the "American system," referred to above. This was not at all new to McPherson, as he followed a long historiographical tradition dating back to the 1920s. Charles A. Beard and Mary Beard originated the modern debate by arguing that the Civil War had been America's second revolution (or even its first) because it shifted the national balance of power from southern planters to northern capitalists. The means for this power shift came from new legislation such as the Morrill Tariffs, Internal Revenue Acts, Legal Tender Act, Public Land Grant College Act, Pacific Railroad Acts, Immigration Act, Homestead Act, and National Bank Act. Mainly passed between 1861 and 1864, these pieces of legislation eroded the power of the states and paved the way for future economic development.

More recent scholars have continued this trend, but with an awareness that these economic benefits were not attained as the result of a conscious plan of any unified business community. Thus, as opposed to the Beards, modern scholars do not see a revolutionary or counter-revolutionary plan because there was no conspiracy on the part of the capitalist class. The opportunity simply arose because southern legislators had withdrawn from Congress where they had blocked economic legislation sought by northern interests. Republicans seized this opportunity not to advance an economic blueprint for industrialization but to enact into legislation the core tenets of their free-labor ideology. In fact, no unified northern business class can be identified, and the new group of finance capitalists spawned by the massive borrowing needs of the federal government during the war generally opposed the attempts of fellow Republicans to pursue an activist policy of Reconstruction in the post-war South. The interests of this group dictated fiscal restraint and the rapid return of the South to its traditional export-oriented role in the national economy.

The most direct challenge to the notion of a second American Revolution comes from those who point to a decline in the rates of growth for most economic indices in the Civil War decade of the 1860s. They conclude that the war, far from accelerating change in a revolutionary way, actually retarded US economic growth and industrial development in the short term. To be sure, the United States' Industrial Revolution cannot be ascribed to the Civil War. None the less, the political and institutional changes of the war years had a significant long-range impact on the economy, and while it might be an exaggeration to suggest that these changes fully underlay US economic development in the Gilded Age, they certainly served a facilitating role. Scholars also have to remember that the southern economy was not revolutionized; rather, it was devastated. And that may have had a retarding effect on the North as compared to the anticipated course of US economic development projected from before the war.

In a sense, therefore, we can conclude that two revolutions were attempted and that while one succeeded, the other failed. Emancipation was a successful and lasting revolution, brought about by the convictions of abolitionists, the courage of leading Republicans, and the actions of individual slaves. From Fort Monroe in May 1861 through the Confiscation Acts of 1861 and 1862, the Emancipation Proclamation, and the Thirteenth Amendment, emancipation was a successful revolution based on limited goals. Reconstruction, on the other hand, had far more wide-ranging goals which it failed to achieve over the long haul. The 1864 Freedmen's Bureau Act, the various Reconstruction Acts, Force Acts, Civil Rights Acts, and the Fourteenth Amendment did not produce equality.

We have seen several revolutionary strands so far; two, emancipation and the American system, were successful and lasting. The third, a reconstruction of race relations and economic and social injustice, was short-lived and ultimately a failure. Another, the revolution in gender relations, also failed, but its effects may have been longer lasting. Northern suffragists failed to include gender equality in the Fourteenth Amendment, but the passage of the amendment freed these women from the cause of abolitionism and black civil rights and acted as a catalyst toward suffrage. In the South, the questioning of traditional gender roles that emerged during the war continued even after the surviving soldiers returned home and helped pave the way for the more active civic involvement of women in the post-war South.

One last point regarding gender studies during the Civil War era should be noted. Before the war, white southerners saw themselves as the masculine counterpoint to the effeminate Yankee. Northern victory reversed this relationship, and the North became the masculine counterpart to the South as handmaiden. Post-war northern fiction and travel literature came to view the South in increasingly romanticized and feminized terms. This gendered imagery was central to a notion of reconciliation in which the defeated, dependent South was welcomed back into the national fold. Here is another instance of a bottom rung reversing positions, only this time with gendered regionalism instead of race.

Such reversals show how the Civil War and Reconstruction do represent a second American Revolution. The revolutionary aspects dealt with here are fourfold: emancipation, the American system, Reconstruction, and women's rights. Two of these revolutionary processes succeeded in dramatically changing American society in the nineteenth century, and those successes have had the most lasting effect on American society. Two – Reconstruction and women's rights – failed but laid a groundwork for a later, twentieth-century revolution.

This brief examination of the literature on the Civil War era is only a sample of major ideas and themes. Scholars have explored so many different topics on the Civil War and Reconstruction that at best a summary can only touch on a few. Nevertheless, this overview of the historiography should show clearly that none of the issues has been definitively resolved. Thus will historians continue to study and interpret this crucial era in American history.

REFERENCES

Beringer, Richard E., Hattaway, Herman, Jones, Archer, and Still Jr, William N. (1986) *Why the South Lost the Civil War.* Athens: University of Georgia Press.

Boles, John B. and Nolen, Evelyn Thomas (eds) (1987) *Interpreting Southern History: Historiographical Essays in Honor of Sanford W. Higginbotham.* Baton Rouge: Louisiana State University Press.

Burton, Orville Vernon (1985) *In my Father's House are Many Mansions: Family and Community in Edgefield, South Carolina.* Chapel Hill, NC: University of North Carolina Press.

Faust, Drew Gilpin (1996) *Mothers of Invention: Women of the Slaveholding South in the American Civil War*. Chapel Hill, NC: University of North Carolina Press.

Foner, Eric (1970) *Free Soil, Free Labor, Free Men: the Ideology of the Republican Party before the Civil War*. New York: Oxford University Press.

Foner, Eric (1988) *Reconstruction: America's Unfinished Revolution, 1863–1877*. New York: Harper and Row.

Ford Jr, Lacy K. (1988) *Origins of Southern Radicalism: the South Carolina Upcountry, 1800–1860*. New York: Oxford University Press.

Freehling, William W. (1994) *The Reintegration of American History: Slavery and the Civil War*. New York: Oxford University Press.

Genovese, Eugene (1965) *The Political Economy of Slavery: Studies in the Economy and Society of the Slave South*. New York: Pantheon.

Harris, William C. (1997) *With Charity for All: Lincoln and the Restoration of the Union*. Lexington: University Press of Kentucky.

Holt, Michael (1978) *The Political Crisis of the 1850s*. New York: Wiley.

Link, Arthur S. and Patrick, Rembert W. (eds) (1965) *Writing Southern History: Essays in Historiography in Honor of Fletcher M. Green*. Baton Rouge: Louisiana State University Press.

McCurry, Stephanie (1995) *Masters of Small Worlds: Yeoman Households, Gender Relations, and the Political Culture of the Antebellum South Carolina Low Country*. New York: Oxford University Press.

McMillan, Malcolm C. (1986) *The Disintegration of a Confederate State: Three Governors and Alabama's Wartime Home Front, 1861–1865*. Macon, Ga.: Mercer University Press.

McPherson, James M. (1988) *Battle Cry of Freedom: the Civil War Era*. New York: Oxford University Press.

McPherson, James M. (1990) *Abraham Lincoln and the Second American Revolution*. New York: Oxford University Press.

Mitchell, Reid (1993) *The Vacant Chair: the Northern Soldier Leaves Home*. New York: Oxford University Press.

Mohr, Clarence L. (1986) *On the Threshold of Freedom: Masters and Slaves in Civil War Georgia*. Athens: University of Georgia Press.

Moore, Barrington (1966) *Social Origins of Dictatorship and Democracy*. Boston: Beacon Press.

Paludan, Phillip Shaw (1988) *"A People's Contest": the Union and Civil War, 1861–1865*. New York: Harper and Row (new edn 1996).

Perman, Michael (1984) *The Road to Redemption: Southern Politics, 1869–1879*. Chapel Hill, NC: University of North Carolina Press.

Vinovskis, Maris (ed.) (1990) *Toward a Social History of the American Civil War: Exploratory Essays*. Cambridge: Cambridge University Press.

CHAPTER FIVE

The Gilded Age, 1878–1900

ROBERT W. CHERNY AND WILLIAM L. BARNEY

T HE political history of the Gilded Age once seemed the preserve of bearded Civil War veterans "waving the bloody shirt" or declaiming on the tariff, while city bosses lined their pockets, spoilsmen sought patronage, and farmers complained. Sandwiched between the fiercely ideological battles of the Civil War–Reconstruction period and the reforming zeal of the Progressive era, politics in the last quarter of the nineteenth century seemed to be long on rhetoric and short on substance. That history was, of course, much more complex than these stereotypes convey, and historians' accounts of it have become much more sophisticated during the past half-century.

Good starting-points for understanding the complexity of Gilded Age politics are H. Wayne Morgan's *From Hayes to McKinley: National Party Politics, 1877–1896* (1969) and Morton Keller's *Affairs of State: Public Life in Late Nineteenth Century America* (1977), which provide detailed overviews of major events and patterns in national politics. Both deserve a careful reading, and Morgan's bibliography warrants attention in its own right. For a shorter overview that synthesizes more recent works, see Robert W. Cherny's *American Politics in the Gilded Age, 1868–1900* (1997).

From Twain to Hofstadter

Some of the initial observers of politics and public life during the Gilded Age delineated them in ways that dominated the thinking of historians throughout the first two-thirds of the twentieth century and that still appear in many treatments today. Charles Dudley Warner and Samuel L. Clemens (Mark Twain) tagged the era with a label that has stuck when they chose *The Gilded Age* as the title for their colorful 1873 novel of political chicanery and corruption in Washington. James Bryce, in his classic analysis of late nineteenth-century America, *The American Common-wealth* (1888), structured his account around the failure of public life to attract the "best men." Bryce's work included much more than a critique of the quality of political leadership. It remains today a valuable account of the structure of American politics at that time, recording details for Bryce's British readership that most American observers found so commonplace as to require no description. Bryce is invaluable for his portrayal of the political parties, election campaigns, and the process of voting in the era before the Australian ballot. Among Bryce's contemporaries, James Ford Rhodes stands out as one whose work still deserves attention. Rhodes, a good Republican from Ohio, provided a wealth of detail on national politics during the Gilded Age but gave little attention to the larger context of social and economic change or to politics at the grassroots. Nevertheless, for detail on presidential and congressional politics, Rhodes remains a valuable reference.

Rhodes's multi-volume, highly detailed, presidentially focused history was already old-fashioned by the time his final volumes appeared in the 1920s. By then, a new generation of professionally trained historians had emerged with their own perspective on the nature of American politics in general and the politics of the Gilded Age in particular. Richard Hofstadter called them "the progressive historians." This Progressive school of history placed sectional and economic conflict at the center of American politics. Combined with earlier views of Gilded Age politics, it pictured national politics as largely devoid of substance, as a rhetorical circus in which orators appealed to Civil War loyalties to distract voters from massive corruption. It often focused on the largely unsuccessful efforts by agrarian radicals in the Middle West and South, sometimes in alliance with urban workers, to secure governmental action against powerful new corporate behemoths. This struggle, most Progressive historians specified, was part of a long-term continuing conflict between the proponents of democracy and opportunity, on the one side, and the forces of privilege on the other. Such a perspective reached a wide popular audience in the works of Matthew Josephson in the 1930s. Drawing upon the concept of the frontier, alert to the role of sections, and focused on economic conflict, a number of other Progressive historians produced works on the politics of the Gilded Age that were characterized by thorough research into primary sources and thoughtful analysis, works that still have a good deal to offer to readers today, especially those works that examined agrarian radicalism.

The heyday of Progressive history had passed by the 1950s, and new approaches to Gilded Age politics were emerging. Richard Hofstadter was in the forefront of these new schools of thought. He argued that previous historians – those of the Progressive school – had emphasized conflict too much and had ignored a cluster of values commonly held by most Americans, values he identified as intensely nationalistic, usually isolationist, fiercely individualistic, and unswervingly capitalist. In *The Age of Reform* (1955), Hofstadter looked at two groups which seemed not to share these consensus values. He drew upon social psychology, rather than sectional or economic analysis, to present the Populists as nostalgic, paranoid, nativist, anti-semitic, and jingoistic, and to portray the Progressives as victims of a revolution in social status produced by industrialization and urbanization that led them into politics as a way to assuage their status anxieties. His view touched off a flurry of historical research as scores of historians sought evidence for Hofstadter's thesis in case studies of particular cities or states.

The "New Political History" and the "Organizational Synthesis"

The response to Hofstadter coincided with two new developments in the historiography of late nineteenth-century politics and public life, one of which was dubbed the "organizational synthesis" and the other the "new political history."

Much of the "new political history" focused on the nineteenth century. While Jacksonian democracy came in for its share of attention, many of the new political historians examined the Gilded Age. These historians, writing during the 1960s and 1970s, drew their initial inspiration from the work of political scientists in analyzing voting behavior. The work of V. O. Key Jr and research conducted at the University of

Michigan's Survey Research Center in the 1950s and 1960s contributed to a reconceptualization of politics that often went under the label "behavioralism." Behavioralists emphasized that individual and group political choices derived from a social and economic context, and they sometimes portrayed political decision-making as little more than the aggregate end-product of many individual or group choices. Political institutions, the favored subject of the previous generation of political scientists – the contemporaries of the Progressive historians – became little more than the arenas within which groups worked out their conflicting objectives through bargaining.

Building on this approach, some historians turned from reviewing arguments over the tariff and bemoaning the vacuousness of Gilded Age politics and followed the lead of Samuel P. Hays in exploring the social basis of political history. In the late 1960s and early 1970s, this new political history of the Gilded Age took shape in monographs that drew upon statistical analysis of voting behavior to present new understandings of voters, parties, and grassroots politics in the late nineteenth century. By 1979, the transformation of historians' thinking was largely complete, with the new view of Gilded Age politics expressed in Paul Kleppner's *The Third Electoral System* (1979).

The work of Samuel P. Hays was central not only to the new political history but also to the "organizational synthesis." Drawing initially upon Hays's *The Response to Industrialism, 1885–1914* (1957) and then upon Robert Wiebe's *The Search for Order, 1877–1920* (1967), this perspective paralleled the emergence of modernization theory in the social sciences and presented the great economic and social transformations of the late nineteenth century as pivotal for understanding all other aspects of American life, including politics and public life. Where political corruption had once been at the center of historians' narratives of Gilded Age politics, Hays now pushed it to the margins, dismissing it as little more than an inconsistency between the formal structure of decision-making and what he saw as the informal influence of local communities. An organizational perspective, Hays specified, required historians to devote less attention to events and more to structure, and to focus on the struggle for dominance among various groups within that structure.

Another defining characteristic of the new political history was the argument that the most important political issues of the Gilded Age were cultural, rooted in ethnic conflict over such issues as the consumption of alcohol. This view held that the basic division among voters was between "pietistic" or "evangelistic" cultural groups and "ritualistic" ones. The pietists were old-stock American Protestants, Calvinist and Wesleyan immigrants from England and Scotland, and Lutherans from Norway and Sweden, all of whom opposed alcohol on religious grounds, favored the political regulation of individual morality, and usually voted Republican. Ritualistic groups included the Irish, southern and eastern European immigrants, and German Catholics and German Lutherans, who saw no sin in a glass of beer or whiskey, opposed political efforts to dictate matters of individual conscience, and usually voted Democratic. The emergence of the anti-Catholic American Protective Association in the 1890s, and its efforts to take over the Republican party in many areas, often intensified this ethnic political conflict. This ethnocultural interpretation of voting behavior became so central to the new political history that some of its adherents (but not Hays) denied the significance of economic or class interests in influencing voting at all.

The contributions of the new political history included not only its emphasis on the importance of ethnicity in understanding voting but also its rediscovery of Bryce's emphasis on the mass nature of politics, characterized by extraordinarily high rates of voter participation and campaign rallies that involved large numbers of males. Detailed studies of voter participation rates, utilizing both quantitative and documentary materials, have concluded that, in most places and at most times, nearly every qualified voter actually voted, barring accident, illness, absence from home, or inclement weather. Furthermore, party loyalty was extremely strong, indeed at the highest point in American history. The result was an incredibly energetic political culture that enshrined parties at the center of public life.

Populism

At the same time that the new political history was taking substantial form, a number of historians responded to Hofstadter's characterization of Populism with detailed case studies of Populism in particular states, and some of these historians employed the concepts and statistical tools of the new political history. First appearing in the 1960s, these studies depicted the Populists as political pragmatists reacting to economic distress. They acted rationally and for the most part were free of the conspiratorial fantasies that Hofstadter claimed were central to their ideological outlook. Continuing to appear and multiply long past the point when Hofstadter's views ceased to be influential, these works have greatly increased our understanding of local and state politics in the 1880s and 1890s, especially in the South and West.

The most direct challenge to Hofstadter came from Norman Pollack. In his *The Populist Response to Industrial America* (1962), a study based on a close reading of the writings of Populist leaders and adherents, he concluded that "Populism was a progressive social force" (1962: 2). Far from nostalgically looking backward and rejecting economic change, the Populists accepted industrialization and formulated an innovative program to curb its excesses. Drawing support from labor leaders and social reformers, they developed a reasoned, powerful critique of industrialism that, Pollack insisted, can still point the way toward a more humanistic and equitable distribution of economic power in the corporate America of the twentieth century.

Unlike the new political historians, Lawrence Goodwyn in *Democratic Promise: the Populist Moment in America* (1976) did not turn to a quantitative analysis of voting for a fresh perspective on Populism. He proceeded instead from a cultural approach in arguing that genuine Populism derived from a "movement culture" of southern farmers that appeared first in Texas and was then challenged and eventually subsumed by a "shadow movement" that lacked the cultural core of genuine Populism. For Goodwyn, the far-reaching democratic goal of the Populists, who originated in the Southern Farmers' Alliance, was "structural reform of the American economic system" (1976: xvii). Although subsequent historians have generally avoided distinguishing between genuine and "shadow" versions of Populism, Goodwyn's work restored the human side of Populism and succeeded in explaining how an agrarian revolt of impoverished farmers became a mass movement that directly challenged late nineteenth-century finance capitalism.

Goodwyn was influential in reviving a debate over Populism that had become trapped in the terms set down by Hofstadter. The emphasis now shifted back to the region identified by John D. Hicks in the 1930s as the heartland of Populism, the wheat-growing states in the trans-Mississippi West.

Spearheading much of this work has been Peter H. Argersinger. His essays, collected in *The Limits of Agrarian Radicalism* (1995), make a strong case for the western Populists as genuine radicals with a vision of a more equitable America. With an indictment of industrial America and an appeal steeped in the moral language of evangelical Protestantism, they sought "an activist state to correct economic injustices" (Argersinger, 1995: 2). What thwarted them was not the shallowness of their commitment but the structural limits of a two-party system that would admit no newcomers. Repeatedly, at both the state and federal levels, entrenched party interests co-opted, blunted, or ignored Populist demands for meaningful reforms. "By the turn of the century," Argersinger concludes, "the structural limits of politics were in many respects more powerful than before the Populists emerged, though by challenging orthodoxy, devising new ideas and criticizing partisan loyalties Populists had at least weakened some of the cultural constraints of politics" (1995: 35–6). Argersinger's Populists, like Goodwyn's in the South, had hoped for much more.

Race, Ethnicity, and Social History

The new political history and the organizational synthesis emerged at about the same time as, and shared some important concepts with, the emergence of social history. The new political history tended to focus on grassroots politics and on cultural values as the basis of voting behavior. Social history, as it developed in the late 1960s and 1970s, sought to understand the experience of particular groups defined by ethnicity, race, gender, or class. Its proponents, like the new political historians, turned to local case studies in an effort to grasp the nature of social relationships and cultural values for a specific place and time. For the Gilded Age, this meant examining the impact of immigration, industrialization, and urbanization on social groups.

Its early critics sometimes derided social history as history with the politics left out, but in fact social historians rarely left politics out, although they did seek to reconceptualize the relationship of politics to society and economy. A typical case study in social history, for example, might begin by describing in detail the social and economic experiences of a group or community, its cultural values, and then its political behavior as influenced by cultural factors. Politics in social history was thus often local, and some social historians disparaged studies of national politics as marginalizing groups who, because of their race, ethnicity, class, or gender, were excluded from the corridors of power.

Works that linked race and ethnicity to politics during the Gilded Age, in addition to those that helped to define the new political history and the many case studies of Populism, appeared in increasing numbers from the late 1960s onward. Bess Beatty, in *A Revolution Gone Backward* (1987), provides the fullest account of the black response to the national administrations from 1876 to 1896. The story she relates is one of almost unrelieved disappointment and frustration for African Americans. Whether Republican or Democratic, the presidents appointed few black office-holders and backed away from vague campaign promises to enhance black rights through new legislation.

Important studies came out in the 1970s from historians specializing in western history that examined the role of race in the development of California's unions and labor parties and in national policy-making. What became clear was that Asian Americans emerged as scapegoats and victims when politicians blamed them for falling wages and unemployment and used pejorative anti-Chinese or anti-Japanese stereotypes to promote white, working-class solidarity. As persuasively argued by Andrew Gyory in *Closing the Gate: Race, Politics, and the Chinese Exclusion Act* (1998), politicians seized on Chinese exclusion to deflect the demands of white workers for a more egalitarian solution to the nation's industrial crisis.

By the late 1980s and 1990s, several authors began to consider political initiatives by Asian Americans and the internal politics of Asian-American groups. The works of Sucheng Chan were especially important for providing a starting-point to explore the nature of politics among members of a community barred from the suffrage and from citizenship itself. As Chan emphasized, one avenue that remained open during the Gilded Age was the courts, and political resistance by Asian Americans often took the form of litigation.

The West, notably the Southwest, was also home to Latino peoples, many of them of Mexican descent who had lived in the Southwest at the time of the Mexican War or who had moved there subsequently. The most thorough overview of politics for these Latinos during the Gilded Age is Juan Gómez-Quiñones's *The Roots of Chicano Politics, 1600–1940* (1994), about a quarter of which deals with the period from 1848 to 1900. Stressing the post-1848 subordination of Mexican Americans under the new Anglo rulers of the region, he uncovers a wealth of new material. Challenging a long-held view, he documents the often significant role of Chicano women in political activities.

One of the thorniest public policy issues of the Gilded Age involved the Native Americans in the West, who were widely seen as either impediments to or victims of a morally and technologically superior Anglo civilization. The solution for politicians and reformers, once the Plains Indians had been militarily pacified and placed on reservations, took the form of the Dawes Act of 1887, legislation that offered individual land holdings to Indians in return for their renunciation of tribal holdings. As shown by Frederick E. Hoxie, the Dawes Act was far more successful in depriving Indians of their land than in assimilating them into American society. Still, in his ambitiously conceived *Parading through History: the Making of the Crow Nation in America, 1805–1935* (1995), Hoxie also demonstrates how Indians could retain and indeed strengthen their identities when faced with divisive issues such as allotment of tribal lands. His study integrates federal policies with the internal dynamics of politics among Crow clans and well might serve as a model for understanding how Native Americans developed their own political techniques for shaping changing circumstances to meet their cultural goals of autonomy and group identity.

Immigrants, Workers, and Urban Politics

Many of the early urban histories focused on bosses and reformers. As if confirming Bryce's claim in the late 1880s that American politics had failed most conspicuously in the cities, historians cast urban politics in the Gilded Age as a morality play between venal bosses and righteous reformers in which the corruption of "boss rule" emerged triumphant. In 1974, Hays called for a new approach to urban politics that dispensed with this old duality and focused instead on structure, ethnicity, and class, and especially on the centrifugal and centripetal forces involved in the rapid urban expansion of the era.

Hays's call reinforced a prior tendency to move away from the machine model of urban politics, and by the 1990s the model lay in ruins. New studies established that most urban machines were short-lived and had little direct impact on municipal expenditures. Moreover, the assumption that immigrant and working-class groups supported expensive urban projects as a source of jobs and patronage proved to be groundless. In fact, as shown by Jon Teaford and others, costly expenditures for such urban services as water, sewerage, parks, and police and fire protection required the creation of new municipal agencies with shifting political constituencies that transcended class and ethnic loyalties.

Working-class immigrants or their children comprised a majority of the urban electorate in the Gilded Age, especially in the large industrial centers of the Northeast and Midwest. In trying to understand the political values and behavior of this urban working class, historians have often talked past each other. Those who embraced the new school of labor history that emerged in the 1960s moved away from the institutional focus of the old Commons school and the rigid structural determinism of a Marxist approach and toward a cultural emphasis associated with the British historian E. P. Thompson. What they found was a vibrant working-class republicanism that workers drew upon to critique American capitalism. Workers pointed to the contradiction between artisanal values of individual autonomy and republican independence and the growing reality of regimented work regimes imposed by the centralization of capital. Reacting to the loss of control over both their labor and their republic, workers turned to farmer–labor alliances, socialist parties, independent labor parties, and fusion movements with local middle-class supporters. At the height of its political influence in the mid-1880s, labor supported 15,000 local assemblies of the Knights of Labor, which, in turn, successfully backed 200 tickets in local elections.

As labor historians, particularly those trained by David Montgomery and Herbert Gutman, were making the case for the political manifestation of working-class consciousness, the new political historians were finding little evidence that class was a determining factor in how Americans were actually voting. The respective ethnocultural alliances of Republicans and Democrats held remarkably firmly during the industrial upheavals of the Gilded Age. Workers, like their employers, appeared to forge their partisan identity from a cluster of cultural and emotional loyalties that transcended class considerations. No strong labor or socialist party ever emerged, and the success of any independent political activity by workers was quite ephemeral. Apparently, any appeal of artisanal republicanism was limited to a small minority of the working class.

The reconciliation of these seemingly contradictory views remains one of the great challenges for historians of the Gilded Age. Richard Schneirov's *Labor and Urban Politics: Class Conflict and the Origins of Modern Liberalism in Chicago: 1864–1897* (1998) suggests one way out of this impasse. He pays special attention to the involvement of unions in party politics at the local level and demonstrates the role of labor in fusing nineteenth-century republicanism into twentieth-century liberalism.

Another approach comes out of Richard J. Oestreicher's *Solidarity and Fragmentation: Working People and Class Consciousness in Detroit, 1875–1900* (1986). More so than most labor or political historians, Oestreicher is concerned with the interaction of class and ethnicity in a specific historical setting. He persuasively argues that these identities or mentalities are not mutually exclusive and that "the extent of class consciousness was a function of concrete opportunities for its expression" (1986: xviii). Although rapid urbanization and new industrial techniques of mass production created a common set of problems for workers, the responses to those problems were filtered through the distinctive social patterns and cultural values of ethnic community life. The resulting tension could reinforce or undercut cross-cultural solidarity as workers assessed how best to redress their grievances in a given setting. The class consciousness that assumed a heightened political form with the rise of the Knights of Labor in the 1880s subsided but did not disappear once the Knights faded into political obscurity after 1886. Workers continued to express their grievances at the workplace, and they responded to any openings that the two-party system offered them for political expression of their class consciousness.

Masculine Politics, Parties, and the New Institutionalism

Most historians have stressed that during the Gilded Age men (that is, the electorate) were expected to hold strong loyalties to a political party. Young males were acculturated into an intensely masculine political world and an often exaggerated masculinity infused political language. Being a party loyalist was considered a mark of masculinity, and women, who could not vote except in a few isolated instances, were seen as having neither politics nor party loyalties. Thus, most accounts have depicted Gilded Age politics – participation in partisan meetings, campaigning, voting, and officeholding – as a highly gendered, highly masculine domain.

Beginning in the late 1950s, a large literature on women and politics in the Gilded Age began to appear, especially on women's suffrage and its leaders. Nearly all of the literature pointed to the emergence of women's political activities within the constraints of domesticity. In addition to exploring how women gained the vote in a number of states and territories in the West, newer studies also broadened the understanding of the female-led drive for prohibition in the Gilded Age by overturning the older view of the prohibitionists as rural, provincial bluenoses.

Some works on women for this period have moved beyond specific campaigns or issues in which women were involved to examine larger cultural patterns involving women and politics. Kathryn Kish Sklar used biography superbly in *Florence Kelley and the Nation's Work: the Rise of Women's Political Culture, 1830–1900* (1995) to limn a broad portrait of women and politics and of the female political culture that developed in the late nineteenth century. However, where Sklar and most others have looked to the separate nature of women's political culture in the Gilded Age, Rebecca Edwards had recently questioned some of these assumptions in *Angels in the Machinery: Gender in American Party Politics from the Civil War to the Progressive Era* (1997). She argues that Republicans incorporated a maternal view of the family into their activist vision of the state and included a role for women.

Edward's inclusion of women is a welcome addition to a field long concerned almost exclusively with male actors and male prerogatives. A main thrust of that concern since the 1950s, aside from investigating the religious and ethnic roots of partisan loyalties, has been a refutation of the Progressives' indictment of the Gilded Age parties as the handmaiden of big business in the pursuit of concrete economic interests. One of the best studies was Robert Marcus's *Grand Old Party: Political Structure in the Gilded Age, 1880–1896* (1971). Traditional political history in its concentration on party leaders and fine-grained analysis of how congressmen used patronage to maintain their base of power at home, *Grand Old Party* none the less develops an important thesis. Marcus finds that party organization remained decentralized at a time when business and professional groups were moving toward centralization. He explains this divergence by the preference of power-seeking politicians to retain control over their state organizations. Power was a goal in and of itself, and only rarely did party alliances with business interests raise sufficient funds to meet party needs. State bosses were in charge until the election of 1896, and only a revolt by voters during the economic depression of the 1890s enabled proponents of more national control to rally behind William J. McKinley. In turn the McKinley candidacy benefited from massive corporate donations sparked by fears of the Populists and the Democrats' call for free silver.

McKinley's administration, as well as those of all the Gilded Age presidents, have been well covered in the American Presidency series published by the University Press of Kansas. Meanwhile, as studies on the role of parties in monetary policy, the tariff, and business regulation continued to appear, the attention of political historians has increasingly been drawn to the transformation in politics that centered on the 1890s.

What has been called "the system of 1896" – the new patterns of politics that developed after a critical realignment in the mid-1890s – resulted in a generation of Republican domination of the electorate and national administrations. Political parties, unrivalled centers of power for most of the nineteenth century, experienced a significant decline in their influence. Voters' party loyalties diminished. Campaign tactics changed from mobilizing loyal voters to advertising candidates. Voter participation rates dropped dramatically. Organized interest groups – from the Anti-Saloon League (formed in 1895) to the National Association of Manufacturers (also 1895) and the German–American Alliance (1901) – began to exercise significant influence in particular policy arenas. All this marked an important change in the most fundamental assumptions of American politics.

New ideals of institutional reform were appearing by 1900 as the Gilded Age gave way to the Progressive era of the early twentieth century. The pursuit of those ideals rested on the institutional process of state-building at the national level that had its origins in the Gilded Age. Scholars have long studied the political institutions of the Gilded Age, beginning with Bryce and his contemporary, Woodrow Wilson, who probed the workings of the US Congress. Institutional studies appeared throughout the twentieth century, often by political scientists rather than historians, and sometimes with little historical analysis. The best of these studies emerged after mid-century and provided solid surveys of the federal bureaucracy, the evolution of policy-related procedures in the US Senate, and the creation and growth of such federal agencies as the Civil Service Commission and the Interstate Commerce Commission.

The 1980s saw the emergence of a "new institutionalism" that raised new and fundamental questions about the origins of the modern federal state. The seminal work here, Stephen Skowronek's *Building a New American State: the Expansion of National Administrative Capacities, 1897–1920*, appeared in 1982. A political scientist, Skowronek combined insights from economists, sociologists, and historians to show how and why the federal government began to reorganize itself around new administrative capacities in the last quarter of the nineteenth century. Grounding his study in an analysis of institutional innovations in civil service reform, army reorganization, and federal railroad legislation, he examines "governmental elites responding to very different kinds of problems presented by the crises, class conflicts, and complexity of the new industrial era" (1982: 15). The result was the gradual, halting evolution of new bureaucratic modes of government at the national level that competed with and undercut the former institutional structure based on the rule-making of the courts and the patronage of the political parties.

Future Directions

In 1986, William E. Leuchtenburg delivered his presidential address to the Organization of American Historians on "The Pertinence of Political History." Responding to the inroads of social history, he argued that historians needed to re-focus their attention on political history. In retrospect, it is clear that at the time of Leuchtenburg's admonition a significant upswing in the study of political history was already underway. One aspect of this has been the new institutionalism and the attention to the nature of federalism in the late nineteenth century. At the same time, many historians of the Gilded Age, without abandoning social history, have moved politics into a more prominent role, treating politics not merely as one expression of cultural values but as the central subject of analysis, as witness such recent work as Sklar's biography of Florence Kelley, Edwards's *Angels in the Machinery*, and Schneirov's study of Chicago labor.

The "new institutionalism" may have run its course so far as examinations of the emergence of the modern federal state is concerned, but other institutional topics, and related topics in legal and constitutional history, are likely to continue to attract attention. More remains to be done on federalism. If social history taught us a great deal about the nature of particular communities and their politics – confirming Thomas "Tip" O'Neill's famous dictum that "all politics is local" – one continuing task is to understand policy not just at the local level but also at state and federal levels. We still have to look more closely at how race, ethnicity, gender, and class have had an impact on the evolution of particular policies. In this regard, the burgeoning field of environmental history has produced some of the most exciting recent work.

During the Gilded Age, new technologies of transportation and communication were shrinking time and space. Historians have begun to explore some of the implications of these for understanding the development of particular political movements or policies: historians of the settlement house movement have looked to its English antecedents; historians of American socialism have studied its European counterparts; and historians of immigration have looked to the influences of the "old country" in understanding American politics. Though both Frances Willard and Ida B. Wells lectured in England to raise funds for their work in the US, we know relatively little about women's international political networks. In 1893, when New Zealand became the first nation to adopt women's suffrage, it was also adopted in Colorado (and was already in place in Wyoming); what sort of communication, if any, existed among the suffrage advocates in the South Pacific and the American West? What did they learn from each other's victories and defeats? Australians read propaganda from the Populists in the 1890s and created their own branch of the Women's Christian Temperance Union. The labor parties of Melbourne, which developed in the 1890s, had a clear parallel in the Union Labor Party of San Francisco, organized in 1901. Students of agrarian radicalism have long understood the porous nature of the border with Canada. All of this suggests the need, at least, for historians of Gilded Age politics to be aware of ways in which the increased ease of international communication and travel produced an increased possibility for the exchange of ideas and organizational models.

One should hesitate to call for synthesis. Calling for synthesis is the usual response when faced with a large and disparate body of work, much of it focused on local communities or specific social groups. Historians have, in fact, been calling for synthesis from the beginning of the change in research agendas produced by social history. But calls for synthesis have sometimes met resistance. Advocates of social history argue that studies of particular places or groups permit greater attention to groups previously overlooked by historians who focused only on national politics, particularly groups disfranchised in law or in practice. Calls for synthesis sometimes meet the response that a "meta-narrative" loses richness and diversity and marginalizes disfranchised groups. Such arguments should not be ignored because it is unquestionably true that social history has vastly enriched our understanding of Gilded Age politics. The conclusion to draw from that diversity and richness, however, is not to avoid synthesis but to construct syntheses that incorporate as much of that diversity and richness as possible, while at the same time seeking the larger patterns that help to put studies of particular groups and places into a larger context. This is, perhaps, the largest task now facing historians of Gilded Age politics.

REFERENCES

Argersinger, Peter H. (1995) *The Limits of Agrarian Radicalism: Western Populism and American Politics*. Lawrence: University Press of Kansas.

Beatty, Bess (1987) *A Revolution Gone Backward: the Black Response to National Politics, 1876–1896*. New York: Greenwood Press.

Bryce, James (1888) *The American Commonwealth*, 3 vols. London and New York: Macmillan.

Cherny, Robert W. (1997) *American Politics in the Gilded Age, 1868–1900*. Wheeling, Ill.: Harlan Davidson.

Edwards, Rebecca (1997) *Angels in the Machinery: Gender in American Party Politics from the Civil War to the Progressive Era*. New York: Oxford University Press.

Gómez-Quiñones, Juan (1994) *Roots of Chicano Politics, 1600–1940*. Albuquerque: University of New Mexico Press.

Goodwyn, Lawrence (1976) *Democratic Promise: the Populist Moment in America*. New York: Oxford University Press.

Gyory, Andrew (1998) *Closing the Gate: Race, Politics, and the Chinese Exclusion Act*. Chapel Hill, NC: University of North Carolina Press.

Hays, Samuel P. (1957) *The Response to Industrialism, 1885–1914*. Chicago: University of Chicago Press.

Hofstadter, Richard (1955) *The Age of Reform: from Bryan to FDR*. New York: Alfred A. Knopf.

Hoxie, Frederick E. (1995) *Parading through History: the Making of the Crow Nation in America, 1805–1935*. New York: Cambridge University Press.

Keller, Morton (1977) *Affairs of State: Public Life in Late Nineteenth Century America*. Cambridge, Mass.: Belknap Press of Harvard University.

Kleppner, Paul (1979) *The Third Electoral System, 1853–1892: Parties, Voters, and Political Cultures*. Chapel Hill, NC: University of North Carolina Press.

Marcus, Robert D. (1971) *Grand Old Party: Political Structure in the Gilded Age, 1880–1896*. New York: Oxford University Press.

Morgan, H. Wayne (1969) *From Hayes to McKinley: National Party Politics, 1877–1896*. Syracuse, NY: Syracuse University Press.

Oestreicher, Richard Jules (1986) *Solidarity and Fragmentation: Working People and Class Consciousness in Detroit, 1875–1900*. Urbana: University of Illinois Press.

Pollack, Norman (1962) *The Populist Response to Industrial America: Midwestern Populist Thought*. Cambridge, Mass.: Harvard University Press.

Schneirov, Richard (1998) *Labor and Urban Politics: Class Conflict and the Origins of Modern Liberalism in Chicago, 1864–1897*. Urbana: University of Illinois Press.

Sklar, Kathryn Kish (1995) *Florence Kelley and the Nation's Work: the Rise of Women's Political Culture, 1830–1900*. New Haven, Conn.: Yale University Press.

Skowronek, Stephen (1982) *Building a New American State: the Expansion of National Administrative Capacities, 1897–1920*. New York: Cambridge University Press.

Wiebe, Robert H. (1967) *The Search for Order, 1877–1920*. New York: Hill and Wang.

CHAPTER SIX

American Law in the Nineteenth Century

JOHN E. SEMONCHE

A GENERATION or so ago a survey of the history of nineteenth-century law would have been centered on public law, primarily the Constitution, and coverage of the broader field of legal history would have been confined to rather limited studies tracing the history of institutions or lending support to some contemporary legal argument. As historians made law their subject, they were aware that they were entering an arena in which there already was an ongoing dialogue between the lawmakers and law interpreters, on the one side, and their critics on the other. That dialogue enabled the historian of law to influence the course of events beyond the academy. An excellent example of this influence can be found in *Erie Railroad Co.* v. *Tompkins* (1938) in which the United States Supreme Court cited historical work done on the Judiciary Act of 1789 as the reason for overturning *Swift* v. *Tyson* (1842), which had spawned the development of a federal common law. The Court said that its now discarded precedent was based upon a misreading of legislative intent that, in fact, had expected the federal courts to follow state common law.

History of this genre, often called law-office or forensic history, even when well done, left its critics wishing for a future when legal history would attract more practitioners and when it would be studied primarily for the purpose of illuminating the past rather than playing the willing handmaiden to present-day controversies. Since that time, these critics have got their wish in that scholars, whose general focus shifted to exploring society in all its ramifications, with particular emphasis upon race, class, and gender, found in the study of law a most fertile field of research. As a result, legal history was redefined and broadened. As more laborers in this particular vineyard appeared, they were less interested in influencing the course of the law than in understanding the role it played in society. They asked questions about its relationship to other forces and interests, such as what it moved in response to, who benefited from doctrinal changes, how neutral was its application, and did law really rule or was it manipulated to serve certain ends? Much of this new work, when it did not treat law as a defining and ordering phenomenon, focused on the area of private, instead of public, law and tended to concentrate on state courts and state legislatures, rather than on the United States Supreme Court or Congress.

How do we explain this new found interest in legal history and the outpouring of work in the field in the past generation or so? Certainly, law schools have become more receptive to legal history than they were in the past, although it still has not become part of the law student's core curriculum. Law school professors who teach and do research in legal history are today more likely than not to have a PhD in history in addition to the JD. This training in history shapes their research in a way that responds more to trends in historical research and writing. The critical legal studies movement, a law school development, has always had a history component, and its critical onslaught clearly mirrors developments and fashions in the social sciences. Also, the way in which the history profession has leaned so substantially in the direction of social history helps explain why legal materials have been so exploited. As historians seek to uncover the life of common people, case records have become important sources in seeking to piece together this life. Whether one is writing social history or legal history depends upon the use of the materials and the questions posed, although the overlap between the areas is apparent.

This new interest is reflected in a number of ways. It is manifested in the growing membership of the American Society for Legal History, which was founded in 1956 but only began publishing its journal, *Law and History Review*, in 1983. This new publication joined *The American Journal of Legal History*, which traces its lineage back to 1957. Recently, these more traditional means of academic communication have been supplemented by the use of the computer, which has not only put much legal source material at the fingertips of historians but also has provided the means for them to interact with each other on an ongoing basis. Yearly conferences of professional organizations continue to serve a useful purpose in terms of providing access to discrete programs that can open new frontiers, but now the Internet has expanded personal access to fellow professionals far beyond the confines of the yearly conference. Michigan State University has instituted a structure called H-Net that provides a series of listserves in various historical areas and specialties by which interested scholars in many disciplines can communicate. For those interested in constitutional and legal history the listserve is called H-LAW, and it is sponsored by the American Society for Legal History. What makes this addition to scholarly communication so valuable is an immediacy that gives even a lone scholar access to a bevy of colleagues who can respond to queries in a timely fashion. Also, by monitoring the network traffic, historians can keep up to date with developments in their field of study and maintain awareness of what questions and issues are generating current interest and attention.

Scholarly activity and production in the field of legal history has surpassed even the most hopeful expectations of the early critics, but, paradoxically, the objectivity that they saw as the goal of new scholarship has been displaced by a new subjectivity. The abundant use of the prefix "post" to characterize the present, whether it be post-industrial or postmodern or any of a myriad of other choices, indicates an indebtedness to the past that normally would gladden the hearts of historians. Are they not the professionals who are expected to chart and explain change over time as they labor to extract the elaborate causal sequence that brought us to this present? Historians, however, have not been immune to developments in the humanities and certain social sciences that have led scholars to embrace indeterminacy as the operative principle, to use interpretations of the past to find meaning in the present, and to exalt conceptualization over the more mundane task of documentation. Squeezing the most meaning from the fewest facts has become a challenging academic game. Logic can be summoned to fill factual gaps: if no evidence can be found that the law was purposefully shaped to achieve the objective it did, then from the fact that certain results were produced one can imply a deliberate causal effect. And since all historians come to their subjects with preconceived ideas, why not boldly announce them and then find support to give them some plausibility? Since law was so often viewed through the lens of economics, scholars in law schools working with this paradigm provided perspectives drawn from critical legal studies, a radical approach that accepted the indeterminacy of law and equated it with politics, and the law and economics movement, a conservative approach that saw a striving for economic efficiency at the heart of legal change. Also, scholars in both history departments and law schools found a new attraction in Marxist interpretations of the operation of law in capitalistic society. So, the new legal history proliferated, and although it could not promise objectivity, it did bring with it an excitement that belied the old view that the study of law's history was a highly technical and boring enterprise.

Another threshold problem in legal history concerned the relationship of law to the political, social, and economic realms; earlier legal history tended to treat law as an entity unto itself, seemingly divorced from the world it sought to order. That a new generation of legal historians would reject such a view was to be expected, but at times the rejection either explicitly or implicitly questioned whether law was even a variable in the social equation. Was it really any more than a simple reflection of the actual determining social variables? For instance, when, in 1973, Lawrence M. Friedman first published his path-breaking history of American law, he confessed that he had surrendered himself "wholeheartedly to some of the insights of social science" in treating "American law... not as a kingdom unto itself... but as a mirror of society" in which all was "relative and molded by economy and society." Despite the outcry of some critics who believed that such an approach to law's history was grossly distortive in that it denied law even a partial life of its own, 12 years later, in a second edition, Friedman reaffirmed his view of law (Friedman, 1985: 12). And when another legal historian, Kermit Hall, wrote a book tying developments in the law to general trends in American history, he entitled it *The Magic Mirror* (1989), borrowing the metaphor from Oliver Wendell Holmes Jr.

That such a total dismissal of legal rules, ideals, and ordering in favor of an instrumentalist or functionalist view would itself stir a reaction might also be expected, and recent literature is filled either with the rediscovery of legal doctrine or testaments to the importance of law in itself. Hall in his history reflects this shift in emphasis by repeatedly using the term "legal culture." Legal historians associated with the critical legal studies movement were extremely critical of instrumentalists, such as Friedman, not only because their histories assumed a socially beneficial effect from changes in the law but also because they had refused to see law itself as a meaningful variable. In fact, not only has legal doctrine been accorded new respect for its explanatory value, but also historians have developed interest in the study of the language of the law and its cultural significance. For instance, Robert Gordon (Gordon and Nelson, 1977) argues that law is ideology with cultural codes embedded in its text and language that constructs the world that judges inhabit. And when Christopher L. Tomlins sought to explain the relationship between law and labor prior to the Civil War, he said that the legal preference for treating citizens as independent units benefiting equally from a protection of their private rights is "not so much... a consequence of the development of a particular political economy, as instrumentalists would have it, but rather as in itself an integral element in that political economy's constitution" (Tomlins, 1993: xv–xvi). So law has again emerged not as independent of the culture but as a most significant constituting factor in its formation. In an unorthodox treatment of the United States Supreme Court, I have traced its history as a culture-defining institution that contributes to the maintenance of a national identity and summons Americans to measure up to the demands of their civil theology (Semonche, 1998).

Legal developments in the nineteenth century have become the primary focal point of the new legal history. This concentration can be attributed, in part, to the characterization of the antebellum period as an era of creativity, a golden age, or the time during which law paved the way for the rise of liberal capitalism. In 1938 Roscoe Pound entitled the collection of his four lectures dealing with the period the "formative era." The challenge posed during that time, he said, was to fashion from "inherited legal materials a general body of law for what was to be a politically and economically unified land" (Pound, 1938: 8). Pound considered legislation and doctrinal writing as well as the common law in his appraisal. This broad approach was furthered by J. Willard Hurst, a Wisconsin law professor, who delivered a series of law lectures at Northwestern University in 1955 that were published under the title *Law and the Conditions of Freedom in the Nineteenth-century United States* (1956). Placing law in all its varieties within the economic environment, Hurst not only produced further work fleshing out his theories but also fathered a Wisconsin school of legal historians that followed the master's lead. They wrote from the perspective that law could be fully explained as a reflection of the social, economic, and political organization of society. Hurst concluded that nineteenth-century changes in the law promoted individual liberty and released the energy necessary for the economic development that benefited the entire society. When Friedman, a Hurst disciple, published his history of American law, he devoted 80 percent of its space to the nineteenth century. This emphasis reflected the fact that much of the new work done by legal historians focused on the 1800s, a focus still in place a quarter of a century later.

When Grant Gilmore delivered his lectures on the history of law at Yale University in 1974, he rechristened Pound's formative period an age of discovery, followed by an age of faith, which then, he said, culminated in an age of anxiety (Gilmore, 1977). Anthony Chase, who contrasted the development of liberal capitalism in the United States with that of authoritarian capitalism in Germany and Japan, added to Gilmore's periods a new one beginning with the end of the Vietnam War (Chase, 1997). Whatever the nomenclature, most scholars accepted the conclusion that the creative period in American law ended with the Civil War. They believed that it was followed by a period beginning in the latter third of the nineteenth century in which a pedestrian formalism dictated legal outcomes: precedent was king and the law seemed to be an obstacle rather than an aid to social change, as talented lawyers were hesitant to don the mantle of reformer. Such consensus existed that the battles were fought not over the paradigm but rather within it. Although certain critics cautioned that painting an unrelieved picture of judges and law-makers basing their decisions on economic calculations distorted the more complex reality, there was general agreement that common law doctrines were modified in the nineteenth century and that the modifications did facilitate capitalistic development. For instance, strict liability in personal injury cases increasingly became liability only with fault; protective devices to prevent impositions upon the less aware fell before *caveat emptor*, let the buyer beware; and property rights were restricted in favor of now more readily available eminent domain proceedings. Where some of the controversy in current scholarship arises is over the question of whom these changes benefited and at whose cost. Was the liberal capitalism that shaped much nineteenth-century American law a conspiracy to oppress the mass of the people for the benefit of the few or was it more generally beneficial to the society as a whole?

Certainly the most provocative and controversial contribution to nineteenth-century legal history has been Morton Horwitz's *The Transformation of American Law, 1780–1860* (1977) in which the author asserted that judges and lawyers had aligned themselves with business interests to extract costs for their capitalistic ventures from the people at large. By manipulating the law, these interests had, in fact, provided themselves with subsidies. In this volume Horwitz, who identified with the critical legal studies movement, focused primarily on private law, primarily in the states, which he saw operating behind a façade of claimed neutrality. Arguing that this private law, the law of property, contracts, and torts, was indeed public in that it distributed benefits and imposed costs, Horwitz exposed what he saw as the intimate bond between politics and law. The conspirators were the judges who reshaped the inherited common law in a manner that would extract the costs from those least able to bear them and confer the benefits upon those who furthered the capitalistic thrust of the economy. Hurst and other writers had included legislators and legislatures as important factors in changing the common law, but Horwitz focused almost exclusively on the judges and what he saw as their concerted attempt to discard common law protections in favor of the economic interests of the capitalists.

That politics and law were related was hardly a surprising conclusion, but Horwitz's relentless insistence that law was no more than politics with no inner life of its own, and that changes in the law could only be understood in terms of a conspiracy against the larger interests of the entire community, obviously invited opposition. Using a limited evidentiary base, given the vast number of American state jurisdictions, Horwitz did provide examples of changes in the common law that seemed to benefit the entrepreneurs to the detriment of the less powerful. However, he found no direct evidence of any conspiracy. One could agree, as most scholars did, that changes in the law had taken place without positing any conspiracy to advance the cause of a rising class at a substantial cost to the majority of the people. For instance, Hurst saw the changes in terms of freeing up energy and encouraging individual liberty. Others saw the transformation in terms of economic efficiency or simple economic growth. Horwitz had little good to say about those who had preceded him in tying changes in the law to the needs of the economy, arguing that their explicit or implicit conclusion that such changes were more widely beneficial or class-neutral was wrong-headed.

Horwitz's second volume, subtitled, "The Crisis of Legal Orthodoxy, 1870–1960" (1992), supposedly a continuation of his earlier work, is a totally different book. Instead of proving his first volume's contention – that the changes made in the common law, subsidizing the few from the pockets of the many, were embedded in a legal formalism that was heavy handedly dispensed by the courts – he simply assumes this result. Although the assumption that an encrusted formalistic approach captured the judiciary after the Civil War is relatively common, it has not been thoroughly tested against the facts. Apparently Horwitz reasoned that, since there was such a constant attack on formalism by its critics, the courts must have provided those critics with the requisite target. So, instead of buttressing the conclusion of volume 1 with research in the decisions of the state courts that had provided the evidentiary base for his first book, Horwitz concentrated on those writers who attacked the formalistic approach. When he cited judicial decisions at all, he used cases drawn from the US Supreme Court, the tribunal that he had avoided in his first volume.

Horwitz's assumption that the instrumentalism of the antebellum period was replaced by a growing formalism in the law thereafter has been questioned by other scholars. To determine whether courts use legal doctrine to resist change, one needs to inspect not only their rhetoric but the decisions themselves. In the very arena where Horwitz looked for evidence, the work of the Supreme Court, his assumption does not meet the test of the evidence. In a comprehensive study of the decisions of the Court from the last decade of the nineteenth century through the first two decades of the twentieth century, when supposedly formalism ruled, I found that the justices, despite some wide-ranging doctrinal pronouncements, usually proceeded pragmatically, shaping results to meet differing fact situations (Semonche, 1978). More work needs to be done to deconstruct the traditional formalistic picture.

Horwitz's first volume won the Bancroft Prize, an award by Columbia University to authors of books on American history of exceptional merit, and although all scholars did not subscribe to his interpretative conclusions, most of them believed that his work had given even greater credibility to the reigning economic paradigm. Most recently that paradigm itself has come under frontal attack in Peter Karsten's *Heart versus Head: Judge-made Law in Nineteenth Century America* (1997). Utilizing a much wider research base in the very material that informed Horwitz's treatment, and looking systematically at judge-made changes in the common law, Karsten argued that the economically oriented paradigm was useless in explaining the changes wrought by common law judges in the nineteenth century. He did not dispute the fact that an entrepreneurial bias characterized certain legislative action during the period, but he found no substantial evidence that the bench had been captured by emerging capitalists or that judges were insensitive to the human costs of their decisions. Furthermore, he discovered more formalism, in the sense that it means adherence to precedent, in the earlier part of the nineteenth century than in the so-called formalistic era following the Civil War. Some of the changes in the common law that Horwitz proclaimed as pro-capitalistic Karsten said were not changes at all, and, when he did find judges departing from precedent, the decisions tended to benefit the weaker rather than the stronger party. What truly characterizes these common law judges, Karsten concluded, was their personal struggle between the head, following precedent, and the heart, responding to the sympathies generated by the real-life drama of the litigants.

By challenging the reigning paradigm, Karsten has made a most significant contribution to the study of nineteenth-century legal history. He speculates on why the economic explanation for changes in the law has become so widely accepted, especially when a balanced reading of the record indicates its severe limitations. From the time of the legal realists in the 1920s until rather recently, he says, legal historians drew upon scholarly traditions that emphasized economic issues; the newer emphasis on cultural and religious values as an important part of nineteenth-century life has only recently become a focal point of historical study.

Such proliferation of work on nineteenth-century private law has not meant the neglect of the century's constitutional history, for in the evolution of the nation's modern constitutional system the century could also be called "formative" or "transformative." The struggle with Great Britain culminating in American independence had, in part, been a struggle for the rule of law. The nineteenth century saw the rejection of the British solution of leaving the protection of a rule of law to the legislative majority in favor of a willingness to trust judges removed from the arena of politics with the task of ensuring the continuation of a rule of law. In no other way can we understand the willingness of the framers and ratifiers of the US Constitution to provide for the lifetime tenure of federal judges.

One of the major stories of nineteenth-century constitutional history is the establishment of judicial review as a distinctive hallmark of the American constitutional and governmental system. The mixed government balance that had protected liberty under the ancient British constitution had succumbed to parliamentary supremacy. Supplementing the protection of a written constitution with a government in which powers were separated and checked, Americans believed that they had responded to the deficiencies that they had perceived in the evolving British constitution. One of Chief Justice John Marshall's tasks in giving the Supreme Court which he headed respect and authority as a keeper of the rule of law was to divorce the Court from partisan politics. After the impeachment of associate justice Samuel Chase, the Court basically withdrew from the partisan politics that had characterized the activity of some justices at the turn of the century. This withdrawal did not mean that the Supreme Court's work was completely separate from politics, for as an independent branch of the federal government it hardly could be, but it did mean that partisan politics would generally not infest the work of the Court.

With the nineteenth century came the start of John Marshall's tenure as chief justice of the US Supreme Court. Although the story of Marshall's significant constitutional opinions for the Court has always been a focal point of scholarly attention – they initiated the judicial review of federal statutes, promoted nationalism over claims of states' rights, and provided security for property in the evolving economy – recent work has focused on judicial review and the Constitution as higher law. In addition to a new round of biographies of Marshall, his long-time colleague on the High Court, Joseph Story, has attracted biographical attention, not only with regard to his work on the Court but also for his treatises in many areas of American law.

Marshall's successor as leader of the Court, Roger Taney, has attracted less study, but the often divided bench he headed was a Court for the times in that it afforded room to the active governing units in the federal system – the states – to legislate and further the entrepreneurial spirit. The potential of the Constitution's nationalizing provisions was not fully realized because of the fear that they would interfere with the peculiar institution of chattel slavery. Despite its support of slavery, the Taney Court in *Ableman* v. *Booth* (1859) provided as forceful a defense of the supremacy of the federal Union as can be found in the reports of the Supreme Court. And Taney's Court extended admiralty jurisdiction, paved the way for a more uniform commercial law to promote the domestic common market, and accommodated the corporate form of organization within the federal judicial system.

Although the Court and the Congress had been accommodating the South with regard to federal governmental action, when the issue of slavery became a moral issue, further compromise became impossible. Varying theories of the Union were posed by North and South, and the conflict was finally decided on the battlefield. The new Union constructed in the wake of the war was different from the old; not only was slavery abolished but the economic and social systems that had been built upon it had to be modified significantly. The fact that it would take another century or so to rid the nation of a social system that hampered the full unification of the country was the result of a commitment to a system of federalism that would survive both secession and Civil War.

The new Union was built in large part on the three Reconstruction amendments: the Thirteenth abolishing slavery; the Fourteenth limiting state action in behalf of individual rights; and the Fifteenth eliminating race and previous condition of servitude as permissible qualifications for the vote. Whether the new amendments radically transformed the Union or simply brought it more fully in line with certain founding premises, such as those expressed in the Declaration of Independence, is a matter still disputed by scholars. Those students of the past who seek to bring historical assistance to the modern civil rights movement tend to view the amendments as writing a new moral imperative into the Constitution that purified a decadent antebellum Union.

Also, since all of the immediate post-war changes in the fundamental law were added only after forcing ratification upon the southern states, which for other purposes were treated as not being in the Union, scholars have intermittently questioned their legitimacy. Bruce Ackerman (1998), in the second volume of three planned to survey aspects of the nation's constitutional history, takes a novel approach to this question by denying that the Constitution's amending procedure, as specified in Article V, is the sole test of legitimacy. He would supplement that process by finding ratification of constitutional change in the political decisions of the American people, who, as they did in displacing the Articles of Confederation with the Constitution, gave their blessing to the Fourteenth Amendment by acting, in conformance with the Preamble, as the architect of their own constitutional destiny.

Although Harold Hyman found in the Thirteenth Amendment all that was needed to complete a reconstruction process had the states only complied with its broad intent to treat all citizens of the American republic equally (Hyman and Wiecek, 1982), the Fourteenth Amendment, in terms of both historical interest and constitutional significance, has always commanded center stage. The first clause of the most significant first section addresses a problem that had existed from the beginning of the Union but now demanded a solution: the absence of a citizenship clause in the Constitution. Federal citizenship no longer would be derivative of state citizenship; instead, it was made primary and conferred by birth within the United States. Addressing by necessity, then, the rights of this federal citizenship, the amendment imposed new general limits upon state action that could interfere with these new rights. Now a state could not abridge the privileges and immunities of citizens of the United States, nor deny to persons the equal protection of the laws or their life, liberty, or property without due process of law.

Just what these terms mean and how broadly they are to be construed has absorbed the interest of constitutional scholars from shortly after their addition to the Constitution to the present. Supreme Court decisions that would stand for the next few generations interpreted the Fourteenth Amendment narrowly to invalidate the first public accommodations law (*Civil Rights Cases*, 1883) and to uphold the practice of racial segregation (*Plessy* v. *Ferguson*, 1896). When the time to reconsider such segregation approached, the Court asked for argument in *Brown* v. *Board of Education* (1954) on the question of whether the framers and ratifiers of the Fourteenth Amendment had left room for racially segregated schools? Despite the forensic attempts on both sides, Chief Justice Earl Warren concluded that the submitted evidence was inconclusive and that the Court's decision would have to be based on other grounds. The Court's conclusion that the historical record of debates left such particular questions unresolved, however, did not stop historians from combing these records and coming to their own conclusions.

Although limiting the civil rights reach of the Fourteenth Amendment by requiring direct state participation in the discriminatory conduct, the Court expanded the amendment's range with regard to protection of the property right. When the argument was mounted in the *Slaughterhouse Cases* (1873) that federal citizenship now embraced all the important individual rights and precluded their invasion by the states, the Court rejected that claim. The decision virtually nullified the privileges and immunities clause, the clause that seemed to promise most in protecting the freedmen in their new status as United States citizens. Insisting that the amendment did nothing to disturb a dual state and federal citizenship in which the most meaningful individual rights were left to the sole protection of the states, the Court seemingly closed the door to any substantial reordering of the federal Union.

With an increase in state regulatory legislation in the industrializing society, however, the losers at the state level sought to find in the new federal amendment some shield against such regulation. In *Munn* v. *Illinois* (1877), the Court rejected a broad-ranging attack on governmental regulation of property, saying that property affected with a public interest was within the state's competence to regulate. Those seeking protection under the new amendment had two approaches left, one to claim that the property was not affected with a public interest and therefore beyond the pale of regulation, or that even property affected with a public interest could not be regulated to deny to its owner a fair rate of return. Although the Court in the nineteenth century repeatedly repulsed the first argument, it began to respond to the second and moved closer and closer to accepting the Fourteenth Amendment as a potential protector of the property right. Then, in 1890 the justices ruled that a state's failure to provide access to a judicial hearing on the question of whether a railroad rate set was confiscatory denied due process (*Chicago, Milwaukee and St Paul Ry* v. *Minnesota*, 1890), and by the end of the decade the Court was invalidating such rates under its new substantive reading of the Fourteenth Amendment's due process clause (i.e. *Smyth* v. *Ames*, 1898).

With this protection of property the Court also associated the protection of a certain individual liberty – the liberty to enter into contracts free of state interference – but to some justices the Court's definition of the liberty promised by the Fourteenth Amendment was far too narrow. During most of his almost 34-year tenure on the high bench, John Marshall Harlan, who was a supporter of the economic rights that his colleagues found protected by the amendment, argued that its first clause also was designed to ensure that the Bill of Rights, in all of its provisions, would now bind the states as well as the federal government. Harlan received virtually no support for his reading of the due process clause. Later in the twentieth century, however, Justice

Hugo L. Black came to the same conclusion in an extensive appendix added to his dissenting opinion in *Adamson* v. *California* (1947).

With the coming of the Warren Court in the mid-twentieth century and its use of the Fourteenth Amendment not only to condemn segregation but to nationalize the protection of individual rights, the scouring of the amendment's history took on greater urgency and attracted much scholarly attention. Did its framers and ratifiers really intend to make the individual rights found in the Bill of Rights binding upon the states as well? Michael Curtis's book, *No State Shall Abridge* (1986), answering the arguments of Raoul Berger, evaluates the way in which evidence is used and how different conclusions can be drawn from the same record. Because the Fourteenth Amendment provides the basis for a reshaping of the American Union, it is the most important and significant addition to the Constitution since the Bill of Rights. It will continue to attract historical attention because of the intrinsic interest generated by any seminal period or event.

Traditional battles between those who read the words of the Constitution narrowly and those who read them broadly, no matter what fashion dictates the two camps should be called, assumed that the words themselves contained only a limited number of meanings. In fact, the text of the Constitution has been at the heart of relatively recent political and scholarly controversy. The question of how to bind or limit the discretion of judges has always attracted interest, and during the presidency of Ronald Reagan, his attorney general Edwin Meese and a defeated candidate for the US Supreme Court, Robert Bork (1990), among others, insisted that judges should be bound by the original intent that informed the constitutional language. The critics on the other side not only argued that such original intent most often could not be discovered but also that the applicable words should be interpreted to apply to new situations that could not have been envisioned at the time the relevant text was framed. In fact, Supreme Court justices have said that in safeguarding individual rights the proper approach to take is to keep in mind the evil that was to be guarded against and not be confined to the manifestations of it that existed when the protective language was framed. This type of controversy has long characterized the study of constitutional history, and the antagonists agree that the text of the fundamental law is all important and must govern.

Other critics, armed with postmodern and deconstructionist theories, however, have challenged the very essentials of a study based upon the Constitution as text. Since it is difficult to imagine a constitutional history written from a perspective that assumes the indeterminacy of all text, such a perspective challenges the viability of the study itself. To make the Constitution's text so malleable as to scrap any possibility of consensus would neglect the simple fact that, in both arguing and interpreting the text, decisions are reached that must stand the test of criticism. Literary scholars might turn their imaginations loose on traditional texts with little practical effect, but judicial interpreters must assume responsibility for what their readings command.

Some scholars, however, manage to write in a linear way and communicate with others who do not share their assumptions. They argue that the Constitution not only has not delivered the rights promised but it has, in fact, frustrated the aspirations of those who seek to achieve their full rights. As with so much of the critical legal studies school, the practitioners come with a clear agenda as to what they want their history to show and how that history can be employed to awaken those who have been cheated by the prevailing system. There is within the movement a powerful frustration at its intellectual core that is impatient with people who do not seem to realize their oppressed condition. This social reconstruction of constitutional history denigrates the written document, finding in it little more than a reflection of an oppressive social organization. The group rights' consciousness, which characterizes this approach, poses a fundamental challenge to the individual rights basis of American constitutionalism. In many ways this radical attack is far from consistent, for on the one hand it argues that the dispossessed have not enjoyed the rights the Constitution promises, while on the other it attacks individual rights as an obstacle to the creation of a just and comfortable society in which the community's welfare is emphasized.

So, in addition to fundamental disputes over text, its interpretation, and supplementation, this new work criticizes the individual rights orientation of constitutional law and history. This interest spills over from the historical work done on the late eighteenth century, especially that dealing with republicanism in the revolutionary and constitution-making period. It poses a conflict between republicanism with its emphasis upon public virtue and community welfare and liberalism with its emphasis upon the rights of the individual. Little controversy exists in the literature over the triumph of liberalism over republicanism, but scholars differ about when this battle was won. For instance, William J. Novak, in *The People's Welfare: Law and Regulation in Nineteenth-century America* (1996), dates the definitive switch much later than earlier writers. What he calls "the well-regulated society," with its implicit limits on individual action, was replaced by the liberal state with its

> simultaneous pursuit of two seemingly antagonistic tendencies – the *centralization of power* and the *individualization of subjects*. The two would be ultimately mediated (and, again simultaneously, promoted) by the *constitutionalization of law*. By the early decades of the twentieth century, a society legally and politically oriented around the relationship of individual subjects to a central nation-state had substantially replaced the well-regulated society's preference for articulating the roles of associative citizens in a confederated republic.   (Novak, 1996: 240–1)

Unlike Anthony Chase (1997), who celebrates the rise of liberal capitalism in opposition to the authoritarian variety, these authors criticize the emphasis upon the individual's property right. A constitution that protects individual rights and encourages individual initiative and acquisition can be quite detrimental to a communal spirit and the creation of civic virtue. Critics, such as Jennifer Nedelsky (1990), lament a system that stresses individual rights and fails to teach a lesson of social responsibility. They yearn for the untraveled road, insisting that the emphasis on individual rights has crowded out what might have been a more humane constitutional vision. Taking a contrary view, I argued, in my study of the Supreme Court as a cultural institution (Semonche, 1998) that the Constitution's focus on individual rights has been an essential bonding agent in what has always been a society composed of very diverse people.

There is no better place to sample the wide-ranging challenges to traditional constitutional history than the special issue of *The Journal of American History* entitled "The Constitution in American Life," volume 74, published in December 1987. In two parts, one centering on the Constitution's significance in American development and the other on rights consciousness in American history, most of the 17 contributors took aim and delivered their critiques, at times questioning the very foundations upon which the field had been built.

However one evaluates the disparate work being published in the legal and constitutional history of the United States in the nineteenth century, it covers not only a wide range of perspectives but genres as well, from intellectual histories to studies of the work of an administrative agency, and from traditional and often absorbing narrative, biographical, and case studies with more general appeal to theory-driven work that can only be digested by professionals on a similar wave length. Further additions to the literature are historical studies of various legal areas, such as torts, contracts, certain aspects of the criminal law, and even family law. In the latter area, Michael Grossberg's *Governing the Hearth: Law and the Family in Nineteenth-century America* (1985) illustrates how this new work can open an area for further profitable study. Such pioneering works may suffer from conclusions that are too broadly drawn, given the necessarily limited research into the sectional and corresponding legal diversity in the country, but their path-breaking nature only stimulates further investigation in areas that have previously been neglected. What characterizes so much of this scholarship is its bold conceptualization and its deliberate attempt to contribute to the more general historical understanding of developments in the nineteenth century. If we are unable to clearly demarcate the line between social history based upon legal sources and legal history drawing larger social conclusions, we can take consolation in the vitality that accompanies such an overflowing of previous boundaries.

Much has been done within a relatively short period of time but the expanded arena still contains many relatively unexplored areas. Willard Hurst's call for an investigation of legislative activity in the states and of the administration of law through agencies as well as the more conventional channels has largely gone unheeded. And with the construction of new models for study we can not only expect such explorations to be easier to undertake but we will likely find new insights and illumination in revisiting previously traversed terrain. Clearly, the leisurely stream that was once legal history has become a river, which, despite variances in its depth and breadth, flows swiftly.

REFERENCES

Ackerman, Bruce (1998) *We the People, 2: Transformations*. Cambridge, Mass.: Belknap Press of Harvard University.
Bork, Robert H. (1990) *The Tempting of America: the Political Seduction of the Law*. New York: Simon and Schuster.
Chase, Anthony (1997) *Law and History: the Evolution of the American Legal System*. New York: The New Press.
Curtis, Michael Kent (1986) *No State Shall Abridge: the 14th Amendment and the Bill of Rights*. Durham, NC: Duke University Press.
Friedman, Lawrence M. (1985) *A History of American Law*, 2nd edn. New York: Simon and Schuster.
Gilmore, Grant (1977) *The Ages of American Law*. New Haven, Conn.: Yale University Press.
Gordon, Robert W. and Nelson, William (1988) "An exchange on critical legal issues between Robert W. Gordon and William Nelson," *Law and History Review*, 6, pp. 139–86.
Grossberg, Michael (1985) *Governing the Hearth: Law and the Family in Nineteenth-century America*. Chapel Hill, NC: University of North Carolina Press.

Hall, Kermit L. (1989) *The Magic Mirror: Law in American History.* New York: Oxford University Press.

Horwitz, Morton J. (1977) *The Transformation of American Law,* vol. 1: *1780–1860.* Cambridge, Mass.: Harvard University Press.

Horwitz, Morton J. (1992) *The Transformation of American Law,* vol. 2: *The Crisis of Legal Orthodoxy, 1870–1960.* New York: Oxford University Press.

Hurst, James Willard (1956) *Law and the Conditions of Freedom: in the Nineteenth-century United States.* Madison: University of Wisconsin Press.

Hyman, Harold M. and Wiecek, William M. (1982) *Equal Justice under Law: Constitutional Development, 1835–1875.* New York: Harper and Row.

Karsten, Peter (1997) *Heart versus Head: Judge-made Law in Nineteenth-century America.* Chapel Hill, NC: University of North Carolina Press.

Nedelsky, Jennifer (1990) *Private Property and the Limits of American Constitutionalism: the Madisonian Framework and its Legacy.* Chicago: University of Chicago Press.

Novak, William J. (1996) *The People's Welfare: Law and Regulation in Nineteenth-century America.* Chapel Hill, NC: University of North Carolina Press.

Pound, Roscoe (1938) *The Formative Era of American Law.* Boston: Little, Brown and Co.

Semonche, John E. (1978) *Charting the Future: the Supreme Court Responds to a Changing Society, 1890–1920.* Westport, Conn.: Greenwood Press.

Semonche, John E. (1998) *Keeping the Faith: a Cultural History of the US Supreme Court.* Lanham, MD: Rowman and Littlefield.

Tomlins, Christopher L. (1993) *Law, Labor, and Ideology in the Early American Republic.* Cambridge: Cambridge University Press.

PART II

Foreign Relations

CHAPTER SEVEN

American Expansion, 1800–1867

JOHN M. BELOHLAVEK

IN the more than half-century between the presidency of Thomas Jefferson and the end of the Civil War the United States underwent a profound physical and psychological transformation. Through a series of land purchases and military conflicts, the country expanded beyond the Mississippi River to the Rio Grande, the Pacific, and the Bering Sea. A series of treaties widened commercial horizons into the Middle East, Latin America, and Asia. And through the crucible of Civil War a union of states metamorphosed into an indivisible nation and hemispheric power. This transformation reveals a young country struggling to align its republican morality with issues of commerce, race, and territorial acquisition.

When Thomas Jefferson assumed the presidency in 1801, the United States had just emerged from the quasi-war with France. The conclusion of this naval conflict permitted the nation a legitimate exit from its only treaty of alliance, the Franco-American pact of 1778, and allowed the "Sage of Monticello" to pursue his foreign policy unencumbered. Jefferson hoped to promote territorial expansion, commercial and neutral rights, and the "two hemispheres" concept. Although he intended to achieve his goals without war, an immediate dilemma presented itself in a Europe aflame in the Napoleonic Wars. Jefferson found himself thrust into the midst of the conflict and his responses – as related to the Barbary Wars, the purchase of Louisiana, the failed effort to obtain the Floridas, and the disastrous embargo policy – produced mixed results.

Jefferson had served as Minister to France and Secretary of State in the 1780s and 1790s. He approvingly observed the rising tide of revolutionary France, but cast a wary eye on Great Britain, the colonial oppressor who dominated the high seas and challenged American free trade. The pre-presidential Jefferson harbored a resentment toward England, but also embraced the concept of "America's success from Europe's distress" as he pragmatically sought to extend the boundaries of empire without involving the nation in war. Jefferson promised a new statecraft, free of the corruption and deceit of the Old World, in which peaceful economic and diplomatic coercion would be founded on natural rights and promulgated by a free and virtuous people. Now ensconced in the White House, Jefferson hoped to use the leverage of American neutrality to promote American commerce and acquire Spanish-held Louisiana, vital to the export of agricultural goods in the trans-Appalachian West and the Floridas.

Jefferson was challenged almost immediately by the Pasha of Tripoli who, along with his North African compatriots, had been harassing Yankee shipping, seizing hostages, and demanding tribute since 1785. When the United States failed to pay the Pasha, he declared virtual war against the United States in May 1801, thus prompting Jefferson to exercise his executive war-making powers by dispatching a squadron to the Mediterranean Sea. The fleet remained off Tripoli bombarding and blockading the city and aiding in a ground assault, which finally brought the conflict to an end in 1805.

The Barbary imbroglio quickly faded from view as the issue of the Napoleonic Wars and American neutrality dominated the scene. Jefferson's strategy regarding both Britain and France on this topic has been the subject of continuing scholarly controversy. Biographers of Jefferson have generally praised their hero for his cautious and skillful diplomacy. Diplomatic historians, led by Alexander de Conde, respect Jefferson's leadership and often view his policies as well planned and consciously imperialistic.

Robert W. Tucker and David C. Hendrickson in *Empire of Liberty: the Statecraft of Thomas Jefferson* present the most formidable recent critique of the president. Contending that Jefferson's "statecraft" was a fraud, they decry his pro-French stance as unrealistic and naïve and attribute the successful conclusion of the Louisiana talks to good fortune resulting from the "Haitian factor," Napoleon's failure to reconquer Santo Domingo between 1801 and 1803. This military and economic disaster compelled the First Consul to refocus temporarily upon Europe and away from the Caribbean. Napoleon's retreat was a boon for the waffling Jefferson who intended neither to ally with Great Britain (a mortal sin) nor provide for the defense of New Orleans with American troops. Jefferson's ministers, James Monroe and Robert Livingston, then successfully purchased the entire Louisiana territory for $15 million in 1803. Having enhanced American security and gained seemingly boundless room to ensure the economic independence of yeomen farmers, Jefferson refused to allow the dubious constitutionality of the purchase to prohibit him from signing the agreement.

Scholars concur that the addition of an "empire of liberty" – one people dedicated to liberty, under republican institutions – was critical to Jefferson's statecraft. The Virginian's idealism, his vision of a world remade in accord with American-centered moral principles, remains vital to understanding his philosophy, if not the practical application of his views. His supporters recognize and excuse the deviation from principle adopted by Jefferson over Louisiana and the failed attempt to pry the Floridas loose from Spain in 1806, even a $2 million appropriation to "facilitate negotiations." While each involved the sacrifice of constitutional ideals, tactics of intimidation, threats of alliance, or bribery, the president compromised to expand American boundaries. Pro-Jeffersonians argue that such trimming was wise, while skeptics suggest that he followed the "law of necessity" and abandoned long-held principles, thus placing "empire" before "liberty" as a priority of his statecraft.

For his critics, Jefferson the realist demonstrated a series of contradictions between ideology and leadership. These contradictions manifested themselves not only on issues of expansion, but also on the question of balance of power. Jefferson's rigid moralism placed a greater emphasis on neutral rights than a European balance. This morality, combined with his anti-English sentiment, fostered an adversarial relationship with the Crown. Instead of viewing Napoleon as a threat to the international order and working with the British to bring him to heel, Jefferson placed Britain in an untenable situation regarding the high seas, a situation that precluded successful negotiations and propelled the two nations down the road of economic retaliation that eventually led to war.

When the Napoleonic contest resumed in 1803 the United States soon found itself in the imperial crossfire. Violations of American commerce resumed on the high seas where hundreds of Yankee ships and thousands of seamen were seized by the British or French. Jefferson, frustrated and embarrassed, persuaded Congress to wage economic warfare against the Europeans by instituting an embargo in 1807 that prohibited American exports. The president might have led the irate Congress and citizenry into a war in June following the attack off the Virginia coast by HMS *Leopard* in search of British deserters on board the USS *Chesapeake*. Jefferson opted instead to avoid a conflict and allow "peaceable coercion" to take effect. Unfortunately, this tactic failed dramatically, damaging American commerce and agriculture far more than the intended European victims.

When Jefferson left office in March 1809 the embargo went with him. The Virginian found himself cursed by friend and foe alike for a policy that was perceived not only as disastrous but as an abusive (and perhaps unconstitutional) use of national power against the states and their citizens. The president's economic measures, especially the embargo of 1807, have few defenders among historians. Many scholars, led by Bradford Perkins (1995) and Donald Hickey (1989), chastise Jefferson for adopting a narrowly conceived policy that was too anti-English, too secretive, and too coercive.

James Madison, Jefferson's friend and Republican successor, found his options similarly limited by the small size of both the army and the navy. Fearing the power of a standing army, the Jeffersonians relied heavily upon state militias, although they had endorsed the concept of an enlarged gunboat navy to protect coastal waters. Gunboats might have provided for harbor defenses, but they could do nothing to defend American ships on the high seas against the might of the British navy. Consequently, Madison followed Jefferson's path of economic coercion against Britain and France for the next two years. However, a non-intercourse measure that restricted trade with Britain and France and Macon's second Bill which permitted commerce with both nations produced no positive results. By 1811, a frustrated president and Congress began seriously to contemplate war against Britain.

The War of 1812 had its roots in a variety of causes: national honor, territorial expansion, neutral rights, Indian problems, and national insecurity. Historians initially traced the origins of the war to the desire on the part of the "war hawks" in Congress for English Canada and Spanish Florida. Those views shifted as scholars re-examined the commercial and naval conflicts with England and settled upon honor and maritime violations as the major causes. More recently, historians have been reconsidering the significance of territorial expansion. J. C. A. Stagg (1993), for example, perceives Canada as an important bargaining chip in resolving issues with Great Britain. Several works have also suggested that Jeffersonians feared for the survival of the republic if ill-fated economic policies prompted desperate voters to return monarchical Federalists to office.

Those fears proved groundless. The Jeffersonians remained in control of the government through "Mr Madison's War" (1812–15). The conflict was marked by a largely inept performance by both the president in providing leadership and the American army in invading and occupying Canada. A financial crisis and political divisions handicapped Congress. Fortunately for the Americans, Napoleon's movements preoccupied the British, who generally treated the war in a cursory fashion. Although they launched a series of coastal assaults along the Atlantic seaboard in 1814, resulting in the destruction of Washington, DC, the British were anxious to end a war they had not wanted. In December 1814, a team of American negotiators, led by John Quincy Adams and Albert Gallatin, signed a peace accord at Ghent, Belgium that restored the status quo antebellum. The Senate ratified the pact in February 1815 by a vote of 35: 0. No issues – neutral rights, impressment, or territorial expansion – were resolved. American national honor had been defended, however, against its former colonial master in what many considered "the second war for independence."

The War of 1812 and the ensuing push north into Canada and south along the Gulf Coast embroiled the Americans in conflicts against the English, Spanish, Indians, and free blacks who stood as obstacles to white American expansion. Historians Frank L. Owsley Jr and Gene A. Smith (1997) have defined this American push as "Jeffersonian manifest destiny." Their study demonstrates that a combination of conventional military forces and assorted filibustering irregulars waged unrelenting warfare in the Old Southwest, especially against the weakened Spanish, with considerable success. These triumphs, however, worsened the growing antagonism between the Federalist urban Northeast and the Republican agrarian South.

The leadership of John Quincy Adams in formulating and executing post-war expansion was critical to American success in the "Era of good feelings." Although Adams's contributions have been recognized by an earlier generation of scholars, his skill has been confirmed by the recent works of historian William Weeks (1992). Adams emerges as the intensely patriotic Puritan, the Hamiltonian realist who understood the limits of the nation's moral authority in world affairs. Accordingly, Adams championed a position of independence from Europe and an aggressive advocacy of union and North American empire for the United States. A former Federalist senator from Massachusetts and diplomat to Prussia, Russia, and England, Adams brought both experience and intelligence to the premier cabinet post. Abrupt and irritable, he argued convincingly that the nation must respond to continental challenges from Great Britain, Spain, and Russia.

Just as Henry Clay's "American system" manifested a domestic nationalism, so the foreign policy of John Quincy Adams mirrored the nation's renewed expansionist mood. In the Convention of 1818, Adams persuaded the English to extend the Canadian–US border at the 49th parallel from the Great Lakes to the Rocky Mountains. The following year, he seized upon the bold and legally dubious invasion of Spanish Florida by General Andrew Jackson to resolve a problem festering for a generation. Amidst heated cabinet debate, Adams single-handedly defended "Old Hickory's" actions and placed the Spanish in a position where they were obliged to cede the Floridas to the US for the payment of $5 million in claims. The 1819 Transcontinental (Adams–Onis) Treaty established the American transcontinental claim to the Oregon territory as well. Adams's decision not to press Spain for the inclusion of Texas, however, would influence sectional politics for the next generation.

Adams duplicated his success of 1819 with the compliant Russians in the Convention of 1824. In that agreement the Czar surrendered claims to Russian territory south of Alaska (54° 40'), granted Americans trade rights in the Northwest, and agreed to language encouraging freedom of the high seas. United States' claims to California and the Pacific Coast had been dramatically strengthened.

Recent historiography praises President James Monroe for his vision and wisdom in foreign affairs, perhaps foremost for his retention of Adams as the energizing force in furthering American expansion. Monroe functioned as the great conciliator and allowed his Secretary of State to operate as the point man in US destiny. Weeks's (1992) praise for the effectiveness of the Monroe–Adams team extends to a suggestion that in some ways the administration marked the birth of the "imperial presidency." Weeks has noted that American destiny was founded on the notions of a unique virtue, a sense of mission, and a divine inspiration. Adams and Monroe traded on this rhetoric to promote a continental destiny and to provide commercial opportunities throughout the hemisphere.

The Monroe Doctrine of December 1823 formed an expansive capstone for Jeffersonian foreign policy by formalizing concepts of Old World political and imperial danger and New World solidarity. Monroe's challenge to the Europeans of non-colonization and non-intervention in the Western hemisphere may have lacked firm military legs in 1823, but his words would eventually resonate soundly with a nation eager to reserve a hemisphere for its own expansion. Scholar John Johnson (1990) notes, however, that the United States did not establish an enduring presence in the antebellum period. He blames this failure on America's focus on internal migration, dominant British presence in the region, and conflicting views regarding race and slavery between the United States and Latin America. If over the next half-century the United States acted in an inconsistent and ill-defined fashion in enforcing the Monroe Doctrine, the foundation for this cornerstone of twentieth-century foreign policy had none the less been laid.

Andrew Jackson entered the presidency in 1829 with an energetic foreign policy and a vision for the Union that would enhance both a commercial and a territorial empire. Jackson held a concern shared by many of his generation: a fear for the security of the country. That security was threatened not only by foreign enemies to the north (England), south and west (Spain), but also by the domestic fifth column comprised of American Indians. The general, who had fought the Creeks in the First Seminole War (1813–14), had observed the Anglo-Indian alliances that formed during the War of 1812 and feared the potential danger to the United States. Indian removal beyond the Mississippi River would eliminate this danger. Relocation would both secure the frontier of the nation and open millions of acres of valuable land for white farmers and planters. Accordingly, Congress agreed to removal in 1830, and by the end of the decade all the tribes east of the Mississippi had been largely dispossessed.

The eastern Indians opposed removal through legal strategies and physical resistance, but the result was ultimately the same: coerced resettlement in the West. Jackson had orchestrated one of the most morally reprehensible episodes in American history. Even so, the blame must be shared by a Congress and citizenry who overwhelmingly agreed that the growth, economic prosperity, and security of the nation should be placed ahead of the interests of the Native American.

Jackson also moved aggressively to advance American commerce around the globe. His agents concluded treaties with Great Britain, Russia, Turkey, Mexico, Chile, Venezuela, and Peru–Bolivia. Missions to South-east Asia, led by Edmund Roberts, and Central America, led by Charles Biddle, proved mostly unsuccessful but reflect Jackson's expansive vision for American trade. The president relentlessly pursued with Denmark, Naples, and Portugal the resolution of longstanding claims over violations of American maritime naval rights during the Napoleonic Wars. His brinkmanship tactics with France in this area took the country along a collision course but, ultimately, the French, too, paid millions of dollars owed to American claimants.

As had President John Quincy Adams in 1827, Jackson failed in his diplomatic efforts to purchase Texas from Mexico. By 1836, Texas was in rebellion, and all hopes for a peaceful transfer of the province to the United States had gone up in flames. The revolutionaries quickly triumphed and the Lone Star Republic applied for admission to the Union in 1837. The presence of slavery in Texas, however, made both Jackson and his successor, Martin Van Buren, wary of absorption. Anti-slavery politicians, such as John Quincy Adams, and reformers, such as Lydia Maria Child, effectively discredited the annexation movement.

While Van Buren focused upon an economic depression triggered by a financial panic in 1837, problems arose with England over the Canadian rebellion and Maine boundary. Issues of power, politics, land ownership, and religion had sparked a revolution in Canada in the summer of 1837. By the end of the year the rebels had been crushed and sent fleeing for sanctuary in the United States. There they found sympathy and support in the form of American "patriot militia" eager to join the cause and fight for Canadian freedom – and perhaps annexation to the United States. Tensions ran especially high along the Niagara River where the rebels made regular supply forays into Canada. On the night of December 29, a party of English soldiers attacked and burned the steamer *Caroline* on the United States side of the river, killing an American in the raid. Anti-British cries reverberated along the border as "patriot militia" units launched ill-fated attacks in support of the rebellion. Anglo-American relations rose to a fever pitch, obliging Van Buren to issue a neutrality proclamation. The president, generally preoccupied with domestic affairs, acted hesitantly to enforce neutrality or to resolve the overall situation with a firm hand.

When John Tyler assumed the presidential office in the spring of 1841, he re-embarked on Jackson's nationalistic path of commercial and territorial expansion. He placed the border issue in the hands of Secretary of State Daniel Webster. Tensions eased with the collapse of the rebellion, the defeat of the American militia, and the not-guilty verdict by a New York jury of the accused murderer in the *Caroline* incident. Kenneth R. Stevens (1989) notes in his *Border Diplomacy* that the result enhanced the power of the national government over the states in foreign affairs and clarified a key point in international law by affirming that aggression was justifiable only if there was an instant and overwhelming need for self-defense.

In 1842, Lord Ashburton, head of the British banking firm of the House of Baring, arrived in the United States to negotiate all differences between the two countries. In the Webster–Ashburton Treaty of that year, the two nations compromised their longstanding controversy over the northeastern boundary between Maine and Canada – awarding most of the disputed territory to the United States – and Webster agreed to assist in ending the international slave trade by posting an American squadron of 80 guns off the African coast. Although the United States rarely lived up to this particular commitment, the treaty served to ease the danger of war with Britain. Recent historiography has given Webster considerable credit for resolving these longstanding issues between the two nations and establishing a *rapprochement* that allowed for a settlement of the Oregon dispute in 1846.

The struggle for the Pacific Northwest began in 1792 when British Captain George Vancouver and Yankee Captain Robert Gray simultaneously explored the Columbia River. The fur trading interests of both nations dominated the contest until after the War of 1812. The Convention of 1818 agreed to extend the United States–Canadian border from Minnesota to the Rocky Mountains, but neither Washington nor London would concede the valuable Columbia. American representatives Richard Rush and Albert Gallatin pressed for a boundary at the 49th parallel, but could gain only a joint occupancy agreement for ten years with the Crown. During that decade, the wily John Quincy Adams maneuvered both Spain and Russia out of their claims to the northwest coast, but he had no success with the British. In 1827, Gallatin renewed the old agreement. By the 1840s, American settlers poured westward in search of fertile land, supplanting the earlier generation of trappers and traders. Oregon became an increasingly emotional issue as both farmers and congressmen asserted American rights to the Willamette Valley and beyond.

The issue, like the Maine border, became one not only of economics but of national honor. By 1843, a confrontation between American settlers and the Hudson's Bay Company became increasingly likely, and both the Peel/Aberdeen ministry and the Tyler administration sought to resolve the issue. A focus on Texas, however, delayed resolution until after James K. Polk took office in March 1845. Polk, elected on a platform of the "reannexation of Texas" and the "reoccupation of Oregon," had rallied the faithful under the banner of "54° 40′ or fight." Over the next year, the president played a dangerous game that involved a variety of players. Extremist senators, encouraged by Polk's strident tone, demanded all of Oregon, while Secretary of State James Buchanan generally counseled moderation.

As posturing continued on both sides of the Atlantic, the Peel ministry moved to repeal the restrictive Corn Laws and promote free trade and greater commerce with the United States. Concurrently, relations with Mexico deteriorated in the spring of 1846, and hostilities commenced along the Texas border in April. The timing was right for compromise. In spite of the anger of "all-Oregon" senators who felt betrayed, Polk approved a British proposal of the 49th parallel in June which gave the United States the Columbia River and Great Britain all of Vancouver Island. The treaty passed the Senate by a vote of 41: 14 on June 18. Either through skill or good fortune (perhaps both), Polk had engineered an Oregon boundary that satisfied the land hunger and national honor of most Americans. Importantly, Polk's ability to maintain a *rapprochement* with Britain and keep the Crown on the sidelines in the existing war with Mexico proved vital to American success.

Polk's ability to extricate himself from a near collision with Britain and into a conflict with Mexico has received mixed reviews from historians. William Weeks (1992) agrees that "Young Hickory" took the Oregon issue to the edge of war, although he really only wanted a settlement at the 49th parallel. Sam Haynes (1997) paints a portrait of a pragmatic Polk who dangerously pushed the British, but then backpedaled to a compromise when his position became untenable. The president knew, however, that the British were more interested in commercial ties, recently enhanced by the low duties of the Walker Tariff of 1846, than the dwindling fur trade of the remote Northwest.

By 1846, America's special mission had come into clear focus. The rising tide of "Manifest Destiny" which rolled over Texas and Oregon prepared to engulf California and the Southwest as well. Many Americans embraced the notion that the United States was divinely ordained to control the continent and, through Protestant Christianity and republican institutions, redeem native populations. This view was compromised, however, by a virulent racism that espoused Anglo-Saxon superiority and denigrated non-white peoples, especially Mexicans. Spurred on by the editorials of the "penny press" and emotionally charged speeches of expansionist politicians, Americans continued to believe in their own special virtue.

James K. Polk shared their vision. Single-mindedly dedicated to this destiny, Polk appeared willing to obtain California and the Southwest at any cost. As historian Norman Graebner (1955) emphasized, Polk was committed to an American "empire on the Pacific." Although scholars disagree over the president's provocative posture with Mexico in early 1846, the evidence suggests that he preferred peace, but prepared for war. Polk dispatched his personal emissary, John Slidell, a former congressman from Louisiana, to Mexico City in November 1845 to offer up to $25 million for California and New Mexico and a settlement of the Texas border at the Rio Grande River. A combination of Slidell's ineptitude and Mexican political divisions resulted in a rejection of Polk's demands. Still, the president remained hopeful of a settlement, even when the Mexican government took on a more anti-American tone in January 1846. While Slidell continued to press American claims, Polk moved Zachary Taylor's 4,000-man army from the Nueces River near Corpus Christi into disputed territory along the Rio Grande.

By mid-March Slidell admitted defeat and returned to Washington where he conferred with the president in early May. Polk, frustrated and weary of delay, moved quickly to call his cabinet together to discuss a declaration of war. With only the dissenting voice of Secretary of the Navy George Bancroft, the cabinet approved war, largely on the grounds of unpaid Mexican debts to American claimants.

Congress might have declined to join the president in so bold a move without an obvious provocation, but events aligned on the side of the Tennesseean. Polk learned on May 9, the same day as the cabinet meeting, that American troops had been attacked and 16 men had been killed or wounded two weeks earlier. American blood had been shed on American soil, or so Polk now claimed. The president could scrap the wafer-thin argument for a war based on claims and go to Congress with a message urging defensive retaliation in response to Mexican aggression. Congress responded overwhelmingly, with only a handful of votes in the House (174: 14) and the Senate (40: 2) in opposition. Mr Polk had his war.

Did Polk conspire to declare war on Mexico to foster American empire or act as a force of moderation among expansionist Democrats and resort to war only when political forces compelled it? Contending that Polk's policies with both Britain and Mexico were "deliberately calculated to escalate tensions rather than minimize them" (1997: 136), Sam Haynes raises serious questions about the president's intentions. Although Polk saw himself, somewhat self-righteously, as motivated by high moral principle, many Whigs disagreed. They suspected the Tennesseean of manipulating events to provoke a conflict which could be used to add slave territory to the Union.

Recent historiography contends that Democrats generally favored expansion in the hope that added territory would foster the Jeffersonian dream of allowing white

Americans to own small farms. For the Democrats, the independent yeoman farmer, freed from the degenerative social forces of the city and the economic control of a factory boss, remained the world's best hope for the preservation of liberty, democracy, and republican institutions. Consequently, Thomas Hietala (1985) argues that American expansion was not "manifest destiny" at all, but "manifest design" – a conscious policy intended to extend the "boundaries of freedom." Many Whigs eagerly eyed the economic possibilities of San Francisco Bay and the window to the Orient provided by ownership of California. However, they believed that waging war to achieve such ends was abhorrent. But their almost uniform opposition to the war – based upon anti-slavery sentiments, racism, moral outrage, and an overriding concern about the loss of liberty that would accompany the extension of American borders – could not stand up to the passionate nationalism engendered by the conflict.

The Mexican–American War, in its military phase, lasted but a year and half (April 1846 to September 1847) and recorded a stream of unbroken United States victories. Americans suffered fewer than 2,000 battlefield deaths, although disease killed more than 10,000 soldiers. The Mexicans, in contrast, lost more than 50,000 troops. While the Mexicans eagerly entered the war, a combination of political instability and the absence of a strong nationalist impulse crippled their efforts. Winfield Scott's campaign of 1847 brought the fall of Mexico City and stirred the imagination of Americans who wanted to annex all of Mexico. Not surprisingly, racist arguments countered these desires by expressing fears about the incorporation of eight million Catholic, Spanish-speaking, dark-skinned Mexicans. While the "All Mexico" debate raged in the fall and winter of 1847–8, Polk focused on negotiating an end to the war.

With peace seemingly within reach, Polk dispatched veteran diplomat Nicholas Trist to accompany Scott's army and seize the moment to negotiate. Unfortunately, Trist's talks with General Santa Anna went awry. Although Mexico City fell to American forces in September, a treaty impasse continued into the new year. By that time the president had grown impatient with the inactivity and recalled Trist. When the discredited diplomat produced the Treaty of Guadalupe Hidalgo that gave Polk everything he had wanted (California, the Southwest, and the Rio Grande border), the president was obliged to retreat and present the agreement to the Senate. On March 10, 1848, the Senate ratified the pact by a vote of 38 to 14. James K. Polk had achieved his "empire on the Pacific."

Polk's triumphs allowed a short-lived patina of nationalist harmony to gloss over a rapidly emerging sectionalism. Seeking to maintain a balance between slave and free states in Congress and to expand the economic frontiers of the "Cotton Kingdom," southerners began to dream seriously of a Caribbean empire. Cuba, of course, presented the greatest lure for expansion, although territories in unstable Central America also offered possibilities. Pro-Cuba forces, including high-profile Democratic senators Stephen A. Douglas and Lewis Cass and editors John L. O'Sullivan and Jane Storms, encouraged presidents from Polk to James Buchanan to annex Cuba. In 1848 Polk attempted to purchase the island from Spain for $100 million, but Queen Isabella II refused to surrender the jewel in the imperial crown.

When Polk departed the presidency in March 1849, the expansionist engine slowed, but did not stop. Many Yankees still dreamed of Canada, some of Cuba, while southerners generally felt frustrated over an unfulfilled Manifest Destiny. Newly elected Mexican War General Zachary Taylor did not want to see the Whig party splintered on the rocks of empire and pulled back from earlier Democratic efforts to gain Caribbean territory. Such caution did not sit well with many southerners who sought to press the Cuba issue. Aligned with the Cuban exile community in New York City and the Democratic party's "Young America" movement, these southerners promoted the cause of the emerging filibustering movement. Filibusters were motivated by many things, including ideology, greed, and adventure; most were soldiers of fortune who sought to provoke revolution in Latin America to further their own personal or political agenda. This agenda frequently dovetailed with that of American expansionists who endorsed illegal filibustering expeditions as a way to accomplish imperial goals outside the strictures of the administration in Washington. Such activities had been integral to American imperialism in the early part of the century along the Gulf Coast from Florida to Texas.

Historian Robert May (1973) has provided the most expansive account of filibustering activities in the 1850s, including the exploits of Narciso Lopez and John Quitman in Cuba and William Walker in Nicaragua. Lopez, a Venezuelan and former colonel in the Spanish army, had intimate connections with the Havana Club, a Masonic coterie of planters and aristocrats in Cuba. This organization, which promoted annexation to the United States, found support and protection for their goals among their Masonic brothers in the South. Although the first Lopez expedition was broken up at Round Island in the waters off Louisiana in 1849, the second (April 1850) and third (August 1851) reached Cuba. Unfortunately for the filibusters, in both cases the populace did not rise up in support. In 1851, Lopez and 50 American mercenaries were captured and executed; hundreds more were imprisoned in Cuban jails. This action, in combination with the unrelenting opposition of the Millard Fillmore administration, temporarily halted the quest for the island.

The election of pro-annexation Democrat Franklin Pierce in 1852 rekindled expansionist hopes. Former Mississippi Governor John Quitman began organizing a force of thousands of men along the Gulf in 1853–4, apparently with sympathy from Washington. The emergence of the sectionally divisive Kansas–Nebraska issue, however, prompted a meeting between Pierce and Quitman in mid-March 1855 that resulted in the filibuster abandoning his invasion plans. The administration had been pursuing its own "carrot and stick" strategy. In April 1854, Minister to Spain Pierre Soule was instructed to offer $130 million for Cuba. When the Spanish again refused, Soule met in October with his European counterparts, James Buchanan in London and John Y. Mason in Paris, and penned the Ostend (Belgium) Manifesto. The document recommended to the president that Cuba be obtained "at any price," but, failing in that, should be taken by force if necessary. The diplomats rationalized that American security and strategic interests justified such bold action. The British or French might seize the island from a weakened Spain, or, worse, Madrid might abandon Cuba to the slaves who would "Africanize" the territory and establish a dangerous example for American slaves. When the Ostend Manifesto appeared in the American press it simply confirmed the worst fears of the anti-slavery forces in the North. With Kansas in tumult and passions in Congress at a fever pitch, the annexation of Cuba was doomed. James Buchanan made Cuba a priority of his administration in 1857, but the rising power of the Republican party in Congress ended any realistic hope of acquiring the "Pearl of the Antilles."

Deteriorating relations with Mexico in the 1850s, however, offered the promise of additional territory. Unpaid claims, Indian problems, continuing border disputes, and raids by American filibusters worsened relations and prompted Franklin Pierce to dispatch South Carolinian James Gadsden as Minister to Mexico in 1853. Gadsden was authorized to purchase as much land as possible from financially strapped Mexican President Antonio Lopez de Santa Anna for a southern route for the transcontinental railroad. He succeeded in obtaining a small strip of land across southern New Mexico and Arizona and the right of transit across the Isthmus of Tehuantepec, but the other issues remained unresolved. Many northern senators saw this as a pro-slavery land grab and reduced the purchase price from $15 million to $10 million and the amount of territory from 45,000 to 30,000 square miles. This strip – the Gadsden Purchase – would be the final land acquisition in the antebellum period.

Southern expansionists also turned their eyes towards Central America. The United States had been active in the region for a generation, largely focusing upon the issue of a transisthmian route that would link the Atlantic and Pacific coasts. The Polk and Taylor administration had dispatched agents who negotiated treaties with Colombia (in Panama), Nicaragua, and Honduras for crossing rights. These rights became critical when the United States added California to the nation in 1848, but the treaties also agitated Great Britain, which had longstanding influence in the area. The Clayton–Bulwer pact of 1850 resolved the immediate competition between the United States and England by denying each the exclusive right to build a canal or to colonize in the region. Tensions remained high, however, both in Washington, where expansionist senators decried the treaty as a sell-out of American interests, and in Central America, where US transit forces came into conflict with both the British and native populations.

At this juncture William Walker, the legendary "gray-eyed man of destiny," appeared on the scene. Physically small, but with a charismatic personality, the Tennessee-born Walker entered Central America at a propitious moment. He had failed in a filibustering effort in Sonora, Mexico in 1853, but then exploited the political chaos of Nicaragua in 1855. Sponsored partly by mining and transit interests, Walker quickly took advantage of the situation and with only 60 men made himself dictator of Nicaragua by October. His reputation rose to heroic proportions in the United States, where he renewed hope for the followers of "Manifest Destiny," especially in the South. Walker's flouting of Great Britain and his proposed reinstitution of slavery in 1856 enhanced his image and won his regime the recognition of the Pierce administration. However, the filibuster could not survive a coalition of Costa Rican and Honduran forces, armed by Great Britian, which ousted him in 1857. Walker organized and launched three more expeditions in 1857, 1858, and 1860 in an effort to regain power in Nicaragua and establish the "slave empire" he promised his southern supporters. Each effort was disastrous, the third resulting in Walker's capture by the British navy and his execution by a Honduran firing squad. Walker's death on the eve of the Civil War spelled not only the demise of antebellum filibustering, but also the end of the southern dream of a Caribbean empire.

As the South awakened to the reality of a failed crusade in the Caribbean and the election of Abraham Lincoln in 1860, a Republican pledged to prohibit the further annexation of slave territory, secession became an option increasingly discussed. During the winter of 1861, the Confederate States of America formed and by April the two sections were at war. Historians generally concur that successful pursuit of foreign policy goals was critical to victory for both sides. They also agree that each side possessed unique diplomatic advantages. The Union, under the leadership of Lincoln and his able Secretary of State William Seward, needed to prevent European intervention and assistance to the Confederacy. Seward had several cards to play, including the possibility of a Yankee invasion of long-sought-after Canada and the critical trade of American grain to Britain. The Confederacy, under the direction of President Jefferson Davis and a series of secretaries of state, most notably Judah P. Benjamin, had the advantage of "King Cotton."

Scholars have often focused upon the talented Seward and his skillful manipulation of people and events, particularly in the early years of the war, to prevent the recognition of the Confederacy by Great Britain and France. He is continually ranked, along with John Quincy Adams, as the most adroit and successful secretary of state in United States history. Seward played a dangerous game, threatening war with the Europeans if they recognized the South, but cagily compromising in the "*Trent* Affair." This unauthorized boarding of a British steamer out of Havana carrying two Confederate diplomats bound for Europe in November 1861 by the USS *San Jacinto* heightened Anglo-American tensions and provoked considerable drumbeating on both sides of the Atlantic. As the British dispatched forces to Canada, Seward tactfully retreated, releasing the captive emissaries, but stopping short of an apology to the Crown.

Seward, subtle and manipulative, demonstrated a marvelous blend of aggressiveness and restraint depending upon the situation. In 1863, he combined with Minister Charles Francis Adams to pressure Foreign Secretary Lord John Russell into halting the construction of Confederate-bound naval rams in Liverpool shipyards. The twin rebel defeats at Vicksburg and Gettysburg in July, coupled with the failure of southern diplomatic efforts in parliament, spelled the end of any serious possibility of recognition. As historian D. P. Crook (1974) has noted, Britain and France had also become increasingly concerned about Russia's role in crushing the Polish insurrection in 1863. The might of the British navy broke the waves and Napoleon III seemed to follow in their wake. Given the balance of power issues on the Continent, the timing was poor for involvement in a North American war whose outcome was unclear.

Historian Charles Hubbard (1998) credits the Union with bold diplomatic leadership, but also blames Jefferson Davis, who he labels "indifferent" to foreign affairs, for the "absence of a well-conceived and implemented diplomatic initiative" (1998: xvi). Hubbard faults the policy-makers in Richmond and their handmaidens in Europe for both arrogance and a lack of vision. He criticizes Davis and his cabinet for a naïve reliance on the economic leverage of "King Cotton" and bungled opportunities abroad. The South's European agents were well intentioned, but inept and inexperienced. In the minds of many scholars, the Confederacy lost the war not only on the battlefields of Virginia and Mississippi, but in the halls of parliament and Versailles.

Continuing political instability in Mexico presented yet another testing ground for Union and Confederate diplomacy. Napoleon III, along with Great Britain and Spain, had intervened in Mexico in 1861, ostensibly to collect debts owed to European creditors. When his compatriots withdrew the next year, Napoleon remained in the hope of establishing an imperial foothold in the region. French troops provided the military support for the overthrow of the government of Benito Juarez in 1863 and the establishment of Austrian Archduke Ferdinand Maximilian as Emperor of Mexico. Confederate diplomats proposed exchanging recognition of Maximilian for that of French recognition of the government in Richmond. Seward countered with his customary carrot-and-stick diplomacy. He suggested that the United States had not closed the door on the recognition of Maximilian, but simultaneously pointed out that French interference in Mexico violated the Monroe Doctrine. Since Napoleon III was reluctant to move without his cross-channel partner, the Civil War ground to a conclusion without the Emperor recognizing the Confederacy. At the war's end, Washington dispatched 50,000 men to the Mexican border and increasingly turned the diplomatic screws on the French adventure. Napoleon wisely withdrew his troops and abandoned the foolhardy Maximilian to his overthrow and death at the hands of the Juaristas in 1867. Seward had demonstrated the power of the Union in 1865 and successfully applied the principles of the Monroe Doctrine.

The purchase of Alaska provided Seward his final opportunity for expansion and empire. Russo-American negotiations for the transfer of the frozen province for $5 million in 1859 were interrupted by the war. When talks resumed in 1866, the sale was easily negotiated for $7.2 million. Fish, furs, ice, timber, and rumors of gold were sufficient to convince a special session of the Senate to ratify the treaty in April 1867 by a 37: 2 vote. Serious problems arose, however, when numerous politicians and editors, led by Horace Greeley of the New York *Tribune*, blasted the acquisition as worthless and unnecessary. Rumors swirled about the capital that both congressmen and editors had been bribed to promote the purchase. A congressional investigation ended inconclusively in 1869, but, significantly, the edge had been dulled on the imperial impulse. The Alaska Scandal aroused suspicion among a skeptical public already preoccupied with Reconstruction.

Seward also pushed the concept of Manifest Destiny beyond the continent into the Pacific and the Caribbean. Although he coveted several islands (Midway and the Hawaiians) in the Pacific, his territorial ambitions stopped short of the Asian mainland. He encouraged cheap Chinese labor into the United States to work on the transcontinental railroad through the Burlingame Treaty of 1868, but Asia remained on the periphery of his vision.

American interest in the Pacific, which dated back to the China trade in teas and silks in the 1780s, had been formalized by a treaty during the Tyler administration. A combination of the depression of 1837, British competition, and pressure from American businessmen and missionaries convinced John Tyler and Daniel Webster to dispatch a minister to China. In 1844, Caleb Cushing, the scion of a Massachusetts shipping family, negotiated the Treaty of Wanghia which granted the Americans most-favored-nation status and extra-territorial privileges. The treaty stood for a half century as the foundation of Sino-American relations.

The navy had traditionally played a major role in aggressively advancing American commercial interests in the antebellum era, particularly in the Pacific Ocean. Captains Thomas ap Catesby Jones and Charles Wilkes led exploratory expeditions to the South Pacific in the 1820s and 1830s which captured the attention of the nation. Merchants were especially interested in the possibilities offered by commerce with the Hawaiian Islands and Japan. When Webster returned to the state department under Fillmore, he dispatched Commodore Matthew C. Perry to Japan to open trade avenues and protect shipwrecked American sailors. Perry utilized the power of his fleet to intimidate the Japanese in 1854 and produce a treaty in 1858 that opened five Japanese ports and provided for extra-territoriality.

Seward's ringing endorsement of the Monroe Doctrine had a measurable impact in Europe and Latin America. But his territorial vision produced Alaska and little else. The navy appropriated Midway Island in 1867, but Seward's dreams of annexing the Virgin Islands, Samana Bay in the Dominican Republic, and the Hawaiian Islands were frustrated by cost, public doubt, and congressional opposition. A canal treaty with Nicaragua was endorsed by the Senate, but a comparable agreement with Colombia for a Panama route died in the Senate. Seward departed the government in 1869 as arguably the most accomplished secretary of state in American history, but a man whose failures must be measured along with his triumphs.

In more than a half-century the United States had transformed itself into a hemispheric power. The addition of Louisiana, Florida, Texas, Oregon, the Mexican Cession, the Gadsden Purchase, and Alaska propelled the nation into a position of domination. American leaders had utilized a variety of rationalizations and justifications to achieve this position, including cries of violated neutral rights, Indian depredations, unpaid claims, national security, unprovoked aggression, the Monroe Doctrine, and "Manifest Destiny". Most struck a responsive chord with an American populace eager to expand at least across the continent and perhaps beyond. Canada and Cuba remained beyond American control, but strong interest remained. Certainly, commercial expansion was reflected in extensive American activity in the Far East and Latin America. Territorial "Manifest Destiny" was slowed by sectional division in the 1850s and by the Civil War and Reconstruction of the 1860s and 1870s. However, by 1867 the United States had the land, population, and resources necessary to emerge as an international power. The country had fought a bloody war that converted a union into a nation. Once the wounds of that conflict had healed, Americans would refocus their energies on redefining their place and mission in the world.

REFERENCES

Belohlavek, John M. (1985) *"Let the Eagle Soar!": the Foreign Policy of Andrew Jackson*. Lincoln: University of Nebraska Press.

de Conde, Alexander (1976) *This Affair of Louisiana*. New York: Scribner.

Crook, D. P. (1974) *The North, the South, and the Powers*. New York: Wiley.

Graebner, Norman (1955) *Empire on the Pacific*. New York: Ronald Press.

Haynes, Sam W. (1997) *James K. Polk and the Expansionist Impulse*. New York: Longman.

Hickey, Donald (1989) *The War of 1812: a Forgotten Conflict*. Urbana: University of Illinois Press.

Hietala, Thomas (1985) *Manifest Design: Anxious Aggrandizement in Late Jacksonian America*. Ithaca, NY: Cornell University Press.

Horsman, Reginald (1981) *Race and Manifest Destiny*. Cambridge, Mass.: Harvard University Press.

Hubbard, Charles (1998) *The Burden of Confederate Diplomacy*. Knoxville: University of Tennessee Press.

Johnson, John (1990) *A Hemisphere Apart: the Foundations of United States Foreign Policy towards Latin America*. Baltimore, MD: Johns Hopkins University Press.

May, Robert E. (1973) *The Southern Dream of a Caribbean Empire, 1854–1861*. Baton Rouge: Louisiana State University Press.

Owsley Jr, Frank L. and Smith, Gene A. (1997) *Filibusters and Expansionists: Jeffersonian Manifest Destiny, 1800–1821*. Tuscaloosa: University of Alabama Press.

Perkins, Bradford (1995) *Creation of a Republican Empire, 1776–1865*. Cambridge, Mass.: Harvard University Press.

Rakestraw, Donald and Jones, Howard (1997) *Prologue to Manifest Destiny: Anglo-American Relations in the 1840s*. New York: Scholarly Resources.

Saul, Norman (1991) *Distant Friends: the United States and Russia, 1763–1867*. Lawrence: University Press of Kansas.

Schroeder, John (1985) *Shaping a Maritime Empire: the Commercial and Diplomatic Role of the American Navy, 1829–1861*. Westport, Conn.: Greenwood Press.

Stagg, J. C. A. (1993) *Mr Madison's War: Politics, Diplomacy, and Warfare in the Early American Republic, 1783–1830*. Princeton, NJ: Princeton University Press.

Stevens, Kenneth R. (1989) *Border Diplomacy: the Caroline and McLeod Affairs in Anglo-American-Canadian Relations, 1837–1842*. Tuscaloosa: University of Alabama Press.

Tucker, Robert W. and Hendrickson, David C. (1990) *Empire of Liberty: the Statecraft of Thomas Jefferson*. New York: Oxford University Press.

Weeks, William (1992) *John Quincy Adams and American Global Empire*. Lexington: University Press of Kentucky.

CHAPTER EIGHT

The Global Emergence of the United States, 1867–1900

Eric Rauchway

THE brute facts of the USA's entrance on to the world stage in the late nineteenth century are undisputed. A population that numbered some 30 million after the Civil War more than doubled to 76 million in 1900, and during that same period far surpassed Great Britain in its accumulated capital. American holdings were in 1865 merely continental in scope, and a French incursion in Mexico threatened the notion of American suzerainty over the hemisphere as embodied in the Monroe Doctrine. In 1867 both of these limits vanished: Secretary of State William Seward arranged for the acquisition of Alaska and the Mexican misadventure of Maximilian came to a close. That year set the American program of landed and commercial expansion on a path that took it through the new states of the West to Midway, Hawaii, Guam, Puerto Rico, Cuba, the Philippines and on to China, which by 1900 enjoyed an uneasy guarantee of its continuing unpartitioned existence owing to an "open door" regime that the Americans supported.

Within the centenary year, Victoria, Queen of Great Britain and Empress of India, would die, and the energies she represented would flow less obviously to her successor than to the rising American president, the distinctly imperial Theodore Roosevelt. The signs were then clear to those who cared to read them and have remained so since: the Americans stood to inherit the imperial mantle from the British. The question that has vexed historians of late nineteenth-century American foreign policy is whether this ascent to eminence represented a break with tradition or a continuous ambition, and if the latter, whose ambition it was.

As any defense lawyer will attest, even when the elements of a crime are conceded, if motive has not been established the nature of the crime – and therefore its severity – cannot be determined. Mitigating or aggravating factors may yet lurk in the determination of intent. Thus, while it is generally clear that during the 1890s American policy more explicitly countenanced expansionist tendencies, extending to the acquisition and government of traditional colonies – foreign populations whose assimilation into the American polity nobody seriously anticipated – historians can still disagree over whether these tendencies in the 1890s represented an incidental change in American foreign policy or an increased commitment to an already extant plan. They further disagree over the question of whose ambition begat the American ascendance. The candidates include elite policy-makers and businessmen, reckless newspapermen inflaming an irrational public, and the mass of Americans of all kinds looking beyond the national borders.

This disagreement among historians derives from factors including present concerns, use of sources, and (perhaps most important) professional fault-lines dividing various subdisciplines of history from each other. A student of American foreign policy looking closely at maneuverings between diplomats will reach interpretations different from those of a historian looking at cultural, economic, or domestic political variables. To suggest the outlines of these interpretations as they developed, it will be useful to begin with the Progressive synthesis of factors weighing on American expansiveness, and the dismantlers of that interpretation.

Synthesis and Dissent: from the Progressives to the Cold War

For Progressive historians reared in the early years of the American historical profession the lines between domestic and international, social and intellectual history were faint traces, not policed borders. Progressive historians answered the airiest of questions by beginning with the earthiest of facts. For example, when Frederick Jackson Turner tried to explain the inmost desires of liberty-loving Americans, he began with the fact of motion – the westward movement of frontier settlements. The simplicity of that fact has, over time and under close investigation, developed complexities – a fate that befell much of Progressive scholarship. But this optimistic comprehensiveness was the hallmark of Progressive thinking.

Consequently, when Charles and Mary Beard wrote their survey of American history in 1927 they did not limit their analysis but instead took for their subject matter everything that fitted under their title, *The Rise of American Civilization*. This ambitious scope and catholic interest gave shape to their explanation of "Imperial America." The United States empire of 1898 and after began, the Beards argued, with the earlier consolidation of Western inland settlements. The rapid settlement and admission to statehood of the Louisiana Purchase lands and the Mexican Cession, the construction of the railroads and the telegraph lines to link the newly re-united East with the resources of the West, the conquest of the Native Americans, and the industrialization of agriculture created a national political economy whose citizens looked with increasing fervor to the markets of "fabled Cathay." This process of consolidation depended not only on the ambitions of individual farmers, manufacturers, and entrepreneurs, but on the creation of a policy framework that allowed them to act on their independent interests. This framework included a high tariff to protect American manufacturers, a sound currency, centralized banking, and a benevolent attitude toward business. It set minimal limits on individual aspirations. By giving Americans license to exploit a "freer field and a richer material endowment" than any older civilization had known, a cooperative government made the emergence of America as a world power only a small matter of time before farmers, manufacturers, missionaries, and big-navy men won control of the necessary markets, heathens, and coaling-stations to spread American influence throughout the world (Beard and Beard, 1927: II, 480, 123, 170).

Despite their courteous agnosticism on the motives for American expansion – they quote, without comment, Andrew Carnegie's hopes for the spread of American liberties, and allow William McKinley his Christian convictions – the Beards, by rooting American expansionism in a combination of the material riches of the continent and a permissive regime of exploitation, implicitly suggest that the overseas spread of American political culture was at best a difficult proposition. The money-making opportunities that global influence could offer were far more certain than the international application of the Declaration of Independence or the Apostles' Creed, especially as the presumptive recipients of these enlightened blessings were after all "half-naked aborigines" ill-equipped to resist "economic competition, whisky, and disease." The rude health of the new continental nation testified not so much to the impending spread of an American-style Rome, but to the shrinking of the world under the inflexible, omnilateral squeeze of industry. American liberties, having resulted from a fortunate combination of the North American environment and the proclivities of a culture that encouraged individual enrichment, were likely to remain robust only within those parameters (Beard and Beard, 1927: II, 354, 357).

The Beardian synthesis enjoyed its widest acceptance through the 1930s. It came apart during the debate over American entry into World War II when Charles Beard's intransigent anti-interventionism left him increasingly alone among even liberal intellectuals. But Beard's rhetorical excesses account only partly for historians' willingness to dismantle the Progressive synthesis. Intellectual and contemporary political currents ran against it as well.

In the early 1930s Perry Miller had begun to argue for a history of ideas independent of social circumstances. He announced his proud disregard of those social and economic factors that the Beards had believed inseparable from intellectual ones. Miller meant for an independent intellectual history to detach historians from their subject matter and prevent the use of the present to judge the past. But his technical innovation of separating ideas from their context helped later historians to see ideological constructs such as liberty and freedom apart from their social and material context – a development with political uses. In reaction to the Nazi horror (and, later, Soviet totalitarianism) Americans mounted a principled defense of rights and liberties where they existed, and furthermore justified trying to spread them abroad. To argue otherwise was to indulge in the cardinal sins of that generation: isolationism and appeasement. If American liberties were the product of an interaction between culture and environment, as the Beards had maintained, efforts to spread them would be likely to fail. But if, on the other hand, these liberties were universally applicable, then wherever they did not thrive the moral duties of power were plain. By removing ideas from their context and by freeing foreign policy from domestic politics, American historians could begin to see America's global emergence as the gradual triumph of American ideas.

At first this interpretation underwrote the idea that the Spanish–American War of 1898 was, in the 1936 work of Samuel Flagg Bemis, "a great aberration." Bemis rested this thesis on his disapproval of what he took to be an unprecedented American example of outright imperialism – colonial rule over a subject people. "After his victory at Manila Bay, Dewey could have sailed right along home, and it is a pity he did not," Bemis wrote. He lay blame for this adventure in "adolescent irresponsibility" at the feet of President William McKinley, rather than on the "American people," whose fault, if any, was that they were unduly aroused by a yellow press. Bemis separated McKinley from the public in order to place blame on the president. But by the late 1940s, with the obvious example of Franklin Roosevelt in immediate hindsight, the president's independent wisdom had become an object of high regard for historians of foreign policy (Bemis, 1936: 463, 467, 475).

For Dexter Perkins in the late 1940s, the consolidation of the American continental nation and the acquisition of overseas territory were not the product of "the imperialist impulse in its naked form." If American statesmen had sometimes acted without public warrant to seize new lands and wage war on their inhabitants, perhaps it was just as well. In language that (intentionally or not) recalled the defense of that moderate plunderer Sir Robert Clive, Perkins remarked on an American "forbearance that is almost unparalleled." Of the most organized American efforts to consolidate territorial gains – the Indian wars of the 1870s – he supposed "even moralistic Americans would not wish to undo their results, or even spend much time in regretting them." Perkins believed "Ideas are a powerful directive of action" in determining the use of American power, and only "cynical foreigners" would attribute American actions to "the acquisitive impulse" (Perkins, 1957: 27, 23, 20, 22).

Some of Perkins's peers advanced more sophisticated arguments, but kept the general terms of his analysis intact. Thomas A. Bailey remarked that "Human motives seldom come unmixed," and if he had to suggest a general-purpose formula for American expansionary motives, he would offer both "Christ and petroleum." In considering "the man in the street," Bailey believed him likely to force the president and Congress into ill-considered action – and, like Bemis, he thought the 1898 war an outstanding example. Also, like Perkins, he was on the whole more impressed with American imperial restraint rather than with its excesses, and those excesses, he believed, came more from a lack of "maturity" in public deportment, not from the representation of rational interests in the acquisition of international power (Bailey, 1948: 195–6, 318).

The focus on ideas, and the mistrust of the public, reflected a general shift in method and address for historians of foreign policy that defined the realist school of interpretation. Where the Beards believed themselves speaking both for and to the American people, illustrating how their government sometimes represented them well and sometimes poorly, their successors had become more sensitive to the error of popular sentiment, especially as it pertained to foreign affairs. The practitioners of diplomacy came naturally to this realization. In a 1950 series of Walgreen Lectures, State Department sovietologist George F. Kennan urged the expulsion of commercial, moral, and other disorderly elements from the realm of foreign policy and reported that American formal imperialism was a bad mis-step undertaken for popular, but not good, reasons. Kennan wished to see foreign policy dissociated from the flighty public and placed in the hands of professionals like himself, who cared only for stability and were little concerned with ideals as such.

Historians who liked Kennan's prescriptions could project them backward into American history. Julius W. Pratt declared in the opening of his 1955 history that the field of diplomatic history ought properly to redress the "vague understanding" of "lay audiences" by exposing them to the processes of expert decision-making in the State Department and foreign service. Where the United States had failed in its pursuit of diplomatic goals – for example, in its willingness to go to war for more territory – it had failed because "humanitarian and sentimental reasons" dominated diplomatic discourse (Pratt, 1955: viii). This focus on diplomatic expertise removed foreign policy from the realm of class- or interest-based politics. For example, Pratt touched on the tariff only as it represented friction between nations, not as it marked the political rise or fall of manufacturing interests. The conquest and consolidation of the West, being an internal matter, bore not at all on the expansionary impulses of the American nation in the 1890s. Alaska fell into the American orbit largely as a favor to a cash-strapped Tsar. And so on: by the mid-1950s, foreign policy history could concern itself with principles – the preservation of security, the defense or spread of liberties – and determine whether a given case study illustrated their application or violation without considering the base matter of social or political affairs (Pratt, 1955: 382).

Tragic Continuity: Cold War Crises

In this climate of astringent analysis, tinged as it still was by an appreciation of American forbearance and decency, William Appleman Williams's work came as a bolt from the blue. Given the Cold War context, Williams struck some commentators and professional historians as a radical or a Marxist. But the major achievement of his 1959 *The Tragedy of American Diplomacy* was not the restoration of economics to the study of nineteenth-century American foreign policy, but rather the forcible reintroduction of American distinctiveness to a debate that had become so largely technical. It is after all only heroic – and heroically flawed – characters who can undergo tragedies, and Williams's America fit this description. It was unfortunate that in the brisk Cold War atmosphere Williams drew attention, including the basilisk gaze of the House Un-American Activities Committee, mainly for the critical elements of his work, rather than for his gropings toward a new synthesis.

In his introductory chapters, Williams argued for the continuity of American expansionist ambitions beginning at least with James Madison's injunction from *Federalist*, no. 10: "Extend the sphere" that liberty might survive the depredations of faction. Since then, Williams argued, the United States had depended on expansion to ensure its own internal stability, and it had acted like a "world power," exercising its influence beyond its borders whenever necessary since its inception. The growing agricultural sector of the 1830s gave rise to new modes of transportation, new methods of capitalization, and a search for new markets to meet supply. Mid-century Americans continued, as their predecessors had, to eye greedily the China market – in one of his rare stabs at humor, Williams remarked that farmers fervently hoped that the Chinese might be "converted from rice to wheat" much as they might convert to Methodism (Williams, 1959: 21–2, 25).

Without making judgments about the economic reality of nineteenth-century America, Williams focused on what American statesmen believed, based on their own observation and contemplation: that the health of America's political institutions depended on prosperity and a consequent comparative absence of class conflict. Nor did he even dispute this thesis. Williams accepted what he called the *Weltanschauung* of his subjects once he had established it. The "tragedy" of his title was one of the consequences that Americans had neither anticipated nor would likely have cared too much about if they had. "In expanding its own economic system throughout much of the world, America had made it very difficult for other nations to retain their economic independence," and thus as difficult, if not impossible, for those other nations to enjoy the blessings of American-style liberty that would come with American-style prosperity (Williams, 1959: 15).

In light of later historiographical developments, it is important to note that Williams did not preclude spreading American political institutions throughout the world, and, if anything, he celebrated the chance. The notion of cultural imperialism would not have fit well in his worldview. What possessed him, and indeed appeared to give him considerable pains of conscience, was his sense of the tragedy of unintended consequences: that in a more or less continuous access of heartfelt idealism, Americans meaning to do good in the world had instead done evil. A more conservative, or at least detached, historian might have called this state of affairs a paradox rather than a tragedy, but Williams believed that the nobility that led to tragedy might resurface in a more just foreign policy – that, as he put it, Americans could through a knowledge of their past errors "transform the tragedy into a new opportunity for great achievement." He recommended that Americans open themselves to other nations' independence rather than urge other nations to open their markets to American goods (Williams, 1959: 16).

It would be at least infelicitous to describe Williams as a neo-Progressive, despite some similarities in the synthetic approaches. Both he and the Beards rooted American motives in an effort to secure domestic benefits. But the Beards remained sensible of the romance of American expansionism and to an evident extent enjoyed relating the spectacles of rascally selfishness that characterized what they called, with a purposive double meaning, "the politics of acquisition." Williams – and his critics too – were sterner. In the Cold War era the debate over what Americans had been doing in the world had to bear the burden of the debate over what Americans were now doing in the world. It would fall to Williams's most adept elaborator to restore some of the Beards' scope and tenor to the theme of American global emergence (Beard and Beard, 1927: II, 285).

Walter LaFeber offered a substantive and thorough new interpretation in his 1963 *The New Empire*. LaFeber drew on three principal sources. First, he relied on the new business history of the 1950s, particularly the work of Edward C. Kirkland, to illustrate both the *modus operandi* and the desiderata of the American business community as it assimilated new technologies and new structural innovations in the world economy. Secondly, he relied on the climate of opinion as expressed by influential figures of the moment: Josiah Strong, Alfred Thayer Mahan, Brooks Adams (whose title he had borrowed), Theodore Roosevelt, and Henry Cabot Lodge. Thirdly, and most important for his case for continuity, he relied on the expressed opinions and evident actions of the secretaries of state and presidents of the period. Even if, as recent historians had argued, actual expansion had been fitful and episodic, the wish for expansion – the ambition and plan for expansion – had been continuous. Thus American expansion came to appear seismic, featuring occasional eruptions driven by constant underlying pressure.

The new American empire required colonial possessions not for trade in themselves – the Samoans would not buy enough shirtings to make much difference in the mills of Massachusetts – but as way-stations to fabled Cathay. Americans required Midway Atoll for precisely what its name implied – not much in itself, but conveniently between here and there. The same held true to a greater or lesser extent for Hawaii, Samoa, Alaska, Guam, and the Philippines, which could in a happier world have been the American Hong Kong (or so the expansionists would have thought). Also, LaFeber (1963) noted, if the Philippine episode represented an aberration of any significant sort, it was an aberration of method rather than ambition. Americans appeared to prefer the absorption of new territory by economic means before sending in troops and flags. Hence the tariff reappeared in historiography as an expansionist tool. Judiciously administered, it could bring Hawaii and Cuba into the American fold with minimal use of military force.

LaFeber also restored the Progressive notion that the integration of the West into the American industrial system constituted a necessary and understood first step to overseas power. "The empire would begin with a strong, consolidated base of power on the American continent and move into the way stations of the Pacific as it approached the final goal of Asia," he wrote, summarizing William Seward's vision as secretary of state in the 1860s. Seward was, for LaFeber's later expansionists, the "prince of players," the ancestral voice crying "open up a highway through your country" that goods might freely flow to the sea. Seward was the first link in "the chain of economic expansion . . . to Theodore Roosevelt and beyond." With Seward's efforts in place, the pattern was set, so that Fish, Evarts, Blaine, Frelinghuysen, Bayard, Blaine redux, Gresham, and Olney all proceeded inexorably to John Hay and the splendid war, which focused, as they had, both on the Caribbean and the Pacific (LaFeber, 1963: 24–6, 32).

As the nineteenth century wore on, LaFeber's statesmen acted increasingly as much out of fear as of ambition. Believing that the depressions of the 1870s through the 1890s resulted from overproduction, and moreover that the closing of the frontier shut off a safety valve for unemployed laborers who might otherwise wreak violent acts of protest, they sought to restore motion to the economy by channeling energies into the discovery of new outlets for American goods. In this respect, as in others, LaFeber's subjects acted not out of bellicosity, idealism, or in reaction to the buffets of public opinion, but "because they feared United States interests were in jeopardy." The policies of expansion were "logical corollaries" of new economic realities, derived by conscientious men applying the sum of their experience. Thus LaFeber kept himself sensible of "the magnificent vision" of Seward, the splendid appeal of James "the Plumed Knight" Blaine, and the stolid persistence of "Major McKinley" in working their effects on foreign policy. He kept his sense of tragedy, if any, subordinate to the spectacle and the irony of unintended consequences. His guiding familiar was the bemused and occasionally delighted voice of Henry Adams, who was, in LaFeber's apt quotation, pleased to see "that the family work of a hundred and fifty years fell at once into the grand perspective of true empire-building" (LaFeber, 1963: 281, 417, 408, 47, 328, 407).

Even LaFeber's strong continuitarian interpretation of post-Civil War expansionism allowed for certain changes in the 1890s. The 1893 panic jolted the Democratic party out of its remaining anti-expansionist prejudices, and the dangerous *démarches* in Venezuela and elsewhere in Latin America convinced American administrations of the need for a stronger military.

Historians following LaFeber tended to focus on these transformations. Over the course of the 1970s historians fleshed out a new periodization and interpretation that characterized the changes in American foreign policy in the 1890s. Taken together these works present a coherent picture of the changes some historians believe marked a watershed in foreign relations.

Robert Beisner, who contributed substantially to the intellectual history of foreign policy through his earlier work on anti-imperialism, proposed in 1975 that renewed attention be paid to the shift "from the old diplomacy to the new." Using Thomas Kuhn's concept of paradigm changes that were the hallmarks of scientific revolutions, Beisner sketched a fairly rapid shift occurring in about 1890 from "amateurish and often maladroit" American efforts at influencing events overseas to a "truly far-sighted" mode of thinking marked by statesmen "prepared to intervene" overseas (Beisner, 1975: 23, 81).

In this interpretation, American expansionists before 1890 were not goal-oriented (if ultimately misguided) actors, as they appeared to be in LaFeber's work, but rather opportunists, and often incompetent ones at that. If Seward's approach had a pattern it was, according to Beisner, that of "buckshot;" Fish's efforts were mere "grabbiness." Blaine's best works amounted to "hasty patch jobs." There was no over-arching intention, no plan, and such efforts as there were toward systematic work were Kuhnian "anomalies," smoothing the way for a fundamental change without themselves constituting fully fledged paradigms. Only the cumulative effects of many cultural changes – a widespread belief in progress, a new generation given to expansionist thinking and accustomed to reading expert opinions in the papers – could yield a new overall system devoted to serious foreign policy (Beisner, 1975: 46, 56, 38).

Beisner's interpretative essay was flanked by about equidistant works that presented before-and-after-1890 views of American foreign policy. Beisner himself relied heavily on Milton Plesur, whose 1971 *America's Outward Thrust*, covering the period from 1865 to 1890, presented a portrait of disorganized pre-1890 American overseas involvement. Plesur looked at culture and intellect, which, in his words, were "awkward to describe, hard to gauge, impossible to concretize, and embarrassingly contradictory and divided." Moreover, the Department of State during this era was "antiquated, inefficient, and poorly suited to meet the needs of a nation which . . . was assuming greater international responsibilities." In such an environment, novelists, essayists, amateurs, explorers, and technicians carried a haphazard and disorganized picture of America to the lands beyond its borders, and returned hawking the romantic, the peculiar, and whatever else seemed commercially viable (Plesur, 1971: vi, 227).

Emily Rosenberg's (1982) *Spreading the American Dream* followed Beisner and complemented Plesur by presenting a picture of American foreign policy after 1890 as an organized, corporatist effort. Rosenberg identified a "liberal-developmental" ideology that "both reflects and is used to affect the social organization." This ideology allowed Americans to combine the liberal tendencies implicit in their political and economic history into a rough-and-ready set of theses about human behavior, theses presumed to be universally applicable. To support the universal applicability of these theses, the new foreign policy apparatus of the American government comprised a "promotional state" willing to work with, and even for, American businesses overseas (Rosenberg, 1982: 7, 48ff). Rosenberg's interpretation comported well with those who saw the emerging American "open door" policy of the 1890s as the parallel to the British anti-colonial imperialism of earlier Victorian decades. The authors of *Sentimental Imperialists* (Thomson et al., 1981: 133) explicitly equated the American "open door" regime with the British "imperialism of free trade."

But if LaFeber over-estimated the conscious designs of American expansionists before 1890, we should take care not to do the same for expansionists after 1890. Nothing quite demonstrates this pitfall so well as the comparison with the British informal empire. The British scholars of free-trade imperialism, John Robinson and Ronald Gallagher, rested their interpretation on what they called Britain's "official mind," which included not only generally applicable sentimental and racist precon-ceptions, but the accumulated habits of Whitehall bureaucrats during roughly two centuries of imperial experience. The Americans had nothing like this official mind – nothing in the way of accumulated experience – when it came to the administration of an empire of free trade, and it is easy to overstate the extent of the American shift toward mindfulness in the 1890s.

To assert that American foreign policy during this period moved toward a more conscientious and organized model is to under-estimate the often wildly haphazard, even bumptious, proceedings of Dollar Diplomats and their compatriots. It was not till late in Theodore Roosevelt's term, and then over some opposition, that he put the consular service on a meritocratic footing, and this reform amounted to the least a president could do to demonstrate his and his country's seriousness. The document-able shift toward institutional competency relies considerably on the establishment in 1897 of the Bureau of Foreign Commerce, responsible for statistics on foreign trade. But economists wishing to quantify the effects of American business cycles and (later on) World War I would have to recalculate such figures from raw data. In the private sphere, American banks could not even engage in the most basic of overseas financial activities – establishing overseas branches and drawing drafts on foreign exchange – until after the Federal Reserve Act of 1913.

Thus during the 1890s, the period of great imperialism, something more than institutional organization may have been afoot because efficiency did not yet amount to much. Historians trying to locate the expansionist impulse within the American heart or mind have long believed that imperialism amounted to more than policy, that it was a set of ambitions, beliefs, and desires – but where they might reside has remained a matter of considerable dispute.

The Location of Desire: the Element of Culture

Diplomatic history, strictly construed, is the province of the powerful. Nevertheless, the story of American expansion and aggrandizement has always contained within it innumerable narratives of settlers, soldiers, homesteaders, trappers, scientists, mer-chants, miners, bankers, and other ordinary citizens seizing the main chance. Seward's highway through the country would have meant nothing if there were no Americans seeking to travel it. In this historiography of American global emergence there is therefore a tension between the decisions of elites and the motives of Americans who act upon or despite them.

In simpler times this tension yielded to the structure of Frederick Jackson Turner's frontier thesis, which lurks behind every continuitarian thesis of American consolida-tion and overseas reach: as the government opened Western lands to settlement, Americans flooded into them, and by a process of "civilization" brought them into the Union, establishing trade routes, towns, and in the process forging a distinctly American character based on the experience. Historians of the West have picked apart key contentions of the Turner thesis as it applied to the actual settlement of the West. But it remains an undeniable proposition that a considerable number of influential thinkers believed a civilizing frontier proceeded westward, and acted accordingly when they thought this process had ended. This observation accounts for the thinking of elites. But as the frontier passed from the West into the imagination of the East, the role of ordinary Americans in pressing for expansion has become less clear. In his essay on civil disobedience, Henry Thoreau scorned the government's utility: after all, he claimed, it was not the government who settled the West. Historians have been less sure than Thoreau of the government's role and plans in the West and further West in comparison with the interest of ordinary Americans.

A useful test of this difficult question is the brass ring of westward expansion, the Asian market. If westward movement had any over-arching purpose, it was to reach, and trade with, the numerous Chinese. As the farthest point West from ordinary Americans, Asia was unlikely to fill up with Americans and their commerce unless the government and business leaders made it possible. As Thomas J. McCormick wrote in 1967, "America's leadership made a conscious, purposeful, integrated effort to solve the economic-social crisis at home by promoting the national interest abroad." In considering the business of the Philippines, as in considering the business of the Aleutians, "America's commercial stake in China played the primary role in the thinking of the business and government elite." Even if the China market never quite materialized (the end of the Qing dynasty would throw China into a political and economic convulsion from which, arguably, it has yet to recover), the idea of the China market remained important, much as the idea of the frontier remained important as a goad (McCormick, 1967: 19, 117).

But ideas liberated from their social context were once again apt to mutate. Thus, as Marilyn B. Young argues in *The Rhetoric of Empire* (1968), where American leaders might have thought to secure America's place in the world by establishing trade links and informal dependencies, they instead imported a worldview in which the United States had increasingly to act unilaterally to oppose the encroachments of Russia on the Asian continent. What began as a deliberate effort to answer domestic economic questions turned, perhaps less consciously, into a self-justifying effort to sustain a balance of power.

McCormick and Young wrote with the Vietnam War in the forefront of their consciousness and so had an obvious point of reference for the pursuit of overseas chimeras and the heavy-handed use of American power abroad. But in addition to the cautionary tales they told about overweening governmental ambition, Young also noted that the American policy toward China in the years before 1900 would more readily suffer characterization as a non-policy. "The United States government remained completely in the background, helpful but not instigating;" having constructed a federally owned highway across the Pacific, the government expected commerce to find its way across on its own. This *laissez-faire* attitude to commerce meant that American entrepreneurs enjoyed little success because the Chinese recognized "the American government was not yet ready to defend the interests of its capitalists or, by extension, of China" (Young, 1968: 56–7). If these characterizations were fair, then how much did American expansion result from the plans of a thinking elite and how much from the ambitions of the missionaries, merchants, and more ordinary Americans who began to travel the international road?

Ernest May, who had earlier hewed more to the realist interpretation, assayed in a 1968 essay on *American Imperialism* a sociological analysis of this murky relation between opinion-makers and the public in the late 1890s. Conceding that the "foreign policy public" was probably as small then as it is today, May set out to discover the "talkers," those who acted as sages for the "suddenly enlarged public" of the newspaper-heavy 1890s. May concluded that "the men who seemed to function as opinion leaders nearly all had close firsthand knowledge of Europe," and that their awareness of European justifications for new imperialist efforts in the 1890s probably affected their opinions. As the question of actually securing colonies grew more acute, and as traditional foreign policy elites divided over this issue, the weight of accumulated opinions and the momentum of those who followed European activities decided the issue in the minds of Americans. Again, it was in the absence of specific leadership that imperialism emerged as the order of the day (May, 1968: 24, 39, 41, 86).

May, like many other historians, limited his discussion of imperialism to the formal acquisition of colonies, and thus was able to exclude "organic growth" on the continent from his analysis. But this organic growth was the only area in which Americans, both elite and ordinary, did have an undeniably continuous experience in the subjugation of peoples whom they considered unassimilable. In this respect, there were important parallels between the consolidation of the West and the turn to insular imperialism as Americans crossed the Pacific. As Walter L. Williams pointed out, the ideas and policy of the Bureau of Indian Affairs, which was responsible for an inland empire, translated reasonably well to the Bureau of Insular Affairs, which was responsible for an overseas empire. Many of the soldiers who went to kill Filipino insurgents had prior experience killing Indian insurgents, and many of the imperialist senators had been leaders in establishing Indian policy (May, 1968: 100; Williams, 1980: 813, n16, 824, n79, 828, n105).

The parallels between these two aspects of late nineteenth-century expansionism extend, in some analyses, beyond actions and personnel to ideology. Arguments by historians of the West like Richard Slotkin have emphasized Americans' need for regeneration through racial violence as exemplified in the conquest of the West. The idea of racism as a driving motor of expansionism has reappeared in more general arguments about American expansionism, such as those that appear in the collection *Cultures of United States Imperialism* (Kaplan and Pease, 1993). Michael Rogin suggests that there has been, overall, a "racial basis for American expansion" (Kaplan and Pease, 1993: 510). At the same time, scholars of racism *per se*, George Fredrickson chief among them, have been skeptical of this claim, believing that "It appears unlikely, in fact, that racial thinking of any kind was an important factor in the original imperialist impulse." This split over the role of racism in American expansion derives directly from Miller's ancient liberation of intellectual history from social and economic factors. Slotkin, Rogin, and other scholars in the *Cultures* collection, though they define themselves politically in opposition to Miller, nevertheless preserve his notion that ideas constitute reality, or at the least an important reality. Fredrickson, and other such scholars who are not the less intellectual historians, nevertheless attribute expansionism and imperialism to "economic motives," albeit along with "concepts of national prestige and influence borrowed from Europe, and the 'psychic crisis' arising from the domestic situation of the 1890s" (Frederickson, 1987: 307).

For the time being it appears as though this schism over the role of ideas and extra-intellectual factors will remain.

The idea of an ideological basis for the peculiarities of American foreign policy persists and carries with it the possibility that elites, even when not reacting to the pressures of public or press, have not acted in a realist or interested manner. Michael Hunt (who in previous work has contributed to the internationalization of American foreign policy history by his facility with foreign-language sources) argues in his 1987 *Ideology and US Foreign Policy* that before 1900 two ideological tenets shaped American foreign relations: the notion of an American mission in the world tied to the ideal of liberty, and the persistent notion of a racial hierarchy. Hunt sees the two elements as unstable and shifting over time in response to a given "season" within the climate of opinion. Though the role of race hierarchy in Hunt's interpretation is clear, the meteorology of the climate of opinion – even the prevailing winds – is not (Hunt, 1987: 69).

Perhaps the most sophisticated scholarly examination of the combined phenomena of racism and America's global emergence is Robert Rydell's 1984 *All the World's a Fair*. Rydell uses a theoretical framework of hegemony and public ceremony to analyze the depiction of the world and its peoples in American World Fairs. The economic and spectacular natures of the fairs exploited racial difference for its exoticism and, Rydell argues, to buttress a notion of American superiority. Because the fairs emerged from networks of ambitious local businessmen hungry for tourist income and equally ambitious social scientists hungry for authority, they represent for Rydell "the exercise of economic and political power in cultural terms by the established leaders of American society." Expansion would not only secure markets for American goods, thus relieving elites of their worries over overproduction and underemployment, it would also assuage psychic anxieties and imbue the most ordinary of Americans (so long as they were white) with pride in the mission of global civilization (Rydell, 1984: 2).

In determining the place of racism and other ideas in the interpretation of American foreign policy, it will likely be helpful in the future to observe a distinction between language that is constitutive and delineates an existing policy regime, and language that is hortatory and meant to motivate changes in policy. If we respect this distinction, we can begin responsibly to address the place of racism and other ideas in American expansiveness. Where does racism belong? It may provide outlines for a sinisterly orderly world, as Hunt's and Rydell's references to an established hierarchy would indicate. On the other hand, it may justify actions taken to secure opportunity in the world, without particular regard for order. Or we may address another difficult concept: where does liberty belong in the American calculus of power? Is it, as the Beards might have suggested, tied to the distinctive path of American economic and social development, and therefore a commodity for domestic consumption only – or is it something to be cultivated overseas in less friendly soil?

These questions remain open in considering the route the US took to global power. Dexter Perkins believed in the paramountcy of ideas, as do many modern historians who have been less impressed with American forbearance. Their place in the framework of an analysis that must at least consider both Christ and petroleum – Locke would be a useful addition – remains unsettled. American historians may become more amenable to unifying these factors as Cold War thinking abates.

Rydell's thesis marks an important step toward examining in combination the operation of culture and of economics in the business of American expansionism, without losing the distinctions between the two. He has also identified an important interaction between American elites and their democracy, a negotiation of the meaning of expansionism. Just as the historiographical tendencies of the 1940s and 1950s resulted as much from new American international responsibilities as they did from new findings, so newer interpretations will likely respond to Americans' interest in the notion of cultural and economic globalization. More synthetic examinations like Rydell's should aid our understanding of America's rise to global power.

As we move toward such syntheses, it will also be wise to preserve such distinctions as we can. For example, it should be clear that the American Indians and the Filipinos shared with the Samoans and the Hawaiians not only the darkness of their skins but also their unfortunate geographical situation: they stood in the way of American progress toward Asia. Thus the Indian and Insular imperialisms that Walter Williams identifies are instructive in so far as they illustrate the means Americans were willing to employ to achieve their end. Keeping this conclusion in mind, we may profit by observing that the Japanese and the Chinese did not possess this same distinction. Rather than being between the Americans and their market, the Chinese were the prospective market, and the Japanese competed for it. Americans' racial attitudes toward Chinese and Japanese may therefore have developed accordingly.

LaFeber's 1997 book *The Clash*, covering US–Japanese relations, takes up precisely this theme, suggesting that Americans' perceptions of Japanese cultural and political difference, and consequent collisions between the two countries, have been based in large measure on the differences between American and Japanese capitalisms. Where Americans have organized a capitalist economy around competitive individual actors, the Japanese have organized a capitalist economy around cooperative networks of combinations, a circumstance that has frustrated Americans who believe, as did the expansionist Alfred Thayer Mahan, that the most common element of human nature is the sensibility of individual improvement. When the Japanese appeared immune to this sensibility, they appeared to Americans irretrievably different. When Mahan looked forward to the twentieth century, he believed that the common motive of individual improvement would ultimately erode notions of racial solidarity in both the East and the West. New interpretations of American expansionism in the late nineteenth century will have to account for the potency of such universalizing and corrosive assumptions about human nature and how they shaped American ambition.

Since the Cold War, the international affairs of the US have appeared to change from state-centered policy initiatives to the less-organized motions of international networks of commerce, industry, science, and information. In such an environment, whose parallels with the international arena at the close of the nineteenth century are more numerous than with that of the mid-twentieth century, historians of the US will have once again to explore the connection between material and ideational factors, domestic and international affairs, and to account for the ways in which Americans from all social strata have made claims on, and participated in the diffusion of, international American power.

REFERENCES

Bailey, T. A. (1948) *The Man in the Street: the Impact of American Public Opinion on Foreign Policy.* New York: Macmillan.

Beard, C. A. and Beard, M. R. (1927) *The Rise of American Civilization*, 2 vols. New York: Macmillan.

Beisner, R. L. (1975) *From the Old Diplomacy to the New, 1865–1900.* New York: Thomas Y. Cowell.

Bemis, S. F. (1936) *A Diplomatic History of the United States.* New York: Henry Holt, 1942.

Fredrickson, G.M. (1971) *The Black Image in the White Mind: the Debate on Afro-American Character and Destiny, 1817–1914.* Hanover, NH: Wesleyan University Press, 1987.

Hunt, M. (1987) *Ideology and US Foreign Policy.* New Haven, Conn.: Yale University Press.

Kaplan, A. and Pease, D. E. (eds) (1993) *Cultures of United States Imperialism.* Durham, NC: Duke University Press.

LaFeber, W. (1963) *The New Empire: an Interpretation of American Expansion, 1860–1898.* Ithaca, NY: Cornell University Press.

LaFeber, W. (1997) *The Clash: US–Japanese Relations Throughout History.* New York: Norton.

McCormick, T. J. (1967) *China Market: America's Quest for Informal Empire, 1893–1901.* Chicago: Quadrangle.

May, E. R. (1968) *American Imperialism: a Speculative Essay.* New York: Atheneum.

Perkins, D. (1957) *Foreign Policy and the American Spirit.* Ithaca, NY: Cornell University Press.

Plesur, M. (1971) *America's Outward Thrust: Approaches to Foreign Affairs, 1865–1890.* DeKalb, Ill.: Northern Illinois University Press.

Pratt, J. W. (1955) *A History of United States Foreign Policy.* Englewood Cliffs, NJ: Prentice-Hall.

Rosenberg, E. S. (1982) *Spreading the American Dream: American Economic and Cultural Expansion, 1890–1945.* New York: Hill and Wang.

Rydell, R. W. (1984) *All the World's a Fair: Visions of Empire at American International Expositions, 1876–1916.* Chicago: University of Chicago Press.

Thomson Jr, J. C., Stanley, P., and Perry, J. C. (1981) *Sentimental Imperialists: the American Experience in East Asia.* New York: Harper.

Williams, W. A. (1959) *The Tragedy of American Diplomacy.* New York: Delta, 1972.

Williams, W. L. (1980) "United States Indian policy and the debate over Philippine annexation: implications for the origins of American imperialism," *Journal of American History,* 66, pp. 810–31.

Young, M. B. (1968) *The Rhetoric of Empire: American China Policy, 1895–1901.* Cambridge, Mass.: Harvard University Press.

Part III

The Economy and Class Formations

CHAPTER NINE

The Emergence of a Market Economy before 1860

STANLEY L. ENGERMAN AND ROBERT E. GALLMAN

THE settlement of mainland North America by the British differed quite significantly from the earlier settlements in Florida and the West by the Spanish.
Whereas the Spanish movement into the New World was primarily a government-
directed operation, with an important military component, the British created institutions that left the actual settlement process to private individuals to seek out the
capital and the labor to be used in conjunction with the land and resources in the
Americas. This was the policy followed in the British settlement of both their mainland and West Indian colonies.

British settlement was influenced by the metropolitan government in its provision
of land grants, corporate charters, and proprietorships to colonists, as well as in the
importance of the military and defense expenditures to establish and maintain the
empire. But, relative to the Spanish and their settlements, market forces and transactions, both in England and in North America, played a considerably greater role.
While the reasons for settlement remain debated – described as a mixture of "God,
gold, and glory" – economic transactions played a major role in the implementation
of the various policies pursued.

There were several different arrangements for colonization (Craven, in Williamson,
1953). Virginia and Massachusetts were initially settled by joint stock companies, with
shares purchased by investors in England. The Virginia Company was a rapid financial
failure. Virginia became a royal Crown colony by 1624 after the failure of the profit-
sharing arrangements between investors and settlers and the use of land grants to
attract labor. More religiously motivated, the Plymouth Company was also a financial
failure. Although a financial loss from the view of overseas investors, these colonies did
succeed in forming permanent, economically viable colonies that were able to attract
population and capital. Most of the other mainland colonies were created as proprietorships based on British government grants to various individuals or groups.

Several key problems needed to be solved to permit successful settlement. It was
important to establish effective relations with the Indians who were already on the
land. This was sometimes accomplished peacefully, through trading relations, particularly for furs, but at times there was military conflict, massacres, and the pushing
westward of Indians. As elsewhere in the Americas, the toll of disease meant a
substantial decline in the Indian population, although the Indian presence in what
was to become the United States and Canada was considerably less than in Mexico
and Peru to begin with.

Europeans sought commodities to produce and to sell in England and elsewhere in Europe in order to pay for imports of manufactured and other goods that the colonists needed or wanted. There was an interest in finding goods that either could not be produced in England or else could be produced there only at considerably higher cost. And there was a desire both for foreign capital, to help pay for the imports that the colonists desired, and for labor, to produce goods for consumption in the colonies and for export.

The need for labor in the settlements was met in several different ways, all involving some form of market transaction, and each with quite different implications for the distribution of income, wealth, and political power. For those in England with sufficient money to pay for transatlantic movement for themselves and their family members, land could be acquired after arrival via cash purchases or land grants from the colony's organizers or proprietors. Or, if neither ownership nor rental of land was possible, the settlers could become wage laborers, working for others, in the hope that this might lead to land ownership in the future. This form of migration was most successful in the New England and Middle Atlantic States, in part because the growing of grains permitted relatively small units of production.

Where, however, the optimal scale of farm production was larger than the family unit, or where the work was rather distasteful, or if the migrants were unable to bear the costs of transatlantic transportation on their own, other forms of labor were important. The institution of indentured servitude was introduced to solve the difficulty of transport costs (Galenson, 1981). Migrants, most frequently young male adults, would sign contracts in England, exchanging transportation for the rights to be sold to farmers or others in the Americas. Terms of service generally ranged from four to seven years, depending on the age, sex, literacy, skills, and related personal characteristics of the servant. The higher the skills, *ceteris paribus*, the shorter the terms of the contract. During the indenture period these contracts could be sold and resold. Probably more than two-thirds of the white migration from England to the thirteen colonies was carried out under indenture contracts. Most indentured laborers went to Maryland and Virginia to grow their leading export crop, tobacco.

When indentured labor became more expensive, due to improved economic conditions in England, and when a new crop with extremely onerous labor conditions (rice) was introduced into South Carolina, the colonies tapped into the slave trade in Africans. The first arrivals of slaves were brought in from the British West Indies, where the population consisted chiefly of black slaves engaged in sugar production. As time passed, however, the labor demands to produce rice in South Carolina increased dramatically, and these demands were further augmented by the continuing requirement for slaves to replace indentured servants in the production of tobacco in the Chesapeake region, and most of the imports of slaves came directly from Africa. All of the colonies received some slaves, but it was only below what was to be the Mason–Dixon line that slavery was economically important. Even then the share of slaves in the South's population (40 percent) was considerably below that of the British West Indies (90 percent). And the thirteen colonies received a relatively small share of the overall slave trade (about 5 percent). The increasing number of slaves in the thirteen colonies reflected the unusual growth of the slave population in the mainland North American colonies. The rate of natural increase, in contrast to the West Indies, was positive and high.

The very high rates of increase of both slave and free population and of labor supplies soon were based on internal population growth, which reflected long-run economic conditions. The high returns to labor and capital possible because of the rich soil and resource base, and the great availability of land for low-cost settlement, influenced marriage and fertility patterns as well as mortality experience. The colonies were unique in the eighteenth (and nineteenth) century world in that their rates of natural increase were probably at least twice as high as the rate in Europe. As Benjamin Franklin and Thomas Malthus recognized, the colonial fertility rate was exceptionally high, the result of an early age of marriage and a high rate of marital fertility, made possible by the great availability of land and high incomes.

Population growth was particularly rapid from early on in settlement in the New England and Middle Atlantic regions, where the basic family pattern of migration led to relatively equal sex ratios from the start. In the South, for whites and blacks, unequal sex ratios and the disease environment meant that it took a generation or two before natural population increase occurred, but then the region experienced the same high rates of growth as did the regions to the north. While the fertility differences with England were most dramatic, the colonies, particularly those in the North, also had lower mortality. The greater life expectation meant more productive years per person, while the greater availability of foodstuffs meant better nutrition, giving rise to taller individuals better able to work long and intensely. The high population growth both reflected a more favorable economic environment in the colonies and provided a larger increase in the labor supply with which to settle the available land.

Farmers had a choice between devoting their own and their family's time to productive purposes or else to enjoy some forms of leisure or non-productive time. Farm output could be consumed on the farm or else sold (or otherwise distributed) to others via market transactions or some other social arrangements. Sales could be within local areas, elsewhere in the particular colony, in other colonies, or to foreign markets. All of these choices occurred, but the market most studied, and for which the most information has been available, has been the overseas market in Britain (and its West Indian colonies) and Europe. Most exports were required to be sent to Britain via British or colonial shipping, after which they might be re-exported to the European continent. Similarly, imports were to come from Britain, also in British or colonial shipping. While these regulations were strictly enforced, it is still debated whether they had a substantial impact on colonial income, given Britain's dominance in the production of the manufactured goods imported by the colonies, the relative size of the British market, and provision of credit and merchant services by the British on colonial goods. The colonial trade was generally an exchange of British manufactured goods for North American agricultural commodities. Since imports into the colonies frequently exceeded their exports, the colonies were required to obtain credit from the British merchants, borrowings that periodically created difficulties when repayment came due in times of unfavourable economic conditions.

It is generally estimated that during the eighteenth century colonial exports were about 10–15 percent of colonial income, a ratio in excess of that of the British at the time. This ratio varied by colony, being higher in the South than in the North, and probably declined somewhat over time. The major colonial exports were tobacco from the Chesapeake region and rice from South Carolina, both produced with either temporarily or permanently coerced labor. The New England and Middle Atlantic colonies exported grains, livestock products, and timber, all of which had important markets in the British West Indian slave possessions (McCusker and Menard, 1985). New capital formation could be financed from borrowings from England, savings by colonists out of their incomes, and, importantly in the early stages of settlement, the direct application of labor time to investment in land improvements, the construction of buildings, and other forms of non-financial investment.

Clearly the colonies had many markets in goods, factors of production (land, labor, and capital), and credit and financial assets. Some production, particularly in the northern colonies, where the commodities marketed were the same as those consumed by the farmers, did not reach markets. Generally, however, in addition to export markets, sales could be in local towns, in regional cities (dependent on farms for their food supplies), or to other colonies. Most farmers were residents in locations where sales to markets were feasible, and while few, if any, sold 100 percent of their output, many sold some fraction of their production to be able to purchase other goods they desired. The shares marketed locally and regionally were probably higher in the Middle Atlantic and New England states, where grains and livestock were the most important agricultural crops, than in the South, where tobacco and rice were sold in overseas markets. Nevertheless, the quantities of goods sold in most colonies suggest that farmers were concerned with production for market sales, and also that opportunities to sell in markets influenced their behavior.

In addition to sales made on credit, not cash, there were local arrangements for borrowings to purchase land, farms, and equipment. Before the revolution, no banks existed in the colonies, but loans would be made from individuals with surplus funds to others who wanted to borrow to acquire assets or consumption goods. These loans were to be repaid in funds, goods, or labor time, under terms that varied with time to repayment and interest rate charged. These borrowings often influenced, or were influenced by, the relations among neighbors since there were often kin or community ties between borrowers and lenders, as well as political interactions. While the absence of banks indicated a more informal set of arrangements than in the nineteenth century, there were frequent opportunities to borrow or to lend in the colonial economy.

Markets and Market Behavior: Conceptual Issues

For many years it was generally held that the existence of markets for goods, factors, and credit was widespread and utilized by most of the colonial population. This attention to the market, it was argued, is what led to the rapid growth and relatively wide distribution of income in the colonial economy. Often described as the Adam Smithian view of colonial development, it presented an optimistic and approving view of the accomplishments of the market system in providing incomes above subsistence in the agricultural sector and elsewhere in the economy. Recently, criticisms of the different strands of the so-called "optimistic" view have arisen. Two of the most important of these arguments, while sometimes linked together, are, however, often based upon quite different contentions.

One critique, based upon assertions about the *mentalité* of the colonial farmer, argues that people were not interested in markets and earnings, preferring to spend time on leisure, communal activities, or non-work concerns, and avoided market transactions in the interest of independence from others and from market changes (Kulikoff, 1992). This choice to reduce potential market activity was often based on a presumed communal concern, emphasizing equality and limited consumption, at the expense of the gains possible from individual decision-making. The difficulty in evaluating the empirical relevance of this argument is that it might regard any constraint, either willed by self or by others, on achieving a "full maximization of financial income" as being an opting out of the market. Few individuals would seek to maximize income fully, given desires for such non-pecuniary benefits as leisure, better working conditions, location near family, and so on. People, even without "full maximization" behavior, often do respond to market and price signals, obtaining some gains, either material or of a non-pecuniary type, via those market transactions they engage in, even if they are not fully convinced of the comprehensive virtues of the market. This interpretation of behavior, emphasizing beliefs as to what are necessities and what luxuries, as well as financial and communal feelings and concerns with the greater welfare of society, may not provide an adequate test of capitalist and non-capitalist belief, since it would seem to be as applicable to nineteenth-century industrial capitalists such as Andrew Carnegie and John D. Rockefeller as to the eighteenth-century New England farmers. A concern with non-economic ends, with the welfare of family members, present and future, with cooperation and giving to communal activities, a distaste for banks and other financial intermediaries and for cut-throat competition, and a deep sense of religious belief and behavior have characterized many individuals after, as well as before, the rise of the market economy.

Further, as was apparently the case in colonial and early nineteenth-century New England, what caused the limited interaction with the market may not have been a set of beliefs about the role of the market but rather cost considerations which limited trading arrangements. In the absence of adequate transportation methods, areas may have been geographically isolated, a situation regarding trade that is reversed when lower-cost transportation is introduced. Because of such cost considerations, farmers in frontier areas tend to be more self-sufficient and do more outside the market than farmers located in more settled areas.

Another criticism of the market is that, while people were initially interested in entering it, they were soon hurt by falling incomes and worsened working conditions (Sellers, 1991). By then, however, they were trapped and continued to lose out in terms of incomes, and possibly perpetually rising debt. Thus, it is argued, the market led to disaster for many of those people who had tried not to avoid it but to benefit from it. Moreover, those who did not desire to enter the market may have suffered losses relative to those wishing to get ahead, who used the market for their own advantage. Any group or individual who elects not to compete in the market when others are willing to do so, will generally suffer a worsening of their relative income position, not because of discrimination or exploitation but because of their current choices.

Whatever the preferences of individuals for or against market involvement, the market clearly has had substantial impacts. Here we want to point briefly to some questions of social and economic impact due to an expanding market sector. It has been argued that the rise of commercial, market society has destroyed what was presumably a more successful earlier society, with more communal behavior and relatively more equal economic and social conditions. Commercial society, by this argument, leads to a narrowing of the benefits of economic change as great inequalities of wealth and political power develop.

A counter-argument to this question usually points to the absence of historical evidence for any such "golden age" society. It is claimed that earlier economic and social conditions were at least as troubled as those that later emerged. Indeed, the rise of a market society provided for an expansion of opportunities for many, particularly the middle and lower classes, and permitted migration from less to more developed areas. Land was available for sale and by grants, leading to a more balanced political system and generating more equality of wealth and income. Proponents of the benefits of the market do not claim that it is in any sense a natural force, independent of individual and social actions. Clearly, not all individuals have the set of beliefs concerning long-term gains that permit a market society to emerge successfully, while legislation and court decisions can obviously impose non-neutral constraints on the market's operation. What is claimed is that for most reasonable political systems, which can prevent great inequities from emerging, the market, with its individual choice and decision-making, has been an effective social and economic institution regarded with favor by the electorate.

The general economic argument against the market was sketched out above. Even when it can promote more rapid measured economic growth, its development, so it is claimed, leads to inequalities and income losses for many, while permitting the wealthy to accumulate more wealth and political power. The wealthy are presumably a relatively unchanged group (or class), and the poorer individuals have fewer opportunities to increase their relative positions over time. More recently, the negative effects of the market (and of industrialization) on the environment and human health have come to be stressed. The counter to this contention has also been described above: that the political and economic beliefs underlying a market system not only provide incentives leading to a more rapid rate of economic growth, but also give opportunities to many members of society to obtain benefits. An expansion of the market can spur increases in specialization and thus in productivity growth (Rothenberg, 1992). If more individuals are given opportunities, then the basic technical and other productivity-increasing changes will be more widespread and growth accelerated. As a result of the process of economic growth, most of the population will experience increased levels of income, even if its relative distribution does not change markedly.

The discussion of the debates on the market is in many ways a major oversimplification. Few would argue for a completely fettered market and, similarly, few for a fully unfettered market, either as preferred policy or as having existed in the past. Much of the practical debate concerns what types of constraints should be introduced for particular problems, and how much political interference is required to ensure better performance of the economy. This said, it is clear that for the period under discussion the market system, with individual choice, was the basic mode followed. Even the aids provided at governmental level were more to promote the market than to regulate it. What the outcome of this system was in the antebellum period is described below.

America in 1800

The future of the American economy in the years of the revolutionary war and the achievement of independence was, to many, uncertain. Writing later in the century (1889), Henry Adams described the economy of 1800 in terms of "slender resources of a kind not easily converted to the ready uses required for rapid development." There was some reasonable degree of prosperity in most states, and if transportation problems could be overcome, primarily by canals, the economy had possibilities for growth and development. The economy of 1800 was still primarily agricultural, dependent upon the British economy for many manufactured goods, and effected negatively by being outside the coverage of the British Navigation Acts. The military and trade dislocations caused by the revolutionary war probably kept the per capita income of the United States, particularly of the southern states, well below pre-revolutionary levels for a decade or two. The post-war economic difficulties influenced the politics of the Articles of Confederation and the Constitution, and played a role in the introduction and implementation of Hamiltonian economic policy.

Hamilton, and government policy in the United States, did not reject mercantilist policy as pursued by the British. Rather, mercantilist policies were generally accepted and adopted, but now were drawn to favor the United States rather than Britain. Hamilton's policies provided an important role for the federal government in creating the institutional framework for growth, with the direct production of goods and services still to take place primarily in the private sector. Put forward in a set of reports and directives, the Hamiltonian policy included tariffs (for revenue and to protect infant manufacturing industries), the creation of a central bank under mixed public and private direction, the use of public debt to provide a form of financial intermediation and to attract foreign capital, patent protection for innovators, encouragement of immigration to attract a labor force for industry, restrictions on the use of foreign vessels for internal and external trade, and related pro-industry, pro-growth measures. Introduced in the early stages of nationhood, these policies helped in the significant growth of American industry and agriculture in the early decades of the nineteenth century. Also promoting growth was the more complete protection effectively proved by the embargos of the first decade and then by the War of 1812. Protection, in its various guises, provided a price incentive to domestic manufacturers, but willing entrepreneurs were still required to bring about successful outcomes.

In 1800, however, the United States economy, as with just about all other countries except Britain, had its labor force primarily in agriculture and the largest share of national output came from the agricultural sector. Over the antebellum period the share of the labor force in agriculture fell, but even on the eve of the Civil War more than one-half of the population lived in rural areas producing primarily agricultural goods. The share of labor in manufacturing rose after 1820, but even by 1860 did not exceed one-sixth of the overall labor force. Distinct regional differences emerged in this period, with the Northeastern share of its labor force in agriculture declining sharply, and the share in manufacturing and services rising. In the South and the newly settled areas of the Midwest the labor force remained primarily agricultural in 1860 (Engerman and Gallman, 1983).

Since measured output per worker in manufacturing and services exceeded that in agriculture, the labor force shift contributed to the measured growth in per capita income (Weiss, in Gallman and Wallis, 1992). Exactly how great the per capita income disparity was depends upon a number of variables not easily measured: for example, the value of non-agricultural output produced by farms, and the hours and intensity of work in agriculture and other sectors. It seems probable, however, that the growth in per capita income in the United States, particularly between 1820 and 1860, rose to rates that exceeded those of the colonial period as well as those for most of the rest of the world at this time. In terms of levels of per capita income, the United States was second to England among the major world economies, a position it was to maintain until it overtook England at the end of the nineteenth century.

What was unique about the United States in the nineteenth century was its exceptionally high rate of population growth which, given the many concerns of the time about the possibilities of over-population and of limits on resources, made the rate of growth of per capita income even more remarkable. Most of the population growth was due to the unusually rapid rate of natural increase, a reflection of the high birth rate and relatively low death rate. Also important, after the 1840s, was the continued increase of immigration from Western Europe, which tended to follow the business cycle pattern in America. By the first decade of the nineteenth century, Congress had ended the external slave trade (but not the internal slave trade), and legal and economic forces had ended indentured servitude. Population growth was accompanied, both North and South, by geographic expansion westward to produce crops similar to those grown in the older parts of the section. Both sections experienced dramatic changes in structure, particularly the South. In 1790 the South's population was generally located in seaboard states, and tobacco and rice were the principal crops. By 1860 cotton had long been the South's (and the nation's) major export crop, and about half the southern population resided in the newer states of the lower South. In the North, agricultural migration left parts of New England desolated, and those families that did not move to new farms in the West would often move into industrial areas, helping to form the manufacturing labor force. Relatively more native-born individuals moved westward into new agricultural regions, while most immigrants located in the urban areas of the Northeast and Middle Atlantic states. Immigration and internal migration were generally the voluntary result of the decisions of individuals made in response to a number of different conditions, of which market signals regarding opportunities for betterment were central.

Rapid population growth due to immigration is one factor that makes any evaluation of the changing distribution of income complicated. Immigrants moved for better material conditions and better opportunities than countries of out-migration provided, whatever may have been their situation in America relative to that of the native-born. Another complicating factor is that the high birth rates meant many children, and this helped to spur the westward movement. The internal migrants may therefore have accepted lower immediate incomes from the land they owned and farmed because they hoped for high capital gains and other future returns and prized independent land ownership. Equal distributions of assets among many children at inheritance (common in the United States) led to rather different future income distributions than would have been the case if the decedent had given his assets to only one individual. For various reasons, the available data indicate no dramatic changes in income and wealth distribution in this period, increased concentration in older areas often being offset by the opportunities available to obtain inexpensive land in newer areas as the result of the government's land policy. Whatever the reality may have been, Tocqueville's discussion of the United States, particularly the northern areas, as a land of opportunity and relative equality of economic reward and political power, does capture widespread contemporary opinion of the comparison between the United States and the rest of the world, including England.

As in the colonial period, most of the goods produced in the United States were sold in domestic markets, with foreign trade generally accounting for only 10–12 percent of GNP. Exports still were predominantly of agricultural goods, of grains and livestock from the North, and tobacco and short-staple cotton from the South. Cotton in the antebellum period generally accounted for about one-half of all United States exports, with most being sold to England for use in its expanding cotton textile industry (North, 1961). Indeed, despite America's increasing political independence of Britain, the flows of international trade resembled those of the colonial period, with American agricultural production being exchanged for British manufactured goods. With the development of American manufacturing under tariff protection, American consumers none the less still purchased British goods, often of better quality than those produced in the United States. And, as befitted what some called a colonial relationship, despite political independence, the United States was to become an important recipient of capital exports from England, mainly to finance the developments of various forms of social overhead capital.

After 1800

The first half of the nineteenth century has been considered the period of "The Cotton Kingdom" of the slave South. After the invention of the cotton gin, and its wide dispersion due to the failure of the patent to protect Eli Whitney, cotton output grew from about zero to account for over one-quarter of southern agricultural output by 1860. The South produced other staple crops utilizing slave labor, but these were generally concentrated in limited geographical areas: tobacco in Virginia, North Carolina, and Kentucky; rice in coastal South Carolina and Georgia; and sugar (with tariff protection) in Louisiana. And the South also produced enough corn and livestock products to become basically self-sufficient in food consumption (Anderson and Gallman, 1977). What was important about cotton was not only the high demand for it in world markets, but its ability to be grown in many parts of the South. Profit-seeking planters were able to migrate with or purchase slaves from the older areas of the South and move them on to more productive land to the south and west. Based on cost considerations, planters usually fed slaves from their own production of corn, pork, and other food products, or else imported supplies from the West. Slaves made up only about 40 percent of the southern population, and only about one-third of all white families owned one or more slaves, with many holdings being quite small. Non-slaveholding whites were generally involved in agricultural production, producing mostly foodstuffs, with limited amounts of cotton and tobacco. The value of their landholdings and wealth placed many in the yeoman class. The southern economy remained very profitable, productive, and expanding up to the Civil War, with slave prices rising to peak levels in the late 1850s. The westward movement and the drive for improved production increased labor productivity. Economic considerations did not suggest that slavery was soon to be ended as an unprofitable institution, at least within what contemporaries regarded as the near future. Slavery's ending was to require intervention of a dramatically different type.

Down to 1860, the economic structure of the North makes it more easily described as two distinct regions, a description that often was as true of its political as of its economic behavior. In the Northeastern states manufacturing was expanding, initially based on a labor force of women and children. In the last decade and a half before the Civil War, immigrants flooded the market and replaced women and children. This region benefited from widespread water power, needed for large factories. Equally important, capital markets developed early, as did bond and stock exchanges and a banking system. How important tariff protection was in the growth of industry, particularly cotton textiles, is still under debate, but there were many other industries, initially small scale, that were able to grow and to experience productivity increases without having received tariff protection against foreign producers. These industries sold manufactured goods to the South and Midwest regions in exchange for food-stuffs and cotton. Many small innovators and manufacturers were able to take advantage of growing markets for goods and labor to profit from the effective American system of patents.

While the growth of the manufacturing sector was what made the Northeast unusual at this time, much of the labor force still remained in agriculture on the eve of the Civil War. It was, however, an agriculture somewhat different from that of colonial times. The production of grains and livestock had moved westward to newer lands where production was at a lower cost than on farms farther east. Eastern farms were then able to shift to commodities such as dairy products and vegetables as a result of their location near to markets in large urban areas.

In the earliest period of their settlement, the Midwestern areas, with their frontier-style agriculture, concentrated on grains, particularly wheat and corn, and livestock. The Midwest was an agricultural exporting region, sending foodstuffs to the South, particularly before the 1840s, to the Northeast, and, mainly after about 1845, to European markets. In exchange, the Midwest generally received manufactured goods from the Northeast and from England. While the region's share of the labor force in manufacturing increased over time, the importance of agriculture persisted. Further-more, the links between Midwestern agriculture and manufacturing remained close: the region's manufacturing was based importantly on the processing of agricultural products (Gates, 1960).

The Midwestern economy was also linked to the Northeast, the latter being the principal source of capital and labor for the newer region. Most of the migrants to the Midwestern states came from the states of the Northeast, very few from the Southeast. While some have argued that the failure of southern migrants to move to the Midwest reflected a desire to maintain residence within slave societies, more important was the fact that farmers tended to move along the same latitude to take advantage of the skills previously developed in raising specific crops and livestock.

Central to the pace and magnitude of settlement of the Midwest and of the lower South were the incentives provided by the government's land policy. As time passed, federal policy eased access to federal lands. The minimum price for land and the minimum plot size were both reduced and, for a small period of time, federal credit was extended. These changes, plus others, increased the small farmer's access to public lands. Most Midwestern farms were involved in production for markets in addition to providing themselves with much of their own food. Productivity on these farms, initially high because of the richness of the region's soil, further increased in the last antebellum decades with the introduction of varieties of mechanization, such as the reaper for grain production, and their adoption by profit-seeking farmers.

The expansion of internal trade in this period reflected the great changes made in the transportation network. These improvements were both intra-regional and inter-regional, providing better connections between units of production and units of consumption. These transportation developments – highways, canals, and railroads – provided for lower-cost, as well as more rapid, links across long distances (Fishlow, 1965). The financing of these transport networks was generally by some variety of government and private funds, including mixtures of government expenditures, guarantees, tax benefits, and other types of subsidy to private investors (Goodrich, 1960). Government aid was sought by farmers and businessmen. In responding to these demands, the government behaved much as did private firms, except that it was easier for government to obtain funds. Government had the taxing power, but it also could more easily borrow, domestically and from overseas, particularly England. The use of subsidies did not differ much across regions, and both North and South followed similar practices regarding funding through much of this period.

There were some changes over time in the mix of public and private expenditures and control that reflected the changing nature of the major transport methods and the changing ability of governments to tax and private firms to borrow. In the pre-canal era, most roads and turnpikes were constructed by state and county governments on the basis of taxes requiring payment in either cash or in labor time. With the development of the canal network in the first half of the nineteenth century, the pattern of contributions by public and private sources became more varied and complex. Some canals, such as New York's Erie Canal, completed in 1825, were state-built and operated; others, such as those in New Jersey, were private. In the period from 1815 to 1860 just about every state constructed canals, in several cases including a number of branches connecting different parts of the state. Of these, however, only one, the Erie Canal was a large success. It helped to increase the commercial advantages of New York City versus its seaboard rivals and to make it the leading city in the transatlantic trade.

The railroad's emergence in the 1830s also depended upon the use of state and local funds in addition to private capital, but over time there was an increase in the relative role of private as opposed to government funds. Most railroads were privately operated and generally used for carrying agricultural goods to markets. Although railroads did help to spur the settlement of the Midwest and the relocation of the South's cotton production, it should be remembered that the initial westward settlement had taken place largely prior to the railroad and that as late as 1860 there was still no railroad crossing the continent (Healy, in Williamson, 1953).

Another important means of transportation, almost exclusively privately owned and operated, was the steamboat. As seen in the Mississippi River traffic, its influence came mainly from the sharp decline in the costs of moving goods upriver from New Orleans, something that the earlier keelboats could not accomplish. The government played only a minor role in the promotion of steamboat traffic. Government cleared debris from the rivers and regulated the dangerous steam engines.

While much of the significant transportation changes concerned long-distance and inter-regional patterns, short-distance, intra-regional developments also played an important role, particularly in allowing the concentration of population and economic activities in towns and cities. Urbanization was of great significance in the states of the New England and Middle Atlantic regions. Their larger cities became important as ports and commercial and financial centers. Manufacturing tended to be more heavily concentrated in medium-sized and smaller cities. Made possible by the agricultural surpluses produced elsewhere – grains and animal products from the Midwest and dairy products and vegetables from their local hinterlands – urban areas became centers of concentrated demand and factor supplies. They had a disproportionate impact upon innovations, patenting, and productivity change. The urban concentrations of banking and financial services had a large impact upon the rate of capital formation in the overall economy.

While cities provided many economic benefits, their high densities and locations on waterways often made them unattractive places to live, and hence a premium had to be paid to urban residents to offset the crowding and dirt. Cities did have features that some preferred to rural life – relief from isolation, access to entertainment, and so on. Certain types of services, such as education and health care, were more available in urban areas. The demography of urban areas differed markedly from that of rural areas, mortality rates being higher and fertility being lower. The continued relative expansion of urban areas required in-migration from domestic and foreign sources. Urban areas contained a disproportionate number of immigrants from Europe, whose poverty contributed to the problems of the cities, but who provided a significant part of the labor force for manufacturing industries.

Important in the economic changes of this period and for the increased rate of measured economic growth was a shift of some consumption from production that had previously taken place within the household, often by women and children and with some seasonal contributions by men, into the market. This shift in the focus of production particularly affected the production of food and textiles. What made it possible were the inter-related effects of improvements in specialized manufacturing and the transportation and distribution of goods, a shift of population from farms to areas of higher density in towns and cities, and the emergence of alternative employment for women, children, and men on a year-round basis. The transfer of female and child labor from farm to factory reflected the nature of demands in agricultural production, the crops of the Northeast being more physically difficult for females and children to grow than was the case for the crops of the southern states. The decline in home production took place throughout this period, but was particularly marked in the decades after the War of 1812 with industrial and transportation improvements. This transformation to market production was never complete, since some functions still remained within the household. The importance of home production remained higher in the frontier areas undergoing settlement than in the older, more densely settled regions.

The initial expansion of market-based industry outside the household took place in the Northeastern states (Clark; Sokoloff, in Gallman and Wallis, 1992). The upward trend in manufacturing output both there and in other states continued throughout the antebellum period, with particularly high rates of growth in the 1820s and the 1840s. The New England cotton textile industry was the first large factory industry. In subsequent years, gains in output and productivity became more pervasive. Advances occurred in a large number of industries, whether characterized by large plants or small, marked by a high capital intensity or by limited mechanization, or with production taking place in factories or in workshops. The growth of most industries was characterized by increases in the input of factors of production (labor and capital) and increased productivity, based on technical, organizational, and institutional changes. As firms grew larger, they were more likely to have more machinery and equipment, and more of their labor force consisted of women, children, and immigrants. There were frequent complaints about the scarcity of labor, since the high returns in agriculture kept labor occupied and reduced the desire to do industrial work. This, it was believed, led to a search for labor-saving technologies and to the greater development of and reliance upon production methods using interchangeable parts than was true elsewhere. Higher productivity helped deal with the industrial labor problem. Nevertheless, the United States was still primarily an exporter of agricultural goods and an importer of manufactured goods, generally from England.

The expansion of manufactures, with its diffusion of growth among industries, and with a wide variety of plants – of different sizes, power sources, and capital requirements – demonstrated the ability of entrepreneurs to respond to the prospects for profits and accumulation. This willingness and ability to enter into industrial pursuits, and to innovate and introduce new techniques of organization and machinery, reflected not only the overall cultural milieu of the United States in the antebellum period and the relative openness of its economic and political system, but also the early growth of state and local support for education at the primary school level. Productivity gains were widely diffused, although probably greatest in those firms located in areas of highest population density along transport facilities. Productivity gains were furthered by government policies that encouraged invention and innovation, particularly the patent system. While tariffs accounted for most federal revenues in this period, the concern to use them for purposes of protecting American industry seemed to have increased after the War of 1812.

The United States had an unusually high literacy rate for its free population as a result of a rather extensive system of primary education financed by state and local taxpayers and by land grants provided for states by the federal government. Levels of schooling of white children, including those of children of immigrants, were high in all sections, particularly in the Northeastern states. Even with a system devoted mainly to primary education, the resulting investment in human capital played a major role in developing skilled labor, entrepreneurial capacity, and the ability to generate technical and organizational innovations.

The average American was several inches taller than the average European. This development reflected the greater nutrition made possible by a more productive agriculture and the better disease environment in the United States, but stature was also related to the magnitude and intensity of labor inputs. The better physical condition meant a greater ability to resist disease, less loss of time due to morbidity, and a longer life expectation. Workers were also able to labor with greater intensity and handle physical labor more productively. There was some decline in height for the cohort born before the Civil War, but such declines were minor. Because of the interaction between nutrition, which is positively related to achieved height, and disease, which can affect achieved heights for given levels of nutrition, it is difficult to establish the precise factors influencing any changes in height over time (Steckel, in Gallman and Wallis, 1992).

Most studies of the economy pay greatest attention to the agricultural and manufacturing sectors that produce tangible goods. The production of such goods, however, represents only one part of the economy. The economy also includes a tertiary sector – the provision of services. One aspect of economic growth experienced in the antebellum United States was a steady increase in the share of the labor force in the service sector, those economic activities providing links between procedures and consumers.

An important component of service output came in response to consumer demand. The largest of these demands in the antebellum period was for domestic services, scarcely a function of the growing modernity of the economy. Within the South these services were often performed by slave labor, but free servants were numerically important. The supply of such laborers was fed by immigration. In particular, Irish young women became housemaids in large numbers. Another important set of outputs came from the construction industry with its production of houses and repair activities of various kinds. Construction techniques differed in rural and urban areas and by region. They also changed as time passed, as new techniques developed (for example, the balloon frame) and as new materials (for example, iron grillwork) were introduced. How far the new techniques changed productivity is not yet clear.

Other parts of the service sector involved production for business, providing key intermediate outputs needed to keep firms operating effectively and to permit an efficient distribution of production. These services included bookkeeping and accounting, and retail and wholesale trade (Porter and Livesay, 1971). Also important was transportation for shipping goods (as well as passengers, a form of consumption expenditure). Canals and railroads had reduced the costs of shipments between producers and consumers. This made possible a geographical separation between place of residence and place of production and also the wider use of natural resources found outside earlier areas of settlement.

Of particular importance for its impact on the economy was the financial sector, including banks and other financial institutions. These firms moved capital funds from those saving to those wishing to invest. Among the key financial institutions, besides banks, were insurance companies and security exchanges. These institutions emerged first in the Northeast by the early nineteenth century, and they had an impact on the structure, if not necessarily the rate, of economic growth (Lamoreaux, 1994). Financial institutions served to reallocate capital not only among individuals, but also among industries and regions. The more effective the financial network, the more likely it was that funds would go where the returns to capital were highest in the industries and regions with the most potential growth. Over the first part of the nineteenth century the number and size of financial intermediaries grew considerably. Banks expanded in all regions. Security exchanges dealt primarily with government bonds rather than industrial stocks and were concentrated in the Northeast. These securities exchanges and banks played a pivotal role in the early industrialization of the Northeastern states.

Most of the funds for investment were raised in the United States, but foreign investment, mainly from England, played some role in economic change, particularly in the 1830s and 1850s. Although a relatively small share of United States capital formation even when at its peak, the inflow of foreign capital was highly specific with regard to sectors, going mostly to banks, canals, and railroads, often in the form of loans to federal, state, and local governments. In these areas, foreign finance could be important, and at various times was.

The American banking and financial system was quite different from that in other western countries. The system was governed by a mixture of federal rules and state regulation of banks. The basic framework of the monetary system was established by the bimetallic standard imposed by the federal government. Since most other countries were also on a metallic standard, this rule linked the international movement of specie to the internal money supply. There were periods, at cyclical troughs, when the United States banking system went off the specie standard for relatively short periods of time, but the goal was always that these suspensions should be only temporary.

The First and Second Banks of the United States were mixed public–private institutions and rather politically controversial. They served, in some measure, as early central banks, influencing the money supply, but, in both cases, political attacks on their potential economic and political impact led to the failure of attempts to recharter them when their twenty-year term of federal corporate charter ran out.

State governments, which also had the power to charter banks, introduced controls in charters and through legislation, including compulsory security backing for money issues, reserve requirements, and restrictions on lending. State regulation led to a system of many small banks each with the ability to issue deposits and currency. Controls over currency issue by banks were also provided by the market, with the choices made by individuals about the acceptability of bank notes. The small size of most banks, and the controls by each state, had certain positive effects on the regional and industrial structure of investment. Smaller banks meant, even given the role of insider lending, more opportunities for investment in different firms and industries, while the absence of national control permitted banks to form in frontier areas, allowing investment to become more geographically dispersed. This American system was quite different from the British system, which consisted of a few large banks with numerous branches. The United States system served the nation by providing a more competitive and flexible banking system, one that helped to contribute to economic growth, despite the pronounced banking crises and financial defaults of the post-War of 1812 years, the 1830s, and 1850s. It is possible, however, that a more controlled growth of banks, with fewer cyclical fluctuations, would have permitted more rapid growth than did the existing system.

The consequences of economic growth in the antebellum period were quite profound in their impact upon American life. All facets of America's political, social, and cultural, as well as economic, life were affected. Only a few of these changes can be discussed here. The period 1800–60 saw a marked redistribution of the population, from a population primarily in states along the Atlantic seaboard to one with significant numbers in the Midwest and lower South regions. Geographical expansion beyond the boundaries of the original colonies was made possible by land purchases and annexations, including the Louisiana Purchase, the purchase of Florida, and the acquisition of Texas, California, and related areas from Mexico. The Native American population was pushed further westward and isolated, increasing the land available for new American settlements. Westward expansion characterized both North and South, and it was only in the 1850s that this gave rise to major political complications as both sections sought to move into the same area.

There was also a significant movement from rural to urban areas, with a relative decline in the agricultural sector and a relative increase in manufacturing and services. Urban areas had more industry, and a generally higher level of measured productivity, and some of the higher income in urban areas may have been a compensation for unpleasant living and working conditions, or an offset for increased hours of intensive labor. The effect of this urban movement on measured incomes was, however, substantial.

The scale of the economy geographically, and in terms of size of population, complexity of inter-industry connections, and the size of firms, increased very dramatically. Manufacturing firms grew larger with the introduction of new power sources and new types of machinery. Mechanization also influenced the size of farms. Distances between producers and consumers increased as the economy covered a larger geographical area, but new means of transport made this economically feasible.

Per capita income growth was high and increasing in this period. Rates of growth were greater than they had been in the colonial period. Growth was reasonably steady, although it was marked by several long swings in economic activity. Growth was particularly rapid in the 1830s and 1850s. Per capita income in 1860 was almost twice what it had been in 1800. Income growth in this period was diffused among regions and individuals, and there is little doubt that this relatively broad diffusion of its benefits made policies encouraging economic growth politically acceptable (Brady; Walsh, in Gallman and Wallis, 1992).

The distribution of income and wealth among factors, sectors, and individuals was also affected by the nature of economic growth, the changing levels of income, and the patterns of consumer demand. Among sectors, agriculture declined relatively as a result of improved productivity and the slower increase in the demand for food as incomes rose. The manufacturing and service sectors increased their shares of national output, a pattern generally described as modernization of the economy. The relative shares of income going to labor and capital did not change dramatically, even with the changing sectoral structure of the economy. Real wages increased, as did the real return to capital, and both labor and capital inputs grew rapidly (Margo, in Gallman and Wallis, 1992). Less is certain about the changing distributions of incomes among individuals, both within the agricultural sector and overall. Even though some large fortunes were accumulated during this period, the generally diffused rise in incomes meant that changes in relative shares of income among individuals were not as dramatic. Important in understanding changes in the distribution of income and wealth was the fluidity of changes. There was ample opportunity to move upward (and downward) over time, less so perhaps for those at the very top and the very bottom of the income scale.

While the American economy at the time has been described as one of *laissez-faire* capitalism, it definitely was not a textbook model. Focus on the revenues, expenditure, and debts of the federal government are misleading about the nature of antebellum governments, given the greater importance of budgets at the state and local levels. While the federal government spent mainly for the military and defense, it had significant impacts on the economy through policies which required minimal levels of expenditure. This included public land policy, tariffs, the patent system, immigration policy, the maintenance of slavery, aid to public education, and so on. The most important roles played by the federal government required very little in the way of expenditures and taxation to finance them.

The state and local levels of government had a different pattern. Their important expenditures were for the provision of education and various types of social overhead capital, particularly canals and railroads. These were frequently paid for by the issuance of public debt (occasionally not repaid.) In addition, local governments provided payment of welfare and relief to the poor. Expenditures were often made for those generally in poverty, as well as to those unemployed or suffering losses of income in cyclical downturns. In New York, for example, much of the public aid went to able-bodied adults who received only short-term assistance during intervals of unemployment or sickness. The present-day distinction between the deserving and undeserving poor in providing relief was generally made at that time. Requirements in some localities included periods of residence prior to being granted relief. This served as a limitation on geographical mobility, as did the payment of relief that served to cushion the impact of economic declines. The absence of a federal relief program did not mean the absence of governmental support for the indigent.

While per capita incomes have been used as one general measure of welfare, various other indices have been used to evaluate other aspects of welfare. Measures of mortality and life expectancy have been used as indices of health and of the consequences of economic growth. There was an increase in life expectancy in the antebellum years during a time of rising per capita income. More ambiguous, however, have been the recent studies of changing heights, a measure of net nutrition and disease conditions, where the increase (from its high colonial level) has been small, and cyclical declines in the late antebellum period pose a contrast with the behavior of per capita incomes. The late antebellum decline in heights took place during a time of a decline in life expectancy, raising questions about the effects of foreign immigration and increased internal migration at that period. Since they describe different aspects of growth, such differences are not usual, but they do serve to remind us of the complexities of the process of economic change.

America in 1860 was quite different from what it had been in 1800, and also quite different from what it would be in 1900. Down to 1860 both North and South were prosperous, growing regions, and the slave South remained an economically viable society. It appeared to contemporaries that these trends would continue. The Civil War ended that, freeing the slaves, and forcing the South into small-scale farming which lacked the productivity of the slave plantation. The South, after 1870, grew as rapidly as did the North, but it took nearly a century for it to recover its relative position in the antebellum period. The antebellum expansion of the North, with productive agriculture as well as manufacturing, placed the North in a position for its great leap forward to surpass Britain and become the world's leading economic power. Earlier interpretations which had the Civil War mark the sharp break into a modern, industrial economy have been replaced by an emphasis on the rapid growth of per capita incomes and the extensive developments in agriculture and manufacturing before the Civil War. Whereas for the South the story is one of war-created discontinuity, for the North there was a greater degree of continuity over the century.

REFERENCES

Anderson, Ralph V. and Gallman, Robert E. (1977) "Slaves as fixed capital: slave labor and southern economic development," *Journal of American History*, 64, pp. 24–46.

Brady, Dorothy S. (1972) "Consumption and the style of life," in Lance Davis et al. (eds), *American Economic Growth: an Economist's History of the United States*, pp. 61–89. New York: Harper and Row.

Clark, Victor S. (1916) *History of Manufacturers in the United States*, vol. 1: *1607–1860*. Washington, DC: Carnegie Institution of Washington.

Danhof, Clarence H. (1969) *Change in Agriculture: the Northern United States, 1820–1870*. Cambridge, Mass.: Harvard University Press.

Engerman, Stanley L. and Gallman, Robert E. (1983) "US economic growth, 1783–1860," *Research in Economic History*, 8, pp. 1–46.

Engerman, Stanley L. and Gallman, Robert E. (eds) (1986) *Long-term Factors in American Economic Growth*. Chicago: University of Chicago Press.

Engerman, Stanley L. and Gallman, Robert E. (eds) (1996–9) *Cambridge Economic History of the United States*, 2 vols. Cambridge: Cambridge University Press.

Fishlow, Albert (1965) *American Railroads and the Transformation of the Antebellum Economy*. Cambridge, Mass.: Harvard University Press.

Galenson, David W. (1981) *White Servitude in Colonial America: an Economic Analysis*. Cambridge: Cambridge University Press.

Gallman, Robert E. and Wallis, John Joseph (eds) (1992) *American Economic Growth and Standards of Living before the Civil War*. Chicago: University of Chicago Press (particularly essays by Weiss, Margo, Walsh, Steckel, and Sokoloff).

Gates, Paul Wallace (1960) *The Farmer's Age: Agriculture, 1815–1860*. New York: Holt, Rinehart and Winston.

Goodrich, Carter (1960) *Government Promotion of American Canals and Railroads, 1800–1890*. New York: Columbia University Press.

Kulikoff, Allan (1992) *The Agrarian Origins of American Capitalism*. Charlottesville: University Press of Virginia.

Lamoreaux, Naomi (1994) *Insider Lending: Banks, Personal Connections and Economic Development in Industrial New England*. Cambridge: Cambridge University Press.

McCusker, John J. and Menard, Russel R. (1985) *The Economy of British America, 1607–1789*. Chapel Hill, NC: University of North Carolina Press.

North, Douglass C. (1961) *The Economic Growth of the United States, 1790–1860*. Englewood Cliffs, NJ: Prentice-Hall.

Porter, Glenn and Livesay, Harold C. (1971) *Merchants and Manufactures: Studies in the Changing Structure of Nineteenth Century Marketing*. Baltimore, MD: Johns Hopkins University Press.

Rothenberg, Winifred Barr (1992) *From Market-places to a Market Economy: the Transformation of Rural Massachusetts, 1750–1850*. Chicago: University of Chicago Press.

Sellers, Charles Grier (1991) *The Market Revolution: Jacksonian America, 1815–1846*. New York: Oxford University Press.

Taylor, George Rogers (1951) *The Transportation Revolution, 1815–1860*. New York: Rinehart.

Williamson, Harold Francis (ed.) (1953) *The Growth of the American Economy*, 2nd edn. New York: Prentice-Hall (particularly essays by Craven and Healy).

Chapter Ten

Industrialization and the Rise of Corporations, 1860–1900

David B. Sicilia

THE closing decades of the nineteenth century were a period of dramatic change at all levels of American society. Central to this change was the rise of a new breed of giant industrial corporation. Internally, these colossal manufacturing firms differed in many ways from their predecessors – in how they were financed, structured, and managed. Externally, they became a central defining feature of American life, the epicenter of key shifts in class relations, in the nature of industrial work, in the legal system, in the role of the federal government as a regulator of economic activity, and even in popular culture, high culture, and the arts.

In general surveys of this period in American history, the rise of giant corporations stands at the center of the story of America's transformation from a localistic, rural, agricultural society into a national, urban, industrial one. Although in actuality the discontinuities were not quite this sharp – industrialization took root well before the Civil War, and the majority of Americans lived on farms or in small towns until the 1920s, for instance – the rate of economic growth and concentration during this period was truly remarkable. In the mid-nineteenth century, the United States was a minor economic player compared with the industrialized nations of Europe. By 1900, America led the world in manufacturing output, and featured more miles of railroad track than all of Europe and Russia combined. Generations of scholars since have tried to understand why the US economy grew so large so quickly after the Civil War, and how American society was transformed in the process.

This research is chiefly the product of scholars working in three distinct disciplines. Business historians have focused on the giant industrial enterprises that so defined the period (Standard Oil, American Tobacco, Carnegie Steel, and the like) and on the entrepreneurs who built those enterprises (in the above-mentioned cases, John D. Rockefeller, James Buchanan Duke, and Andrew Carnegie). A general trend in this work has been from biography toward more analytical approaches. Economic historians, the second group, have tried to understand both the nature of the "factor inputs" that went into late nineteenth-century industrialization (labor, capital, natural resources, and so on) and the resulting social benefits and costs of the industrializing process. In recent decades, economic historians trained in the advanced quantitative and econometric techniques of economics have dominated this field. Finally, and most recently, a growing number of social and cultural historians have been investigating social relations, power, and gender within large and small firms alike, as well as the cultural, social, and aesthetic consequences of large-scale incorporation and industrialization for the larger society. Although these three groups of scholars often seem to speak past one another in the questions they pose and the methodologies they employ, their work, taken as a whole, is refreshingly complementary.

The Rise of the Modern Industrial Enterprise

The field of business history has made enormous strides in the last generation or so, thanks in large measure to the pioneering work of Alfred D. Chandler Jr, who introduced a compelling analytical framework for understanding the rise of big business in the late nineteenth century. To understand Chandler's contributions and impact on the field and its current directions, it is useful to review briefly the trajectory of this historiography over the past century.

In their own day, the "captains of industry" who built the nation's leading railroads and manufactories after the Civil War frequently were targets of harsh social commentary by "muckraking" journalists such as E. L. Godkin of *The Nation* and Ida M. Tarbell, whose vivid and scathing indictment of the business practices of J. D. Rockefeller's Standard Oil Company (*History of the Standard Oil Company*, 1904) gained a wide readership. Such critiques were broadened and refined, beginning in the 1930s by Progressive historian Charles Beard (*The Rise of American Civilization*, 1927), quasi-socialist Matthew Josephson (*Robber Barons*, 1934), and popular writer Frederick Lewis Allen (*The Lords of Creation*, 1935).

These and like-minded historians defined what became known as the "robber baron" tradition in American business history. In their accounts, Rockefeller (oil), Andrew Carnegie (steel), Cornelius Vanderbilt (railroads and steamships), Jay Gould (railroads, telegraph companies, and newspapers), J. P. Morgan (finance), and their ilk became extraordinarily wealthy because they were more aggressive, cunning, ruthless, and, in many cases, more downright dishonest than their rivals. Whereas Carnegie and other members of the new industrial elite embraced the "social Darwinism" espoused by Herbert Spencer of England in an effort to justify the enormous new disparities between America's richest and poorest citizens, the "robber baron" historians saw a kind of reverse social Darwinism at work, in which those with the lowest moral character in the society amassed the greatest wealth and power. While this work struck a chord with readers anxious about the unprecedented concentration of economic power in the hands of a relatively small number of corporations and individuals, the "robber baron" writings of the early 1900s have been largely discredited in recent years by archivally based, rigorously researched biographies of leading entrepreneurs and their firms.

The terms of the debate about late nineteenth-century industrialization began to shift dramatically during and after World War II. In 1942, Thomas Cochran and William Miller published *The Age of Enterprise: a Social History of Industrial America*, a beautifully written synthetic treatment of the impact of big business on Gilded Age America. In their attempt to tell "the story of business . . . institutions and their impact upon American society," Cochran and Miller (1942: 2) ranged widely into labor relations, urban life, business and religion, business and politics, social philosophy, commercial farming, and aesthetics. Although *The Age of Enterprise* had little secondary literature upon which to draw, it was ambitious, eloquent, and passionately critical of big business, and no one scholar has attempted a similar synthesis since.

Following World War II – as American business recaptured much of the stature and respect it had lost as a result of the crippling Great Depression, and as more onservative winds began to blow through the nation (including its colleges and universities) – the history of Gilded Age industrialization received more positive treatment. Journalist turned Columbia University history professor Alan Nevins wrote laudatory multi-volume histories of Standard Oil and the Ford Motor Company in the 1950s and 1960s. Other historians began to employ sociological methods in their work, which produced some interesting findings – for example, that the "rags-to-riches" scenario was largely a myth – but which washed out much of the passion, power, and flesh and blood from the story of America's rapid industrialization. Between 1948 and 1958, the Research Center in Entrepreneurial History at Harvard University served as an intellectual forum for a group of scholars interested in understanding the role of entrepreneurs in American economic history more from an economic and sociological perspective than one geared to politics and power.

One member of the center was Alfred D. Chandler Jr. Influenced by the "structural functionalism" of sociologist Talcott Parsons (who had joined Harvard's faculty in 1926), Chandler examined big business as a system that needed to develop an internal structure in order to adapt to and compete successfully within its competitive environment. In 1962, Chandler published *Strategy and Structure*, an enormously influential study of several major twentieth-century firms, in which he argued that, in the evolution of big business, "strategy follows structure," that is, a firm's internal structure – the scheme by which it organized its departments and divisions – must be fashioned to meet its particular competitive strategy. Fifteen years later, Chandler elaborated this thesis in a magisterial study of the rise of big business in the late nineteenth century, *The Visible Hand: the Managerial Revolution in American Business* (1977), which won the Pulitzer Prize in history. It is difficult to over-emphasize the influence of that book on the study of business history in general and on the historiography of late nineteenth-century industrialization in particular. Virtually every interpretative work for the next generation made reference to what became known as the "Chandlerian school" of business history.

Chandler's central thesis in *The Visible Hand* was that, beginning with the railroads in the middle of the nineteenth century and spreading to large manufacturing firms after the Civil War, a new kind of enterprise appeared in which professional managers rather than owners made the key decisions about the allocation of resources. This shift in power and agency came about as a result of the unprecedented scale, complexity, and capital requirements of these giant firms. Whereas the nation's largest businesses in the early nineteenth century could be funded privately by wealthy families, the railroads by the 1850s and sprawling manufactories by the postbellum period were so capital intensive that they could be financed only through the sale of millions or tens of millions of dollars of bonds or stocks. Moreover, these enterprises (again, first the railroads and then the giant manufacturing companies) were so large and complex – by 1874, the Pennsylvania Railroad, with some 6,000 miles of track and capital of $400 million, was the largest corporation in the world – that their operations could not be overseen by a single owner-manager or even his extended family. What was needed were scores of managers, each assigned a discrete set of responsibilities for which he was held accountable. For Chandler, the appearance of these bureaucratic hierarchies was one of the defining features of modern "big business."

Chandler's discussion of the rise of giant manufacturing after the Civil War unfolds with a clean and compelling logic. In some manufacturing industries, new technologies were developed that allowed producers to capture dramatic economies of scale, that is, to manufacture goods more cheaply (per unit) by expanding the size of their factories. By capturing large economies of scale, giant manufacturing firms were able to produce and sell their mass-produced goods *much* more cheaply than smaller competitors. In this way, they transformed the nature of competition in certain industries from a contest open to many modestly funded players into one that could be played only on an enormous scale. Moreover, explained Chandler, the "first movers" in big business did not leave much room for latecomers. National and international markets simply were not large enough to absorb the output from more than a handful of mass producers.

Chandler also charted the way in which the typical giant manufacturing firm evolved strategically after the Civil War. Many grew larger by buying up competitors and then rationalizing their production facilities, a process that typically involved shuttering less efficient operations and expanding and modernizing the more efficient plants. Now commanding a larger percentage of their industry's market share (an astounding 90 percent in the case of Standard Oil), these firms then took over the distribution of their products by buying or building wholesale and retail operations. They did so in order to handle special marketing problems associated with their products better than independent wholesalers and retailers had been handling them. For example, Swift and Company, the giant Chicago-based meat packer, opened a chain of refrigerated storage facilities (to augment its famous refrigerated railroad cars) in order to ensure that its very perishable products were brought to market properly. The Singer Sewing Machine Company operated more than 500 retail outlets by the late 1870s; prior to that, sewing machines were sold chiefly in hardware stores, whose clerks had neither the expertise nor the inclination to educate customers in the use of the complicated machines.

Along with, and often following, this strategy of "forward integration," the giant industrial corporations of the late nineteeth century also pursued a strategy of "backward integration" toward their sources of supply. By controlling through direct ownership the extraction (for example, mining, logging, harvesting) and primary processing stages prior to manufacturing, these firms were better able to ensure steady supplies of materials at affordable prices than if they depended on many independent suppliers.

In short, the giant manufactories of the postbellum period pursued a strategy of horizontal combination (or merger) to limit competition through economies of scale; a strategy of forward integration to ensure that the massive output from their plants would be distributed properly and on a large scale; and a strategy of backward integration to ensure that their mass-production factories were supplied with a steady diet of raw or semi-processed materials. In stark contrast to their depiction in the "robber baron" literature, Chandler's industrial leaders gained wealth and power, not because they were scoundrels, but because they understood the economic realities of their businesses and took the steps necessary – mainly heavy investment in modern manufacturing facilities and in managerial staff – to achieve early dominance. Thus, Chandler focused on business strategy and organization rather than on power and morality.

More than any other work in the field, *The Visible Hand* defined the research agenda of a generation of business historians writing in the last quarter of the twentieth century. Some tested Chandler's model in other industrialized nations in order to see when the "modern industrial enterprise" appeared in those settings and how similar it was to the American model. (Chandler himself later undertook this task for Germany, Great Britain, and the United States in *Scale and Scope*, 1990.)

Others built on Chandler's work by viewing through a Chandlerian lens aspects of late nineteenth-century industrialization that Chandler had not addressed or had given but minor attention in *The Visible Hand*. Olivier Zunz (1990), a social historian, delved into the backgrounds of the middle managers who staffed Chandlerian firms. His portrait of that cohort, based on research into the careers of individual middle managers in several key firms, showed many of the flesh and blood realities that critics charged had been lacking in the more clinical *Visible Hand*. Moreover, in contrast to Chandler's largely top-down model of leadership, Zunz presented a messier view of managerial hierarchy, one in which middle managers possessed more independence and agency to define corporate culture than could be found in *The Visible Hand*.

Several other scholars have added rooms on to the house that Chandler built. To fill *The Visible Hand*'s labor history void, William Lazonick (1990) argued that American firms did a poor job of capturing the shop-floor-level knowhow of their workers compared with other major economies, particularly Japan. Thomas K. McCraw (1984) investigated nineteenth- and twentieth-century business regulation within a Chandlerian framework of core and peripheral firms, and argued that regulators have done best – for business and for the larger society – when they have understood the structures of the industries and the internal economics of the firms that they are regulating. McCraw and other students of the anti-trust movement of the late nineteenth century have been influenced by Chandler's argument that the Sherman Anti-Trust Act of 1890 encouraged rather than discouraged industry concentration because it made informal agreements among competitors illegal.

Whether the regulation of big business *should* have been left to the economists is debatable. Even so, some remain uncomfortable with Chandler's view of managers as hyper-rational maximizers of efficiency. Naomi Lamoreaux's (1985) study of the great merger movement of the late 1890s, for example, argues that corporate leaders were driven more by a desire to limit price competition (as classical monopoly theory suggests) than by a wish to improve the efficiency of their operations. The strategy worked, Lamoreaux concludes, but only for a short while.

Chandler's strongest critics have come from the ranks of economics and the history of technology. Among the former, Oliver Williamson has explained the creation of late nineteenth-century big business as a move to lower "transactions costs" by internalizing many functions within the firm. Stated differently, manufacturers bought up suppliers and distributors in order to capture their profit margins. It should be noted that Williamson's critique of Chandler reflects a deeper rift between neoclassical economics, which questions whether firms need to exist at all, and business historians, who see firms as the most important unit of economic analysis.

Among historians of technology, some have accused Chandler of being a techno-logical determinist because of the primacy that he gives to economies of scale, and because he does not explore the "social construction" of those technologies. And a few historians of late nineteenth-century industrialization disagree fundamentally with Chandler's thesis and offer alternative explanations. The two most notable con-tributions to this literature – by Michael Piore and Charles Sabel (1984) and by Philip Scranton (1997) – differ in many ways but share the premise that Chandlerian-style mass production was neither the only nor the best path for American industry. According to Piore and Sabel (1984), the decision of American manufacturers to embrace capital-intensive mass production at the expense of labor-intensive craft production established a trajectory that has become increasingly anachronistic in an increasingly segmented global market in which flexibility com-mands a premium.

For his part, Philip Scranton (1997) aspires to revise our fundamental understand-ing of large-scale industrialization rather than redirect the future (Piore and Sabel advocate that American industries spurn mass production as they cross today's "sec-ond industrial divide"). Rather than an industrial domain bifurcated into core and peripheral firms, Scranton sees a more complex reality in which many large-scale producers simultaneously operated high throughput processes to produce standard-ized commodities *and* skill-based batch operations to produce specialized goods. To this mix Scranton adds other operational categories, such as the "networked special-ists," batch producers of similar goods who operated in close proximity, and "special-ist auxiliaries," who provided goods and services to locally clustered producers. As these categories suggest, Scranton's work features a strong geographical component. It also engages gender, consumerism, urban history, and other topics related to industrialization that are usually ignored. But his evidence that large batch producers roughly equalled mass producers in value-added, revenues, and employment is the most compelling finding in this complex and ambitious reinterpretation.

Still, Chandler's thesis has remained remarkably durable, and (unlike a great deal of scholarly work) it has thoroughly infiltrated the field. Most textbook treatments of the Gilded Age now include a discussion of the rise of big business that owes a large debt to *The Visible Hand*. Nor has the "robber baron" tradition vanished from sight. Indeed, survey treatments of Carnegie and his steel company, Rockefeller and Stand-ard Oil, Duke's American Tobacco, and other industrial giants of the late nineteenth century now typically discuss the power and morality of those figures as well as their industrial strategies. They conclude by posing the question of whether those men were "robber barons" or "industrial statesmen."

Industrialization as a Macroeconomic Problem

Economic historians have brought a different intellectual agenda to the study of late nineteenth-century industrialization. The key distinction between their interests and questions and those of business historians is roughly akin to the difference between macroeconomics and microeconomics. In very broad terms, macroeconomics is the study of national-level variables that affect the overall performance of an economy and the welfare of its people, such as investment (public and private), interest rates, tax policies, unemployment levels, tariffs, and the distribution of wealth and income.

Microeconomics, on the other hand, is concerned with the behavior of firms and industries by sector or region.

Economic history originated as a branch of political history, and like political history it relied on the narrative form. Following the rise of the United States to industrial pre-eminence in the late nineteenth century, economic historians focused on growth: how did the American economy grow so large and so quickly? Much of this literature described the "triumph" of individual entrepreneurs and firms and offered a counterpoint to the "robber baron" tradition in business history.

All of that began to change in the 1960s and early 1970s. For one thing, thousands of American historians began to embrace the "new social history" pioneered in Europe by French historians from the *Annales* school and by labor historians, most notably E. P. Thompson, author of the enormously influential *The Making of the English Working Class*, 1963. The new social historians rebelled against what they saw as deeply embedded biases in the dominant traditions of historical writing. This "top-down" view of the past, they said, was written by and for literate, white elites, and it consequently left out the experiences of less powerful and less well-educated members of society such as women, people of color, the poor, and the otherwise dispossessed. Accordingly, the new social historians advocated and practiced history "from the bottom up." Many of these scholars were inspired by and sympathetic to the coun-ter-cultural movement of the 1960s, with its emphasis on the empowerment of previously marginalized members of society.

At the same time, computers were beginning to find their way into the historical profession. Working originally with punch cards and user unfriendly (by today's norms) mainframe database programs, a few historians began to build large databases from census records, probate and tax records, and similar sources, and to integrate that data to discover general patterns of economic, occupational, and geographical mobility. Computers enabled those historians to compile and analyze in a few months or years volumes of data that would have taken lifetimes to manipulate.

A "new economic history" sprang directly out of these larger trends. While many scholars continued to focus on the "growth" question, an increasing number also oriented their research toward questions of "welfare" and "equity;" that is, patterns in the *distribution* (not merely the *accumulation*) of wealth and income. Not surpris-ingly, economic historians were among the first to utilize computers in their research. There was another component of the new economic history as well, but one that was unique to that discipline and that reflected the influence of the *economics* profession rather than the *historical* profession. In the 1950s, economists developed new tech-niques for "quantification" that involved the assembly and analysis of data and the estimation of data for incomplete series. By the 1960s, some of these techniques evolved into "econometrics," a set of highly sophisticated techniques for modeling the behavior of economic systems while controlling for independent variables. The small number of historians who began to apply these methods to the study of economic history – all of them trained as economists – became known as "clio-metricians." More broadly within the discipline, economic historians who were trained as economists became more influential than those trained as historians, to the point where the majority of articles published in the leading economic history journals by the 1980s were filled with elaborate equations and other econometric apparatus that were inaccessible to the non-economist.

The cliometricians were dedicated to a mission of adding precision to discussions of economic growth and welfare. They pointed to the vague qualifiers that riddled traditional historical narratives – such as "few," "many," and "most" – and argued that, since "most" could mean anywhere between 51 and 99 percent, it was better to quantify where possible. They also argued that the application of econometrics promised to bring about new interpretations of some fundamentally important questions in American economic history. The questions on which most cliometric research focused initially were: the economic burden of the Navigation Acts (was it severe or benign?); the economic costs and benefits of canals and railroads (did all of the private profiteering benefit the larger society?); the economics of slavery (how profitable was slavery, was it economically moribund by the time of the Civil War, and were slaves better or worse off than Gilded Age industrial workers?); and the Great Depression (what were its causes and economic consequences?).

The late nineteenth century received relatively less attention from the new economic historians, but they nevertheless made important contributions in at least four main areas of US economic history from 1860 to 1900: (a) the role of railroads as engines of economic growth; (b) the nature of "finance capitalism;" (c) postbellum agriculture (especially the transition from slave-based to market production in the South); and (d) the growth and structure of American industry. I will review key works in each of these areas, with emphasis on the fourth.

Many US historians were introduced to cliometrics through the work of Robert Fogel, whose massively funded study of the economics of American slavery, co-authored with Stanley Engerman in the 1970s, generated a firestorm of controversy by arguing (among other things) that the economic hardships endured by American slaves were less severe than those of industrial workers. With a penchant for challenging long-held beliefs and assumptions about the past, Fogel also turned his attention to the railroads, specifically to the question of whether railroads were "indispensable" to nineteenth-century economic growth. In *Railroads and American Economic Growth* (1964), he attempted to calculate what the US economy would have looked like in 1890 without railroads (econometric history often employs such "counterfactual" suppositions). Fogel concluded that the railroads had contributed only about 5 percent to America's gross national product. His argument produced a small cottage industry of detractors. Some claimed that Fogel had hypothesized a national economy in which railroads were present and then were magically removed from the scene, rather than never having existed in the first place; that his counterfactual scenario included canals in the arid Great Plains; and that even if one accepted the 5 percent GNP figure, no other single industry had contributed more to economic growth.

Those who were not ready to downplay the railroad's economic role in American history found comfort in the work of econometrician Albert Fishlow, who emphasized the importance of the railroad's "backward linkages" with other key industries such as iron and steel, lumber, coal, and leather. Although Fishlow's *American Railroads and the Transformation of the Ante-Bellum Economy* (1965) focused on the period from 1830 to 1860, its argument about backward linkages is quite relevant to the postbellum era, a period about which Fogel wrote in several important articles.

Some of the most interesting revisionist work by econometricians focused on the massive land grants made by municipalities, states, and especially the federal government to encourage railroad building. Because these grants totaled roughly a tenth of the land area of the continental United States, and because many railroad builders (especially those who controlled the transcontinental lines) were notorious for earning exorbitant profits, many historians saw the land grants as a necessary form of government subsidy that was often abused by greedy railroad barons. Fishlow, Fogel, and others, however, have shown that land grants made up but a small portion of total railroad investment, and that the railroads probably would have been built at roughly the same time and on the same scale without them.

How much "social savings" did late nineteenth-century railroads contribute to the economy by reducing the amount of resources needed for transportation? This question has sustained a lively debate. As noted, Fogel's estimates are low. But most econometric studies put the social savings rate at somewhere between 12 and 30 percent – a hefty rate indeed. And although Chandler focused on the railroads as wellsprings of modern management practice, his additional argument that the rail-road, telegraph, and steamship forged a national economy that made the rise of giant manufacturing possible helped restore some of the railroad's lustre as an engine of economic growth. It remains difficult to discount the importance of the 200,000 mile-long railroad web that wove together America's far-flung regions at the turn of the twentieth century.

A prime example of the way in which business historians and economic historians approach the same topic with different questions and methodologies is the subject of Gilded Age finance. For business historians, the 1870s to the 1890s were an era of "finance capitalism" in which powerful investment bankers – epitomized by J. Pier-pont Morgan – harnessed massive sums of investment capital to underwrite – and, in larger measure, control – the building of the nation's giant railroads and industrial firms. Economic historians, on the other hand, have asked questions about the changing structure of banking and about trends in interest rates and bank profits.

As a new industrial order took shape, money and banking were leading national controversies between 1870 and 1900. Should America remain on the gold standard or become bi-metalist by backing its currency with silver as well? Did Eastern bankers exploit Western farmers by charging exorbitant interest rates, as many farmers claimed at the time? These are compelling questions. Most of the quantitative work by economic historians, however, has focused on the convergence of regional interest rates that is one of the striking features of late nineteenth-century finance. Whether this was a result of improved infrastructure, increased competition in banking (especially at the state level) or the interventions of the National Banking Act – the debates rage on – economic historians are nevertheless enriching our understanding of the chaotic world of nineteenth-century money and banking.

Economic historians have found late nineteenth-century US agriculture, which shrank in size relative to industry between 1870 and 1900 but still remained domin-ant, to be a rich field to plow. This work, more than the above-mentioned research on converging interest rates, has shed new light on the period's farmer uprisings. In spite of the loud complaints of Populists, quantitative analysis undermines their contention that railroads, banks, and land speculators exploited farmers by gouging prices. Comparisons of crop prices and railroad shipping rates, for instance, show the two falling at roughly parallel rates (in inflation-adjusted dollars) between 1860 and 1900. Mortgage lending rates appear to have been competitive nationwide, and bankers had strong disincentives to foreclose. Why, then, the widespread disenchant-ment among farmers? Some had very real reasons to complain; in some regions, farmers experienced absolute losses during this period. Overall, however, American farmers seem to have suffered the most from a loss of control and a *relative* decline in their wealth and income. The nationalization and globalization of agricultural products made prices increasingly dependent on distant markets. The expansion of farm size and the mechanization of planting and harvesting made farmers more dependent on moneylenders. Perhaps most importantly, although Northern farmers increased their wealth after the Civil War, industrial workers were moving up economically at a much faster pace.

Not surprisingly, agricultural change was much more dramatic in the South in the aftermath of the Civil War. With the shattering of the region's economic foundation – slave-based commercial crop farming – enormous upheaval followed. The most important book-length investigation of this phenomenon remains Roger Ransom and Richard Sutch's *One Kind of Freedom* (1977), which helps explain the harrowing economic depression into which the South plunged after the Civil War. In 1880, southern per capita income, slightly higher than the North's before the Civil War, stood at a mere 60 percent of the national average. Whereas white southern racists ascribed those declines to "laziness" on the part of blacks, Ransom and Sutch show how African-Americans restructured their labor within the family (women tended to switch from fieldwork to household work) and – no longer threatened with corporal punishment or death – assumed work schedules that were more in line with their white yeomen counterparts. At the heart of *One Kind of Freedom* is a compelling argument about how an insidious system of "debt peonage" locked most freedmen into sharecropping rather than bringing about open labor markets.

In explaining southern economic decline, Gavin Wright (1978) emphasizes the growing competition from foreign producers of cotton after the Civil War – India especially, but also Brazil and Egypt. According to Wright, demand for southern cotton grew at an average of 5 percent per year in the three decades before the war, but fell to 1.3 percent per annum between 1866 and 1895. Fortunately, these two explanations (by Ransom and Sutch, and by Wright) are complementary rather than contradictory; both the supply of and the demand for southern cotton plunged after the Civil War, dragging down the region's cash-crop economy in the process.

A laudable trend in the literature of the period is that agriculture is no longer segregated from industry in explanations of economic growth. Rather, the two are seen as mutually interdependent, especially in the last four decades of the century and in the Midwest. Chicago, for example, was a center for the marketing and shipping of the region's grains as well as home to the International Harvester Company and other large producers of agricultural machinery and implements. By any definition, these were big businesses.

It took decades for the slave-labor-based Old South to transform itself into the more industrialized and service-based New South. With that transformation, the South would compete fiercely with the North and West for industrial workers and manufacturing plants in the twentieth century. But in the late nineteenth century, there was no contest: the Northeast was the industrial powerhouse of the nation, with the Midwest an aspiring but distant second. As they have done in other areas of American economic history, economic historians have brought fascinating new insights to the study of Gilded Age industrialization, some of which challenge long-standing interpretations. Taken as a whole, their work paints a much more complex picture of what factors went into the mix, and how they interacted.

New England – birthplace of the Slater and Lowell textile mills, of giant boot and shoe manufactories, and of the nation's first railroad network – is strongly associated with industrialization. But as quantitative historian Albert W. Neimi Jr (1974) has shown, manufacturing spread rapidly from the Northeast to the South and West (especially Illinois and Ohio) after 1860, and mobile factors of production (such as labor and capital) were less important than non-mobile factors (demand and natural resources) in determining these regional patterns.

Economic historians also have tried to explain the rapidity and scale of postbellum industrialization in terms of relative factors of production or "factor inputs." In an influential work on this subject, Gavin Wright (1990) concludes that natural resources played a key role, but not merely because America was a land of plenty. Rather, it was the great facility with which American manufacturers exploited non-reproducible resources that drove the industrial juggernaut. Other nations had abundant natural resources, but none was more efficient at cutting, drilling, mining, and processing them. But other research on this question emphasizes capital intensity, especially the high investment in machinery and other physical capital per worker, as a defining feature of late nineteenth-century economic growth (Abramovitz, 1993). These explanations are not mutually exclusive, and together they suggest that Gilded Age entrepreneurs invested aggressively to develop the nation's vast resources.

Industrialization as a Social and Cultural Phenomenon

Although it has been decades since "race, class, and gender" became watchwords in most fields of American history, business and economic history only recently have begun to apply these categories to their analysis of Gilded Age America. The same is true of deconstruction and postmodernism, which quickly gained a foothold in some fields of US history (particularly intellectual and cultural history) but have barely poked their noses into the economic and business tent.

This is not to say that historians have completely neglected the social and cultural dimensions of postbellum industrialization. Beginning with Cochran and Miller (1942) and running through James Gilbert (1972), Alan Trachtenberg (1982), and Olivier Zunz (1990), historians have grappled with the complex relationship between the newly emergent industrial behemoths and the society that both produced and was irrevocably transformed by them. But these scholars have been outliers in a literature long dominated by Chandlerian organizationalists and neo-classical econometricians.

Very recently, however, the historiography seems to be shifting, or at least broadening, in the direction of social and cultural studies. In part, this is because a growing number of scholars trained in anthropology, American studies, intellectual and cultural history, African-American history, and the history of women and gender have begun to write about business and economic subjects. Angel Kwolek-Folland (1994), for example, has explored the gender dimensions of big business in the late nineteenth century. She argues that gender definitions more than market forces defined occupational roles, office space and design, modes of social interaction, and other salient characteristics of corporate life in the banking and insurance industries between 1880 and 1930. Juliett E. K. Walker (1998) and Robert Weems (1996) view big business through the lens of racial identity in their studies of African-American business. Their accounts challenge long-standing notions that African-Americans were anti-capitalist, and show how exclusion from many mainstream, white-dominated firms and industries frequently sparked black entrepreneurial initiative.

There are other signs that business and economic historians are shifting toward a cultural orientation, from the dissertation topics previewed at historical conferences to the recent founding of a new journal by the leading international organization of business historians (the Business History Conference) with the revealing title *Enterprise and Society*. If the trend continues, more and more students of late nineteenth-century America will be revisiting the terrain scouted out by Cochran and Miller more than half a century ago, but with a much deeper understanding of the dynamics of the tumultuous era's firms and markets, thanks to the many expeditions of the Chandlerian business historians and econometricians who came later. The greatest advances will come, of course, from up-and-coming scholars whose work builds upon and extends the best historical traditions of the past. If the result is a richer, more complex, more multi-disciplinary understanding of the great transformations in American economic life between 1860 and 1900, so much the better.

REFERENCES

Abramovitz, M. (1993) "The search for sources of economic growth: areas of ignorance, old and new," *Journal of Economic History*, 53, pp. 217–43.

Chandler, A. D. (1977) *The Visible Hand: the Managerial Revolution in American Business*. Cambridge, Mass.: Harvard University Press.

Chandler, A. D. (1990) *Scale and Scope: the Dynamics of Industrial Capitalism*. Cambridge, Mass.: Harvard University Press.

Cochran, T. C. and Miller, W. (1942) *The Age of Enterprise: a Social History of Industrial America*. New York: Macmillan.

Fishlow, A. (1965) *American Railroads and the Transformation of the Antebellum Economy*. Cambridge, Mass.: Harvard University Press.

Fogel, R. W. (1964) *Railroads and American Economic Growth: Essays in Econometric History*. Baltimore, MD: Johns Hopkins University Press.

Gilbert, J. B. (1972) *Designing the Industrial State: the Intellectual Pursuit of Collectivism in America, 1880–1940*. Chicago: Quadrangle.

Kwolek-Folland, A. (1994) *Engendering Business: Men and Women in the Corporate Office, 1870–1930*. Baltimore, MD: Johns Hopkins University Press.

Lamoreaux, N. (1985) *The Great Merger Movement in American Business, 1895–1904*. New York: Cambridge University Press.

Lazonick, W. (1990) *Competitive Advantage on the Shop Floor*. Cambridge, Mass.: Harvard University Press.

McCraw, T. K. (1984) *Prophets of Regulation: Charles Francis Adams, Louis D. Brandeis, James M. Landis, Alfred E. Kahn*. Cambridge, Mass.: Harvard University Press.

Neimi, A. W. (1974) *State and Regional Patterns in American Manufacturing, 1850–1900*. Westport, Conn.: Greenwood Press.

Piore, M. J. and Sabel, C. F. (1984) *The Second Industrial Divide: Possibilities for Prosperity*. New York: Basic Books.

Ransom, R. L. and Sutch, R. (1977) *One Kind of Freedom: the Economic Consequences of Emancipation*. New York: Cambridge University Press.

Scranton, P. (1997) *Endless Novelty: Specialty Production and American Industrialization, 1865–1925*. Princeton, NJ: Princeton University Press.

Trachtenberg, A. (1982) *The Incorporation of America: Culture and Society in the Gilded Age*. New York: Hill and Wang.

Walker, J. E. K. (1998) *A History of Black Business in American Capitalism*. New York: Twayne.

Weems, R. (1996) *Black Business in the Black Metropolis: the Chicago Metropolitan Assurance Company*. Bloomington, Ind: Indiana University Press.

Wright, G. (1978) *The Political Economy of the Cotton South: Households, Markets, and Wealth in the Nineteenth Century*. New York: Norton.

Wright, G. (1986) *Old South, New South: Revolutions in the Southern Economy since the Civil War*. New York: Basic Books.

Wright, G. (1990) "The origins of American industrial success, 1879–1940," *American Economic Review*, 80, pp. 651–68.

Zunz, O. (1990) *Making America Corporate, 1870–1920*. Chicago: University of Chicago Press.

CHAPTER ELEVEN

Urbanization

TIMOTHY J. GILFOYLE

A generation ago Richard Hofstadter (1955: 23) proclaimed that the "United States was born in the country and has moved to the city." Few questioned Hofstadter's urban manifesto. Indeed, it long remained a mantra in American history textbooks: the United States populace was 95 percent agrarian in 1790; by 1920, over half the citizenry lived in cities or towns; and by 1990, less than 3 percent of all Americans were employed in agriculture. Much of American history, Hofstadter and others argued, could be understood through the *longue durée* of urbanization. American democracy may have been nurtured on the rural frontier, as Frederick Jackson Turner (1894) theorized, but modern America was embodied in the growth of cities.

Today it is not so simple. Urbanists can hardly agree on the definition of a city and whether size, population, density, physical extent, or function are reliable yardsticks. Ancient Greek cities contained populations numbering only 1,000. Aristotle argued that 5,000 was the ideal size (excluding, of course, women, freedmen, and slaves). By contrast, ancient Rome had one million at its peak, whereas the inhabitants of medieval German and French cities numbered only 2,000–3,000. In 1872, Dodge City, Kansas had under 1,000 residents. When Miami, Florida was incorporated in 1896, there were only 343 voters. Others argue that urban areas are physically and functionally separate from the countryside. Indeed, the term "pagan" originated from *pagus*, Latin for "uncivilized countryside." Yet foraging pigs were common in nineteenth-century US cities, as were truck farmers raising crops on the outer edge of the city. Some, like Max Weber and Jane Jacobs, define cities as places of trade, commercial exchange, and industry. But Lewis Mumford (1961) contends that some Greek cities of antiquity explicitly forbade commerce: Delphi was a religious center; Cos a sanatorium, hospital, and spa; and Olympia a site of athletic contests. For much of their history, Rome, Jerusalem and Mecca thrived as religious, not commercial, centers. Historically, cities in the Western world were equated with "civilization." For these reasons, Mumford defines cities as central sites of art, culture and, most importantly, power. A more accurate (but less alliterative) rewording of Hofstadter might announce that the United States was born in the small city and has moved to the suburbs.

The earliest studies located the origins of North American urbanization in the nineteenth century. Most focused primarily on population growth, physical expansion, and the relationship between city and agrarian life. Before 1930, city biographies and regional studies adhered to a celebratory or "booster" ideology that equated urbanization with demographic increase, often emphasizing the emergence and demographic expansion of large cities in the age of industrialization. Many writers contrasted urban and rural life, frequently equating urbanization with modernization. Louis Wirth, Robert E. Park, Ernest W. Burgess, Roderick D. McKenzie and their disciples in the Chicago school of sociology were the most influential. "There is a city mentality which is clearly differentiated from the rural mind," wrote Wirth. "The city man thinks in mechanistic terms, in rational terms, while the rustic thinks in naturalistic, magical terms" (Park et al., 1925: 219).

The shadow of Frederick Jackson Turner loomed large over initial studies of American urbanization. In 1933, Arthur M. Schlesinger Sr juxtaposed city and rural life, arguing that urbanization epitomized modernity and the rejection of agrarian values. According to Schlesinger, growing nineteenth-century cities assimilated immigrants, created new cultural institutions, stimulated the growth of political parties, nourished a continuing debate between urban creditors and rural debtors, produced social reform, and fostered a collective belief in social responsibility. The modern, nineteenth-century metropolis, in effect, defined the American experience. Schlesinger's metropolitan argument offered a positive view of urbanization while directly attacking Turner's famed frontier thesis.

Schlesinger's metropolitan thesis influenced historians of urbanization for more than a generation. Lewis Mumford (1961) similarly viewed cities as the cultural epicenter of any leading civilization. Mumford never directly attacked Turner, but none the less argued that urbanization emancipated humankind from the primitive, irrational life of rural society. Indeed, reason and order were the ideological linchpins infusing much of modern urban planning. Mumford traced large shifts in economic organization, alterations in city geography and the built environment, and the transformation of social life. Mumford assumed that urban structures were the product of technology, indeed the domain of reason. Historians like Richard C. Wade (1959) elaborated on Schlesinger's thesis, arguing that cities not only preceded settlers in the development of the West, but were the real pioneers or "spearheads" in peopling the nineteenth-century continent. Similarly, John W. Reps (1965) showed that cities and towns were the earliest organized institutions in the Euroamerican settlement process. Nineteenth-century railroad companies, responsible for much of the urban, town, and community planning in North America, were in fact part of a four-hundred-year process dating back to Samuel de Champlain in New France, William Penn in British North America and Spanish missionaries in the Southwest.

The prominence of such figures as Mumford and Schlesinger, however, did little to attract interest in the field of urban history, much less urbanization. By 1950, only five historians taught university or college courses on urban history: Allan Nevins, Arthur Schlesinger, W. Stull Holt, Bessie L. Pierce, and Bayard Still. As late as 1965, urban history was considered a recent and largely unestablished field among professional American historians. Much early work was dismissed as antiquarian or local history. The first comprehensive synthesis did not appear until Charles Glaab and Theodore Brown's *A History of Urban America* (1967).

At that moment, however, a "new urban history" emerged. Like the "new social history" of the 1960s and 1970s, it drew inspiration from the *Annales* school in Europe, the Chicago school of sociology, and new methods of quantification that were employed in case studies of local communities, neighborhoods, and subcultures. Abandoning narrative and consensus, this historical literature emphasized empirical methodologies, historical continuities over time, and the evolution of various urban social structures. The popularity of the computer and the initial enthusiasm for quantification generated new studies employing manuscript censuses, tax rolls, building permits, city directories, conveyance records, court indictments, and other unpublished manuscripts that allowed a level of measure and study previously unimaginable. Urbanization was treated as a societal and ecological process, synthesizing the forces of population growth, social organization, physical environment, and technological change. Interdisciplinary studies precisely analyzed the spatial makeup of the nineteenth-century city and the link between urbanization and industrialization. Indeed, the most significant advances in the literature of social history were frequently focused on those processes linked to urbanization: migration, industrialization, and family life.

Several aspects of urbanization were dramatically reinterpreted. First, the origins of North American urbanization – the "urban threshold" – were pushed back in time. Numerous studies of colonial towns explored the form, social structures, and settlement patterns of the earliest European settlements in North America. Rather than identifying the beginnings of North American urbanization with nineteenth-century expansion and growth, this literature located it in the colonial era. After 1970, historians argued that urbanization involved a complex multi-cultural makeup of English, Spanish, Indian, and French influences. More recent examinations of cities as ecological systems relocate the roots of urbanization in the precolumbian period. The origins of St Louis, for example, lay not with the eighteenth-century European settlement, or nineteenth-century growth, but with the Indian city of Cahokia near present-day East St Louis. Between the tenth and thirteenth centuries, archaeologists estimate that Cahokia's 20,000–40,000 residents made it one of the world's largest cities. Over the course of the past three decades, scholars increasingly moved the beginnings of urbanization back in time, recognizing various precolumbian urban systems that provided geographical and other foundations for later nineteenth-century urbanization. North America before 1800 may have had low levels of urbanization, but small urban settlements nevertheless dotted the landscape.

Secondly, these studies disclosed that few urban groups stayed in the same place for very long. High levels of residential and physical mobility defined much of American urbanization for most of the nineteenth and twentieth centuries. American cities were characterized by high levels of physical transiency. Even in the colonial period, about half the residents moved every decade. Only the federal housing programs after 1933 slowed the rate of geographical mobility, cementing Franklin Roosevelt's vision of a modern social compact dependent upon a residentially stable citizenry. None the less, the persistent image of cities organized around neighborhoods with consecutive generations of families living in the same physical space simply proved untrue.

Thirdly, since nineteenth-century urbanization was fueled by internal and foreign migration, numerous studies of immigrants appeared. Before 1970, the bulk of immigration history reflected the influence of Schlesinger and argued that the gulf between the urban and the rural, between the city and the country, was rigid, deep, and pervasive. Early historians of urban migration applied Ferdinand Tonnies's (1963) theory of modernization organized around *gemeinschaft* and *gesellschaft* and portrayed a stark dichotomy separating urban and agrarian subcultures – in essence the "premodern" and "modern" worlds. So acute was the presumed cultural divide between tradition and change that historians characterized migration as debilitating and destabilizing.

Beginning in the 1960s, historians began questioning this description of urbanization. Indeed, the physically dense and culturally intense setting in many urbanizing communities *reinforced* certain rural and traditional patterns of behavior. Comparative studies of mid-nineteenth-century cities, for example, showed how Germans were highly diverse and enjoyed considerable opportunities that enabled them to leave their "premodern" ethnic world if they wanted. By contrast, the Irish tended to be more limited by class and a narrower range of opportunities, making them more economically and residentially constrained. Examining Detroit a generation later, Olivier Zunz (1982) found that ethnicity remained a decisive element in organizing urban life between 1880 and 1900. By the early twentieth century, however, class increasingly replaced ethnicity as a formative influence. The one group who did not follow this pattern was African-American migrants.

Thomas C. Bender (1978) was among the earliest to expose the weaknesses embedded in the Tonnies model. Too often, historians ignored how elements of both worlds – the traditional and non-traditional, the premodern and modern – coexisted in urbanizing communities. Influenced by anthropological theory, historians increasingly emphasized the persistence and adaptability of premigration cultures over time. From Italians in the tenements of East Harlem to Mexicans in the bungalows of Los Angeles, migrant groups shaped and controlled their lives, even within the harsh economic, spatial, and social limits of the dominant culture. Vastly different kinds of migrants were active agents in choosing among different courses of action, not simply subjects of social control. Rather than positing a picture of complete assimilation or constant ethnic/racial persistence, historians now envision a continuous, pluralistic process blending multiple elements over time.

Much of the recent literature on urban migration details the "construction" of certain social identities. Historians of urban social groups have replaced "modernization" and Marxism with a variety of subcultural theories that concentrate on the social structures generated by urbanization. Labor historians, for example, frequently locate the source of class consciousness and group identity in the workplace. By contrast, urban cultural historians emphasize domestic and leisure-time activities. Urbanization in the nineteenth century spawned male working-class identities defined around neighborhood networks, street gangs, and saloons, not simply in the place of employment. Antebellum elites and Protestant institutions separated themselves by physically constructing "patches of elegance" in their urbanizing neighborhoods – renaming specific blocks, planting trees, and erecting picket fences to concretely extend the domestic space outward. Geography became equated with gentility.

Finally, case studies and "thick descriptions" of various social groups and their identities overturned the "textile" and "Coketown" paradigms of the industrial city (Mumford, 1961: 446–81). Historians now argue that the evolution of industrial capitalism followed a complex, multifaceted, even pluralistic pattern. Variated models stretching from Lowell to Los Angeles have replaced older, linear theories of industrialization. Despite their large populations and simultaneous industrial development, cities like Philadelphia, New York and Cincinnati witnessed multiple forms of industrialization: factories, manufactories, sweatshops, households, outwork, and small artisan shops. Industrialization was never uniform but evolved in different ways based upon levels of mechanization, wages, female employment, specific craft, and shop size. In sum, industrialization of certain sectors generated distinctive urban forms for different cities depending on a variety of local contingencies.

Sam Bass Warner Jr (1962) offered one of the initial and most compelling syntheses of urbanization. In a case study of late nineteenth-century streetcar suburbs, Warner found that transit-line contractors developed communities according to their own private, entrepreneurial goals rather than publicly mandated ones. American cities grew according to the secular, economic imperatives of individual citizens pursuing personal independence and wealth. Urbanization was structured around an ideological and cultural paradigm which Warner labelled "privatism": an emphasis on the individual and the accretion of wealth. Urban communities were created, organized, and, in essence, defined as a fusion of money-making, accumulating citizens, not as a collectivity of public or political participation. Urbanization, in effect, was the aggregate success and failure of thousands of individual, autonomous enterprises. By 1900, American cities displayed a fragmented physical and social development that served as a foundation for the "centerless" form of the twentieth-century metropolis (Warner, 1968: 3–5).

Much literature on urbanization focused on the three dominant metropolises, New York, Chicago, and Los Angeles, and for good reason. In the nineteenth century, New York and Chicago were the dominant urban centers on the North American continent. New York and its surrounding territory, in particular, ultimately attracted the largest population in the United States and, by some measures, the entire world. New York's economic institutions eclipsed not only American competitors by the early nineteenth century, but the rest of the planet after World War I. The centralization of capital in the region attracted an ever-growing population that was the most polyglot in world history. At various times, New York was the largest Irish, Jewish, Italian, and African city in the world. As in medieval Bruges and Venice and early modern Paris and London, textile production proved a key stimulus. Between 1850 and 1950, clothing and garment manufacturing employed 25–50 percent of the city's workforce. Manhattan was and is the most intensely developed piece of American real estate, making New York the most densely populated city in world history. By 1894, New York south of 110th Street had a density of 143 people per acre, surpassing second-place Paris at 125 per acre. Lower Manhattan's Eleventh Ward had 986 people in each of its 32 acres, a figure overwhelming the most densely populated slums in Asia (Bombay at 760 per acre in 1881) and Europe (Prague at 485 per acre in the 1890s). By every important measure – from population to density to industrial output to bank deposits to wholesale trade – New York ranked first in the country. And unlike other world cities, such as London, Paris, Berlin, Tokyo, and Vienna, New York was not a national or even state capital.

In the three decades since Warner first articulated his theory of "privatism," historians have supported and refuted different elements of it. Case studies of nineteenth-century Chicago reveal that physical improvements were the responsibility of individual property-owners or private development companies. Private real-estate forces thus dominated municipal government, excluding propertyless citizens and delaying the construction of streets, sidewalks, and sewers. Ironically, because they were privately developed, working-class Pullman and Harvey enjoyed better streets, sewers, and gas than the more affluent Wicker Park. Even residents in older New England communities demanded more and better services as cities grew larger, but refused to pay for them. Only at the turn of the twentieth century did municipalities begin assuming such responsibilities. Even then "reformers" created less-represent-ative political bodies – commissions, special districts, city manager governments, strong-mayor systems, at-large councils – to ensure efficient delivery of services.

At the same time, some find that citizen activism preceded infrastructure improve-ments. Von Hoffman (1995) found that middle-class residents moved into the Boston suburb of Jamaica Plain before streetcar lines linked them to the central city. Indeed, residents organized, petitioned, and fought for physical improvements. Rather than transportation technology triggering urban growth or developers acting on their own entrepreneurial whims, urban transit networks followed the settlement of newly developed neighborhoods. Still others like Eric Monkkonen (1988) maintain that focusing on the urbanization of the largest cities ignores how the medium-sized community (or suburb) was and is the typical American city. While the nation became increasingly urban after 1800, and cities like New York, Chicago, and Los Angeles grew into "global" metropolises, much of that urbanization occurred in much smaller cities. In fact, big, central-city growth peaked in the late 1920s, making this form of urbanization largely a nineteenth-century phenomenon. Twentieth-century urbaniza-tion emerged as a mosaic of governments in metropolitan areas. By 1990, for ex-ample, Los Angeles County comprised 86 cities, some dating back to the eighteenth century and others incorporated after 1950.

Studies which de-emphasize the large central city increasingly equate urbanization with suburbanization. While some theorists still argue that suburbs or "multi-nucleated metropolitan regions" represent new, twentieth-century forms of urban space, historians locate the source of American suburbanization in the eighteenth and nineteenth centuries. Indeed, American suburbs enjoy transatlantic origins as histor-ians increasingly situate their ideological roots in European Romanticism and British town planning. Kenneth T. Jackson (1985) demonstrates that suburbanization not only has a long history in the United States, but embodies a paradoxical element of urbanization. The largest American cities experienced "urban population deconcen-tration" in the first half of the nineteenth century. By 1830, for example, "suburban" Brooklyn was growing faster than Manhattan. Three decades later, the largest cities had idyllic, romantic suburbs populated by the affluent on their peripheries: Chestnut Hill outside Boston, the North Shore above Chicago, Germantown outside Philadel-phia, Llewellyn Park near Newark, Glendale outside Cincinnati. Metropolitan areas like New York witnessed population and physical growth while the older, interior core simultaneously experienced population decline and physical deterioration. Suburban-ization, in effect, represents continuing urbanization alongside the rejection of the large metropolis, or the inner-city core.

Social and technological change propelled a distinctive American suburban form. Cultural values like Jeffersonian agrarianism favored rural living and thus drove suburbanization. Nineteenth-century suburbs, alongside the pioneering landscape designs of cemeteries and parks, exemplified key elements of American romanticism, naturalism and domesticity. Efforts to incorporate nature into city life not only produced a "new urban landscape," but distinguished American suburban design well into the twentieth century. Transportation technologies also facilitated suburban growth. The ferry service established by Robert Fulton in 1814 made Brooklyn the first commuting suburb in the United States. New and multiple transit systems emerged throughout the century: the horse-drawn omnibus from 1827 to the 1850s; the horsecar from 1832 to 1927; the steam railroad from the 1830s to 1900; the elevated railroad after 1868; the electrified streetcar (or trolley) after 1887. In the 1890s, Boston opened the nation's first subway system, while the gasoline-combustion automobile made its first appearance on city streets in 1893 (Jackson, 1985).

The railroad, in effect, dramatically reorganized urban space in the nineteenth-century American city. Commuter railways enabled urbanites to more easily reside on the periphery of the metropolis, effectively separating work and home and creating new urban forms called "streetcar suburbs" (Warner, 1962). Transportation systems not only facilitated suburban growth, but turned North American cities inside out. In European cities, the affluent and the elite resided in or near the center of the metropolis, leaving the suburban fringe for lower income and working-class groups. American cities, by contrast, were configured differently. Comparatively cheap land offered a practical incentive for the middle classes to create residential districts and thereby avoid the crime, congestion, and ethnic diversity of the older, inner city. The bulk of American elite and middle-class families "suburbanized" throughout the course of the nineteenth century, creating a distinctive "North American pattern" of urbanization (Jackson, 1985).

Municipal officials sought to control urbanization by annexing outlying suburbs. In 1854, for example, Philadelphia expanded its municipal boundaries from 2 square miles to 129 square miles. Chicago grew from 43 square miles to 133 square miles when Lakeview and Hyde Park were added in 1889. The most significant political expansion came in 1898 when five counties (including Brooklyn, then the fourth largest city in the US) merged to create Greater New York City, increasing Gotham's square mileage from 40 to 300 and its population by 2 million. Other annexations took place in Boston, Baltimore, Pittsburgh, Cleveland, Minneapolis, St Louis, and New Orleans. Thus, suburbs that began as outlying villages evolved into inner-city neighborhoods: Harlem and Brooklyn in New York, Old Irving Park in Chicago, the San Fernando Valley in Los Angeles. In effect, suburbs have no single or easy definition, much like cities themselves. In the nineteenth century, railroad suburbs had *both* rich and poor, sometimes duplicating the spatial and employment plans of inner cities. While these patterns accelerated after World War II, their foundations lay in the nineteenth century.

Finally, American suburbs are distinctive in their political independence. In contrast to Europe, incorporated suburbs thwarted movements toward metropolitan governance and central city control of urbanization. A multitude of affluent suburbs not only fought annexation, but evolved as distinct municipalities in opposition to central cities. In Massachusetts, Brookline in 1873, Cambridge in 1892, and Somerville in 1893 rejected plans for incorporation into Boston. Evanston, Illinois, did the same in 1894. American urban growth was historically unique in its low residential density, strong penchant for home-ownership with big lawns, and the tendency of middle and wealthy classes to live on the periphery and suffer a long journey to work (Jackson, 1985).

Analysis of suburbanization has generated greater attention to regional forms of urbanization in the South and West. Most significantly, the American West has replaced the Midwest and East Coast as the centerpoint of many urban narratives. Although most of this research concentrates on the late twentieth-century "megalopolis" of Southern California, reinterpretations of Western history increasingly highlight the region's nineteenth-century urban character. Much of the earlier literature on urbanization and planning omitted the South and Southwest in their histories. Yet, as early as 1880, the West was more urban than the rest of the US (30 percent versus 28 percent). California, in fact, was 50 percent urban by the 1880s, long before the rest of the United States reached that threshold in 1920.

Recent historians of the urbanizing West and South emphasize several themes. First, the study of Western cities has shifted from "frontier" questions to issues concerning ecology, urbanity, and the metropolitan periphery. Just as earlier generations of urban historians documented the emerging economic and communication networks in the nineteenth century linking the Northeast, Mid-Atlantic and Midwestern regions of the US, historians of the frontier West increasingly describe rural and "peripheral areas" becoming ever more integrated into an urban–industrial economy. Secondly, the diversity of individual cities is comprehensible only by regional comparisons of urban systems, thereby emphasizing interactions among towns and cities. For example, Mississippi River communities experienced similar patterns of growth in their early histories before factors individual to each city caused them to diverge in the twentieth century. Finally, Western urbanization rarely imitated Eastern competitors. Some locales, notably Portland and San Francisco, reproduced and physically reflected East Coast influences. But these were exceptional. More often, as Carol O'Connor (1994) shows, the metropolitan expansion in "sunbelt cities" throughout the West witnessed business-dominated politics, hostility to organized labor, suburban spatial form, and federally subsidized growth.

Distinctive, regional patterns of urbanization similarly apply to the South. David Goldfield (1982) maintains that southern city building was "urbanization without cities." Even after four centuries, southern cities remained closer in spirit to antebellum plantations than their northern counterparts. While transportation and communication systems integrated some southern cities into regional networks, distinctive southern characteristics grew more pronounced as the South "modernized without northernizing." Yet, contrary to Goldfield, the post-Civil War South also increasingly replicated the North with growing boosterism, physical infrastructures, planned suburbs, new and dominating business elites, and the emergence of an urban network of southern cities.

Questions regarding the physical evolution of nineteenth-century cities generated questions concerning ecological development. Students of the built environment focus on "technological networks" – roads, bridges, water and sewer systems, disposal facilities, power grids, transit and communication structures. As part of their attention to environmental questions, recent studies treat urban technologies as the material embodiment of people's values and culture. Some even redefine long-held assumptions in urban history. For example, nineteenth-century nuisance regulations alter the standard chronology of municipal politics. Women reformers, acting as "municipal housekeepers" after 1890, used environmental issues like smoke abatement to affect public policy and generate reform movements. William Cronon's (1991) study of nineteenth-century Chicago, in particular, examines the environmental impact of urbanization. Cronon reintroduces themes that dominated the study of urbanization earlier in the century. Like Arthur Schlesinger's work in 1933, *Nature's Metropolis* (1991) represents part of a periodic attempt by urbanists to refute Frederick Jackson

Turner and locate cities at the center of US history. Like Richard Wade (1959), Cronon offers a "frontier" history from a metropolitan perspective. And, like Lewis Mumford (1961), Cronon sees the city and country landscape as symbiotic components of an interdependent regional economy and ecosystem. Urban and rural are one thing, not two things.

By his own admission, Cronon "reads Turner backwards." Whereas Turner viewed agrarian life and urban growth in conflictual terms, Cronon insists that urbanization made rural development possible. The growth of cities was the motor force of agrarian change. The frontier was not an isolated rural society, but rather the edge of an expanding urban empire built upon the destruction of the original ecosystem by farming, lumbering, and grazing. In societies organized around market exchange, trade between city and country serves as the most powerful force influencing cultural geography and environmental change. The frontier and Chicago represented mutually dependent markets. The rural landscape was determined by the value urbanites attached to the products of the soil and the cost of getting those products to urban markets (Cronon, 1991: 47–51). At the same time, urban commodity markets – grain, meat, and lumber – had a greater impact in determining rural community life and related ecosystems than any other economic institution. Chicago thus played the most important role in shaping the economy and landscape of the Midwest. Whereas earlier writers like Schlesinger, Wade, and Reps positioned cities and rural hinterlands in opposition to each other, Cronon ultimately renders such dichotomies false. Rural, agrarian landscapes often defined as "natural" were the product of human forces like cities themselves.

While Cronon innovatively reinterprets urbanization through the prism of ecology, he was not the first to explore the impact of technology. Indeed, studies of technological change forced the earliest students in urban history to abandon traditional "political" chronologies. In their place, urban historians substituted an "urban" chronology based on technological, spatial, and social change. Most recently, examinations of technological reactions to urbanization generated an important reinterpretation of city politics. For more than a century, the narrative of municipal government was framed by two words: "boss" and "machine." Even before New York's William Marcy Tweed was convicted and sent to prison in 1871, most of the literature on urban politics described that world as divided between native-born, middle-class groups (often labelled "reformers") and foreign-born, working-class groups (associated with "machine" politics).

Since 1980, the politics of urbanization has been dramatically reinterpreted. Rather than focusing on electoral politics and rhetoric, historians increasingly examine the political results of urbanization: budgets, physical infrastructures, bureaucratic behavior, and the provision of city services. Late nineteenth-century American cities so successfully developed new urban services and infrastructures that Jon Teaford (1979) has depicted an "unheralded triumph." Engineers thus replace the ward boss in the political narrative of urbanization. Furthermore, urbanists increasingly argue that modern city services and physical infrastructures associated with urbanization created new municipal agencies and special-interest factions that transcended neighborhood and ethnic loyalties. The result was pluralistic and contested forms of municipal authority. Even elites were never monolithic. Rather, they were internally divided, constantly competing and shifting alliances depending upon the issues.

Examinations of urban political institutions conclude that the "local state" was relatively autonomous from social and cultural patterns. Nineteenth-century municipalities spent far more money than state and federal counterparts and enjoyed considerable control over their destinies. Estimates suggest that between 1820 and 1930 the breakdown of governmental expenditures was 33 percent for federal, 11 percent for state, and 56 percent for local. Forced to compete against one another for the best revenue-generating activities, municipalities adopted policies of "boosterism," acted as "economic adventurers," and relied on residential property-owners for support, not immigrant or working-class masses looking for patronage or social services. Much of this growth was financed by debt. No state limited municipal borrowing before 1870; by 1881, 23 states still had no limits. By investing in new technologies and physical infrastructures, municipalities underwrote urbanization and the expansion of a capitalist urban economy.

More significantly, immigrant and working-class groups, traditionally identified as proponents of patronage, actually resisted municipal expansion. In a case study of San Francisco, Terrence McDonald (1986) discovered that municipal taxes and expenditures reached historic lows under administrations dominated by Irish politicians (in part because home-ownership increased among immigrants and workers). Progressive reformers and ward bosses alike espoused "pay as you go" philosophies and minimal expenditures. The pattern of low per capita municipal expenditures from 1890 to 1910, years when allegedly patronage-driven machines were powerful, is repeated in other studies. The watchwords of urban growth were not "spend, spend, spend" but "economy, economy."

This interpretative framework relegates the machine model of urban politics to myth. While 80 percent of the 30 largest cities had "machines" from 1880 to 1914, few enjoyed a long hegemony, most were "factional," and endured only through two or three elections. Even the prototypical boss, George Washington Plunkitt, suffered a loyal opposition throughout his political career before three defeats finally drove him out of office. Most significantly, battles between bosses and reformers in cities like San Francisco little affected city expenditures. Ideology and institutional structure did. A bi-partisan commitment to fiscal conservatism was shared by both "patronage-hungry" ward bosses and economy-minded reformers. The squandering boss is simply a caricature, the political machine a social construct.

For most of the twentieth century, urbanists accepted Frederick Jackson Turner's cultural assumption that a sharp polarity separated urban and rural life. Cities were congested and complicated; rural life was dispersed and simple. Cities were functionally mixed; farms singularly uniform. Urban streetscapes were physically dense but geographically modest; rural landscapes were open and expansive. Urbanites inhabited a largely human-made world; agrarians shared their physical space with "nature." Cities were the domain of reason and civilization; rural life was the realm of ignorance and superstition.

Since 1970, historians of urbanization have rejected most of these dichotomies. Analytical categories such as "premodern" and "modern," "traditional" and "modernity," "consensus and conflict," *gemeinschaft* and *gesellschaft* are viewed as simplistic. Such classifications fail to adequately explain the past because elements of "urban" and "agrarian" life appear in both milieux. For example, the stark divide between urban and non-urban worlds embodied in the "textile" and "Coketown" patterns of urbanization (Mumford, 1961: 446–81) represent at least over-simplification, if not misrepresentation. Studies of suburbanization have forced urbanists to abandon urbanization models organized around archetypes of "city versus country" for more nuanced and complicated paradigms. Indeed, the old vocabulary of suburbanization and urbanization is now supplanted by terms like "megalopolis," "spread cities," "technoburbs," "edge cities," "disurbs" and "post-suburbs." Political models pitting bosses against reformers are viewed as myth rather than accurate history. As William Cronon (1991) forcefully argues, dichotomies separating cities and rural hinterlands only create false boundaries. Rural, agrarian landscapes, often defined as "natural," were in fact created by humans just as cities were. Even the traditional divisions between "the city as site" and "the city as process," or the sociological and spatial "imaginations," now seem outdated and over-simplified. "Urbanization," long focused on geography and physical growth, increasingly intersects with the "urbanism" of metropolitan life, social groups, and subcultures.

For over three decades, students of urbanization have abandoned the "Mumfordian" meta-narrative. Fragmentation defines the way historians now envision urbanization. Case study, subcultural, interdisciplinary, and postmodern methodologies prove that urban growth defies easy generalization. Lewis Mumford offered a comprehensive and attractive narrative of urbanization linking culture, politics, and technology. Recent research, however, renders much of Mumford's "organic" view romantic. Urbanists have even foregone Sam Bass Warner Jr's call for a comparative, synthesizing "scaffolding" approach because few believe "all the world was Philadelphia." Philadelphia in 1775, New York in 1860, Chicago in 1900, and Los Angeles in 1950 represent distinctive cities having less, not more, in common with urban counterparts. Consequently, urbanization, like urban history itself, remains a field with no totalizing theory, hegemonic interpretation, or universal paradigm. A plurality of micro-theories now characterizes the history of nineteenth-century American urban development.

REFERENCES

Bender, Thomas C. (1978) *Community and Social Change in America*. New Brunswick, NJ: Rutgers University Press.

Cronon, William (1991) *Nature's Metropolis: Chicago and the Great West*. New York: W. W. Norton.

Glaab, Charles N. and Brown, A. Theodore (1967) *A History of Urban America*. New York: Macmillan.

Goldfield, David (1982) *Cottonfields and Skyscrapers: Southern City and Region, 1607–1980*. Baton Rouge: Louisiana State University Press.

Hofstadter, Richard (1955) *The Age of Reform: from Bryan to FDR*. New York: Alfred A. Knopf.

Jackson, Kenneth T. (1985) *Crabgrass Frontier*. New York: Oxford University Press.

McDonald, Terrence J. (1986) *The Parameters of Urban Fiscal Policy: Socioeconomic Change and Political Culture in San Francisco, 1860–1906*. Berkeley, CA: University of California Press.

Monkkonen, Eric H. (1988) *America Becomes Urban: the Development of US Cities and Towns*. Berkeley, CA: University of California Press.

Mumford, Lewis (1961) *The City in History*. New York: Harcourt, Brace.

O'Connor, Carol A. (1994) "A region of cities," in Clyde A. Milner II, Carol A. O'Connor, and Martha Sandweiss (eds), *The Oxford History of the American West*, pp. 534–63. New York: Oxford University Press.

Park, Robert, Burgess, Ernest W., McKenzie, Roderick D., and Wirth, Louis (1925) *The City.* Chicago: University of Chicago Press.

Reps, John W. (1965) *The Making of Urban America: a History of City Planning in the United States.* Princeton, NJ: Princeton University Press.

Schlesinger, Arthur M. (1933) *The Rise of the City, 1878–1898.* New York: Macmillan.

Teaford, Jon C. (1979) *The Unheralded Triumph: City Government in America, 1870–1900.* Baltimore, MD: Johns Hopkins University Press.

Tonnies, Ferdinand (1963) *Community and Society,* trans. Charles P. Loomis. New York: Harper and Row.

Turner, Frederick Jackson (1894) "The significance of the frontier in American history," *Annual Report of the American Historical Association for the Year 1893*, pp. 199–227. Washington: Government Printing Office.

Von Hoffman, Alexander (1995) *Local Attachments: the Making of an American Urban Neighborhood.* Baltimore, MD: Johns Hopkins University Press.

Wade, Richard C. (1959) *The Urban Frontier: Pioneer Life in Early Pittsburgh, Cincinnati, Lexington, Louisville, and St Louis.* Cambridge, Mass.: Harvard University Press.

Warner Jr, Sam Bass (1962) *Streetcar Suburbs: the Process of Growth in Boston, 1870–1900.* Cambridge, Mass.: Harvard University Press.

Warner Jr, Sam Bass, (1968) *The Private City: Philadelphia in Three Periods of its Growth.* Philadelphia: University of Pennsylvania Press.

Zunz, Olivier (1982) *The Changing Face of Inequality: Urbanization, Industrial Development, and Immigrants in Detroit, 1880–1920.* Chicago: University of Chicago Press.

CHAPTER TWELVE

The Development of the Working Classes

KEVIN KENNY

THE historiography of the nineteenth-century American working classes has gone through three principal phases. The first phase lasted from the emergence of labor history as a separate subdiscipline at the end of the nineteenth century to the late 1950s and is known as the "old" labor history. This "old" labor history, typified by the Wisconsin school of John R. Commons, concentrated on the study of institutions, trade unions, collective bargaining, party politics, and public policy. From about 1960 onward, the "old" labor history gave way to an innovative "new" labor history which, in the hands of its finest practitioners, E. P. Thompson and Herbert Gutman, exercised a considerable influence on American historiography as a whole, especially through its central concepts of culture and human agency. More recently, since the 1980s, the "new" labor history has in turn given way to an as yet undefined school of labor historiography that takes gender, race, and discourse as its central categories. This most recent phase of scholarship has overturned the certainties of much previous writing on nineteenth-century labor, though without as yet producing a coherent overall interpretation of its own.

Before turning to the first of these three schools of interpretation, that of John Commons and his associates, it will be helpful to have some sense of how the subdiscipline of labor history emerged in the first place. Scholarly study of American labor had its origins in the 1870s, just as American historical study as a whole was beginning to emerge as a professional discipline. What made the 1870s especially relevant in the case of labor history, however, was that it was the decade when questions of labor and capital began to take center stage over questions of race and Reconstruction on the national agenda. The year 1877 is usually seen as an important turning-point in American history, for the withdrawal of the last troops from the reconstructed South in that year coincided with the first national strike in the United States. Indeed, some of the troops in question were deployed to put down this "great uprising" of railroad workers, and after 1877 armories were built in the major cities of the Northeast to protect against similar outbreaks of violence in the future. It was in this context that the serious investigation of American labor history began.

The intellectual roots of US labor history lie in the field of economics, rather than history proper. The prevailing "classical" school of economics in the late nineteenth century worked within a highly abstract and deductive paradigm of enquiry which drew its conclusions from supposedly immutable laws. A discipline based on such timeless laws and abstractions was by its very nature ahistorical. At the same time, it was politically conservative, taking the economic status quo to be natural, normal, and inevitable, and arguing against any intrusion by government into the workings of the marketplace for the protection of workers or consumers. Trade unions and collective bargaining, predictably, were dismissed as unnatural obstacles to freedom of competition, trade, and production.

The new historical study of labor that emerged in the United States from the 1870s onward broke from all these premises. Derived from a rival school of economics based in Germany, where many American students began to attend graduate school after the Civil War, its emphasis was empirical rather than theoretical. It focused on the practical workings of the economy rather than deducing laws of economic activity from general principles. As such, it was inevitably historical in focus, breaking from the timeless abstractions of classical economics and searching instead for the social origins of quotidian practice, especially the formation of trade unions and the enactment of social and labor legislation. This new historical economics was often consciously political, seeking to validate trade unions and labor legislation, in sharp contrast to the prevailing classical school. By the 1880s, historical enquiry into American labor was well under way. But it was based in the discipline of economics rather than in the historical profession, which was only just emerging in the United States (also under a heavy German influence).

The great pioneer of American labor history was John R. Commons of the University of Wisconsin. Commons and his associates focused on the institutional history of labor, gathering together the various records left by American workers to produce the multi-volume *A History of Industrial Society.* On this basis, Commons and his students proceeded to write *A History of Labor in the United States,* published in four volumes between 1918 and 1935, which remains the most comprehensive account of the history of the American labor movement in its formative years. The practitioners of this so-called Wisconsin school of labor history were mainly labor economists, and their interest lay almost exclusively in labor institutions rather than work or culture. Many of them were themselves practitioners in the field of labor relations, serving as arbitrators or consultants. They produced a vast monographic literature on the history of individual unions and their practices of collective bargaining, which remains a useful source of reference.

One important exception to the dominance of the Wisconsin school before the rise of new labor history in the 1960s was the remarkably prolific historian Philip Foner, who published more than 50 original works and edited collections on US labor history, including a multi-volume *History of the Labor Movement in the United States,* and several pioneering books on the labor history of African Americans. As a committed Marxist, Foner brought to the history of labor an ideological approach that was in some ways diametrically opposed to the Wisconsin school. Both Foner and the Commons school wrote detailed histories of how the American labor movement had evolved, in an apparently necessary progression, from the utopian, impractical, intermittent, and poorly coordinated organizations of the antebellum and Civil War eras, into the national labor movements of the late nineteenth and early twentieth centuries. They were especially concerned with how the movement had developed into its dominant form, the practical, business-like, non-radical unionism of the American Federation of Labor (AFL), founded in 1886. The primary emphasis of the AFL was on securing better wages and conditions for workers, especially skilled workers, rather than offering an over-arching critique of wage labor or the capitalist system as such. This approach is often referred to as "bread and butter" unionism or "pure and simple" unionism.

For historians like John R. Commons and Selig Perlman of the Wisconsin school, the AFL was the embodiment of an organic, job-conscious, American-style trade unionism, whose rise to power their work chronicled and celebrated. But, precisely because the AFL was so conservative, it was an abomination to Philip Foner, who traced its rise to power in order to lament what he saw as a debilitating accommodationism between American labor and capital, stifling the potentially revolutionary activity of workers in the United States. Unlike the Wisconsin school, then, Foner told the story of American trade unionism in pessimistic rather than celebratory tones. But, like them, his focus was on institutional history, marked by detailed accounts of the evolution of trade unions and their practices. Despite its radical ideological position, Foner's methodology was very much that of the "old" labor history.

If the "new" labor history of the period since 1960 can be summarized by a single characteristic, it is the concerted effort by historians to move beyond the study of institutions to the study of workers themselves, in all the various aspects of their lives. The towering figures in this "new" American labor history were the British historian E. P. Thompson, one of the most influential historians of the English-speaking world in the second half of the twentieth century, and three historians of the United States, Herbert Gutman, David Montgomery, and David Brody. Brody's *Steelworkers in America: the Nonunion Era* (1960) inaugurated one strand of the "new" labor history. As the subtitle indicated, his work was anything but an institutional history of a trade union. Instead, Brody tried to understand the lives of the steelworkers by looking at, on the one hand, the type of work they did, and, on the other hand, the structure and values of the ethnic communities they lived in. These two themes – the nature of the labor process, and the nature of the working-class and typically immigrant community – would dominate the "new" labor history.

The hallmark of David Montgomery's scholarship has been his emphasis on the nature of work, on traditions of shop-floor militancy, and on the position of workers as citizens in a republican democracy. Montgomery's path-breaking book *Beyond Equality: Labor and the Radical Republicans 1862–1872* (1967) exposed the emerging fissures in Republican ideology during the era of Reconstruction by demonstrating the failure of the Radicals to come to terms with the meaning and content of freedom and equality as defined by working people. Most of his subsequent work, which concentrated on the classic period of American labor history between the Civil War and World War I, dealt with similar questions of shop-floor militancy and worker democracy.

If the themes pioneered by Brody and Montgomery constituted one principal strand in the new labor history, the other strand was a new emphasis on what workers did when they were not working or organizing, in other words on their culture and community life. Without ignoring either the labor process or the history of trade unions, the most influential (and readable) of the "new" labor historians concentrated on issues of class and culture, typically in a local community setting. The focus of labor history was broadened considerably, to include questions of religion, ethnicity, family structure, and leisure, in an attempt to capture the entirety of working-class lives and culture, not just work and trade union activities. In this way, much of the "new" labor history typified, *par excellence*, the "new" social history that began to emerge in the United States and Europe in the 1960s.

The single most influential figure in this new project was E. P. Thompson, whose *The Making of the English Working Class* (1963) inspired a generation of labor and social historians on both sides of the Atlantic. Thompson's great appeal to Americans was that he offered a version of Marxism with a human face. Having broken with the rigid dogmatism of the Stalinist Communist Party in Britain in 1956 (at the age of 33, as he later put it, he "commenced to reason"), Thompson developed a brand of humanist Marxism that stood in sharp contrast to the more rigidly deterministic approaches typified by much of the "old left" and by many of his "structuralist" Marxist contemporaries in continental Europe. The hallmark of Thompson's Marxism was his emphasis on human agency, hence the label *humanist* Marxism (as distinct from a *structuralist* approach emphasizing how people's lives are determined by forces larger than themselves).

The English working class, Thompson insisted in his most famous work, had not simply been created by the vast, impersonal forces of socio-economic change known as the Industrial Revolution. It had, instead, been "present at its own making," by which Thompson meant that working people had brought to the process of industrialization a rich cultural heritage which enabled them to shape the content of their emerging class consciousness. Class, in Thompson's formulation, was a dynamic social and cultural process embodied in the lives of real, active human beings. Though it was ultimately determined by economic (specifically, productive) relations, class for Thompson was as much "a cultural as an economic formation." Working people were born into and labored in worlds that were not ultimately of their own making, but in the midst of great social and economic dislocation they possessed rich resources of plebeian politics and culture, thereby shaping the course of history as well as being shaped by it. Workers, in short, were exploited but not powerless and degraded.

Subsequent critics would complain that Thompson did not distinguish clearly enough between class and class consciousness, i.e. between an objective social structure, on the one hand, and apprehension of that objectivity by workers, on the other. Thompson's point was to reject the deterministic notion that modes of production mechanically determined people's consciousness. But in downplaying economic determinism, it has recently been suggested by some historians that he (quite unwittingly) cleared a path for recent "post-structuralist" theory which collapses the distinction between the representation and the real, between "discourse" and "society." When it appeared, however, Thompson's work was hailed throughout the English-speaking world for its reinvigoration of the category of class, which offered a powerful new approach to labor history. This approach quickly transformed the historiography of the nineteenth-century American working classes.

The principal exponent of the Thompsonian approach to labor history in the United States was Herbert Gutman, whose single most influential work was perhaps the long essay, "Work, Culture, and Society in Industrializing America, 1815–1819," written in 1968 and published in a collection of essays bearing the same title in 1977. This essay was in some ways a Thompsonian manifesto, outlining the extent to which American workers had maintained a rich and autonomous culture of their own, deploying it to resist the demands and imperatives of their capitalist employers. Gutman's enduring belief throughout his career was in the power and dignity of working people to fight back. The important topic for historians to study, he insisted, was not what was done to working people by others, but what they did for themselves.

As well as borrowing from Thompson, Gutman's work highlighted the single characteristic that has always distinguished American labor history most sharply from British labor history, its multi-ethnic and multi-racial character. Unlike Britain, the United States was a land built by slaves and immigrants. Extending the Thompsonian theme of agency under adversity to American slavery, Gutman wrote some of his most influential work on that topic. It was typical of his vision as a historian that he included slaves as part of the overall narrative of the nineteenth-century working classes. At the same time, Gutman astutely observed that Thompson's story of the English working class, which had a single "making" between 1780 and 1830, could not be applied to the United States, where the "working class" made itself over and over again throughout the nineteenth century, its structure and consciousness being repeatedly modified by the infusion of pre-industrial immigrants. The richest and most innovative of the "new" labor history pioneered by Herbert Gutman, therefore, was concerned with questions of ethnicity and race as well as class.

This scheme of things made American historical development considerably more complex than British. In his attempt to come to terms with this complexity, Gutman rejected the standard chronology of nineteenth-century United States history, with the Civil War at its center, insisting that it was incapable of grasping the sailent aspects of American working-class history and culture. He disrupted conventional chronology still further with the provocative suggestion that, in terms of labor history at least, early nineteenth- and late nineteenth-century American history were strikingly similar, each period being marked by an abrupt transition to industrial capitalism for a large group of workers. In the first case these workers were native-born (mostly women initially) and Irish; while in the second they were immigrants from eastern and southern Europe.

While Herbert Gutman necessarily modified the Thompsonian model in applying it to multi-ethnic America, his greatest impact on American labor historiography was his emphasis on Thompson's central categories of culture and agency. In a long series of essays investigating working-class culture, Gutman argued that American workers in the nineteenth century had rejected a middle-class ideology of "possessive individualism" in favor of a working-class ethic of "mutualism" and solidarity. This idea of an autonomous working-class culture became the central theme in the post-1960 generation of American historiography that came to be known as the "new" labor history. The culture in question was typically most discernible in nineteenth-century industrial communities, the in-depth study of which provided the basis for a new type of historical monograph.

What exactly did Gutman and his fellow-practitioners of the "new" labor history mean by an autonomous worker culture? They meant, first and foremost, that nineteenth-century workers were not simply lesser versions of their employers, men and women who had failed to become capitalists and were envious and embittered as a result. It followed that the "working class" was not simply a way-station to the "middle class." Contrary to the perspective of their employers, not to mention many subsequent historians, American workers in the nineteenth century did not spend their lives wishing they were somebody else. They may have been exploited, but they had not been robbed of their dignity; the last thing most of them wanted was to embrace the values of those who were exploiting them. They had their own values, and for Gutman these values provided an alternative moral basis on which to resist the efforts of employers and their allies to impose their will, discipline, and ideology on workers.

Gutman and other historians of the nineteenth-century working classes have since faced the charge that they were being romantic and idealistic in their conception of an autonomous working-class culture. In Gutman's defense, it should first be noted that he was *not* arguing that nineteenth-century workers were averse to earning money, owning property, or looking after the material welfare of their families. Instead, they drew an important distinction between two types of property: that which every man needed, and had a right to, so that he might retain his dignity and provide for his family, and that which was accumulated by capitalists and speculators for the sake of accumulation, through the exploitation of others. This question of property aside, however, many historians today would agree that there is so much "worker culture" in Gutman's writing, and this "culture" is often so autonomous from the power of any ruling or dominant class, that one tends to forget the extent of exploitation and degradation that was necessarily inherent in wage labor during the Industrial Revolution. This point raises several possible criticisms of the "new" labor history, which will be addressed below. These criticisms will not make proper sense, however, without prior consideration of the category of "labor republicanism" which has lain at the heart of nineteenth-century labor historiography for most of the past generation. Among the most influential proponents of this approach have been David Montgomery (1993) and Sean Wilentz, (1984a, b), whose work inspired a host of other studies.

While all Americans in the nineteenth century could claim to be republicans in some sense, American workers (especially native-born "artisans," or skilled workers) developed a distinctive brand of this philosophy for themselves. Worker republicanism, according to Wilentz, was a distinctively American form of class consciousness. Historians have often wondered why the United States failed to develop radical labor movements and political parties of the European sort. The question is most often posed as follows: why no socialism in America? But as Wilentz and several other historians have persuasively argued, this is not really a useful question with which to frame a historical enquiry. While many European countries have certainly had stronger labor parties than the United States, it is by no means clear that any pure form of radical class consciousness, abstracted from the writings of Marx, ever took root there either. More to the point, Wilentz urges historians to stop asking what did not happen in American labor history and turn instead to the question of what *did* happen. Instead of searching in vain for signs of some abstract and theoretical form of class-conscious activity, why not concentrate instead on what American workers really did do and think?

Approaching the history of nineteenth-century American workers in this way, historians have found abundant evidence of a form of consciousness they label "labor" or "artisanal" republicanism. The ideology in question was based on five principal assumptions: that (a) the goal of society should be to preserve the common good, or *commonwealth*; (b) in order to do so, citizens had to be *virtuous*, that is, able to subordinate their private wants to public needs; (c) the virtue of all citizens was contingent upon their *independence* from the control of others; (d) to guard against "tyrants" (as well as for individuals to realize full selfhood), all citizens had to *participate* in public life; and (e) as part of the radical heritage of the American Revolution, citizens were entitled to certain *natural, inalienable rights* under a representative system of government.

What did these ideas mean in practice? They meant that the goal of society was the promotion of the common good rather than individual greed. They meant that the activities of large employers and bankers, and especially the "robber barons" of the late nineteenth century, contradicted this ideal of commonwealth and virtue in the most direct and blatant ways. They meant that the accumulation of wealth for its own sake, through the progressive impoverishment of some of the citizenry, violated their sense of republican democracy. At the same time, the health of republican democracy depended on the ability of the citizenry to participate in its political life in an independent fashion. By the second half of the nineteenth century, however, this ability was being undermined in all sorts of ways.

The ideal citizen of the early republic had been an independent craftsman or a yeoman farmer. The world of the late nineteenth-century industrial worker was a far cry from both. Men and women who worked for wages in nineteenth-century America were in some ways more independent than their predecessors a century earlier (whether farmers, craftsmen, servants, or slaves): they could move from place to place more freely, and in theory at least they were free to work for whom they chose. The problem, however, is that this freedom was double-edged: people were not only free to work for wages, they increasingly *had* to do so in order to survive. In this sense, wage labor represented a simultaneous loss and gain in independence. Dependent on wage labor in order to live, working people protested that the material basis of their political independence had been undermined. Democracy was further threatened, workers of the postbellum era protested, by railroads and other corporations, who controlled vast amounts of wealth and wielded unprecedented political influence on state and national government.

The nineteenth-century ideology of labor republicanism, at its most developed and articulate, offered a coherent critique of the workings of American industrial capitalist society as a whole. American workers insisted on a restoration of commonwealth, virtue, and independence. They referred to their type of work as nothing more than a form of "wage slavery." They invoked the American Revolution to insist that, among their inalienable rights was the right to control the fruits of their own labor, rather than having this wealth taken away by their employers. Nothing less than the fate of the republic was at stake.

The category of labor republicanism is at its most useful when applied to skilled, white workers. In the early nineteenth century the system of production in many skilled crafts broke down under the pressure of an emerging market economy. Apprentices who had hoped to become master craftsmen found their path blocked, as their masters moved upward into large-scale manufacturing based on wage labor, or downward into the ranks of wage work if they could not adapt to the new conditions. Production of a wide variety of goods moved from individual households headed by a master craftsman and staffed by live-in trainees called journeymen to centralized shops organized on the basis of extensive division of labor and the "putting out" of work on piece rates to domestic-based workers. Whereas the old masters had produced individual goods to order, the new entrepreneurs were mass producers who sold their goods in bulk on the open market. By the time of the Civil War, this centralized production was giving way to a full-scale factory system. The first of these factories, founded in Massachusetts as early as the 1820s, recruited their young women from farms and rural villages, and then turned to immigrant labor (mainly Irish) in the 1840s and 1850s. By the early postbellum era, industrial production was increasingly organized on the factory model, huge corporations were controlling vast amounts of wealth and exercising enormous political power, and the age of waged labor was well under way.

Not surprisingly, American workers fought back against the havoc and degradation wrought in their lives by this momentous transformation. By the 1830s, skilled working men from Boston to New York and Philadelphia were lamenting the decline of republican democracy, while invoking the radical principles of the American Revolution to support their case. The result was the formation of city-wide trade unions and working men's political parties in the Northeast, uniting workers across the lines of craft, ethnicity, and religion in a coherent critique of the emerging ethic of industrial capitalism. Demanding higher wages, shorter hours, safer conditions, universal white manhood suffrage, free public education, reform of the banking system, and cheap access to federally owned land (in the form of "homesteads"), they presented an alternative perspective on the meaning of republican democracy, based on the premise that labor was the ultimate creator of all wealth and was entitled to a just portion of its own fruits. This labor republicanism, which is often referred to as a "producerist" ideology, reached its peak with the Knights of Labor, which united some 750,000 workers of all backgrounds in the 1880s.

While the concept of "labor republicanism" yielded important insights into the history of the nineteenth-century American working classes, its limitations became increasingly evident to historians in the 1990s. Daniel T. Rodgers (1992), for example, pointed to the potentially vague and amorphous character of the category "republicanism" when applied loosely or uncritically to nineteenth-century labor history. As a concept in modern historiography, it was introduced to study the city-states of Renaissance Italy, was subsequently employed to study the American Revolution, then colonized the historiography of nineteenth-century labor, and even began to creep into the study of the early twentieth century. If the term is to be used by historians, it must therefore be used precisely, with specific reference to time and place.

Historians of nineteenth-century American labor fulfilled this obligation well enough, pointing to a particular vocabulary of commonwealth, virtue, independence, and the revolutionary heritage. But the problem remains that nearly all Americans, not just workers, participated in a national culture based on these precepts. Andrew Carnegie, for example, could, and did, claim to be every bit as much a republican as the workers who opposed him in Homestead, Pennsylvania, in 1892. And the category of "independence" that was central to the notion of labor republicanism could be, and was, defined by capitalists as the right to accumulate as much wealth as possible, and to be free from the restraints imposed by organized labor and the state (just as the owners of slaves, another form of labor in antebellum America, insisted on their right to own human property independent of government interference).

Proponents of the "republican synthesis" of nineteenth-century labor historiography, however, argued that the different meanings assigned by different Americans to the same key words support rather than contradict their case. In other words, workers had their own distinctive perspective on what the republic meant, just as capitalists or slaveowners did. The vocabulary of "republicanism" was contested, and the different positions on republican democracy advanced by different social groups are therefore excellent guides to their overall ideology and consciousness. This point is well taken, but it raises another, more difficult objection. How much resistance or opposition is possible without stepping outside the terms of a dominant political vocabulary? The point is important because the advocates of labor republicanism saw it not simply as a worldview but as a coherent ideology articulating a serious critique of industrial capitalism as a way of life.

The most commonly voiced objection to the "republican synthesis" in recent years is that the model of working-class culture and consciousness it employs is ultimately very narrow. It simply excludes too many people to be able to fulfill its claim to represent the American working class. As Peter Way (1993) has forcefully argued in his work on Irish canal construction laborers, the world of artisanal republicanism was far removed from that of the hundreds of thousands of Irish immigrants who worked at manual labor in nineteenth-century America in conditions of appalling poverty and degradation. Coming from a peasant culture disintegrating under the pressures of colonialism and commercialization, these Irish manual laborers differed sharply from native-born artisans in that they had no skilled or privileged position from which to fall. Their emergence as a class-conscious group of wage workers, therefore, involved not the erosion of a once secure and privileged position but transplantation from one system of social oppression to another. These canal workers belonged to a largely untold narrative of American labor history, that of the unskilled immigrant worker, a narrative that also includes the Molly Maguires of Pennsylvania. The story of these voiceless millions who built the infrastructure of industrializing America inevitably differs from that of the skilled minority who emerged as a conscious group of organized workers through the degradation of their craft. Why, then, should only the latter and not the former be taken as representative of the "American working class?"

Part of the answer, surely, lies in the different modes of protest these two groups of workers adopted. Both were fighting for much the same thing – at the very least, decent wages and humane conditions – but the manner in which they went about it was very different. The trade union, with its strategy of negotiation between the representatives of workers and their employers, was the standard form of labor organization in industrial capitalist societies such as those that emerged in nine-teenth-century United States. The unskilled Irish masses, however, brought to America a rather different strategy, rooted in the Irish countryside, which they adapted to the new industrial conditions in which they found themselves. The Irish canal laborers of the antebellum period became notorious for their faction fighting, whereby gangs of Irishmen affiliated according to county or region in their homeland did battle along the trenches and public works from Canada to New Orleans. They also banded together in secret societies, called Ribbonmen or Whiteboys, to threaten their employers and intimidate workers of other nationalities. In neither case were the Irish fighting for the sake of it, as contemporaries charged. Instead, they were fighting for access to work, driving their competitors away from the works, and using the Irish secret society tradition to enforce what they believed to be fair and just conditions of employment.

The purest example of this secret society tradition of the Irish type were the Molly Maguires of the 1860s and 1870s, 20 of whom were hanged for the assassination of 16 mine officials in northeastern Pennsylvania. The Molly Maguires coexisted with a formally organized trade-union movement, but the union leaders (most of them British-born or British-raised) were unequivocal in their condemnation of violence, claiming it could only backfire against the labor movement. The divisions between these two very different sides of the labor movement in Pennsylvania reveal the complexities in any labor history that seeks to do justice to the unskilled laborer and the immigrant as well as the skilled worker and the native-born. While the trade-union movement united Pennsylvania's mine workers across lines of religion, nativity, and skill, the divisions between Irish laborers and British miners and mine bosses resurfaced violently when the trade union was defeated in the 1870s. At the same time, the enemies of organized labor conveniently ignored the differences between the Molly Maguires and the trade union, lumping them together in a single category of terrorist conspiracy in order to ensure the destruction of both.

The complexity of nineteenth-century American labor history is greatly magnified once the analysis is pushed beyond white male labor to include women, African Americans, and various other ethnic and racial groups. The "new labor history" did not simply exclude these groups, of course; on the contrary, it produced many excellent studies of these topics. None the less, the groups in question did not always fit into the "republican synthesis" all that well. Women, African Americans, and immigrants might, with a fair amount of pushing and shoving, be slotted into the dominant narrative of class and class consciousness, though at other times – as slaves, or domestic servants, or immigrant menial laborers – they were rather unlikely candidates for such inclusion. Yet they worked for a living, and hence were a necessary component of any comprehensive labor historiography.

The challenge of how to include them as part of the dominant narrative was never really solved by the "new" labor history, and this failure led in the 1990s to its gradual replacement by diverse new approaches to the history of nineteenth-century workers. The process has been uneven and incomplete, and, by the end of the decade, has not produced any single new interpretation to rival the coherence of the Thompsonian and Gutmanesque approaches it debunks. It has, however, added important new dimensions of diversity and complexity to the study of labor history, with the categories of gender, race, and discourse at the heart of its enquiry.

The historiography of the 1990s used these categories to demonstrate that the very concept of a universal class consciousness, which the "new" labor historians took directly from the evidence left by nineteenth-century workers, was in fact particularist and exclusive. In racial terms, nineteenth-century class consciousness was almost exclusively white and, in gender terms, it was almost exclusively masculine. Far from representing "the working class" as a whole, this concept of class referred mainly to the elite of skilled white workers. The primary direction of recent historiography, moving beyond the "new" labor history, is to dismantle this old category of class, exposing its racial and gender exclusiveness, and in so doing to open the way to a more genuinely inclusive labor history.

Many historians would agree that the most innovative area in American historical scholarship over the past two decades has been the history of women and gender. Much of the initial work in this area involved restoring a voice to silenced women, putting them back in the historical narrative as agents of their own history. More innovative than this approach (often referred to as "herstory") has been work which moves beyond the history of women to the history of gender, locating gender throughout the field of labor history as a whole. Instead of writing the history of women, or adding a few token women to the existing narrative (an approach known as "add women and stir"), recent historians have pointed out that social relations and social meanings are themselves encoded with gendered meanings.

The most influential work in this regard has been done by Joan Scott (1988) and Ava Baron (1991). Gender, for these historians, is a form of meaning based on perceived differences between the sexes: men and women are biologically different, but the meanings we attach to those differences are the basis of gender. Gender is at the heart of all social relationships, and searching for it is an excellent way of discerning how power works in any society. Gender is not just a matter of women in history, or their relationship with men; it is a question of how masculine and feminine meanings are socially ascribed to all sorts of activities, whether politics or war or homemaking. Gender is unstable rather than fixed. It changes with time, rather than standing outside history. Thus, people's understanding of class is also based on certain assumptions about gender, and a new task for labor historians is to study how the meaning of "class" was constituted and how it changed over time.

Using this powerful and flexible approach, recent historians of labor have begun to dismantle the universalist claims of class consciousness at the heart of much of the "new" labor history. Not only do some of the classic works, such as Thompson's *The Making of the English Working Class*, contain very little information on women, they take for granted that class is by definition a masculine category. But what about women who worked? Were they without a class position, without class consciousness? Related to this, historians of gender have dismantled old distinctions between public and private, between waged work and unpaid housework, asking why only waged work conducted outside the home has traditionally been taken as the proper subject of labor history. On what grounds can this exclusion be justified, other than the same forms of exclusion which confined women to the private realm in the first place? If women, in all their varieties of work, are to be properly included in labor history, then what sense is to be made of the type of work they have always done most often, unpaid work within the home? How is this sort of work to be included in the narrative of labor history, and how does it relate to the traditional category of class? These were only some of the fruitful questions about gender, recently posed and yet to be adequately addressed, as historians moved in the 1990s into the largely uncharted territory lying beyond the "new" labor history.

In much the same way, historians in the 1980s and 1990s began to ask new questions about the significance of race in nineteenth-century American labor history. Part of this project was the equivalent of "herstory," a much-needed reconstruction of the lives of black, Asian, and other "minority" Americans in a fairly conventional form of labor history, based on the usual categories of culture, community, and agency. More innovative, and increasingly influential, was the approach of historians like David Roediger (1991) who concentrated on the new area of white racial formation, examining how white workers came to have a sense of their racial identity in the nineteenth century. This insistence that white people, and not just so-called "minorities," have a racial identity served as the basis for some of the best labor historiography of the 1990s. Roediger persuasively demonstrated that the nineteenth-century conception of class was not only masculine in its gender coding but white (or better yet Anglo-Saxon) in its racial coding. The starting-point for this analysis was the assumption that exploited white workers in the nineteenth century (who described themselves as wage slaves) might have made common cause with another group of exploited workers, the African American slaves. That they did not could be explained by what Roediger called "the wages of whiteness:" by embracing whiteness, workers gained various social and cultural benefits, while at the same time inserting a tragic and ever-widening gulf between themselves and black Americans. The history of the American working classes, therefore, was intimately bound up with the formation of a white racial identity.

This argument was applied by several historians, including Roediger, to Irish immigrant laborers in the antebellum era, whose extreme poverty held out an even greater promise of solidarity with African Americans and whose gradual absorption into the ranks of "whiteness" and consequent virulent racism reveal "the wages of whiteness" in its starkest form. While this line of enquiry in nineteenth-century labor history has opened up an important new investigation into white racial identity, some have criticized its implicit assumption that white and black workers *ought* to have united, and its related tendency at times to blame white workers, especially Irish ones, for not doing so.

The re-writing of labor history along the lines suggested here only began to get under way in the 1990s. Much of what has been written is as yet theoretical rather than empirical in form; historians have produced numerous essays suggesting where labor history now needs to go, but they are only just beginning to write books taking us in that direction. The new emphasis on language, discourse, and identity that emerged in American history generally from the 1980s onward (sometimes referred to as "post-structuralism" or the "linguistic" turn) posed a major challenge to nineteenth-century labor history. The guiding assumption of most labor historians until the 1980s (and many since that time) was that there existed a separate, identifiable, social world, composed of objective social classes determined by relations of production, and that individuals became conscious of that world through class struggle. Class consciousness, in short, was perception of the social world as it really was, a perception that historians of nineteenth-century labor could gain for themselves by studying the words of the workers who lived at that time.

Beginning in the 1980s, the tidy certainties of this approach to history were quickly undermined. Historians no longer agreed that language, in this case the evidence left by past workers, simply reflects and describes the world in some transparent and uncomplicated way. Instead, they emphasized how "discourse" worked to produce meaning. The term "discourse" can mean many different things; in the hands of recent critics of labor history, inspired by the work of Michel Foucault via Joan Scott, it signified forms of knowledge (for example, gender or race) permeating society as a whole. Discourse, in this sense, was "non-referential:" far from being a mere representation of objective social relations existing somehow prior to or outside it, discourse was itself the medium of social power. In this scheme of things the distinction between the social world and how it is represented in language is rendered invalid; discourse alone becomes the proper subject of historical enquiry. How do discourses work? How do they produce meaning? Above all, how did the discourse of class in nineteenth-century America work? How was it constituted, what were its rules and assumptions? These were among the central questions of labor history in the 1990s, as a new generation of historians cogently argued that the nineteenth-century concept of class had staked its claim to universality only by excluding women and racial and ethnic minorities, placing them beyond the pale of organized labor. Like all forms of identity, in other words, nineteenth-century class identity was constructed in terms of the exclusion and suppression of alternatives.

What, then, became of the master category of "social class"? If everybody who worked in nineteenth-century America – waged and un-waged, skilled and unskilled, male and female, white and non-white – was now included as a legitimate subject for enquiry by labor historians, then the category of class would quickly lose most of its coherence and analytical bite. Yet if the category were limited to include only skilled workers, or white workers, or even wage workers, then it would fail to represent the majority of people who worked in the nineteenth (or any other) century.

At stake is the question of what the proper subject matter of labor history should be. As the study of largely male industrial workers, nineteenth-century labor history made central contributions to American historiography as a whole. As a history of everybody – waged and un-waged, skilled and unskilled, native-born and immigrant, white and "minority" – who worked for a living, labor history would be in danger of becoming the study of society generally. As a genuinely inclusive history, would it be able to retain its identity as a separate subdiscipline? Although this dilemma is perhaps especially acute in nineteenth-century labor history, the question is relevant to many other subdisciplines within the larger field of American historiography. Can a subfield retain a coherent identity if it becomes too inclusive? No solution to this dilemma is in sight, but few practitioners of nineteenth-century US labor history today would be willing to sacrifice the new inclusiveness of their field in the name of disciplinary coherence.

REFERENCES

American Social History Project (1989) *Who Built America? Working People and the Nation's Economy: Politics, Culture and Society*, 2 vols. New York: Pantheon.

Baron, Ava (ed.) (1991) *Work Engendered: Toward a New History of American Labor*. Ithaca, NY: Cornell University Press.

Boydston, Jeanne (1990) *Home and Work: Housework, Wages, and the Ideology of Labor in the Early Republic*. New York: Oxford University Press.

Brody, David (1960) *Steelworkers in America: the Nonunion Era*. Cambridge, Mass.: Harvard University Press.

Commons, John et al. (1918–35) *A History of Labor in the United States*, 4 vols. New York: Augustus M. Kelley, 1966.

Dublin, Thomas (1979) *Women at Work: the Transformation of Work and Community in Lowell, Massachusetts, 1826–1860*. New York: Columbia University Press.

Fink, Leon (1983) *Workingmen's Democracy: the Knights of Labor and American Politics*. Urbana: University of Illinois Press.

Foner, Philip (1947–87) *History of the Labor Movement in the United States*, 8 vols. New York: International Publishers.

Gutman, Herbert (1977) *Work, Culture, and Society in Industrializing America: Essays in American Working-class History*. New York: Vintage.

Kenny, Kevin (1998) *Making Sense of the Molly Maguires*. New York: Oxford University Press.

Krause, Paul (1984) *The Battle for Homestead, 1880–1892: Politics, Culture, and Steel*. Pittsburgh: University of Pittsburgh Press.

Montgomery, David (1967) *Beyond Equality: Labor and the Radical Republicans, 1862–1872*. New York: Alfred A. Knopf.

Montgomery, David (1993) *Citizen Worker: the Experience of Workers in the United States with Democracy and the Free Market during the Nineteenth Century*. New York: Cambridge University Press.

Prude, Jonathan (1983) *The Coming of Industrial Order: Town and Factory Life in Rural Massachusetts, 1810–1860*. New York: Cambridge University Press.

Rachleff, Peter (1984) *Black Labor in the South: Richmond, Virginia, 1865–1900*. Philadelphia: Temple University Press.

Rodgers, Daniel T. (1992) "Republicanism: the career of a concept," *The Journal of American History*, 78, pp. 11–38.

Roediger, David (1991) *The Wages of Whiteness: Race and the Making of the American Working Class*. New York: Verso.

Saxton, Alexander (1971) *The Indispensable Enemy: Labor and the Anti-Chinese Movement in California*. Berkeley, CA: University of California Press.

Scott, Joan W. (1988) *Gender and the Politics of History*. New York: Columbia University Press.

Thompson, E. P. (1963) *The Making of the English Working Class*. London: Gollancz.

Way, Peter (1993) *Common Labour: Workers and the Digging of North American Canals, 1780–1860*. Cambridge: Cambridge University Press.

Wilentz, Sean (1984a) "Against exceptionalism: class consciousness and the American labor movement, 1790–1920," *International Labor and Working Class History*, 26, pp. 1–24.

Wilentz, Sean (1984b) *Chants Democratic: New York City and the Rise of the American Working Class, 1788–1850*. New York: Oxford University Press.

CHAPTER THIRTEEN

The Evolution of the Middle Class

CINDY S. ARON

ALTHOUGH the middle class has played a critical role in American politics and culture since the early nineteenth century, only during the past few decades have historians accorded it serious scholarly attention as a subject worthy of study in its own right. Until about 25 years ago, historians tended to take the middle class as a given – assuming rather than analyzing it. During the 1950s consensus historians, attempting to challenge the claims of an earlier generation of Progressive historians, maintained that what distinguished the history of the United States was the absence of feudalism, the strength of a liberal tradition, the weakness of aristocracy, the limits of working-class discontent, and the failure of socialism. Implicit in such an explanation was the belief that conflict in America did not stem from disagreements between economic classes and that, in some unexamined but fundamental way, Americans were all middle class.

During the 1970s historians began to realize that the nineteenth-century middle class deserved closer investigation, and the source of this new interest lay partly in the political and social ferment of the late 1960s. Young New Left historians, interested in uncovering the history of the "inarticulate," brought renewed attention to the issue of class analysis. E. P. Thompson's magisterial work, *The Making of the English Working Class* (1963), helped to inspire a new generation of American social historians and labor historians who focused their attention first on the development of the American working class. These historians – often searching for sources of working-class consciousness – examined the process of working-class formation and explored the political, economic, and social dimensions of working-class life. It did not take long, however, before scholars realized that understanding how class operated in nineteenth-century America required, as well, an analysis of the formation of the middle class.

Interest in the history of the middle class also emerged from new scholarship in women's history. Many of the early works in American women's history concentrated on Northeastern, white, middle-class women. Historians who grappled to understand the lives of these women needed to explain what it was that made such women middle class. That most nineteenth-century women derived their class standing from either their husbands or fathers proved only a partial answer. As scholars analyzed the economic, family, and cultural experiences of nineteenth-century middle-class women, they invariably raised new questions about the nature of the middle class itself.

Social and labor historians of the late 1960s made class a central concern, while pioneering scholarship in women's history raised questions about the middle class specifically. Still, one of the first studies of the 1970s to deal specifically with the middle class bore the marks of neither the new social history nor the history of women. In his 1976 book, *The Culture of Professionalism*, Burton Bledstein reminded readers that the middle class was, itself, a new social construct in nineteenth-century America. Even the term "middle class" did not appear in an American dictionary until 1889. Most nineteenth-century people would, rather, have used the words "middling sort," "men of middling interests," or the "middling classes." Bledstein's book concentrated on the professional middle class, pointing to the ambition, drive, relentless competitiveness, and energy that characterized middle-class men: people who saw "the individual as an 'escalator,' moving vertically between the floors of the poor and the rich" (Bledstein, 1976: 20). Bledstein explored the means by which ambitious middle-class men sought "a professional basis for an institutional order, a basis in universal and predictable rules to provide a formal context for the competitive spirit of individual egos" (1976: 31). *The Culture of Professionalism* examined the professional and educational institutions that served to create that order and, in the process, to enhance the authority and prestige of middle-class men.

Bledstein was interested primarily in the professionals who inhabited the upper reaches of the middle class during the last half of the nineteenth century. His book, therefore, offered little help in understanding how a middle class originally took shape in early nineteenth-century America. Moreover, when Bledstein wrote "middle class" what he really meant was "middle-class men." Half the middle class remained absent from his analysis.

Much of the scholarship that followed Bledstein made the question of middle-class formation central and focused on the first half of the nineteenth century, a period of dynamic economic and social change. As expanding transportation networks helped to create an internal domestic market, towns and cities emerged where produce of the countryside could be marketed, turned into finished goods, and exchanged for needed services. At the same time the development of commercial and early industrial capitalism brought changes in the organization of work and in the relationship between workers and employers. It was in these new towns and growing cities, particularly in the Northeast, that a recognizable middle class first developed in the United States. And it was here that many historians turned their attention.

In his 1978 book, *A Shopkeeper's Millennium*, Paul Johnson found evidence of a middle class taking shape in Rochester, New York, in the decades of the 1820s and 1830s. Johnson discovered important changes in the behavior of master craftsmen and merchants that suggested a new, "middle-class" outlook on life:

> In 1825 a northern businessman dominated his wife and children, worked irregular hours, consumed enormous amounts of alcohol, and seldom voted or went to church. Ten years later the same man went to church twice a week, treated his family with gentleness and love, drank nothing but water, worked steady hours and forced his employees to do the same, campaigned for the Whig Party, and spent his spare time convincing others that if they organized their lives in similar ways, the world would be perfect. (Johnson, 1978: 8)

What wrought these changes, according to Johnson, were the evangelical revivals of the Second Great Awakening that swept through the state of New York in the 1820s and 1830s. The reforms, particularly temperance, advocated by revivalist preachers such as Charles Grandison Finney, fitted the needs of a group of ambitious and upcoming entrepreneurs. These newly evangelized Christian employers, recognizing the financial benefits that would accrue from a workshop of orderly and sober employees, dispensed or withheld patronage and jobs on the basis of workers' willingness to forgo drink, to behave industriously, and to embrace the revivalists' brand of evangelical Protestantism. In the process, two classes formed in Rochester: a middle class of businessmen and employer-artisans devoted to frugality, abstinence, and religion, and a class of workers who thwarted efforts to control them. For Johnson (1978: 8), revivalism was "the moral imperative around which the northern middle class became a class."

Johnson's book broke interesting new ground, but suffered from one of the same problems as the work of Bledstein. For Johnson, too, middle class meant middle-class men – whether the merchants and master craftsmen who embraced the revival or the workers who resisted the evangelical impulses of their employers. There was little recognition or understanding of what being middle class meant for women or, more importantly, of the role that women played in shaping the American middle class.

By the 1970s historians of women had begun to elaborate an important characteristic of the nineteenth-century middle class: that it defined itself in specifically gendered terms. Historians found a well-articulated domestic ideology in the periodicals, sermons, and advice literature of the 1820s and 1830s. Respectable women were being advised to remain within the domestic arena where they would nurture children, raise virtuous and patriotic sons, soothe their harried and work-weary husbands, preserve morality, and promote religious devotion. Men were assigned the tasks of supporting their families, exercising the franchise, and participating in the market. More prescriptive than descriptive, these ideas nevertheless fitted a world in which some women were losing the important productive function they had once filled within their homes. Instead of women furnishing the food and making the clothing for their families (as they had done for generations), men increasingly worked outside their homes to earn the money necessary to buy what the family needed to eat or to wear. Being middle class increasingly came to be defined as being able to follow this sexual division of labor and abide by the dictates of the domestic ideology. Women who needed to earn wages to help support their families crossed the boundaries that separated the male public sphere from the female domestic sphere. By so doing they failed to meet middle-class standards.

If engaging in forms of wage work disqualified most women from the ranks of the middle class, other women could nevertheless venture beyond the strict confines of their home and still maintain middle-class status. Middle-class women found that they could stretch and manipulate norms of domesticity to include a vast array of activities outside the home. Over the course of the antebellum period large numbers of middle-class women participated in a variety of reform, charitable, religious, and voluntary organizations – often dispensing aid or advice to poorer members of the community. In so doing, such women established and reaffirmed their middle-class identity as they differentiated themselves from the less-fortunate women who were often objects of their ministering and charity.

Women's role within their families also had a significant impact on the formation of an American middle class. Mary Ryan's 1981 study of Oneida County, New York, *The*

Cradle of the Middle Class, posited the following hypothesis: "Early in the nineteenth century the American middle class molded its distinctive identity around domestic values and family practices" (Ryan, 1981: 15). For Ryan, changes in social reproduction – specifically the demise of the patriarchal and community-oriented family of the eighteenth century and its replacement with a more privatized, Victorian family – were instrumental in the development of a middle class. Within such families mothers taught their children (and, more specifically, their sons) to be honest, prudent, and hard-working, character traits that they would need to succeed in the commercial marketplace. Would-be members of the middle class discovered, as well, the importance of limiting the size of their families so they could offer each child sufficient educational, emotional, and financial assistance to maintain and secure middle-class status. The children raised in these families understood what it would take to sustain themselves within the middle class.

Evangelical ferment, ideological dictates about gender roles, and new family patterns were certainly crucial to the development of an American middle class. Combined with important changes in the economy, they went a long way toward explaining how and why a middle class took shape. There were, however, other important elements that contributed to middle-class formation. Stuart Blumin's 1989 book, *The Emergence of the Middle Class*, sought to identify the various components of an "emerging middle-class way of life" and to understand how these various "patterns of experience" made some people conscious of themselves as different from those above and below them on the social ladder (Blumin, 1989: 11).

Blumin, like other scholars, located the cities of the Northeast as the place where middle-class formation first occurred. He found that one of the important determinants of an urban man's middle-class status was his ability to make a living without performing manual labor. Where once the independent artisan had been comfortably situated within the "middling sort" of American society, during the second quarter of the nineteenth century class distinctions were increasingly drawn between manual and non-manual laborers. Small entrepreneurs, clerks, wholesalers, jobbers, and agents – all non-manual workers – frequently earned enough income to enjoy a variety of other "patterns of experience" that, in turn, contributed to and reinforced their class status. Blumin's emerging middle class was distinguished by its higher incomes, its habits of consumption, its ability to enjoy a fairly comfortable standard of living, its tendency to reside in class-segregated neighborhoods, and its emphasis on keeping home separate from the workplace. Ethnicity served to reinforce class boundaries since most immigrant men (primarily Irish and German) worked as manual laborers.

But did this emerging middle class think of itself as a class? Here Blumin (1989: 9–10) revealed "a central paradox in the question of middle-class formation, the building of a class that binds itself together as a social group in part through the common embrace of an ideology of social atomism." The shared experiences of middle-class life, he maintained, created a class awareness – one that did not rely on strictly political manifestations for its coherence. Blumin suggested that the confidence in individualism and distrust of collectivism served, ironically enough, as a unifying ideological structure. The middle class, thus, was "most likely to express awareness of its common attitudes and beliefs as a denial of the significance of class" (Blumin, 1989: 9). It was, according to Blumin, a range of shared experiences rather than a distinct or coherent political agenda that distinguished the emerging middle class.

Blumin's work offered a persuasive explanation of the formation of the middle class in the antebellum years. His book, however, concentrated on the first half of the nineteenth century, devoting only one chapter to the postbellum years – the period when industrialization became more widespread and corporate capitalism came to dominate the economic landscape. These changes had a significant impact on a middle class that had only recently begun to take shape. New to the commercial capitalist economy of the early nineteenth century, the middle class was barely formed before it was already being re-formed.

During the first half of the nineteenth century, the middle class had come to include men who were small entrepreneurs, professionals, clerks, wholesalers, agents, salesmen, and even some skilled artisans and comfortably placed farmers. Diverse as these occupations were, they had shared one characteristic: all had either allowed for or at least held out the promise of independence, autonomy, and self-employment. The small scale of most American businesses had meant that even those men who were employees – clerks, bookkeepers, salesmen – would not have felt as though self-employment and independence were out of reach. A clerk in a small business, for example, would be likely to have seen himself as an apprentice, learning the trade so that he might one day become a partner, open his own establishment, or perhaps marry the boss's daughter and inherit the business. Either the fact or the reasonable expectation of autonomy in the form of self-employment had differentiated middle-class men from their working-class counterparts who, by the second quarter of the nineteenth century, were being relegated to the position of permanent wage workers.

The growth of a corporate economy in the last three decades of the century altered the work of many middle-class men, turning them into white-collar employees. Moreover, the companies for which such men worked were often large establishments, places where hierarchies and bureaucracies replaced the informal structure of the antebellum office. It was highly unlikely that a clerk or bookkeeper would one day become the owner or president of a large corporation. The division of labor that accompanied the bureaucratization of white-collar work meant that these men no longer possessed broad knowledge of the businesses for which they worked. The chances for autonomy and independence – characteristics that had once been vital to the definition of middle-class masculinity – receded as middle-class men joined the ranks of salaried workers.

In the early 1950s sociologist C. Wright Mills offered a dismal picture of what he considered the legacy of this change. The "new middle class," a product of the late nineteenth century, had by the mid-twentieth century become, according to Mills, an army of men in gray-flannel suits. Mills saw white-collar workers as alienated, exploited, powerless, and materialistic, "living out in slow misery their yearning for the quick American climb" (Mills, 1951: xii.)

Historian Olivier Zunz suggested a much less dismal perspective on the creation of this new, salaried middle class. In *Making America Corporate* (1990), Zunz explained the important and dynamic role that the new group of salaried employees played in the development of the economy and culture of the United States. Mid-level managers and white-collar workers, Zunz maintained, were not simply brainless cogs, following orders and fulfilling endless rounds of mind-numbing tasks. They were, rather, instrumental in devising new corporate systems and then in disseminating these innovations throughout the country. In the process they enlarged the size of the middle class and created "modern work culture," a culture from which they drew significant individual rewards and benefits.

The development of the "new middle class" brought with it, as Zunz and others have recognized, significant changes for middle-class women. The expansion of corporate bureaucracies and, with them, the amount of paper to be processed, created the need for a new sort of middle-class worker. In an effort to keep costs down and profits up, corporate managers continued to rationalize and subdivide white-collar labor. As a result, there emerged a new, bottom layer to the white-collar workforce: people responsible for the most routine, repetitive, and least intellectually demanding jobs. File clerks, stenographers, copyists, and typists became part of the white-collar workforce.

Middle-class women proved the ideal candidates for such positions. Schooled in grammar and penmanship, women possessed the necessary literary skills for the jobs. Moreover, culturally prescribed norms made them willing to accept low pay and to demand little in the way of promotion. As middle-class men substituted a climb up the corporate ladder for the increasingly unlikely prospect of self-employment, middle-class women became the recipients of dead-end jobs. Some scholars have argued that such work, while still nominally middle class, had in fact become proletarianized, as machines like typewriters and counting machines contributed to the degradation of middle-class labor. Low paid, repetitive, sometimes mechanized, and with no chance for advancement, such work had more in common with the labor of working-class wage-earners than with that of salaried, middle-class employees.

However problematic the nature of this work, it is clear that by the late nineteenth century increasing numbers of middle-class women were not only willing but eager to become white-collar workers. Despite the widespread belief that middle-class women enjoyed the financial support of husbands or fathers, in fact many such women faced the necessity of earning money. Families where male breadwinners had died, were ill, or had suffered financial reverses found themselves relying upon female members. And women without male protectors – widows and needy but respectable single women – needed to find means of support. Until the federal government began to employ women as clerical workers in the early 1860s, teaching school, often for very low salaries, remained the main wage-earning opportunity for such women. Consequently, when corporate and government bureaucracies began to offer jobs to women, they found an enthusiastic response.

Middle-class women had proceeded far beyond the boundaries of the home by the late decades of the nineteenth century, engaging in a wide range of reform and community organizations. But women's entrance into office work breached the divide between men's and women's spheres in a more direct and challenging way. Women were placing themselves in a formerly all-male environment, and the presence of women in corporate and government offices forced the middle class to rewrite many of its old rules. In newly sexually integrated offices, middle-class men had to alter how they behaved at work. The spittoons that had once graced many offices began to disappear and men were sometimes forbidden to smoke at work. In other words, women succeeded in bringing some of the standards and decorum of the parlor into their new workplaces. At the same time, female office workers were forced to relin-quish certain protections that the middle class had traditionally afforded to women. Women clerks learned, for example, to interact with strange men, to negotiate the streets of urban business districts, and to compete in the business environment. The "new" white-collar middle class of the late nineteenth century thus went a long way toward revising the tenets of the domestic ideology that had attended the formation of the "old" middle class.

What, then, did it mean to be middle class and how did that meaning change over the course of the nineteenth century? For antebellum men, it meant not performing manual labor and, if possible, remaining independent and self-employed. For early nineteenth-century women, it meant abiding by the dictates of the domestic ideology and remaining, if possible, out of the world of waged work. The growth of the white-collar labor force in the decades after the Civil War altered these standards somewhat. Middle-class men were forced to relinquish self-employment for salaried labor in growing bureaucracies, and it became possible for women with financial needs to maintain their middle-class standing while entering corporate and government offices.

Although the nature of middle-class work changed over the course of the century, many other characteristics of the middle class remained constant. Middle-class people continued to limit the number of children they had, to guard and privilege the privacy of their families, to live in increasingly class-segregated parts of the city, and to enjoy the benefits of a fairly comfortable standard of living. Being middle class also meant ascribing to certain values, many of which were inherited from eighteenth-century republican thought and reinforced in the evangelical Protestant revivals of the Second Great Awakening. Middle-class men and women endorsed hard work, frugality, integrity, virtue, discipline, and individualism. Moreover, they took pains to teach these values to their children.

But this picture suggests a stability and security that much of the middle class in all likelihood did not feel. Middle-class people were on the move, both socially and geographically. Throughout the century would-be members of the middle class migrated from countryside to towns, in the process turning those towns into cities. Members of the middle class were certainly aware that their lives differed in marked ways from that of the working class that was taking shape around them. Working-class people, many of them immigrants, worked at manual labor, relied on the wages and productive work of many members of the household (including women and children), and often were still unable to meet basic needs. The definition of middle class derived its meaning, in part, from the contrast with the conditions of the people at the bottom of the social ladder. Middle-class people were imbued with the possibilities for social advancement, but also understood the ever-present possibility of financial decline.

The sources of insecurity for members of the urban middle class were not only economic but cultural. As numerous scholars in the early 1980s began to examine the economic, familial, and occupational dimensions of middle-class life, a few turned their attention to the cultural history of the middle class. In *Confidence Men and Painted Women* (1982), Karen Halttunen found that the urban middle class was disquieted by the problems of pretense and hypocrisy. In small villages or rural areas people had looked to families, communities, and churches to patrol boundaries and keep unwanted or potentially troublesome people away. But the cities in which middle-class people increasingly lived were populated by strangers. How was one to protect oneself from unsavory or dangerous people who might cheat, steal, or – worse – lead the young astray? Members of the middle class worried about the ease with which people could (and indeed sometimes did) pretend to be who they were not. In such an environment hypocrisy was not merely a harmless personal foible but a potentially dangerous threat to the social fabric.

Advice literature attempted to solve the problem by stressing the importance of sincerity. If people behaved with absolute sincerity in the marketplace, the street, and the parlor, then the security of small-town or rural life could be transferred to the social interactions of the city. By the 1850s, however, it was becoming clear that urging people to behave sincerely would neither solve the problems nor eliminate the dangers that an increasingly mobile, urban culture presented. The middle class came, instead, to rely upon a detailed code of rituals and manners. John Kasson's book, *Rudeness and Civility* (1990), offers a fascinating account of the role and function of etiquette in middle-class urban life. In "the anonymous metropolis," middle-class people came to realize that they would have to withstand public scrutiny and win public approval (Kasson, 1990: 7). Middle-class status rested, in part, on claims to a publicly recognized respectability, a respectability gained by adhering to elaborate and complicated rules of etiquette that governed every minute aspect of life. Reliance on etiquette signalled the middle class's capitulation to a culture that privileged outward forms of behavior, despite their knowledge that polite conduct might mask inner deficiencies. Respectable middle-class people would understand the proper ways to dress, speak, pay social calls, and write letters, as well as how to stifle a sneeze or a yawn, to walk with dignity, and to avert their gaze when necessary.

The rules of etiquette pointed to middle-class concerns with self-control – not only social but physical. And perhaps no form of physical self-control was more important to the middle class than the sexual. Scholars remain in some dispute about how best to characterize Victorian sexuality. Some have maintained that nineteenth-century men and women were extremely sexually repressed and that the need for sexual self-control manifested itself in both public and private matters – from the 1873 Comstock Law that forbade obscene material from being sent through the mail to widespread fears about the dangers of masturbation. Nineteenth-century medical opinion allegedly held that proper middle-class women were devoid of sexual desires and that they submitted to sexual intercourse only to fulfill wifely duties.

Other historians dispute such findings. These scholars point to scattered but persuasive evidence that many respectable, middle-class people indulged in and enjoyed sexual activity without experiencing guilt or censure and that nineteenth-century physicians were divided on whether or not respectable women experienced sexual needs. Since most middle-class people were loath to write about their sexual lives, the sources remain sketchy and definitive answers elusive. Still, it seems clear that one of the definitions of middle-class respectability in the nineteenth century remained at least a public adherence to strict codes of sexual conduct.

The most thorough and sweeping exploration of the importance of respectability in the process of middle-class formation comes from the fine work of Richard Bushman. In *The Refinement of America* (1992), Bushman examined the cultural world that the emerging middle class created in the early nineteenth century. Using both literary sources and evidence of material culture, Bushman explained how middling folks made themselves middle class by appropriating forms of gentility that had character-ized the eighteenth-century gentry. Bushman identified a "vernacular gentility" that took numerous forms among the early nineteenth-century middle class: rugs for their floors, parlors for their homes, schools and libraries for their communities. The process of class differentiation, however, derived not just from acquiring possessions but from the meaning that those possessions imparted:

> The parlors meant more than that the owners were rich . . . Creating parlors as a site for a refined life implied a spiritual superiority. Parlor people claimed to live on a higher plain than the vulgar and coarse populace, to excel them in their inner beings. Pecuniary display was outward and by definition superficial; refinement was inward and profound. (Bushman, 1992: 182)

Having both the outward trappings of gentility and the title to inner refinement served to differentiate middle-class people from those below them and, moreover, gave them a claim to similarity with those above them. Bushman (1992: 274) explained: "The great divide in American society as refinement diffused into the middling ranks lay not between the small and great parlor houses, but between houses with parlors and those with none." Members of the lower orders found themselves isolated and marginalized. People who could or would not attempt to participate in the culture of respectability – by learning the rules of polite behavior and by bringing some of the accoutrements of refinement into their homes – had no place among the company of the genteel. At the same time, those people who possessed a slight modicum of resources *and* who were willing to put those resources toward the acquisition of refinement could lay claim toward respectability and, with it, middle-class status.

Refined culture spread in the early nineteenth century in a variety of ways. Etiquette books and sentimental literature informed people how to behave, but the increasingly commercial, industrial economy also played a critical role. Many of the trappings of refinement needed to be purchased, and savvy entrepreneurs quickly learned to manufacture and sell what the would-be middle class required. Capitalism, according to Bushman (1992: 408), "did not invent genteel culture, rather it exploited it."

The acquisition of refinement, however, posed definite problems for the middle class. After all, gentility and refinement had their source in an aristocratic order – one that prized luxury and idleness. The emerging nineteenth-century middle class, however, deplored those qualities. Hard work, discipline, and self-control – the very things that allowed for the accumulation of resources necessary for the purchase of refinement – remained the cardinal middle-class virtues. Middle-class people were, after all, suspicious of luxury and fearful of idleness. Numerous middle-class writers and commentators recognized these contradictions and offered various ways to solve the problems that gentility posed. But, as Bushman's book revealed, the tensions inherent in the quest for gentility remained central to middle-class culture.

Bushman's work not only explored the critically important cultural dimension of middle-class life, but offered compelling evidence of a middle class living beyond the boundaries of cities. Most scholarship on the nineteenth-century middle class has maintained that middle-class formation was primarily an urban phenomenon. Cities, after all, offered the sorts of non-manual, white-collar labor that characterized middle-class work, the reform and voluntary organizations that drew middle-class interests, and the consumer and cultural amenities that defined middle-class culture.

Bushman's work revealed how middling folks in small villages and rural areas embraced refinement and, in the process, made themselves middle class. The small village of Smyrna, Delaware, for example, lay 15 miles south of Dover and claimed a population of only 1,800 people. By the mid-nineteenth century, Smyrna had established "the institutions of refinement essential to the self-respect of the aspiring middle class": a boarding school, a library, two hotels, and stores that sold jewelry, carriages, and fine china (Bushman, 1992: 225–6). And places like Smyrna appeared throughout the landscape; predominantly in the Northeast but in rural areas of the West and (less frequently) the South. It was, in fact, this widespread embrace of genteel culture that helped to create a "national market for genteel goods and fashions, a market large enough to power industrialization" (Bushman, 1992: 399).

If Bushman challenged the notion that the middle class was necessarily urban, other historians have recently questioned another longstanding assumption: that the nineteenth-century middle class was white. Until the beginning of this decade most scholars, in fact, ignored the issue of race almost entirely and took for granted that middle class meant white. But important recent scholarship reveals that an African-American middle class emerged in the last half of the nineteenth century. Examining the African-American middle class requires looking at the category of class both within and across racial boundaries.

In the decades after the Civil War the majority of African Americans remained poor – often desperately poor – as they struggled for education, economic stability, and political rights. These goals eluded most African Americans, who worked as tenant farmers or labored in white people's kitchens. A small minority of freedmen and women, however, succeeded in accumulating enough skills, education, property, or financial resources to establish the lifestyle of the middle class. In the immediate post-Civil War years this class drew some of its members from antebellum free blacks and others from the ranks of more advantaged former slaves – house slaves or slave children of white masters. By the 1880s a younger generation of African Americans, educated in the missionary and government schools of Reconstruction, made their way into the ranks.

Historians differ over how to identify or understand this population. Indeed, many dispute whether "middle class" is, in fact, an apt characterization. These African-American men and women were clearly not in the middle. They were, rather, the elite within African-American society, hence historian William Gatewood's identification of them as "aristocrats of color." Gatewood's 1990 book of the same name explored the importance of class within the African-American community. In a dominant white culture that designated all blacks as degraded, immoral, and inferior, class distinctions offered one avenue for disproving white racist theories. Those who could accumulate wealth and display respectability could prove that all blacks were not the same, that some clearly had proven their right to full economic and political citizenship.

Gatewood's "aristocrats of color" lived primarily in cities where they comprised an elite within the black community. They were distinguished by their wealth, the lightness of their skin color, their educational achievements, and their mastery of the codes of gentility. But unlike white aristocrats, members of the African-American elite were not people of leisure. They resembled the white middle class both in the necessity that they worked and in some of the occupations they held. Many were professionals or government employees. Some, however, worked at occupations that, by the late nineteenth century, were no longer considered middle class in the white community. Successful barbers, tailors, and caterers, for example, accumulated enough wealth to climb into the ranks of the African-American elite. At the same time the considerable wealth that some blacks accumulated in these occupations, combined with successful investments in real estate, made them far richer than many members of the white middle class. Thus, race affected the criteria for membership of the middle class.

Janette Greenwood's 1994 study of Charlotte, North Carolina, *Bittersweet Legacy*, also examined the formation of a small class of prosperous and respectable African Americans. But for a number of reasons she, too, preferred not to call them "middle class." For Greenwood, the term "middle class" connoted a group with "significant economic and political power," the sort of power that blacks never possessed in New South Charlotte. Moreover, "middle" implied a group "sandwiched between an elite and a working class." The social structure of black Charlotte, however, was "two-tiered" (Greenwood, 1994: 5). Greenwood found the term "better class" a more useful way to designate the important group of African-American business and professional people.

Charlotte's black "better class" differed in significant ways from the big city "aristocrats of color." They were less concerned with skin tones and less likely to have had free black ancestors. The black "better class," rather, had been born in the last decade of slavery and had been the beneficiaries of the educational opportunities of Reconstruction. Often taught in schools of northern white missionaries, they had embraced the values of self-discipline and morality that their teachers had promoted. By the mid-1880s they had become professionals, merchants, teachers, ministers, and artisans and had formed a network of educational, self-improvement, and social organizations.

Before Jim Crow came to North Carolina in the late 1890s, many members of Charlotte's black "better class" worked actively with their white counterparts in local and state-wide prohibition campaigns. The effort for prohibition was critically important to members of the black "better class," offering them an opportunity to make alliances with white prohibitionists, to reaffirm their commitment to standards of discipline and propriety, and to distance themselves from the black lower orders. As they worked with white counterparts, African-American prohibition-ists hoped to disprove racist ideas and to assert their claim to a place among the better classes.

Neither Gatewood's "aristocrats of color" nor Greenwood's "better class" were technically in the middle of the African-American social structure, but they still shared many of the cultural values and styles of living that characterized the white middle class during the last half of the nineteenth century. These were people, for example, who knew the importance of education. Perhaps more so than their white counter-parts, African-American parents took great pains to make sure that their children received the best education available.

Most importantly, African Americans subscribed to a range of values and codes that were widely embraced by the white middle class. Gentility, respectability, self-disci-pline, virtue, thrift, morality – these were critically important guides to how African-American middle-class people governed their lives. Culturally, then, it makes sense to speak of a nineteenth-century black middle class, although it is important to recognize that the middle-class values blacks and whites shared served somewhat different purposes for the two races. While both whites and blacks used middle-class norms as tools to achieve economic security and upward mobility, blacks saw that the adoption of these ideals served a political purpose as well. As historian Glenda Gilmore (1996: 3) has explained, "By embracing a constellation of Victorian middle-class values – temperance, thrift, hard work, piety, learning – African Americans believed that they could carve out space for dignified and successful lives and that their examples would wear away prejudice." By behaving respectably, middle-class African Americans hoped that they could disprove white racist ideas, eliminate bigotry, and allow African Americans to claim a full range of political and economic rights.

There was, however, a persistent tension within the black middle class that attended their embrace of white norms of respectability. Middle-class blacks were consciously trying to separate themselves from the black lower orders in order to prove to whites that all blacks were not ignorant, degraded, and inferior. They also, however, felt a responsibility to uplift those very masses from whom they were working to distance themselves.

African-American middle-class men and women worked actively on behalf of the less fortunate members of their communities. If their efforts sometimes belied a patronizing attitude, they nevertheless were laboring in what they thought were the best interests of their race. Historian Evelyn Brooks Higginbotham (1993) has elaborated a "politics of respectability" that particularly characterized the reform efforts of middle-class black women. Working through the Baptist Women's Convention, African-American women worked hard to "implant middle-class values and behavioral patterns among the masses of urban blacks." Such efforts took on special significance for women because of dominant white stereotypes that characterized all black women as sexually immoral (Higginbotham, 1993: 195–6). Mary Church Terrel, a leader in the community of African-American women, knew that "colored women of education and culture . . . cannot escape altogether the consequences of their most depraved sisters," and so she urged women of her class to work diligently on behalf of the less fortunate (quoted in Gatewood, 1990: 244). Lower-class African Americans sometimes resented the patronizing attitudes, elite airs, and reforming campaigns of middle-class blacks. As a result, class could and sometimes did become a divisive wedge within the African-American community.

While middle-class blacks hoped that uplifting the masses would help to ensure their own success in a culture dominated by white racist ideas, their tenacious and determined efforts at reform and uplift were far more than self-serving. Middle-class African Americans went beyond imploring the masses to adopt codes of genteel behavior. They engaged in a wide range of educational and social service endeavors designed to improve the lives of vast numbers of African Americans. Middle-class African Americans were less enamored of the value of individualism than were their white counterparts, understanding that individualism was one middle-class ideal that they did not have the luxury to embrace. Living in a society dominated by extreme forms of racism, African Americans understood the importance of taking collective responsibility for improvement within their communities.

By the end of the nineteenth century a small but growing number of African Americans had assumed their place within the ranks of an emerging black middle class. Despite the racism that they witnessed and experienced, many had hopes that by working hard and embracing white middle-class virtues they could translate their economic gains into full political rights. The arrival of Jim Crow in the late years of the century dashed those hopes, and forced many middle-class blacks to accept

Booker T. Washington's compromise, settling for a modicum of economic stability but seeing the promise of full citizenship fade.

The scholarship of the past 25 years has revealed that the middle class was a product of the early nineteenth century, formed initially in the flush of an expanding domestic market economy and early industrialization, and then re-formed as large-scale corporate capitalism came to dominate the American landscape. More importantly, the rich historiography of the past decade has shown that the middle class was far more complex than even its varied occupational or financial profile suggests. The cultural ideals of the middle class held out the democratizing promise that anyone could, with a little effort, achieve middle-class status. At the same time, those who either declined or were unable to do so were blamed for their failure – suffering not just the hardships of poverty but the onus of disrespectability as well. Moreover, the cultural history of the past decade has uncovered deep tensions within both the black and white middle class. Genteel lifestyles to which middle-class people aspired conflicted, for African Americans, with the need for collective efforts at racial progress and, for whites, with the values of self-control, hard work, frugality, and discipline that they held most dear.

Connecting the rich cultural, social, and economic history of the middle class to the issue of politics remains a central challenge for historians of the nineteenth century. It seems time, perhaps, to question Blumin's contention that the middle class was, by its very nature, non-political. An excellent, recent book by Rebecca Edwards, *Angels in the Machinery* (1997), has enriched the study of the nineteenth century by pointing to the importance of gender and the role of middle-class women in party politics. Edwards's work reveals that these women were motivated both by class and gender issues to participate actively in Republican, Democratic, and Populist party campaigns. How middle-class values, tensions, and issues informed American politics, and how politics shaped the middle class are questions that loom on the historiographical horizon.

REFERENCES

Aron, Cindy Sondik (1987) *Ladies and Gentlemen of the Civil Service: Middle-class Workers in Victorian America*. New York: Oxford University Press.

Bledstein, Burton J. (1976) *The Culture of Professionalism: the Middle Class and the Development of Higher Education in America*. New York: W. W. Norton.

Blumin, Stuart M. (1989) *The Emergence of the Middle Class: Social Experience in the American City, 1769–1900*. Cambridge: Cambridge University Press.

Bushman, Richard L. (1992) *The Refinement of America: Persons, Houses, Cities*. New York: Vintage.

D'Emilio, John and Freedman, Estelle B. (1988) *Intimate Matters: a History of Sexuality in America*. New York: Harper and Row.

Edwards, Rebecca B. (1997) *Angels in the Machinery: Gender in American Party Politics from the Civil War to the Progressive Era*. New York: Oxford University Press.

Gatewood, Willard B. (1990) *Aristocrats of Color: the Black Elite, 1880–1920*. Bloomington, Ind: Indiana University Press.

Gilkeson Jr, John S. (1986) *Middle-class Providence, 1820–1940*. Princeton, NJ: Princeton University Press.

Gilmore, Glenda Elizabeth (1996) *Gender and Jim Crow: Women and the Politics of White Supremacy in North Carolina, 1896–1920*. Chapel Hill, NC: University of North Carolina Press.

Greenwood, Janette Thomas (1994) *Bittersweet Legacy: the Black and White "Better Classes" in Charlotte, 1850–1910*. Chapel Hill, NC: University of North Carolina Press.

Halttunen, Karen (1982) *Confidence Men and Painted Women: a Study of Middle-class Culture in America, 1830–1870*. New Haven, Conn.: Yale University Press.

Hartz, Louis (1955) *The Liberal Tradition in America: an Interpretation of American Political Thought since the Revolution*. New York: Harcourt, Brace.

Hewitt, Nancy (1984) *Women's Activism and Social Change: Rochester, New York, 1822–1872*. Ithaca, NY: Cornell University Press.

Higginbotham, Evelyn Brooks (1993) *Righteous Discontent: the Women's Movement in the Black Baptists Church, 1880–1920*. Cambridge, Mass.: Harvard University Press.

Johnson, Paul E. (1978) *A Shopkeeper's Millennium: Society and Revival in Rochester, New York, 1815–1837*. New York: Hill and Wang.

Kasson, John F. (1990) *Rudeness and Civility: Manners in Nineteenth-century Urban America*. New York: Hill and Wang.

Lystra, Karen (1989) *Searching the Heart: Women, Men and Romantic Life in Nineteenth-century America*. New York: Oxford University Press.

Mills, C. Wright (1951) *White Collar: the American Middle Classes*. New York: Oxford University Press.

Ryan, Mary P. (1981) *The Cradle of the Middle Class: the Family in Oneida County, New York, 1790–1865*. Cambridge: Cambridge University Press.

Thompson, E. P. (1963) *The Making of the English Working Class*. New York: Vintage.

Zunz, Olivier (1990) *Making America Corporate, 1870–1920*. Chicago: University of Chicago Press.

PART IV

Race, Gender, and Ethnicity

CHAPTER FOURTEEN

African Americans

DONALD R. WRIGHT

T WO groups of experiences, one in slavery and one in freedom, underlie the
history of African Americans in the nineteenth century. Prior to the Civil War,
most blacks were slaves in a young country struggling to find its place in an Atlantic-
oriented world involved in slave-based production for a European market. Most
struggled after the war as free men and women to create decent lives in a country
increasingly involved in industrial and agricultural production for a larger market in
which the white majority embraced popular notions of black inferiority. One of the
telling points of nineteenty-century African-American history is that the experiences
in slavery and freedom held so many similarities.

But recent scholarship has shown that mere focus on African Americans as slaves
and then as free persons hides enormous individual variety. Slave or free, urban or
rural, North or South, old or young, accommodating or rebellious, content with their
lot or enterprising and ambitious, African Americans had differing experiences in the
same locales throughout the nineteenth century. Questions about how they became
involved in, and reacted to, such experiences defy simple answers. African-American
men and women were complex individuals, sometimes rational and sometimes not, in
situations that nearly always were difficult in the extreme, but were far more complex
than we have led ourselves to believe.

Formative Times during the Early Republic

At the beginning of the nineteenth century, African Americans in the United States,
though nearly all slaves, had reasons to be optimistic. The libertarian underpinnings of
the American Revolution had started the ending of slavery north of Maryland and had
brought a wave of individual emancipation in the upper South that created the first
noticeable body of free persons of African descent in the country. With a sense that the
Atlantic slave trade would end after 1807 as soon as the Constitution allowed; with an
idea that Congress might ban slavery in new territories, as it had done with the
Northwest Territory in 1787; with a sense that more white landowners might yield
to humanitarian pressures for manumission; and with a growing sense of themselves as
part of an African-American community, close in identity to freedom-seeking blacks
on Saint Domingue (soon to be Haiti) in the Caribbean, there was hope that greater
freedom and opportunity might be in the wind.

But such optimism was necessarily short lived. In fact, a larger number of blacks in
the United States had equally good reason to hold a grim outlook on their future. The
Constitution, in respecting rights to property above all, recognized and sanctioned

slavery without naming it. The racism prevalent at the time was evident in some of the early acts of Congress, one limiting acquisition of citizenship to white immigrants and another restricting militia participation to white men. Particularly prescient blacks may have realized that the institution of slavery that bound so many of their lives was not dying away where it was most profitable in the lower South. In that part of the new country, where prominent citizens opposed entering a Union that threatened their right to own human beings, budding white elites were perpetuating a slave regime as they extended settlement westward. The continuing importation of African slaves – over 100,000 between 1783 and 1808 – showed the country's willingness to allow its system of slave-based agriculture to recover following the revolution and then to extend into new areas of settlement in the South.

If these signs were not ominous enough to make American blacks dread for their future, the slow, steady expansion of cotton production should have tipped the scale. The nineteenth century dawned on an African-American population that was not far away, geographically or chronologically, from participating in one of the greatest booms in commercial agriculture of its time: the rise of America's Cotton Kingdom. Industrial technology was at the heart of slave-based cotton production in the United States. England's Industrial Revolution had begun in the textile mills in the last half of the eighteenth century, and by the start of the nineteenth such factories were dependent on huge supplies of raw cotton. The invention and improvement of cotton gins to clean raw cotton made its production in the United States feasible. Then, steady acquisition of new lands in the South and their opening to settlement following the Creek Wars in 1814 brought a growing stream of white planters to carve out cotton plantations. Through the first half of the nineteenth century American cotton production soared, and Louisiana experienced a sugar boom. With enslaved African-American men and women comprising the major group of laborers on the plantations and smaller farms, demand for slaves seemed almost insatiable across the American South from the end of the War of 1812 to the 1850s.

The Atlantic trade helped meet early slave demand in America until 1808. But, then, where were laborers to come from? The answer, ultimately, was through a domestic slave trade. The systematic buying, transporting, and selling of slaves, from the old centers of tobacco and rice production along the Eastern seaboard to the new centers of cotton production in the lower South, became a dreaded annual phenomenon for many. On average, every decade between 1820 and 1860 saw over 200,000 enslaved men, women, and children of African descent uprooted and sent south. Michael Tadman (1989) provides an account of the domestic slave trade that bursts many a myth about the kindliness of slaveowners. Profit rather than paternalism ruled in the marketplace, and thus the trade broke marriages and separated parents from children. For the enslaved humans involved, it was the wrenching experience of a lifetime.

The expansion of cotton production in the American South and the domestic slave trade set the stage for much of nineteenth-century African-American history. Slavery's move south strengthened the institution and made it a sectional matter, establishing the basis for the Civil War that would end slavery in the country. The domestic slave trade rapidly turned the Black Belt, running from central Georgia through Alabama and Mississippi to Louisiana, into the center of the country's black population and the place where America's distinct African-American culture would be reshaped into a form that would carry it into the twentieth century. And in large part it was the actions of masters, who separated families and sold off faithful hands in the domestic trade, that convinced blacks of the cruel insensitivity of whites and made black and white relations all the more difficult over the years following emancipation.

The time of the early republic was formative for free African Americans as well. There had been free persons of African descent in the colonies since the middle of the seventeenth century, but not many – perhaps 30,000 in 1770, not 5 percent of the black population. But the years of the American Revolution witnessed the ending of slavery in the North and enough manumission in the upper South to create a sizeable free black population, numbering nearly a quarter of a million by 1820. In the early decades of the nineteenth century this self-aware group discovered the racial limits on its freedom. At this time, too, free African Americans developed ways to cope with what seemed like life in a tunnel, lined with discrimination and unequal opportunity, without much of a glimmer of light at the end.

Antebellum Slavery

If there has been a great debate in African-American historiography, it has been about the nature of the slave experience. The long-accepted interpretation of America's peculiar institution was racist, based on the assumption of the inherent inferiority of peoples of African descent. Ulrich B. Phillips, in *American Negro Slavery* (1918), used evidence from plantation records to support ideas that on the whole masters were benevolent; that enslaved men and women were shiftless and sensual, loyal but lazy; and that the plantation was "in fact, a school constantly training and controlling pupils who were in a backward state of civilization" (Phillips, 1918: 342). The first widely accepted revision of Phillips's interpretation did not appear until after the landmark Supreme Court ruling against segregated education and midway through Montgomery, Alabama's bus boycott. Using many of the same records as Phillips, Kenneth M. Stampp in *The Peculiar Institution: Slavery in the Antebellum South* (1956) exposed as myth the idea of harmonious race relations in slavery and con-demned the institution for its brutality. A scholar who took Stampp's arguments a step further was Stanley Elkins, whose *Slavery: a Problem in American Institutional and Intellectual Life* (1959) used interpersonal theory from sociology and psychology to argue that the southern plantation was so harsh, with the master being the slaves' only "significant other," that enslaved men and women were rendered docile and childlike, an experience Elkins compared with that of the Jews in the Nazi concentra-tion camps of World War II. Subsequent revisions in the early 1970s, in books by John W. Blassingame (1972) and Leslie Howard Owens (1976), using evidence provided by slaves as well as masters, showed a strong black culture in the slave quarters, away from the masters' eyes, and a range of personality types among individuals. More recently, studies have emphasized the variety in the slave experience, with important regional and temporal differences reflecting the general complexity of life itself.

It seems unnecessary to point out that, since slavery was an institution of forced labor, the kind of work the slaves did had the biggest effect on the way they led their lives. Yet, for a time historians placed so much emphasis on slave society, religion, and culture that they tended to overlook what life in bondage was all about – which was hard work. A 1989 conference at the University of Maryland, papers from which were published, with an insightful introduction by the editors Ira Berlin and Philip D.

Morgan, as *Cultivation and Culture: Labor and the Shaping of Slave Life in the Americas* (1993), helped right this imbalance. Masters wanted their slaves to work as much as humanly possible, and they had the law and brute force on their side; slaves resisted these efforts by malingering, breaking tools or damaging crops, running off, or refusing to work. What came out of the continuous, if often tacit, negotiations were mutually agreed-upon standards of how much work was "enough." Of course, "enough" varied according to crop, season, demand, size of slaveholdings, even individual personality. Work in sugar, as in Louisiana, was the most taxing; work in rice, in the South Carolina and Georgia low country, was next; cotton in the central Deep South required more work than the tobacco and grain production of Virginia and Maryland.

Most crops had seasons of peak labor – sugar cane, once harvested, required nearly constant work for a month to prevent spoilage, for instance – and of less intense work. The crop tended to dictate the organization of the workforce: slaves on rice plantations worked on a task system, where individual men and women had specific tasks to complete in a working day; most other crops lent themselves to gang labor, slaves working in groups under close supervision throughout the day. Slave artisans existed on larger holdings; skilled labor was reserved for men. Enslaved men and women often had enterprises of their own, working to produce additional food or something to sell. Depending on prices for exports versus prices for food crops, masters sometimes encouraged slaves to grow their own provisions.

Following a trend in many fields, some recent work on antebellum slavery has focused on women's issues and health. Women were at a disadvantage in slavery. They did a disproportionate amount of work in the fields (contrary to common notions) because they had only domestic work to take them away from the hard work with staple crops (whereas men had many more out-of-field jobs); they bore and reared children and did family cooking and tending in addition to their work for their masters; and they often were at the mercy of white men, some of whom were sexual predators. As for health, that of slaves was not good, for their day or any day. The American South was a difficult disease environment. People of African descent had their own particular physiological and nutritional problems, notions of hygiene were primitive, and slave diets were grossly deficient. Thus, what many observers viewed as lazy or slow-moving slaves were ill or malnourished human beings. Infants and children suffered most. At mid-century, over half of all slave children died before they reached the age of five – a figure twice that for the United States population at the same time.

What recent study offers of subtle importance is that while slavery was a collective experience, it was, as most of life's situations, one that held room for individual difference. African-American men and women who were enslaved had to work hard and eke out an existence under difficult circumstances. They found a variety of ways of doing so, so that generalizing about everything from personality types to methods of dealing with harsh masters is difficult to do.

Free African Americans

The evolution of scholarship on free blacks over the last third of the century is evident in a comparison of Leon Litwack's *North of Slavery: the Negro in the Free States* (1961) with Ira Berlin's *Slaves without Masters: the Free Negro in the Antebellum South* (1974) and James O. Horton and Lois E. Horton's *In Hope of Liberty: Culture, Community and Protest among Northern Free Blacks, 1700–1860* (1997). Litwack's book was a revelation to whites in that, as he put it, "discrimination against the Negro and a firmly held belief in the superiority of the white race were not restricted to one section but were shared by an overwhelming majority of white Americans in both the North and South" (Litwack, 1961: vii). Though he includes a chapter on African Americans' efforts toward abolition of slavery, Litwack's focus is clearly on what was *done unto* free blacks in the northern states. Berlin's and the Hortons' books also point out the extensive white racism and the severe restrictions under which free blacks lived and worked in the different sections of the country, but their work treats African Americans in the subjective, as opposed to the objective, case. These authors of the post-civil rights movements era emphasize black activities within racist constraints: the establishment of extended families and households; the creation of an African-American community, identity, and culture; and sustained efforts on the part of African Americans to win freedom for all people of African descent.

Litwack's book was startling to northern whites, many of whom were supportive of the sit-ins and freedom rides taking place in southern states at the time the book was published. They identified historically with the abolitionists and the side that had fought to end slavery. Litwack shows how federal and northern state governments, all backed by white opinion, viewed blacks as inferior and carved out a legal status for free blacks that made certain a degraded status, poverty, and humiliation. Some northern states restricted black immigration, disfranchised black citizens, curtailed their legal protections, and permitted extra-legal measures that relegated African Americans to society's lowest level. Even the most religious northerners held strong racist sentiments, and the vaunted abolitionists were ambiguous about race in ways that made them less than admirable. Free African Americans south of the Mason–Dixon line had it worse, because, in Berlin's words (1974: 89), "In a slave society, the free Negro was an incorrigible subversive." Race lumped together southern free blacks with slaves and brought added limits to their liberty. No matter where they lived, however, free blacks had to walk a particularly rough road.

What helped them in their walk was one another. Like most Americans, free blacks developed a sense of community. Theirs was founded in households that included extended families, boarders, and friends. As the nineteenth century progressed, identification with an African-American community broadened steadily as mutual aid societies, fraternal orders, schools, and churches proliferated. The black church, with memberships overlapping with the other organizations, became central to African-American culture. Although some churches dated to the refusal of blacks to accept mistreatment in white-dominated churches, African Americans clearly wanted a religious expression that reflected their culture. Increasingly, as free blacks recognized that their quest for freedom was tied to all others of their race, black churches became places where African Americans led an attack on slavery. In these efforts, churches served as training grounds for black leaders as well as venues where free blacks could gain some education.

One issue that free blacks had to contend with and decide on in both the North and South involved colonization. In the first half of the nineteenth century blacks and whites alike recognized the immense problems surrounding African Americans.

Increasingly denied rights of citizenship, African Americans early in the century attempted to colonize some in their midst along Africa's West Coast. Paul Cuffe, a black Massachusetts shipower and businessman, took one shipload of blacks to Sierra Leone in 1816. Then, white efforts to rid the United States of its free black population under the newly formed American Colonization Society brought money, power, and authority to colonization. Settlement of Liberia on Africa's West Coast was the eventual result. Free African Americans in upper South cities, where slaveowners recognized a threat to the institution of slavery and where opportunities for free blacks were limited most severely, were the ones most interested in emigration. For most blacks born in the United States, however, Africa was part of their heritage, but America was their home. As the Hortons put it (1997: 202), "By the late 1830s most free blacks, while maintaining a delicate balance between seemingly conflicting identities, had declared themselves willing to stand together to demand recognition as colored Americans."

It was at least by that time also that free African Americans were willing to stand together with other blacks to work toward the ending of slavery. The first generation of African Americans in freedom may rightfully have focused on the personal uplift they had been denied. By the 1820s, though, as white colonization efforts grew, as it became clear with Missouri's admission to the Union as a slave state that the federal government was willing to allow slavery's expansion, as white mob violence against blacks worsened, and as American society generally drew clearer racial limits around full citizenship, more and more free blacks recognized that their own liberty was tied to those of their race who remained enslaved. Thus, gradually, African Americans focused more on efforts to bring about the ending of slavery in America.

African Americans and the End of Slavery

African Americans were critical to slavery's demise. Books of a generation ago that wrote about the abolition movement, the coming of the Civil War, and the war itself tended to focus on whites, sectionalism, and political discord. More recently, historians have brought out the critical role free blacks and slaves played in bringing the issue to a head and then turning the war into one to end slavery and winning it.

Frustration at being denied access to meaningful work, education, and other roads to advancement, coupled with anger over discrimination and public humiliation, brought concerted action on the part of blacks. At the same time as Bostonian David Walker was calling upon slaves in 1829 to "kill or be killed" and warning free blacks that their "full glory and happiness . . . shall never be fully consummated, but with the *entire emancipation of your enslaved brethren all over the world*," the first black editors of newspapers were calling for national meetings to address the growing problems of the African-American community. Such meetings reflected the growing sentiment among some to press for judgment on the slavery issue. As a result of his associations with African Americans in Baltimore, William Lloyd Garrison commited himself in 1830 to immediate abolition. The same year, the literate and pious slave Nat Turner led slaves on a rampage of killing in Southampton County, Virginia that brought growing numbers of southern planters and small farmers to believe themselves under seige by slaves, free blacks, and northern sectional interests. More and more, the small but growing number of educated African Americans focused their energies on resolving the slavery issue, sometimes in concert with whites (Frederick Douglass being just one of scores of former slaves who faced danger to spread awareness of slavery's evils) and sometimes by themselves in writings and convention speeches. They pushed for racial uplift and moral reform in their long-range attack on slavery. Through the 1840s, more militant voices at African-American conventions spoke to slaves: New Yorker David Ruggles exhorted, "Rise, brethren, rise! Strike for freedom or die slaves" in 1841, and two years later, in Buffalo, Henry Highland Garnet echoed the same refrain: "Strike for your lives and liberties. Now is the day and the hour. Let every slave throughout the land do this, and the days of slavery are numbered."

Every slave did not strike for his or her liberty, but growing numbers of slaves began striking out on their own to escape, and free blacks helped. Though white abolition-ists did not operate an underground railroad extending deep into the South to spirit away the region's enslaved labor force, as legend holds, the bold, often lone actions of slaves themselves in escaping and then, once in the North, looking mainly to fellow African Americans for assistance led southern planters to believe that such a secretive apparatus did exist. The southern push for a stricter Fugitive Slave Act in 1850 was the result. This brutal law, intended to douse sectional fires as part of the Compromise of 1850 following the admission of California as a free state and the ending of the slave trade in the District of Columbia, led to African-American "vigilance" activities in northern cities. Such activities involved the thwarting of slave hunters to the point of kidnapping alleged fugitives from federal authorities. It was almost as if a war had begun already, pitting these slaves, free blacks, and their white abolitionist allies fighting on the side of a higher moral law against the slaveholders of the South and representatives of the federal government, fighting to uphold the immoral legalities supporting slavery.

This "war" broadened in the 1850s. When the Kansas–Nebraska Act of 1854 opened new territories to slavery on the basis of popular sovereignty, fighting over the extension of slavery into Kansas erupted. The decision of the Supreme Court in [Dred] Scott v. Sanford in 1857 that slaves were not citizens and that "a black man has no rights which a white man is bound to respect" brought African Americans to consider more desperate measures in their struggle against slavery and white racism. As prospects for all blacks seemed to worsen, some turned again to considerations of emigration while others formed military organizations, ready to defend themselves or participate in armed conflict. Douglass was one of a number of black and white abolitionists who lent John Brown support as the white anti-slavery fighter planned an armed strike against slavery. Brown's 13 whites and five blacks failed in their assault on the federal arsenal in Harper's Ferry, Virginia in 1859, intended as the first step toward a massive slave rebellion, but for southerners it was almost the last straw. Republican Abraham Lincoln's victory in the 1860 election brought the secession of southern states and the formation of the Confederate States of America; Confederate firing on the federal Fort Sumter, off Charleston, South Carolina, in April 1861 led Lincoln to call for volunteers to preserve the Union; and then the real war was on. Most African Americans, slave and free, had been waiting for such an occurrence.

Quickly, the actions of large numbers of slaves forced Lincoln's hand and helped make a war to preserve the Union into one that would end slavery. Not long after the war began, slaves began fleeing their masters' domains and seeking refuge with Union armies. What to do with the fugitives was a problem for Lincoln, who dared not irritate slaveowners in the still loyal border states. Congress eventually passed two Confiscation Acts, the first freeing fugitive slaves whom Confederates had used in the war effort, and the second freeing the slaves of all disloyal masters. The farther Union armies pushed into the South, the more slaves fled – in their thousands – to Union lines. In June and July 1862, Congress passed bills abolishing slavery in United States territories and freeing fugitive slaves of disloyal masters; then, following the Union victory at Antietam in September, Lincoln issued the Emancipation Proclamation, directing that on January 1, 1863 "all persons held as slaves within any State, or designated part of the State, the people whereof shall be in rebellion against the United States, shall be then, thenceforward, and forever free." The character of the war had decisively changed: as Lincoln noted at Gettysburg in the fall of 1863, the Union dead would bring forth "a new birth of freedom" in the 87-year-old nation, and most knew to whom that freedom would extend.

By the time Lincoln spoke at Gettysburg, many of the Union dead were African American. Early government opposition to the enlistment of blacks fell in the face of military necessity. Congress authorized Lincoln to enlist black troops in July 1862, and by 1863 African Americans were pouring into the Union army, despite discrimination in pay that was not equalized until 1864 and despite mortality rates one-third or more higher than among white Union troops. By the war's end, 186,000 black troops had enlisted; over 38,000 of them died in the effort. The Constitutional guarantee of the freedom for which they had fought came with adoption of the Thirteenth Amendment late in 1865.

Reconstruction

Reconstruction involved putting the nation back together. The war had devastated the South: its economy was at a standstill, its society in chaos. In the midst of this destruction were the four million African-American men, women, and children whom the war had freed. These "freedmen" were largely illiterate, without property, and inexperienced in important aspects of life. Congress already had created a bureau to begin tackling massive problems associated with refugees, freedmen, and abandoned lands – the so-called Freedmen's Bureau. No one believed it would have an easy time.

For years, emphasis among historians of Reconstruction was on its political aspects. The racist Dunning school of historiography (named after William Archibald Dunning, who, along with John W. Burgess, trained many Reconstruction historians at Columbia University) presumed African-American inferiority and thus argued that Radical Republicans, who forced the black vote and office-holding on white southerners, were men intent on punishing the defeated Confederacy as well as unethical politicians who would do anything to ensure Republican ascendancy. Not until the 1960s did revisionists John Hope Franklin (1961) and Kenneth M. Stampp (1965) argue successfully that the Radicals were men who sincerely cared about blacks and their future and made honest efforts to establish the basis for full African-American citizenship. More recent studies (Foner, 1988, for example) suggest that Radical Reconstruction was basically conservative in its failure to provide African Americans with economic self-sufficiency.

The political history of Reconstruction is straightforward. Lincoln spoke of lenient terms for returning the southern states to their former status. His assassination precluded such efforts, but they were taken up by his successor, Andrew Johnson, a Tennesseean who harbored not-so-latent racist notions. Johnson permitted the southern states to create new governments over the summer and fall of 1865, and these states' new, all-white governments rapidly passed a body of laws, the "Black Codes," designed to place the freedmen as close as possible to the subordinate and servile position they had held before the war. Binding labor contracts, vagrancy laws, and denial of blacks' rights to bear arms were basic to these statutes. When Congress convened in December 1865, its Republican majorities would have none of presidential Reconstruction. Spurred on by growing popular support in the North, Congressional Republicans took control of the Reconstruction process, carved the defeated South into military districts under control of the federal army, placed more difficult terms on southern states for re-entry, and passed legislation (soon incorporated into a Fourteenth Amendment) intended to guarantee civil rights for blacks. On such terms, the southern states re-entered the Union, most with Republican governments and with African Americans voting and holding office. Radical Reconstruction's high tide was ratification of a Fifteenth Amendment in 1870, solidifying blacks' right to vote.

Southern, conservative, white Democrats won control of their states from the Republicans over the next half-dozen years. They did so in some states merely by organizing Democratic voting majorities. In the Deep South, where African-American voters were in a majority, conservatives resorted to violence, intimidation, and fraud, none of which state or federal governments could quell. The final southern states were "redeemed" (a loaded, shorthand term for the winning back of political control by southern Democrats) in the corrupt and violence-filled election of 1876, which resulted nationally in the election of Rutherford B. Hayes to the presidency. Hayes removed federal troops from the remaining southern states as part of a deal that sealed his election – the Compromise of 1877, it is termed – and the southern states were thenceforth left alone to deal with their own, internal issues. The biggest issue, of course, was how to treat the large, mostly rural, poor, and under-educated black population. Within two decades the southern state governments, unmolested by federal supervision, would devise their ways.

How and why the conservative white regimes in the southern states could so quickly regain political control over the bi-racial Republican governments set on more fully integrating African Americans into the political process has long been a thorny question. Eric Foner (1988) summarizes a body of arguments that point outside the South – toward industrialization and conflict between wealthy capitalists and lower-class workers in the North. By the 1870s, industrialism, progress (as it was perceived), and class issues took the place of sectional matters in northern thinking. Northern industrialists, Republican in their politics, had more affinity with southern planters and businessmen than with poor workers. Thus, they were less concerned with the status and interests of the freedmen and more likely to sit idly when conservative southerners used violence to suppress black labor and overthrow Republican governments. After 1877, northern whites were involved enough in their own social and economic issues to leave the white South alone in dealing with its peculiar problems involving African Americans.

Of course, no discussion of Reconstruction politics tells us much about how blacks eked out a living and tried to move ahead during the period. With emancipation, some African Americans, long bound to the plantation, headed off toward southern cities – if only because they could. Unwelcome in the central, residential parts of urban areas, indigent blacks congregated on the edges of towns, most in squatter colonies. It was there that the Freedmen's Bureau found many in the greatest need of relief. Such groupings of African-American former slaves, almost none with more property than he or she could wear and carry and few with any means of support, heightened whites' fears of the black masses and helped bring along notions of the desirability of separating the races that had been necessarily absent in the days of slavery. Edward L. Ayers (1992) writes that, between 1865 and 1877, "Blacks and whites withdrew into their own houses, churches, and neighborhoods, watching each other warily." What whites saw their former slaves doing, mainly, was struggling to survive and find a way to advance in a society in flux and lacking a stable economy. Ambitious freedmen, who recognized education as the key to their rise, too often floundered in schools that were segregated and unequal from the start. Always too few in number, usually in session only 2–5 months per year, and moving toward instruction in manual training, these schools became the foundation for what DuBois (1903) would term the "enforced ignorance" of African Americans.

When white southern landowners failed initially in their efforts to turn emancipation back toward legalized black subservience, they opted for the next-best thing: low-paying wage labor. Freedmen's Bureau functionaries, wanting to get something moving economically, were eager to get former slaves into such arrangements. Rather quickly, between 1866 and 1868, working for wages in agriculture for white landowners became the norm for African Americans across the South. But the men and women not long out of slavery did not like these circumstances. In addition to paltry pay, the black farmers did not like the work in gangs, often from dawn to dusk, as before. They desired the independence they thought should accompany their new, free status and saw its existence tied to possession of the means of production – land. A decent-sized plot could provide economic security that would undergird their freedom and would give them something to work on and improve which they could pass on to their children. Thus, there came rapidly into the minds of individual African-American farmers a desire to "set up for himself" – to own a small plot of land.

But freedmen did not have the means to "set up" – the 40 acres and a mule often rumored to be coming from the Freedmen's Bureau would have cost the dirt-poor former slaves some $250 – and whites would not be willing to sell them land, anyway. So, in place of setting up for himself, the capital-deficient African American opted for something as close as possible. The system that evolved over the decade following 1868, most accurately referred to as farm tenancy, is known popularly as "sharecropping." Large landowners would divide their plantations into plots of between 30 and 50 acres. They would allow black families to live on and work such plots and would provide seed, tools, and a mule. For this, the tenant would pledge a portion of the crop at harvest, usually half. Beyond this, the tenant would need food, perhaps articles of clothing, and other necessities before harvest and sale of the crop. He might receive this "furnish" from the landowner or from a nearby merchant, on credit, to be paid for out of the tenant's share of the crop. At harvest, the landlord weighed the crop and took his half; then the tenant paid off his furnish. In theory, in a good crop year, when market prices were strong, the tenant would be able to make enough on his share to furnish himself the next season and perhaps even salt away cash for the eventual renting or purchase of his own land. In practice, it almost never worked that way. Landowners frequently cheated tenants in weighing the crop; merchants charged exorbitant rates of interest; and croppers had little recourse. Laws prevented their leaving so long as they owed money and prescribed inheritance of debt upon death. The result was an endless cycle of work, debt, and poverty that meant dismal lives without hope. By 1880 African Americans owned only 1.6 percent of the South's taxable land and wage laborers worked only 8.9 percent of the South's cotton. Roughly half of all southern black farmers were tenants or sharecroppers in 1880, three-quarters by 1900.

The economic dependence that characterized the lives of southern blacks, when combined with the lack of any support from the federal government, rendered them unable to stand in the way of whatever southern whites might want to do. And what southern whites ended up wanting to do was to separate the races and place African Americans in a position of absolute subordinance and servility. Such a position was the foundation for the Jim Crow era that would last into the middle of the twentieth century.

Toward Jim Crow

Some inclinations of southern whites changed over the third of a century following the Civil War, but one that did not involved their desire to place and keep African Americans in a perpetual position of economic, social, and political subordination. That had been the goal of the post-war Black Codes, and it was the goal of the violence, disfranchisement, and legislated separation of the races that marked the onset of the Jim Crow era in the 1890s. The major difference for African Americans between the two periods was that by the century's final decade almost no influential supporters of black equality existed. Those whites interested in African-American advancement cast their lots, and their philanthropical donations, with accommodationists. By 1890 the only "radicals" in race relations were the racist southern whites intent on driving blacks down into, and keeping them in, their lowly "place."

That legally sanctioned segregation and disfranchisement did not descend on southern African Americans immediately following the removal of federal troops in 1877 lent support for C. Vann Woodward's argument, in *The Strange Career of Jim Crow* (1955), that such was not inevitable. Writing in the 1950s, when liberal Americans were hoping to end segregation, Woodward pointed to forgotten alternatives of inter-racial co-existence and cooperation in the 1870s and 1880s and blamed white aggression rooted in the political frustrations of the Populist era of the 1890s for the rush to disfranchisement and segregation after 1895. Three decades later, Joel Williamson, in *The Crucible of Race: Black–White Relations in the American South since Emancipation* (1984), took a psychoanalytical approach, arguing that the economic depression of the 1890s prevented white males from fulfilling their prescribed roles as providers for white women, prompting men to create a perceived threat, the "black rapist beast." The economically emasculated men could provide women with protection from this beast and maintain the supposed purity of the white race through violence, intimidation, and ultimately segregation. Supporting such action was the rising tide of pseudo-scientific racism that was sweeping intellectual America at the end of the century. From the white pulpit to the college lectern, from the political stump to the dime novel, what one heard about people of African descent was that they were dangerous to American civilization, incapable of self-government, and impossible to educate.

Whites used cyclical logic to justify their dealings with African Americans as the century neared its end. Society respected success generally; white society argued that blacks could not succeed because of their inferior nature, but when blacks did succeed, whites felt threatened and reacted violently by beating, burning, and lynching blacks who had moved beyond their "place." So blacks who showed ambition and enterprise, who held anything beyond servile jobs, who began to accumulate, or who showed evidence of uplift placed themselves in real danger. African Americans thus had to learn to bank their ambitions and limit their success; then, their lack of success confirmed white ideas of their inferiority.

What is particularly remarkable in this situation is that African Americans clung to a faith in progress. "The literature and rhetoric of uplift and self-help proliferated almost in direct proportion to its irrelevance to the working lives of most black Southerners" writes Litwack (1998: 148). Those blacks who championed the fruitless doctrine most eloquently – like Booker T. Washington, builder of Tuskegee Institute in Alabama, who gained special notice following his 1895 address in Atlanta in which he encouraged blacks to work hard in agriculture and manual labor, to accept white assistance where it appeared, and to accommodate to the segregation and disfranchisement that were spreading like a wind-driven fire – were championed as race leaders. Those who opposed the doctrine – like Harvard-educated W. E. B. DuBois, who advocated the highest education for the "stewards" of the race and constant agitation for equal rights – were considered dangerous radicals. And those ordinary African Americans who did not follow the doctrine faced terror and the potential of violence – like the 754 African Americans lynched over the first decade of the twentieth century.

Outside the South, African Americans faced only a marginally better situation. The northern black population remained largely urban. In growing cities, a black middle class continued to exist by providing services for whites or members of their own communities. As more white artisans worked to exclude blacks from their trades, the skill levels of African-American workers declined generally. Most northern blacks congregated in such urban areas as New York's "Tenderloin" or "Hell's Kitchen." The segregation of urban blacks into massive ghettoes awaited the large black exodus out of the South later in the twentieth century. Through the last part of the nineteenth century, black women, who got jobs more easily as domestics, outnumbered men in northern cities. Black urban dwellers had to compete with the growing tide of European immigrants, and their status as under-educated, unskilled laborers considered incapable of advancement made it difficult for them to do so.

Thus, 1900 dawned on an African-American population one-third of a century removed from slavery, but still at the lowest rung of America's social ladder. As the country took over and ruled the Philippines, whites seemed to increase their contempt for darker peoples at home. Looking back over the century that began with most African Americans living in slavery and ended with most living in poverty under the threat of violence, DuBois (1903) would recognize more clearly than others that "The problem of the twentieth century is the problem of the color line . . . ."

Directions

Historians may be on the threshold of a new era in examining the history of African Americans in the nineteenth century. In the 1950s and 1960s, scholars did exemplary work overturning the blatantly racist interpretations of the previous half-century; in the 1970s and 1980s they developed a body of scholarship to demonstrate that, in the midst of remarkable difficulties brought about by slavery, racism, and social and economic subordination, blacks were not mere ciphers, consigned to the objective case, but participants in noteworthy efforts to improve their lives. They showed, too, how much the experience of African Americans informs the central narrative of American history. In all of these studies, race was the foundation of African-American identity and community life.

A new book that deals with the earliest years of nineteenth-century African-American history may point to the direction that scholarship covering the whole century is most likely to take. James Sidbury, in *Ploughshares into Swords: Race, Rebellion, and Identity in Gabriel's Virginia, 1730–1810* (1997), relies on a critical reading of evidence from the 1800 trial of conspirators in Gabriel's rebellion in Richmond, Virginia to draw conclusions about black Americans' individual and collective identity. He shows generally how much more complex were such matters than previously recognized – how African Americans, with roots in different cultures and broad contacts across the Atlantic world, crossed racial lines to form "crosscutting identities" at once Virginian and Atlantic, American and racial, urban and partly autonomous, yet still bound by slavery. Sidbury's findings apply broadly to African-American communities and culture. Throughout the nineteenth century, while struggling to overcome the restraints of slavery and racism (as shown so clearly by a generation of exceptional historical scholarship), African-American communities consisted of multifaceted individuals in complex situations, with ideas affecting their actions and personal and community identities that came from their varied circumstances and rested on a variety of cultural traditions. Race was an overwhelmingly important factor in their lives, but, still, only one of many. The scholarship of the coming generation is likely to bear this out.

REFERENCES

Ayers, Edward L. (1992) *The Promise of the New South: Life after Reconstruction*. New York: Oxford University Press.

Berlin, Ira (1974) *Slaves without Masters: the Free Negro in the Antebellum South*. New York: Pantheon.

Berlin, Ira and Morgan, Philip D. (eds) (1993) *Cultivation and Culture: Labor and the Shaping of Slave Life in the Americas*. Charlottesville: University Press of Virginia.

Blassingame, John W. (1972) *The Slave Community: Plantation Life in the American South*. New York: Oxford University Press.

DuBois, W. E. B. (1903) *The Souls of Black Folk: Essays and Sketches*. New York: Fawcett, 1961.

Elkins, Stanley (1959) *Slavery: a Problem in American Institutional and Intellectual Life*. Chicago: University of Chicago Press, 2nd edn, 1968.

Foner, Eric. (1988) *Reconstruction: America's Unfinished Revolution, 1863–1877*. New York: Harper and Row.

Franklin, John Hope (1961) *Reconstruction after the Civil War*. Chicago: University of Chicago Press.

Horton, James O. and Horton, Lois E. (1997) *In Hope of Liberty: Culture, Community, and Protest among Northern Free Blacks, 1700–1860*. New York: Oxford University Press.

Litwack, Leon F. (1961) *North of Slavery: the Negro in the Free States*. Chicago: University of Chicago Press.

Litwack, Leon F. (1979) *Been in the Storm so Long: the Aftermath of Slavery*. New York: Random House.

Litwack, Leon F. (1998) *Trouble in Mind: Black Southerners in the Age of Jim Crow*. New York: Alfred A. Knopf.

Owens, Leslie Howard (1976) *This Species of Property: Slave Life and Culture in the Old South*. New York: Oxford University Press.

Phillips, Ulrich B. (1918) *American Negro Slavery: a Survey of the Supply, Employment and Control of Negro Labor as Determined by the Plantation Regime*. New York: Appleton.

Sidbury, James (1997) *Ploughshares into Swords: Race, Rebellion, and Identity in Gabriel's Virginia, 1730–1810*. New York: Cambridge University Press.

Stampp, Kenneth M. (1956) *The Peculiar Institution: Slavery in the Antebellum South*. New York: Vintage.

Stampp, Kenneth M. (1965) *The Era of Reconstruction, 1865–1877*. New York: Alfred A. Knopf.

Tadman, Michael (1989) *Speculators and Slaves: Masters, Traders and Slaves in the Old South*. Madison: University of Wisconsin Press.

Williamson, Joel (1984) *The Crucible of Race: Black–White Relations in the American South since Emancipation*. New York: Oxford University Press.

Woodward, C. Vann (1955) *The Strange Career of Jim Crow*. New York: Oxford University Press, 3rd rev. edn, 1974.

CHAPTER FIFTEEN

Native-American History

MICHAEL D. GREEN AND THEDA PERDUE

NATIVE American historiography has undergone dramatic changes in the past two or three decades. Once understood as the history of Indian relations with non-Indians, the literature was influenced by a Turnerian model of Euro-American frontier expansion. Scholars depicted Indians as obstacles to be overcome, enemies to be subdued, and impediments to the progress of American society. It was a natural interpretative conclusion considering the sources available to historians. The documents at their disposal were almost entirely the product of the Euro-American side of the contact experience. Government reports, missionary records, military accounts, diplomatic minutes, the correspondence, diaries, and memoirs of various non-Indian participants, all agreed in their portrayal of Indians as people who behaved badly, thought wrongly, believed strangely, and fought savagely. Deficient either because of cultural or racial weaknesses, Indians could only be understood in the terms used by those who had known them.

Gradually, scholars rejected such simplistic characterizations. Sensitive to culture and rejecting race as a category of analysis, "Indian–white" relations came to be understood in terms of the conflict that naturally occurs when very different people come together. In this view, culture became the determinant of thought and action, and the outcome was the measure of cultural characteristics. Strong, adaptive, imaginative traits won out over weak, brittle, close-minded ones. The outcome of the inevitable clash of cultures was thus predetermined and history became little more than the recounting of the steps taken to reach the only possible result.

Equally simplistic, this approach had the virtue of calling attention to culture. As historians explored cultural questions, they discovered the literature of anthropology and began to learn something about what students of culture did. Out of this interaction between history and anthropology came ethnohistory, a methodology used by both historians and anthropologists to explain a different kind of Native American history. The records of analysis remain the same documents, reports, and correspondence that previous generations of scholars used, but ethnohistorians use them differently. They ask questions framed in cultural contexts, they interpret the evidence from the perspectives of cultural awareness and sensitivity, and they assume things about Native-American societies that their predecessors never did.

Ethnohistory permits Native-American history to be presented from the inside out. Sometimes called the "new Indian history," it focuses on Indian people themselves, their societies, their economic and political systems, their diplomatic and military activities, their lives, their habits, and their interests. This is, of course, nothing more than what history has always been about. The novelty is that it has become what Native-American history is about. The intricacies of Indian–white relations no longer pose the questions or drive the interpretations. Rather, the problems are those that were intimate and pressing in the lives of Indian people in the past. Without written Indian languages, literatures, and documents at their disposal, ethnohistorians have made remarkable, even astonishing, progress in their efforts to tease understanding about Native Americans from the flawed, biased, incomplete, and ethnocentric records of non-Indians.

Several themes have emerged as central to the histories of Native groups in the eighteenth and nineteenth centuries. Most importantly, perhaps, is the realization that Indians, who had control over their lives and histories prior to the arrival of Europeans, did not willingly or easily surrender that control after the inundation occurred. Beset by a host of novel, often deadly, experiences that included epidemic disease, manufactured goods, guns, and people in rapidly growing numbers, Indians lost neither their wits nor their will. Rather, they confronted these phenomena with decisions and creative responses that made sense within the contexts of their cultures and experiences. Furthermore, as time passed and their knowledge deepened, they reassessed their responses, experimented with new ideas, and adapted continuously to changing circumstances. This logical and sensible pattern of behavior represents a theme of central importance in the new historiography of Native America that differs dramatically from the perspective of an earlier historiography that had presented Native people as bewildered and helpless victims of forces set in motion elsewhere.

Other themes that characterize the literature on nineteenth-century Native Americans relate directly to the birth and growth of the independent United States and expand on the idea that Indians continued to seek control over their own destinies. The fur-trade economy of the eighteenth-century withered, producing in the nineteenth-century economic collapse, hardship, and dependency. At the same time, growing American populations encroached on Indian lands, competed with Indians for resources, and squeezed Indian communities in an ever-tightening grip. In the face of lost land, resources, and space, tribes fought both militarily and politically to preserve and protect their sovereignty, territory, and economic autonomy. These became the central issues of relations between Native groups and the United States, but more importantly to the new ethnohistoriography, they also became the central issues of Native-American history.

George Washington's Indian policy committed the United States to acquire Indian-owned land and resources and to eradicate Indian cultures. Using federal officers and Christian mission organizations, the government planned to educate Native people into becoming culturally Anglo-American and thus suitably civilized to be integrated into American society. At the same time, Washington committed the United States to the acquisition of what he considered to be "surplus" Indian land. The intensity of the administration of this program varied with the shifting winds of American politics, but throughout the century the forced cultural transformation of Native people and the acquisition of their lands remained near the center of federal policy. Thus the Native struggle for sovereignty, territory, and economic autonomy became fully entangled in the culture wars waged wherever federal agents and missionaries went. By the 1820s, policy-makers had abandoned Washington's goal of rapid assimilation and sought instead to segregate Native populations in discrete areas where they could acculturate more slowly. A policy of remarkable cruelty, the resettlement of Native peoples in Indian territory and on reservations resulted in thousands of deaths through forced migration, prolonged wars, and disruptions in ancient subsistence patterns. Through all of this, however, Native people retained a strong sense of tribal identity and cultural worth, and they exercised agency by directing their own lives, adapting to changed circumstances, and making decisions about the future.

Ethnohistorians have tried to understand the exercise of agency in several different ways. Acculturation, the process by which Native people adopted aspects of the dominant culture, helps explain rapid cultural transformation. Revitalization, attempts to make Native cultures more meaningful and effective for beleaguered peoples, is perhaps the most overt and easily documented expression of Native agency. Many Native peoples divided between those who preferred traditional values and practices, usually called traditionalists or conservatives, and those who advocated change, frequently referred to as progressives. Unfortunately, some scholars have resorted to a kind of racial shorthand and termed these two groups "full-bloods" and "mixed-bloods," but ancestry was no certain determinant of the cultural choices people made. These divisions produced factionalism, which provides another analytical model by which scholars have tried to understand the internal dynamics of Native societies. More recently, scholars have moved away from these dualistic approaches to the Native-American past and focused on cultural syncretism, the blending of Native and European cultures in ways that permitted Native people to physically survive Euro-American expansion without relinquishing key components of their cultures. With a new awareness of the role of Native people in their own history, scholars also have made more culturally sensitive attempts to understand the relationship between Natives and non-Natives.

Early tribal histories tended to focus on acculturation because treaties, mission reports, and other historical documents charted change. These studies often presented the process of acculturation as predetermined because of Euro-American cultural superiority and military might or divine providence. Furthermore, they often implied uniformity among a particular people and used the cultural choices of leaders to characterize all the members of a tribe. More recently, historians have used acculturation far more circumspectly to examine the process by which some Native people adopted certain Euro-American practices and to delineate issues that divided Native peoples. The Cherokees have been the subject of much of this work because nineteenth-century observers, modern scholars, and the Cherokees themselves have regarded them as the most "civilized," that is, highly acculturated, of all Native people.

In *Slavery and the Evolution of Cherokee Society, 1540–1866* (1979), Theda Perdue examined the Cherokee elite's adoption of plantation slavery. The Cherokees traditionally held individuals whom Europeans called slaves. Eventually ransomed, adopted, tortured, or merely held in a kind of social limbo, these people held little economic value for Cherokees until Europeans provided a market for them. Europeans redeemed their own nationals or the suspected spies of their enemies, and they purchased Native captives for use alongside Africans on their plantations. By the end of the eighteenth century, however, the market for war captives had collapsed, and Cherokee leaders had embraced the United States' policy of "civilization," which included commercial agriculture. Since Cherokees, like most Native peoples, held land in common and permitted any tribal member to use unoccupied land, individuals who had accumulated capital and acquired acquisitive values began to purchase African-American slaves in order to bring more land under cultivation, and they implemented political changes to protect their property and provide for its inheritance. Many Cherokees, however, had little use for such legislation or the economic values that these laws embodied. The ownership of slaves, therefore, both distanced a Cherokee elite from the majority of Cherokees and served as a marker of cultural differences within the tribe.

William G. McLoughlin's *Cherokee Renascence in the New Republic* (1986) has more broadly addressed the massive changes in Cherokee society in the first three decades of the nineteenth century. Having focused on the impact of missions in an earlier book, McLoughlin tended to concentrate on political acculturation in this work. The Cherokees centralized their government in the early nineteenth century. They established electoral districts that sent delegates to an annual general council, and an executive committee which, along with the principal chief, managed Cherokee affairs in the interim. District courts and a supreme court heard cases arising from the laws passed by the council. In 1827, the Cherokees wrote a constitution that embodied the separation and balance of powers, but to Georgia this act represented a violation of state sovereignty and precipitated the Cherokee removal crisis. Cherokee nationalism and United States nationalism collided; ultimately, the United States triumphed and forced the Cherokee Nation west of the Mississippi.

McLoughlin regarded the rise of Cherokee nationalism as imitative, in some respects, of a similar process in the United States, but he also placed that development firmly in the context of cultural revitalization, an analytical model normally applied to cultural persistence rather than change. The Cherokee elite, McLoughlin argued, adopted Anglo-American political forms in order to save their society, which threatened to disintegrate with the decline of an eighteenth-century economy based on hunting and a political system that grew out of almost constant warfare. These new political forms, along with the skills and values learned from US agents and missionaries, enabled the Cherokees to survive as a people and mount a credible, though unsuccessful, defense of their homeland.

Most scholars have been reluctant to offer an explanation for the Cherokees' apparent exceptionalism, but sociologist Duane Champagne suggested a plausible theory for the Cherokees' unique political developments in *Social Order and Political Change* (1992). Choctaws, Chickasaws, and Creeks viewed their social and political organizations as interwoven and interpreted governance in religious terms. Political office derived in large part from one's place in the tribe's social organization, in particular, clan affiliation. Furthermore, government represented the social units of clan and town, a feature that made other forms of political apportionment and the delegation of power unthinkable. Additionally, religion and politics were considered inseparable. Because Cherokee social organization played a far more limited role in their political system, and Cherokees did not see governance as religious behavior, they were able to change their government structure without challenging more deeply embedded cultural practices. Therefore, the Cherokees could centralize their government, spark a sense of national identity, and withstand the onslaught of Euro-Americans in the nineteenth century somewhat better than their neighbors. Cultural expressions are interconnected, as Champagne has shown us, and fundamental changes were enormously difficult for most Native people.

Anthropologist Anthony F. C. Wallace developed revitalization theory to help explain how Native people, under circumstances of extreme cultural crisis, systematically and deliberately reshaped their cultures. He illustrated this process in *Death and Rebirth of the Seneca* (1970), a cultural history of the Senecas. After the American Revolution, which devastated the Seneca Nation, there was a period marked by land loss, economic depression, political upheaval, and widespread social collapse. Quaker missionaries and government officials encouraged the Senecas to adopt American cultural values, but most Senecas sank into a sea of despair. In 1799, Handsome Lake, a Seneca political leader, had the first of many visions. Wallace groups the visions into two categories, the first or "Apocalyptic Gospel," and the second or "Social Gospel." The apocalyptic visions were concerned with sin, damnation, and the destruction of the world. The Creator warned Handsome Lake that evil behavior had brought the Senecas to the brink of ruin and that without repentance they would be destroyed. In particular, the Creator denounced drunkenness and witchcraft and demanded that Handsome Lake instruct the people to confess their sins, reform, and find salvation.

The social gospel contained the prescription for salvation by emphasizing the importance of temperance, peace, the retention of land, English language education, domestic harmony built on stable monogamous marriage, and changed gender roles that assumed men farmed and women kept house. This program was an amalgam of Seneca and American values that assumed continued culture change. As Handsome Lake presented it, however, the Senecas under his guidance would select from American culture according to their needs, not as dictated by government agents and missionaries. Handsome Lake's message of controlled change and survival attracted large numbers of Senecas and continues to be a vital religion to this day.

In two biographies, one of Tenskwatawa, the Shawnee prophet, the other of his brother Tecumseh, R. David Edmunds (1983, 1984) detailed the histories of the leaders of a pan-Indian revitalization movement that bears a similarity to that of Handsome Lake except that it had inter-tribal appeal and a militaristic tone. In 1805, Tenskwatawa had his first vision. Followed by several more visions, they formed a coherent message that promised salvation for those who reformed their personal lives and faithfully followed the prescribed regimen of ritual and ceremony. Influenced in part by Christian teachings, the message also threatened a hell of perpetual torment for those who refused to follow the prophet.

The prophet's message resonated throughout the Old Northwest and beyond. Disciples from as far away as the Blackfeet from the northern Plains journeyed to the Shawnee country to listen and learn. Tecumseh, the prophet's elder brother and a village leader, was also converted, but most civil leaders, labeled "government chiefs" by Edmunds, rejected the prophecy and clung to their political and economic ties with the United States. As the number of Tenskwatawa's followers grew, and as his message spread from tribe to tribe, adherents openly challenged their civil leaders.

Edmunds identified a significant change beginning in 1807 with the emergence of Tecumseh. In that year he announced at a conference at Chillicothe the proposition that there was no such thing as tribal land. Rather, all land belonged to all the people. This was not a novel claim. Indian leaders in the Great Lakes country had made it as early as the 1780s, nor was it an illogical argument. The most meaningful political unit in the country north of the Ohio River was the village, most of which were multi-ethnic, and they were scattered so widely that it was virtually impossible to block out a tract belonging exclusively to any single tribe. Shawnee country had Potawatomi villages in it, and so forth. Tecumseh's point, however, was to denounce the actions of United States agents who purchased lands from tribal leaders. His argument, of course, also denied the authority of the government chiefs to conduct business. By 1809, following the massive cession made by Potawatomi, Miami, and Delaware government chiefs at Fort Wayne, Tecumseh stepped out from Tenskwatawa's shadow to assume a dominant role as political and military leader of a rapidly growing alliance system that included most of the Native population north of the Ohio. Tenskwatawa continued to be important, his message was the glue that held the alliance together, but Tecumseh was rapidly turning it into a war machine which, allied to the British during the War of 1812, ultimately killed him.

In his *Spirited Resistance* (1992), Gregory Evans Dowd put Tenskwatawa, Tecumseh, and other prophets into historical context. He argued that the Indians living east of the Mississippi River shared a common Woodlands religious tradition based on the belief in a binding connection between the spiritual and temporal worlds which was interpreted by prophets. Between 1745 and 1815, this understanding underlay a split into two trans-tribal divisions in response to the combined territorial and cultural assaults of Euro-Americans. The two groups, which Dowd labeled "accommodationists" and "nativists," shared the anxieties produced by land loss, military defeats, and cultural change, and agreed that to survive Native people had to find new sources of power. The disagreement arose over where this power was to be found. Accommodationists, Dowd wrote, looked to the Euro-Americans. They had the clothes, tools, weapons, and other goods upon which their people depended, and their rapidly growing numbers guaranteed that these foreigners were in America to stay. These accommodationists, who tended to be tribal leaders and thus responsible for the well-being of their people, argued for policies that linked their groups to the outsiders, assured the flow of goods, achieved assurances of future independence, and made the best of the difficult situation in which they found themselves. During periods when more than one imperial power contended for tribal alliances, accommodationists embraced play-off diplomacy to minimize political interference. At other times, they relied on their skills as politicians and diplomats to look after the needs of their people. Throughout, the vision of the accommodationists was tribal.

Nativists sought power elsewhere. Influenced, often led, by a succession of prophets, they looked to the spiritual realm for salvation. Many of the prophets, including the Delaware Neolin, Tenskwatawa of the Shawnees, and several Creek holy men, attained notoriety through highly publicized visions. Dowd argued that a central element in the attempts at spiritual reinvigoration through prophecy was a vision of the world that de-emphasized tribal identity in favor of pan-Indian unity. The prophets addressed the problems of economic dependency and depression by urging their listeners to refuse to purchase liquor and to reduce their consumption of foreign goods. A message that some have called reactionary, it also made good economic sense. The traditional economy of subsistence agriculture and hunting had been the basis of economic autonomy, after all, and in the midst of widespread depression caused by the collapse of the fur and hide trade and mounting indebtedness, reducing consumption was a rational recommendation. Prophetic denunciation of the sale of land and condemnation of all future sales reaffirmed the spiritual link between Native people and the land the Creator had given them even as it sought to assure a future for the people.

Some scholars have argued that the study of factionalism, such as that which Dowd described, could be the key to understanding the debates over how to protect sovereignty, territory, and economic autonomy. These were political questions of such extreme importance that people had powerful and differing views about them. Uncover and understand the differences of opinion, the points of debate, the interests of the proponents, and the focus of history will be directed into the community. Such a focus gives us insight into Native community political and social systems as well as issues of critical importance. Two scholars, Michael D. Green and Joel Martin, have found factionalism a useful model for explaining the history of the Creeks. Given the character of the Creek confederacy, a multi-ethnic, multi-lingual amalgam of tribal remnants with a history that emphasized local community autonomy rather than tribal identity, the Creeks are perhaps particularly susceptible to an interpretative model that stresses disagreement. In his *The Politics of Indian Removal* (1982), Green used factionalism to explain Creek history from the Creek War to removal in 1836. Martin's *Sacred Revolt* (1991) looked at the period ending with the Creek War of 1813–14.

The removal crisis began in the years after the War of 1812 and intensified during the 1820s as Americans pressed against Indian country in search of land and resources. Nowhere were these encroachments more persistent than on the border between the Creek Nation and Georgia. By the early 1820s, the power of the state was increasingly directed toward the expulsion of the Creeks, thus making their land available for its citizens. Georgia's demands, supported by the federal government, presented the Creeks with a serious political crisis. At the same time, the Creek Nation had never been weaker. The Creek War, concluded in 1814, had been devastating. Recovery demanded extraordinary political skills and generated profound disagreements over the proper courses of action.

The lines of political cleavage in the Creek Nation reflected, in part, the growing cultural gulf that had precipitated the Creek civil war. Many Creeks remained outside the direct influence of the federal civilization policy and its program of culture change, but some had found market agriculture, ranching, slavery, and American-style education attractive. These Creeks also often accepted bribes from federal officials. The factional division was also in part geographical, however, with the eastern or lower Creeks more responsive to the culture change demanded by the Americans and the western or upper Creeks less inclined to do so. After a decade of political and economic reconstruction, during the mid-1820s the growing cultural tensions became critical. In 1825, William McIntosh, a lower Creek headman, agreed to a land cession to benefit Georgia despite the resolve of the national council, dominated by upper Creeks, against it. The council, citing a law forbidding unauthorized sales of tribal land, ordered his execution and launched a program of political centralization designed to head off further cessions and removal to the West. Over the next ten years, as the removal crisis intensified, factional disagreement over removal, the propriety of centralist national government, and the future of Creek society persisted. Removal in 1836 carried these conflicts west to Indian territory.

Joel Martin's *Sacred Revolt* (1991), published a decade after Green's book, interpreted the period in Creek history that culminated in the Creek War of 1813–14. That conflict, he argued, was fundamentally a civil war rooted in a cultural division that had religious overtones. While perhaps influenced by Tenskwatawa's message and Tecumseh's vision of a political and military alliance, the Creeks, Martin demonstrated, had both problems and prophets of their own. Tecumseh's 1811 recruiting trip may have been timely, but the Creeks did not join his pan-Indian alliance. They did, however, divide themselves along cultural and political lines that conform to Dowd's nativist–accommodationist model. Between the mid-1790s and the outbreak of civil conflict in 1813, enough Creeks embraced enough of the American civilization policy to become noticeable as an alternative to traditional ways of life. This cultural gulf had deep political implications. Those Creeks who did not select from the array of "civilized" attributes found themselves increasingly dissatisfied with both the changes in their world and the apparent unwillingness of the civil leaders to show them a better way. Continued land cessions, persistent economic hardship, settlers and travelers in growing numbers, and leaders who seemed primarily interested in personal gain all threatened the natural order of things and demanded redress. Several prophets, armed with spiritual power, taught that the Creator abhorred these changes and demanded that the people repel the invaders and crush their Creek allies. This message, Martin argued, was designed to replace the chaos of invasion, collapse, and political and cultural disharmony with a new spiritual order and balance. The prophets gained followers, their movement became political, and in the face of opposition from civil leaders, the movement became a revolt.

Martin characterized the prophetic rebellion as a millenarian movement. The prophets and their followers sought to take control of their world by expelling from it those who would remake it wrongly. In a massive effort of cultural cleansing, they attacked and destroyed the herds and plantations of their Creek opponents, burned their towns, and tried to kill their leaders. Unable to defend themselves, the government chiefs appealed to the United States for help, American armies invaded the Creek Nation, and the Creek civil war became the Creek War. Coincidental with the War of 1812, Martin showed that what happened in the Creek Nation was not connected to that conflict. Rather, it represented a prophetic upheaval that sought through ritual and ceremony to re-establish spiritual order and control. While many scholars believe that factionalism defines much of Native political life, this episode of Creek history was uniquely violent.

While factional conflict in the Cherokee Nation did not reach the level of civil war, it threatened to. As William McLoughlin has shown in his *After the Trail of Tears* (1993), Cherokee history in Indian territory was marked by a succession of factional divisions. Until the mid-1840s, the argument was over the nature and composition of tribal government. The new arrivals from the east brought their constitutional system with them and expected to re-establish the Cherokee republic. The Old Settlers, in the west for many years, opposed constitutionalism. This dispute became violent when several of the men who had signed the removal treaty were murdered. It did not become civil war, according to McLoughlin, because both factions were fully committed to the preservation of Cherokee sovereignty, but the Nation was in turmoil for nearly a decade.

Once the constitutional division was healed, a new controversy arose over the question of slavery. Here, McLoughlin argued, "full-bloods" who spoke only Cherokee and did not own slaves were arrayed against "mixed-bloods" who spoke English and did own slaves. While the division targeted slavery, deeper cultural differences underlay the dispute and led, by the mid-1850s, to organized political confrontation. At issue in particular was the extent to which Cherokees should adopt American cultural elements. As occurred repeatedly, the cultural assaults launched in the name of "civilization" and integration by the federal government primarily stimulated division and discord in Native America.

With the outbreak of the American Civil War, slaveholders dominated the government and the Nation allied with the Confederacy, but during the course of the war the anti-slavery faction gained predominance and the Cherokees switched allegiance to the Union. After the Civil War, the lines of faction continued to mark Cherokee public affairs. No longer divided on slavery, the deeper cultural distinctions that had earlier characterized the full-blood/mixed-blood division continued. It is important to note, however, that "blood" determined neither attitudes nor actions. The division was cultural, not genetic, and McLoughlin unfortunately chose to use an old and easy but flawed terminology to describe cultural differences.

Green, Martin, and McLoughlin agreed that factionalism among the Creeks and Cherokees resulted from the efforts of Native people to protect sovereignty, territory, and economic autonomy from the Euro-American onslaught. Some believed that by carefully selecting particular elements from American culture they could empower themselves to do so, others did not. In *To Be the Main Leaders of our People* (1998), Rebecca Kugel delved deeply into the history of Ojibwe political and social organization and demonstrated how ancient divisions became factions in the nineteenth century. Like many Native nations, the Ojibwe respected two sources of power. One group, the civil leaders, represented age, wisdom, experience. Through decisions in council they charted the course for the people. The other group comprised the warriors. Young, brash, impatient to win war honors, and by training militant, they were responsible for the protection and defense of the community. As they shared the primary goal of serving the best interests of the people, the two groups respected one another, but there was also a tension between them. Under normal circumstances, the warriors deferred to the leadership of the elders, but in the mid-nineteenth century crisis conditions changed that norm. Economic collapse and the American assault on Ojibwe culture demanded response. The civil leaders chose commercial agriculture and looked to the missionaries and government agents for technical aid and instruction. The warriors rejected this path, called for resistance, and in their outrage over the decisions of the civil leaders demanded a formal and institutionalized voice in governance. To counter the alliance between the civil leaders and the agents and missionaries, the warriors enlisted the aid of the traders and nearby Metis groups, thus magnifying the degree of foreign interference in Ojibwe domestic affairs. The result, Kugel argued, was a deep and contentious split in the nation. Toward the end of the nineteenth century, however, Ojibwe factions reunited in defense of political and economic autonomy and preservation of social control.

While factionalism provided political expression for the diversity that existed within most tribes in the nineteenth century, ethnohistorians realize that cultural choices were often more complex on both the individual and societal level than factional dichotomies imply. Several scholars have explored the ways in which Native people borrowed selectively from Euro-American culture and adapted Euro-American practices and beliefs to suit their particular society or circumstance. They have revealed remarkable complexity and creativity in the responses of Native people to the demands of Euro-Americans.

William McLoughlin employed the concept of syncretism in *Champions of the Cherokees: Evan and John B. Jones* (1990) to explain why these Baptist missionaries, father and son, enjoyed far greater success among culturally conservative Cherokees between 1821 and 1826 than did their competitors in the mission field. He concluded that the Joneses did not insist on the complete cultural transformation that other missionaries made mandatory for converts. They recognized that Native religion involved a number of beneficial beliefs and practices, such as medical treatment, that Christian doctrine neither contradicted nor replaced. Consequently, they demanded only limited compliance with the "civilization" program that other missionaries saw as an essential component of conversion. The Joneses also enlisted individual Cherokees to become preachers. These new religious leaders, preaching in Cherokee, excelled in blending Christianity with Cherokee beliefs. After removal to Indian territory, they were instrumental in turning Christianity into a Cherokee religion. The Joneses also adopted aspects of Cherokee culture in order to become genuine members of the community to which they ministered. They learned the Cherokee language, lived modestly, and suffered an occasional moral lapse. While McLoughlin's book focused on the missionaries, he revealed a syncretic Christianity that provided Cherokees with substantial cultural continuity.

George Phillips, in *Indians and Intruders in Central California, 1769–1849* (1993), argued that many Native Californians, contrary to the general assumption, turned the lessons learned in the Franciscan missions against their former tutors. In an example of syncretism that linked economic opportunity with resistance, coastal Indians who had been swept up into the Spanish mission system often found refuge in the central valleys of California. Neophytes who either escaped from the missions or were expelled when the Mexican government secularized the mission system in 1834, they introduced aspects of Spanish culture to the valley people who had been outside the scope of Spanish power. The valley Indians had long enjoyed a complex trading network that linked the various communities into an economic system, but with the entry into the Rocky Mountains of American trappers and the development of a large and vigorous trade with New Mexico, the ancient trade relations changed. The foreigners introduced both new goods and new demands, the chief of which was for horses and mules. Exploiting their familiarity with Euro-California and command of the Spanish language, the refugee neophytes soon established an organized raiding and trading operation. They led raiding parties into the rancho districts, making off with large numbers of stock which they then traded with buyers from New Mexico. Simultaneously, the neophytes introduced into the valley communities a brand of political organization that reflected Spanish practice. Bands became villages, neophytes became leaders, and a strange kind of Hispanicized culture as modified by neophyte interests and the needs of valley Indians came to characterize the new world of central California Native people. At the same time, the Indians damaged the rancho economy of Mexican California and preserved their autonomy, at least until the gold rush period.

Sidney Harring, a legal scholar, studied a different kind of syncretism in *Crow Dog's Case* (1994). A legal history of two kinds of law, federal Indian law and tribal law, in the nineteenth century, Harring's book demonstrates that both could be turned to the benefit of Native people. Harring sought to understand the principles of tribal law and to explain how it could be marshaled to defend sovereignty. He considered examples from many tribes, but the title case and the heart of the book explores the relation between Lakota and US law. In 1881, when Crow Dog killed Spotted Tail, Lakota law required that Crow Dog's family compensate Spotted Tail's people for their loss. This was done. But federal agents wanted to make an example of Crow Dog, and then tried and convicted him for murder in a Dakota Territory court. The US Supreme Court reversed Crow Dog's conviction on the grounds that federal law had no jurisdiction in the matter. The Court recognized and accepted the sovereign right of the Lakotas to govern themselves and adjudicate their own affairs. A rare moment in American legal history: tribal and federal law coincided.

Crow Dog's case represented to Harring an example of the importance of tribal law to the history of federal law. Tribal law structured the reactions of the tribes to federal law, Harring asserted, by instructing Native people in their adaptations to culture change imposed by the United States. Harring's discussion of the tribal law of the Creeks, Cherokees, and several Alaska groups, along with his analysis of Lakota law, shows how knowledge of Native legal systems supplements our efforts to understand the legal development of tribal sovereignty. Often in collision, but not always, frequently adaptive, but always firmly reflective of basic tribal sovereignty, together Native legal systems constitute the full body of Indian law that defined nineteenth-century relations between Indians and the government.

As Phillips, Harring, and others have demonstrated, the relations of Indians with outside forces took many forms, and syncretism, the blending of tribal and foreign ideas, covered a wide range. In *Parading through History* (1995), Frederick Hoxie explored how Crow history from the early nineteenth century to 1935 exemplifies such a cultural mixing. Through most of the nineteenth century, observers repeatedly predicted with confidence that the Crows were on the verge of extinction. The fact that they survived provides the central question of Hoxie's book. How did it happen? Through careful resistance, persistence tempered by adaptability, a judicious borrowing from American culture, and the ability to take advantage of unexpected opportunity, Hoxie concluded, the Crows turned their reservation into a modern Indian nation.

The Crows were reservationized in 1884. Their buffalo-hunting economy destroyed, surrounded by potentially hostile neighbors, and thrust into a sedentary way of life for which history had not prepared them, Crow leaders found new ways to protect and rebuild their society. The locus of power lay with government agents, necessitating the development of a working relationship between the Crows and the agents that maximized opportunity while minimizing interference. Exploiting the inefficiencies of the cumbersome federal bureaucracy and the absence of any clear federal program for the Crows beyond confining them to a reservation, a new generation of leaders, young men raised after the demise of buffalo hunting who had attended American boarding schools, led in the forging of new institutions rooted in the past but capable of guiding the people into the twentieth century. The Crow Act of 1920 was the culminating demonstration of this sophisticated new brand of Crow politician. The result of negotiations between Crow spokesmen and Congress that grew out of the heyday of allotment, the bill assigned all the unallotted lands of the reservation to Crow individuals. The alternative was to throw the land on to the open market and inundate the people with American settlers. The outcome was a compromise in that many preferred that the lands should be retained in tribal ownership. As this was impossible, the Crows struck a bargain for the best alternative. The importance of this, Hoxie maintained, was that Crow leaders designed the arrangement. Responsive to the wishes and needs of the people and mindful of the political realities, they forged out of the American concept of the private ownership of land the means for the continued survival of the Crow Nation. In the process they set an example that other tribes in similar situations embraced.

In *Cherokee Women* (1998), Theda Perdue examined the ways in which gender enabled the Cherokees to blend two disparate cultures and to interact with Euro-Americans while retaining their own cultural moorings. In the nineteenth century, Cherokee women became the conservators of many traditional Cherokee beliefs and practices. Despite the attempts of US agents and missionaries to transform the Cherokees into replicas of Anglo-Americans, Cherokee women continued to farm just as they had for hundreds of years. They exercised control over their children under the Cherokees' traditional matrilineal kinship system, and they insisted on common title to land which embodied the communitarian values that were central to women's lives. In the early nineteenth century, Cherokee men could no longer be hunters and warriors, the traditional roles of men, and so the traditions that persisted in Cherokee culture were deeply rooted in the roles of women. Perdue also demonstrated how critics of the Cherokees used the persistence of traditional women's roles to define Cherokees as the "other" and to justify Cherokee removal. The Cherokees, however, had created a syncretic culture in which women's traditional ways blended with, moderated, and even made possible the new lifestyles of Cherokee men.

As historians have come to terms with Native culture and acknowledged that culture both persists and changes, they have recognized that Euro-American culture also organized knowledge in ways that served social, economic, and political ends. The most influential work on the Euro-American construction of "Indian" is Robert Berkhofer's *The White Man's Indian* (1978). The core of this book focuses on the nineteenth century when Euro-Americans moved from a depiction of Native people as fundamentally the same as Europeans to a view that they were inherently different. Euro-Americans developed the "civilization" policy on the assumption that the conversion of Indians into replicas of themselves was both possible and practical. As long as the pacification of Native peoples and the piecemeal acquisition of some of their land were the primary goals of United States Indian policy, this construction served Euro-Americans well. When rapid population growth and geographical expansion mandated a more draconian policy, Euro-Americans transformed their view of Native people and came to regard cultural practices, beliefs, and values as immutable. Inherent inferiority condemned Native people to subordination and dispossession.

More recently, historians have found Immanuel Wallerstein's world systems theory useful in explaining how Native people became so marginalized. In *The Roots of Dependency* (1983), Richard White examined the collapse of the subsistence systems of three very different Native peoples in three different periods. Only the Pawnee story fits firmly into the nineteenth century, but the consequences of Choctaw dependency – loss of their homeland and removal to the West – and the roots of Navajo dependency – environmental degradation caused by expanding sheep herds – occurred in the nineteenth century. The Pawnees became enmeshed in world markets through the trade in buffalo hides. When demand was high, they altered subsistence patterns that had included horticulture in order to obtain more hides, a decision that rendered them increasingly dependent on Euro-Americans and the market. When the buffalo herds were decimated, they no longer had a role to play in world markets and found themselves powerless.

Albert L. Hurtado plotted a similar story of peripheralization in *Indian Survival on the California Frontier* (1988). First Mexico and then the United States needed Native labor to exploit the agricultural and mineral wealth of California. Native Californians entered the market as workers, sometimes willingly but often as slaves or debt bondsmen. When citizens of the United States began to pour into California to fill the demand for labor themselves, they squeezed Native people out of the market and left them destitute and demoralized. Indians survived in California, but most often as individuals. Their communities, Hurtado concluded, often did not.

Such marginalization and peripheralization, however, needs to be understood in context. Frederick Hoxie's *A Final Promise* (1984), an ethnohistorical analysis of federal Indian policy between 1880 and 1920, shows that the seeds of cultural survival can be found in peripheralization. The period of Hoxie's study begins with the development of the policy of allotment, a program that assumed the integration of Native people into American society as fully equal citizens. The period ends with the replacement of the goal of integration with peripheralization. Ironically, Hoxie argued, peripheralization meant a lifting of the American demands for total cultural change. As the federal government lost interest in the culture wars, Indians found ways to extend a degree of control over their lives. Reservation conditions were appalling, but culture survived, leaving scholars with the perplexing problem of interpreting cultural victories at the cost of economic defeats.

In approaching this problem, ethnohistorians must once again confront the centrality of culture and acknowledge that culture shapes the decisions people make. Furthermore, in even the most straightened circumstances, Native people have exercised agency, that is, control over their lives. At the same time, however, practitioners of the new Indian history must be careful that an emphasis on culture and agency does not obscure the tragedies of the Native American past. That Native people managed to acculturate to Euro-America, revitalize their cultures, debate courses of action, and blend disparate cultural traditions does not negate the invasion of their homeland and assault on their culture that mandated these responses. While most modern scholarship pays tribute to Native resourcefulness, creativity, and endurance, it also overtly condemns both the historical events of European conquest and colonization and the historiography that glorified those events. In this sense, nineteenth-century Native American history is politically charged. But then, it always has been. In turning to ethnohistory and focusing on Native societies and cultures, scholars of the past three decades have effectively challenged intellectual colonialism and eurocentric Native-American history.

REFERENCES

Berkhofer Jr, Robert F. (1978) *The White Man's Indian: Images of the American Indian from Columbus to the Present*. New York: Alfred A. Knopf.

Champagne, Duane (1992) *Social Order and Political Change: Constitutional Governments among the Cherokee, the Choctaw, the Chickasaw, and the Creek*. Stanford, CA: Stanford University Press.

Dowd, Gregory Evans (1992) *A Spirited Resistance: the North American Indian Struggle for Unity, 1745–1815*. Baltimore, MD: Johns Hopkins University Press.

Edmunds, R. David (1983) *The Shawnee Prophet*. Lincoln: University of Nebraska Press.

Edmunds, R. David (1984) *Tecumseh and the Quest for Indian Leadership*. Boston: Little, Brown.

Green, Michael D. (1982) *The Politics of Indian Removal: Creek Government and Society in Crisis*. Lincoln: University of Nebraska Press.

Harring, Sidney L. (1994) *Crow Dog's Case: American Indian Sovereignty, Tribal Law, and United States Law in the Nineteenth Century*. Cambridge: Cambridge University Press.

Hoxie, Frederick E. (1984) *A Final Promise: the Campaign to Assimilate the Indians, 1880–1920*. Lincoln: University of Nebraska Press.

Hoxie, Frederick E. (1995) *Parading through History: the Making of the Crow Nation in America, 1805–1935*. Cambridge: Cambridge University Press.

Hurtado, Albert L. (1988) *Indian Survival on the California Frontier*. New Haven, Conn.: Yale University Press.

Kugel, Rebecca (1998) *To Be the Main Leaders of our People: a History of Minnesota Ojibwe Politics, 1825–1898*. East Lansing: Michigan State University Press.

McLoughlin, William G. (1986) *Cherokee Renascence in the New Republic*. Princeton, NJ: Princeton University Press.

McLoughlin, William G. (1990) *Champions of the Cherokees: Evan and John B. Jones*. Princeton, NJ: Princeton University Press.

McLoughlin, William G. (1993) *After the Trail of Tears: the Cherokees' Struggle for Sovereignty, 1839–1880*. Chapel Hill, NC: University of North Carolina Press.

Martin, Joel W. (1991) *Sacred Revolt: the Muscogees' Struggle for a New World*. Boston: Beacon Press.

Perdue, Theda (1979) *Slavery and the Evolution of Cherokee Society, 1540–1866*. Knoxville: University of Tennessee Press.

Perdue, Theda (1998) *Cherokee Women: Gender and Culture Change, 1700–1835*. Lincoln: University of Nebraska Press.

Phillips, George Harwood (1993) *Indians and Intruders in Central California, 1769–1849*. Norman: University of Oklahoma Press.

Wallace, Anthony F. C. (1970) *The Death and Rebirth of the Seneca*. New York: Alfred A. Knopf.

White, Richard (1983) *The Roots of Dependency: Subsistence, Environment, and Social Change among the Choctaws, Pawnees, and Navajos*. Lincoln: University of Nebraska Press.

CHAPTER SIXTEEN

Gender and the Changing Roles of Women

LAURA F. EDWARDS

JUST 25 years ago, neither women nor their work figured prominently in the historiography of nineteenth-century America. While occasionally noting sentimental expressions of domesticity, historians generally passed by hearth and home to locate the dynamics of change in factories, polling places, and statehouses. It seemed obvious that significant historical events originated with men in public arenas. After all, how could anything momentous come out of the mundane routine of domestic labor? Because women were so closely associated with the home, they were relegated to the historical margins as well. Historians generally treated those women who ventured out into paid work or politics as exceptions that proved the rule. These historiographical assumptions actually duplicated a distinctly nineteenth-century conceptual framework that divided society into two separate spheres: a private, female world, centered on domesticity and affective family ties, and a public, male world of production and politics. In this sense, nineteenth-century historiography remained trapped within the very century it sought to explain.

Recently, however, the intellectual foundations that supported this historiographical edifice have begun to crumble. The process began with efforts to recover women's pasts and place them in history. It continued with concurrent work in labor history, which looked within families and communities to explore worker's participation and resistance to capitalist economic change. And it grew as historians began extending these insights to other racial, ethnic, and sexually marginalized groups, revealing that women were more different than they were similar and that the domestic sphere took multiple forms. As the various strands of the scholarship intertwined, historians began questioning the assumption that women's lives and labor really were "separate", "domestic," and "private." The analytical concept of gender, which distinguishes the social traits labeled "female" and "male" from biological sex, was particularly influential. Although first applied to women, historians refined and expanded their use of gender to "male" attributes and responsibilities to posit a relationship between men's and women's roles, and to reveal the ways in which gender ideology shaped the economy and politics. As the boundary that separated private homes from the public world became more historical, it also become less stable. Of course, the use of gender has generated new conceptual problems. Still, the implications have transformed our understanding of women's relationship to nineteenth-century history.

Neither the distinction between private and public nor the differentiation of women from men was new to the nineteenth century. But in this century the dichotomies took on meanings that continue to shape the historiographical view of women. In the colonial period, notions of governmental authority were based on analogies between individual patriarchs' private power over their own families and the king's public power over all his subjects. The private realm of individual households and the public realm of the state were both distinct and inseparable, just as the subordination of wives was both different from and comparable to male subjects' relation to the king. The same logic that gave an individual man authority within his own household also made him subject to authority outside it.

Even in the early colonial period, however, a body of thought was emerging that recast authority and the relationship between private and public. This work included a range of thinkers with varied political goals, from relatively staid liberals, such as John Locke, to more radical thinkers, such as Tom Paine. But all questioned absolute authority, by bringing individual men into the public realm, granting them a bundle of inalienable rights, and insisting that governments were formed by their consent. More radical theorists pushed the logic further, elevating individual men from the status of private subjects to public citizens and asserting their right to participate in governance. These ideas animated the American Revolution. By this logic, it was British rule, not the revolutionary challenge to it, that was illegitimate. Similarly, revolutionary leaders and their supporters became righteous citizens defending the public good, instead of unruly subjects who threatened public order. Afterward, the new republic's leaders put these same ideas at the center of the nation's governing structures, replacing the king with a common brotherhood of sovereign men who now represented the public interest. Exactly which men would be included within this brotherhood produced conflicts that continued over the next two centuries. But the position of women was particularly tenuous. The same political theories that reconstructed the public realm remained silent about relations in the private sphere. Consequently, male household heads retained authority within their homes after the revolution. In fact, once individual rights and political conflict became so closely associated with the public sphere, they seemed that much more inapplicable to domestic relations.

Popular culture, particularly the middle-class "cult of domesticity," then reinforced this separation, giving the two spheres distinctly male and female faces and attaching specific kinds of work to them. Beginning in the early nineteenth century, domestic writers bombarded their audiences with practical advice, heavy-handed prescriptions on appropriate womanly conduct, and syrupy sentimental fiction. Although it is easy to mistake the genre's melodramatic superficialities for historical insignificance, domestic writers were engaged in a profound ideological project. The best-selling advice manuals of Catharine Beecher, for instance, blended practical household advice with theoretical explanations of domesticity and women's roles. According to Beecher, men's new public responsibilities left women to tend to a private sphere centered around home and family. She located this separation of spheres in historical events, namely the creation of the new republic's political structures and the development of market capitalism. Still, she conflated domestic labor with female nature, in assuming that household management and motherhood were women's destiny. Beecher thus attributed to nature what were, in fact, the results of particular historical processes. Yet, by uniting women through this natural bond of domesticity, Beecher created a female counterpart to the liberal brotherhood of men: just as "all men" possessed a bundle of "natural" rights that suited them for public governance, "all women" had "natural" traits that uniquely fitted them for governance at home. These two complementary spheres, according to Beecher, were of equal importance, because the domestic realm was necessary to sustain the public sphere. It provided a haven where women nurtured the nation's citizens and the values necessary for public order.

Not all women in the early nineteenth century agreed with Catharine Beecher. Other female activists, including Elizabeth Cady Stanton and Susan B. Anthony, were not so sure that women's historical mission lay within the home. Nor did they think that domesticity and motherhood rendered women unfit for full civil and political rights. Instead, they used elements of natural rights philosophy to emphasize women's similarities to men as abstract individuals with inalienable rights. Other activists used recent economic changes that brought women into the paid labor force to argue for civil and political rights. If women were taking on male obligations and doing men's work, then they deserved men's rights as well. None the less, most activists still believed that domestic responsibilities and motherhood differentiated women from men. Although they did not think that this situation should limit women's rights, they accepted the notion of a separate, domestic arena and located women within it.

Separate spheres also found expression in nineteenth-century conceptions of labor and economic relations. The rhetoric and images of free-labor ideology, for example, posited a series of dichotomies: free laborers and slaves, white and black, men and women, North and South. Within these dichotomies, slaves, African Americans, women, and the South represented dependence and unfreedom, while white, laboring, men in the North represented independence and freedom. The ideology obscured, but did not erase, inequalities among white northern men. In the early part of the century, the term referred primarily to those who owned productive property, directed their own labor, and controlled the fruits of their labor. But even when the category "free labor" did not include all white northern men, only these people could comfortably assume places within its borders. In the process, the ideology eliminated everyone else, including all women, from the category "labor."

Nineteenth-century studies in political economy revealed the logic behind free-labor ideology's exclusion of women. The work of Karl Marx and Friedrich Engels is particularly suggestive. Although best known for their condemnation of private property and their call for democratic revolution, their arguments also incorporated very conventional assumptions about women and the domestic sphere. According to Marx and Engels, individual households lost control of the means of production as the economic forces of capitalism commodified all things, including labor. People were first drawn into the market economy when they could purchase items for less than they could produce them. Eventually, these forces undermined the household economy completely. Those who once worked for themselves were forced to sell their labor for wages, forfeiting the surplus value to their employers who now owned the means of production. Shorn of all productive value and severed from the economic relations around which future political action would revolve, the household became a separate, private realm of reproduction and consumption. As a result, neither the domestic realm nor women figured prominently in Marx's work.

Engels, however, did deal directly with these issues in *The Origin of the Family, Private Property, and the State* (1884/1990). Not surprisingly, Engels identified women's changing relationship to the means of production as the source of their marginality in industrializing societies. In fact, his faith in this explanatory framework led Engels to de-emphasize obvious inequalities between men and women in the pre-industrial period. Then, he maintained, women had more power and greater social status because they had participated directly in the production process and their labor had economic value. It was capitalist economic change that robbed them of productive labor and left them isolated within the diminished, devalued domestic sphere. Engels was obviously critical of these changes. Moreover, rather than portraying the home in terms of domestic tranquility, he characterized it as the site of struggle between the sexes. But his analysis still had a great deal in common with domestic writers and liberal theorists. Like them, he located women within the private sphere, defined this arena in terms of domesticity and motherhood, and labeled such labor qualitatively different from that done in the public realm. In the process, Engels removed nineteenth-century women from the dynamics of history.

These combined elements of nineteenth-century ideology have had a profound impact on historians, in directing their attention away from women and their labor. The trend intensified in the late nineteenth century as the discipline began to professionalize and to distinguish itself from genealogists and antiquarians, who focused on families and communities. It continued into the 1980s. Despite the fact that women's history was one of the fastest growing fields in these decades, it made few inroads into the traditional areas of law, economics, or politics. Until recently, nineteenth-century political history remained focused on traditional party politics and male leaders. Similarly, nineteenth-century labor history centered on the organizing efforts of men who engaged in paid work outside the home. The proliferation of historical subfields suggests the tendency to separate certain topics – particularly women's history, but also various categories of social history – from "real" history. Condemnation of the resulting historiographical balkanization and calls for building connections among fields circulated continually within the profession during the 1980s. But the proposed solutions tended to reinforce the underlying problem. The perceived need for connections, for instance, assumed that the fields were, in fact, discrete entities. Just as suspension bridges bring together two distant shores, so these intellectual bridges would facilitate historical crossing where it would otherwise be impossible.

The nineteenth-century separation of spheres also influenced the work of those who challenged both the distinction and its effects – from domestic writers in the early nineteenth century, to advocates of women's rights and labor reform at the turn of the twentieth century, to historians in the late twentieth century. These activists and scholars pushed at the spheres' borders, working in different ways to bring women and their domestic labor into the public and into history. Yet, they never completely escaped the ideological confines of the nineteenth century. In fact, they often built their political and scholarly agendas on the domestic sphere's distinctiveness, thus reinforcing the ideology and extending its historical legacy.

The now extensive scholarship on women's organizations and reform efforts, for instance, has emphasized the various ways in which women activists asserted their special knowledge of children and all things domestic to assume public roles throughout the nineteenth century. By the century's last decades, even the woman suffrage movement had adopted this approach. Arguing that governmental neglect of domestic concerns was leading to the nation's ruin, suffrage leaders maintained that men were unfit to handle these issues because they lacked women's nurturing qualities and their practical experience. Women thus needed the vote *because* of their separate sphere of interests. Indeed, as Paula Baker has claimed in her influential article, "The domestication of American politics" (1984), women reformers were so success-ful in promoting their reform vision that they had reshaped the nation's political culture long before they received the vote in 1920.

Meanwhile, the labor movement in the nineteenth and early twentieth centuries tended to assume that workers were white men. Recent work in labor history has demonstrated that white working men in the North established their own independ-ence by distancing themselves from all African Americans, men and women. Similarly, they also used feminine dependence to naturalize masculine independence. In fact, white farmers and working-class men in both sections of the country relied on their gendered position as household heads with responsibilities for women and children to legitimize their claims for better wages and working conditions, more autonomy on the job, and greater political rights. Perhaps the best example is the "family wage:" wage rates high enough so that one man could support his entire family through his labor alone.

Labor initiatives and social welfare policy in the late nineteenth and early twentieth centuries continued to exclude women from the category of "labor." Proponents of protective legislation at the turn of the twentieth century thus argued that female laborers were, in fact, mothers with different interests from other workers. Long hours and dangerous work left women unable to fulfill their natural maternal role, which was crucial to the health of the nation. Placing public health and welfare over an individual's liberty to contract, reformers reversed the logic the courts often used to strike down labor regulations. But they did so by emphasizing women's anomalous place within the labor force.

Academic work on women and labor in the early twentieth century reflected and reinforced these same assumptions. These studies began to diverge from earlier work in the nineteenth century by problematizing the association between women, domes-ticity, and motherhood. Some social scientists were beginning to see the different roles of men and women as the product of socialization, not biology or nature. A few took the next logical step, arguing that men and women were more similar than they were different. If social barriers made women different and kept them within the domestic realm, then these not only could, but should, be removed. Yet the work pointing toward the importance of socialization did not necessarily alter the deeply embedded gendered premise that a separate domestic realm was essential to the public order. Instead, the emphasis on socialization legitimized the idea that social programs and governmental intervention could produce better homes and better mothers.

To this end, reformers produced a profusion of statistics, facts, and findings with which to prod reluctant legislators and jurists. Actually, activists and academics in this period were closely linked. Some of the best scholarship on and by women was produced outside academia because the lack of academic positions led many college-educated women to pursue scholarly work in other venues. As a result, key decisions in the reform agenda, such as *Muller* v. *Oregon* (208 US 412 [1908]), which upheld maximum working hours for women, rested as much on research in the social sciences as they did on legal precedent. The popular and influential Children's Bureau provides another example of this mixing of academia and political activism. The Bureau sponsored research to further its mission of improving women's status by addressing the problems of mothers and young children. A 1916 study in North Carolina, for instance, found that rural African-American women preferred fieldwork to housework. It paid better, brought women more social recognition, and offered an escape from the isolation and tedium of housework by allowing for more sociability. Yet these findings, which confounded the Bureau's conflation of women and motherhood and the universality of its brand of domesticity, did not alter the study's focus on pregnancy, child birth, and the care of young children within the home.

As the era of Progressive reform faded, historical accounts of women moved to the background. History and other disciplines began drawing a sharper line between academics and activists, prioritizing "hard" scholarly research directed toward the acquisition of objective knowledge over "soft" research designed to promote particular social agendas. As a result, scholarship by and about women disappeared within the academy. The Depression accentuated this trend. With jobs so scarce, men were given precedence. Women, it was assumed, did not "need" paid labor because they were economically dependent on men.

The Cold War and the economic boom of the 1950s presented new obstacles to women in academia. De-emphasizing conflict of every kind, this era's "consensus school" stressed the expansiveness and widespread acceptance of liberalism and capitalism. Most work credited liberal capitalism with spreading democracy and prosperity, although some historians, such as Richard Hofstadter and Louis Hartz, found the absence of more radical political alternatives deeply disturbing. Women, however, figured as neither historical subjects nor historians. Because consensus historians tended to represent the past from a single point of view, they subsumed women's lives within those of men and the private within the public, just as they represented working-class people within a middle-class experience. Of course, as recent work suggests, the line between private and public was much less clear in the popular culture of this period, which constantly worried over outside forces impinging on domestic space and domestic disorder producing social unrest. But, unlike Progressive era scholars, consensus historians tended to romanticize women and the home out of history altogether. Only the suffrage movement, which promised to incorporate women into institutional party politics, received much attention. The few works that dealt directly with women tended to be contribution history, concerned with recovering notable women whose accomplishments could be evaluated by the same standards as those applied to men. These same assumptions also made it difficult for women to break into the historical profession.

As late as the 1970s, few US historians recognized women as legitimate subjects of study, and fewer still thought that a focus on the domestic sphere would alter the terms of historical analysis. That situation soon changed as a growing body of work in women's history emerged to question the assumptions that had banished women and domestic issues from the historiography. The revived feminist movement, in particular, ignited the field, as women who gained access to the historical profession responded to the call to recover women's pasts. So too did the concurrent growth of social history, particularly its focus on ordinary working people. Many women's historians embraced social history because it illuminated women's lives in a way traditional historical paradigms, with their focus on formal politics and paid labor, did not. Social history's emphasis on "ordinary" people held the potential to make more women visible, while its insistence that history was made from the bottom up defined a much broader range of issues as historically significant. From this perspective, both women and their domestic realm became legitimate, historical topics.

As the field of women's history developed in the 1970s and 1980s, it departed from previous work by viewing the distinction between private and public as the question, not the answer. Women's historians began examining the creation of a separate, female sphere as a continuing historical process with results that required critical explanation. Work in the 1960s laid the foundations by locating the creation of a separate, woman's sphere in the early nineteenth century. Barbara Welter blazed the way in her influential essay, "The cult of true womanhood, 1820–1860" (1966), which did for the nineteenth century what Betty Friedan had done for the twentieth. Bringing a critical eye to that century's domestic literature, Welter argued that the insistence on women's piety, purity, submissiveness, and domestic isolation constrained them at the very moment when social, economic, and political opportunities of all kinds were expanding for men. In the introduction to her documents collection, *Up from the Pedestal*, Aileen Kraditor (1968) also noted the increased emphasis on separate spheres in the nineteenth century and linked it to economic changes that "broadened the distinctions between men's and women's occupations" and "provoked new thinking about the significance and permanence of their respective 'spheres'" (Kraditor, 1968: 10). Gerda Lerner's "The lady and the mill girl" (1969) then extended the analysis beyond the middle class by introducing differences among women. According to Lerner, it was no accident that calls for women's domestic confinement intensified at the same time that industrialization was drawing poorer women out of the home and into paid labor. Against this historical backdrop, Lerner saw "the cult of true womanhood" as the means through which middle-class women marked their class status. Yet, regardless of these studies' conclusions, they opened up new historiographical possibilities by revealing the domestic sphere as the product of a specific moment in history.

Even as this work brought the domestic sphere into history, it tended to leave women behind. Women did not make history. It happened *to* them: whether in the form of culture, ideology, or economics, history pushed them into the private sphere and imposed domesticity on them. Subsequent work addressed this issue by using the concept of "women's culture" to show how women's efforts could give meaning to their own lives and effect change in the world around them. Although focusing on one particularly influential woman, Kathryn Kish Sklar's influential biography of Catharine Beecher highlighted the role of women in creating, propagating, and using domestic ideology (Sklar, 1973). Beecher shunned the idea of women's direct political action. None the less, she still opened up new possibilities with her emphasis on women's dominion over the home, their responsibility for children, and their need for education. Indeed, as Sklar's work suggested, domesticity could be liberating as well as limiting. Carroll Smith-Rosenberg expanded this idea in her pioneering article, "The female world of love and ritual" (1975). Relying on women's diaries and letters, Smith-Rosenberg found a powerful female world, where women nurtured and supported each other and developed a different "women's culture" based in motherhood and domesticity.

In *The Bonds of Womanhood*, Nancy Cott (1977) also outlined a distinct female culture based on shared patterns of domestic labor and an increased emphasis on motherhood. But Cott took these findings in a different direction, arguing that women defined their work within the home in opposition to capitalist economic changes that were transforming the outside world. Women and the domestic realm, Cott maintained, came to represent everything – love, purity, piety, and morality – that men and the public world had abandoned. As such, this separate, female culture lay the groundwork for the feminist movement by not only providing an organizational network but also positioning women as critics of social and economic change. In fact, as Cott suggested, women's experience within their separate sphere was a necessary precondition of feminism, which rested on the "bonds" of womanhood in the sense of women identifying with each other as a distinct group with common interest that were different from those of men.

A series of books and articles on women's organizations followed, which traced women's reform activities and their public uses of domesticity from one end of the nineteenth century to the other. In the early decades, for instance, female reformers began addressing the problems of poor women in urban areas. They visited homes, gave advice about motherhood and housekeeping, and distributed material aid to those deemed worthy and deserving. Some reformers even confronted the sensitive issue of prostitution, linking it to women's economic marginality and their exploitation by men. Domestic ideology also figured in women's participation in the abolition movement. Identifying with enslaved women on the basis of an imagined sense of common womanhood, abolitionist women attacked slavery as an institution that perverted family ties and prevented women from fulfilling their roles as wives and mothers.

Women's reform efforts expanded in the years following the Civil War, as did the issues they included within the domestic sphere. In these years, Frances Willard built the Women's Christian Temperance Union (WCTU) into a national organization. As the WCTU maintained, temperance was a woman's issue because chronic drunkenness destroyed the home and made it impossible for women to perform their domestic duties. Later, the WCTU and other groups used the same logic in other areas. In general, women's reformers of this period criticized what they labeled the excesses of social and economic change: overcrowding, sanitation problems, unplanned urban growth, and the vulnerability of women and children to the vagaries of the market. Their solutions included child labor laws, literacy and education, changes in the legal status of married women, pure food laws, as well as better housing, health care, and other social services. The scholarship in these areas not only challenged the traditional historiographical emphasis on party politics but also significantly expanded notions of "the political." What emerged were strong, vocal women who fought hard for women's issues, sought to ameliorate the poverty and despair of others, shaped public policy, and directed the course of history. More than that, this work also established the public importance of women's labor and domestic responsibilities.

The implications, however, reinforced as well as recast key elements of nineteenth-century ideology and historiography. Not only did this work tend to privilege institutional politics and formally organized reform movements, but it also centered the historical narrative around the experience of middle-class whites. Positing the common experience of domestic work as the basis of women's action, it did not linger on the actual details of women's labor. The lives of these women, moreover, seemed to be too good to be true: studies emphasized women's efforts to create positive identities for themselves and to shape their lives *within* their separate sphere, not the oppressive practices that confined them to this sphere. Even enslaved women's supportive networks, as described in Deborah Gray White's influential *Ar'n't I a Woman?* (1985), seemed oddly insulated from the coercion of the slave system.

Ellen DuBois, Mari Jo Buhle, Temma Kaplan, Gerda Lerner, and Carroll Smith-Rosenberg took up this issue in a *Feminist Studies* forum, "Politics and culture in women's history" (Du Bois et al., 1980). In it, DuBois warned that the celebratory approach to women's culture obscured its limitations. While taking DuBois's point, the other participants tended to draw a distinction between the ideology imposed on women and women's positive uses of domesticity to foster creativity, self-worth, and political action. Revisiting this debate eight years later in a historiographical piece on women's history, "Separate spheres, female worlds, woman's place," Linda Kerber (1988) argued that the "need to break out of the restrictive dualism of an oppressive term (women's sphere) and a liberating term (women's culture)" resulted in new work that considered the ways in which "that sphere was socially constructed both *for* and *by* women" (Kerber, 1988: 18).

Although concurrent with the work on "women's culture" and influenced by it, another strand of the scholarship moved in a different direction that built more directly on insights and methodology from the "new" social history. Labor history's application of these concepts was particularly influential. Following the work of E. P. Thompson and Herbert Gutman, US labor historians became less preoccupied with the internal politics of labor unions in heavy industry and began looking more broadly at working people's experience with economic change. They explored, for instance, the transition from the seasonal rhythms of pre-industrial labor to the routinized discipline of factory work; informal efforts on the shopfloor to control the production process; and the culture, nurtured within families and communities, that supported workers' political action.

Some labor historians also began looking outside industrial areas to explore the roots of capitalist economic change and the culture that people brought with them to industrial work. Previously, the historiography had linked both "labor" and "capitalism" to urban industrial areas. Indeed, the terms still conjure up images of the belching smokestacks, huge factories, and noise, filth, and stench of cities that grew too rapidly and too haphazardly to accommodate all those who flocked there. As new studies revealed, capitalism began transforming rural households in the nation's isolated farms and quiet country hamlets long before it produced urban, industrial centers. The process was slow and uneven, varying according to specific conditions of time and place. But the effects were already visible in many areas in the first decades of the century. The expansion of markets beyond local areas placed small producers in competition with larger producers elsewhere, who experienced efficiencies of scale and could better absorb downturns in prices. Unable to compete, many men lost their farms and their workshops and became wage workers. Those who persisted turned to intensive production techniques that would allow them to compete successfully. For artisans, this meant increasing the size of their operations, hiring more workers, and making them more efficient through machinery and segmentation of the work process. For farmers, it meant more attention to marketable, cash crops in order to produce a surplus that could be invested in the kinds of improvements necessary to stay competitive. In fact, men and women in the US and abroad gravitated to cities and sought paid employment because of market-induced changes within their households.

By shifting the focus to families and communities, this approach had the potential to make women and their labor more visible. Yet, following in Marx's footsteps, many labor and social historians still conflated the experiences of working-class women with those of working-class men. Women's historians, however, began taking this assumption apart. Picking up the threads of Cott's (1977) economic analysis of women's domestic labor, some historians explored the changes in housework, cooking, and child care in more detail. As these studies showed, improvements in technology and rising expectations made women's work more, rather than less, demanding over time. Others took the analysis a step further by questioning the widely held view that production left the home and relegated women to consumption and child care. Joan Jensen's *Loosening the Bonds* (1986) demonstrated that women's butter and egg production was crucial to middle-Atlantic farm families and even carried them through years when staple crop prices were low. Urban working-class housewives also continued productive labor at home, taking in boarders and piecework that they could combine with domestic responsibilities.

Studies on wage-earning women directly challenged the notion that only men were "workers." As they revealed, women's experiences paralleled those of men in important ways. In the early nineteenth century, many of the cheap manufactured goods – yarn, cloth, hats, linens, shirts, and other basic articles of clothing – replaced items that women had produced at home. But poor women still needed to contribute economically to their families because the same changes also lowered the prices of the crops and products their menfolk were still trying to produce. To make up the difference, growing numbers of women worked for wages, either in factories or as outworkers. Indeed, contrary to the impression created by nineteenth-century domestic ideology and historians' application of it, women were among the first to experience the effects of capitalism. After laying out this economic transformation in early nineteenth-century New England, Thomas Dublin's *Women at Work* (1979) followed displaced rural women into the textile factories. Women's experience with factory labor was marked by difficulties adapting to a pace of work set by the clock and machines. Yet if these experiences were similar to those of men, wage labor ultimately had different implications for women in that it fostered a sense of independence and camaraderie that had been impossible working in their fathers' houses or as domestic servants.

Other studies departed from Dublin in offering much bleaker conclusions of the impact of wage labor on women. Tracing women's labor-force participation from the colonial period to the twentieth century, Alice Kessler-Harris's *Out to Work* (1982) showed how the notion of a separate, domestic sphere shaped women's work both within and outside the home. Although many women had to work for wages, their families, employers, and the state never acknowledged women as "workers" who supported themselves and their families on their wages. Even working women did not see themselves that way. The results pushed them into lower-paying, sex-segregated work on the basis that they did not really "need" higher wages. At the same time, this marginalization buttressed both the social constraints that forced women to perform unpaid domestic work and the economic constraints that led so many to seek paid labor.

Work on African-American and immigrant women highlighted the racial and ethnic inequalities that also defined this experience. All women may have faced barriers in the labor force, but they were far greater for ethnic women and, in particular, African-American women. In slavery, African-American women had no choice but to combine motherhood with field work and other productive labor. After emancipation, entrenched racism simultaneously forced them into wage work and excluded them from most jobs except domestic service. Indeed, work on African-American and other ethnic women revealed the home as a workplace. Domestic servants relieved white middle-class women of the heaviest, dirtiest housework. Yet white middle-class women refused to treat or pay domestic servants as skilled laborers, thus perpetuating the assumptions that constrained all women.

As other studies on unionization and radical labor reform indicated, it was not just employers who erected and maintained the barriers that kept women on the economic fringes. Working-class men also ignored working women's particular economic problems and resisted their entry into the "men's" work and labor organizations.

Just as it became more difficult to use men's experiences to stand in for the entire working class, it also became more difficult to use middle-class white women's experience to represent all women. Indeed, scholars of African-American women and other women of color had been voicing such complaints for some time. What emerged was a powerful critique of paradigms that emphasized a common women's experience defined by certain kinds of domestic labor and a sense of shared sisterhood. This approach, the critics maintained, had subordinated differences and conflicts among women to a transcendent female experience that was actually exclusive to middle-class white women in the industrial Northeast. By failing to examine the racial and class components of women's lives, women's history was homogenized and a whole host of women ignored. Although this critique was shaped by political concerns both inside and outside the academy, it also owed a great deal to the growing quantity, sophistication, and diversity of the work generated by social history. As social history developed and revealed more about how traditional historical paradigms made "ordinary" people invisible, it became clear how women's history had similarly rendered "ordinary" women invisible.

The result was new work that reached beyond white women in the middle class and beyond the Northeast. Drawing in the South, Midwest, and West, these studies highlighted diversity and conflict among women and developed a much more sophisticated, complicated view of the domestic sphere. As they revealed, the notion of a separate, domestic sphere made little sense for poor women and women of color who had always juggled work inside and outside the home. These women's domestic standards and concerns also differed considerably from those of middle-class white women. As Christine Stansell argued in *City of Women* (1987), middle-class notions of domestic privacy and women's confinement within the home did not apply to working-class women in antebellum New York City. For young women, participation in the emerging consumer culture of the city streets and even occasional forays into prostitution were compatible with their future roles as wives and mothers. Married women spent time in these same streets – as paid workers, scavengers, and shoppers – to provide basic necessities for their families. Despite the attempts of middle-class reformers to convince them otherwise, the concept of domestic isolation held little attraction for women who depended so much on each other to survive the harsh realities of urban poverty. Studies on African-American women explored their duel experience with racial and gender inequality and their efforts to combine paid work and public service with their roles as wives and mothers. According to Elsa Barkley Brown (1989), in her widely cited article "Womanist consciousness," black women in the late nineteenth century did not separate their problems from those of black men because of the way in which race both circumscribed their lives and connected them to the African-American community. But neither did black women subsume their interests within those of men. To the contrary, they believed that elevating black women was integral to the larger project of racial uplift. Borrowing from novelist Alice Walker, Brown used the term "womanist" to distinguish African-American women reformers from white feminists who tended to define women's interests in opposition to those of men.

Other historians showed how working-class women collaborated with their menfolk in strikes and labor protests, while also marking out their own interests as women. This body of work also placed the political agendas of poor women and women of color in conflict with those of middle-class white women, who appeared not as sisters but as slaveowners, employers, white supremacists, and representatives of agencies with the power to enforce unwanted restrictions on their lives. By implication, studies of middle-class and elite white women also began to change. Elizabeth Fox-Genovese's *Within the Plantation Household* (1988) emphasized the centrality of class authority and racial privilege to slaveholding women's social role and sense of womanhood. Similarly, studies of middle-class women's organizations increasingly stressed female reformers' power over the poor people they sought to aid.

Even as women's historians debated, complicated, and even rejected the notion of a domestic, woman's sphere, they could not completely escape the ideology that made the separation of spheres so powerful. Recovering women's pasts and placing them in history had the ironic effect of reinforcing the anomalous place of women in historical scholarship. Despite the growing sophistication of the work, women's experiences figured as an optional digression that could be added or discarded without altering the "real" historical narrative of men's experiences with party politics, public policy, and business. Mounting frustration with the inability of women's history to make inroads into the historical mainstream ultimately resulted in the refinement of the analytical category "gender." Much of the scholarship on women since the late 1960s had been built around the idea that male and female roles are socially constructed, not biologically determined – a distinction characterized as "gender." Historicizing practices considered "natural" had provided the critical wedge to question dichotomies – "nature" versus "culture," "production" versus "reproduction," and "private" versus "public" – that had placed women on the historical borders and devalued their lives. But, as some women's historians began to point out, revealing these dichotomies as "false" did not necessarily negate their power. Establishing the value of women's labor and their presence in the public sphere, for instance, did not alter power arrangements that continued to minimize women's contributions and to structure this arena in ways that discounted women's participation there. Most closely associated with Joan Scott (1986), this critique contended that gender had been needlessly confined to the analytical work of interpreting women's lives, leaving the "male" side unexamined as the standard against which the "female" side was explained. More than that, gender was about the broader meanings attached to perceived differences between men and women, with effects reaching into every aspect of social, political, and economic relations. Not only did gender apply to men, but it was embedded in all social relations and the exercise of power generally.

This formulation of gender opened up new ways of understanding the historical connections between women and men and, by extension, between the domestic sphere and the public arenas of traditional historical scholarship. Women's historians are now bringing these insights, often in combination with race, sexuality, class, and ethnicity, to traditional topics in the nineteenth century. These studies problematize the distinction between a female, domestic sphere and the male arena of work and politics by approaching it as the result of specific political struggles rather than the outcome of economic forces. The focus tends to be on the process by which this separation is maintained in different times and contexts rather than on the results of the separation.

These new studies have asked, for instance, how the category "labor" was structured as "male," how men's claims as workers excluded women, and how women themselves participated in this process. Some historians have used these questions to address wage-earning women's problematic place in labor history. Surveying the literature in women's history and labor history in the introduction to the important essay collection, *Work Engendered: Toward a New History of American Labor* (1991), Ava Baron noted how little effect the two fields had on each other. Labor historians either subsumed women's experiences within those of men or, when that was impossible, treated women as exceptional cases, while women's historians tended to treat women in isolation from men. The solution, Baron argued, was for both groups to step back and consider gendered meanings embedded in the categories "labor" and "laborer." The essays included in the collection provided suggestive models. Subsequent work has taken up Baron's call, showing how central manhood was to men's identities as workers, how public policy assumed and reinforced the assumption that workers were men, how the gendered categorization of certain jobs changed over time, and how difficult it was for women to claim the title "worker" or claim the rights and wages of "workers" when that category was so gender-laden. By locating oppression broadly in social structures and ideological practices instead of in men themselves, these studies have shed new light on the resilience and varieties of patriarchal oppression faced by different groups of working women.

Other historians have begun to dissolve the distinction between home and work in ways that also make women's labor seem less "domestic," that is, substantively different from the kinds of labor that men performed. In *Home and Work*, Jeanne Boydston (1990) took issue with the traditional Marxist assumption that capitalism removed production from the home. She argued that the distinction between reproduction and production is a theoretical abstraction that reveals more about the relative social standing of men and women than it does about the actual value or even the actual history of women's labor. As Boydston maintained, production never left the household completely in the nineteenth century, although the productive work that women did was increasingly categorized as something other than "labor." Not only did housework, childrearing, and even shopping have economic value in industrializing societies, but that labor enabled the growth of capitalism by allowing employers to pay their workers less than a living wage. As Stephanie McCurry's *Masters of Small Worlds* (1995) suggests, the pervasive effects of the separate spheres ideology have led historians to confuse all women's subordinate status with economic insignificance. According to McCurry, the economic viability of yeoman households in the ante-bellum South rested on women's labor. Yeoman women, particularly those in house-holds without grown children or slaves, regularly did field work. Their other chores, including the important task of bearing more laborers, were no less "productive."

In its current form, gender can limit as well as expand the boundaries of women's history. Some women's historians initially resisted "gender history" on the grounds that it undermined the field's fundamental goals. As they argued, gender marginalized women by casting them as victims whose lives were wholly constructed by outside forces. Moreover, they maintained, the application of gender to men would have similar results, transforming them into victims and, as such, absolving them from responsibility for oppressing women. Recent critics have echoed some of these con-cerns, pointing out that the rush to analyze the ideology and institutions of the powerful has left women on the sidelines. Once again, women, particularly poor women and women of color, have become the objects of, rather than participants in, history. Other historians, particularly those interested in sexuality and gay and lesbian studies, question analytical conceptions of gender that first assume a dichot-omy in which "male" and "female" form two mutually exclusive positions and then uncritically transpose this binary structure on to all social relations. Such an approach, these critics argue, ultimately limits our ability to understand the complexity of human behavior in the past, the range of positions that men and women may have occupied, and the social and political meanings attached to them.

None the less, current work on gender has begun to transform nineteenth-century historiography by finally breaking out of the confines of nineteenth-century ideology. These studies have revealed the links between the domestic, female sphere and the male, public work so successfully that the distinction itself is now beginning to look very different. As these studies suggest, the problem with previous scholarship was that it misconstrued cause and effect. The ideology of separate spheres, with its sharp distinction between men's and women's work, did not just reflect the results of economic and political change. It was also a powerful political tool that different groups of people marshaled to shape the course of historical events. The results, in turn, reinforced the distinctions in social practice and lent them an air of inevitability. Previous work, in other words, mistook the struggle to shape history for the outcome of history. As the ideology that created separate spheres has begun to loosen its grip on the historiography, it has cast the project of connecting the historical subfield of women's history to "real" history in a different light. Instead of thinking in terms of finding ways to bring women over the domestic divide into history, it is now possible for historians to conceive of the nineteenth century as a place that always included women.

REFERENCES

Baker, Paula (1984) "The domestication of American politics: women and American political society, 1780–1920," *American Historical Review*, 89, pp. 620–47.

Baron, Ava (ed.) (1991) *Work Engendered: Toward a New History of American Labor.* Ithaca, NY: Cornell University Press.

Boydston, Jeanne (1990) *Home and Work: Housework, Wages, and the Ideology of Labor in the Early Republic.* New York: Oxford University Press.

Brown, Elsa Barkley (1989) "Womanist consciousness: Maggie Lena Walker and the Independent Order of Saint Luke," *Signs,* 14, pp. 610–33.

Cott, Nancy F. (1977) *The Bonds of Womanhood: "Woman's Sphere" in New England, 1780–1835.* New Haven, Conn.: Yale University Press.

Dublin, Thomas (1979) *Women at Work: the Transformation of Work and Community in Lowell, Massachusetts, 1826–1860.* New York: Columbia University Press.

DuBois, Ellen, Buhle, Mari Jo, Kaplan, Temma, Lerner, Gerda, and Smith-Rosenberg, Carroll (1980) "Politics and culture in women's history: a symposium," *Feminist Studies,* 6, pp. 26–64.

Engels, Friedrich (1884) *The Origin of the Family, Private Property, and the State,* ed. Eleanor Burke Leacock. New York: International Publishers, 1990.

Fox-Genovese, Elizabeth (1988) *Within the Plantation Household: Black and White Women of the Old South.* Chapel Hill, NC: University of North Carolina Press.

Jensen, Joan (1986) *Loosening the Bonds: Mid-Atlantic Farm Women, 1750–1850.* New Haven, Conn: Yale University Press.

Kerber, Linda (1988) "Separate spheres, female worlds, women's place: the rhetoric of women's history," *Journal of American History,* 75, pp. 9–39.

Kessler-Harris, Alice (1982) *Out to Work: a History of Wage-earning Women in the United States.* New York: Oxford University Press.

Kraditor, Aileen (1968) *Up from the Pedestal: Selected Writings in the History of American Feminism.* Chicago: University of Chicago Press.

Lerner, Gerda (1969) "The lady and the mill girl: changes in the status of women in the age of Jackson," *Midcontinent American Studies Journal,* 10, pp. 5–15.

McCurry, Stephanie (1995) *Masters of Small Worlds: Yeoman Households, Gender Relations, and the Political Culture of the Antebellum South Carolina Low Country.* New York: Oxford University Press.

Scott, Joan W. (1986) "Is gender a useful category of analysis?," *American Historical Review,* 91, pp. 1053–75.

Sklar, Kathryn Kish (1973) *Catharine Beecher: a Study in American Domesticity.* New Haven, Conn.: Yale University Press.

Smith-Rosenberg, Carroll (1975) "The female world of love and ritual: relations between women in nineteenth-century America," *Signs,* 1, pp. 1–29.

Stansell, Christine (1987) *City of Women: Sex and Class in New York, 1789–1860.* Urbana: University of Illinois Press.

Welter, Barbara (1966) "The cult of true womanhood: 1820–1860," *American Quarterly,* 18, pp. 151–74.

White, Deborah Gray (1985) *Ar'n't I a Woman? Female Slaves in the Plantation South.* New York: Norton.

CHAPTER SEVENTEEN

Immigration and Ethnicity

NORA FAIRES

O N May 9, 1983, the *Wall Street Journal* ran a front-page story of what Salt Lake City authorities referred to as a "cultural misunderstanding." A local man advertised a pony for sale; a prospective buyer examined the pony; and the two struck a deal. The inquisitive seller, much attached to the pony, asked the buyer the purpose of the purchase. For his son's thirteenth birthday, the buyer responded. The buyer then took a piece of 2×4 out of his pick-up truck, clubbed the pony to death, loaded the carcass in the truck, and drove away. Shortly thereafter, the horrified seller, accompanied by police, descended on the buyer's home. In the backyard, a birthday party was in full swing, complete with men and boys crowded around the dead pony roasting on a spit. The seller screamed at the buyer, "I thought you bought the pony for your son to ride." The startled buyer replied, with obvious confusion and sincerity, "We don't *ride* horses, we *eat* them."

What does this late twentieth-century incident involving a native-born seller and a foreign-born buyer have to do with the historiography of nineteenth-century United States immigration? Much more than a case of purported "cultural misunderstanding," this episode provides an opportunity to explicate several key contributions to this scholarship and to discuss challenges that continue to face this field of enquiry. For in order to appreciate the multiple dimensions of this story requires both using the lenses of gender and religion and employing such concepts as assimilation, cultural pluralism, cultural adaptation, imperialism, and the constructions of state policy and of ritual. Class relations *per se* do not illuminate this event, yet clearly market relations, including the expectations and rights of buyer and seller, play a critical role; so, too, does the nature of the commodity exchanged, for differences in food ways have long represented a visible, contested, appropriated, and commodified source of ethnic diversity in the United States. In sum, a close interrogation and interpretation of this incident can illuminate the varied analytical perspectives that historians of immigration and ethnic studies have developed to investigate the experiences of immigrants (and internal migrants) and their descendants. Such finely grained reading of a single ethnic interaction clearly cannot resolve what many practitioners believe constitutes a crisis in the field, but may demonstrate how concepts derived from seemingly antagonistic perspectives might be deployed to fashion a more comprehensive discourse on immigrant and ethnic life.

The episode's site, Salt Lake City, provides a clue to the religion of the principals: both belonged to the Church of Jesus Christ of Latter-day Saints, more commonly known as Mormonism, a faith founded in upstate New York in the 1830s and thence brought by westward migrants to Utah (via Illinois) and by immigrant missionaries to much of the rest of the globe during the remainder of the nineteenth century. Citizens of England numbered among those converted to Mormonism and they, in turn, and in the style of the nineteenth-century's most far-flung empire, brought their religion (and their language) to Tonga, a set of small islands in the Micronesian region of the South Pacific. After the Great War Tongans came under Britain's "protection," and during World War II US forces were stationed there. In the post-war years, Tongans have migrated across the Pacific to the land of the GIs, with many Mormon Tongans settling in Utah, the state of their co-religionists. Notably, the eating of roast pony constitutes no centuries-old custom, but a tradition Tongans created by adapting the food ways of the British newcomers to their island. The early missionaries had found the islanders' diet of vegetables, fruit, and fish unsatisfactory to their roast-beef-and-potatoes palate, and so had imported livestock as a source of meat; first cattle, then, when these animals fared badly, horses. The English immigrants' adaptation of food ways led Tongans to their own adaptation (some might say acculturation). Young horseflesh roasted over an open pit became a culinary delicacy, assuming a central place in the celebration of a Tongan boy's passage to manhood.

A pony and a boy's coming of age: as the burly, brown-skinned Tongan immigrant buyer and "white," native-born seller concluded their deal, whatever cultural gap may have separated the two men must have seemed bridged by their mutual anticipation of the birthday party and the pony's key role in its success. What more home-grown American image than a boy, glowing with happiness, astride his very own pony? And what could be more obliterating to this imagined assimilation than the clubbing, cooking, and eating of the pony, as the immigrants literally ingested this symbol of Western Americana (itself a sixteenth-century import of the Spanish to the conquered "New World")? As the seller and buyer eyed each other across the roasting carcass, racial/ethnic lines must have been redrawn, with whatever belief in cultural pluralism the seller may have had now probably as dead as the pony. Moreover, the presence of the police must have prompted each co-religionist to wonder whether, and how, the state might intervene, to re-broker the sale, to protect the property rights of the buyer, or to enforce the "prevailing community norms," those of the culturally, socially, and presumably politically privileged seller. "They" (the dominant) *ride* horses, don't they?

"They" – the dominant – also figured prominently in producing the early studies of nineteenth-century immigration. Significantly, over the course of the twentieth century, as the struggles of subordinate groups for rights in American society altered the composition of the academy, this "they" came to comprehend an increasingly diverse demography of historians and ethnic studies scholars. As I discuss below, in conjunction with other developments, this re-formation of those who create scholarship has refashioned the study of immigration and ethnicity in the United States. The result has been more subtle, more varied, and more contingent readings of events like that delineated above; in sum, more complex, more nuanced, and sometimes more oppositional narratives of the nation's – and its peoples' – nineteenth-century pasts.

The "Immigrant Paradigm"

The United States as uniquely a "nation of immigrants," a "melting pot," and a haven for the "tired," "poor," "homeless," and "tempest-tost" has long proved a staple of self-referential and global discourse and iconography. In a twenty-first century world, increasingly marked both by racial, ethnic, and religious strife (often bound up with efforts to forge new nationalisms) and by the growing mobility of populations across regional, national, and continental boundaries, the myth of American demographic exceptionalism persists in the public mind, if significantly less so in contemporary scholarship. Not so during the early days of immigration studies, when the explicit or implicit assumption of American exceptionalism undergirded the field – a field that emerged in the early twentieth century in an era characterized, much like the present, by heightened cultural conflict and large-scale population movements.

One source for this field of enquiry lay in the city, specifically Chicago. During the 1920s sociologists under the leadership of Robert Park at the University of Chicago embarked on a self-consciously scientific study of the social functioning and spatial "ecology" of immigrants in this rapidly industrializing and culturally diversifying urban center. Using Chicago as a laboratory and employing metaphors from the natural sciences, especially botany, Park, his colleagues, and their students investigated myriad aspects of immigrant life, focusing especially on a pattern they termed "ethnic succession": as foreign newcomers arrived, they "invaded" existing neighborhoods, prompting the residents of these neighborhoods to resettle in adjacent city blocks where they in turn both formed a new ethnic enclave and displaced this second area's current inhabitants. From the viewpoint of the sociologists observing these spatial transformations, if not of the urban residents participating in them, immigration consequently spurred a continuing, regular, and predictable cycle of residential change. Influenced by the massive outpourings from southern and eastern Europe that so transformed Chicago in the late nineteenth and early twentieth centuries (and largely ignoring other vast contemporaneous migrations to the city such as those of African Americans), practitioners of the Chicago School concentrated on immigrants from Europe. Writing as the era of relatively unrestricted immigration from such European areas came to an end, Park and his colleagues produced pioneering works that placed the issue of immigration firmly and enduringly on the scholarly agenda. If their clinical gaze objectified those they observed, it also raised immigrants and their children to the realm of subjects worthy of study, a bracing change from the prevailing academic attitude that sentimentalized or, more commonly, dismissed or derogated the nation's foreign born.

The urban immigrant saga advanced by Park and his co-investigators had pessimistic and optimistic facets. Immigration, they maintained, ripped people from the soil of their homelands and left them rootless and alienated in their new land, thus inclining individual immigrants to personal pathologies, and immigrants, as a group, to social disorganization. Yet hope for these newcomers' adjustment and faith in their material improvement brightened this gloomy tale: America was exceptional not only for its welcome to Europe's "wretched refuse," but, integrally, for its capacity to absorb them and provide them with unprecedented opportunity.

The second wellspring of the field of immigration history shared this view of American uniqueness, grounding it, figuratively and literally, in the countryside rather than the city. Frederick Jackson Turner's famous frontier thesis, first put forward in the 1890s, posited the creation of a uniquely American democracy via the interaction of waves of newcomers, expressly including immigrant settlers, with the environment, the wide, "open" spaces of the US West. As narrowly European in its focus as the

Chicago School, Turner's sweeping synthesis ignored the West's conquered, then colonized, Mexicans and decimated, then displaced, indigenous peoples. Comprehending varieties of European newcomers (though emphasizing those from northern and western Europe) within a tale of adaptation and modernization, Turner and those whom he influenced envisioned the frontier as crucible, forging a new American character and a distinctive American polity. In 1908, little more than a decade after Turner first postulated this view, Israel Zangwill, an immigrant English Jew, popularized the phrase "melting pot" in his enthusiastically received play of the same name. In the midst of a great tide of migration to the United States, what scholars would later dub the "immigrant paradigm" – America as a "Land of Promise" for "immigrants, all!" – had found a prominent exponent in a non-Christian, foreign-born playwright.

Assimilation, Cultural Pluralism, and Community

Like Zangwill (and unlike Turner or Park), many of the next generation of immigration scholars were themselves children of immigrants. Marcus Lee Hansen, student of Turner and son of Danish and Norwegian immigrants, exemplified this trend. Proud of his ethnic heritage and cosmopolitan in his outlook, Hansen intended to write a sweeping three-volume "history of the continuing settlement of the United States" (Hansen, 1940: v) from its colonial years onward; his untimely death dashed this ambitious plan. Nevertheless, the first volume of the projected trilogy, *The Atlantic Migration, 1607–1860*, proved pathbreaking. Published posthumously in 1940, Hansen's work rested on meticulous research in both Europe and the United States and told a saga that included the trials of the humble as well as the triumphs of the prominent. In clear, vivid prose, he recast America's economic and political history through its "peopling," first of the 13 distinct British colonies, then of the vibrant new republic, and finally of a reunited nation in which "[a]ll who lived in America, alien-born and native-born, were resolved to become one people" (Hansen, 1940: 306). Bridging the Old World and the New, Hansen portrayed the homeland situations that prompted Europeans to emigrate, the conditions they endured on long oceanic voyages, and the circumstances they confronted upon settlement. In a foreword to the original edition of the book, its editor, Arthur M. Schlesinger, used terms strikingly evocative of contemporary work in immigration history to describe this volume written in the late 1930s: Hansen's history, Schlesinger declared, "deals with the great transatlantic migration of white peoples" (Hansen, 1940: xix).

Like Hansen, Schlesinger had immigrant parents, and, like Turner (a Harvard colleague), one of his students, Oscar Handlin, would become the next major figure in the field of immigration history. Hansen's saga had reached print as World War II erupted across Europe, Asia, and Africa; Handlin's masterwork, *The Uprooted: the Epic Story of the Great Migrations that Made the American People*, appeared in 1951, to a world transformed by war and increasingly remade in the image of the now-dominant United States. If, by then, the Soviets had exploded "the bomb," a "hot" proxy war had broken out in Korea between Cold War powers, and domestic anti-communists had begun a sordid witch hunt, for most (white) Americans the post-war years constituted an expansive and upbeat era, dubbed at the time the onset of "The American Century." In the midst of this triumphalist national mood, Handlin, the son of immigrant Jews from Russia, published his Pulitzer prize-winning book, an alternately mournful and extolling paean to those brave and bereft Europeans who had made a "painful break with their past" (Handlin, 1951: 307) by journeying to the United States, only to encounter a harsh new life and become culturally alien to those for whom they had sacrificed so much – their American-born children. Recapitulating and extending the Chicago School's theory of psychological and social "disorganization," Handlin stressed the deep shock immigrants experienced at being torn from their homelands and lamented the destructive impact that this wrenching process had even "on generations which themselves never paid the cost of crossing" (Handlin, 1951: 6).

Remarkably popular, *The Uprooted* introduced to a wide audience the testimonies of immigrants themselves and acquainted this public (many undoubtedly second- and third-generation Americans) with the works of ethnic writers. To portray the minds, hearts, and souls of his subjects more accessibly, Handlin published his chronicle without documentation, to powerful literary, if frustrating scholarly, effect. Although depicting immigrants primarily as downtrodden ("the uprooted" surely qualified as the "tempest-tost" for whom Miss Liberty lifted her lamp in New York harbor), Handlin represented nineteenth- and early twentieth-century European immigrants not as victims so much as peasant-heroes, enduring enormous hardships in their quest for a better life for themselves and their children. In his account, moreover, the heretofore marginal field of immigration history not only moved to the discipline's center, it rightfully *became* that center. Handlin's initial sentences of the volume boldly proclaimed: "Once I thought to write a history of the immigrants in America. Then I discovered that the immigrants *were* American history" (Handlin, 1951: 3).

Heady words indeed for toilers in an academic field traditionally provoking little interest. By such lights, historians of immigration became scholar-heroes, rescuing and retelling the stories of those who truly made America and thereby bringing the nation's "right stuff" to the forefront of academic notice. Perhaps to the disappointment of the small but growing number of immigration historians, the discipline neither immediately nor overwhelmingly endorsed Handlin's redefinition of the field. In the generally consensus-oriented 1950s, the discipline's focus remained on formal politics and those wielding power in and deriving privilege from mainstream culture and its institutions. Thus post-war historiography continued largely to exclude immigrants and their descendants, among others, from scholarly view. Not until the 1960s, when the attention of American society became riveted on some of those "others" (particularly as they struggled for civil rights and economic opportunities) and as the "new social history" emerged within this conflictual social context, would immigration and ethnic history become an important area of historical enquiry. When it did, it would do so in opposition to the assimilationist assumptions and ethos that had undergirded much of the work to date, including that of Handlin. Fittingly, the first major broadside in this historiographical campaign emerged from a study of immigrants in Chicago, the city where four decades previously sociologists had sought to measure the degree of immigrants' pathology and extent of acculturation.

In 1964 Rudolph J. Vecoli published "*Contadini* in Chicago," a landmark article he pointedly subtitled "A critique of *The Uprooted*." Vecoli's deft, incisive examination of the enduring cultural patterns of southern Italian immigrants to Chicago took precise aim at historians who maintained that immigrants to the United States had assimilated uniformly and uncritically as well as at those scholars who championed this process as a positive national goal. These immigrants, Vecoli contended, demonstrated agency, rather than alienation; cultural durability and selective adaptability, rather than acculturation; community building, rather than social disorganization. Hence, claimed this ethnically identified second-generation southern Italian, the United States neither erased Old World patterns nor effaced immigrants and their children as human actors. Expressive in part of the larger critique of modernization theory animating the disciplines of sociology and anthropology during the 1960s – a critique itself reflective of the intellectual underpinnings of the era's anti-colonial movements – Vecoli's article brought a neglected oppositional tradition to the fore in the study of immigration and ethnicity: cultural pluralism. In myriad, sometimes contradictory forms, this analytical tradition, repudiating assimilation and explicitly stressing ethnic group survival and distinctiveness, dominated historians' study of nineteenth-century mass migrations to the United States for the next three decades.

John Bodnar's *The Transplanted: a History of Immigrants in Urban America* (1985) illustrates this pattern, its title signaling the historiographical sea change. In purposeful counterpoint, Handlin's "uprooted' becomes Bodnar's "transplanted": those who left for the United States brought with them practices, outlooks, dispositions, and values, and upon arrival in America re-established many of these in the soil of their new homeland. Published in 1985, Bodnar's concise and readable synthesis relied on the extraordinary outpouring of work on immigration history that had appeared in the 20 years following Vecoli's denunciation of assimilation. The book's lengthy bibliography provided a valuable overview of the state of the art, attesting to the welter of journal articles, monographs, and, especially, doctoral dissertations completed during these two decades, as immigration historians (zealously incorporating immigrants and their children in the "new social history's" reinterpretation of "history from the bottom up") examined groups ranging, if not quite from A to Z, at least from Armenians through Finns, Germans, Italians, Latvians, Poles, and Slovaks to Ukrainians. Notably, Bodnar's account, focused predominantly on immigrants from Europe, paid some attention to those from the Mediterranean basin and Asia and, within the western hemisphere, from Mexico and the Caribbean. His influential survey thus accurately reflected the substantially broadened scope of the field by the mid-1980s and inscribed into the canon this geographically more expansive and culturally more inclusive vision.

The contribution of *The Transplanted*, however, extended beyond presenting a narrative of immigration history grounded in recent scholarship, for the book's contents proved more analytically multi-dimensional than its title. In particular, Bodnar's overview sought to advance two significant conceptual concerns: to replace monolithic views both of individual immigrant groups and of American culture with conceptions of each as fragmented and frequently conflictual; and to examine the connections between immigrants and the forces of capitalism and modernity. According to Bodnar, earlier views, including many written within a cultural pluralist framework, portrayed immigration as a "clash of cultures"; he suggested presenting it as "innumerable points of contact between various categories and beliefs" in order to observe the "process of social changes stimulated almost incessantly by the changing imperatives of the marketplace and the diverse responses of human beings themselves" (Bodnar, 1985: xx). Bodnar's "transplanted," then, might more accurately be deemed the "transformed." That the former term became the book's title may signify a particular historiographical juncture, a moment when conceptualization outstripped language. In any case, Bodnar's attempt to reorient the field fore-shadowed some of the concerns that in the 1990s prompted reassessments of cultural pluralism. Moreover, his organizing question – how did immigrants' encounter with capitalism and a varied American culture shape their experiences and values? – assumed prominence among both contemporary and subsequent immigration schol-ars, many of whom arrived at the query independently and endeavored to answer it more fully.

Community studies of particular immigrant groups constituted the most common works in the flourishing literature that Bodnar synthesized. In 1989, four years after the publication of *The Transplanted*, one such work appeared that demonstrated many of the strengths and avoided many of the limitations of the genre, while pointing to new directions in the field. David A. Gerber's analytically sophisticated, gracefully written, and hefty *The Making of an American Pluralism: Buffalo, New York, 1825–60* rested on extensive and painstaking research in sources commonly used in such studies, including city directories, manuscript population censuses, and immigrant newspapers, and those less frequently consulted, including parish histories and pol-itical leaders' personal papers. Interweaving the history of antebellum Buffalo and that of its immigrant settlers (especially the Irish and Germans) within the framework of an evolving polity, Gerber traced the dynamics that resulted in immigrants' integration – not assimilation – into a stratified center of commercial capitalism. Subtly writing immigration history back into intellectual, political, and economic history, Gerber concluded that Buffalo's "pluralistic social system" had a "formidable absorptive" capacity to "preserve order by balancing competing claims and interests, and by holding out visions of a good life in a just society to those allowed, willing, and able to take advantage of opportunity" (Gerber, 1989: 412). In analyzing the changing relations within and among immigrant groups, Gerber eschewed the assumption that ethnic groups existed in antebellum Buffalo, instead employing the anthropological notion of "ethnicization" (1989: xiv) to trace their formation. Admittedly eclectic in its approach, Gerber's book commingled assimilationist and cultural pluralist view-points, demonstrating through the detailed analysis of one city the fashioning and refashioning both of ethnic communities and of the larger society that reciprocally comprehended and constituted them.

Through the Lenses of Class and Gender

The theme of making and re-making that coursed through Gerber's volume owed much to a pioneering 1973 journal article by labor historian Herbert G. Gutman. In "Work, culture, and society in industrializing America, 1815–1919" Gutman had introduced a broad range of historians in the United States to the analysis of class formation put forward by renowned British labor historian E. P. Thompson, an analysis infusing Marxism with cultural anthropology. Historians of American workers long had struggled with their own brand of American exceptionalism, a reading of the past in which the United States had become a modern, industrial power without the conflict between labor and capital that had characterized European nations (for better or worse, depending on the historian's political proclivities). Cleverly turning the notion of labor exceptionalism inside out, Gutman combined it with a modified version of the nation's immigrant exceptionalism to craft a new story of what might be termed America's "long nineteenth century." Pointing to the waves of "diverse premodern native and foreign born peoples" who successively entered factory work in the United States from 1815 to 1919, he argued that a "state of tension" cyclically developed between workers and industry (Gutman, 1977 edn: 13).

By assuming that immigrants and migrants had "premodern" pasts, Gutman endorsed a version of the "clash of cultures" model that ten years later Bodnar's synthesis would debunk. Still, his account treated these native- and foreign-born peasants-cum-workers with dignity, investing them with the ability to challenge and reorganize American economic and social life. Furthermore, while he discussed only European immigrants, Gutman emphasized that a fuller account should incorporate the study of "bound workers (factory slaves in the Old South)" and "nonwhite free laborers, mostly blacks and Asian immigrants" (Gutman, 1977 edn: 13). Ambitious, bold, and crisply written, Gutman's lengthy essay remains compelling; its major arguments are now refined, significantly revised, or substantially rejected, but the article's approach and vitality arguably contribute enduringly to both labor and immigration history.

If Gutman's essay exemplifies the intertwining of labor and ethnic history that invigorated both fields from the 1960s on, Hasia Diner's *Erin's Daughters in America: Irish Immigrant Women in the Nineteenth Century* illustrates the crucial conjuncture of women's history and ethnic history that began in the late 1970s. Published in 1983, in the wake of the second wave of twentieth-century American feminism, Diner's thoughtful and imaginative book demonstrated the power of using gender, in addition to class, as a lens through which to view immigration. The Irish had long occupied a prominent place in immigrant historiography, with scholars generally aware that Irish emigration included proportionately larger numbers of women than did other nineteenth-century immigrations. Yet no student of the Irish before Diner had systematically examined the causes or consequences of the migration's demography. *Erin's Daughters*, however, went further, focusing on Irish women themselves and their agency, especially in shaping their lives as workers. Her optic revealed that many single Irish women migrated alone, particularly after the famine years. Like their male counterparts, Irish women sought economic opportunities for themselves and the families they left behind; unlike their brethren, they also sought relief from the restrictions that gender placed upon them in their homeland. Moreover, while Gutman had stressed differences between the society and culture of immigrant peasants and that of industrializing America, Diner traced important pre- and post-migration continuities. In nineteenth-century Ireland, for example, a prolonged, severe agricultural crisis had led to low rates of marriage, especially in rural counties; in the United States a different mix of factors resulted in Irish women marrying at lower rates and at higher ages than other women, whether native- or foreign-born.

Diner's study also broadened the study of immigrant worklife beyond factory labor, bringing particular attention to domestic service, the most common occupation of immigrant women throughout the nineteenth century. Most significantly, the scholarship on women immigrants represented by *Erin's Daughters* exposed the patriarchal conflation of "immigrants" with "men" that had limited and distorted much previous work. While analysis of gender relations would not come to assume as high a place on many (mostly male) immigration historians' scholarly agendas as had the examination of class relations, by the mid-1980s the field had changed profoundly: more studies included women, and those authors who overlooked them had difficulty defending the omission.

From Emigration and Immigration to Migration

In addition to incorporating the insights of labor and women's historians into their scholarship, immigration historians during the 1980s increasingly adopted a more holistic and processual conception of their field: not just *immigration* (arrival) or even immigration plus *emigration* (departure), but *migration*. Building (often unknowingly) on works by Hansen and Handlin that had examined both homeland and destination, many practitioners explicitly broke with the teleological view undergirding this same literature, which tended to depict immigrants as heretofore sedentary individuals who journeyed on one-way tickets from the Old World (with its old ways) to the New (with its promise of being a "common man's utopia"). Many of those historians who began exploring migration as a multi-faceted, non-linear process invoked as inspiration an article written 20 years before by British historian Frank Thistlethwaite.

In "Migration from Europe overseas in the nineteenth and twentieth centuries" (1960) Thistlethwaite had urged scholars, in a now well-known phrase, to rend the "salt-water curtain inhibiting [American] understanding of European origins" (Thistlethwaite, 1991 edn: 20). This essay had implored scholars to delineate the various circumstances that prompted Europeans to emigrate from particular locales, to compare the various countries these migrants chose as destinations, and to trace the multiple connections between population movements within Europe and beyond. Delivered during the salad days of "the American century," Thistlethwaite's call to decenter the United States as immigrant destination largely fell on deaf ears; it would continue to do so throughout much of the 1970s, a decade during which the nation's bicentennial celebration consecrated the "immigrant paradigm" as a tenet of civil religion. But in the following decade, as Americans faced a world in which their nation's global hegemony seemed less secure and as immigration historians searched for more nuanced and more geographically comprehensive approaches, Thistlethwaite's plea found a more receptive audience.

One noteworthy study motivated by his challenge focused on immigrants from a region in north-western Germany who settled in the American Midwest. In 1987 Walter D. Kamphoefner published *The Westfalians: from Germany to Missouri*, a spare, cogent, and copiously researched monograph. Bearing the title "Not uprooting but reunion: the significance of chain migration in the immigrant experience", Kamphoefner's introduction (1987: 3) announced his major theme and outlined the painstaking methodology he used to find evidence for it. According to Kamphoefner, Westfalians who settled in rural Missouri came not as individuals but as links in a chain that connected particular homeland villages and neighborhoods to particular sites in the American countryside; hence, on arrival, these immigrants faced not a sea of strangers but clusters of familiar faces, some kin. To demonstrate this thesis, Kamphoefner, a descendant of Westfalian Missourians, researched not only regions of emigration and areas of settlement but tracked individual migrants from one place to the other. Contrary to the belief that peasants formed the backbone of nineteenth-century emigration, Kamphoefner found that in Westfalia "emigration was highest where there was little agriculture" (Kamphoefner, 1987: 27); instead, outflow was greatest from those rural districts that had seen the rise and collapse of proto-industry, primarily linen-making.

Three other studies completed in the mid-1980s differently and consequentially extended and embellished aspects of Thistlethwaite's views; each, in turn, knocked another prop from the tottering "immigrant paradigm," at least for historians. In 1985 Kerby A. Miller published the massive *Emigrants and Exiles: Ireland and the Irish Exodus to North America*. Based on voluminous research in both Ireland and the United States, Miller's study drew on sources ranging from government reports to poetry and song in order to demonstrate that many who left Ireland did so with great reluctance and, whether settling in the United States or Canada, remained estranged in North America. For many "emigrants and exiles," return migration to Ireland, rather than assimilation or integration into American culture, became the ultimate goal. Some achieved it; others maintained or reinforced their ties to Ireland by reinstituting cultural practices or participating in political movements, thus seeking continuing membership in an Irish nation they materially and imaginatively attempted to create.

Two macro-historical analyses, attending more to process and structure than the experiences of individual migrants or immigrant groups, represent important counter-parts to Miller's finely grained account. In 1985 prolific German historian Dirk Hoerder published "An introduction to labor migration in the Atlantic economies, 1815–1914," the sweeping conceptual overview to his edited book, *Labor Migration in the Atlantic Economies: the European and North American Working Classes during the Period of Industrialization*. Relying on and critiquing a broad American and European literature, Hoerder offered a synthetic, century-long re-examination of diverse European migrants as workers, sketching elaborate systems of intra-European and two-way transatlantic labor markets and labor pools, then comparing these migrants' acculturation in their varied destinations. His account complicated the narrative of European migrants' itineraries, further decentering the United States as the only obvious or even favored destination. Partially in response to the second macro-historical synthesis, Hoerder soon expanded his already wide vision, embedding his examination of the Atlantic economies of migration into a world-system model and extending his investigation of European migrations back to the twelfth century.

Notably, this second synthesis had appeared less than a year before Hoerder's. Lucie Cheng and Edna Bonacich published their imposing edited volume, *Labor Migration under Capitalism: Asian Workers in the United States before World War II*, in 1984. Like Hoerder, they provided a powerful, challenging introduction to the essays they collected, entitling theirs "A theoretical orientation to international labor migration" (Cheng and Bonacich, 1984: 1–56). Dense, abstract, and studded with diagrams that hinted at the authors' social science expertise, Cheng and Bonacich focused on Pacific economies, rather than Atlantic ones, and eastward and northward movements of peoples, rather than westward migrations. Employing a Marxist perspective to place migration in a global frame, their volume considered various Asian immigrant groups, but also America's colonized workers, such as Mexicans and Puerto Ricans, and the nation's formerly enslaved, African Americans. In their conceptualization, structural forces of political economy largely determined the timing and nature of mass migrations: the rise of American capitalism and the spread of American imperialism together organized and reorganized a shifting and truly international labor market during the nineteenth century.

Immigration historians familiar with Cheng and Bonacich's analysis could see in it a criticism of a key theme in the "immigrant paradigm": that America, as beacon, beckoned the "huddled masses" to a life of freedom and opportunity. But Cheng and Bonacich themselves did not advance this view; indeed, their work neither explicitly engaged this paradigm nor its critics. A glance at the bibliography to their introduction reveals that Cheng and Bonacich placed themselves in a different scholarly lineage to that discussed above and, consequently, engaged a different discourse. Rather than the discipline of history, their theoretical orientation derived overwhelmingly from the social sciences and from interdisciplinary programs in American studies and ethnic studies, the latter a field that has proliferated in several branches since the 1970s. As discussed below, work since the 1980s stemming from the social sciences and interdisciplinary programs as well as from the field of immigration history has increasingly contributed to a remarkable flowering of literature on a wide variety of what scholars (following Gramsci) now term "subaltern" groups in nineteenth-century America. Yet too often scholars of these two traditions – those (more or less) outside the discipline of history and those (more or less) inside it – continue to write in isolation from each other, thus prompting, in part, what some regard as a crisis in the field of immigration history (or perhaps the field of ethnic studies).

Contestation in the Constructions of Race and Ethnicity

In the 1990s, much of the best work on immigrants and migration emerging from both these scholarly traditions focused on "race" and "ethnicity" as changing social constructions. Published in 1991, historian David R. Roediger's highly influential *The Wages of Whiteness: Race and the Making of the American Working Class* constituted a cornerstone of such investigations. Influenced by such disparate frameworks as Marxism and psychoanalysis and inspired especially by the writings of W. E. B. DuBois, Roediger argued that antebellum white workers forged identities and developed class consciousness in opposition to black Americans. Interrogating class and race as constructions expressed through lived experience, cultural forms, and language, *The Wages of Whiteness* demonstrated how Irish immigrants, in particular, garnered substantial social, economic, and psychic benefits – "wages" – from the race they came to occupy, "whiteness." Roediger's trenchant work sparked a spate of "whiteness studies" during the 1990s (few of them recognizing that 50 years previously immigration historians Hansen and Schlesinger had written of Europeans expressly both as "white" and as "peoples").

By the end of the decade more comprehensive studies of racial construction appeared, including Matthew Frye Jacobson's *Whiteness of a Different Color: European Immigrants and the Alchemy of Race (1998)*, a disquisition on the evolution of racial categories from the founding of the republic in the eighteenth century through the advent of the civil rights movement in the twentieth. Critical of Roediger's economic focus although expressly building on his work, Jacobson proposed a broader nexus for examination: the "complex crosscurrents at the confluence of capitalism, republicanism, and the diasporic sensibilities of various racially defined groups themselves" (Jacobson, 1998: 19). To assess the "historical fabrication, the changeability, and the contingencies of whiteness" (1998: 280), he looked to popular culture (fiction, theater, travelers' accounts, cartoons) as well as to law and other varieties of formal speech. Using such sources creatively to craft a "political history of whiteness" (1998: 13), Jacobson surveyed the shifting identities and mainstream constructions of groups whose ancestors ranged geographically from England to Africa, India to Japan, Mexico to the Caribbean. His approach to the realm of the public and political, even more than Roediger's concentration on the waged economy, led Jacobson away from a systematic analysis of gender. Consequently, it would fall to other writers to trace the connections between fabrications of race, ethnicity, and class and contingent and relational constructions of men, women, and sexuality during the nineteenth century.

In the meantime, other studies, by scholars both inside and outside the discipline of history, significantly advanced understanding of the social construction of race and ethnicity. Two representative articles appeared at mid-decade. Directly engaging the emerging literature on "whiteness," in 1994 Gary Y. Okihiro, a scholar of Asian-American studies, asked an especially provocative question in an essay entitled: "Is yellow black or white?" Confronting the tendency among scholars to portray the American past (and present) as two-toned, Okihiro demonstrated that historians' preoccupation with "black" and "white" erased diverse Asians – and Latinos and indigenous peoples – from the national narrative and thereby falsified accounts of racial and ethnic dynamics in the United States. The following year, Earl Lewis, a historian of African Americans, further problematized the idea of race by unpacking the idea of "black." Deeming the historical study of African Americans at a "conceptual crossroads," Lewis suggested in the subtitle of his essay one path scholars might follow: by "Writing African Americans into a history of overlapping diasporas" historians more fully could comprehend the "diversity in black life" (Lewis, 1995: 782, 786). This perspective would clarify "how racial identity informs individual identity and how identity formation in turn informs racial construction," while reconnecting the history of "African-descended immigrants" with that of "American blacks" (1995: 783, 786), especially important for understanding the post-emancipation history of African Americans. Significantly, Lewis's use of the noun "diaspora" – dispersed communities – called attention to the common geographical home, Africa, from which blacks had emanated, while his modifier for that noun, "overlapping," underscored the multiplicity of evolving populations emanating from this continent.

Toward a New Paradigm

In addition to furthering the reformulation of "race," Lewis's prescription and Okihiro's question each implicitly engaged other significant themes in the historiography of nineteenth-century American immigration and ethnicity, notably cultural pluralism. Specifically, diasporic studies, like those endorsed by Lewis, recalled the theme of "community-building," a motif dominating work on immigration history from the 1960s through the 1980s. Similarly, many of the studies (like Okihiro's) of diverse groups of Asian Americans, Native Americans, Latinos, and African Americans (members of "racial ethnic groups" or "peoples of color," as they increasingly became known) delineated the continuities in these groups' experiences in the United States and the durability of their cultures.

Despite such cultural pluralist resonances, the work of Lewis, Okihiro, and numerous other scholars of racial ethnic groups differed substantially from that in the mainstream of immigration and ethnic history before the advent of whiteness studies. Exposing, then deposing, the eurocentrism that characterized much of this earlier work, scholars of peoples of color moved the study of race from the periphery to the core, formulating around this center new views of race and ethnicity in nineteenth-century America. Focusing on the ways in which American society excluded rather than incorporated peoples of color, ranging from state-supported efforts (notably the Chinese Exclusion Act of 1882 and Jim Crow laws used against various "non-whites") to less formal and more quotidian discrimination (in employment and social relations, for instance), these studies detailed American society's reluctance to consider immigrants and migrants of color as candidates for absorption, assimilation, or acculturation. Explicitly or implicitly rejecting the "immigrant paradigm" because it denies the salience of race in the process of migration, this scholarship metaphorically replaced the lamp raised by a beckoning Miss Liberty with a searchlight held by a sentinel guarding the American landscape from unwanted intruders (or a torch clutched by a white-robed Klansman in a smoldering African-American neighborhood, "Chinatown," or "Little Mexico"). More generally, the growing evidence that racial ethnic migrants typically encountered resistance and oppression during what both scholars and the public widely have regarded as America's heyday of unrestricted immigration substantially revises and advances our understanding of the nineteenth-century republic.

Significantly, many of those writing on the experiences of these subaltern groups (including historian Lewis and Asian-American studies scholar Okihiro) themselves claim membership of such groups. Thus, as obtained in the earlier decades of the twentieth century, subject and object within the field of immigration and ethnicity often are joined in complicated ways. Concomitantly, the continued transformation of the American ethnic and racial present, however constructed, contributes to the evolving analysis of the differently constructed and constituted American past.

In that vein it may be appropriate to conclude this brief historiographical survey by examining three works, all published in 1997, that focus on immigration and ethnicity in the West, a region that for centuries has witnessed a distinct demography. Moreover, during the nineteenth century the progressive conquest, annexation, and incorporation of this region into a United States fulfilling its continental "manifest destiny" forced issues of immigration, ethnicity, and race to the top of the nation's agenda. The conflict over expansion of the institution of chattel slavery constitutes the most obvious example, but issues of "Indian" policy and of laws governing such seemingly disparate areas as citizenship, land ownership, contract labor, prostitution, and alcohol consumption, to cite but a few, centrally concerned migration, ethnicity, and race (and, alliedly, culture and religion). Scholars of the West thus necessarily engage these topics and long have done so; it was Frederick Jackson Turner, we recall, who posited the "frontier" as immigrant crucible. More recently, students of ethnicity and race, exemplified by the authors discussed below, have increasingly found the

"West," variously defined, an especially appropriate physical and cultural space for exploring the experiences of migration, immigration, colonization, and settlement and the consequent formation and re-formation of identities.

Neil Foley's incisive study of central Texas from the late nineteenth century through the early decades of the twentieth century conceptualized this geographical area as a borderland where the West, South, and Mexico met, overlapped, and produced a distinctive cultural region. His gracefully written monograph, *The White Scourge: Mexicans, Blacks, and Poor Whites in Texas Cotton Culture* (1997), demonstrated the wisdom of Okihiro's (and others') admonition to abandon a binary black/white model of ethnic and racial construction. Carefully and creatively mapping the changing ethnic, racial, and class identities in this region, Foley (1997: 5) explicated how Mexicans "ruptur[ed] the black–white polarity of southern race relations," thereby complicating the maintenance of the "color line" in a region of *de jure* segregation, and explored the "heterogeneity and hybridity of whiteness," particularly the emergence of race consciousness among whites who "feared that if they fell to the bottom [of the economic and social scale] they would lose the racial privileges that came with being accepted for what they were *not* – black, Mexican, or foreign born" (Foley, 1997: 7). Alert to issues of gender and family relations, and interweaving local events with national patterns, Foley traced the complex, often structurally overdetermined struggles that various persons and groups in central Texas waged against their racialization.

Foley's work takes on heightened significance when placed alongside Cynthia Radding's *Wandering Peoples: Colonialism, Ethnic Spaces, and Ecological Frontiers in Northwest Mexico, 1700–1850* (1997). Technically not a study of ethnicity in the United States, Radding's conceptually sophisticated study focused on ethnic frontiers in far north-west Mexico, a part of which the United States annexed in 1848 (constituting the southernmost counties of modern-day New Mexico, Arizona, and California). A historian extensively trained in anthropology, Radding (1997: 8) demonstrated the emergence of "ambivalent ethnicity, reconstituted through the convergence of Amerindian and Hispanic traditions" in these borderlands. Delineating the variety of cultures in this region and attending to structures of political economy and to the contours of intimate lives, she examined a peasant class-information, as indigenous peoples struggled for land and autonomy, and analyzed how the "transition from colonial to national rule" (1997: 168), in conjunction with missionary policies, influenced kin and community relations in mining and farming settlements. Falling outside the standard periodization of nineteenth-century American history (which follows the formation of the nation-state that emerges from the British North American colonies' revolt against their empire), Radding's work reminds us that the evolution of ethnicity and race in territories that became part of the American nation preceded by centuries the arrival of the US cavalry in vanquished Mexico.

Each in its own right a first-rate, if very different, study, taken together Radding's and Foley's works serve as bookends, territorially and temporally bracketing the complicated narratives of conquest, colonization, migration, settlement, and ethnic/racial transformation in the vast, evolving cultural borderlands of the American South/West from the beginning of the eighteenth century through the early decades of the twentieth. A third book provides something of a sampler of these multiple narratives, hinting at the scale and complexity of the sagas in this evolving region.

Writing the Range: Race, Class, and Culture in the Women's West, edited by Elizabeth Jameson and Susan Armitage (1997), tellingly does not include the terms "immigration" or "ethnicity" in its title, yet this fine collection of essays contributed substantially to this field. In the introduction to what they intend to be "an inclusive history" of Western women, Jameson and Armitage note that the "various ways people label race tell us a great deal about how race and ethnicity function in different cultures," indicating that throughout the West "racial boundaries were drawn differently," with definitions of who belonged to the category "white," for example, varying according to place, time, and situation (Jameson and Armitage, 1997: 3, 6, 7). Using gender as their primary but not exclusive lens, the authors of *Writing the Range* demonstrate the malleability of racial/ethnic construction, untangle complex ethnic and racial dynamics of institutional and familial power, and, in general, illuminate an expansive array of experiences of culturally diverse women and men in the nineteenth-century American West (from Basque sheep-herders in isolated areas of California and Irish laundry workers in a Montana smelter town to Anglo and Hispano agriculturalists in a New Mexico county renowned for its violence). Testifying to the breadth of scholarship in the subfield of western women, the volume concludes with bibliographies listing the literature on five groups: Latinas/Hispanas, African American, Asian American, Native American, and Euro-American ethnic women.

Like the bibliography on urban immigrants published in John Bodnar's (1985) synthesis, the bibliographies appended to Jameson and Armitage's (1997) collection provide an insightful survey of recent developments in an important segment of the field of immigration and ethnic history. If Bodnar's work, with its focus on cities and immigrants, revisited and revised the urban wellspring of immigration and ethnic history – Robert Park and the Chicago School of sociology of the 1920s – Jameson and Armitage similarly re-imagine and re-order the century-old immigrant and ethnic West of Frederick Jackson Turner. By any measure, the field has come a long way since the era of its founders.

Conclusion

The above constitutes one reading of the historiography of nineteenth-century American immigration and ethnicity. Yet in the current scholarly moment, when postmodernism has rocked the foundations of an already shaky ivory tower while heightening the self-reflexiveness of its denizens, locating oneself in a particular scholarly discourse borders on the compulsory. So, who am I to assay this field? A self-proclaimed, if no longer "new," social (and cultural) historian; an advocate of multi-culturalism rooted in inclusive social justice; a practitioner who constructs the field as "migration" history and endorses a comprehensive and contingent view of "ethnicity" and "race" – and a daughter of working-class Ontarian immigrants who identified deeply, if differently, with England, Canada's colonial power. To some, my reading of the field of immigration history may be as distinct and disturbing as was my answer to an ostensibly easy question asked on my very first day at elementary school. Pointing to the portrait on the classroom wall, my teacher asked, "Who is this man?" "George Washington," I piped up, "a traitor to his country."

Perhaps my first-grade teacher regarded this breakdown in the Socratic method as a product of "cultural misunderstanding," just as the Salt Lake City authorities years later regarded the menu of the Tongan birthday party. Yet in both these twentieth-century episodes – George-Washington-as-traitor and pony-as-taste-treat – more was going on than some intercultural "failure to communicate." Both episodes reveal the contextually contingent nature of ethnic constructions. Yes, some people consume horses rather than comb and curry them; and, yes, Washington led a rebel army to overthrow British rule. But here, in the United States of America, we *ride* horses and we *revere* Washington (even as we acknowledge that the patrimony of this Father of his Country included slaves), or at least "we, the people," as nation, uphold such norms.

Scholars such as those discussed in this chapter have demonstrated that, throughout the nineteenth century, ethnic and racial groups constructed myriad identities and cast aside, expunged, transplanted, altered, appropriated, and invented sundry practices and beliefs, and that they did so in the overlapping contexts of pre-migration/pre-conquest experiences, of intra-group diversity, of inter-group interactions, and of gender, class, sexuality, culture, and religion. But, saliently, individuals and groups experienced American society within evolving structures of power that somewhat arbitrarily and often contradictorily permitted, facilitated, ignored, or thwarted their agency. Whatever it may be at a particular historical moment and whoever may be shaping it, safeguarding it, undermining it, or manipulating it, some would-be hegemonic "American" discourse and structure exists which subaltern groups some-times must engage.

Ultimately, writing the history of immigration and ethnicity in nineteenth-century America requires weaving together multitudinous narratives told in multiple voices. Bringing these complicated stories together remains a major challenge in the field, despite the major advances this chapter has sought to highlight. As historians and other practitioners of the field work toward a new paradigm, they must strive, perhaps even more than those in other domains of nineteenth-century American history, to produce an emerging narrative that represents more than the sum of its fascinating, wonderfully diverse, and still-to-be-explored parts.

REFERENCES

Bodnar, John (1985) *The Transplanted: a History of Immigrants in Urban America*. Bloom-ington, Ind.: University of Indiana Press.

Cheng, Lucie and Bonacich, Edna (eds) (1984) *Labor Migration under Capitalism: Asian Workers in the United States before World War II*. Berkeley, CA: University of California Press.

Diner, Hasia (1983) *Erin's Daughters in America: Irish Immigrant Women in the Nineteenth Century*. Baltimore, MD: Johns Hopkins University Press.

Foley, Neil (1997) *The White Scourge: Mexicans, Blacks, and Poor Whites in Texas Cotton Culture*. Berkeley, CA: University of California Press.

Gerber, David A. (1989) *The Making of an American Pluralism: Buffalo, New York, 1825–60*. Urbana: University of Illinois Press.

Gutman, Herbert G. (1973) "Work, culture, and society in industrializing America, 1815–1919," in Herbert G. Gutman (ed.), *Work, Culture, and Society in Industrializing Amer-*

ica: Essays in American Working-class and Social History, pp. 3–78. New York: Vintage, 1977 edn.

Handlin, Oscar (1951) *The Uprooted: the Epic Story of the Great Migrations that Made the American People*. Boston: Little, Brown, 1990.

Hansen, Marcus (1940) *The Atlantic Migration, 1607–1860: a History of the Continuing Settlement of the United States*. New York: Harper, 1961.

Hoerder, Dirk (1985) "An introduction to labor migration in the Atlantic economies, 1815–1914," in Dirk Hoerder (ed.), *Labor Migration in the Atlantic Economies: the European and North American Working Classes during the Period of Industrialization*, pp. 3–31. Westport, Conn.: Greenwood Press.

Jacobson, Matthew Frye (1998) *Whiteness of a Different Color: European Immigrants and the Alchemy of Race*. Cambridge, Mass.: Harvard University Press.

Jameson, Elizabeth and Armitage, Susan (eds) (1997) *Writing the Range: Race, Class, and Culture in the Women's West*. Norman: University of Oklahoma Press.

Kamphoefner, Walter D. (1987) *The Westfalians: from Germany to Missouri*. Princeton, NJ: Princeton University Press.

Lewis, Earl (1995) "To turn as on a pivot: writing African Americans into a history of overlapping diasporas," *American Historical Review*, 100, pp. 765–87.

Miller, Kerby A. (1985) *Emigrants and Exiles: Ireland and the Irish Exodus to North America*. New York: Oxford University Press.

Okihiro, Gary Y. (1994) "Is yellow black or white?", in Gary Y. Okihiro (ed.), *Margins and Mainstreams: Asians in American History and Culture*, pp. 31–63. Seattle: University of Washington Press.

Radding, Cynthia (1997) *Wandering Peoples: Colonialism, Ethnic Spaces, and Ecological Frontiers in Northwest Mexico, 1700–1850*. Durham, NC: Duke University Press.

Roediger, David R. (1991) *The Wages of Whiteness: Race and the Making of the American Working Class*. London: Verso.

Thistlethwaite, Frank (1960) "Migration from Europe overseas in the nineteenth and twentieth centuries," in Rudolph J. Vecoli and Suzanne Sinke (eds), *A Century of European Migration, 1830–1930*, pp. 17–49. Urbana: University of Illinois Press, 1991.

Vecoli, Rudolph J. (1964) "*Contadini* in Chicago: a critique of *The Uprooted*," *Journal of American Ethnic History*, 51, pp. 404–17.

PART V

Regional Perspectives

CHAPTER EIGHTEEN

The South: From Old to New

STEPHEN W. BERRY

THE South, C. Vann Woodward (1951) argued, has experienced something the rest of the American nation has not – military and psychic defeat, occupation, humiliation, and reconstruction. Like most of the rest of the world, the South has felt the sting of over-extension and failure, of fighting and dying on the wrong side of a moral cause. These experiences created at one and the same time William Faulkner and the Klan, each in their own way dealing with a uniquely southern angst. The North and West, by contrast, have for the most part enjoyed the comforts and confidence that comes with an undefeated, transcontinental empire. The great promise of America, ordained by God and sustained through revolutions in agriculture, industry, and commerce, has come to fruition, at least in the North. When Woodward made these observations in the post-World War II era, the South was still the nation's "number one economic problem," and its racial policies of segregation and disfranchisement were coming under increased scrutiny and activist criticism. The burdens of southern history had perhaps never been so heavily borne, even as the nation as a whole had secured the status of a superpower; the South, for some good and much ill, seemed a glaring exception to the American rule. But the past 40 years have remade the North, the South, and the Woodward thesis. With Vietnam and the discovery of racism and sexism above the Mason–Dixon line, the North has come to understand that it shares many supposedly southern burdens. Then, too, the decomposing steel mills of the rust belt, standing like the ruins of a failed civilization, are but one reminder that the North has undergone a reconstruction of its own, with all that that means for the psyche of a people. The South, in the meanwhile, has become the nation's economic boombelt; it has elected presidents and vice-presidents; its cities play host to conglomerates and bank mergers and Olympic games.

For the past 30 years, the South's historians have sought to engage these very issues. The 1960s' challenge to the white, male, middle-class mainstream ushered in a host of studies which examined society from the bottom rail up. Once marginalized, the lives of African Americans, Native Americans, women, and the lower classes became the subject of sustained concern. More impressively, the latest work has ensured that these groups can never be marginalized again. The history of "out-groups" has given way to the history of concepts central to all human identity and interaction: race (blackness *and* whiteness), gender (femininity *and* masculinity), and class dynamics (lower *and* upper). And, through it all, southern historians have kept a walleye keenly focused on a question in which they have a vested interest – how distinctive was (is) the South?

Politics and Class

Most historiographies of the Old South begin with the work of Eugene Genovese. The reasons for this are manifold, but, most important, he is one of the few scholars to have come up with a "universal field theory" for the South, complete in its parts and consistent in its particulars. His "rightness" has been significantly less important to the discipline than the degree to which his work has set the terms of the debate. The Old South, Genovese contended, was an organic society, in but not of the liberal capitalist transatlantic world. The hierarchy and deference to elites that had inhered in an earlier period persisted and matured in the South, reinforced and softened by an economic system in which planters provided yeomen with loans and food during economic downturns and cotton gins and rental slaves during economic booms. In the North, such services were impersonal and market-driven; in the less commercial, less urban, less centralized South, they were filtered through neighbor-hoods, churches, and handshakes. As the two societies both diverged and sought their perpetuity in the West, the Civil War became inevitable.

Genovese's Old South has a consistency, a resiliency, and a motive force that has kept it relevant for more than two decades. But it has tended to dominate the historiography not as a reigning paradigm but as a reigning straw man – whole articles, books, and dissertations have been dedicated to the refutation of some of Genovese's individual contentions. Econometricians, for instance, have taken pains to challenge his notion that the slave economy inhibited the capitalization of manufac-turing that was transforming the North. Far from being arrested in its development, they suggest, the slave South was prospering at the same rate as the rest of the country. The planters' disinclination to engage in large-scale manufacturing had little to do with an aversion to capitalism; rather as proper capitalists they invested their money where it could command the greatest profits – plantation agriculture. North and South may have been in different places in their economic development, the scholars contend, but they were both on the same road.

Another, and perhaps more effective, assault against the centrality of Genovese's planters has been mounted by historians of southern Jacksonianism. Looking at state constitutions, legislative journals, statute books, county rosters, court and census records, historians have long noted that the forms of democracy, at least, were alive and well in the South. J. Mills Thornton III pushed this argument even further, suggesting that the substance of democracy could be found as well. In *Politics and Power in a Slave Society: Alabama 1820–1860* (1978), Thornton moved the focus of study from Genovese's tidewater to the Old Southwest and discovered not a planta-tion aristocracy but a democracy so run amok that politicians could not control or shape it. Paying particularly careful attention to debates over economic development in the late antebellum period, Thornton argued that common white male Alabamians were unnerved by the dislocations of the southern economy during the cotton, railroad, banking, and urban booms of the 1850s and that it was this yeoman ambival-ence to market change that drove the politics of the region. Deeply distrusting the new concentrations of money and power, deeply fearful that such forces might intrude on their liberties or worse yet "enslave" them, Thornton's Alabamians demanded and got a politics that safeguarded common white liberty and scapegoated the privileged, pretentious, and northern as the source of their problems. Finally, in 1982, James Oakes took on the heart of Genovese's model – paternalism – in *Ruling Race: a History of American Slaveholders*. The trajectory of southern life, Oakes claimed, was not toward a plantation economy and paternalist culture but away from it; Genovese's tidewater aristocrats were small in number *and* small in influence, mere anachronisms in a larger society committed to an aggressive and acquisitive individualism. Slave-holding, after all, was not limited to a few pretentious patriarchs but extended to a much larger class of middling farmers who preferred material success to moral postur-ing. The politically relevant sector of southern society, Oakes concluded, viewed slavery not as an aristocratic office but as an economic opportunity, and they viewed their laborers less as family than as commodity.

But it was precisely here that Genovese's argument held, a straw man with an iron spine. If Genovese had failed to appreciate the degree to which the South was under-going the same economic transformation as the North, the solution was not to make industrialists of planters or factories of fields. The attempt to minimize planter influence and maximize their market-mindedness reached its high-water mark in the mid-1980s, and it seems now as if Genovese and his critics have reached a kind of accommodation. In his latest work, Genovese has come to agree that market inroads in the South were historically significant and hotly debated among the differing sectors of southern society. In *his* latest work, James Oakes has come to agree that slavery was ultimately incompatible with liberal capitalism and yet also central to a peculiarly southern version of modernization. Jacksonianism, it seems, came equally to North and South. Both regions began in the 1830s to embrace optimistic materi-alism, aggressive individualism, a democratized politics and religion, and progressive attitudes toward social betterment. The legitimacy of the North's political culture was based on the dignity it offered the common white laborer, on the sanctified import-ance of the hard, white working day for the economic and moral advancement of society. The legitimacy of the South's political culture was based on the dignity *it* offered the common white farmer, on the sanctified importance of black slavery as the guarantor of all that it meant to be white and free. While debates over the nature of political cultures and class relations North and South continue, most scholars now agree that the problem was not that the regions were fundamentally different but rather that they responded differently to the fundamental transformation they shared.

Slavery and Race

No aspect of the South's historiography has matured more rapidly than the study of slavery. As Charles Dew has noted, no lesser scholars than David Potter in 1967 and Orlando Patterson in 1977 have declared the subject surfeited only to witness another and another outpouring of studies. The interest in the subject, it seems, will never wane, and for good reasons. So long as contemporary American society is marked by racial inequality, historians will search for the roots of that inequality in its most glaring American expression – plantation slavery. Then, too, the debate over southern distinctiveness, itself perennial and interminable, will continue to encourage scholars to search for cultural spin-offs from the South's peculiar institution. But once more a trend seems to be emerging: slavery is increasingly understood in a transatlantic context in which northerners and Africans are themselves implicated. Moreover, recent studies on the racial attitudes of northern whites have demonstrated that while slavery did not exist in northern climes, the racism that undergirded the institution ran just as deep. Another seemingly southern burden is being shifted to a wider group of shoulders, making the South seem more normative in its historical experience.

Eugene Genovese was one of the first (with John Blassingame and George Rawick) to complicate our understanding of slavery, positing a complex system of accommodation and resistance wherein the will of blacks was circumscribed but never snuffed out. The slaves did not have to rise in arms to maintain their self-respect, Genovese concluded; the smaller rebellions of sabotage, work stoppage, subversive gestures, and black Christianity signaled a population which, while never granting the legitimacy of slavery, nevertheless took up the practical questions of making the best of a bad lot. Herbert Gutman's *The Black Family in Slavery and Freedom, 1750–1925* (1976) pushed the historiography further still in its appreciation of black activism under slavery. Gutman contended that, despite the system's cruelties, the black nuclear family survived intact to anchor a community unique to, and respecting of, itself. The psychic space necessary to build such communities, Gutman argued, was not granted by paternalistic masters, as Genovese had claimed, but seized by blacks whose sense of family was too strong to be subsumed. In *Black Culture and Black Consciousness* (1977), Lawrence Levine corroborated Gutman's findings in a study of black culture under slavery. In their music, storytelling, humor, medicine, and spiritualism, Levine argued, slaves created an expressive folk culture so strong and vibrant that it anchored and dignified black communities during and after slavery.

All three works were important refutations of Stanley Elkins's central contention that slavery had been so harsh as to reduce slaves to child-like Sambos. Then, too, all three books were written at a time when the emphasis of the civil rights movement had shifted from black–white cooperation to black activism and even militancy, and when the celebration of Afro-American cultural distinctiveness had reached a high ebb. As the civil rights movement began to collapse, however, and it became clear that no single, decisive move, whether militant or cooperationist, would eradicate racism, the emphasis of slavery studies shifted back toward the malevolence of the institution and the intractability of the problems blacks faced. Books like Gutman's and Levine's were criticized for over-reading black cultural freedoms, and the historiography drifted toward a modified Genovesean model: African Americans under slavery were severely compromised but not crushed; masters were paternalistic *and* materialistic depending on their needs of the moment. They might pose as patriarchs of families black and white; they might even mean it; either way they might turn and sell the underpinnings of that patriarchy down the river for railroad stock.

The relative consensus on this model (such as it is) has sent the historiography in two separate directions: toward grand syntheses (only possible because fundamental questions are for the moment stalemated) and toward smaller monographic treatments of specific slave populations (drivers, house servants, field hands, artisans, women, children) in their specific locales and circumstances (upper South, lower South, tidewater, mountains, cities). Not having to haggle over sweeping interpretations and reinterpretations, historians of slavery have moved to solidify the gains of the past 30 years and to flesh out the details. Robert Fogel, for instance, has recently completed a four-volume last word on the subject of the economics of slavery. Other deans of slavery studies have been similarly synthetic in their recent treatments. Closer to the bone, archival research into slave life has resulted in an incredible proliferation of the details so necessary to humanize a historical subject. We now know a great deal, for instance, about how slaves felt not only about slavery and work and freedom and leisure but about fashion, pets, holidays, hunting, fishing, childrearing, love, death, and the afterlife. More important, we are beginning to hear about these things in the terms and words of those who experienced them. The publication and wide reading, for instance, of Harriet Jacobs's diary, chronicling the story of a young slave woman subjected to sexual indignities at the hands of her master, has helped to give a personal dimension to what we already knew as an unfortunately common plantation pattern.

But a driving impulse of recent studies has been to examine the duality of slavery and freedom in a context far wider than the plantation South. In *Slavery and Social Death* (1982), Orlando Patterson surveyed more than 60 different slave societies, from antiquity to modernity, from Europe and the Americas to Africa and the Far East. In each he discovered what he thought was a defining tendency of human bondage: the alienation of the individual from that most natural means of engaging and measuring the full meaning of life – as a member of a blood family, with all its inherited dignity and history, responsibility and friendship. Similarly, the extensive work on northern racial attitudes has enriched our appreciation of the degree to which black unfreedom was an American, not a southern, phenomenon. Most northern whites, after all, were significantly less interested in black freedoms in America than in establishing a relatively black-free America, significantly less concerned that slavery might degrade blacks as human beings than that it might degrade whites as laborers, significantly less put out by the unfair disadvantages heaped on the slave than by the unfair advantages enjoyed by the master. In *Slavery and Freedom: an Interpretation of the Old South* (1990), James Oakes has attempted to combine the insights of comparative studies like Patterson's with the recent work on northern race relations and southern modernization to forge a synthetic reinterpretation of the Old South's peculiar institution. Here America races pell-mell toward modernity with the South right alongside, struggling to keep up, striving to explain why it is bringing black bondage – an institution it had itself decried before 1830 – into a liberal and progressive new age. And the Civil War emerges just as Lincoln would have hoped – not as a struggle over the death of slavery in the South but over the rebirth of freedom in America.

What remains for southern historians now that slavery studies seem to be percolating along so well? We need a much, much better account of racism and racial thinking in different periods among different classes within different regions of the South. Race is so omnipresent and immense in our own time that it tends to take on a trans-historical aspect in our study of the past; the charge of racism is so stigmatizing that it seems to permit no variations or degrees – Lincoln and the Grand Wizard stand equally condemned before the charge. But since we can all admit that racism is a learned response, perhaps we can admit that throughout history the lessons have been taught differently, the students have drawn different things from the lessons, and the teachers have been occasionally reluctant, tired, and even subversive in drawing up their plans. So long as racism remains a monolith it will be insuperable; it does not deserve this advantage and historians should be the first to say so. We have inadvertently celebrated the monolithic and transhistorical power of racism in our exuberant appreciation of its evils; we need now to hold it in contempt, to render its history in all its fractious and pathetic parts.

Women and Gender

The most dramatic outpouring of southern slavery studies occurred in the 1970s, ten years after the high point of the civil rights movement. The most dramatic outpouring of southern women's studies occurred in the 1980s, ten years after the high crest of the feminist movement. Why it should take a decade for historians to respond to such momentous events is curious. Perhaps it takes ten years to establish some historical perspective. Perhaps it takes ten years to get the people transformed by such a movement through graduate school. Regardless, it is somewhat gratifying to note that having waited so long for their historians, southern women have received some of the very best. More gratifying still, the study of women has resulted not merely in the addition of a chapter but in the rewriting of the book. As Jacquelyn Hall and Anne Scott have noted, "[i]n no way has the historical landscape changed more radically in the past two decades than in the emergence from the deep shadows of the other half of the population" (Hall and Scott, 1987: 455).

And, of course, Anne Scott should know. Her *The Southern Lady: from Pedestal to Politics, 1830–1930* (1970) was the first modern monograph to focus on the lives of southern women, and it kick-started a concern for the subject that has shown no sign of abating. Scott's major contribution was to penetrate the façade of the South's idealized belle to find hard-working planter women, harried by household and farm management, discontented with the unavailability of education and birth control. Written in 1970, the book had a presentist ring; Scott's antebellum planter women had the same demands as modern feminists, though antebellum disgruntlement was less shouted than muttered. Most of the early works on southern women were similarly preoccupied with a concern dominating the more advanced historiography of northern women – the construction and politicization of a distinctively reformist female culture, of something that could be called a sisterhood. Inasmuch as such a culture was formative to modern feminism, the search for its antecedents became an important historical project, but it has never been clear that any such culture existed in the antebellum South. In two influential articles and an influential book, Carroll Smith-Rosenberg, Barbara Welter, and Nancy Cott laid out the northern model. Welter argued that in a farm or small-shop-based economy, a moral culture of family virtue and a business culture of equitable dealings coexist in the home, the site of production and reproduction. With the capitalization of an economy, the cultures are polarized and gendered: an aggressively male ethos of self-interested competition dominates the world outside the home; a piously female ethos of virtuous rehumanization dominates the world within. The female sphere may confine women, but it also provides them with a moral legitimacy and a moral model for reform should the excesses of the outer world threaten to intrude on the inner. Confinement to, and activism within, that sphere, Smith-Rosenberg and Cott argued, gave women a common experiential base from which they formed first homosocial support groups, then a reform-minded culture.

Elizabeth Fox-Genovese's *Within the Plantation Household* (1988), while not necessarily the first or best refutation of the northern model for the South, is certainly the most complete. Slavery and rural isolation, Fox-Genovese believes, defined southern women's experience in ways significantly different from that of their northern counterparts. In the South, the plantation household remained the locus of production and moral inculcation, and it was generally presided over by both a patriarch and a faithful lieutenant, his wife. Isolated within such households, southern women did not have access to the education or the urban camaraderie that had provided the substrate for the growth of northern reform cultures. More important, as fully a part of the administration of the southern slave economy, plantation mistresses could not as readily, nor as legitimately, stand outside their culture to criticize it.

While agreeing in the main with Fox-Genovese's broadest claims – that southern women faced challenges and opportunities peculiar to their region – the latest work follows the general trend in the discipline of collapsing the fundamental differences between North and South. A few works can provide a sense of the whole. Somewhat ahead of her time, Suzanne Lebsock (1984) found some, though not all, of the elements of a distinctly female culture in Petersburg, Virginia. In *The Free Women of Petersburg: Status and Culture in a Southern Town, 1784–1860*, Lebsock claimed that by the 1850s women had an increasing amount of economic autonomy, were drawn more deeply and in greater numbers into associational relationships and projects, and had developed a standard of behavior – personalism – that lent their feminine culture a distinctive cast. More recently, Christie Farnham has discovered that, for a small group of southern white women, at least, the educational opportunities in the South were relatively robust. Schooling their charges in classics, mathematics, and science, the female academies of the South in many ways outpaced their northern counterparts in curricula reform. In *We Mean to be Counted: White Women and Politics in Antebellum Virginia* (1998), Elizabeth Varon has noted that, contrary to our deeply held assumptions, women were involved in southern politics, even in the antebellum period, through their voluntary associations, legislative petitions, published appeals, and physical presence at rallies, meetings, and proceedings. Non-elite white women are also coming into view. In *Unruly Women: the Politics of Social and Sexual Control in the Old South* (1992), Victoria Bynum documents an inter-racial subculture of women who, in their drinking, stealing, gambling, and fornicating, operated well outside the proscriptions of the southern lady. In all of these works, Fox-Genovese's included, the goal is to understand women on their own terms and in their full complexity – the surest sign that the historiography has matured past stereotyping, imported models, and imposed arguments. But in all of these works, Fox-Genovese's excepted, one has the sense that southern women had more in common with their white northern sisters than with their own southern men.

Oddly, what is most missing from the historiography on southern gender is a nuanced study of masculinity. The story of manliness in the Old South has been often and poorly told, understood more, in its posturing and in its preening, for what it claimed to be than for what it was. This should not surprise us. Men of the nineteenth century were encouraged to cloak their hearts, to stifle their doubts, to so carefully groom their public persona as to become it. The result is a staggering amount of evidence for the public, external, and projected parts of men's lives and significantly less evidence for the private, internal, and introspective aspects. Scholars,

however, have compounded the problem. For centuries, historians studied men without consciously studying masculinity. Thanks to a revolution in women's studies,
gender has become *a* if not *the* analytical category of choice, and writers ignore it at
their peril. But the fact remains that the historiography of southern men is somewhat
paltry and what *has* been written focuses on public culture, on dueling, hunting,
gambling, and drinking, on activities, however compelling, that represent better what
fronted for manliness than what lurked behind. More important still, we need to
better understand how the sexes related to each other and how that relating has
changed over time. Steven Stowe may well be right that it required a small act of
rebellion for a man and woman to break through the heavy gender proscriptions of
the antebellum period to find each other whole, but it is the kind of great question
that can only be answered when we begin to examine gender relations in all their
richness.

Southern Cultures

With most of the South's historiography leaning toward the fundamental similarities
between North and South, scholars of southern distinctiveness have tended to seek
refuge in cultural studies, where shades of meaning can be parsed out without fear of
being contradicted by despotic facts and figures. The sharpest cultural historians have,
of course, like Faulkner, brushed this imputation aside, noting that facts and figures
can be a crashing bore when one has got hold of the truth. As might be expected of a
subdiscipline with so much freedom, the study of southern culture has produced some
of the flakiest work but also some of the most penetrating. The South's peculiar
Zeitgeist was laid out first and most forcefully in W.J. Cash's brilliant *Mind of the South*
(1941), an oddly titled work considering its core contention that the South had less
mind than mood. Conflicted in his relationship with the region, burdened by psychological issues of his own, Cash depicted the South as a brooding Hamlet, petulant
and hedonistic, sinning helplessly, dreaming savagely, picking constantly at its own
self-inflicted wounds. Cash believed that the South had come late and reluctantly to
self-consciousness and then only because the North's loud litany of southern sins was
too much to sleep through. Born prematurely, defensive and sinning from the womb,
the South became a perpetual infant, mewling over things it was not, did not, and
could not. While Cash has been criticized rightly as presenting too impressionistic a
portrait of the region, his determination to see the South as myth and symbol, image
and invention, paved the way for other scholars to test and ground his impressions.

Other historians, however, have sought more concrete sources for separate regional
cultures. In *Southern Honor: Ethics and Behavior in the Old South* (1982), Bertram
Wyatt-Brown claimed that an older, more primal, code of honor governed southern
social interaction while a more supple system of internalized morality prevailed in the
North. Honor, as Wyatt-Brown defined it, was more or less synonymous with public
reputation, a sense of self-worth not internal to the human being but established in
the clash of wills in a wider community. This system had been common to all the
colonies before the revolution, but in the more liberal North it gradually dissolved
into the modern, self-policing notions of respectability, responsibility, civic-minded-
ness, and domestic virtue. The older system persisted in the South for several reasons:
white southerners tended to be Celtic in origin where northerners tended to be

British; slavery reinforced affections for hierarchy and violence; and the intertwining of families in the South's rural culture tended to make society more organic and more touchy about personal alignments. Like Cash before him, however, Wyatt-Brown did not romanticize these differences; his version of southern honor had less to do with aristocratic poise than mismanaged rage.

While agreeing with Wyatt-Brown that the South was a distinctive place, intellectual historian Michael O'Brien has attempted over the past decade or so to locate a more high-toned source for those distinctions. The South's antebellum intellectuals were neither barren nor completely preoccupied with slavery, O'Brien has claimed; rather, stumbling and somewhat desperate, they developed a telling critique of free labor, capitalism, and the essential soul-sickness of modernity. The whole nation might have profited from a wider discussion of the southern position, but the more important work of ending slavery and laying out the dead interceded.

Secession and Civil War

He has not analyzed this subject aright nor probed it to the bottom who supposes that the real quarrel between the North and the South is about the Territories, or the decision of the Supreme Court, or even of the Constitution itself; and that, consequently, the issues may be stayed and the dangers arrested by the drawing of new lines and the signing of new compacts. The division is broader and deeper and more incurable than this. The antagonism is fundamental and ineradicable. The true secret of it lies in the total reversion of public opinion which has occurred in both sections of the country in the last quarter of a century on the subject of slavery.

This was the judgment in February 1861 of a writer for the city of Richmond's *Southern Literary Messenger*. Since that time southern apologists have demurred and a handful of southern scholars have sought to relieve the monotony of such simple causality, but most reconstructed historians have always returned, whether headlong or with feet dragging, to the notion that so impressed the writer for the *Messenger* – the North and South went to war over slavery. Far from ending debate on Civil War causality, however, this relative consensus has over the past 20 years provided a jumping-off point for an astounding variety of interpretations.

Granting that a fundamental disagreement over slavery lay at the root of the war, historians have haggled over questions of timing – why did that disagreement reach such a critical pass in 1860? – and questions of meaning – what did slavery mean to the societies that fought for and against it? Hardly matters of dickering fustiness, these questions have cut to the core of what America was and is. Historians of northern exceptionalism, for instance, have noted that slavery stood condemned in the North only after the notion of society as stable, hierarchical, and organic had been challenged and rendered absurd in a region increasingly committed to individualism, democracy, progress, and capitalism. Historians of southern modernization, on the other hand, have argued that these commitments were hardly unique to the North; the Civil War, they claim, should be rooted not in the North's successful development of a coherent and multi-faceted critique of slavery as a response to its own liberalization but in the South's successful development of a coherent and multi-faceted defense of slavery as a response to *its* own liberalization.

Turning on its head the notion that two fundamentally different societies went to war – industrial and capitalistic *v.* agricultural and seigniorial – the latest scholars have tended to view secession as a southern response to crises of modernization too long associated exclusively with the North. Some have argued that the South seceded to shore up internal race and class fault lines strained by its quick economic diversification in the immediate pre-war period. More still have argued for the relative cohesiveness of the South as planter and poor white locked arms and marched out of a Union threatening to undermine their whiteness and their maleness. Others with a taste for the irrational in human motivation have argued that both sections of the country made scapegoats of each other rather than confront the faceless forces transforming the Fathers' fragile republic into an imperial behemoth. Regardless, in the best recent interpretations a dynamic not a timeless South takes center stage and the conflict is less one of North against South than America against itself.

Political Economy of the Post-war South (1865–1900)

We don't call the Old South old and the New South new for nothing – 250,000 dead southerners and 4 million freed southerners are, most would agree, worthy of the major milestone. But just what of the Old continued in the New and what of the New departed from the Old is a matter of no little debate. For most of this century, the historiographical stress has fallen on the discontinuous elements of the ante- and postbellum Souths, and, seemingly for most of this century, C. Vann Woodward has been at the forefront of the discontinuity argument. While not going so far as Charles and Mary Beard in presenting the Civil War as a second American revolution, Woodward adapted the Beards' interpretation to the South in arguing that (a) the twin tolls of Civil War and emancipation left the planter class in ruins; and (b) the men who rose to rebuild were new men, business-oriented and bourgeois, struggling to find new solutions to the new problems that confronted them.

Given the latest appreciation, as discussed above, of the degree to which the antebellum planter class was itself business-oriented and bourgeois, it should not surprise us that for the past 20 years the continuity forces have had the upper hand. Econometricians have noted that planter families for the most part "persisted" in the same counties and same relative status they had commanded in the pre-war period. The capitalization of businesses they set in motion in the 1840s and 1850s continued after Reconstruction; the South's chronic postbellum poverty was less a matter of an anti-industrial mind-set than a legacy of the crushing one-time loss of the billions of dollars once invested in slaves. Even those who argue that the South took a "Prussian road" to industrialization – coming to it late with an agricultural elite at the helm who favored a closed and coercive society to one liberal and *laissez faire* – situate themselves firmly in the continuity camp; unable to stave off modernity in war the planters co-opted it in peace, and brought to it some of the same peculiar notions that had marked their society in its antebellum heyday. Finally, many continuity scholars have agreed with U. B. Phillips that race control has always been the South's central preoccupation: with slavery defeated, white southerners moved quickly to establish a system that could give them much of what emancipation had taken away – labor control, convenient scapegoats, and a sense of their own superiority to something, anything.

But the latest scholarship has begun to regard the continuity–discontinuity question as a paper tiger. Most history, after all, is concerned with change over time, continuity and discontinuity; in many historiographies this is tacit, unspoken, given. Why should it so dominate the historiography of the post-war South? Because the Civil War draws us in and in again, forcing some to believe that it remade the region and others to rise and challenge them. The truth is that many southerners' goals remained the same as they had been before the war – planters sought affluence and sway, yeomen sought to engage the market without foundering on it, blacks sought a freedom they knew they were worthy of – but the world these groups confronted was very different than it had been, calling for adjustment and experimentation, rebuilding and rethinking. As Edward Ayers's somewhat thesis-less *The Promise of the New South* (1992) reminds us, however much of the antebellum remained, the dislocations of the post-war period were very real and very profound for the participants themselves, even as, and perhaps precisely because, they sought with such mixed success to understand their new world in terms comfortable, familiar, and often, ill-fitting. While some critics have complained that Ayers's synthetic treatment is too post-modern in its gamboling attentions, *Promise* fits snugly within the new fashion of portraying the postbellum period in all its dynamic muddle. To the work of adapting itself to a free-labor economy and culture, Ayers might suggest, the South brought no little baggage and no little experimentation and mixed them liberally, helplessly; and while this muddle model may lack Woodward's interpretative verve, it compensates with a better sense of the cross-cutting contingencies, the trials and errors, that constitute human life.

At the core of the continuity–discontinuity issue has always lurked the question Woodward framed so well: did former planters or a new class of industrialists lead the South through its rough modernization? The Woodward camp preferred the latter; the Cash camp the former; today's muddle-modelers prefer both, if they answer at all, given their proper reluctance to generalize about the region as a whole. As James Cobb (1988) has noted, the notion of factories versus fields may have mythic power, but in reality industrialists and planters, businessmen and agri-businessmen, can and have tended to proceed hand in hand. "So long as industrial-development initiatives posed no threat to white supremacy, labor control, fiscal conservatism, and political stability," he has written, "the interest of the region's planters were in no danger of compromise" (Cobb, 1988: 56). Indeed, Cobb could have continued, this was the precise environment in which the commerce suited to the South, agricultural *and* industrial, would be most likely to thrive. The notion of a muddlingly allied planter/industrialist class, moreover, helps make sense of the peculiar dynamics of Populism and Progressivism in the South. In the four planks of the planter/industrial policy, blacks had the least to gain. It was their labor being controlled, their supposedly equal, certainly separate, facilities sacrificed to financial stringency, their race buttressing white supremacy, and their disfranchisement providing one of the props of political stabilization. Yeomen fared a little better, but not much. Labor control was of little consequence to them, except when they slipped into the laboring class; fiscal conservatism could be celebrated for lowering taxes but decried for its reliance on cash crops; and white supremacy was occasionally small compensation for the yeomen's support of a politics that rarely had their best interest at heart. All these were, of course, good reasons for blacks and yeomen to huddle together under the Populist umbrella, except that Populism ultimately would not, and perhaps could not, deliver effective agricultural reform; even the reluctant whites and blacks had little choice but to part company to find their separate shelters. And while it is beyond the scope of this chapter to comment at length on an impulse that found its fullest expression in the twentieth century, Dewey Grantham is probably right that in its southern expression, at least, Progressivism blended industrial and planter interests in a pastiche of progress and tradition. In the South, reform's emphasis fell on social control more than social welfare, business boosterism more than moral uplift, an emphasis that represented the broad, conservative consensus of the South's hybrid elite.

But the real problem with the continuity question may not merely be that notions of continuity and discontinuity, industrialists and planters, are too cut and dried. Such questions suffer most from their frame of reference, from their own stiflingly southern focus. Just as the historiography of the antebellum South has profited from an understanding that North and South had similar experiences and slightly dissimilar reactions to those experiences, so the latest scholars have profitably applied a quasi-comparative perspective to the postbellum era. Whatever an elite's preference as regards modernization and change, the technological and market circumstances of its society will always be the prevailing factors. The South could pursue best those industries and opportunities in which it had a comparative advantage with the North – labor-intensive agriculture and enterprises that could effectively exploit the South's raw materials, cheap labor, and low taxes. By situating the South in its national and international markets, William Parker (1980) has noted, elite preferences become a matter of secondary importance; the South's economic development could only have been other than it was if the nation's labor and capital had been redistributed "without regard to race, locality, or previous social structure" (Parker, 1980: 1045). The South's economic policy, in other words, grew out of its economic circumstances, not the other way round.

Race Relations in the New South

In *The Strange Career of Jim Crow* (1955), C. Vann Woodward sought out the origins of southern segregation, implying that the key to the system's defeat lay in understanding why it was created in the first place. The 1870s and 1880s, Woodward claimed, had been a time of relatively fluid race relations: blacks were unevenly oppressed, a conservative and condescending paternalist impulse still reigned in the minds of many upper-class whites, and a streak of racial cooperation ran through the ideology of a new breed of radicals (Populists, Fusionists, and Readjustors). With the brutal economic downturn of the 1890s, however, fluidity turned to chaos; white leaders moved to formally lock blacks out of power, both to stabilize the system and to underscore to the now poorest voters that their leaders remained committed to white dignity even in troubled times. Less a white aversion to black freedom than a white aversion to white unfreedom, then, Woodward's version of segregation had strong implications for his civil rights-minded contemporaries. If segregation was the legal legacy of a bygone era and a created solution to a problem that no longer existed, then sweeping away the laws and pointing white southerners toward the truer traditions of radicalism and paternalism would start the South on the road to real integration.

The failure of this programmatic has, of course, caused successive waves of historians to rethink the Woodward thesis. Some have questioned the true commitment of
the third parties to racial cooperationism. Others have noted that, particularly in the
cities of the South, segregation antedated the economic crisis of the 1890s and was in
a few areas firmly established in the immediate post-war period. More surprising,
some scholars have argued that when compared to what came before, *de jure* segregation had a (P/p)rogressive impulse and was a sign of improving not declining race
relations. Separate but (purportedly) equal is, after all, at least marginally better than
separate and flatly unequal. Finally, recent scholars have suggested that segregation
cannot be divorced from a technological context; its most glaring expressions coincided with the rise and development of mass facilities such as train cars, cable cars,
buses, restaurants, movie theaters, and schools. In *The Crucible of Race* (1982), Joel
Williamson confirmed (and added to) many of these criticisms of the Woodward
thesis, but he also showed that *The Strange Career of Jim Crow* had got one thing
perfectly right: the 1890s marked the "turn time" in southern race relations that
forged a new regime for the South. Looking particularly at the marked increase in
incidents of racial violence in the period, Williamson concluded that a concatenation
of circumstances – an economic downturn, the withdrawal of northern support for
blacks, the threat of renewed support and further meddling in southern affairs, the
success of blacks themselves in raising their own status – all encouraged a sea change in
white attitudes toward whiteness and blackness. While some might quarrel with a few
of Williamson's conclusions, his relegation of segregation to a matter of secondary
importance and call for a history of a larger white worldview in which racism – and its
formalized expressions – was integral, partial, and malleable has set the tone for most
recent works on southern race relations from the white perspective.

The black perspective on these issues is finally getting some attention as well. In
Gender and Jim Crow (1996), for instance, Glenda Gilmore tells the story of the
gendered politics by which middle-class blacks first gained and then lost their socio-
economic status in the redemptive South. While other scholars, Joel Williamson
included, have impressed upon us the degree to which gender – in most cases the
politicized threat of black freedom to white womanhood – was an important part of
the New South foundation, Gilmore does the kind of study scholars have called for for
years, examining the cross-cutting and shifting intersection of classes, races, and
sexes as they haggle over how class, race, and gender will order their world. Like
Lebsock's (1984) work on town women or Bynum's (1992) on unruly women,
Gilmore's attention to a subgroup *within* race, *within* class, helps us get past the
transhistories and monoliths that marked the earliest work in these areas.

Conclusion

"The South will exist," John Reed has noted, "for as long as people think and talk
about it." Mostly to their credit, southern historians have done a lot of talking, and
that talking has come to support foundations and prop up chairs and endow professorships. The South, most would agree, has never been so fertile a field nor one so
deeply plowed. But it is showing signs, too, of a super-abundance of fertilizer. The
"distinctive" elements of a regional culture can tend to triteness, particularly when
that culture is in the last stages of its co-optation, and the South's tiresome homilies

on hominy are no exception. The problem with talking so much, after all, is that when that first brave soul tells you to shut up a thousand people have already thought it and the wave you have ridden so long and so well breaks and crashes in a blink. To avoid this, southern historians must continue to do what C. Vann Woodward has done better than anyone else – tie regional studies to fundamental questions bigger than the region itself. One of the biggest may sound "touchy-feely," but at least, unlike the South, it is not going to disappear anytime soon: what does America mean? The delight and débâcle of this country has always been its consistent and rank hypocrisy, but its guilt before this charge is only possible because America is supposed to stand for something. Forcing it to live up to itself is the job of every citizen, and more certainly the job of every American historian. The South ought to situate itself both humble and assured at the very center of this project. The South's colossal failures, most historians now agree, have been fundamentally American ones; its successes, though limited, have been some of the country's most painful and hardest won. Human decency and human darkness have been knotted here like nowhere else; if they can be untied here then we know they can be untied. Will southern history be subsumed within the larger rubric of regional history? A quarter of a million dead men suggest not (no such number, after all, ever died trying to establish the independence of the Pacific Northwest or the Fergus Falls flood basin). But will that history (those dead) continue to be an integral part of some project larger than the foundations and the chairs and the professorships? The works reviewed here offer a positive sign.

REFERENCES

Ayers, Edward (1992) *The Promise of the New South: Life after Reconstruction*. New York: Oxford University Press.

Bynum, Victoria E. (1992) *Unruly Women: the Politics of Social and Sexual Control in the Old South*. Chapel Hill, NC: University of North Carolina Press.

Cash, Wilbur (1941) *Mind of the South*. New York: Alfred A. Knopf.

Cobb, James C. (1988) "Beyond planters and industrialists: a new perspective on the New South," *Journal of Southern History*, 54, pp. 45–68.

Fox-Genovese, Elizabeth (1988) *Within the Plantation Household: Black and White Women of the Old South*. Chapel Hill, NC: University of North Carolina Press.

Gilmore, Glenda (1996) *Gender and Jim Crow: Women and the Politics of White Supremacy in North Carolina, 1896–1920*. Chapel Hill, NC: University of North Carolina Press.

Gutman, Herbert (1976) *The Black Family in Slavery and Freedom, 1750–1925*. New York: Pantheon.

Hall, Jacquelyn Dowd and Scott, Anne Frior (1987) "Women in the South," in John B. Boles and Evelyn Thomas Nolen (eds), *Interpreting Southern History: Historiographical Essays in Honor of Sanford W. Higginbotham*, pp. 454–509. Baton Rouge: Louisiana State University Press.

Lebsock, Suzanne (1984) *The Free Women of Petersburg: Status and Culture in a Southern Town, 1784–1860*. New York: W. W. Norton.

Levine, Lawrence (1977) *Black Culture and Black Consciousness: African American Folk Thought from Slavery to Freedom*. New York: Oxford University Press.

Oakes, James (1982) *Ruling Race: a History of American Slaveholders*. New York: Random House.

Oakes, James (1990) *Slavery and Freedom: an Interpretation of the Old South*. New York: Random House.

Parker, William N. (1980) "The South in the national economy, 1865–1970," *Southern Economic Journal*, 46, pp. 1019–48.

Patterson, Orlando (1982) *Slavery and Social Death*. Cambridge, Mass.: Harvard University Press.

Scott, Anne Frior (1970) *The Southern Lady: from Pedestal to Politics, 1830–1930*. Chicago: University of Chicago Press.

Thornton III, J. Mills (1978) *Politics and Power in a Slave Society: Alabama 1820–1860*. Baton Rouge: Louisiana State University Press.

Varon, Elizabeth R. (1998) *We Mean to be Counted: White Women and Politics in Antebellum Virginia*. Chapel Hill, NC: University of North Carolina Press.

Williamson, Joel (1984) *The Crucible of Race: Black–White Relations in the American South since Emancipation*. New York: Oxford University Press.

Woodward, C. Vann (1951) *Origins of the New South, 1877–1913*. Baton Rouge: Louisiana State University Press.

Woodward, C. Vann (1955) *The Strange Career of Jim Crow*. New York: Oxford University Press.

Wyatt-Brown, Bertram (1982) *Southern Honor: Ethics and Behavior in the Old South*. New York: Oxford University Press.

CHAPTER NINETEEN

The Middle West

ANDREW R. L. CAYTON

THE American Middle West was a creation of the nineteenth century. In 1800, no such entity, real or imagined, existed. American Indians, French men and women, and métis populated the territory that would eventually comprise the region: the land north of the Ohio River, south of the Great Lakes, and west to roughly the 98th meridian, encompassing all or parts of the present-day states of Ohio, Indiana, Illinois, Michigan, Wisconsin, Minnesota, Iowa, Missouri, Kansas, Nebraska, and the Dakotas. Although Great Britain had surrendered its claim to the region in the Jay Treaty of 1795 and France would surrender its claim as part of the Louisiana Purchase of 1803, the United States did not exercise uncontested sovereignty over the area, and would not do so for several more decades.

In fact, the Middle West was on the far edges of the westward expansion of the United States until the middle of the nineteenth century. If people applied any kind of label to the region, they called it the Northwest or the West. According to the geographer James Shortridge, the use of the term Middle West achieved universal acceptance only around 1912. Then people merged the states of the Old Northwest (Ohio, Indiana, Illinois, Michigan, and Wisconsin) with the more recently settled northern plains states (Minnesota, Iowa, Missouri, Nebraska, Kansas, South Dakota, and North Dakota) into a conceptualization of a Middle West as a coherent region.

Whatever it was called, the area was flourishing in 1900. In the astonishingly short span of a single century, European Americans, operating as citizens of the United States and embracing the culture of market capitalism, conquered and transformed the region into one of the most prosperous and powerful places in the world. By 1900, railroads, telegraphs, and telephones criss-crossed the Middle West, linking millions of square miles of family farms with huge industrial and commercial centers. Home to over 26 million people in 1900, the region made up about one-third of the total population of the United States. Chicago, founded in the 1830s, was the undisputed metropolis of the region; with a population of 1,698,575, it was the second largest city in the United States. Other major cities included St Louis (575,238), Cleveland (381,768), Cincinnati (325,902), Detroit (285,704), Milwaukee (285,315), and Indianapolis (169,164). The Middle West had long since succeeded the South as the dominant region in national politics. Meanwhile, it provided the United States with an extraordinary number of artists, activists, and entrepreneurs, from William Dean Howells and Theodore Dreiser to Frank Lloyd Wright and Wilbur and Orville Wright to Jane Addams and Eugene Debs.

A Region without Borders

As striking as the rapid emergence of the Middle West was the lack of regional consciousness that accompanied it. The people who lived there rarely identified themselves in regional terms. More commonly, they imagined their identities – their participation in larger communities – in terms of ethnicity, religion, political partisanship, nationalism, or state citizenship. Midwesterners have never been as self-consciously regional as southerners or westerners.

Traditionally, Americans think of midwesterners in a very vague fashion, using generic adjectives such as solid, friendly, stable, and respectable. Rarely do they employ colorful, eccentric, unusual, or peculiar. The dominant image of the region was and is one of a place in the middle: a mature, pastoral area located somewhere between the extremes of east and west, urban and rural, civilization and barbarism, young and old. The virtues and flaws of the people are similar to those associated with the emerging nineteenth-century bourgeoisie; they are not intrinsic to a specific place.

Some historians have suggested that it is more useful to think of the Middle West as the antithesis of a region. To the extent that residents discussed regionalism, they did so in the manner of local boosters. Many midwesterners came to pride themselves on their normalcy, on their lack of peculiarity, on the absence of distinctiveness. The Middle West was Middletown (as the sociologists Robert and Helen Lynd would call Muncie, Indiana in the 1920s), the typical American place.

Critics often characterize midwestern culture as flat, like a prairie landscape, unbroken by diversity or dissonance. The Middle West in American myth is a world of small towns and family farms, unstintingly homogeneous and predictable as a diet of meat loaf and mashed potatoes, constricting and suffocating in its resistance to innovation and diversity. It is a world from which intelligent, sensitive people flee whenever they are given the opportunity, as in Sherwood Anderson's *Winesburg, Ohio*, or suppress their distinctiveness in the pressure to conform, as in Steve Tesich and Peter Yates's 1979 film, *Breaking Away*.

Given the lack of self-conscious writing about what it means to be midwestern and the emphasis on the essential normalcy of the place, it is hardly surprising that its historians have given very little thought to regionalism. Few scholars have even considered the idea, let alone taken it seriously, and almost no one has thought it through in any kind of formal, rigorous fashion. Which is not to say that historians have not written about the Middle West. To the contrary, they have produced a steadily growing stack of excellent monographs.

But almost none of these works are regional in their construction. Most historians write about subjects of trans-local interest – gender, race, unionization, urbanization, resistance to capitalism, and so on – that are set in the Middle West but are not particularly of the Middle West. That is, rhetorical bows aside, place and a sense of regional identity play a minimal role in the collective work of historians of the Middle West. Most would not even accept that label; rather, they are scholars of other topics who happen to be writing about them in a midwestern context. The nature of that context is rarely sketched out in any detail, certainly not in the way that a southern or western historian would be very conscious of how a regional culture, or milieu, suffuses what she or he is studying.

The major reason for the lack of midwestern regionalism is that the peoples who lived there have rarely needed to think of themselves as having much in common. Like all articulated identities, regionalism tends to flourish in the face of perceived persecution by others. People in the Middle West in the nineteenth century resented a great deal: there were periods of "western" resentment in the agrarian protests of the late nineteenth century, most notably the Populist movement, and episodes of violence and resistance among working-class peoples in urban areas. Taken as a whole, however, the Middle West as a region did remarkably well in the nineteenth century. In terms of their position in the nation as a whole, midwesterners had less to complain about than conquered southerners, neglected New Englanders, and exploited westerners. They perceived their grievances more often than not in terms of ethnicity, religion, occupations, and class. Only occasionally did they locate their resistance to national or economic developments in terms of a regionalism that transcended all other identities.

Because the historical literature almost never confronts the question of midwestern regionalism head on, we have to tease regional identity from works that were never intended to serve that purpose at all. Running through the work of historians are recurring themes or questions that help us to begin to discuss the existence of distinctive regional qualities. They include location, landscape, demographic diversity, identification with market capitalism, and a peculiar relationship between governments and economic and social development. It was the peculiarly midwestern configuration of these issues, ironically, which made it so difficult for its residents to imagine themselves as members of a regional community.

An Interior Region

The most important thing about the Middle West is that it is an interior region. It is essentially the place where the drainage area of the upper Mississippi River meets the drainage area of the Great Lakes. As William Cronon (1991) has observed, Chicago became significant not because it was a central place but because it was on the peripheries of other regions. In the nineteenth century, there were two major natural outlets to the ocean, the St Lawrence River and the Mississippi River. Americans then built their own outlets, starting with the Erie Canal and various state canals and finishing with the great railroads that linked the region, particularly with New York City. These improvements could not disguise the fact that access to and from the Middle West required travel through another kind of place.

The landscape itself was well watered and accommodated agriculture on a grand scale. The hilly countryside of southern Ohio and Indiana aside, the terrain is relatively horizontal. The soil is generally fertile, though difficult to plow. Farmers in the Middle West had to contend with neither deserts nor mountains. Somewhat surprisingly, the highest points are in the western portions of the region, in South Dakota, Nebraska, and Kansas. The highest point of land east of those states is in Michigan at 1,979 feet above sea level; the lowest is 230 feet in Missouri. Land in Illinois ranges between 279 and 1,235 feet above sea level.

Settlers of the Middle West had their problems but, relatively speaking, they were pretty well off. There were few places in the region, its reputation for isolated towns and farms notwithstanding, that were truly very far from a major urban center or transportation network. Although the absence of distinctive topographical features may make the landscape boring to late twentieth-century sensibilities in need of diversion, they made them enticing to immigrant families looking to feed and shelter themselves.

Demographic Diversity

The lack of irregularities in the landscape contributed to the constant intermingling of peoples in the Middle West. Few communities could escape the major economic and social developments of the nineteenth century. The Middle West has no Appalachia, no high plains towns miles from major rivers and cities. One of the unique features of the region was the extent to which the landscape encouraged communication as well as agriculture, interaction as well as divergence.

Contact was important, for the Middle West was one of the most demographically diverse regions in the world in the nineteenth century. To be sure, other American regions attracted tens of thousands of European, Asian, and Hispanic immigrants. But, belying its flat image, a bewildering array of peoples called the Middle West home by the end of the nineteenth century.

Numbers give some sense of the complexity of the story. In 1880, the majority of farmers in Wisconsin, Minnesota, and the Dakota Territory had been born outside the United States as had approximately one-third of the farmers in Michigan, Iowa, and Nebraska. Cities had even higher proportions of European-born peoples. In 1900, around 75 percent of Cleveland's population were first- or second-generation immigrants, mainly from eastern Europe; they spoke some 40 different languages. In 1890, Milwaukee had the smallest percentage (less than 13 percent) of white citizens whose grandparents had been born in the United States of any city of 100,000 or more in the United States. Chicago was third and Detroit fourth with about 21 percent each. Of the major midwestern cities, only in Indianapolis had the majority of the population been born to native-born Americans. In fact, until the 1880s, the proportion of foreign-born residents in the upper Middle West was roughly similar to that in the great cities of the East.

The population of the Middle West thus included a wide variety of peoples. In addition to those Native Americans who had not been removed to Oklahoma and the French and métis who had been there when others arrived, there were Germans, Scandinavians, Poles, Italians, Russians, Irish, Scots, Yankees from New England, and migrants from the upland South. They spoke different languages, ate different foods, wore different kinds of clothes. Scholars such as Kathleen Neils Conzen (1976) and Jon Gjerde (1997) have stressed the traditional character of many of these immigrants. They often moved as part of chains of relatives or friends. More often than not, people from similar backgrounds settled and developed their own urban and rural enclaves, hoping to preserve and extend household relationships by migrating from Europe to the Middle West in groups and settling near each other.

Many of the communities in the region both within and outside large cities were ethnic enclaves in which immigrants and their children could recreate and perpetuate a sense of community through language, food, clothes, and leisure activities. Milwaukee, Cincinnati, and St Louis have been indelibly marked by their great abundance of German cultural events, buildings, periodicals, and businesses.

Crucial to virtually all nineteenth-century midwesterners was religion. For many, it was the defining feature of their lives. Overwhelmingly, they were Christian with small but influential pockets of Jews, especially in major cities. Within the parameters of Christianity, there were Catholics, Lutherans, Presbyterians, Quakers, Methodists, Baptists, and a host of other denominations. In 1895, Iowa, a largely rural state, had 397,000 residents who claimed to be Methodists, 344,000 Catholics, 258,000 Lutherans (divided into German, English, Swedish, Norwegian, and Danish), 132,000 Presbyterians, 105,000 Disciples, 103,000 Baptists, 79,000 Congregationalists, 29,000 United Brethren, 31,000 Evangelical Synod, 23,100 Reformed (both German and Dutch), 20,100 Quakers, 4,420 Jews, 73,500 in other denominations, and 428,000 people who identified themselves as Protestant. If these ethnic and religious differences seem to pale before those of the late twentieth century, they were real enough in their time and place. The nineteenth-century Middle West was an exceedingly heterogeneous place.

Capitalism and Communities

Whatever their background, midwesterners had a unique relationship with market capitalism. The burden of much scholarship has been to show ambivalence about the impact of capitalist modes of production and attitudes on their lives. Historians have labored hard to demonstrate the persistence of household forms of organization and to stress the importance of religious and ethnic traditions in tempering the attractions of individualism and competition. Thanks to their work, we have a much more nuanced understanding of the market revolution in the Middle West and the ambiguous participation in it of tens of thousands of people.

One of the central works in this literature is John Mack Faragher's *Sugar Creek: Life on the Illinois Prairie* (1986). Faragher wanted to "understand more about Americans of the early-nineteenth century-West, the region now called the Midwest" (Faragher, 1986: xiii). To do so, he focused on an open country settlement in central Illinois. Combining the texture of local history with the questions of academic scholarship, Faragher found a complex relationship between traditional modes of social organization – such as the household, kinship networks, and religion – and the expansion of democratic politics and capitalism. Faragher insisted that dramatic changes had come to the Illinois prairie in the nineteenth century. He also insisted that those changes had not caused a disintegration of households into individuals; rather, "community...provided a means of making the transition to" the modern world. "Like the society that bound the households together, cultural sentiments along the creek were essentially traditional and conservative. Family and household remained the essential social building blocks; community continued to be constructed from the relations among kinship, neighborhood, and church" (Faragher, 1986: 237).

Susan Gray's book, *The Yankee West: Community Life on the Michigan Frontier* (1996), makes somewhat similar points. Although she is at great pains to explode traditional myths about New England settlements in the Middle West, she is just as interested in showing the ways in which families and markets intersected with each other. Yankee settlers were committed to the preservation and extension of their families' collective fortunes over a number of generations; they were unwilling to accept subsistence agriculture as the limits of economic production. Few, however, saw any contradiction between means and ends. According to Gray (1996: 12), "capitalism for Yankees seemed to promise not the destruction but the intensification of familial and communal ties. The commodification of land did not challenge but eased the potability of status." Yankees did not see the market as a threat to their worlds. Their "objective was fundamentally ambivalent: to create traditional rural communities of unlimited potential for economic growth. They wanted more of the same, only better" (Gray, 1996: 15).

Jane Marie Pederson's *Between Memory and Reality: Family and Community in Rural Wisconsin, 1870–1970* (1992) suggests that "most farmers may not have been aware of the dichotomy between farming as a way of life and farming as a business or means to a living; to them, farming probably has seemed to be both and not exclusively one or the other" (Pederson, 1992: 229). Mary Neth's (1995) work on farm families in the early twentieth century upper Mississippi Valley shows how patriarchal household organization and capitalist development were complementary, rather than exclusionary. In the upper Mississippi Valley in the early twentieth century, farm families were not collections of autonomous individuals cut off from each other by an all-encompassing capitalist transformation. They preserved kin and personal relationships, within and beyond their households, as ways of coping with huge changes in their lives.

In books such as *Agrarian Women: Wives and Mothers in Rural Nebraska, 1880–1940* (1992), Deborah Fink has offered a different perspective on these issues. She has stressed not just the economic importance of rural women but their relative isolation and their lack of protection from "violence and exploitation" (Fink, 1992: 190). She emphasizes how the ideology of agrarianism and the centrality of family life meant that their "primary adult relations were with men." Women may have resisted their exploitation but they generally "muted and censored their talk with other women, thereby depriving themselves of the chance to mirror each other's wisdom, pool their knowledge, pull together common threads, and express their common condition in stories, songs, poems, speeches, paintings, and essays that would give meaning to the specificity of their experiences" (Fink, 1992: 191).

As Jon Gjerde (1997) has argued in *The Minds of the West*, there was no reason why commercialization had to destroy traditional ways of living. Household production continued, as did sexual divisions of labor and intergenerational relationships. Still, if capitalism occasionally worked to reinforce community values, it was more likely to strengthen the individual *vis-á-vis* the community. Women tended to work in fields less and children's sense of obligation to families was weakened. The result was a society that was more secular, more concerned with debating issues of gender and moral power in public than in private. Kathleen Neils Conzen (1976) has rightly stressed the local nature of the transformation of life in the Middle West, arguing that communities united by ethnic and religious ties evolved, rather than disappeared. Some adopted "Yankee" ways to a greater extent than others. From the broadest chronological perspective, however, there is no doubt about the tremendous impact of capitalism on the region. As people became more enmeshed in the market, the most basic aspects of their lives were affected, if not transformed, by it. That impact may not have been fully evident until the Great Depression. But it had been building for a very long time.

The same thing was true for working-class peoples in nineteenth-century midwestern cities. In Chicago, St Louis, Cincinnati, and Detroit, people constructed residential enclaves centered on ethnicity and religion, the remnants of which persist at the end of the twentieth century. Men and women found respite from work in a wide range of increasingly commercialized leisure activities. They participated in fairs and parades and joined a broad spectrum of clubs and other organizations. Many worked hard to preserve family ties and personal relationships with people from similar backgrounds.

The primary factor in their lives, however, was the nature of their work, much of which was dismal. The dynamic industries of the Middle West created thousands of jobs, many of them requiring little in the way of skill or craft. Workers spent long days in dirty and dangerous factories away from homes and communities engaged in monotonous manual labor for low wages and with virtually no protection from debilitating injuries and old age. No wonder, then, that labor unrest was so much a part of the landscape of the Middle West in the second half of the nineteenth century, from miners in southern Ohio to factory workers in Chicago to railroad workers throughout the region. Or that workers found solidarity and community in organizations such as the Knights of Labor that promised to value them as people as well as commodities. Strikes and protests were not uncommon, especially in the deflationary decades of the 1870s, 1880s, and 1890s; the names Haymarket and Pullman signify prominent and violent episodes in the region's history. More generally, throughout the region workers often dealt creatively with the brutal aspects of industrial work by drawing upon and modifying traditional relationships in a world transformed by technology.

Yet popular unrest against the vagaries and inequities of market capitalism in both rural and urban settings was generally dependent upon the state of the market. Minnesota, Iowa, and Illinois were centers of the Grange movement and other protests against the tyranny of American railroads in an era of declining prices for virtually all commodities. Workers in the cities organized to resist falling prices and falling status in the 1880s. Whether urban or rural, the protests, indeed the rage, against the tentacles of an international market intruding into their lives were strong testimony to the dominance of market capitalism in the lives of midwesterners.

As historians such as Steven J. Ross (1985) have argued, protest movements in the Middle West were generally undone by the other characteristics of regional society. Its great diversity, for example, made it difficult for workers to overcome ethnic and religious disagreements and unite in common cause. Another challenge to effective protest was the tendency of so many people in the Middle West to see themselves as middle class. They wanted to own their own homes, improve the lot of their children, and enjoy leisure activities and consumerism. In all these ways, they were more supportive of the goals of the American Federation of Labor than the Knights of Labor. These were people looking to share the benefits of capitalism, not destroy it.

The Triumph of the Market

If there is a danger in the tendency of scholars to highlight widespread ambivalence and occasional resistance to the market, it is that it deflects attention from the triumph of capitalism in the Middle West. To write of triumph is not to celebrate but to underscore the pervasiveness of the conquest of the market. Nowhere else in the world did human beings find their lives more fully and precisely defined by their relationship to the business of buying and selling. Whatever their origins or their purposes, immigrants transformed an eighteenth-century environment that had supported subsistence agriculture and a long-distance trade in furs and peltries into a capitalist's dream come true. Indians, in the words of the geographer John C. Hudson in *Making the Corn Belt: a Geographical History of Middle-Western Agriculture* (1994), bequeathed to the Europeans who "would eventually destroy them a country much improved over what nature alone had provided, one that was ready for the plow immediately... The expanses of rolling grassland left no doubt what should be done there, at least in the minds of men who envisioned farming on a grand scale" (Hudson, 1994: 30).

European Americans proceeded, in the wake of the defeat and removal of the Indians, to cut down trees, lay out rectangular lines on maps in order to facilitate the location and transfer of lands, and construct roads, canals, and trains. They put thousands of acres into extensive cultivation with grains that nurtured an explosion in the number of hogs and cows which would ultimately feed people all over the world. They constructed small towns whose primary purpose was to facilitate the exchange of crops and animals for finished goods, whose distinguishing architectural features by the end of the nineteenth century were the practical, straightforward façades of banks, general stores, and railway stations.

They developed large metropolitan areas around commercial centers and processing plants. Cincinnati flourished with the hogs raised on the corn of the central Ohio Valley, which were then slaughtered and turned into all kinds of products to be shipped to New Orleans, Philadelphia, and beyond. Even as its gentry strove to make the "Queen City of the West" notable for its educational and cultural achievements, Cincinnati remained "Porkopolis." Its emergent industries in the middle of the nineteenth century produced massive quantities of packed meats, and related products such as candles and soaps. Procter and Gamble was well on its way to becoming the city's dominant business corporation by the 1880s when its 500 workers made 20,000 bars of soap and 100,000 candles a day.

Milwaukee also had diverse manufactures, but it made its reputation (along with St Louis) as the center of the brewing industry. There the relatively easily grown and relatively easily transported grains of the upper Middle West became the beer that was sold not only to the Germans and other immigrants of the region but throughout the world, carried away by ships across the inland waterways of the Great Lakes. In 1895, the first and third largest brewers in the United States were Pabst and Schlitz with Anheuser-Busch of St Louis in second place.

The quintessential example of the merging of landscape and city in the Middle West was Chicago. In *Nature's Metropolis: Chicago and the Great West*, William Cronon (1991) has detailed the extensive appropriation of the natural resources of the city's vast hinterland which lay behind the remarkable expansion of the metropolis in the second half of the nineteenth century. Cronon sees Chicago and other cities as the engines of regional growth. He interprets Frederick Jackson Turner's frontier as "the ongoing extension of market relations into the ways human beings used land – and each other – in the Great West" (Cronon, 1991: 53). Cronon's Chicago obviously fits that description, a city that grew phenomenally on a vast network of railroads and ships that brought grains and animals from Iowa, Nebraska, and beyond, as well as timber from Wisconsin and Minnesota into the regional metropolis.

Hundreds of thousands of laborers in Chicago transformed these resources into packaged meats, flour, and other processed goods for companies such as Armour and Swift and sent them back on trains and ships for destinations throughout North America and the world. Paralleling and fueling the growth of these industries was the expansion of banks and commercial institutions that provided credit and insurance, organizations such as the Chicago Board of Trade that strove to regularize some of the rampant and often chaotic exchanges of goods and capital, a whole host of lawyers and clerks to deal with the details and inevitable conflicts, and mail-order companies such as Montgomery Ward and Sears, Roebuck and Company to tempt people in rural areas to send the money they made on selling their crops in the first place back to Chicago for cloth, tools, and trinkets. So successful was the last business that by the end of the nineteenth century, Montgomery Ward was blanketing the region and much of the nation with a 1,200 page catalogue that offered 70,000 separate items for sale. The company shipped an average of 13,000 packages a day.

Daniel Nelson (1995) and Jon Teaford (1993) have amply demonstrated that one of the peculiar characteristics of the Middle West is that it is a region of both family farms and great cities. In the Northeastern United States, cities and industry dominated, while in the South, agriculture and farms remained pre-eminent until well into the twentieth century. But the midwestern states tended to have great metropolitan areas that were both commercial and industrial centers in the middle of huge expanses of farmland. Of all the states in the region, only Indiana and Iowa did not have a great industrial city by the end of the twentieth century. Ohio and Missouri, on the other hand, had two: Cincinnati and Cleveland, St Louis and Kansas City. In other states, one city dwarfed all others: Chicago in Illinois, Detroit in Michigan.

This bifurcation of the landscape, in which people traveled for hundreds of miles through prairie farmland interrupted at regular intervals by incredible concentrations of people and industry, meant that the Middle West was both pastoral and highly developed. The regional economy was neither completely colonial nor completely industrial. Midwesterners grew enormous amounts of raw materials, most of which was processed and marketed within their region.

The point is not to deny that many people on farms and in factories actively resisted the intrusion of the market into their personal lives. It is simply to emphasize that, from the broadest perspective, the transformation of an interior region whose inhabitants were largely scattered and diffuse into one of the most significant commercial regions in the history of the world in the course of a few decades was a remarkable event. It is also the defining phenomenon in the history of the American Middle West. Nowhere else in the United States was capitalism embraced so fully.

Free Labor

With this economic transformation came equally important social changes. One of the primary ways the region defined itself was in its celebration of free labor. Although *de facto* slavery was widely practiced in southern Ohio, Indiana, and Illinois in the late eighteenth and early nineteenth centuries, efforts to overturn the Northwest Ordinance's 1787 prohibition of slavery north of the Ohio River failed. In addition, many of the upland southerners who migrated to the Old Northwest in the early 1800s were Methodists and Quakers who were opposed to slavery for religious reasons; one of the reasons they chose to move to Ohio or Indiana rather than Kentucky or Tennessee was its supposedly free soil. Yankee immigrants who began to swarm into the Old Northwest with the opening of the Erie Canal in the 1820s completed the free labor mentality. Mixing evangelical zeal with a strident distaste for the southerners and slavery, the residents of northern Ohio and Michigan became supporters of moral and political reform movements designed to promote self-discipline and destroy institutional control over all human beings.

Despite the presence of a few enlightened souls, particularly Quakers, even the opponents of slavery in the Old Northwest were decidedly racist in their assumptions about African Americans. The new states in the region moved quickly, and with little opposition, to create legal barriers both to the settlement of free blacks and to their enjoyment of the full range of legal rights. Black codes in Ohio, Indiana, and Michigan severely restricted the activity of African Americans. Successful stories of free blacks in urban areas and in rural communities, such as Free Frank's Illinois town, should not divert our attention from the fact that blacks were not welcome in the Old Northwest in the nineteenth century. At the time of the Civil War, less than 1 percent of the population was African American, a percentage that would not dramatically change until the Great Migration of the twentieth century. There were virtually no blacks in the rural Midwest beyond isolated pockets of people in southern Indiana, Illinois, Ohio, and Missouri. The census of 1900 showed that while 11.6 percent of the national population were black, in most midwestern states the percentage was below 1 percent. Even in the border states, the black share of the population was small: in Missouri it stood at 5.2 percent, Kansas, 3.5 percent, Indiana and Ohio, 2.3 percent, and Illinois, 1.8 percent. As late as 1910, the African-American population of every major midwestern city was under 10 percent of the total; only in St Louis, Indianapolis, Cincinnati, and Columbus did it exceed 5 percent. The black population of Chicago was 2 percent.

There was a direct correlation between these figures and politics in the region. The vast majority of white midwesterners had no desire to see widespread black migration into the region. Indeed, the most potent political issue Democrats had during the Civil War and Reconstruction was their claim that a vote for a Republican candidate meant opening the gates to a flood of black immigrants, bringing miscegenation, low wages, and declining standards of living for white workers in their wake.

For the most part, these were not serious fears. The Republican party, which was organized in the Old Northwest in the 1850s and found many of its most powerful national candidates in the region, was not committed to either racial mixture or true racial equality. Rather, the party of Abraham Lincoln stood for the lifting of any and all restraints on the freedom of individuals to compete. White men should be free to settle where they wished and compete for land and jobs in as free a market as possible. The great problem with slavery was not so much that it was inhumane to blacks as that it threatened the livelihood and privileges of all white men by introducing unfair competition and elevating some white nabobs to a privileged position created by the work of enslaved blacks.

The 1850s and 1860s marked the coming of age of the Old Northwest as a region. The sectional crisis and the Civil War brought midwestern men such as Lincoln,

Stephen Douglas, Ulysses S. Grant, Salmon P. Chase, William Tecumseh Sherman, and John Sherman to national prominence. They made visible the numerical and economic power of the Old Northwest in the nation as a whole, shifting dominance away from the Northeastern states. Above all, they forced midwesterners to define themselves in terms of a place committed to commercial capitalism, free labor, free soil, and free men. They did so largely by contrasting themselves with the southerners they despised and defeated. The prosperity of the Old Northwest rested on its rejection of slavery, first in 1787, and then in subsequent elections.

Originally the basic artery into the trans-Appalachian West, draining its resources and peoples into a common stream, the Ohio River became a border between free and slave, North and South. In this sense, the regional significance of the 1857 Dred Scott case, which held that Congress could not prohibit slavery in the territories, was that it threatened to blend the Northwest and Southwest together into one unit. The overwhelming majority of the people in the Old Northwest wanted none of that.

The Politics of Development

More broadly, the politics of the region reflected the diversity in the economic and demographic patterns of the Middle West. Political organizations were critical to the acquisition and maintenance of power and the distribution of patronage and resources. As important, partisanship was intense, embodying serious differences among the diverse peoples of the Middle West about economic development and cultural values. There are few places in which values and structures have been so thoroughly and persistently *contested* by its inhabitants. Nothing have they contested more consistently than the role of government – at the local, state, and national levels – in the economic, social, and cultural development of the region.

To a considerable extent, the national government created the Middle West as much as rivers, plains, immigrants, or railroads. The Congress of the United States made the region with the passage of the Northwest Ordinance of 1787. Its provisions insured that Congress would have immense influence in the kinds of states that emerged in the region and that federally appointed officials would direct development until elected officials were ready to take over. The ordinance assumed that territories would be like children to a wiser, older federal father. As I have argued with Peter S. Onuf in *The Midwest and the Nation: Rethinking the History of an American Region* (1990), its articles amounted to a "charter document" for the Middle West (Cayton and Onuf, 1990: 2). They established certain basic principles as *sine qua nons* of regional development: the importance of exercising the freedom to worship God "in a peaceable and orderly manner;" the importance of protection from laws "that shall in any manner whatever interfere with, or affect private contracts or engagements;" that "There shall be neither Slavery nor involuntary Servitude in the said territory," although all escaped slaves and servants had to be returned to their owners; that government had the duty to encourage civility and social order through schools and churches; and that the states formed from the Northwest Territory were forever parts of, and subject to the authority of, the United States. No state could sell or tax federal lands nor could it treat rivers and lakes as anything other than "common highways, and forever free." Although the people of the territory had the right to form states, they could only do so if their "constitutions and governments" were "republican," in line with the provisions of the ordinance, and "consistent with the general interest of the Confederacy."

The ordinance constructed the uneasy balance between freedom and conformity, desire and duty, which is at the center of the midwestern culture that evolved throughout the nineteenth century. Unlike the Declaration of Independence, the ordinance did not talk exclusively about liberty. Unlike the Constitution of 1787, it emphasized values as much as structures. What the articles of the ordinance described was a world in which freedom had to coexist with responsibility. People could worship as they pleased, *if* they behaved in a "peaceable and orderly manner." People could enjoy protection from government, *if* they built schools and encouraged morality. People could buy land, *if* they treated dispossessed Indians with dignity and respect. People could experience the blessings of citizenship in the United States of America, including the ownership of private property, *if* they agreed to pay their taxes and bear their share of the financial burdens of its government.

The provisions of the Northwest Ordinance were honored more often in the breach than in the observance. Settlers squatted on Indian lands and treaties were ignored even as they were signed; settlers who could not see the value of education in local, rural settings resisted for decades paying taxes to support schools whose curricula would be determined by state-appointed bureaucrats. Still, the document established a charter of principles and values that have distinguished the Middle West ever since. The classic example is the prohibition of slavery, which was above all else a political decision. Congressmen decided that the Northwest Territory would not have slaves and, in so doing, they defined the Middle West as sharply as glaciers and rainfall.

If the Northwest Ordinance did not dictate the direction of midwestern society, it did establish a commitment, a tone, a set of principles that has distinguished the region for over two centuries. In many ways, the political history of the Middle West in the nineteenth century was a debate over the meaning of these principles and the degree to which one group could enforce its interpretation on others. Nowhere was this tension more obvious than in what the Northwest Ordinance referred to as the relationship between "morality" and "good government." Nowhere else did the diverse peoples of the Middle West disagree more violently than on the meaning of morality; over nothing else did they contest more fiercely than over the power of government in their lives. As the historians Paul Kleppner and Richard Jensen (1971) have shown, temperance and education became the quintessential midwestern political issues in the second half of the nineteenth century. The region was evenly divided between Republicans, who drew strongly on middle-class Protestant voters and advocated restrictions on liberties that threatened to become licentious (such as drinking) and the need for education as the best way to inculcate values, and Democrats, who tended to be supported by voters of southern ancestry and immigrants who wanted no part of Republican plans for orderly society interfering with their own local cultures.

Politics was the point of intersection between the great demographic diversity of the region and its larger commitment to economic and social development, between tradition and progress, between localism and nationalism. As members of the Democratic party and as participants in third party movements, many midwesterners strove to protect local autonomy, to preserve and defend their particular traditions from the homogenization of the market and the notions of economic and social development embedded in the Northwest Ordinance. In the second half of the nineteenth century, their efforts meant that the politics of morality was fought out over a wide variety of cultural issues (prohibition in Iowa, public education in Wisconsin) on the local or state level. It was virtually impossible to discuss them on any higher level. Bourgeois morality was to the Middle West what racism was to the South, the central, defining issue in people's lives. As Jensen (1971) has vividly demonstrated, politics was an intense, popular, all-involving business. People acted as if their way of life was at stake in nearly every election because it was.

Needs and Opportunities

The cornucopia of literature on midwestern topics does not mean that the subject has been exhausted. The great achievement of historians in the second half of the twentieth century has been to move beyond filiopietistic local studies and celebratory state histories and to emphasize the larger significance of the Middle West. No longer can the authors of textbooks write about the North in the nineteenth century as an undifferentiated whole, anymore than they would write about the South in that fashion. Minnesota was no more an unmodified extension of New York than Louisiana was of Virginia. All American historians must take the peoples of the Middle West seriously, accepting the notion that understanding their lives and work is central to understanding the economic, political, and social development of the United States. The Middle West was more than a place of farmers and middle-class entrepreneurs, more than a place that pops up in historians' consciousness when they want to discuss Populist protests at the end of the nineteenth century. Historians of the Middle West are reorienting the history of the region so that it is told on its own terms, not from local or national perspectives.

What is lacking, however, is any rigorous study of the question of regionalism. Historians have only begun to consider cultural aspects of life in the Middle West and they have done so almost exclusively from the perspective of class, ethnicity, or locality. We might profit from broadening our investigations beyond politics, economics, and religion to include literature, art, music, architecture, parades, or festivals as windows into the world of the nineteenth-century Middle West. More generally, we might think much more formally about what it meant to be from or of the Middle West, about creative and political expressions as regional phenomena, and about how growing up in or living in such an unabashedly capitalist environment in the middle of such immense diversity and rapid change affected human beings' sense of themselves and their relationships with other people. In other words, we might focus squarely on the question of midwestern identity, or what I will call, borrowing the word of Benedict Anderson, the contested construction of an "imagined" regional community.

In short, historians ought to begin writing about the region as a whole. Most of the best work in recent decades has centered on cities, states, or local areas. It is past time for scholars to step back and to address the growing literature on the Middle West from a broader perspective, to write articles and books that have regional rather than local parameters. One of the most promising ways to do this would be to think beyond the region, to write comparative history, or at least midwestern history informed by serious reflection on the origins and development of other regions, not only in North America, but throughout the world.

REFERENCES

Cayton, Andrew R. L. and Onuf, Peter S. (1990) *The Midwest and the Nation: Rethinking the History of an American Region*. Bloomington, Ind: Indiana University Press.

Conzen, Kathleen Neils (1976) *Immigrant Milwaukee, 1836–1860: Accommodation and Community in a Frontier City*. Cambridge, Mass.: Harvard University Press.

Cronon, William (1991) *Nature's Metropolis: Chicago and the Great West*. New York: W. W. Norton.

Etcheson, Nicole (1996) *The Emerging Midwest: Upland Southerners and the Political Culture of the Old Northwest, 1787–1861*. Bloomington, Ind.: Indiana University Press.

Faragher, John Mack (1986) *Sugar Creek: Life on the Illinois Prairie*. New Haven, Conn.: Yale University Press.

Fink, Deborah (1992) *Agrarian Women: Wives and Mothers in Rural Nebraska, 1880–1940*. Chapel Hill, NC: University of North Carolina Press.

Gjerde, Jon (1997) *The Minds of the West: Ethnocultural Evolution in the Rural Middle West, 1830–1917*. Chapel Hill, NC: University of North Carolina Press.

Gray, Susan E. (1996) *The Yankee West: Community Life on the Michigan Frontier*. Chapel Hill, NC: University of North Carolina Press.

Hudson, John C. (1994) *Making the Corn Belt: A Geographical History of Middle-Western Agriculture*. Bloomington, Ind.: Indiana University Press.

Jensen, Richard (1971) *The Winning of the Midwest: Social and Political Conflict, 1888–1896*. Chicago: University of Chicago Press.

Murphy, Lucy Eldersveld and Venet, Wendy Hamand (eds) (1997) *Midwestern Women: Work, Community, and Leadership at the Crossroads*. Bloomington, Ind.: Indiana University Press.

Nelson, Daniel (1995) *Farm and Factory: Workers in the Midwest, 1880–1990*. Bloomington, Ind.: Indiana University Press.

Neth, Mary (1995) *Preserving the Family Farm: Women, Community, and the Foundations of Agribusiness in the Midwest, 1900–1940*. Baltimore, MD: Johns Hopkins University Press.

Oestreicher, Richard Jules (1986) *Solidarity and Fragmentation: Working People and Class Consciousness in Detroit, 1875–1900*. Urbana: University of Illinois Press.

Pederson, Jane Marie (1992) *Between Memory and Reality: Family and Community in Rural Wisconsin, 1870–1970*. Madison: University of Wisconsin Press.

Ross, Steven J. (1985) *Workers on the Edge: Work, Leisure, and Politics in Industrializing Cincinnati, 1788–1890*. New York: Columbia University Press.

Sawislak, Karen (1995) *Smoldering City: Chicagoans and the Great Fire, 1871–1874*. Chicago: University of Chicago Press.

Shortridge, James R. (1989) *The Middle West: its Meaning in American Culture*. Lawrence, Kansas: University Press of Kansas.

Teaford, Jon (1993) *Cities of the Heartland: the Rise and Fall of the Industrial Midwest*. Bloomington, Ind.: Indiana University Press.

Winkle, Kenneth J. (1988) *The Politics of Community: Migration and Politics in Antebellum Ohio*. Cambridge: Cambridge University Press.

CHAPTER TWENTY

The Relational West

MOLLY P. ROZUM

RECENT scholars of western history have given the field a self-conscious "region-al" definition, revisionist public goals, and a movement called "new western history." The rise of this rigorous and vital movement has resulted in a huge literature concerning the western field's founding ideas and its historians. Even *when* western history became "new" remains contested. In the past 30 years the field's "diversity project" has gradually expanded from exploring how race, ethnicity, class, gender, and place identities shape western experience to examining relationships among these identities as they affect and displace one another within and in response to historic intercultural and intracultural relationships. This survey of scholarship begins with the reorienting synthesis in western history and continues with several important edited collections that, taken together, set the larger context for the most recent interpret-ative wave of the nineteenth-century West.

The story of "new western history" begins in 1987 with the publication of Patricia Nelson Limerick's literary, synthetic *The Legacy of Conquest: the Unbroken Past of the American West*. She emphasized the West of the twentieth century as a dynamic "place," a geographical region, almost a century after Frederick Jackson Turner declared the western frontier "closed." The "settlement" of the West was not an orderly, entirely rural, sequential process of categorical man – explorer, trader-trapper, rancher, pioneer, farmer – subduing nature. Nor was it an experience that shaped some unified "American character." Nor did it create political democracy. For Turn-er's linear, celebrated process, Limerick substituted the West as *region*, a specific place with continuing colonial, international, national, and regional histories. If any single process marked American history, moreover, it was one of "conquest," the seizure of someone else's land, euphemistically obscured on Turner's "frontier." Native-Amer-ican reservations and increasing Latino populations, Limerick maintained, served to remind contemporary American society that the legacy of nineteenth-century con-quest still burdened a twentieth-century western present. Euro-American cultural dominance, asserted through government policies of assimilation and paternalism, had not white-washed the American West's first inhabitants. Nor had they vanished. Moreover, consistent waves of new immigrants had defied exclusionary legislation and relentless discrimination to make the American West of the twentieth century even more multi-cultural than the nineteenth-century West.

Legacy of Conquest actually emerged at the confluence of several new rivers of scholarship to announce "new western history" to public audiences. In essence, Limerick's western synthesis can be viewed as a seismic after-shock to an earthquake that took place 20 years earlier and had multiple epicenters at the major research universities that trained her and her contemporaries. She explained that the roots of *Legacy* lay in an "intellectual revolution" (Limerick, 1987: 22). New Indian history and the growth of Chicano, women's, urban, and environmental history fertilized this flowering. More by coincidence than regional design, many of the publications from these rising fields of American history centered on western minorities and/or western spaces.

In addition, in 1961, a new professional association and its journal, the *Western Historical Quarterly*, began to revitalize "frontier" western history. The Western History Association and its journal started out with a much reduced place for their "founding father." Detailed research had challenged aspects of Turner's "frontier" idea since the turn of the century, but became especially vigorous after his death in 1932. Attempting to correct the idea's most obvious defects – vagueness, geographical imprecision, neglect of minorities, and grand, meta-narrative explanations – the Western History Association had begun to promote new conceptions of "frontier" and to develop connections between a growing group of professionals and an always large group of western enthusiasts. *The Oxford History of the American West* (1994), edited by Clyde A. Milner, Carol A. O'Connor, and Martha A. Sandweiss, comprehensively maps this important and continuing, post-1950s' scholarship. Limerick drew on this new work but laced her emphasis on the field's geographical identity with a bold idea: instead of quietly redefining "frontier," carrying Turner's baggage along, she argued, historians should finally "go public" in an all-out disavowal of Frederick Jackson Turner and his ubiquitous thesis. She wished her colleagues to speak out as contemporary public, cultural critics because the "message has not gotten through" (Limerick, 1987: 31). Public audiences, from western hobbyists, to tourists, to western regional residents themselves, still believed in the heroic, mythic "frontier."

Important proponents of what by 1989 had become known as "new western history" summarized the scope of this bolder enquiry and assessed its potential problems in *Trails: Toward a New Western History* (1991), edited by Limerick, Charles E. Rankin, and Clyde A. Milner. Donald Worster writes on the western rural myth; Richard White on how environmental history has reoriented concepts of western nature; and Peggy Pascoe on the key role historians of western women have played in the rise of new thinking about the West. Alongside these original essays appear critical assessments of the "new western history" by Gerald Thompson, Elliott West, and Michael Malone and several essays that explain recent "global" directions in the field. Limerick's two short contributions to the collection are important for specific descriptions of western regional coherence. The West-as-region can be identified, she argues, from its aridity, its long-time large American Indian and Hispanic presence, its preponderance of Indian reservations and federally administered lands, its borders with Mexico and the Pacific Ocean (and through these borders continuing links with Latino and Asian populations), and by its historic position as an inhabited place undergoing conquest by the United States as a fully constituted nation.

Under an Open Sky: Rethinking America's Western Past (1992), edited by William Cronon, George Miles, and Jay Gitlin, both supplements and supplants the *Trails* collection. In their collaborative introduction, the editors maintain that a modern, trans-Mississippi, regional West should remain a vital research project. They add several regional unifiers: low population density, the development of a rural–urban dichotomy in overall landscape appearance, and, most importantly, the western region's unbroken commitment to embracing the nation's mythic frontier past. But they would not dismiss Frederick Jackson Turner. Instead, they agree with Turner's insight that "'the colonization of the Great West' by Euro-African-Asian invaders remains *the* event of importance for American history" (Cronon et al., 1992: 6). They propose, however, to ground the field of western history with six "Non-Turnerian," non-linear, non-sequential "frontier processes" that are "inextricably entangled" in the "movement toward regional identity" (Cronon et al., 1992: 23, 11). The core of these processes is the invasion by peoples, their cultures, the ecosystems of the places from which they moved, and their daily mingling in varied geographical spaces with similar migrations of other cultures. This motion arises from patterns of eco-species distribution, trade markets, land use, and nation-state formation, with the "self-shaping" of multiple identities saturating all of the processes. Drawing, maintaining, and shifting boundaries in daily acts, they emphasize, is the "very essence of frontier life" for invaders; it is through these acts over time, over generations, that a growing "sense of entitlement to the landscape" occurs that shifts personal identity from that of invader-pioneer to that of regional resident (Cronon et al., 1992: 15). Regional residents live in turn amidst the legacy of conflicts set in motion by the moral ambiguity of these frontier processes. In short, the authors extract Turner's "frontier" from its old Darwinian, "hierarchy of culture" moorings, leaving only his basic original insight that "frontier" and "section" or region constitute important and linked processes in the conquest and colonization of North America.

Richard W. Etulain's *Writing Western History: Essays on Major Western Historians* (1991) uses recent scholarship to sort out a century of complicated shuffling within the western field. The collection as a whole stresses the antecedents of the field's current orientation. Contributions analyze Josiah Royce's early regional theory of "Provincialism;" Turner's "Frontier" and "Section" essays; Walter Prescott Webb's geographical regionalism and systems of Euro-world expansion; Herbert Eugene Bolton's Spanish-Mexican "Borderlands" West; and James Malin's creative use of earth sciences. Patricia Nelson Limerick explores the process by which Ray Allen Billington almost single-handedly kept the "frontier thesis" current until recent times. William Cronon places Turnerian thought – nationalist, "probably imperialist," "potentially racist," Eurocentric, and Darwinian – securely in a turn-of-the-century historical context (Etulain, 1991: 91). He historicizes Turner's discourse by defining what phrases like "free land," "Old West," "West," and "Far West" meant in late nineteenth-century America. Turner emerges as a Progressive scientific historian, trained in the "new," German professional methods of primary source analysis. He shines, however, when active in the nineteenth-century role of public orator. Cronon shows that Turner's most remembered works were speeches created to be read aloud to public audiences and constructed according to the logic of "grand" oratory, with all the tricks of rhetoric, metaphor, and image. The value of Turnerian ideas in the late twentieth-century context, Cronon argues, lies *only* in his repeating frontier: it forms a useful geographical, temporal plot for constructing multiple, regionally linked American history narratives.

The debates over "frontier" and "region" have left the field of western history with two distinct, but overlapping, projects. The first, its "frontier" wing, analyzes the West as the history of United States colonization "processes" and the diverse peoples it involved. The West in this sense is a place that shifts over time and jumps around the space of North America until, by the 1930s, it has left a continent of regions in its wake. Not all inhabitants migrated in a westerly direction to arrive in these many historic Wests, but all peoples who lived in these changing Wests came under the powerful influence of the federal government and an expanding commercial, international economy, both located in the Eastern United States. The location of this relationship of influence made all inhabitants part of "westernness." The second wing focuses on "region" and analyzes a geographical, trans-Mississippi North American western "place" and the diverse populations which met there in conquest and through migration. Its geographical reach more often includes borderland areas of Mexico and Canada, as well as Hawaii and Alaska. The temporal scope of this wing is continuing and antedates US history. The geographical West suggests an implicit "difference" between the continent's western nature – its landscape, ecology, geology, and atmosphere – and historical development and those of the continent's East. These separate western wings, however, remain attached to the same bird. The "geographical-regional" West analyzes frontier because the regional West has become the repository of the nation's frontier myth, while the "moving-frontier" West analyzes the geographical West as the location of the nation's last western frontiers. Both explore continuing relationships of conquest. Environmental history also grounds both wings and they share the commitment to complex multi-cultural analysis.

A recognition of the West's diversity – cultural, geographical, and disciplinary – more than any other factor unifies current scholarship. The "diversity project" started with the "excavation" and "recovery" of western voices once ignored: women's, Native-American Indian, Hispanic-Mexican American, and Asian American. But diversity also has grown to mean structuring historical narratives according to multi-cultural perspectives and intercultural relations, with identities of race, ethnicity, class, gender, and place forming central categories of analysis. Diversity for western historians in particular includes the implicit voice of environment. The importance of the environment – understood as an actively changing, surrounding terrain and atmosphere – may be western history's most important contribution to the field of United States history at large. The field has also ensured that region, the cultural corollary of environment, is treated as a category of historical analysis, whether one studies the South, New England, or the Midwest. Finally, western writers seek diversity through interdisciplinary work; they often view historical evidence through the eyes of cultural geographers and geologists, literary and cultural theorists, anthropologists and folklorists, and ecologists, botanists, and biologists. The selections chosen here to illustrate the main developments in recent western history arise from the place where the two wings of the western field overlap: the nineteenth-century geographical West. The important interpretations discussed below take the western history to the edge of a new landing on which a fully realized "relational West," based on relationships among North America's historic populations in their environmental contexts, will likely emerge in the twenty-first century.

Historians of western women are at the center of western history's "diversity project." As historians began to understand the extent to which gender exclusiveness had limited older interpretations of western history, they recognized the kinds of limitations their own racial exclusiveness might place on their efforts to describe a complex western historical experience. Editors Elizabeth Jameson and Susan Armitage view their recent collection, *Writing the Range: Race, Class, and Culture in the Women's West* (1997), as fulfillment of the commitment to inclusiveness that their older edited volume on western women had attempted, but did not realize in full. *Writing the Range* includes essays on diverse intra- and intercultural relations involving African-American, Asian, Euro-American Ethnic, Native-American, and Latina/Hispaña women. Advances made by the collection as a whole are visible in the essays on Latino culture. Yolanda Chávez Leyva and James F. Brooks, respectively, show how Hispaña women used land ownership and their precarious place in a "captive-exchange" system to forge intracultural gendered generational bonds and syncretic intercultural bonds among colonial Hispaños and Native Americans. Darlis Miller describes how Hispanic villagers forged intercultural bonds with later migrating white women based on their common roles in reproduction and food producing. Advances in theory include Peggy Pascoe's suggestion that the phrase "race difference" might be used, as "gender" is distinguished from biological "sex," to separate biological categories and social relations from their conflation in the category of "race." Finally, Jameson and Armitage propose a subtle shift in the emphasis of American history from the "history-of-the-United-States" to the "history-of-United-States-peoples." With this shift, they argue, the "frontier" metamorphoses from a zone at the outer-edge of nationally claimed lands to any location within the mid-drift of the North American continent where intercultural relationships were or are formed.

Published ten years earlier than the *Range* collection, Sarah Deutsch's *No Separate Refuge: Culture, Class, and Gender on an Anglo-Hispanic Frontier in the American Southwest, 1880–1940* (1987) signaled the early commitment of western historians to both gender and cultural diversity. Deutsch redefines "frontier." She views US and Mexican frontiers as "interlocked" on southwestern landscapes already shaped by Native Americans. Rather than marking Turner's line between savagery and civilization, Deutsch's "frontier" is both an interactive process and a zone where cultures meet in a range of situations and spaces and form a spectrum of responses. From this angle of vision, the military victory of the Mexican–American War of 1846–8 did not bring Anglo-cultural dominance. Rather, Deutsch's research has shown that Spanish-founded villages actually increased in population and expanded north with the establishment of new villages until at least 1880, regardless of far-off imperial machinations. Deutsch's detailed descriptions of pre-1880 Hispano-Mexican village formation, arrangement, and daily life demonstrate a growing movement in western history toward analyzing diverse cultures autonomously rather than solely in relation to dominant Anglo culture.

Historians of the West also look for the cultural agency of peoples formerly presented as passive. To this end, Deutsch shows how Anglo conquest of Spanish Mexicans remained incomplete for several generations, even beyond World War I, as rural villagers retained a measure of cultural autonomy through processes of "selective adaptation." Deutsch describes a "regional system" that allowed villager identity to flow freely back and forth between rural and urban spaces. Male villagers migrated for occasional wage labor in the railroad, coal mining, and sugar-beet industries that fueled the growth of urban islands located in New Mexico and Colorado. Trade and seasonal work had long been cultural traditions for men. Hispanic women selected imported material culture, such as cook-stoves or iron beds, as well as ideas from Protestant missionaries, and adapted them to village culture. In their roles as owners of land and gardens, and keepers of Catholic religious ritual, women already formed the cultural center of village life. The regional system allowed men and women to work in tandem to resist cultural conquest; men provided income to support the village system, while women maintained a cultural life in which men could take "refuge." Anglo conquest, however, reached a new level (but was by no means complete) when intracultural gender roles among Mexican women reorganized as the village semi-subsistence "refuge" role gave way to non-village wage dependence in the twentieth century.

Peggy Pascoe's *Relations of Rescue: the Search for Female Moral Authority in the American West, 1874–1939* (1990) typifies new western studies that weave cultural analysis of race, class, gender, and place through inter- and intracultural relations. Pascoe's study begins by examining the Victorian gender roles that white middle-class women carried with them into the post-Civil War West. She then proceeds to show how these benevolent women created a new "female moral authority" derived from the power of their presumed piety and purity. Western cities, with their large male populations and problems of vice, gambling, and prostitution, appeared needy of feminine influence. Migrating missionary women, Pascoe argues, carved urban leadership spaces for themselves out of this opportunity by founding "rescue homes" to save women who, in their view, were the victims of male immorality.

Such institutions also became centers for women's public voice and power opportunities. Because it was recognized nationwide as a middle- to upper-class and female activity, benevolent work, for example, could be used by women to "mark" a new (higher) class position for themselves in the West. Benevolent women, Pascoe found, also situated a critique of patriarchal power within a racial hierarchy; this was the case in one San Francisco "home" designed to save Chinese prostitutes. White women argued that Chinese men abused Chinese women, in both California and China. In doing so, these women voiced discontent at male gender power in general, which their middle-class husbands could choose to hear as a racial critique. Because benevolent women believed in an essentialized "woman's culture," positive, warm, cross-cultural bonds often formed among matrons and residents. Such bonds led benevolent women to challenge racial discrimination by fighting for integrated education and against immigration restrictions such as the 1882 Chinese exclusion law. As white women, however, their convictions lacked legal, political, and social power; gender constraints trumped racial liberalism. Women's race-encased gender critique also obscured their own cultural economic dependence on patriarchy. But their position as superior in the period's racial order empowered them in relation to "rescued" Chinese women; even those Chinese women who fully accepted "Protestant true womanhood" remained underlings.

For their part, "rescued" Chinese women often used the "homes" not as vehicles of religious conversion but as a means to find marriage partners, social services, and their footing in US society. Nor did former prostitutes and otherwise troubled young women always set aside Chinese or Chinese-American notions of morality. Female converts, however, became liminal in both Chinese-American communities, which had their own gender systems and sense of morality, and the larger San Francisco society, in which they could not be hired into middle-class jobs reserved for white women. Assimilation resulted, then, in limited marriage prospects within the Chinese community and only low-paying domestic jobs in the larger culture. While patterns of shifting hierarchies no doubt existed in Eastern benevolent work, the uneven sexual demography of the western context, Pascoe argues, allows historians to see more clearly how and in what ways middle-class women could push against the limits of their power within Victorian gender ideology.

Revisionist "new" Indian history, like women's history, contributed early to diversifying western "frontier" history. Two among many important studies illustrate the "new" Indian history as it emerged in the 1970s to 1980s. The first, James P. Ronda's *Lewis and Clark among the Indians* (1984), traces an early nineteenth-century intercultural journey from St Louis along the Missouri River up through the Dakotas and Montana to the Pacific Coast. Ronda's interpretation relies on information from anthropology and material culture studies to supplement European manuscript sources; this allows him to secure complex points of view. His strategy centers on detailed analysis of relationships forged out of daily life experiences between Lewis, Clark, their military corps, and the Otos, Omahas, Yankton and Teton Sioux, Mandan, Hidatsa, Arikara, Assiniboine, Blackfeet, and Chinookan peoples, among others. According to Ronda's reading, all explored each other's cultures equally, even though Lewis and Clark deemed their own culture superior to that of Native Nations. They shared food, meals, sex, stories, rituals, dancing, hunting, and cultural knowledge. Military men took notes on earthlodge, hide, and plank homes, burial rites, and other material cultural of various Nations; Native peoples, these same notes describe, almost daily watched whites build forts, inspected white-constructed boats, and handled the numerous material goods inside both. Out of daily life grew friendships between Native leaders – Sheheke (Big White), Kagohhami (Little Raven), and Posecopsahe (Black Cat), for example – and Lewis and Clark; all emerge in Ronda's presentation as historical actors with developed, idiosyncratic adult personalities. Military men participated in "Buffalo calling" rituals and gave prizes to adolescent Native boys who demonstrated their bow-and-arrow skills. Native men requested fiddle dancing and were welcomed to sleepovers at Fort Mandan. These men together formed multicultural hunting parties and no cultural blinders blocked them from recognizing a good hunter. The experiences on the journey varied with individuals and Native cultural groups and thereby exploded simple historical stereotypes.

Ronda also reminds readers that the mission of Lewis and Clark and their military entourage centered on an expansion of a US trade-centered empire, and *not* one for further European-American western settlement. Ronda makes clear that, despite Lewis and Clark's own view of Natives as inferior children in adult bodies, Native-American leaders demanded treatment as equals in recognition of their numerical and cultural dominance. Sometimes cultural encounters mutually missed their marks. Ronda explains Lewis and Clark's difficulty in understanding the Native politics lying beneath intricate patterns of warfare and long-standing webs of trading alliances among western Indian groups and representatives of British, Spanish, and French imperial powers. Lewis and Clark also failed to recognize Indian leadership customs when more than one individual held authority to make decisions. For their part, the previous experience Native groups had with white men preconditioned them to view Lewis and Clark as traders and to expect negotiation for long-term trade alliances. Natives did not understand the occupation of exploration or the shifting nature of imperial claims to their land bases that Lewis tried to convey through "peace" medals, good behavior certificates, military uniforms, and US flags.

A second theme in the "new" Indian history attempted to show Native people's cultural persistence in spite of disease, dispossession of land, starvation, and assimilation policies. In California only some 15,000, or 5 percent of the pre-Spanish period Native population, remained alive in 1900, with dramatic losses occurring in the gold rush years. Despite this worst-case scenario, Albert L. Hurtado's *Indian Survival on the California Frontier* (1988) found paths of cultural maintenance hidden in manuscript sources, Spanish-Mexican and United States government records, and census records. Even while they suffered from indiscriminate violence and grievous government policies, Native Californians were not passive victims of gold-camp aggression. Hurtado charts Native cultural survival through adaptation. California Indians traded, raided camps, resisted with violence, and intermarried among various new ethnic immigrants. Natives also entered wage labor to work in gold mines, on ranches, or within households. An early federal reservation system designed to "civilize" Natives by making them farmers supplemented, but did not replace, traditional hunting and gathering subsistence. Such reservations lacked sufficient food supplies and land area to provide ample work opportunities; and while Natives welcomed reservation provisions, few wanted to leave their traditional home locations. Seasonal work, as with the Hispanic villagers Deutsch (1987) analyzed, functioned, then, as a middle ground. Hurtado speculates using census evidence that, by 1860, reproduction rates within California Native groups had plummeted because of high death rates in the female Native population in comparison to males and because of Native isolation caused by gender-specific work places.

Most California Natives retreated from the gold rush camps by the end of 1849. They were pushed out of wage positions by the multi-ethnic, multi-racial tide of gold-dreaming newcomers described in Malcolm J. Rohrbough's recent study, *Days of Gold: the California Gold Rush and the American Nation* (1997). Euro-Americans came from every state and territory by ship and overland to California to join native Californios (Mexicans) and the diverse Native peoples studied by Hurtado. So, too, came Chileans, Peruvians, French, English, Welsh, Scottish, Irish, Chinese, Hawaiian Islanders, Sonora-area Mexicans, Australians (including some Irish, black, and Chinese), free blacks and black slaves, all to dig for gold or to profit from serving this instant, cosmopolitan community. Anxieties over debt and family left at home, loss of self-respect due to failure in mining ventures, fear and weariness from new experiences in labor, landscape, and living in this male-dominant setting pushed some men over the edge. Rohrbough suggests how such frustration often pitted one minority group against another, a picture that new work by Susan Lee Johnson complicates by detailing the emergence of a male domesticity in which the "mark" of race chased some men into new gender roles (in Matsumoto and Allmendinger, 1999).

The national framework of Rohrbough's study furthers the attempts of the "new western history" to draw together the nation's eastern and western experiences. He argues that this massive migration rent the cultural fabric of the nation, disrupting and destroying family life and gender norms. His evidence suggests that women who took over farm and business responsibilities in their husbands' absences found that women's rights and suffrage suddenly made more sense. Rohrbough also charts how the gold rush carried issues of wealth and class to the fore of national culture and public discourse at a time when increasing industrialization began to affect the nature of work, reordering national class structure along the way. Some of these men would emerge as part of the generation who reconfigured national attention from Reconstruction to issues of capital and labor. Finally, the dissemination of the gold rush in print and first-person experience across the nation and down through generations of family "gold rush" and "overland" stories suggests how enduring national myths took shape.

Gold has had perennial multi-cultural appeal; the picture of mid-century California as a multi-ethnic, multi-racial West, therefore, has been longstanding. A multi-racial West, however, did not begin with the thousands lured by gold to cross continents and oceans. It began much earlier in the reality of a mestizo population arising within the bounds of the Spanish North American empire. Quintard Taylor's *In Search of the Racial Frontier: African Americans in the American West, 1528–1990* (1998) reveals the pre-nineteenth century, multi-cultural foundation of North America's West by recovering the long over-looked and little analyzed black western experience. Visiting northern New Spain in Texas in the early nineteenth century, one would find, according to Taylor, a mestizo culture already in place, the result of long-term, large-scale intermarriage and sexual encounters among Spanish, African, and Indian peoples. Attention to historical constructions of race shows how in the complicated mestizo culture, class rather than color determined racial orientation. For this reason, and because of independent Mexico's constitutional commitment to the abolition of slavery, Texas became an attractive place for both free blacks and fugitive slaves. Even after a "perpetual" contract labor system allowed slaveholding settlers to continue on as they had in the southern United States, Texas experienced "abolition scares" throughout the antebellum period as Mexicanos assisted thousands of fugitive slaves across the Rio Grande.

In the far western Spanish-Mexican lands, California hosted several thousand of the West's free African Americans in the antebellum years. This free black population had either migrated north from Mexico or escaped from ships competing in the Pacific coast's commercial sea-otter and fur trade during the early nineteenth century. In 1863, a growing middle-class black community began the western tradition of challenging racial exclusion with lawsuits when the driver of a San Francisco streetcar unlawfully refused to let a black woman ride the line. Some 30 years later, just before segregation became entrenched in the Jim Crow South, middle-class blacks succeeded in securing the passage of a California anti-discrimination law. Although the South and the Far West seemed to be heading in two different directions at the turn of the twentieth century, Taylor (1998) concludes that, while slavery and segregation generally remained illegal, both institutions existed in *de facto*, insidious forms all over the nineteenth-century West. The application of slave labor to cattle ranching in Texas and gold mining in California proved slavery's adaptability. Ultimately, Taylor argues, the choice to limit slavery in the United States was political rather than based on regional differences.

One of Taylor's key observations about the black western experience goes to the heart of a "new western history" project. Undercutting the stereotypes of the lone "rugged black cowboy" and the "sturdy, silent black woman" and the myth of the "rural frontier," Taylor (1998: 22) concludes that an urban setting helped shape black western life. Every western state and territory had some African-American residents, usually in small towns and growing cities. In turn, race laws in some states influenced urban culture. Oregon and California, for example, refused blacks home-steading privileges, the source, along with railroad lands, of much of the rural settle-ment around which the western "rural" myth centers. Active city cores, with their institutions and newspapers, also linked rural blacks to city communities across the West, suggesting that city–country ties may have been stronger for African Americans than for other westerners.

Taylor's analysis supplements the work of David M. Emmons in *The Butte Irish: Class and Ethnicity in an American Mining Town, 1875–1925* (1989), which also addresses an urban racial ethnic culture in the late nineteenth-century West. From almost its earliest days, and in opposition to the "rural frontier" myth, Butte formed an urban "industrial island" within the spacious sea of Montana (Emmons, 1989: 62). Emmons analyzes how Irish ethnic ties of Catholic culture, mining work, and enclave neighborhoods connected Montana Irish identity with the labor force con-tinuously migrating from Ireland to make the labor rounds from US city to city. Irish nationalism and transient, single, male laborers knit national urban areas into a net-work parallel to the regional city–country community network of African Americans. Irish town residents located themselves in Butte, America, *not* Butte, Montana. Despite these ethnic links, Emmons observes also that an (anti-British) "anglopho-bia" divided nineteenth-century Irish Americans via race. The largely unskilled and continually arriving Irish labor force fits perfectly into the basic needs of a town Emmons describes as "born industrializing." The strength of the Irish hold on Butte, a city that in 1900 had the largest percentage of Irish population in the nation, mirrored transformations within the shifting of capitalism in the nation at large. The Irish lost cultural control of the town and mining jobs when Irish mine ownership ended with the turn-of-century rise of monopoly investment capitalism.

As the nineteenth-century western region has become more *urban* in recent histori-ography, ironically it has also become more *rural*. Environmental historian William Cronon's *Nature's Metropolis: Chicago and the Great West* (1991) best illustrates this merging of rural and urban historiographies. Cronon analyzes the relationship between country and city landscapes using as his example the reshaping of the ecological prairie, plains, and forest habitants, or "second natures" laid over "first natures," as he explains the singular process of Chicago's rise in the second half of the nineteenth century. Capital from both the Eastern US and a maturing international economy flowed through the hands of Chicago boosters to the "Gate City" and out on railroads to a countryside that would become its "regional hinterland." Symbiotic relationships between country and city transformed "nature" into grain, lumber, and meat. Cronon's specific analysis of time and place rests on the application of newly conceived "frontier processes." He describes processes of development that end in regional formation: Chicago moved from the edge of the nation in the middle of the nineteenth century to a "central place" in the Midwest by the beginning of the twentieth century.

In "Bison ecology and bison diplomacy" (1992), Dan Flores analyzes Native-American environmental adaptation to North America's southern grasslands from 1800 to 1850 – at the dawn of Chicago's reach to pull this environment within its orbit. He weaves together the diverse histories of the Comanche, Kiowa, Cheyenne, and Arapaho Nations to argue for a major Native role in the depletion of southern

Plains bison herds, which was formerly attributed to the 1870s developments of railroad expansion, overkill by sportsmen, and spiraling market demands. Pollen analysis, archeological data, and cultural anthropology help Flores to build an eco-logical context, from the Pleistocene extinctions of 10,000 years ago to 200 years after the Pueblo Revolt of 1680. A host of complicated calculations allows him to conclude that Native Americans needed nearly 6.5 bison and 10–15 horses per person per year, both of which fueled the power of Indian culture through absorbing the energy contained in the Plains' most common resource: grass. Flores concludes that Indians had already placed considerable stress on the ecological equilibrium of their horse and bison culture by the time industrial culture blew through in the form of steel rails and gun shots in the 1870s. Yet conquest still looms large in the decline of bison herds, for it was the 1680 revolt of Pueblos against Spanish-imposed missions that sent horses diffusing north, increasing the chance of Native adaptation to horse culture. The expansion and fast pace of change demanded by capitalist culture and trade, moreover, halted pre-commercial, incremental styles of change in which the horse–bison complex might have achieved successful adaptation to grassland habitats. Central to making these kinds of arguments is the environmental framework or the *longue durée*, which brings into view long-term change not apparent in mere decades of analysis.

The environmental frame of the *longue durée* also encourages multi-cultural analysis through the centuries of evidence that exist layered and mixed in any given geogra-phical setting. Elliott West builds on Flores's arguments in *The Contested Plains: Indians, Goldseekers, and the Rush to Colorado* (1998) by analyzing the stories of the aboriginal peoples of the same central Plains alongside the stories of some hundred thousand southerners, northerners, midwesterners, and others who streamed to Colorado for gold from 1859. West's larger historical project foregrounds the process by which multiple dynamic histories entangle so that their "narrative roots" grow together. For a generation, the central Plains became two regions at one time: the "Middle Border" or internal borderland region separating North America's geogra-phical east from its geographical west and a "homeland" for Native Americans. West describes how each culture storied itself across space and time from 1700 through the 1860s, eventually to meet at mid-century with clashing "visions" of life. When necessary, West dips through 120 centuries of change in the grasslands setting. Concentrating first on the Cheyenne, West analyzes their unique development from forest dwellers, then earthlodge builders along the Missouri River, through their movement on to the northern Plains, a spiritual awakening at Bear Butte in the Black Hills, and their subsequent split in the 1830s into northern and southern bands. By the mid-nineteenth century, the return of drought and some 20 years of overland migrations for gold and land joined the southern Cheyenne and other Native groups on the central Plains. Instead of periodic, seasonal use of grasses and river tree-stands, these important sheltering, fuel, building, and feeding resources were in constant demand all year long, first by "gold-seeking" overlanders and Colorado town-builders from late spring through fall, and then by Native American bands from fall through winter. Eventually, gold rushers and the service entourage left in their wake weaned themselves from dependence on the grasslands. Natives, however, were left with a severely stressed grasslands resource in which to carry on their own environmentally demanding culture. The trails and rails of new cross-Plains connec-tions, West eloquently argues, tied the Rocky Mountains, the Plains and Prairies grasslands, and the Missouri River edge towns together into a "seamless region" in the minds of migrating territorial invaders. Severe environmental stress resulted for Native Nations in a further fracturing into complex traditionalist and accommodationist groups.

Elliot West's (1998) cultural analysis suggests how "place" begins in the mind, but is imagined out of the content of specific ecological habitats. A growing "sense of place" or "regional identity" specialization in western history has begun to emerge out of the realization that "environment" and "region" are separate but reinforcing concepts. Leading environmental historians such as Donald Worster have begun to suggest that regional identity emerges from "the way people *think* about each other and about the place where they live" as well as from a landed, material perspective (Worster, 1992: 230). William Deverell has argued that the West's scenery is so powerful that its grandeur, space, and landscapes have the power to imprint minds with "dreamscapes" on which people enact real life. He advises historians to dislodge the cultural power hidden in historic geographical spaces and constructs of beauty even as they recognize the pleasures historical actors felt in their surroundings (in Milner, 1996). Richard Maxwell Brown, among others, has identified Wallace Stegner as a foundation of Western emotional history, or what Elliot West has called history from the "inside out" (in Milner, 1996; Limerick et al., 1991). Stegner emerges in this specialization because his life as a westerner, as the son of a failed homesteader, and as a western writer suggests the blending of environmental encounter and regional identity at the crux of "sense of place" issues.

Place analysis also involves what David M. Wrobel and Michael C. Steiner have called a "regionalizing" of the "One Great West." This, too, is related to the frame of the *longue durée* that encourages a narrowing of analysis to subregion as it promotes increased temporal analysis. The authors included in Wrobel and Steiner's edited collection, *Many Wests: Place, Culture, and Regional Identity* (1997), explore different kinds of regional formation within the West – state, commercial, ecological, "ethno," and "bio" – and suggest a range of concepts and processes identified by the editors as forces of "internal" and "external" regionalism. The collection as a whole demonstrates that historians have begun to consider the core theories of cultural geographers such as Yi-Fu Tuan and John Brinckerhoff Jackson alongside the more familiar theories developed by ecologists and geologists. Tuan's ideas about "space" and "place" and Jackson's work with "built" landscapes offer new ways to think about relationships among environment, culture, and regional identity.

The turn to cultural geography and "sense of place" resulted in part from the difficulty that early environmental historians seemed to have in placing human beings *naturally* in geographical spaces: people always seemed only to destabilize some ecological equilibrium. As Elliott West (1998) described how multiple cultures became inextricably entangled through cultural imagination enacted on the same spaces, Richard White (1995) describes how the constant physical intertwining of people and environments, their work and energy, makes their place *together* in nature more apparent. In his *The Organic Machine: the Remaking of the Columbia River*, White (1995) argues that through labor people come to know nature. White explains that working with nature allows for intimate knowledge of its surfaces; hidden energy flows emerge with new cultural relationships built over time. Pacific Coast Native Americans knew the workings of the Columbia River through dip-net fishing;

Hudson's Bay Company traders felt the river's power as they canoed through fierce flows; boiler-room workers knew the river's force as they shoveled coal for steam power; Chinese, then Norwegians, Italians, and Finns, knew the river through canning varieties of salmon that swam in it; and dam-builders in the twentieth century knew the properties of river rock and textures of the river bed. While the Columbia River responds in adaptation to new energies shaping it, the river never stops "being" nature as a result of the larger organic cycles – of the *longue durée* – that envelop human cultural energy back into nature.

If nature persists, differently organized cultural economies can change the form of nature rapidly. Most historians argue that, as the United States began the process of incorporating much of North America's western territory into its political borders at the beginning of the nineteenth century, a concomitant incorporation into modern capitalism also occurred. In his synthesis, *Colony and Empire: the Capitalist Transformation of the American West* (1994), William G. Robbins provides a bird's-eye view of a host of local or area studies to demonstrate the regional linkages of nineteenth-century industrialization in the post-Civil War era. The timing of the West's conquest and resettlement, he argues, makes it an ideal case study of modern capitalism and its social power relationships. Western mythology, he also argues, masks the capitalist nature of the conquest. Contrary to the dominant image of the "lone prospector," for example, western mining was shaped by corporate industrialism. Similarly, the often-told story of the demise of open-range ranching in the aftermath of the 1886–7 blizzards on the Great Plains masks the capitalist restructuring underneath the land-use shift. As the power of the rural dream indicates to Robbins, almost all social classes wanted land in the West. But those wanting the typical family farm, he argues, could not compete with the accumulated capital resources of Eastern corporate speculation. Moreover, the federal government worked with eastern schemes of exploitation: it subsidized multiple conquests of Native-American Nations, military forts, railroad expansion, investment capital for resource extraction, and bureaucracies for resettlement of contested rural landscapes.

In addition to discussing East–West international economic relationships, Robbins also addresses the US West's regional relationships with Mexico and Canada, illustrating in each case that capitalism does not recognize political boundaries. More interesting, the inclusion of the United States' western neighbors is suggestive of the subtle, recent rise of a North American emphasis in the study of the West. International framing in part continues the longstanding tradition of Spanish "Borderlands" history (most recently synthesized by David J. Weber). But the inclusion of the West's northern neighbor, Canada, is a distinctly contemporary departure. In part, the historical ties arise naturally, as with Mary Murphy's "Making men in the West," which studies manhood ideals and behavior in the late nineteenth-century Montana–Alberta borderland area (in Masumoto and Allmendinger, 1999). Also, in looking for ways to move beyond the mythic US West, scholars have looked to Canada for comparative purposes because of its similar chronological development and its geographical continuities. This is evident, for example, in William Cronon's recent, modified Chicago application of the Canadian "metropolitan thesis" developed by historian Harold Innis. Moreover, it is plainly inaccurate for historians working in Native-American history to split narrative settings when their subjects acknowledged no such border. And, for almost half of the nineteenth century, there existed in the geographical west of the continent neither northern or southern United States political borders. Finally, ecological habitats do not recognize political boundaries; therefore, nor do environmental historians. For these reasons and others, many recent western studies refer to a "North American West" instead of a "US West" or "American West." Whether either a Canadian-American fully fledged "Northern Borderlands" or a "North American West" will emerge with a depth to match that of the longstanding Southern Borderlands school are questions for the future.

In conclusion, the main interest of the field of western history as it moves into the twenty-first century might be termed the "relational West." Not only diverse western peoples, but their relationships with each other and/or their environment frame the "relational West," as the region's peoples, lands, and even (for "frontier" historians) the West all change over time. The "relational West" rests on what William Cronon and others (1992) have called "connectedness;" what Peggy Pascoe (1990) has referred to as multi-cultural encounters at the "cultural cross-roads;" and what Richard White (1995) has described as the history of diverse "series of relationships" located in western places. Elliott West (1998) has shown that it also involves envisioning new relationships, "whole" regions, from formerly disconnected "parts," until those visions become naturalized, the taken-for-granted relationships of place in particular historical periods. How detailed knowledge of power relationships will reorient the field of western history, however, remains for future synthetic work to determine. For now, the field remains seriously engaged in the task of understanding the shifting nature of these historic western relationships among people and place.

ACKNOWLEDGMENTS

I would like to thank William L. Barney for inviting me to contribute to this project and for his comments on this chapter. I would also like to thank Laura Moore, Jennifer Ritterhouse, Roger W. Lotchin, John Herd Thompson, and Jacquelyn Dowd Hall for their comments on various versions of this chapter and for their encouragement, each in their own way.

REFERENCES

Cronon, William (1991) *Nature's Metropolis: Chicago and the Great West*. New York: W. W. Norton.

Cronon, William, Miles, George and Gitlin, Jay (1992) *Under an Open Sky: Rethinking America's Western Past*. New York: W. W. Norton.

Deutsch, Sarah (1987) *No Separate Refuge: Culture, Class, and Gender on an Anglo-Hispanic Frontier in the American Southwest, 1880–1940*. New York: Oxford University Press.

Emmons, David M. (1989) *The Butte Irish: Class and Ethnicity in an American Mining Town, 1875–1925*. Urbana, Ill.: University of Illinois Press.

Etulain, Richard W. (ed.) (1991) *Writing Western History: Essays on Major Western Historians*. Albuquerque: University of New Mexico Press.

Flores, Dan (1992) "Bison ecology and bison diplomacy: the southern Plains from 1800 to 1850," *Journal of American History*, 78, pp. 465–85.

Hurtado, Albert L. (1988) *Indian Survival on the California Frontier*. New Haven, Conn.: Yale University Press.

Jameson, Elizabeth and Armitage, Susan (eds) (1997) *Writing the Range: Race, Class, and Culture in the Women's West*. Norman: University of Oklahoma Press.

Limerick, Patricia Nelson (1987) *The Legacy of Conquest: the Unbroken Past of the American West*. New York: W. W. Norton.

Limerick, Patricia Nelson, Milner II, Clyde A., and Rankin, Charles E. (1991) *Trails: Toward a New Western History*. Lawrence: University Press of Kansas.

Matsumoto, Valerie J. and Allmendinger, Blake (eds) (1999) *Over the Edge: Remapping the American West*. Berkeley, CA: University of California Press.

Milner II, Clyde A. (ed.) (1996) *A New Significance: Re-envisioning the History of the American West*. New York: Oxford University Press.

Milner II, Clyde A., O'Connor, Carol A., and Sandweiss, Martha A. (eds) (1994) *The Oxford History of the American West*. New York: Oxford University Press.

Pascoe, Peggy (1990) *Relations of Rescue: the Search for Female Moral Authority in the American West, 1874–1939*. New York: Oxford University Press.

Robbins, William G. (1994) *Colony and Empire: the Capitalist Transformation of the American West*. Lawrence: University Press of Kansas.

Rohrbough, Malcolm J. (1997) *Days of Gold: the California Gold Rush and the American Nation*. Berkeley, CA: University of California Press.

Ronda, James P. (1984) *Lewis and Clark among the Indians*. Lincoln: University of Nebraska Press.

Taylor, Quintard (1998) *In Search of the Racial Frontier: African Americans in the American West, 1528–1990*. New York: W. W. Norton.

West, Elliott (1998) *The Contested Plains: Indians, Goldseekers, and the Rush to Colorado*. Lawrence: University Press of Kansas.

White, Richard (1995) *The Organic Machine: the Remaking of the Columbia River*. New York: Hill and Wang.

Worster, Donald (1992) *Under Western Skies: Nature and History in the American West*. New York: Oxford University Press.

Wrobel, David M. and Steiner, Michael C. (eds) (1997) *Many Wests: Place, Culture, and Regional Identity*. Lawrence: University Press of Kansas.

PART VI

Cultures and Ideas

CHAPTER TWENTY-ONE

The Communications Revolution and Popular Culture

DAVID HOCHFELDER

A SHLEY Bowen, a rigger and sailmaker born in 1728, lived his entire life in the small port town of Marblehead, Massachusetts some dozen miles from Boston. He kept a meticulous journal between 1766 and 1795 in which he noted important news, especially local events such as harbor entries and clearings which directly affected his livelihood. Yet he also recorded garbled and incomplete accounts of key regional and national events such as the British march on nearby Lexington and Concord in April 1775, which he described simply as a "hubbub about soldiers." Although Bowen was literate and found ample time to write in his journal, he was little interested in current events or popular culture. He seldom bought a newspaper and read little other than his copy of the Anglican Book of Common Prayer (Brown, 1989: 122–6).

Edward Jenner Carpenter, a western Massachusetts cabinet-maker born in 1825, also kept a diary in which he recorded important news and his participation in the cultural institutions of his day. His experiences, which he recorded in 1844 and 1845, differed markedly from Bowen's. Although Carpenter worked about 50 hours a week and had little disposable income, he still found the time and money to attend lectures and concerts, to subscribe to two monthly newspapers, to borrow books and magazines frequently from friends and local lending libraries, and sometimes to buy a few books of his own. Carpenter even exchanged newspapers through the mail with friends and family as far away as Michigan and New Orleans (Brown, 1989: 230–5).

Although Carpenter kept current with the news, he only learned of distant events many hours or even days after they had occurred. Until the widespread extension of the telegraph network, information could travel no faster than about 30 miles per hour, the typical speed of the era's steam locomotives. Twenty years later, however, Americans throughout the country learned of the assassination of Abraham Lincoln almost instantly. At 3 o'clock in the morning of April 15, 1865 the telegraph operator at Worcester, Massachusetts informed the town's officials of the shooting of the president earlier that night, and they immediately tolled the church bells to inform residents of the sad and shocking news. Although most town fathers did not rouse their citizens from bed, nearly all Americans in places with a telegraph office learned of the assassination sometime during the morning of April 15th. In Indianapolis, for instance, the prominent attorney Calvin Fletcher heard the news from his son as they sat down to breakfast at 6.30 a.m. A few hours later Fletcher read a full account in a local newspaper (Brown, 1989: 260–3).

As the experiences of Bowen, Carpenter, and Fletcher showed, Americans witnessed a thoroughgoing communications revolution between the revolutionary war and the last third of the nineteenth century. This revolution occurred in two overlapping phases. The first phase, roughly bracketed by the diaries of Bowen and Carpenter, began in the 1790s and continued until about 1850. During this period Americans enjoyed easier access to more diverse sources of information. This transformation took place without the introduction of any new communications technology, and arose mainly through improved transportation, the expansion of the postal system, and the rise of new forms of popular culture.

This first phase of the communications revolution was largely complete when the second one began in 1844, the year that Carpenter began his diary and Samuel F. B. Morse opened his first telegraph line between Washington and Baltimore. Telegraphy possessed one attribute – its ability to transmit information instantly across long distances – which set it apart from previous communications technologies. Prior to its invention the transmission of information depended upon the transportation of physical objects. By severing this link between communication and transportation the telegraph helped to reshape American society and culture, although its full impact would not become apparent until after the Civil War.

The Pre-telegraphic Communications Revolution

Before 1844 information travelled no faster than the pace at which goods and people moved. Yet the speed at which information moved through space, the amount and diversity of available information, and access to information networks all increased dramatically in the half-century before the advent of telegraphy. These processes occurred without the invention of any new communication technology *per se*, although advances in transportation such as canals, steamboats, and railroads did improve the speed and reliability of information flow. Nevertheless, political ideology, cultural institutions, and administrative improvements in existing communications networks mainly shaped the pre-telegraphic communications revolution.

Americans in this period believed that the maintenance of national unity and the preservation of republican institutions depended on communications. James W. Carey (1989: 4–5) argues that citizens of the early republic hoped that communications and transportation networks would unite the nation in an imagined community by creating "a tissue of relations in space and time, relations expressed in the basic terms of republican existence – citizen and patriot." They looked to the "space-binding potential" of communications networks to knit together the regions of the country and to fuse individual citizens into a national polity. Similarly, the "time-binding power" of educational and cultural institutions promised to inculcate a sense of patriotism by preserving the republican ideals of the founders and by transmitting them to future generations.

In concrete terms, Americans sought to unite their vast national territory through an extensive program of internal improvements. Sponsors of these projects argued that a comprehensive transportation network would act as a channel for the transmission of ideas as well as commerce. They claimed that such links would foster commercial and personal contacts between the country's sections and would thereby create a national community of interest and sentiment. Similarly, many Americans hoped that improved access to information would preserve republican institutions over time by fostering a sense of patriotism. As Richard D. Brown (1996: xv–xvi) points out, this hope provided an important impetus for the establishment of many public and private institutions in the early republic, including a free and competitive press, an extensive postal service, government support for internal improvements and public education, and a wide array of local schools, libraries, museums, and lecture halls.

In terms of sheer speed, communications improved dramatically between 1790 and 1840. Geographer Allan R. Pred found that it took seven days for New York newspapers to publish news of George Washington's death in Alexandria, Virginia in December 1799; in 1830, New York papers published Andrew Jackson's State of the Union address to Congress $15\frac{1}{2}$ hours after he had delivered it. Seven years later, this time improved to 11 hours (Pred, 1973: 13). Pred claims that the period's increased trade and commercial activity, which created a demand for faster and more reliable communications, was the main factor which contributed to this acceleration of information flow, but these improvements were far from uniform throughout all regions of the country (Pred, 1973: 19). Because of the connection between information flow and commerce, towns located along established trading routes, especially on the Atlantic seaboard between Boston and Washington, enjoyed faster and more reliable communication than did interior points in the South and West.

Historians of transportation have also examined the close connection between trade and the flow of personal correspondence and news. They have shown that the transportation revolution that occurred between 1815 and 1860 was a necessary (but insufficient) condition for both the market and communications revolutions which occurred in the same period. George Rogers Taylor's (1951) comprehensive survey remains the definitive account of the transportation revolution and its effects on American commerce and communications. Carter Goodrich (1960) adopts an economic-development perspective, characterizing the growth of the American canal and railroad networks as a successful example of mixed private and government enterprise which benefited both the public and investors. Goodrich (1960: 268–71) shows that government funding provided crucial support for internal improvements projects, and he estimates that public investment before the Civil War accounted for about 70 percent of the $195 million spent on canal-building and about 30 percent of the $1.145 billion spent on railroad construction. Ronald E. Shaw (1990) has emphasized the connections between internal improvements projects and nationalism. He argues that Americans not only regarded internal improvements as a means to facilitate commerce and to promote national prosperity, but that they also hoped that improved transportation would preserve republican values and would bind the different regions of the country into a unified whole. This mix of motives – the desire to spur commerce and prosperity and the belief that internal improvements would unify and preserve the republic – provided much of the rationale for government assistance for such projects until the Civil War.

Similar motives lay at the heart of American postal policy after the passage of the Post Office Act of 1792. Richard R. John (1995: 24) has credited the act with ushering in "the single most revolutionary era in the entire history of American communications." By the early 1830s the postal network had indeed reached an impressive size; it operated about 8,450 post offices and transmitted nearly 14 million letters and 16 million newspapers (John, 1995: 3–4, 51). John uses these figures to claim that the Post Office was the most important communications medium of the pre-telegraphic era. He argues that the postal system was crucial in establishing integrated markets for both goods and information, and in establishing both a political sphere and a civil society, all of national extent.

The Post Office Act of 1792 contained two far-reaching provisions (John, 1995: 30–53): a mechanism for the rapid expansion of the system into the trans-Appalachian West and a system of subsidies for the newspaper press. Together, these provisions established the principle of universal access to information networks as the central feature of American communications policy throughout the nineteenth century and well into the twentieth (John, 1998: 191–2).

The act facilitated the growth of the postal system by placing the authority for establishing post offices and post roads with Congress rather than with the executive branch. This allowed local interests to pressure the national government for the rapid expansion of facilities and for the reduction of postage rates. Reformers during the 1830s and 1840s argued that cheap postage would both promote national unity and preserve affectionate ties in an era of increasing sectional tension and heightened geographical mobility. They succeeded in securing passage of the Post Office Acts of 1845 and 1851, which reduced letter postage from up to 25 cents per sheet, depending on distance, to a mere 3 cents per half-ounce, a rate which would remain in place for a century. Prior to this rate reduction, the postal system was primarily a commercial medium; afterward, it became a social medium as well. For instance, the mails made possible the extensive networks of female friendships identified by Carroll Smith-Rosenberg and other women's historians; the frequent exchange of letters allowed nineteenth-century women to sustain intimate connections across wide distances and over time (John, 1995: 156–61).

The second important provision of the Post Office Act of 1792 was its favorable rate structure for the transmission of newspapers through the mails. This intended subsidy of the press facilitated a dramatic growth in the number of newspapers and subscribers between 1792 and 1840. Richard B. Kielbowicz (1989: 2) argues that "the post office and press together constituted the most important mechanism for the dissemination of public information at least until the Civil War." Postal policy assisted the growth of the press in two important ways. First, low postage on periodicals allowed religious, political, and reform organizations to flourish during the Jacksonian era by providing them with the means to reach a national audience (Kielbowicz, 1989: 107–8). Secondly, the postal law allowed newspaper editors to exchange postage-free copies with the editors of all other newspapers in the country. Before the rise of telegraphic news reporting in the 1840s, these exchanges were the primary means by which newspapers obtained regional and national news. They were instrumental in disseminating political and financial information throughout the country, and thus helped to build the mass political party and an integrated inter-regional economy (Kielbowicz, 1989: 149).

Improvements in communication not only helped Americans to build national civic and political institutions, but they also transformed individual experience. Richard D. Brown (1989: 270, 286) claims that before the American Revolution information was scarce and possessed a narrow topical range. Access to information networks was hierarchical and largely dependent on social status. But by the 1840s, Brown argues, information had become abundant, diverse, and available to a vast mass audience. He suggests (1989: 274) that this transformation was responsible for two broad processes in American history during the second quarter of the nineteenth century: the rise of mass politics, which required an individualistic, competitive marketplace of ideas; and the development of a popular culture which diffused knowledge in the liberal arts and the natural sciences throughout the population.

Donald M. Scott (1980) reaches a similar conclusion in his examination of the public lecture circuit between 1830 and 1860, which he claims was instrumental in the formation of an egalitarian mass culture in this period. The lecture system began in earnest in the late 1820s, as an outgrowth of the lyceum and mechanics' education movements. By the early 1830s, lectures delivered by local or regional figures and aimed at the broad public were common; in the following decade, lectures by nationally known speakers had become a central feature of American popular culture. By the early 1840s, Scott (1980: 791, 800) estimates that 3,500–4,000 towns boasted societies which sponsored public lectures, and that about 400,000 people attended lectures each week at the peak of their popularity in the 1850s. Audiences throughout the country, particularly in the Northeast and Midwest, heard lectures on similar topics delivered by a corps of professional speakers, recognized figures whom lecture-goers regarded as bearers of a national culture. Although most lectures possessed an educational or informative character, audiences also expected entertainment and spectacle. By the 1850s, Scott concludes, the lecture circuit helped to create a mass public of national extent which "transcended sectarian, partisan, and social division" (Scott, 1980: 808).

Ronald J. Zboray (1993) outlines both the extent and the limits of this public, which he labels "a fictive people," in his work on reading and the antebellum publishing industry. While he shows (Zboray, 1993: xvi) that the explosion in printed matter during the second quarter of the nineteenth century helped to build a mass reading audience, he also cautions (1993: 15) that this audience was fractured along the lines of sex, class, region, and religion. Zboray argues that both contemporary commentators and historians of literacy have overstated the presence of a unified print literature and its attendant democratization of culture. In short, he concludes (1993: 16) that printed matter followed "the same geographical and social patterns of dissemination as other luxury commodities."

During the half-century between the passage of the Post Office Act of 1792 and the construction of Samuel F. B. Morse's first telegraph line in 1844, Americans experienced an intensive broadening and deepening of the information available to them. This communications revolution proceeded along political, administrative, and cultural lines of development. The framers of the Constitution regarded a well-informed citizenry as a necessary bulwark for the preservation of republican institutions; the transmission of newspapers via the Post Office at low cost was the primary means by which citizens obtained their news (Kielbowicz, 1989; John, 1995; Brown, 1996). Indeed, the development of the Post Office between 1792 and 1840 made unprecedented amounts of public information widely available to literate Americans. In this period businessmen increasingly used the postal system to communicate with distant trading partners, and so the Post Office widened the range of commercial activity. Finally, the expansion of the postal system, along with the growth of a transportation infrastructure, enabled the creation of a mass popular culture, consisting especially of a diverse print literature (Zboray, 1993) and a widespread public lecture circuit (Scott, 1980).

Non-electrical communications networks retained their importance for many years after the commercial introduction of the telegraph in 1844. By way of comparison, the postal system carried over 70 million pieces of mail in 1840, four years before Morse's first telegraph line; over 13,000 post offices and nearly 156,000 miles of post roads handled this volume. The telegraph industry attained a comparable level of message traffic, office facilities, and miles of line only in the 1880s. While businessmen and reporters quickly adopted the telegraph as an ideal medium for the rapid transmission of quantitative and time-sensitive information (Thompson, 1947; Blondheim, 1994), they still used the Post Office for much of their correspondence. Newspaper editors, for example, continued to rely heavily on postal exchanges and correspondents' written reports to obtain full coverage of distant news stories (Kielbowicz, 1989: 151–5; Schwartzlose, 1989: 137–42). The Post Office also remained the primary medium through which Americans exchanged personal and social correspondence, especially after the introduction of pre-paid postage stamps and the drastic slashing of postal rates in 1845 and 1851 (John, 1995: 156–61).

The Significance of the Telegraph

Despite the persistence of non-electrical forms of communication, telegraphy was an important advance in the transmission of information and ideas. The leading attribute of the telegraph which distinguished it from older, non-electrical forms of communication was its instantaneous operation across vast distances. It was the first technology to sever communication from its dependence upon transportation (Carey, 1989: 203–4). This decoupling had at least five important consequences for American culture, society, and economy after the telegraph's introduction in 1844; however, these consequences only became clear after the new technology had been in operation for two decades or so.

In the most general terms, telegraphic transmission encouraged Americans to reconceptualize communication and information (Czitrom, 1982: 10–11). Prior to the telegraph, the meanings of "communication," "intercourse," and "community" were closely linked; all referred to the mutual exchange of ideas and goods between individuals or groups, usually at a distance from each other. The language which Secretary of the Treasury Albert Gallatin used in 1808 to garner support for an extensive program of federally funded internal improvements aptly revealed the connection between these terms. Because of the country's size and geography, Gallatin argued, federal support was necessary for "opening speedy and easy communications through all its parts. Good roads and canals will shorten distances, facilitate commercial and personal intercourse, and unite, by a still more intimate community of interests, the most remote quarters of the United States" (quoted in Goodrich, 1960: 28–9). After the telegraph, the term "communication" increasingly lost its meaning as the mutual or communal exchange of goods and ideas; it began to take on its modern meaning as the one-way transmission of information for private purposes.

From its introduction in 1844 until at least the Civil War, Americans regarded the telegraph as a powerful agent of social and cultural change. Indeed, telegraphy was one of the most mythologized technologies in American history. In the middle third of the nineteenth century Americans employed a common rhetorical framework which yoked technological innovations to moral and material progress. This framework consisted of two broad ideologies about technology and its effects. The first was what Leo Marx (1964) and David Nye (1994) have both labeled the "technological sublime," which Nye defines as "the awe induced by seeing an immense or dynamic technological object" in action. Advances in speed, like the telegraph and the railroad, elicited "the collective realization of the power of human intellect" over nature. Instant telegraphic communication, in particular, was "literally dislocating, violating the sense of the possible" (Nye, 1994: 60, 62). Furthermore, Americans almost universally embraced a positive form of determinism; they believed that technological advances inexorably led to social improvement. While they regarded progress as a natural feature of modern Western civilization, they claimed that American republican institutions and market capitalism made the best environment in which both technological and social progress thrived (Kasson, 1976).

Yet these two intertwined conceptions of technological advances – as sublime triumphs of human reason over brute nature and as beneficent engines of social progress – were insufficient to capture the sense of awe that many Americans held for telegraphy (Czitrom, 1982: 8–14; Carey, 1989: 113–41). Americans particularly pointed to three characteristics of the telegraph which set it apart from other technologies. Its instantaneous transmission of electrical signals promised to annihilate time and space. Thus, contemporaries hoped that it would preserve ties of affection over great distances, check the centrifugal forces of sectionalism and westward expansion, and foster commerce and prosperity. While Americans invested prior improvements in transportation and communications with similar hopes, instant communication over the "lightning lines" promised organic unity. For example, telegraph inventor and physician William F. Channing described telegraphy as "the nervous system of this nation and of modern society." Telegraph wires "spread like nerves over the surface of the land, interlinking distant parts, and making possible a perpetually higher cooperation among men, and higher social forms than have hitherto existed. By means of its life-like functions the social body becomes a living whole" (quoted in Thompson, 1947: 253).

Telegraphic brevity, through clipped businessmen's dispatches and wire-service journalism, promised to replace bloated, aristocratic English with lean, democratic expression. Telegraphy was the first technology since the printing press to interact extensively with the written word; both the expense and urgency of the typical message encouraged a certain brevity. Many observers hoped that this condensation would perfect language as a medium for the clear and direct exposition of thought and would lead to terse and uncluttered writing. They looked to telegraphic brevity to help establish a uniquely American literary style.

The telegraph's use of electricity, a poorly understood and awe-inspiring force, especially excited the wonder of contemporaries (Czitrom, 1982: 8–10; Carey, 1989: 206–9). Americans invested electricity with a spiritual character and invoked a wide array of religious imagery to describe it. The telegraph and its use of electricity even served as a foundation for spiritualism, an occult movement which began in 1848 and which boasted as many as 3 million adherents during the 1850s. Many contemporaries equated the harnessing of electricity for utilitarian ends with human control over the elemental violence of lightning; for them such control confirmed humanity's place at the pinnacle of creation and even granted it a share of God's omnipotence. For others, such sentiments smacked of blasphemy and hubris.

Samuel Morse chose a biblical query from the Book of Numbers, "What hath God wrought?," to inaugurate his first telegraph line between Washington and Baltimore on May 25, 1844. Immediately afterward he enquired of his Baltimore operator, "Have you any news?" (Blondheim, 1994: 33). Morse's second question suggests that the telegraph and the press enjoyed a symbiotic relationship from the beginning. In particular, telegraphic reporting was responsible for imparting an objective and detached tone to news coverage (Carey, 1989: 210–11). Wire-service journalism redefined news as the rapid and factual reporting of events, and transformed the newspaper from a vehicle for the editor's personal and political views into a neutral source of factual information about current events (Czitrom, 1982: 18).

As early as the mid-1850s instant telegraphic reporting of distant events had established the principles of objectivity and news-worthiness as integral parts of modern journalistic practice. Daniel Craig, the head of the Associated Press (AP), gave the fullest expression to these principles in an 1854 circular to AP reporters (Schwartzlose, 1989: 142–6). He instructed them to transmit "only the *material facts*" and to omit "all expressions of opinion . . . all political, religious, and social biases; and especially all *personal feelings* on any subject." Whatever Craig's other motives may have been, his insistence on objectivity and impartiality made good business sense. Stripped-down dispatches required far fewer words to transmit, thus reducing the AP's telegraph expenses. Furthermore, the bland and factual AP reports appealed to newspapers of all political stripes and increased the number of potential customers; publishers, if they wished, could offer editorial comment upon the dispatches. Menahem Blondheim (1994: 195) concludes that by the mid-1850s Associated Press reporters were no longer journalists but had become "news vendors" who regarded the news as a commodity sold over the telegraph wires.

Shortly after the Civil War, the New York Associated Press and the Western Union Telegraph Company secured monopolies over their respective industries. The two organizations forged an alliance which gave them nearly complete control over the flow of news and information. Many Americans regarded this double-headed monopoly as a menace to republican institutions. Between 1866 and 1900 reformers repeatedly called upon the government to establish a postal telegraph network to compete with Western Union or to nationalize the telegraph industry completely; Congress considered over 70 such bills in this period (Lindley, 1975; Czitrom, 1982: 21–9).

Advocates of a government telegraph regarded congressional refusal to purchase Samuel F. B. Morse's patent in the 1840s as a tragic lost opportunity. Morse and many of his contemporaries had believed that the telegraph lay within the sphere of the Post Office's responsibilities; they had interpreted the Constitution as granting that department an exclusive monopoly on the transmission of intelligence. Despite Morse's repeated offers, Congress failed to purchase his patent, and the telegraph remained a privately owned enterprise. After passing through a chaotic period of wasteful competition during the 1850s, the telegraph industry attained a great degree of stability by 1860 under a cartel of six companies, including Western Union. In 1866 Western Union bought out its two remaining rivals and became the nation's first industrial monopoly (Thompson, 1947).

Reformers objected to the Western Union monopoly for two main reasons. Most importantly, they regarded its alliance with the Associated Press as a menace to two key republican institutions: the independent press and the informed citizen. In 1867 the two organizations signed a contract which strengthened each other's dominant positions in their respective industries. Western Union gave the AP preferential discounts on its press dispatches, while it charged rival press associations and individual newspapers seeking to compete with established AP members a much higher rate for their telegraph service. This discriminatory rate structure effectively maintained the Associated Press's monopoly over the collection and distribution of news into the 1890s (Schwartzlose, 1990: 54–62, 144–7). In return, the Associated Press pledged to give all its business to Western Union and not to patronize its smaller competitors. The AP and its member newspapers also agreed not to advocate in print the patronage of opposition telegraph lines or the entry of the government into the telegraph industry (Blondheim, 1994: 150–1). Many Americans feared that this dual monopoly compromised the freedom of the press by cutting off independent newspapers from the AP wire service and by dictating the editorial stance of member newspapers on the postal telegraph issue. Reformers argued that the Western Union / Associated Press grip on the country's news betrayed "the telegraph's original promise to be the common carrier of intelligence" (Czitrom, 1982: 21).

Advocates of postal telegraphy also sought to break Western Union's monopoly because of its high rates for private messages. Reformers claimed that these rates effectively barred the vast majority of Americans from using the telegraph for social and personal messages. They argued that Western Union's rates made the telegraph primarily a medium for press and business correspondence, whereas social and family messages made up only a small percentage of telegraph traffic. Reformers admitted that the American telegraph network worked admirably as a business system, but they wished to reduce rates and to extend facilities in order to bring telegraphing within the reach of all citizens. They drew a parallel between the Gilded Age telegraph network and the Jacksonian postal system. Before the Post Office Acts of 1845 and 1851, postal rates had been prohibitively high for ordinary citizens, and the Post Office had been a network used primarily by the press and businessmen. After the two acts reduced postage to 3 cents a letter, the postal system also became a medium for social correspondence. Advocates of a government telegraph service wished to guarantee universal access to the network and to transform it into a social medium as well as a business medium, just as antebellum reformers had done for the postal system.

At a deeper level, the debate over the telegraph in the last third of the nineteenth century was a contest between two competing notions of the relationship between communication and citizenship. The two positions were similar to what James W. Carey (1989: 14–19) has called the "ritual" and "transmission" models of communication. Those who advocated a government telegraph service used as a social medium espoused a unitary and organic vision of citizenship. They saw national communications networks as systems which cemented ties of sentiment and affection and which embedded individuals in a cooperative economic and social order. Such a vision harked back to an older view of communication, similar to that which Secretary of the Treasury Albert Gallatin had espoused in his 1808 report on internal improvements and which the postal reformers of the 1840s drew upon to argue for cheap postage. This "ritual" view was somewhat utopian and emphasized the use of

communications networks to forge and maintain a community of interests and sentiment among citizens of all classes and regions. Those who fought to maintain a
privately owned telegraph used primarily as a business medium put forward a more
atomistic vision of citizenship in which individuals used communication as an instru-
ment to pursue private ends. Those who were satisfied with the telegraph as a business
medium adhered to the "transmission" view, which saw communication as the
transmission of information used for political and economic control or for personal
financial gain.

Although reformers failed to reach their ultimate goal, the end of Western Union's
monopoly over telegraphic communication, they achieved some lasting success. By
calling for increased government involvement in economic affairs and in securing
citizens' access to communications networks, they constructed an important part of
Progressive economic thought. By the 1890s, their efforts helped to establish regulation as an acceptable middle ground between state ownership of a networked technology and its operation by untrammeled private capitalists. Regulation was a
pervasive and persistent notion which Progressives relied upon to work out the proper
economic role of federal government after the turn of the century, especially in the
communication, transportation, and electrical power sectors.

Just as the telegraph made possible the Associated Press's monopoly over the
collection and distribution of news, it also facilitated the concentration of economic
power on the floors of the large stock and commodity exchanges (Carey, 1989: 216–
22). After the late 1840s the telegraph transmitted instant news of market conditions
in important trading centers and helped to create a national market for agricultural
products. Furthermore, as regional price convergence eliminated opportunities for
geographical speculation between local markets, the telegraph opened up futures
trading as a new realm of speculation. During the late 1840s and 1850s businessmen
in several cities set up commodity exchanges to standardize and regulate the expanding grain trade. The brokers who traded on the floors of these exchanges relied on
market information sent over the telegraph to set prices for agricultural products and
to coordinate their sale and distribution. By the outbreak of the Civil War, the
telegraph network helped to set in motion an unmistakable trend toward the centralization of commodities trading on the floors of the large boards of trade.

The introduction of the ticker in 1868 dramatically accelerated this trend. The
ticker provided brokers across the country with a printed transcript of trades on
exchange floors almost immediately after they had happened, and allowed them to
react in a matter of minutes to price movements occurring hundreds of miles away. In
this way the telegraph network and the ticker abetted the rise of speculation and
finance capitalism during the Gilded Age. The ticker actuated a latent demand for
real-time news and financial information, a major growth market of the telegraph
industry in the final third of the nineteenth century. By the 1880s several thousand
bankers and brokers across the country subscribed to Western Union's ticker service
which broadcast up-to-the-minute stock, gold, grain, cotton, and oil quotations as
well as general financial and political news.

Western Union's ticker service was in many ways the first mass news and entertainment broadcast medium. As a news medium, it supplied identical real-time financial
information to countless brokers, bankers, and exchange-floor traders across the
country. As an entertainment medium, however, the ticker had an intimate connec-

tion to illicit economic activities, especially gambling. After the mid-1870s Western Union transmitted sporting news of all varieties, including the results of horse races, rowing matches, boxing bouts, and baseball games. Most subscribers to this service were establishments of questionable morality and legality, like saloons and betting parlors, located in working-class neighborhoods of the large cities. By the turn of the century, the tickers carried play-by-play or blow-by-blow coverage of sports events, and Western Union paid generously for their exclusive broadcast rights. Although its designers originally intended it as a tool for speculators and financiers, the ticker also played an important role in the formation of urban working-class mass culture in the late nineteenth and early twentieth centuries.

Conclusion

The communications revolution which occurred between the 1790s and the last third of the nineteenth century presents three broad interpretative issues for historians. Most importantly, it forces us to reconsider the role of technology as an agent of social and cultural change. It is tempting to adopt a technologically deterministic standpoint which identifies technical innovations as the dominant factor in improving the speed, reliability, and accessibility of information media. But the differences in the experiences of Ashley Bowen in the revolutionary era and Edward Jenner Carpenter during the mid-1840s show that new information technologies were not necessary to effect dramatic improvements in communications. Both Richard R. John (1995) and Richard B. Kielbowicz (1989) demonstrate that the postal system had become a rapid, regular, and accessible national network for the transmission of private and public information by 1830, and that it did so without the aid of innovations in communications or transportation technology. Instead, administrative initiative and political will were the sources of greater speed, volume, and reliability – attributes ordinarily associated with technical advances.

In the middle third of the nineteenth century Americans like Carpenter participated in a dramatic expansion of cultural institutions which gave them unprecedented access to information about current events, the liberal arts, and the natural sciences. Carpenter's diary outlined many of the forms of this popular culture, including the widespread diffusion of newspapers, access to a diverse print literature, and an extensive popular lecture circuit (Scott, 1980; Brown, 1989; Zboray, 1993). The rise and popularity of these institutions rested on political and cultural ideologies such as the ethos of an informed citizenry and the promise of upward economic mobility through self-improvement and education (Brown, 1989, 1996). Technological innovations – like the high-speed rotary printing press and the railroad – played a secondary role in the formation of these institutions.

As the rapid dissemination of the news of Lincoln's assassination demonstrated, technology played a larger transformative role after the advent of commercial telegraphy in 1844. An important new technology like the telegraph contains the potential to act as an agent of social and cultural change, but only as the outcome of a series of conscious choices made by its owners and users. Morse and most Americans first regarded the telegraph network as similar to the postal system, simply a means for the rapid transmission of intelligence, a viewpoint which muted its transformative potential. But the telegraph's customers and managers soon put it to two particular uses –

wire-service journalism and financial news reporting – which unlocked this potential. By the mid-1850s telegraphic news reporting had transformed journalistic practice. Shortly after the Civil War, the Associated Press and Western Union together controlled the production and distribution of national and international news. The ticker, invented in 1868, allowed Western Union to broadcast stock and commodities quotations to several thousand brokers across the country. This new service aided the formation of a new economic structure, the stock and commodity exchange, and the creation of a new set of economic relations, finance capitalism. The ways in which journalists and financiers used the telegraph thus helped to create two new institutions: large media organizations which centrally produced and distributed news and entertainment and stock and commodities exchanges which coordinated economic activity. Both institutions became permanent and distinctive features of late nineteenth- and twentieth-century American society.

The history of American communications during the nineteenth century also reveals a tension between centralization and decentralization, or between the concentration of political and economic power and its dispersal. The postal system, for instance, helped to forge a national community of interests and sentiment; yet it also acted as a force for cultural hegemony and sectional conflict. Richard R. John (1995: 260, 264, 281–3) argues that this tension first appeared when southerners seized and burned abolitionist tracts at the Charleston post office in July 1835, an incident which prompted the Post Office to ban anti-slavery publications from southern mail routes. This ban remained in place until the Civil War and prevented abolitionist groups from using the mails to establish a national dialogue on slavery. Nevertheless, southern defenders of slavery increasingly worried that improvements in communication and transportation tended toward the concentration of economic and political power in the North, a concentration which eroded the South's autonomy. This fear was an important nucleus around which southern sectionalism coalesced in the 1850s and which fueled the secession movement following Lincoln's election in 1860.

In general, new communications media since the printing press have tended to centralize the production of information while diffusing it more widely. The post-Civil War monopoly of the Associated Press on national and international news sent over Western Union's telegraph lines is a good example of this dual process. Associated Press dispatches gave Americans like Calvin Fletcher more rapid and intensive access to national and international news than ever before. Yet the Associated Press maintained strict control over the production and distribution of its dispatches, leading to two forms of *de facto* censorship: the AP decided which newspapers received its reports and which did not, and it constricted the editorial stance of member newspapers on the government telegraph issue.

Finally, the nineteenth-century communications revolution recast individual experience and realigned the relationship of the individual to society. Both Brown (1989, 1996) and Scott (1980) suggest that the communications revolution was a leveling influence which helped democratize both political power and cultural authority. Brown (1989) especially argues that the increased amount and diversity of information between the American Revolution and about 1840 was instrumental in eroding the hierarchical and deferential basis of elite authority. Yet elites remained. By the 1840s the basis of elite authority had shifted from hierarchy and deference to the control of expert, specialized knowledge unavailable to or unintelligible to lay audiences. The professionalization of the legal, medical, and scientific communities after about 1840 was perhaps the most visible part of this reconstitution of elite authority.

Brown and Scott also describe the expansion of popular culture in the middle third of the nineteenth century as a process that paralleled – and in important ways assisted – the concurrent rise and growth of American democratic and free-market institutions. The heightened scope and depth of information in this period was indeed a positive development for Americans like Edward Jenner Carpenter, who enjoyed full access to communications media and cultural institutions. But Zboray (1993) reminds us that race, class, gender, and region shaped this access; northern white men, most of them urban and with some education, participated most fully in the communications revolution.

ACKNOWLEDGMENTS

I would like to thank Richard R. John, David Morton, and Ann Pfau for incisive readings of earlier drafts of this chapter.

REFERENCES

Blondheim, Menahem (1994) *News over the Wires: the Telegraph and the Flow of Public Information in America, 1844–1897.* Cambridge, Mass.: Harvard University Press.

Brown, Richard D. (1989) *Knowledge is Power: the Diffusion of Information in Early America, 1700–1865.* New York: Oxford University Press.

Brown, Richard D. (1996) *The Strength of a People: the Idea of an Informed Citizenry in America, 1650–1870.* Chapel Hill, NC: University of North Carolina Press.

Carey, James W. (1989) *Communication as Culture: Essays on Media and Society.* Boston: Unwin Hyman.

Czitrom, Daniel J. (1982) *Media and the American Mind: from Morse to McLuhan.* Chapel Hill, NC: University of North Carolina Press.

Goodrich, Carter (1960) *Government Promotion of American Canals and Railroads, 1800–1890.* New York: Columbia University Press.

John, Richard R. (1995) *Spreading the News: the American Postal System from Franklin to Morse.* Cambridge, Mass.: Harvard University Press.

John, Richard R. (1998) "The politics of innovation," *Daedalus: Journal of the American Academy of Arts and Sciences,* 127, pp. 187–214.

Kasson, John F. (1976) *Civilizing the Machine: Technology and Republican Values in America, 1776–1900.* New York: Penguin.

Kielbowicz, Richard B. (1989) *News in the Mail: the Press, Post Office, and Public Information, 1700–1860s.* New York: Greenwood Press.

Lindley, Lester (1975) *The Constitution Faces Technology: the Relationship of the National Government to the Telegraph, 1866–1884.* New York: Arno Press.

Marx, Leo (1964) *The Machine in the Garden: Technology and the Pastoral Ideal in America.* Oxford: Oxford University Press.

Nye, David (1994) *American Technological Sublime.* Cambridge, Mass.: MIT Press.

Pred, Allan R. (1973) *Urban Growth and the Circulation of Information: the United States System of Cities, 1790–1840.* Cambridge, Mass.: Harvard University Press.

Schwartzlose, Richard A. (1989, 1990) *The Nation's Newsbrokers,* 2 vols. Evanston, Ill.: Northwestern University Press.

Scott, Donald M. (1980) "The popular lecture and the creation of a public in mid-nineteenth-century America," *Journal of American History,* 66, pp. 791–809.

Shaw, Ronald E. (1990) *Canals for a Nation: the Canal Era in the United States, 1790–1860.* Lexington: University Press of Kentucky.

Taylor, George Rogers (1951) *The Transportation Revolution, 1815–1860.* New York: Rinehart.

Thompson, Robert Luther (1947) *Wiring a Continent: the History of the Telegraph Industry in the United States, 1832–1866.* Princeton, NJ: Princeton University Press.

Zboray, Ronald J. (1993) *A Fictive People: Antebellum Economic Development and the American Reading Public.* New York: Oxford University Press.

CHAPTER TWENTY-TWO

Interpreting American Religion

CATHERINE A. BREKUS

THERE was a time not very long ago when American historians interpreted America's religious history as a triumphant story of Protestant progress. The nineteenth century, they claimed, was an age of Protestant consensus that was unsurpassed in its commitment to religious liberty. Under the guidance of God, Protestants had succeeded in making America into the most Christian country on earth, a "new Israel" that beckoned as a promised land.

In recent years, however, historians have told a much different story about America's religious past. Instead of portraying America as a Protestant country that was unified by a set of common values, they have emphasized the diversity of nineteenth-century religion. Influenced by the rise of social history, multi-culturalism, and the feminist and civil rights movements, they have chosen religious pluralism, not unity, as the main theme of their narratives. An older history of mainstream Protestants has been replaced by a new history of Roman Catholics, Jews, slaves, Native Americans, and Mormons – a history of conflict rather than consensus.

This chapter explores the changes in the writing of American religious history from 1844, when Robert Baird published his groundbreaking *Religion in the United States of America*, to the present day. Most scholars today have shown little interest in earlier interpretations of American religious history, but before they can develop new questions to bring to their study of the past, they must try to understand the strengths and weaknesses of the old narrative of Protestant unity as well as the new narrative of religious pluralism. Although these two interpretative traditions cannot be completely reconciled, each offers insights that might help historians create a richer, more complex account of religion in nineteenth-century America.

A History of Protestant Unity

The first major interpreter of nineteenth-century American religion was Robert Baird, a Presbyterian minister who published *Religion in the United States of America* (1844) after spending several months in Europe. Faced with questions about whether religion could survive in a republican society, he hoped to show that the constitutional separation of church and state had not weakened American churches but, on the contrary, strengthened them. First and foremost, his book was a defense of America's revolutionary experiment in religious freedom. Before the revolution, as Baird explained, most colonies had forced people – no matter what their personal beliefs – to pay taxes to support churches and ministers. (Ever since the fourth century, when Constantine had established Christianity as the official religion of the Roman empire, most Westerners had assumed that governments should enforce religious worship.) After the American Revolution, however, the founders shattered traditional patterns of church–state relationships by defending the principle of religious liberty. In 1791, when the First Amendment to the Constitution guaranteed that "Congress shall make no law respecting an establishment of religion or prohibiting the free exercise thereof," individual states began to disestablish the colonial churches. In the new republic, churches which had once depended on state support (particularly the Congregationalists in New England and the Anglicans in the South) were forced to rely on persuasion, not coercion, to attract new members. The result, as Baird argued, was exactly the opposite of what fearful clergymen had predicted: churches did not decline, but flourished. Inspired by the new climate of religious freedom, growing numbers of people chose to join churches and religious associations. Voluntarism, according to Baird, was America's greatest religious achievement.

To illustrate America's religious vitality, Baird provided an exhaustive survey of the country's churches. Bewildered by their sheer number and variety, he divided them into two categories: the "evangelical" and the "unevangelical." According to his interpretation, the evangelical churches were responsible for the best features of American life. Despite doctrinal differences, the Presbyterians, Congregationalists, Episcopalians, Baptists, and Methodists shared a common desire to transform America into the most Christian country on earth. They founded reform societies to combat intemperance, prostitution, and slavery; they sent foreign missionaries to convert the "heathen;" they created orphanages and charities to care for the poor; and they established Sunday schools to teach children the truths of the Bible. Although Baird admitted that Protestants often quarreled with one another, he insisted that they saw themselves as "branches of one great body." With common roots in the Protestant Reformation, they were "divisions of one vast army" who marched in separate regiments under God's direction (Baird, 1844: 606).

The "unevangelicals," in contrast, were a blight on America's religious landscape. Lumping together Roman Catholics, Jews, Shakers, Swedenborgians, Unitarians, Mormons, Deists, and atheists, Baird condemned them for rejecting "true" Christianity. Roman Catholics, for example, had "buried the truth amid a heap of corruptions of heathenish origin," while Mormons were "a body of ignorant dupes" (Baird, 1844: 649, 654). Although Baird claimed that all of these groups were too small, weak, or disorganized to pose a significant threat to the evangelical majority, he still worried that they might undermine America's identity as a Protestant nation. Despite his defense of religious voluntarism, he hoped that "unevangelicals" would eventually become mainstream Protestants.

"Unevangelicals" were not the only people whom Baird slighted in his book. Even though many southerners belonged to evangelical churches, Baird claimed that few of them were truly Christian. Writing 20 years before the outbreak of the Civil War, he complained that northerners and southerners were separated by insurmountable cultural differences. Tracing these differences all the way back to the Norman Conquest of 1066, he argued that southerners were inferior by "blood:" while the first New England colonists had been "Anglo-Saxon in character," the earliest southern colonists had been "Norman in spirit." In contrast to New England Puritans, who prized freedom, independence, and hard work, southern Anglicans were supposedly aristocratic and lazy by nature. Although Baird must have known that eighteenth-century New York was home to one of the largest slave populations in America, he chose to describe slavery as a peculiarly southern sin. The most faithful Christians, he implied, lived in the North.

What was at stake for Baird in his harsh condemnations of southerners and "un-evangelicals" was nothing less than the definition of what it meant to be American. America's "national religion," according to his interpretation, was "evangelical Chris-tianity," and its "national character" was "Anglo-Saxon" (Baird, 1844: 42–3, 663). Despite his recognition of America's religious pluralism, Baird insisted that "true" Americans were Anglo-Saxon Protestants. All others – including southerners, Jews, Catholics, and slaves – were peripheral to American culture. Certain that God had chosen America to be "a great Protestant empire," he assumed that "outsiders" exerted no influence on historical events (Baird, 1844: 16).

Although Baird's focus on mainline Protestants may seem biased to modern-day historians, he gave voice to assumptions that many people in his culture shared. Despite its flaws, his interpretation of nineteenth-century religion was echoed by several generations of historians, including Daniel Dorchester in the 1880s, William Warren Sweet in the 1930s, and even Sydney Ahlstrom in the 1970s. Although each of these scholars tried to expand Baird's categories in order to pay closer attention to "unevangelicals," all of them identified Protestant consensus, not conflict, as the key theme for understanding nineteenth-century religion. Dismissing groups outside the Protestant mainstream as "divergent currents," "strange and unusual movements," or "countervailing religion," they chose to tell the story of nineteenth-century American religion as the story of Protestantism. Even though these historians pub-lished their books during years of increasing American religious diversity, they pre-ferred to ignore the influence of the utopian reformers, Christian Scientists, and fundamentalists who competed for public attention. As R. Laurence Moore has noted, their books are best understood as expressions of desire: they longed for a Protestant oneness that eluded them. Indeed, they seem to have been motivated by "the fear, never entirely suppressed in their books, that they were not in control" (Moore, 1986: 21).

After Baird, the most important historian of nineteenth-century American religion was Daniel Dorchester, who published his encyclopedic *Christianity in the United States* in 1888. His book is one of the most comprehensive surveys of American religious history ever written. Celebrating the growth of religious liberty, Dorchester argued that voluntarism was responsible for America's high rates of church member-ship. "The purely voluntary are the best, the purest, and most favorable conditions for the religious life of any people," he affirmed (Dorchester, 1888: 777). Compiling detailed statistics on the number of churches, missionary societies, Sunday schools, and denominational colleges, he traced Protestants' powerful influence on American culture.

Like Baird, Dorchester distinguished between mainstream Protestants and "diver-gent currents," but because of the large numbers of German and Irish immigrants who arrived after the 1840s, he also added a separate, third category for Roman Catholics. Just as he treated Mormons, Unitarians, Shakers, and Jews as infidels on the fringes of American culture, however, he also refused to identify Catholics as true Americans. Echoing the antagonistic language of nativist groups such as the American Protective Association, he expressed fears that the Catholic church was involved in a conspiracy to subvert American democracy. "Its magnificent cathedrals, artistic music, subtle logic, and political patronage have captivated and led away some of the Protestant population," he warned. "Never was it plotting more deeply and determinedly than now, and some persons have grave fears for the safety of our free institutions" (Dorchester, 1888: 614). Fearful of the millions of Catholic immigrants from Germany and Ireland who had flooded America's ports, Dorchester branded them as "foreigners" who were hostile to American values. Like Baird, he assumed that America was a Protestant country: real Americans were Protestant.

From his vantage point at the end of the nineteenth century, Dorchester was even more concerned about "divergent currents" than Baird had been 40 years earlier. Despite Baird's hopeful prediction that sectarian movements would eventually disappear, groups such as the Mormons and Universalists had only grown larger and more assertive. In addition, the expansion of cities, the arrival of thousands of poor, uneducated immigrants, and the modern assault on tradition all seemed to pose a threat to Protestant unity. Influenced by higher criticism, theologians questioned the literal truth of the Bible, and after the publication of Charles Darwin's *The Origin of Species* in 1859 scientists struggled to reconcile the theory of evolution with the biblical account of creation. During the tumultuous decades of the 1870s and 1880s, many Protestants feared that they were losing their earlier power and prestige.

Yet Dorchester, like Baird, ended his book on a note of triumph. Because of his unwavering faith that evangelical Protestants had been "intended by Providence to found in the New World a great Christian Republic," he interpreted their difficulties as nothing more than temporary setbacks (Dorchester, 1888: 25). God would never allow his chosen nation to fail. According to Dorchester's rosy view of the 1880s, every "divergent current" was being countered by a "convergent current:" atheism and skepticism had begun to yield to theism, and science had begun to make peace with religion. In his closing pages, Dorchester confidently proclaimed the dawn of a new age of Protestant ascendancy. Not only had "Romanism" begun to lose its "hideous character" under Protestant influence, but Mormonism, which he described as "an ecclesiastical despotism," was only "a local ulcer" that could not slow American progress. Despite his worries about America's growing ethnic and religious diversity, he believed that he could see the beginnings of "the majestic unfolding of Providence" (Dorchester, 1888: 646, 779–80).

Like many other nineteenth-century historians, Baird and Dorchester wrote their books out of profound religious conviction. Before the rise of "scientific" history in the late nineteenth century, most historians were amateurs who wrote for the general public, not a specialized audience of academics, and they hoped their books would be morally instructive. As ordained clergy, both Baird (a Presbyterian) and Dorchester (a Methodist) saw their books as an extension of their ministry. Baird, for example, confessed his desire to "promote the extension of the Messiah's kingdom in the world" (Baird, 1844: ix). Although he and Dorchester certainly tried to be fair-minded, they believed historians had a religious duty to make moral judgments on the past. As a result, they not only condemned groups whom they believed were not truly Christian, but they insisted that America's national identity was – and always should be – Protestant. God had chosen America to be a new Israel, a city set on a hill.

Although many later historians were as committed to the Christian faith as Baird and Dorchester, they became more circumspect about expressing their beliefs as they sought greater professional recognition. Beginning in the late nineteenth century, many groups, including lawyers, doctors, businessmen, and scholars, tried to enhance their prestige by founding national organizations that set formal standards for conduct and membership. Reflecting this trend toward professionalization, historians created the American Historical Association in 1884, an organization devoted to the pursuit of historical truth. At a time when newspapers were filled with stories of remarkable scientific advances, including the invention of the telephone and electric lighting, historians emphasized their impartial, "scientific" commitment to gathering information. Their ideal, however illusory, was to let the facts "speak for themselves." Instead of beginning their research with a hypothesis they hoped to substantiate, they refused to offer an interpretation until examining all of the evidence. Whether their subject was politics, the economy, or religion, they cultivated an air of empirical detachment.

By 1930, when William Warren Sweet published *The Story of Religions in America*, most religious historians no longer explained historical events as the product of divine intervention, and they took pains not to be seen as Protestant apologists. Trained as a professional historian, Sweet carefully distanced himself from earlier generations of amateurs. As he complained on the very first page of his book: "American religious history has been written by the denominational historian and in denominational terms.... Too frequently it has been written in a denominational spirit, for the purpose of exalting the denomination or of praising its leaders." In contrast, Sweet promised to write a more critical, objective book that would identify the common themes in American religious history. Whatever his personal beliefs, he chose to analyze religious history in the context of "economic, social, and political influences" (Sweet, 1930: 1).

When it appeared in 1930, Sweet's book was hailed as the most incisive treatment of nineteenth-century religion yet published. On the surface, it seemed remarkably different from what had come before. Fascinated by what he perceived as America's religious uniqueness, Sweet emphasized the interaction between churches and American culture. According to his interpretation, several "creative forces" had combined to give American religion a distinctive cast, including the revolutionary commitment to religious freedom, the tragedy of slavery, the cycles of revivalism, and the centralization of the national government. Building on the pathbreaking work of Frederick Jackson Turner, who saw the frontier as the cradle of American democracy, Sweet argued that westward expansion had fostered a uniquely American spirit of religious individualism. To explain the remarkable growth of the Methodists, for example, he explained that they preached a "democratic gospel" that appealed to ordinary Americans (Sweet, 1930: 319).

Despite his commitment to writing a more "scientific" history of American religion, however, Sweet shared many of Baird and Dorchester's underlying assumptions. Most important, he took Protestant dominance for granted, relegating Catholics, Jews, and other non-Protestants to the margins of his narrative. Although he tried his best to treat them fairly, he found it impossible to imagine them as agents of historical change: he simply did not believe that they had contributed anything to the national character. At best, like the Catholics, they retreated into their own separate neighborhoods and institutions; at worst, like the Mormons and the Millerites (a millennial sect that predicted the world would end in 1844), they provided a refuge for "uncouth and unstable people pitifully eager for signs and wonders" (Sweet, 1930: 397). In contrast to the "great Protestant churches," which were busy "adding tens of thousands of sane Christians to their membership," these "strange and unusual religious movements" attracted only the irrational or the deranged (Sweet, 1930: 411, 395).

Although his statistics showed that millions of people belonged to these "strange" movements, Sweet insisted that American religion was characterized by growing consensus rather than by controversy. On one hand, he lamented that nineteenth-century Protestant churches were filled with strife: Reconstruction heightened sectional and racial tensions; the flood of Catholic immigrants sharpened religious intolerance; and, perhaps most disturbing, Protestant liberals and conservatives fought over how to interpret the Bible, laying the foundation for the fundamentalist movement. On the other hand, Sweet also saw evidence of growing interdenominational harmony and cooperation. Like Baird and Dorchester, he ended his book by assuring his readers that Protestants would soon overcome their differences. In his words, "there is every indication among all the Protestant churches, great and small, that the day of contented separation is fully passed and there is undoubtedly a growing will to, as well as an enlarging expectation of, union" (Sweet, 1930: 523).

This consensus view of nineteenth-century religion did not begin to break down until the 1960s and 1970s, one of the most turbulent times in American history. As historians witnessed (or participated in) civil rights demonstrations, the Black Power movement, student riots, protests against the Vietnam War, and women's liberation groups, they inevitably brought new questions to their study of the past. Gradually they began to change the way in which they wrote about nineteenth-century America by emphasizing conflict over consensus. Instead of focusing on white male Protestants, growing numbers of them chose to write articles and books about African Americans, Native Americans, women of all races, and Catholic and Jewish immigrants. Connecting past and present, they resolved to write a new history that would help them explain America's racial and class divisions, sexual inequalities, religious turmoil, and political unrest. An older history of Protestant unity, they believed, could no longer answer the country's most pressing questions.

These were the concerns that framed Sydney Ahlstrom's award-winning book, *A Religious History of the American People* (1972), which is still widely assigned in undergraduate and graduate courses today. Ahlstrom's book supplanted Dorchester's *Christianity in the United States* as the longest, most comprehensive, and most detailed survey of American religious history ever published. Struggling to understand how America had seemingly lost its historic identity as a Protestant nation during the 1960s, Ahlstrom decided to write a more inclusive, pluralistic narrative that would help Americans make sense of both their past and their present. "Post-Protestant America requires an account of its spiritual past that seeks to clarify its spiritual present," he explained. "And such an account should above all do justice to the fundamentally pluralistic situation which has been struggling to be born ever since this country was formally dedicated to the proposition that all men are created equal" (Ahlstrom, 1972: 12). Criticizing Baird, Dorchester, and Sweet for being part of the "consensus tradition," he promised to move beyond "the great Protestant tradition of historiography" (Ahlstrom, 1972: 10).

In order to recapture the multiplicity of nineteenth-century American religion, Ahlstrom filled his book with a dizzying array of characters: Presbyterians and Spiritualists, German Pietists and Jews, Seventh-day Adventists and communitarians. Fascinated by religious pluralism, he paired his discussion of Protestant, "democratic evangelicalism" with a section on "countervailing religion," a category that encompassed Catholicism, Lutheranism, Judaism, transcendentalism, and the Mercersburg and Oxford Movements. (These two movements represented conservative Protestant attempts to reclaim parts of Roman Catholic theology.) With the notable exception of his treatment of Joseph Smith, the founder of the Mormons, whom he scornfully described as a "megalomaniac," his analysis of churches outside the Protestant mainstream was remarkably balanced (Ahlstrom, 1972: 506). In addition, he deliberately set himself apart from earlier historians by emphasizing that all nineteenth-century Protestants had not been white. Influenced by the civil rights movement, he devoted a full chapter to African-American churches after the Civil War.

Although Ahlstrom was careful to emphasize religious diversity, he still argued that nineteenth-century Protestants, not "countervailing churches," were responsible for shaping America's national character. Tracing the distinctiveness of American religion back to the colonial Puritans, who had believed that America was God's chosen nation, he argued that nineteenth-century Protestants inherited a belief in America's providential identity as a beacon to the world. "Beneath American denominationalism," he wrote, "lay a large Protestant consensus, Puritan and Reformed in spirit" (Ahlstrom, 1972: 381). Despite his interest in "countervailing trends" (a phrase that echoed Dorchester's "divergent currents"), he assumed that the lines of religious influence pointed in only one direction: all religious "outsiders" absorbed Protestant values, but few Protestants were affected by the Mormons, Catholics, and Jews in their midst. Even though Ahlstrom was intrigued by religious figures such as Mary Baker Eddy, who believed in malicious animal magnetism, or Phineas Quimby, who practiced faith healing, he did not believe that their stories were central to understanding American religious history. He assumed that only *Protestants* made things happen; other groups simply added drama and color to the Protestant landscape.

Contrary to what he intended, Ahlstrom wrote the crowning book in the interpretative tradition that Robert Baird had begun in 1844. Even though he argued that Puritanism, not voluntarism or the frontier, had given American religion its distinctive flavor, he echoed Baird, Dorchester, and Sweet by claiming that Protestantism was the glue that held the republic together. Ironically, Ahlstrom had hoped that his book would serve as a model for a more pluralistic religious history, but instead he ended up reinforcing Baird's emphasis on consensus. By the end of the nineteenth century, he explained, the dominant American religion was a homogeneous, "common-core Protestantism" that linked diverse Christians together despite denominational schisms (Ahlstrom, 1972: 843). Even though this unity seemed to be threatened by immigration, the growth of cities, and industrialization, it remained strong until the emergence of a new "post-Protestant America" during the 1960s. The nineteenth century, in Ahlstrom's view, had been an oasis of calm before the storms of twentieth-century pluralism.

Considered in its broadest outlines, the consensus interpretation of nineteenth-century religion was marked by both strengths and weaknesses. On the positive side,

Baird, Dorchester, Sweet, and Ahlstrom convincingly demonstrated the immense power that Protestants wielded in shaping nineteenth-century American culture: most politicians, business leaders, and university professors were evangelical Protestants who believed in spreading their faith to the rest of the nation. More negatively, however, these historians also ignored or belittled large segments of the population, especially slaves, free blacks, Native Americans, immigrants, southerners, and women. Indeed, even though women made up the majority of most nineteenth-century Protestant churches, no one except for Ahlstrom mentioned the women's rights movement or the controversies over female ordination. (And even Ahlstrom limited his discussion of women to a few short pages.) Like all historians, these men were shaped by the assumptions of their times, and despite their genuine desire to be fair, they imagined nineteenth-century American religion as white, middle-class, male, Anglo-Saxon, northern, and Protestant.

What lay behind all these books was the fear that America's democratic experiment might collapse without the support of a common faith. Since Baird, Dorchester, Sweet, and Ahlstrom were all Protestant, they had theological reasons for emphasizing Christian unity, but even apart from their commitment to the ideal of a universal church, they were influenced by political concerns. Quoting from Joseph Story, a Supreme Court justice, Dorchester worried "whether any free government can be permanent where the public worship of God and the support of religion constitute no part of the policy or duty of the State in any assignable shape" (Dorchester, 1888: 773). Despite his belief that people should be free to choose their own churches, he lamented that the Constitution did not explicitly identify the United States as a Protestant country. Politically, he feared that Americans would split into warring factions if they did not share a common set of religious beliefs. Even Ahlstrom, who saw the separation of church and state as an absolute good, voiced misgivings about the political viability of "post-Protestant America." Fearful of what the future might hold, he and other historians offered their readers a reassuring message: previous generations of Americans also had been religiously diverse, but despite their differences, they had managed to forge a common worldview. Consensus, not conflict, was the American way.

Toward a More Pluralistic History

As Ahlstrom's book illustrates, the upheavals of the 1960s and 1970s did not transform the writing of American history overnight. Despite their desire to broaden the study of American religion, historians were deeply influenced by the classic books that had defined the "great Protestant tradition." Gradually, however, they began to create a new paradigm for understanding the past – a paradigm that turned traditional interpretations upside-down. In contrast to Ahlstrom, who had tried to include more material on "divergent currents" while still salvaging the remnants of the older narrative, they began to question its basic premises. Reorganizing the field around three new assumptions, they claimed that minority religious groups (Baird's "unevangelicals") had influenced American culture as much as mainstream Protestants; they affirmed that slaves, Native Americans, and women had been important historical actors; and they insisted that nineteenth-century religion had been characterized more by conflict than by consensus. Although they shared many of the same interests in revivalism and voluntarism as earlier authors, they self-consciously embraced a more inclusive, pluralistic definition of American religion.

Martin E. Marty's *Righteous Empire: the Protestant Experience in America* (1970), a broad survey of American Protestantism between 1776 and 1970, represented one of the first and most influential attempts to move beyond the consensus tradition. Marty's book stands between an older history of Protestant unity and a newer history of religious dissent. Since Marty focused on Protestantism, most of his readers probably did not expect to read about conflict, but he offered a far more pluralistic narrative than earlier historians who had claimed to write about all of American religion. On one hand, he was linked to Baird, Dorchester, Sweet, and Ahlstrom by his assumption that mainstream Protestants, not religious "outsiders," wielded the most influence in nineteenth-century American culture. In his words, "Protestantism was the dominating spiritual force in the American past" (Marty, 1970: foreword). Yet, unlike other historians, Marty emphasized Protestant divisions more than unity, and he presented a sharper, more critical picture of the Protestants' "righteous empire." With a keen sense of historical irony, he compared their rhetoric of chosenness to the reality of their racism and their "decorous worldliness."

Marty's most important contribution was his focus on the regional, racial, and class divisions that splintered nineteenth-century Protestantism. During the 1830s and 1840s, as he pointed out, Protestants argued so bitterly over the morality of slavery that they divided along regional lines: the Baptists, Methodists, and Presbyterians all split into northern and southern branches. After the Civil War, Protestants seemed to be united by their faith in America's divine destiny, their defense of personal property, and their sanctification of wealth, but deeper strains lay underneath the surface (Marty, 1970: 146). In contrast to Dorchester and Ahlstrom, Marty claimed that the closing decades of the nineteenth century were not marked by growing unity, but by controversy and dissent. By the turn of the century, Protestants had divided into two competing parties, one private and individualistic and the other public and reform-minded. Anticipating later divisions between modernists and evangelicals, Protestants argued over whether churches should try to save individual souls or the entire social order. Ironically, the most divisive forces within nineteenth-century Protestantism did not come from without, but from within. As Marty explained, "Protestants often spent more time fighting each other than they did fighting Catholics, Jews, and infidels" (Marty, 1970: 181). Despite their desire to create a "righteous empire," Protestants battled over how to spread their faith in an increasingly industrial, urban, and pluralistic culture.

Righteous Empire was one of several books that challenged the traditional narrative of nineteenth-century religious history. Inspired by both the political upheavals of the 1960s and the rise of the "new social history," a new approach to studying the past that focused more on ordinary people than elites, scholars gradually developed a new model of historical change: they argued that change did not come only from the top down, but also from the bottom up. Promising to rewrite American history from the perspective of subordinate groups (whom they unfortunately chose to describe in patronizing terms as the "inarticulate"), they increasingly turned their attention away from the pulpit to the pew. Unlike Baird, who had assumed that "unevangelicals" had contributed little to the making of history, they insisted that slaves, women, and other minority groups had profoundly shaped American culture.

Reflecting these changes in the profession, historians began to study slave religion, a topic that had attracted little notice before the 1960s. Although earlier scholars, including William Warren Sweet, had recognized the importance of the northern anti-slavery movement (which had been dominated by white abolitionists such as William Lloyd Garrison), they portrayed slaves as the objects of white action rather than as historical actors in their own right. With the notable exceptions of Sidney Ahlstrom and Martin Marty, few chose to examine the dramatic rise of Christianity in the slave quarters. Yet as Albert Raboteau argued in his groundbreaking book, *Slave Religion: the "Invisible Institution" in the Antebellum South*, which was published in 1978, large numbers of slaves converted to Christianity in the early nineteenth century, creating a vibrant religious culture of their own. Drawing on an impressive variety of records, including church and plantation records, travel accounts, ex-slave narratives, and missionary reports, Raboteau revealed a world of slave preachers and religious resistance that few historians had ever seen before. Emphasizing the slaves' spiritual independence from their white masters, he argued that "slaves did not simply become Christians; they creatively fashioned a Christian tradition to fit their own peculiar experience of enslavement in America" (Raboteau, 1978: 209). Although most slaves were Protestant, especially Methodist and Baptist, they deliberately set themselves apart from the values of the white "righteous empire." Instead of building an inter-racial Protestant consensus, they fought with white masters over the meaning of religious "liberty."

Although Raboteau was more concerned with recovering the history of slave religion than writing a new narrative of nineteenth-century America, his book made it clear that slaves could not simply be incorporated into an older paradigm of Protestant unity. In contrast to Baird, Dorchester, and Ahlstrom, who had empha-sized Americans' common identity as a "new Israel," Raboteau argued that blacks and whites found different meanings in the biblical story of Exodus. For whites, America was Canaan, the promised land of milk and honey. For blacks, however, it was Egypt, the brutal land of captivity and oppression. As Raboteau (1978: 251) explained, "White Christians saw themselves as a new Israel; slaves identified themselves as the old." If historians wanted to write an inclusive history of nineteenth-century Amer-ican religion – a history that examined the experiences of both blacks and whites – then they would have to rethink their assumptions about America's identity as a "redeemer nation." Despite the power of the older interpretative tradition, it could not be stretched to include slaves.

Nor, as many historians argued, could it be expanded to fit the experiences of Native Americans, who had been ruthlessly uprooted from their tribal lands in the nineteenth century in order to make room for white settlers. Understandably, Native Americans had not shared the Protestant faith in America's destiny as a chosen nation; nor had they accepted white understandings of religion. As William G. McLoughlin explained in his 1984 book *Cherokees and Missionaries, 1789–1839*, thousands of Native Americans were exposed to Christianity in the early nineteenth century, but they fused Protestantism with their traditional religious beliefs. Fearful of losing their distinctive way of life, many Cherokees borrowed parts of Christian theology without ever fully renouncing the "old ways" of seasonal religious festivals, communal living, and conjuring (McLoughlin, 1984: 332). In McLoughlin's (1984: 334) words, "the message many Cherokees took from the Bible was not the message the missionaries preached." Like slaves, Native Americans adapted Protestantism to suit their own distinctive needs, splintering it along racial and class lines.

Challenging the assumptions of earlier historians, McLoughlin emphasized not only the divisions within nineteenth-century Protestantism, but also the importance of Native Americans in shaping American culture. Unlike Robert Baird, who had belittled Indians as "squaws" and "savages" whose "crude theology" was unworthy of serious study, he argued that the interaction between Cherokees and missionaries had been a "two-way street:" not only had many Cherokees converted to Christianity, but missionaries had been "forced to make critical reevaluations of their own culture" after living in Indian villages (Baird, 1844: 13; McLoughlin, 1984: 2). According to McLoughlin's model, religious influence never flowed in only one direction, but eddied between the powerful and the subordinate. Even though the missionaries were wealthier and politically more powerful than the Cherokees, both groups were profoundly changed by their religious encounter.

As part of their crusade to recover the stories of overlooked groups, religious historians not only explored the lives of Native Americans and slaves, but women of all classes and races. Criticizing earlier scholars for writing as if all nineteenth-century Americans had been male, they argued that women had been the backbone of most churches and synagogues. Not only had they been the majority of members, but they had founded charities and orphanages, joined reform and benevolence organizations, and served as home and foreign missionaries. Even though religious leaders urged women to stay within their own "separate sphere," more than one hundred evangelical female preachers criss-crossed the country between 1800 and 1845, and, beginning in the 1850s, scores of Spiritualist women spoke publicly as "mediums" who supposedly communicated with the dead (Braude, 1989: 82; Brekus, 1998: 3). Whether conservative or radical, women were active participants in religious life, but because they were excluded from positions of official leadership, historians dismissed them as peripheral to Protestant culture.

Much of the recent scholarship on women, like the scholarship on slaves and Native Americans, has focused on their religious resilience and creativity. Without ignoring women's inequality in nineteenth-century America – they could not vote, hold political office, or, until late in the century, be ordained – historians have argued that women transformed the repressive ideology of domesticity into a justification of their essential worth and dignity. For example, many evangelical female preachers (both white and black) defended their right to preach by describing themselves in domestic language as "Mothers in Israel" or "Sisters in Christ" (Brekus, 1998: 151). More radically, Spiritualist women insisted that their "feminine" virtue not only qualified them to speak publicly, but to vote in political elections. Rather than simply reinforcing women's subordination, "the identification of piety with femininity could aid in the expansion of women's options and contribute to the potency of a comprehensive moral idealism" (Braude, 1989: 201). Even though nineteenth-century women were taught that God had ordained their subordination to men, they managed to find a more liberating, egalitarian message in their faith.

Alongside this new interest in women, slaves, and Native Americans came a wealth of scholarship on the experiences of other religious "outsiders," especially groups outside the Protestant mainstream. Like Ann Braude (1989), who used the Spiritualists to examine nineteenth-century attitudes toward marriage, the women's rights movement, and the medical establishment, other historians claimed that sectarian movements offered a valuable window on nineteenth-century America despite their relatively small membership. For example, even though earlier historians scorned the Mormons as religious deviants, especially because of their defense of polygamy, Jan Shipps argued that their religious concerns linked them to many other antebellum Americans. The Mormons, like the Disciples of Christ, were primitivists who hoped to recapture the purity of the early Christian church, but they eventually moved in more radical directions (Shipps, 1985: 68). Instead of seeing themselves in symbolic terms as a new Israel, they claimed to be the literal restoration of the *old* Israel (1985: 83). Ultimately they created a new religious tradition that was as different from Christianity as early Christianity had been from Judaism, but their history was rooted in the religious disorder of the 1820s and 1830s. At a time of theological debate and political uncertainty, the Mormons offered a compelling interpretation of America's past and its future.

Other historians focused on how religious "outsiders" tried to preserve their distinctive identities within a largely Protestant culture. Like Baird and Dorchester, they noted that Catholics and Jews tended to cluster in their own institutions and neighborhoods, but, reversing earlier interpretations, they saw this as a strength rather than a weakness. Although Catholics and Jews were influenced by Protestant culture, they also took pains to separate themselves from the religious mainstream. In some ways, they had no choice: they were constantly reminded of their "otherness" by discrimination against them in the workplace and in public schools. More positively, however, they insisted that their religious loyalties did not prevent them from being genuinely American. For example, Reform Jews tried to make their worship more modern and "Protestant" by abandoning traditional dietary and Sabbath laws, but as Hasia R. Diner has explained, their hope was to build a *"Jewish American* culture" that would allow them to remain true "to their own sense of self" (Diner, 1992: 203). Similarly, Catholics imitated Protestants by holding emotional revival meetings (known as "parish missions"), but they also clung to their traditional beliefs in saints and miracles. According to Jay Dolan, devotional Catholicism flourished in the nineteenth century because it "became a means of social identity; it gave people a specifically Catholic identity in a Protestant society" (Dolan, 1985: 238). No matter how much Catholics and Jews may have assimilated to the dominant culture, they did not believe (as did Baird and Dorchester) that being "American" meant being Protestant.

Besides expanding the definition of American religion to include "outsiders" such as Catholics, Mormons, women, and slaves, historians also began to question the identification of "America" with New England. In contrast to Baird, Dorchester, and Ahlstrom, who had assumed that the moral center of the nation lay in the North, they argued that the unique cultures of the South and the West had also shaped American identity. According to Donald Mathews (1977), for example, southern evangelicals had not only developed a "slaveholding ethic" that justified racial inequality, but an egalitarian ethic that laid the foundation for the civil rights movement. Ironically, the same evangelicals who insisted that slaveholding was "a positive, Christian responsibility" also gave slaves the language to demand their liberty as children of God (Mathews, 1977: 174). Although earlier historians had tried to erase the painful legacy of slavery by dismissing southern religion as "unAmerican," Mathews argued that they had distorted the past. By focusing on "the inability of whites to be true to the liberating promises of Evangelical Christianity," they had failed to see "the admirable accomplishments of black Christianity" (Mathews, 1977: 238). Southerners – both white and black – had left an indelible imprint on American culture, subtly influencing debates about religion and race long after the end of the Civil War.

Examining the history of religion in frontier California, Laurie Maffly-Kipp (1994) tried to stretch the geographical boundaries of American religious history even further. Criticizing earlier scholars for treating "eastern patterns of religiosity as normative for religious developments in other regions," she argued that the West should be seen as "a distinctive area contributing unique but related pieces to a broader picture of American religion" (Maffly-Kipp, 1994: 6). For example, although western settlers brought traditional Protestant understandings of wealth and community to the frontier with them, the chaos of the gold rush forced them to construct a new "moral world" around the values of self-control and ethical behavior. Decades before the late nineteenth-century controversies between Protestant conservatives and modernists, California gold miners had begun to articulate a more liberal understanding of theology. Although precise lines of influence are hard to trace, the frontier experience may have contributed to the development of a more privatized, liberal Protestantism (Maffly-Kipp, 1994: 184). Religious innovation did not come only from New England, but from the West as well.

No single historian has challenged the older narrative tradition more forcefully than R. Laurence Moore, whose 1986 book, *Religious Outsiders and the Making of Americans*, became the manifesto of the "new religious history." Although Moore built on the work of many other scholars, he clarified their assumptions about the importance of religious "outsiders," offering a sweeping new interpretation of the field. According to Moore, "nineteenth-century historians, and many who followed them, got the meaning of American religious experience almost exactly backwards. The trend was never toward unity. American religious experience began as dissent, and invented oppositions remained the major source of liveliness in American religion both in the nineteenth and twentieth centuries" (Moore, 1986: 46). Like earlier historians who had divided American religion into Protestants and "divergent currents," Moore labeled several groups as "outsiders," but, instead of dismissing them as inconsequential, he saw them as the key to understanding America's religious vitality. Rather than emphasizing Protestant unity, he argued that pluralism, competition, and conflict were intrinsic to American religion: every American religious group, from the Methodists to the Mormons, first became popular by dissenting from the Protestant establishment. "Outsiderhood," Moore (1986: xi) explained, "is a characteristic way of inventing one's Americanness."

Inspired by Moore's book, the "new religious historians" of the 1980s and 1990s argued that the most important religious groups had been on the fringes of American culture. Ironically, Moore himself had explicitly cautioned scholars not to treat "all religious groups, no matter what their size, no matter how ephemeral, [as] equally significant in accounts of American religion," but few heeded his warning. Inverting earlier arguments about Protestant dominance, they published groundbreaking books about Spiritualists, Mormons, Native-American religion, and slave religion, but relatively little about Presbyterians or Methodists. In a development that would have bewildered Robert Baird, they no longer imagined American religious history as the history of Protestant consensus, but of oppression and resistance.

Despite all these new developments, however, the "new" religious history still bore a strong resemblance to the "old." Whatever the flaws of the earlier scholarship, especially its focus on white Protestants as the sole agents of historical change, it was marked by notable strengths as well. Ironically, many of the most creative books that have been published in recent years have explored the same themes as earlier classics in the field. For example, in *Holy Fairs: Scottish Communions and American Revivals in the Early Modern Period* (1989), Leigh Schmidt unintentionally repeated one of Robert Baird's most important insights: American religious history could not be separated from its transatlantic context. Just as Baird had argued that American Christianity was rooted in the Protestant Reformation, Schmidt traced the origins of Presbyterian communion festivals back to religious reforms in sixteenth-century Scotland. Instead of emphasizing America's uniqueness, a favorite theme of historians during the 1950s and early 1960s, he argued that revivalism was deeply rooted in the Old World. Since nineteenth-century America was home to large numbers of immigrants and slaves, Schmidt and other historians have begun to seek connections between the history of religion in America and the history of religion in Europe, Asia, and West Africa.

Other "new" historians echoed the older tradition by focusing on revivalism, a topic that has inspired countless numbers of books and articles over the past 150 years. Not surprisingly, different generations of historians have interpreted the revivals of the "Second Great Awakening" in contradictory ways, but most have seen them as a microcosm of early nineteenth-century religion as a whole. For Baird, Dorchester, and Sweet, they symbolized the best features of Protestant worship: the revivals were orderly, rational, and marked by "very few extravagances" (Dorchester, 1888: 375). For Jon Butler (1990) and Nathan Hatch (1989), in contrast, the revivals were anti-intellectual, emotional, and even crude at times. Instead of focusing on Timothy Dwight, the genteel leader of the revival at Yale College, they recounted the exploits of popular evangelists such as Lorenzo Dow, a charismatic preacher who claimed to have received direct revelations from God. For example, Butler linked the revivals to popular beliefs in dreams and visions, describing nineteenth-century America as a "spiritual hothouse" where Spiritualists and Methodists competed for converts (Butler, 1990: 225–56). Although he and Hatch argued over whether the revivals represented the coerciveness or the "democratization" of early nineteenth-century Christianity, they agreed that the revivals had Christianized the republic, giving America a new identity as a "righteous empire." On one hand, they challenged Baird by questioning whether America had always been a Protestant country. At the same time, however, they echoed earlier historians by interpreting the revivals as a crucial part of American nation-building, a religious response to the political upheavals of the early national period.

In another parallel to the past, scholars have asserted that the early nineteenth century was the most critical period in American religious history. Despite the tumultuous events of the second half of the century – the Civil War, large-scale industrialization and urbanization, the beginnings of the fundamentalist movement, and the rise of the social gospel – most historians have focused on the years between 1800 and 1850. Ever since Robert Baird published *Religion in the United States of America* in

1844, historians have persistently identified revivalism, voluntarism, and disestablishment as the most important themes for understanding the century as a whole. Yet as William Hutchison (1976) and George Marsden (1980) have argued (building on the work of Martin Marty), the 1880s and 1890s were marked by controversies that reverberated into the twentieth century. As liberal modernists and conservative fundamentalists debated over the role of churches in American culture, they created a rift in Protestantism that clergy found impossible to heal. Fundamentalists, Marsden explained, were fiercely opposed "to modernist attempts to bring Christianity into line with modern thought" (Marsden, 1980: 4). Despite these religious crises, however, historians have written far more books about religion in the early republic than they have about religion during or after the Civil War. Even though they have deliberately tried to dismantle the older narrative tradition, traces of it still remain.

Looking Ahead

The history of religion in nineteenth-century America, like all histories, remains incomplete. Whenever historians shift their interpretations in order to incorporate new themes and questions, they inevitably privilege one kind of evidence over another. As a result, even though recent scholars have prided themselves on their inclusiveness, they have ignored many topics that deserve greater attention. First, they have been so interested in the experiences of ordinary believers that they have written very few books about theology, a subject that may seem too "elite." Although they have been fascinated by popular beliefs in magic and divination, they have often ignored the creeds that most people actually heard in their churches and synagogues each week. Instead of examining how lay people made sense of formal theology, they have dismissed it as an abstraction that had little effect on everyday life. (Exceptions include Leigh Schmidt, who has carefully analyzed the ceremony of the Lord's Supper, and William Hutchison, who has explored the ideas of liberal theologians such as Walter Rauschenbusch.) Since many nineteenth-century Americans were well schooled in their particular religious traditions, heatedly debating with one another about the divinity of Christ or the doctrine of transubstantiation, historians must take their beliefs seriously. It is impossible to understand the quarrels between Methodists and Congregationalists or modernists and fundamentalists without grasping the theological issues at stake.

Although it may sound surprising, historians should also devote more attention to mainstream Protestants, the group that dominated history books for generations. Ironically, recent scholars have been so eager to distance themselves from the consensus tradition that they have virtually ignored the majority of Protestant believers. The balance may have tipped too far: although Spiritualists and Transcendentalists are certainly worthy of study, so are Methodists, Congregationalists, Lutherans, and Presbyterians. If historians are interested in religious pluralism, then they should not only focus on the tensions between "insiders" and "outsiders," but on the quarrels within the Protestant mainstream. The religious history of the Civil War, a topic that has received surprisingly little attention, offers a dramatic example of the regional and racial divisions that splintered the Protestant establishment. Although Baird and Dorchester tried to ignore the controversies that divided Unitarians from

Presbyterians, or black slaves from white masters, nineteenth-century Protestantism was never a monolith.

Last but not least, religious historians must continue to explore the experiences of overlooked groups. Even though historians have published more books about "outsiders" in the past 25 years than ever before, they still have not charted the stunning diversity of nineteenth-century beliefs and practices. For example, women's historians have written many books about white, middle-class, and Protestant women, but relatively few about slave, Mormon, immigrant, Catholic, Jewish, or lower-class women. Historians of Catholicism and Judaism have written extensively about immigration and assimilation, but very little about ritual or devotion. African-American historians have presented a riveting portrait of slave religion, but have only begun to explore the rise of independent black churches after the Civil War. Historians of the frontier have tried to move beyond William Warren Sweet's celebration of religion as a civilizing influence, but they still know little about the clash between Anglo-American and Native-American cultures. And the list could go on.

The greatest challenge facing historians today is synthesizing the "old" history with the "new." Few would like to return to the old paradigm, which identified anyone outside the Protestant mainstream as "unAmerican," but few completely accept the new paradigm either, which treats mainstream Protestants only as the foil for religious "outsiders." Unfortunately, neither the older interpretative tradition nor the newer one provides a full, sophisticated account of religious diversity in nineteenth-century America. What is needed – and what future historians must struggle to achieve – is a new history that weaves together the experiences of men and women, Native Americans and Anglo-Americans, Catholics and Protestants, blacks and whites. Like William McLoughlin, who emphasized that the encounter between Protestant missionaries and Indians changed *both* groups, historians should explore how nineteenth-century American culture was shaped by the complicated interactions between "insiders" and "outsiders." Instead of longing for an elusive Protestant unity, they must write narratives that wrestle with the reality of religious pluralism in both the past and the present.

REFERENCES

Ahlstrom, Sydney (1972) *A Religious History of the American People*. New Haven, Conn.: Yale University Press.
Baird, Robert (1844) *Religion in the United States of America*. Glasgow: Blackie.
Braude, Ann (1989) *Radical Spirits: Spiritualism and Women's Rights in Nineteenth-century America*. Boston: Beacon Press.
Brekus, Catherine A. (1998) *Strangers and Pilgrims: Female Preaching in America, 1740–1845*. Chapel Hill, NC: University of North Carolina Press.
Butler, Jon (1990) *Awash in a Sea of Faith: Christianizing the American People*. Cambridge, Mass.: Harvard University Press.
Diner, Hasia R. (1992) *The Jewish People in America*, vol. 2: *A Time for Gathering: the Second Migration, 1820–1880*. Baltimore, MD: Johns Hopkins University Press.
Dolan, Jay P. (1985) *The American Catholic Experience: a History from Colonial Times to the Present*. Garden City, NY: Doubleday.
Dorchester, Daniel (1888) *Christianity in the United States from the First Settlement down to the Present Time*. New York: Phillips and Hunt.

Hatch, Nathan O. (1989) *The Democratization of American Christianity.* New Haven, Conn.: Yale University Press.

Hutchison, William R. (1976) *The Modernist Impulse in American Protestantism.* Cambridge, Mass.: Harvard University Press.

McLoughlin, William G. (1984) *Cherokees and Missionaries, 1789–1839.* New Haven, Conn.: Yale University Press.

Maffly-Kipp, Laurie F. (1994) *Religion and Society in Frontier California.* New Haven, Conn.: Yale University Press.

Marsden, George M. (1980) *Fundamentalism and American Culture: the Shaping of Twentieth-century Evangelicalism, 1870–1925.* New York: Oxford University Press.

Marty, Martin E. (1970) *Righteous Empire: the Protestant Experience in America.* New York: Dial Press.

Mathews, Donald G. (1977) *Religion in the Old South.* Chicago: University of Chicago Press.

Moore, R. Laurence (1986) *Religious Outsiders and the Making of Americans.* New York: Oxford University Press.

Raboteau, Albert J. (1978) *Slave Religion: the "Invisible Institution" in the Antebellum South.* Oxford: Oxford University Press.

Schmidt, Leigh Eric (1989) *Holy Fairs: Scottish Communions and American Revivals in the Early Modern Period.* Princeton, NJ: Princeton University Press.

Shipps, Jan (1985) *Mormonism: the Story of a New Religious Tradition.* Urbana: University of Illinois Press.

Sweet, William Warren (1930) *The Story of Religions in America.* New York: Harper and Brothers.

CHAPTER TWENTY-THREE

Science and Technology

ALAN I. MARCUS

HISTORICAL studies of nineteenth-century America's science and technology undertaken during the past 30 or more years reflect their postmodern origins and differ markedly from their modernist ancestors. Historians of technology and science prior to the 1960s tended to frame questions and issues that would elucidate or have implications for modernism. In that regard, the early history of science in America took its inspiration from Europe as exemplified by A. O. Lovejoy's *Great Chain of Being* and Alexandre Koyre's *From the Closed World to the Infinite Universe*. Following European precedent, this early history of science in America was dominated by two questions. The first concentrated on individuals identified as great men and asked how these geniuses reasoned when they achieved their greatness. A fine example of this approach was Edward Lurie's *Louis Agassiz: a Life in Science* (1960), which was framed to show genius in action and practice. The second question revolved around then current knowledge and asked what were the positive and therefore relevant steps that were taken in the march that led to this particular enlightenment. A. Hunter Dupree's *Asa Gray, 1810–1888* (1959), for instance, was more interested in Gray's involvement in bringing Darwinism to America than in other aspects of Gray's career.

History of technology questions were equally formalized. Historians wanted to know how great inventors and great companies achieved their greatness. They sought to identify the seminal insights that produced technological progress and tended to equate progress with the then contemporary situation. Roger Burlingame's *March of the Iron Men* (1938) and Nelson Blake's *Water for the Cities: a History of the Urban Water Supply Problem in the United States* (1956) are classic examples of this thrust to accentuate the origins of the technological present in their analyses of the technological past.

The subtitles of Lurie and Blake's works serve as modernist fingerprints and reveal the penetration of modernist assumptions. When Lurie identifies his biography as "a life in science," he is in effect acknowledging that the whole idea of an American science or technology is untenable. In Lurie's modernist view, science and technology are universal constructs transcending geopolitical borders, local arrangements, or even time. Science and technology are timeless, intellectual endeavors that proceed from great person to great person. For Lurie's generation, the history of science in America was possible but inconvenient, but the history of American science was utterly nonsensical.

Blake's *Water for the Cities* also embraces timelessness but in another sense. It demands that an urban water supply was a continuing and continuous problem and that the identification of the problem in that fashion holds out the real and likely possibility of insight. By lumping together a functional activity without respect to time or place, Blake assumes the universal validity of the categorization, especially its persistence to the present.

In both the history of science and the history of technology in America, initial concerns were modernist and best characterized as internalist. Historians wondered what went on inside the heads of geniuses or what were the milestones on the road to modern knowledge and application. The focus was what the unique individual, the scientific or technological diva if you will, understood and how that insight shaped others and ultimately the present.

It is ironic, perhaps, that as modernist historians asked the same fundamental questions in the history of science and technology, they did not consider science and technology all of one piece. Those focusing on science looked at technology as applied science, a spin-off of science and degraded at that. To these men and a few women, technology was, unlike science, not the product of great conceptions but rather application or practicality, which they deemed common and therefore considered a lesser state. Persons primarily studying technology reacted to the rebuff by splitting with the historians of science and establishing their own professional institutions to mark their unique professional identity.

In the past several decades, the postmodernist tableau emerged first to challenge and then to oppose the modernist program. Perhaps the first important postmodern statement came from the physicist turned historian of science, Thomas S. Kuhn. In his now classic *Structure of Scientific Revolutions* (1962), Kuhn asserted that scientific knowledge was not the province of and did not reflect simply the genius of individuals but rather it was the product of communities of scientists. Scientific theories reflected agreed-upon assumptions about the then available data as accepted by members of a self-defined community. Many historians of science cited the work of Kuhn, who ironically became the American academe's patron saint of postmodernity, as they shifted their gaze from individuals to nominal scientific communities. Each sought first and foremost to elucidate, identify, and name the critical community it detected.

Historians of science at the Smithsonian Institution, such as Nathan Reingold, were central to inaugurating this program. Through much of the 1960s and 1970s (and to a lesser degree to the present day), Smithsonian fellowships provided financial support and intellectual direction to generations of aspiring historians of science. At the Smithsonian they learned of science and scientific communities as international entities, not the product of a single nation. But they also were taught that the only creditable nineteenth-century American science was based in Washington and in communities within Washington institutions. In short, these agencies and institutions controlled what was good and significant about American science within the international scientific community. The US Geological Survey's exploration of the American West, the establishment of the National Academy of Science and of the American Association for the Advancement of Science, and even the creation of the Smithsonian itself were products of that Washington agenda. So too was the identification of Washington-based scientific communities not affiliated with a single government or government-supported institution. The Cosmos Club, a late nineteenth-century gentlemen's club that counted as its members the heads of many Washington-situated scientific bureaux, and the Lazaroni, a shadowy, informal gathering of Washington-located bureaucrats at mid-century, both received attention as dominant and dominating forces that ensured that the nation's science would contribute to international scientific knowledge.

Emphasis on communitarianism in science led the same postmodernist generations to search for and develop rules and procedures by which these newly identified American communities behaved. In a series of essays on the evolution of professionalism in early nineteenth-century America, George Daniels provided the first definitive statements. Daniels's professionalization process did not please everyone, however, and subsequent efforts aimed to modify his schema. His first book, *American Science in the Age of Jackson* (1968), proved an even more telling proposition. Operating from a Kuhnian framework, Daniels showed something that Kuhn never dared to broach and possibly did not even recognize: he demonstrated that scientific communities could fail and gave a cogent example of that failure by depicting mid-nineteenth-century American science. According to Daniels, infatuation with description, allegedly without a priori assumptions, marked the sole acceptable scientific form during that early era. Called Baconianism after Sir Francis Bacon, this descriptive regimen netted virtually no productive work and was different from and out of step with contemporary European science. In short, Daniels had extended Kuhn's argument by replacing the idea of an international scientific community with a "local" one. He talked of an American scientific context and thus carried Kuhnian presumptions to a new conclusion. If science at any given time and/or place was an agreed-upon understanding and that understanding could be changed at subsequent times and/or in subsequent places, need those agreed-upon understandings have any intrinsic merit in themselves? Might they not simply be agreed-upon premises with no more validity than other agreed-upon premises? Could they not simply be wrong rather than less or differently right?

That realization opened a new form of postmodernist enquiry. If the premises were in fact arbitrary, the focus necessarily shifted on to the formulators of and adherents to the premises. New issues abounded in this reconstructed view. Why did these particular premises suffice? How did they suffice? Put another way, the question that emerged turned on a rather simple and simplistic assumption, namely that who these formulators were was in fact deterministic (although how historians defined who their scientists "were" – what was the crucial experience – differed). Who were the formulators of the premises? What did they suppose and how was their frame of reference similar so that they could construct such a scientific understanding?

This new enquiry reoriented discussion from premises to context. It was not what was believed that was truly important in science and technology but rather who formulated belief and why and how that particular belief was formulated. To signal their differences from the previous generations, these generally young historians of science quickly and initially called themselves social historians of science. Daniels himself wrote an ill-fated book, *Science in American Society: a Social History* (1971), which incorporated social history and American science in a single title.

A National Science Foundation-funded project, inspired by the American Academy of Arts and Sciences, marked the apex of this approach. In preparation for its two hundredth anniversary, the Academy appointed a group of prominent historians of science to develop a plan to commemorate the event. Their selection of a series of essays on learned societies in American life was itself a product of the new history of science. By demarcating these groups as "learned societies," they characterized the groups by their memberships – learned men – rather than by their productions. Moreover, the term "learned societies" was a tacit acknowledgment that the "science" produced by these groups need not be science at all by some late twentieth-century definition but rather the focus of a nineteenth-century scientific society. Even more telling were the questions essayists were to ask. Contributors were to discuss the organization of knowledge, not knowledge itself. Coordinators wanted to know if there were some regional patterns of development for scientific societies and what was the nature and composition of their membership. The influence of public and private support on the formation and growth of learned societies and the difference in terms of various social and geographical communities they were to serve were to be discussed. Essayists were invited to compare the ages, occupations, and geographical distributions of leaders and members and to explore the social, political, and intellectual rewards of membership. Finally, they were told to search for overlapping memberships between learned societies and other educational institutions.

Well over 50 historians of science were involved in the project and nearly as many essays on the nineteenth century were published in two hefty volumes. But even before the second volume was published, some historians of science began to have second thoughts about the project. The people they were analyzing were elites. But if scientific theories and knowledge were essentially arbitrary, why focus exclusively on elites. Why privilege a particular group? Historians of science had already deconstructed science in one important way. They shunned the text of science – scientific ideas – for an examination of the subtext of science – who these scientists were and why they did what they did. To move to the next logical step proved a relatively easy task. Simply put, many historians of science asked why focus on scientists, privileged people? Why not consider popular science or at least the agenda of elites seeking to have others conform to their templates? To these historians, knowledge and power went together. But it was authority, not knowledge, that remained the seat of power.

Well before 1980, the deconstructionists had come to dominate the American history of science profession. Dismissing the internal, they accentuated what they initially termed the external, the forces operating and impacting on science and scientists. Among the first manifestations of this new externalism was a curious union of history and sociology. Traditionally, the history of science had been linked to the philosophy of science. Several academic departments had long functioned under that twin rubric and the vast majority of practitioners had shared an extensive commonality. But with the emphasis now on the forces that shaped scientists and yielded scientific events, philosophy seemed antiquated, at best interested in issues foreign to postmodern historians of science. Sociology, the laws of group interactions taken without regard to time, culture, or place, became the panacea. This sociology sometimes took a cue from functionalist anthropology, which supposed the existence of rigid categories of action and sought to identify within each culture the agencies that performed those specified, required functions.

In a number of instances, historians of science refined the sociological model to make it even more suitable for the history of science. Two major formulations gained some currency. Both were post-structural and owed some inspiration to a thread of thought of the French historian, Michel Foucault. The first, the "ecology of knowledge," was interested in a dynamic between persons claiming to possess special knowledge, their social institutions, and the social institutions of society at large. Adoption of the term "ecology" suggested just how embedded concepts of the social environment – sociological concepts – were within this formulation. More extreme was the social constructionist school, which at its most daring argued that all science (and social reality) was in effect negotiated by persons and groups seeking to maintain or extend their authority or dominance. To these scholars, reality was not perceived but real and objective. But reality as social constructionists viewed it did not exist in physical nature but rather only in social space. Social matrices defined reality, which was characterized by boundaries and other geographical constructions that helped circumscribe social space. From this analysis emerged functionalist communities: learner, user, and consumer among others. Each owed its existence to the supposed social cleavages axiomatically creating it.

After 1980, a modified form of social constructionism also began to resonate with historians of technology. To a large degree, historians of science had been correct in their portrait of historians of technology up to that time. Historians of technology dealt with applications or productions – tangible artefacts, not theories – and this focus on material things translated into a lack of consideration about methodological issues in their scholarship. Even Daniels, who explicitly tried to set an agenda of the "big issues in the history of technology," failed to generate methodological or topical unity or even much attention, let alone excitement. Until about 1980, historians of technology were pleased that anyone would be interested and involved in the study of technology and welcomed any and all approaches. In fact, the famous novelist Norman Mailer, who belonged to the professional organization and subscribed to the journal, counted himself as a member of the professional history of technology group in America. During this era of disinterest in methodology, historians published a number of useful history of technology books, including Louis Hunter, *Steamboats on the Western Rivers: an Economic and Technological History* (1949); Edwin Layton Jr, *The Revolt of the Engineers* (1971); W. David Lewis, *Iron and Steel in America* (1976); Alfred Chandler, *The Visible Hand: the Managerial Revolution in American Business* (1977); and A. F. C. Wallace, *Rockdale* (1978). Yet they did so without any concentrated attempt to establish what approach the history of technology necessarily needed to adopt.

Rejection of efforts to forge an explicit history of technology methodology was an ironic casualty of the sociology/history of science nexus. History and sociology of science departments hired historians to work up the history and sociology of technology to serve as a sort of mirror image twin of the history and sociology of science. The ideology of social constructionism reigned there, although not with the methodological purity that extremists in the history of science demanded. Historians now sought to elucidate the nature of technology and technological change, which invariably brought to the forefront issues such as the social orgins of innovation; sociological explanations for production bottlenecks; and studies of specific engineering communities, especially the forces external to these groups. Virtually all consideration of the technology *per se* was absent, supplanted by social constructionist thought. Thomas P. Hughes's *Networks of Power: Electrification in Western Society, 1880–1930* (1983) became the first acknowledged classic of this type and a model for this sort of approach. Here, almost without reference to time or place, Hughes considered who electrified Western Europe and America and how they did it. What mattered to

Hughes was pattern, the identification of a sociological process that occurred in country after country and entailed the same parameters. Indeed, within this socio-logical perspective, pattern – law – necessarily was the end product. It could not be any other way and there could be no exceptions.

Social constructionism continues to hold sway over the history of technology and the history of science. But a particular variant has gained increasing attention during the past decade. Like social constructionism itself, the variant emerged from the recognition that if scientific and technological truth were indeed community-invented or community-negotiated events, then community members had no special claim – genius or profound knowledge – to account for their authority. They were simply another group who seized upon social position to exert authority and power over others. Demystification of this community as arbitrarily privileged made it just another Eurocentric, patriarchal elite of dead white males, who fostered competition rather than cooperation. Combating this privilege required a two-fold agenda: that the stories of those excluded should be told and that the stories of how those privileged gained their privilege and domination should be exposed. Overturning this privilege, itself a goal of postmodern pluralism and diversity, necessitated the construction of the history of science/scientists and technology/technologists in and of under-represented groups (or its resurrection if the elites had conspired to bury it). Women and African Americans, the two largest nineteenth-century American groups that were not white or male, became the focus of this alternative history approach.

This new discourse revolved around a few central questions. First and foremost was how the privileged discriminated against and marginalized the minority. Almost as important was acknowledging and demonstrating that the minority had in some fashion managed to overcome the privileged to do good work, even as the virtues of that work were hampered by discrimination. This history of science and technology of identity sought specifically to empower and entitle groups long thought to be ignored by science and technology historians. Donna Haraway was among the first to bring attention to women and science, but Evelyn Fox Keller's *A Feeling for the Organism: the Life and Work of Barbara McClintock* (1983) and Margaret Rossiter's *Women Scientists in America: Struggles and Strategies to 1940* (1982) were the initial touchstones, although neither was specifically about nineteenth-century American science and technology. Similarly, the recurring interest in George Washington Carver could be attributed to his ability to have withstood racial prejudice and achieved scientific prominence.

For nineteenth-century studies, historians of science have tended to focus on how certain groups were discriminated against. These studies suggest how elites used barriers or reformulated disciplines to restrict entrance, forcing some to labor on the boundaries of disciplines. History of technology questions have been framed rather differently. They have stressed how particular technologies or technologists have discriminated against or hampered a group. Ruth Schwartz Cowan's *More Work for Mother: the Ironies of Household Technology from the Open Hearth to the Microwave* (1983) is the classic work of this genre. Cowan's volume concentrates less on the inspiration for new domestic technologies than exploring the sociological process of moving from a pre-industrial to industrial society and the ramifications of that socio-logical reality for the status and work of women, especially in the twentieth-century home. Others have extended the analysis to telephone operators, seamstresses, and office workers, the three most prevalent occupations for women outside the home in the nineteenth century (aside from work as domestics).

While explorations of social caste have been plentiful in both the history of technology and of science, consideration of social class has been a predominantly history of technology issue. In fact, within the postmodernist tableau, where elites are merely the result of bias and privilege, issues of class, even more than gender and race, assume importance. As do colleagues in business, labor, and economic history, postmodern historians of technology examine what they see as a de-skilling process which occurred in the nineteenth century as workers lost control of the means of production. But historians of technology often broaden the analysis to discuss business culture and a culture of consumption or a consumer culture. To these scholars, it is not simply the aggrieved group that deserves consideration. The technological juggernaut influenced entire communities, which are said to include labor, ownership, management, government, and consumers.

Social constructionist history of science and technology and the history of science and technology of identity have dictated what are acceptable questions for the disciplines and erected a relatively straightforward if mundane sociological methodology as their agenda. In that sense, both constrain scholarship and narrow vision. But postmodernism in the two fields generally, at least since Daniels's *American Science in the Age of Jackson*, has also had a somewhat contradictory effect. Indeed, it has helped accomplish something modernist historians of science and technology could never manage. Postmodernism has opened entire new vistas for the history of science and technology of nineteenth-century America to explore, if only from one particular vision. Ironically, postmodernism's reduction of science from a true proposition – the modernist platform – to merely the agreed-upon conclusions of a self-defined community transformed the past's usability for the present; it converted what persons in nineteenth-century America actually considered science and technology into fair game, fit topics for research for contemporary historians of science and technology. No longer was study restricted to modernist heroes. No longer were the internationally prominent physicist Joseph Henry, a few equally well-regarded astronomers, and some early advocates of Darwinism the sole suitable subjects for the history of nineteenth-century science in America. Postmodernist scholars saw a technological history of nineteenth-century America that included more than Edison and the railroads. As in the case of Daniels's elaboration of Baconianism, postmodern history of science and technology now had an entire, virtually unexamined, century to investigate. Put baldly, postmodernist thought made it conceivable to rediscover premodern phenomena and possible to write their history.

In some cases, this thrust simply meant that scientific communities, formerly ignored as not dealing with international issues or not meaningful in some way, were resurrected. Such was the case with American natural history and geology, including the surveying of the West and expeditions to other lands. From Lewis and Clark on, Americans retained an active interest in describing and defining the West and identifying those forces that contributed to its distinctive formation and striking fauna and flora. That many of these American investigators adopted a sort of Lamarckianism, rather than Darwinianism, was now less important than that they functioned as a scientific community.

More telling, however, was the recognition of American exceptionalism. Just what constituted and should constitute American science and technology in nineteenth-century America itself became a vital and viable question. That America was conceived as a democratic republic, a break from, rather than replication of, Europe, had tremendous implications for its science and technology. This great experiment in democracy, situated on a continent relatively new to Europeans, produced a science of discovery, a science of a New World, as well as a science of democracy and improvement. Questions of monopoly versus merit, opportunity and privilege, the role of education and educational institutions, and the responsibility of federal, state, and local governments flavored the new nation's science and technology.

Historians of science have dealt with several of these intellectual ramifications, even as they overlook their genesis. Perhaps the most extensively detailed aspect has been the history of agricultural science. Proceeding from the belief that an informed, prosperous yeomanry provided the backbone of democracy, nineteenth-century Americans worried about maintaining that yeomanry in the face of what they recognized as a series of pressures seeking to reduce those persons to a dependent state. They often gravitated to science and persons claiming special scientific knowledge to keep the yeomanry strong. Early nineteenth-century agricultural societies and newspapers spread the latest techniques and theories. Soil analysts, using the newest chemical methods and understandings, tested farmers' mid-century soils and later the quality of the fertilizers they purchased. The federal government also got involved in protecting (in effect, privileging) its yeomanry. In 1862, it created the first agency, the United States Department of Agriculture (USDA), dedicated to providing scientific information and material to a particular group, and established tuition-fee land-grant colleges, where knowledge, including technological and scientific knowledge, could be passed to successive generations, "the sons and daughters of farmers and mechanics." From the USDA would come support for entomologists, meteorologists, pomologists, ornithologists, and a host of other scientists working in areas that pertained to agriculture. Finally, through a federal–state partnership, Americans created and provided funding for an institution for agricultural experimentation and research, the agricultural experiment station. These stations proved so important that virtually every life science initiative undertaken in the United States down to the 1950s was done at least in part through experiment stations.

Historians of science have also noted the nineteenth-century desire to learn the sciences of democracy. Considerable work has been done on sketching out communities dealing with and developing sciences of collective and group behavior. Histories of the various social science communities, especially their late-century origins, have been explored for economics, sociology, and political science. Several education and educational psychology communities also have been identified. Historians have proved less willing to examine the early nineteenth-century sciences of individual improvement, such as phrenology and physiognomy, which captured at least as much attention and interest in their time as did the more familiar social sciences some half-century later.

The postmodernist reorientation has also redefined the topics that historians of technology scrutinize, converting technological America into a subject worthy of study before it assumed international prominence in the twentieth century. Indeed, there was published in 1989 a fully fledged professional history of technology in

America from the nation's colonial origins to the present day. Publication of *Technology in America: a Brief History* (Marcus and Segal, 1989) would have been an event inconceivable to modernists. The idea of a nineteenth-century democratic republic frames the volume's discussion of nineteenth-century American technology. What constituted appropriate production and production techniques for a then contemporary democracy? What did it mean to produce at best advantage? What were the appropriate relations among those producing and those designing or sustaining production facilities? Should each necessarily be different or should they all be the same? What was a democratic infrastructure – canals, railroads, turnpikes, gas, sewer, and electricity, telegraphy, and telephony – and on whose responsibility rested its creation and maintenance? The United States Constitution specified that the national defense was the province of the federal government, but what were the ramifications of that power?

But *Technology in America* has been an exception, perhaps even an aberration. Historians of technology have repeatedly ignored the spirit and substance of these questions, even as they, as good postmodernists, embrace the material manifestations. Historians of technology have tended to explore areas such as production, formation of technological organizations, military technology, government involvement in the private sector, and the like as if these phenomena occurred regardless of time or place. They have treated them as universal phenomena, simply the confluence of sociological forces. In practice, historians of technology first strained to identify the social forces and functionalist groups that constitute the parameters of the community which they chose to study. Then they claimed to undertake an analysis, which they have seen as inter- or multi-disciplinary because it employs insights generated from business history, labor history, consumer history, and advertising history. In reality, however, historians of technology merely adopted sociological concepts similar to their own from scholars who have successfully erected and maintained boundaries around their bailiwicks; rather than representing a different methodology or technique, each of these outsiders was and is nothing more than a functionalist sociologist of a particular topic and thrust.

At a meeting of the History of Science Society two years ago, the noted historian of science Charles Rosenberg fretted that his social constructionist colleagues had gone too far. He warned that they had abandoned all pretense of interest in scientific ideas in their zeal to examine the intricate union and intersection of social forces that engendered or circumscribed a particular science. Finding this a fatal flaw, Rosenberg urged others to redress this balance without forsaking the social constructionist approach. That few have tried to take up Rosenberg's challenge suggests just how difficult merging scientific ideas and social constructionism is. Subtext continues to vanquish text.

Even more difficult but perhaps more fruitful is employing ideas more generally, not just of science but of social organization. Although it may be less intellectually satisfying or neat than reducing everything to a series of simply stated axioms, there exists abundant evidence to suggest that sociological forces are simply manifestations of ideas. Rather than operating outside of time and place, interpretations of the situations and conditions often called forces are time- and place-dependent. It is time to treat the history of science and technology of nineteenth-century America within the context of the specific breed of premodernism that generated them. By deconstructing nineteenth-century American science and technology, postmodern social constructionists make what happened in the premodern an appropriate subject for study and thus legitimate it. But by forcing these premodernist events into some kind of timeless, placeless template – the inevitable consequence of social forces operating on thoroughly malleable humankind – they refuse to consider why these nineteenth-century men and women did what they did. This willful neglect renders their historical efforts essentially ahistorical as they remove time from any meaningful role in the analysis.

Practitioners of technology and science in nineteenth-century America investigated phenomena and established processes as solutions to problems – conditions and situations – they understood around them. In that sense, their ideas, assumptions, and beliefs made a "problem" a problem and also pointed to potential and suitable solutions. This was not just some simple expression of social situation; social position, ethnicity, and gender are not and never have been unalterably deterministic. Each is and has always been the product of ideas. Culture, a series of ideas, notions, and customs, binds together diverse groups of persons in seemingly unexplainable ways and provides a common perspective from which to interpret and reason, even to argue. Culture, in short, gives meaning to social discriminants.

What is necessary for the further study of science and technology in nineteenth-century America is not sociology but a more sophisticated anthropology, bordering on historical particularism. Specific, dominant cultural notions and social themes dominate different eras in the American past. It is these cultural notions and social themes that make a series of years a distinct era. But cultures change. In this regard, culture is not simply a phenomenon of people and place. Cultures rarely emerge from the settlement of geographical areas and persist inviolate; instead, a culture has distinctive epochs, each characterized by a particular set of assumptions locked in time. In effect, nineteenth-century America was but a series of cultures, each of which succeeded and was markedly different from its predecessor. True cross-cultural study, then, is not only the study of different geographical units. It is also the study of the same geographical unit at different times. In that sense, what makes and has made technology and science in nineteenth-century America distinct from technology and science someplace else or at some other time is and was the cultural epochs through which America has passed. Science and technology in nineteenth-century America were a manifestation and explication of particularistic culture-based ideas. That approach to the past is radically at odds with social constructionism, and as long as social constructionism persists as the reigning paradigm, it will remain virtually untapped.

REFERENCES

Blake, N. M. (1956) *Water for the Cities: a History of the Urban Water Supply Problem in the United States*. Syracuse, NY: Syracuse University Press.

Burlingame, R. (1938) *March of the Iron Men: a Social History of Union through Invention*. New York: Scribner.

Chandler, A. D. (1977) *The Visible Hand: the Managerial Revolution in American Business*. Cambridge, Mass.: Belknap Press of Harvard University.

Cowan, R. S. (1983) *More Work for Mother: the Ironies of Household Technology from the Open Hearth to the Microwave*. New York: Basic Books.

Daniels, G. H. (1968) *American Science in the Age of Jackson*. New York: Columbia University Press.

Daniels, G. H. (1971) *Science in American Society: a Social History*. New York: Alfred A. Knopf.

Dupree, A. H. (1959) *Asa Gray, 1810–1888*. Cambridge, Mass.: Belknap Press of Harvard University.

Hughes, T. P. (1983) *Networks of Power: Electrification in Western Society, 1880–1930*. Baltimore, MD: Johns Hopkins University Press.

Hunter, L. C. (1949) *Steamboats on the Western Rivers: an Economic and Technological History*. New York: Octagon Books, 1969.

Keller, E. F. (1983) *A Feeling for the Organism: the Life and Work of Barbara McClintock*. San Francisco: W. H. Freeman.

Kuhn, Thomas S. (1962) *Structure of Scientific Revolutions*. Chicago: University of Chicago Press.

Layton, E. T. (1971) *The Revolt of the Engineers: Social Responsibility and the American Engineering Profession*. Cleveland, Ohio: Press of Case Western Reserve University.

Lewis, W. D. (1976) *Iron and Steel in America*. Greenville: Eleutherian Mills-Hagley Foundation.

Lurie, E. (1960) *Louis Agassiz: a Life in Science*. Chicago: University of Chicago Press.

Marcus, A. I. and Segal, Howard P. (1989) *Technology in America: a Brief History*. San Diego: Harcourt Brace Jovanovich.

Miller, H. S. (1970) *Dollars for Research: Science and its Patrons in Nineteenth-century America*. Seattle: University of Washington Press.

Oleson, A. and Brown, S. C. (eds) (1976) *The Pursuit of Knowledge in the Early American Republic: American Scientific and Learned Societies from Colonial Times to the Civil War*. Baltimore, MD: Johns Hopkins University Press.

Oleson, A. and Voss, J. (eds) (1979) *The Organization of Knowledge in Modern America, 1860–1920*. Baltimore, MD: Johns Hopkins University Press.

Rossiter, Margaret W. (1982) *Women Scientists in America: Struggles and Strategies to 1940*. Baltimore, MD: Johns Hopkins University Press.

Wallace, Anthony F. C. (1978) *Rockdale: the Growth of an American Village in the Early Industrial Revolution*. New York: Alfred A. Knopf.

CHAPTER TWENTY-FOUR

A History/Historiography of Representations of America

BARBARA GROSECLOSE

IN 1893, thanks to the Columbian World's Exposition in Chicago, the satirical magazine *Puck* would seem to have been over-supplied with topical items regarding United States' materialism, entrepreneurialism, insularity, ingenuity, *naïveté*, intelligence, stupidity – qualities any capitalist country puts on display when it hosts a world fair and, likewise, makes available for the language of caricature. The fair merely whetted *Puck*'s appetite for American foibles that year, it turns out, as other problematic areas, notably immigration, were gleefully and regularly skewered. In one such cartoon (figure 23.1), a genial Uncle Sam and a carelessly confident Columbia, familiar to viewers as representations of "America," preside at the anniversary of the arrival of their "best child," the German immigrant. The party is well attended by a

Figure 23.1 "A Family Party" (*Puck*, 1893)

tableful of immigrant stereotypes: a turbulent-looking Irishman, a buffoonish Italian organ-grinder, monkey-like Asians, sleeping baby Africans, and so forth.

The nativist implication of the cartoon – a polyglot America comprised of various nationalities being "brought up" by two white, middle-class, and presumably Protestant parents who favor the child like themselves – is not why it provides a germane starting-point for a consideration of nineteenth-century representations of America in art. Rather, the cartoon reveals not only the absence of a single image which stands for "America" but also an abundance of potential additions to, or permutations of, a visually conceptualized "America." But was there ever a single personification of America? If so, why is there more than one in the 1890s?

To answer this question requires looking at nineteenth-century examples of representations of America in the visual arts and, in so doing, delving into the ways in which scholars past and present have assessed these representations. The types of query found in modern art-historical scholarship range from the specific to the general: Who are "Uncle Sam" and "Columbia?" – to name the two most familiar images associated with the United States. Why do they look like they do and how did they get their names? What alternatives to Uncle Sam and Columbia have been attempted and why have they been unsuccessful? What is the relationship between these or any visual national embodiment and the individuals and communities which comprise the nation?

In truth, no nation of people, homogeneous or not, can be reduced to a single image, so Uncle Sam no more represents "America" or "Americans," say, than John Bull stands for some monolithic notion of the British. On the other hand, most nations in the modern period have used visual symbols for themselves, and/or have had them devised by outsiders. Representations of a royal personage or a historical figure, a trait (negative or positive), even architecture can embody the idea of "nation," as may a flag or a document. According to the comprehensive analyses of these and other "places of memory" by Pierre Nora (1989) and his collaborators, such items shape a national culture as much as they are shaped by it. Nora offers historians of the United States a complicated and current model for thinking about representation of the nation, as emblem or as material culture, but his lead has not been followed with enthusiasm. Instead, although scholars throughout the humanities (art history not excepted) have been thinking about issues in terms of religious, ethnic, geographical, and gender perspectives, past and present researches on representations of America in art only rarely integrate these methodologies and viewpoints in writing about symbols of national culture.

Female Geniuses

The first personification of the United States took the form of a Native-American woman and one does not have to look very far for the reason: she descends from imagery personifying the continent(s) of America. As knowledge of the western hemisphere spread throughout Europe during the sixteenth century, the "old cosmography" of three continents of Europe, Africa, and Asia personified as regal women grew to four, and, Hugh Honour (1976: 112) reminds us, this "allegorical representation . . . [reflected] the growing self-awareness of Europeans as they confronted the rest of the world." With the convention of geographical personification, *genius loci*, European artists answered the question, "If I am I, who are you?" with a dichotomized visual and verbal terminology, both extremes of that terminology being frequently swollen by exaggeration.

For example, from Spanish reports of the Tupinamba and Caribes encountered in what is now Brazil and the West Indies came the sixteenth-century emblem of the Americas as a nude woman warrior, known as an "Indian queen," her muscular body decorated with feathers and usually accompanied by a parrot and other animals then unknown to Europe. Her weapons only partially account for the severed heads or limbs with which she also was depicted. Instead, they allude to the practice of cannibalism imputed to the Tupinamba and Caribes. Thus it is that European representations of *America* in the late sixteenth century include attributes such as a feathered head-dress, bow and arrow, exotic beast, and pieces of a corpse.

For the important initial personifications of the new American republic, the United States Congress perforce turned to European artists, French in particular, and they in turn, drew upon the tradition of personifying the new world as a majestic Native-American woman. Congress commissioned Augustin Dupré to design commemorative medals shortly after the Peace of Paris was concluded. In one of these, struck in 1789, the Native woman who bestows a laurel crown upon Brigadier General Daniel Burgen appears barefoot, wearing a feathered cap and skirt-like wrap; in another, executed a year later, a similar figure holding a cornucopia indicates to Mercury wares ready to export. For her American diplomatic function, Europe's Indian queen shed a few years and a few pounds. She became, in fact, a girl, a princess rather than a queen, perhaps in sympathy with the youth of the new nation she now represented.

Pioneering efforts in the mid-1960s by E. McClung Fleming, which were published in *Winterthur Portfolio* (1967), track the image of America as continent(s) in the visual arts from the colonial period to 1815. Fleming concluded that in the years surrounding the revolutionary war personifications multiplied and overlapped. A neoclassical Greek goddess with vestiges of the Indian princess shared the stage in/ as North America with "newly minted" Columbia and Liberty, the latter an emblem much in use in Europe. His point, and it is worth emphasizing for comparison with more recent interpretations, was that the female embodiments constituted "polite fancies of gentlemen of the genteel tradition" closely tied to the eighteenth century and that the "vernacular spirit" of the nineteenth would bring "earthiness and colloquialism" (Fleming, 1967: 38) to the imagery in the bodies of men, Brother Jonathan and Uncle Sam.

"Columbia," declares the *Oxford English Dictionary*, serves as a poetical name for America, specifically the United States, and it was first used in 1757. The adjective "Columbian" the *OED* defines as "of or belonging to America or (esp.) the United States," thus etymologically affirming the popular understanding of Christopher Columbus's so-called discovery of the New World as one which led ineluctably to the founding of the United States. As an image, an idea, and a word Columbia owes her existence therefore to the explorer and navigator Columbus and notions about his achievements, but her visualizations have always been grounded in European female personifications. In eighteenth-century political cartoons, for instance, she shows up as the "genius" of the US accompanied by cornucopia, liberty caps, a shield, or other traditional accoutrements. Whether she took a maternalized, personalized form – dressed in a robe of red, white, and blue, for instance, mourning the death of her "son," George Washington – or whether she donned a helmet and took on military airs – as happened around the time of the War of 1812 – Columbia's image persisted, most likely because the convention of female personification was already in place, a familiar thing visually (figure 23.2).

Unlike the Indian queen/princess, Columbia's race matched that of the United States' dominant culture; even so, she never functioned as an ideologically empty vessel. Occasionally, a residue of the initial personification reminded the viewer of the roots of blonde, white-skinned, white-gowned Columbia, as in paintings and engravings in which the demure European damsel wears a feathered head-dress. Dismissed by Fleming (1967) as the apolitical workings of classical taste, the elimination of a female Indian as a personification of America occurs at the same time as Columbia receives a new pictorial attribute: a child of uncertain gender, sometimes black and other times Native American, in Indian dress. In this regard, it seems likely that this child of color represents exactly what she looks like, that is, an attribute or *possession* of the figure standing for the United States itself. That the "possession" should be a child is not difficult to understand; both Indians and Africans received infantalizing characterizations in literature and the fine arts to denote the "primitive" state of their cultural condition from a Euramerican point of view. (Infantilizations of indigenous peoples by colonizers occurs throughout the history of imperialism as a comforting rationale.)

What the transformation of Indian queen to child suggests is that representations of America are produced by its hegemonic culture in a mode that rationalizes and supports its hegemony. This perhaps obvious point needs to be emphasized, for until very recently one of the most often overlooked aspects in the study of personifications or other types of national representations had to do with agency: somebody produces them and somebody has the power or the opportunity to ensure that they be viewed and, to a certain extent, to control the conditions of their viewing. Neither conspiratorial nor yet innocuous, the hegemonic control of national representation remains its most obvious feature and the one taken most for granted.

What can be learned about agency and iconography by tracing Columbia's transformations? No specifics are offered by Fleming (1967), who, as we have seen, favored an explanation with a Jacksonian tinge: the Federalist eighteenth century, centered on a well-bred, European-trained elite giving way to a Populist nineteenth century with mass, homespun tastes. Although he acknowledges the appearance of Columbia's sister personifications, America and Liberty, Fleming does not indicate that their potency and prevalence extended nearly to the end of the century.

Liberty or "Libertas," a Roman goddess who appeared on coins during the reign of Julius Caesar, was far more ancient than the four-continent personifications. She furnished the emblem not only of the American Revolution but the French as well, the latter with visible accoutrements such as a Phrygian cap that were then adapted in representations of Liberty as the United States. According to Vivien Green Fryd (1992), Liberty tends to be militaristic in association, in so far as she triumphs over despotism of all stripes, a victory frequently symbolized by broken chains, manacles, swords, or other instruments of oppression under Liberty's heel. In suggesting that images of Liberty associated with the United States be identified as "the American Liberty," Fleming (1967) points to accoutrements or inscriptions specifically twinning Liberty with the United States and consequently divesting her of any European,

Figure 23.2 Thomas Nast, "Columbia in a Dilemma" (*Harper's Weekly*, March 15, 1884)

specifically French, associations. Of interest in this regard are Liberty figures in the Capitol, such as the 13ft 7in plaster monument, 1817–19, by Enrico Causici. Causici's "Liberty" holds the Constitution in her outstretched right hand, a gesture presaging the now indelible, globally famous equation of America and Liberty: Frederic-Auguste Bartholdi's 1886 *Liberty Enlightening the World* (Figure 23.3). What irony or prescience is there in the fact that the most universally recognized monument in the US was not created by an American artist?

In some respects Bartholdi's 151 ft giantess (of thin copper sheeting stretched, or rather hammered out, and assembled on a scaffold-like armature) reproduces traditional inscriptions of American Liberty, among them not only her classical mien but also the tablet dated "July 4, 1776," and the broken chain under her foot. In other ways, she introduces elements new to the personification, especially the seven-rayed crown (for the seven seas and continents) and the torch of enlightenment (the statue was intended originally as a lighthouse). Both of these new elements took on added meaning when read in conjunction with lines from Emma Lazarus's poem, "The New Colossus," which were inscribed on a bronze plaque and put inside the base of the statue in 1903, when immigration was at its height: "Give me your tired, your poor, / your huddled masses yearning to breathe free, / the wretched refuse of your teeming shore / Send these, the homeless, tempest-tossed to me: / I lift my lamp beside the golden door!"

Agency and iconography follow a mostly forgotten path through the thickets of bureaucracy in the production and reception of the Statue of Liberty. Bartholdi proposed *Liberté Eclairant le Monde* in 1876 as the gift of France to mark the two republics' ties of friendship on the occasion of the United States' centennial. He built the statue in Paris under the aegis of the Franco-American Union, the American branch of which was to raise funds for the gigantic pedestal on which the monument would be placed. Bartholdi finished it in 1884, but he was forced to wait two more years before enough money could be raised to complete the pedestal project, an achievement credited to newspaper publisher Joseph Pulitzer's appeal to "the people" after he excoriated selfish "plutocrats" who would not contribute the necessary funds.

"The people" apparently referred exclusively to an American-born public, since years were to pass before Liberty's light shined very brightly on the foreign-born population. Although Lazarus's poem was written in 1883, it was not read at the statue's unveiling, an event which made, in fact, no reference to immigration. Indeed, plans to use Bedloe's Island, where the Statue of Liberty stands, as an immigration receiving station were not able to be put into operation for decades as a result of heavy opposition to the idea of linking the monument with foreigners. Thus, while many people associate Lazarus's words so closely with the Statue of Liberty that they would not, I think, be surprised if they issued from her lips, in fact isolationist sentiment time and again tried to sever the mental coupling of the representation with immigration, opportunity, or asylum. Only the national government's eagerness to present the monument as a symbol of freedom during World War II and the Cold War which followed finally overcame the resistance. Unlike the Statue of Liberty, Hiram Powers's *America*, the marble version of which dates from 1848 to 1865 (when fire destroyed it), maintains a fame, art-historically speaking, in the present that it never acquired in the sculptor's own day. That fact alone might be grounds for including the image in this chapter because one of the explanations tendered for its inability to attract a buyer

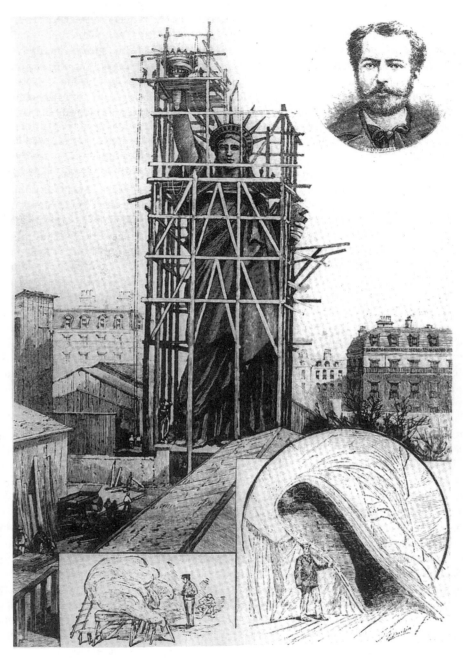

Figure 23.3   "Construction of the Statue of Liberty in Paris"
(*Harper's Weekly*, January 19, 1884).

has to do with how closely Powers veered toward denouncing slavery via the broken chains under *America*'s foot. In American art, such an explicit exposure of a core inconsistency in American self-identification would not readily be tolerated. Another reason might be that, unlike both Columbia and Liberty, Powers's *America* depended openly on a Greek prototype, the renowned second century BC marble known as the Venus de Milo, and emulated its nudity and muscular strength, though neither were qualities Americans were wont to attach to women. As will be seen in discussions of Uncle Sam, and as already encountered in the peculiar iconographic episodes in which Columbia is accompanied by a black child in Indian dress, imagining the nation in visual form often took a quite literal turn – cause enough to reject a nude in this case.

Males and Men

With the exception of the Statue of Liberty, Uncle Sam today is more familiar to viewers around the world than now recondite allegorical figures like Columbia or America. Uncle Sam also embodies the male personification of the United States most accessible to mass audiences and most easily deployed in graphic art for commercial or propagandistic purposes. His accessibility derives from his heritage: as Columbia is related to four-continent personifications from the Renaissance onward, Uncle Sam's kin include the fictional Brother Jonathan, a brash nineteenth-century reworking of Yankee Doodle, and the historical Davy Crockett, "b'ar killer" and Congressman in coonskin cap. Boisterous, local types, these fellows rise out of, or create, folklore and folk theater. When the incarnation of Brother Jonathan known as Jonathan Plough-boy, a cunning farmer whose eternal joke was to outsmart city folk, spoke in American theaters, his diction could only be described as colloquial and his accent hewed as nearly as possible to regional variations. Joshua C. Taylor (1976: 44) points out that because there was no "synthesized American," one was forced "to adopt the manners and speech of a particular locale, preferably rural," to "be American." The visual typology of Uncle Sam enhances this folk element of his make-up and explains his graphic, mass appeal to an audience still mostly rural. Despite fantastical garb of red and white striped pants, blue jacket, and star-trimmed hat, Uncle Sam looks like a folk hero, with his gangling body and clever, alert face (figure 23.4).

The name "Uncle Sam," though not his figure or demeanor, has been attached to a real person, "Uncle Sam" Wilson of Troy, New York. He sold provisions to the American military in 1812 in crates stamped "US," which initiated the wordplay Uncle Sam/United States. Even his name contributed to his popularity among the general public. Lacking in either poetical association or refinement, it sounded distinctly homely, reinforcing Uncle Sam's character traits: in cartoons he was quick to anger, smart but not academic, boastful, and independent.

In contrast to Uncle Sam, neither George Washington nor Christopher Columbus has qualified as a national representation of America. Both Washington, especially in Emanuel Leutze's 1852 *Washington Crossing the Delaware* (Metropolitan Museum of Art, New York), and Columbus, visually known to Americans primarily through his incarnations in the United States Capitol Rotunda mural (by John Vanderlyn, installed 1847) and bronze doors (by Randolph Rogers, installed 1863), are linked with the United States in ways that allow their names or faces to be instantly associated with "America." However, as historical personages, they can never incar-

Figure 23.4 Thomas Nast, "Scaly Justice (Uncle Sam)" (*Harper's Weekly*, March 9, 1878).

nate or personify the nation, for that is the job of rhetoric and allegorical abstraction (or, in the case of Uncle Sam, metaphor), not history. For this reason, classes of people, like colonists or Puritans, normally do not represent America as a personification.

Indian males occasionally do serve as such a personification, but their presence as *genius loci* requires some qualification. Both the art historian Hugh Honour and the historian John Higham have written about European proclivities for projecting on to the Native American a vision of noble savage-ness, a state in which the Indian's presumed innocence of worldly experience and uncorrupted manner of living are exalted. Perhaps even more than the female, the male Native American was read into this role, especially in literature, not as specifier of place so much as of position in an evolutionary scale of development in which pre-twentieth-century anthropology invested much credence. None the less male personifications of four-continent im-agery did exist, in sculpture particularly, and in one memorable instance in modern painting.

Benjamin West's *Death of General Wolfe*, 1770, drafts a kneeling Mohawk in neoclassical design to call attention to the Canadian region where Wolfe's death took place. By endowing the Mohawk with a heroic musculature, West, claims Vivien Green Fryd (1995), calls attention to the Indian's nobility as well as his exoticism. Fryd goes on to argue that the Native American in this painting "symbolizes the masculinity of an alien culture, that of the natural, uncivilized man," a masculinity undermined by the Mohawk's "nakedness" which makes him "vulnerable" (Fryd, 1995: 75). West's contemporaries put it differently: "Women can have nothing to do here; all is war; the allegory therefore, if taken from our species, must be a man, and that man must be a warrior," opined philosopher and man of letters Robert Bromley in 1793. If these readings, old and new, are combined, a reason for the male Native American's infrequent assumption of the role of personification of America becomes evident. Associated with war and possessed of a suspect masculinity, the noble male Indian provided an almost irresistible synecdoche for the extinction of his race; as with the female Native American, race rather than place overtook the Indian's metaphorical potential.

Points of View

Perhaps because American art history, a discipline distinctly junior to the study of American history (see Corn, 1998), devoted much of its initial time and energy trying to answer a question – what is American about American art? – that most scholars today consider not only unanswerable but pointless or irrelevant as well, the study of representations of America in the visual arts has not been high on the list of crucial investigation. The history of American art history probably also accounts for the fact that the most comprehensive studies of the topic come from scholars outside the American academy: Hugh Honour, the gifted British author, and E. McClung Fleming, an antiquarian by profession. Commemorating the United States' bicentennial in 1976, Honour wrote *The European Vision of America*, a catalogue for an exhibition that toured Washington, Cleveland, and Paris. This work remains the most exhaustive study of imagery of Native Americans as noble savages and incorporates some of the finest examples of the typologies discussed in this chapter; for example, "fourth-continent" personifications, Native Americans of both genders, and "libertas Americana." Fleming (1967) has emphasized medallions, handkerchiefs, engravings, and other examples far from the art-historical mainstream as it has been conceived in the United States. This may explain why his work is not cited as frequently as Honour's contributions.

Neither author considered the gender implications of the images about which he wrote, and it has since been the case that gender studies have informed art history rather than the other way around. Literary historian Martha Banta (1987: xxvii) comments that, in the last half of the nineteenth century, "occasions for the making of pictorial public statements" were "assigned symbolic value on the spot" by the "habitual" cultural interchangeability of the idea of "American" and the body of woman. In a cogent analysis of the power of this interchangeability, Judy Sund (1993) has hypothesized that the rhetoric which exalted the contribution of American women to the cultural life of the United States was subsumed and made negligible by the images of women in allegorical sculpture (among other media) at the 1893

World's Columbian Exposition in Chicago. When race is added to the mix, as happens when the allegorical representation takes the form of a Native American, the shift from geography to condition as the denotational element of the representation of nation grows exponentially. As an illustration, one thinks of a statue (1837–44) by Luigi Persico that stood to the left of the staircase on the east façade of the United States Capitol (until 1958, when Native-American groups succeeded in having it permanently removed). Composed of a globe-wielding, triumphant Columbus and a half-naked, weak, and frightened Indian woman who cowers at his side, the monument, called *Discovery of America*, uses the woman's figure to forecast a narrative with an inevitable denouement. Such combinations of gender and race in personification imagery await a scholarly assessment.

Likewise, despite great contributions in other subdisciplines of American history, ethnic studies have not been utilized as fully or as specifically as they might be in American art history, with the study of personifications being a case in point. It is true, indeed, that historians of American art have been concerned with the portrayal of Native Americans in painting and sculpture. They have not, for the most part, addressed this issue from any theoretical perspective, although studies of post-colonialism, for instance, would seem to offer access to thinking about how the Native-American image could do double duty as a personification of the country and as its nemesis. Likewise, ethnography and social histories harbor analyses of inter-ethnic stereotyping as well as the more common extrinsic forms of visual prejudice that could freshen the kinds of thinking now attending representations of America. One of the most important characteristics of personification in the alternation from place to race has to do with social condition, a factor crucial to ethnic stereotyping in descriptive categorizations. Thus, for example, the famous nineteenth-century print firm of Currier and Ives produced cozy pictures of "the American farm" that linked a healthy American yeomanry with Nordic races rather than, say, Italian immigrants who owned farms in New Jersey, or Mexicans who worked the land in California.

The American Land

On the other hand, a special case should be made for representations of America as landscape, and the land itself, since both rhetorically and visually Americans metaphorically identified the land as the nation. As Stein (1968: 10) has noted, "American nature argued, by its very existence, the case for the new nation, and . . . to paint it well would release to a receptive beholder its latent, intrinsic significance."

In representing America, landscape imagery stretched American metaphors to their limit and beyond. Pride is paraded, and national identity is pieced together constructively and oppositionally. In the nineteenth century, imagining the United States as its land/nature involved anthropomorphizing waterfalls, prairies, and the wilderness in the sense that their traits or dominant qualities mimic those desired (if not actually possessed) by "Americans" (usually unspecified). Thus Niagara Falls, painted by dozens of artists and engraved by many more, was thought by Americans and foreigners alike to convey the energy and expansiveness characteristic of the people of the United States. Landscape imagery qualified the wilderness as "an American wilderness," unknown in Europe and so unique to America (other measures held no attraction for Americans), its basic appeal an openness and toughness found in its plains and in its inhabitants. The wilderness thereby became the proper sphere of democracy, a difficult concept to pictorialize.

Frederick Jackson Turner, in his 1893 essay on the closing of the American frontier, deemed wilderness an essential ingredient of democracy: "The wilderness masters the colonist. It finds him a European in dress, industries, tools, modes of travel and thought... He must accept the conditions which it furnishes, or perish, and so... little by little he transforms the wilderness, but the outcome is not the old Europe... here is a new product that is American" (1962 [1893]: 30). If representations of America in art include landscape/nature as wilderness, then one comes close, perhaps too close, to the essence of an idea presently under scrutiny: American exceptionalism. Malcolm Bradbury (1995: 7) explains it thus:

> Americans, looking westward, had to think of Europe to triangulate their own situation against the wilderness, the savage, the Pacific. Newly positioned in history, they required the credit of origins and a past, and these they ascribed back to Europe, therefore reserving the new life and the great historical future for themselves. The Europe they imagined was not so much a nation, or even a complex of nations. It was an idea, an opposite, a polar contrast.

In art this dependence–independence duality plays out in landscape paintings composed in modes that subscribe, at least superficially, to European tradition, while inscribing a difference through wilderness imagery. The American subjects of painter Thomas Cole may be taken as exemplar of this relentlessly repeated feature of American landscape painting history. Believing wilderness unique to American nature, Cole, in the 1830s, set about depicting scenery that was very close to disappearing before his very eyes as tourism and development exploited forest and field. Through beautiful scenes of wilderness, Cole thought, he could slow the countryside's destruction or at least cause material-minded Americans to reconsider the loss of a harmonious relationship with nature and the idyllic relationship (that he so ardently desired) of farmers to land. In the sense that Cole's images, such as his famous *Oxbow (View of the Connecticut River near Northampton)* (1836, Metropolitan Museum of Art), actually *were* regarded as representations of America, with a knowing exchange on the part of his Northeastern viewers of the local for the national, Cole succeeded in his aim. From another perspective, as we so well know, his paintings had no discernible effect on what he called "the ravages of the axe."

The nineteenth-century sense, at least among an East coast intellectual elite, that some sort of national representation could be achieved in landscape painting has been the hook on which much American art history has been snared. For almost two decades following the publication in 1969 of Barbara Novak's *American Painting of the Nineteenth Century*, scholars generally followed her lead in asserting the primacy of landscape painting to American art history and to national identity. Only recently has this assertion been subjected to scrutiny, most insightfully in the work of Angela Miller, whose 1993 book, *Empire of the Eye: Landscape Representation and American Cultural Politics, 1825–1875*, dissects the origins of the idea of a national landscape, for whom the idea carried import and why, and what other course they might have followed – how, in other words, the national representation came to be located in landscape. Unlike Novak (1969), who posits an "American" mind that naturalizes the combination of national and land, Miller analyzes national = land as a politicized construction and finds that underneath public rhetoric ran an ambivalence springing from an antagonism between local and national. "National," she wants to say, is and always has been a contested concept; the implications for reading national representation in landscape painting, then, break down not so much into sectionalism, as into the dominance of a single section, the Northeast.

Conclusion

The image with which this chapter began was not only produced in New York but also reproduces it, and much of the Northeast at the end of the nineteenth century. Immigrants settled all over the United States, to be sure, but during the time of the greatest influx New York and other urban centers in the region experienced a denser concentration of newcomers and a more heterogeneous mixture than other areas. Like landscape painting, imaging the United States in popular graphic arts almost invariably was precipitated by events in the Northeast. Uncle Sam and Columbia represent the whole of America but, as it were, kept their residence in New York.

Miller's (1993) sense that "national" has always been a contested concept is at once belied and affirmed by representations of America such as Columbia and Uncle Sam: belied because together and individually they naturalize and incorporate a response that the entity *is* a whole, a unity, and affirmed because, however you cut it, there can be no single concept, America, and especially not if it is pictorialized as rural and male, or female and Europeanized. How will all the other members of the "family" be represented? In the late twentieth century, no answer is forthcoming. As an example, one might take the exhibition, *The West as America*. It was mounted at the National Museum of American Art in 1992 and offered a reading of imagery of the American West as, basically, colonialized (or perhaps appropriated) land, a reading that puts a disagreeably imperial face on traditional affirmations of landscape, and the history of the American West itself, as quintessentially "American." Outrage reached the highest levels of government – a senator, who later admitted he had not seen the show, muttered darkly in the press about convening a congressional inquiry to sort out the show's politics in relation to the museum's funding – and the resulting *brouhaha* proved, if not conclusively at least dramatically, that the issue of how America is to be represented simply won't go away.

REFERENCES

Abrams, Ann Uhry and Palumbo, Anne Cannon (1986) *Goddess, Guardian and Grand Old Gal*. Atlanta: Emory University Press.

Banta, Martha (1987) *Imaging American Women: Idea and Ideals in Cultural History*. New York: Columbia University Press.

Bradbury, Malcolm (1995) *Dangerous Pilgrimages: Trans-Atlantic Mythologies and the Novel*. London: Secker and Warburg.

Corn, Charles (1998) *The Scents of Eden*. New York: Kodanshai International.

Fleming, E. McClung (1967) "From Indian princess to Greek goddess: the American image, 1783–1815," *Winterthur Portfolio*, 3, pp. 37–66.

Fryd, Vivien Green (1986) "Hiram Powers's *America*: "Triumphant as liberty and in unity,"" *American Art Journal*, 18(2), pp. 54–75.

Fryd, Vivien Green (1992) *Art and Empire: the Politics of Ethnicity in the United States Capitol, 1815–1860.* New Haven, Conn.: Yale University Press.

Fryd, Vivien Green (1995) "Rereading the Indian in Benjamin West's *Death of General Wolfe*," *American Art*, spring, pp. 73–85.

Honour, Hugh (1976) *The European Vision of America.* Cleveland: The Cleveland Museum of Art.

Ketchum, Alton (1959) *Uncle Sam: the Man and the Legend.* New York: Hill and Wang.

Miller, Angela (1993) *Empire of the Eye: Landscape Representation and American Cultural Politics, 1825–1875.* Ithaca, NY: Cornell University Press.

Nora, Pierre (1989) "Between memory and history: *les lieux de memoire*," *Representations*, 26, pp. 7–25.

Novak, Barbara (1969) *American Painting of the Nineteenth Century.* New York: Praeger.

Novak, Barbara (1980) *Nature and Culture: American Landscape and Painting, 1825–1875.* New York: Oxford University Press.

Pohl, Frances K. (1994) "Old world, new world: the encounter of cultures on the American frontier," in Stephen F. Eisenman (ed.), *Nineteenth Century Art: a Critical History*, pp. 144–62. London: Thames and Hudson.

Pravoyeur, Pierre and Hargrove, June (1986) *Liberty: the French–American Statue in Art and History.* Philadelphia: Perennial Library.

Stein, Roger (1968) *View and the Vision: Landscape Painting in Nineteenth-century America.* Seattle: Henry Gallery.

Sund, Judy (1993) "Columbus and Columbia in Chicago, 1893: man of genius meets generic woman," *Art Bulletin*, 75(3), pp. 443–66.

Taylor, Joshua C. (1976) "The American cousin," in *America as Art*, pp. 37–94. Washington: Smithsonian Institution Press.

Trachtenberg, Marvin (1986) *The Statue of Liberty.* New York: Penguin.

Turner, Frederick Jackson (1893/1962) *The Frontier in American History.* New York: Holt, Rinehart and Winston.

Bibliography

Politics and Public Life

Abbott, Richard H. (1986) *The Republican Party and the South, 1855–1877: the First Southern Strategy*. Chapel Hill, NC: University of North Carolina Press.

Ackerman, Bruce (1998) *We the People, 2: Transformations*. Cambridge, Mass.: Belknap Press of Harvard University.

Anbinder, Tyler (1992) *Nativism and Slavery: the Northern Know Nothings and the Politics of the 1850s*. New York: Oxford University Press.

Appleby, Joyce O. (1984) *Capitalism and a New Social Order: the Republican Vision of the 1790s*. New York: New York University Press.

Argersinger, Peter H. (1995) *The Limits of Agrarian Radicalism: Western Populism and American Politics*. Lawrence: University Press of Kansas.

Ashworth, John (1983) *"Agrarians" and "Aristocrats": Party Political Ideology in the United States, 1837–1846*. Cambridge: Cambridge University Press.

Ashworth, John (1995) *Slavery, Capitalism, and Politics in the Antebellum Republic*. Cambridge: Cambridge University Press.

Ashworth, John (1996) "Free labor, wage labor, and the slave power: republicanism and the Republican party in the 1850s," in Melvyn Stokes and Stephen Conway (eds), *The Market Revolution in America: Social, Political and Religious Expressions, 1800–1880*, pp. 128–46. Charlottesville: University of Virginia Press.

Atkins, Jonathan M. (1997) *Parties, Politics, and the Sectional Conflict in Tennessee, 1832–1861*. Knoxville: University of Tennessee Press.

Baker, Jean H. (1983) *Affairs of Party: the Political Culture of Northern Democrats in the Mid-nineteenth Century*. Ithaca, NY: Cornell University Press.

Banner, James M. (1967) *To the Hartford Convention: the Federalists and the Origins of Party Politics in the Early Republic, 1789–1815*. New York: Alfred A. Knopf.

Banning, Lance (1978) *The Jeffersonian Persuasion: Evolution of a Party Ideology*. Ithaca, NY: Cornell University Press.

Bardaglio, Peter W. (1995) *Reconstructing the Household: Families, Sex, and the Law in the Nineteenth-century South*. Chapel Hill, NC: University of North Carolina Press.

Barney, William L. (1974) *The Secessionist Impulse: Alabama and Mississippi in 1860*. Princeton, NJ: Princeton University Press.

Baum, Dale (1984) *The Civil War Party System: the Case of Massachusetts, 1848–1876*. Chapel Hill, NC: University of North Carolina Press.

Baxter, Maurice G. (1995) *Henry Clay and the American System*. Lexington: University Press of Kentucky.

Beard, Charles A. and Beard, Mary R. (1933) *The Rise of American Civilization*, 2 vols. New York: Macmillan.

Beatty, Bess (1987) *A Revolution Gone Backward: the Black Response to National Politics, 1876–1896*. New York: Greenwood Press.

Bender, Thomas A. (ed.) (1992) *The Antislavery Debate: Capitalism and Abolitionism as a Problem in Historical Materialism*. Berkeley, CA: University of California Press.

Bensel, Richard F. (1990) *Yankee Leviathan: the Origins of Central State Authority in America, 1859–1877*. Cambridge: Cambridge University Press.

Benson, Lee (1961) *The Concept of Jacksonian Democracy: New York as a Test Case*. Princeton, NJ: Princeton University Press.

Bergeron, Paul A. (1987) *The Presidency of James K. Polk*. Lawrence: University Press of Kansas.

Bergstrom, Randolph E. (1992) *Courting Danger: Inquiry and Law in New York City, 1870–1910*. Ithaca, NY: Cornell University Press.

Beringer, Richard E., Hattaway, Herman, Jones, Archer, and Still Jr, William N. (1986) *Why the South Lost the Civil War*. Athens: University of Georgia Press.

Bernstein, Ivar (1990) *The New York City Draft Riots: their Significance for American Society and Politics in the Age of the Civil War*. New York: Oxford University Press.

Blair, William (1998) *Virginia's Private Civil War: Feeding Body and Soul in the Confederacy, 1861–1865*. New York: Oxford University Press.

Blue, Frederick J. (1973) *The Free Soilers: Third Party Politics, 1848–54*. Urbana: University of Illinois Press.

Boles, John B. and Nolen, Evelyn Thomas (eds) (1987) *Interpreting Southern History: Historiographical Essays in Honor of Sanford W. Higginbotham*. Baton Rouge: Louisiana State University Press.

Bork, Robert H. (1990) *The Tempting of America: the Political Seduction of the Law*. New York: Simon and Schuster.

Bourke, Paul and Debats, Donald (1995) *Washington County: Politics and Community in Antebellum America*. Baltimore, MD: Johns Hopkins University Press.

Bridges, Amy (1984) *A City in the Republic: Antebellum New York and the Origins of Machine Politics*. Cambridge: Cambridge University Press.

Brock, William R. (1973) *Conflict and Transformation: the United States, 1844–1877*. Baltimore, MD: Penguin.

Brock, William R. (1979) *Parties and Political Conscience: American Dilemmas, 1840–1850*. Millwood, NY: KTO Press.

Brown, Roger H. (1964) *The Republic in Peril: 1812*. New York: Columbia University Press.

Brown, Thomas (1985) *Politics and Statesmanship: Essays on the American Whig Party*. New York: Columbia University Press.

Bryce, James (1888) *The American Commonwealth*, 3 vols. London and New York: Macmillan.

Buel Jr, Richard (1972) *Securing the Revolution: Ideology in American Politics, 1789–1815*. Ithaca, NY: Cornell University Press.

Burton, Orville Vernon (1985) *In my Father's House are Many Mansions: Family and Community in Edgefield, South Carolina*. Chapel Hill, NC: University of North Carolina Press.

Bushman, Richard L. (1992) *The Refinement of America: Persons, Houses, Crises*. New York. Alfred A. Knofp.

Campbell, Stanley W. (1970) *The Slave Catchers: Enforcement of the Fugitive Slave Law, 1850–1860*. Chapel Hill, NC: University of North Carolina Press.

Carwardine, Richard J. (1993) *Evangelicals and Politics in Antebellum America*. New Haven, Conn.: Yale University Press.

Chase, Anthony (1997) *Law and History: the Evolution of the American Legal System*. New York: The New Press.

Cherny, Robert W. (1997) *American Politics in the Gilded Age, 1868–1900*. Wheeling, Ill.: Harlan Davidson.

Chused, Richard H. (1994) *Private Acts in Public Places: a Social History of Divorce in the Formative Era of American Family Law.* Philadelphia: University of Pennsylvania Press.

Cole, Donald B. (1984) *Martin Van Buren and the American Political System.* Princeton, NJ: Princeton University Press.

Cole, Donald B. (1993) *The Presidency of Andrew Jackson.* Lawrence: University Press of Kansas.

Cortner, Richard C. (1993) *The Iron Horse and the Constitution: the Railroads and the Transformation of the Fourteenth Amendment.* Westport, Conn.: Greenwood Press.

Cox, Lawanda and Cox, John H. (1961) *Politics, Principles, and Prejudice, 1865–1866: Dilemma of Reconstruction America.* Glencoe, Ill.: The Free Press.

Craven, Avery (1939) *The Repressible Conflict, 1830–1861.* Baton Rouge: Louisiana State University Press.

Crofts, Daniel (1989) *Reluctant Confederates: Upper South Unionists in the Secession Crisis.* Chapel Hill, NC: University of North Carolina Press.

Cunningham Jr, Noble E. (1963) *The Jeffersonian Republicans in Power: Party Operations, 1801–1809.* Chapel Hill, NC: University of North Carolina Press.

Cunningham Jr, Noble E. (1996) *The Presidency of James Monroe.* Lawrence: University Press of Kansas.

Curtis, James C. (1970) *The Fox at Bay: Martin Van Buren and the Presidency, 1837–1841.* Lexington: University Press of Kentucky.

Curtis, Michael Kent (1986) *No State Shall Abridge: the 14th Amendment and the Bill of Rights.* Durham, NC: Duke University Press.

Dalzell Jr, Robert F. (1973) *Daniel Webster and the Trial of American Nationalism, 1843–1852.* Boston, Mass.: Houghton Mifflin.

Dangerfield, George (1952) *The Era of Good Feelings.* New York: Harcourt, Brace and World.

Davidson, Cathy N. (1986) *Revolution and the Word: the Rise of the Novel in America.* New York: Oxford University Press.

Davis, David Brion (1975) *The Problem of Slavery in the Age of Revolution.* Ithaca, NY: Cornell University Press.

Davis, Peggy Cooper (1997) *Neglected Stories: the Constitution and Family Values.* New York: Hill and Wang.

Diggins, John P. (1984) *The Lost Soul of American Politics: Virtue, Self-interest, and the Foundations of Liberalism.* New York: Basic Books.

Doenecke, Justus D. (1981) *The Presidencies of James A. Garfield and Chester A. Arthur.* Lawrence: University Press of Kansas.

Donald, David (1960) *Charles Sumner and the Coming of the Civil War.* New York: Alfred A. Knopf.

Donald, David (1961) *Lincoln Reconsidered: Essays on the Civil War Era.* New York: Vintage Books.

Dykstra, Robert R. (1993) *Bright Radical Star: Black Freedom and White Supremacy on the Hawkeye Frontier.* Cambridge, Mass.: Harvard University Press.

Edwards, Rebecca (1997) *Angels in the Machinery: Gender in American Party Politics from the Civil War to the Progressive Era.* New York: Oxford University Press.

Ellis, Richard E. (1971) *The Jeffersonian Crisis: Courts and Politics in the Young Republic.* New York: Oxford University Press.

Ellis, Richard E. (1987) *The Union at Risk: Jacksonian Democracy, States' Rights and the Nullification Crisis.* New York: Oxford University Press.

Ely Jr, James W. (1995) *The Chief Justiceship of Melville W. Fuller, 1888–1910.* Columbia: University of South Carolina Press.

Faust, Drew Gilpin (1996) *Mothers of Invention: Women of the Slaveholding South in the American Civil War.* Chapel Hill, NC: University of North Carolina Press.

Feller, Daniel (1984) *The Public Lands in Jacksonian Politics*. Madison: University of Wisconsin Press.

Fischer, David Hackett (1965) *The Revolution of American Conservatism: the Federalist Party in the Era of Jeffersonian Democracy*. New York: Harper and Row.

Fitzgerald, Michael W. (1989) *The Union League Movement in the Deep South: Political and Agricultural Change during Reconstruction*. Baton Rouge: Louisiana State University Press.

Foner, Eric (1970) *Free Soil, Free Labor, Free Men: the Ideology of the Republican Party before the Civil War*. New York: Oxford University Press.

Foner, Eric (1986) *Politics and Ideology in the Age of the Civil War*. New York: Oxford University Press.

Foner, Eric (1988) *Reconstruction: America's Unfinished Revolution, 1863–1877*. New York: Harper and Row.

Foner, Philip S. (1941) *Business and Slavery: the New York Merchants and the Irrepressible Conflict*. Chapel Hill, NC: University of North Carolina Press.

Ford Jr, Lacy K. (1988) *Origins of Southern Radicalism: the South Carolina Upcountry, 1800–1860*. New York: Oxford University Press.

Forgie, George (1979) *Patricide in the House Divided: a Psychological Interpretation of Lincoln and his Age*. New York: W. W. Norton.

Formisano, Ronald P. (1971) *The Birth of Mass Political Parties: Michigan, 1827–1861*. Princeton, NJ: Princeton University Press.

Formisano, Ronald P. (1983) *The Transformation of Political Culture: Massachusetts Parties, 1790s–1840s*. New York: Oxford University Press.

Freehling, William W. (1966) *Prelude to Civil War: the Nullification Controversy in South Carolina, 1816–1836*. New York: Harper and Row.

Freehling, William W. (1990) *The Road to Disunion*, vol. 1: *Secessionists at Bay*. New York: Oxford University Press.

Freehling, William W. (1994) *The Reintegration of American History: Slavery and the Civil War*. New York: Oxford University Press.

Freyer, Tony A. (1994) *Producers versus Capitalists: Constitutional Conflict in Antebellum America*. Princeton, NJ: Princeton University Press.

Friedman, Lawrence M. (1985) *A History of American Law*, 2nd edn. New York: Simon and Schuster.

Gallagher, Gary W. (1977) *The Confederate War*. Cambridge, Mass.: Harvard University Press.

Gara, Larry (1991) *The Presidency of Franklin Pierce*. Lawrence: University Press of Kansas.

Genovese, Eugene D. (1965) *The Political Economy of Slavery: Studies in the Economy and Society of the Slave South*. New York: Pantheon.

Gienapp, William E. (1987) *The Origins of the Republican Party, 1852–1856*. New York: Oxford University Press.

Gilmore, Grant (1977) *The Ages of American Law*. New Haven, Conn.: Yale University Press.

Gómez-Quiñones, Juan (1994) *Roots of Chicano Politics, 1600–1940*. Albuquerque: University of New Mexico Press.

Goodman, Nan (1998) *Shifting the Blame: Literature, Law, and the Theory of Accidents in Nineteenth-century America*. Princeton, NJ: Princeton University Press.

Goodman, Paul (1988) *Towards a Christian Republic: Antimasonry and the Great Transition in New England, 1816–1836*. New York: Oxford University Press.

Goodman, Paul (1998) *Of One Blood: Abolitionism and the Origins of Racial Equality*. Berkeley, CA: University of California Press.

Goodwyn, Lawrence (1976) *Democratic Promise: the Populist Moment in America*. New York: Oxford University Press.

Gordon, Robert W. and Nelson, William (1988) "An exchange on critical legal issues between Robert W. Gordon and William Nelson," *Law and History Review*, 6, pp. 139–86.

Gould, Lewis L. (1980) *The Presidency of William McKinley.* Lawrence: University Press of Kansas.

Grossberg, Michael (1985) *Governing the Hearth: Law and the Family in Nineteenth-century America.* Chapel Hill, NC: University of North Carolina Press.

Gyory, Andrew (1998) *Closing the Gate: Race, Politics, and the Chinese Exclusion Act.* Chapel Hill, NC: University of North Carolina Press.

Hall, Kermit L. (1989) *The Magic Mirror: Law in American History.* New York: Oxford University Press.

Hamilton, Holman (1964) *Prologue to Conflict: the Crisis and Compromise of 1850.* New York: W. W. Norton.

Hammond, Bray (1957) *Banks and Politics in America from the Revolution to the Civil War.* Princeton, NJ: Princeton University Press.

Hargraves, Mary W. M. (1985) *The Presidency of John Quincy Adams.* Lawrence: University Press of Kansas.

Harris, William C. (1997) *With Charity for All: Lincoln and the Restoration of the Union.* Lexington: University Press of Kentucky.

Hatch, Nathan O. (1989) *The Democratization of American Christianity.* New Haven, Conn.: Yale University Press.

Hays, Samuel P. (1957) *The Response to Industrialism, 1885–1914.* Chicago: University of Chicago Press.

Heale, M. J. (1982) *The Presidential Quest: Candidates and Images in American Political Culture.* New York: Longman.

Hicks, John D. (1931) *The Populist Revolt: a History of the Farmers' Alliance and the People's Party.* Minneapolis: University of Minnesota Press.

Hobson, Charles E. (1996) *The Great Chief Justice: John Marshall and the Rule of Law.* Lawrence: University Press of Kansas.

Hofstadter, Richard (1948/1973) *The American Political Tradition and the Men who Made It.* New York: Vintage Books.

Hofstadter, Richard (1955) *The Age of Reform: from Bryan to FDR.* New York: Alfred A. Knopf.

Hofstadter, Richard (1969) *The Idea of a Party System: the Rise of Legitimate Opposition in the United States, 1780–1840.* Berkeley, CA: University of California Press.

Hollingsworth, J. Rogers (1963) *The Whirligig of Politics: the Democracy of Cleveland and Bryan.* Chicago: University of Chicago Press.

Holt, Michael F. (1978) *The Political Crisis of the 1850s.* New York: Wiley.

Holt, Michael F. (1999) *The Rise and Fall of the American Whig Party: Jacksonian Politics and the Onset of the Civil War.* New York: Oxford University Press.

Hoogenboom, Ari (1995) *Rutherford B. Hayes: Warrior and President.* Lawrence: University Press of Kansas.

Horwitz, Morton J. (1977) *The Transformation of American Law,* vol. 1: *1780–1860.* Cambridge, Mass.: Harvard University Press.

Horwitz, Morton J. (1992) *The Transformation of American Law,* vol. 2: *The Crisis of Legal Orthodoxy, 1870–1960.* New York: Oxford University Press.

Hovenkamp, Herbert (1991) *Enterprise and American Law, 1836–1937.* Cambridge, Mass.: Harvard University Press.

Howe, Daniel Walker (1979) *The Political Culture of the American Whigs.* Chicago: University of Chicago Press.

Howe, Daniel Walker (1997) *Making the American Self: from Jonathan Edwards to Abraham Lincoln.* Cambridge, Mass.: Harvard University Press.

Hoxie, Frederick E. (1995) *Parading through History: the Making of the Crow Nation in America, 1805–1935.* Cambridge: Cambridge University Press.

Hurst, James Willard (1956) *Law and the Conditions of Freedom: in the Nineteenth-century United States*. Madison: University of Wisconsin Press.

Hyman, Harold M. and Wiecek, William M. (1982) *Equal Justice under Law: Constitutional Development, 1835–1875*. New York: Harper and Row.

Hyman, Michael R. (1990) *The Anti-Redeemers: Hill-country Political Dissenters in the Lower South from Redemption to Populism*. Baton Rouge: Louisiana State University Press.

Johannsen, Robert W. (1989) *The Frontier, the Union, and Stephen A. Douglas*. Urbana: University of Illinois Press.

John, Richard R. (1995) *Spreading the News: the American Postal System from Franklin to Morse*. Cambridge, Mass.: Harvard University Press.

Johnson, Michael P. (1977) *Toward a Patriarchal Republic: the Secession of Georgia*. Baton Rouge: Louisiana State University Press.

Johnstone Jr, Robert M. (1978) *Jefferson and the Presidency: Leadership in the Young Republic*. Ithaca, NY: Cornell University Press.

Jordan, Daniel P. (1983) *Political Leadership in Jefferson's Virginia*. Charlottesville: University Press of Virginia.

Karsten, Peter (1997) *Heart versus Head: Judge-made Law in Nineteenth-century America*. Chapel Hill, NC: University of North Carolina Press.

Keller, Morton (1977) *Affairs of State: Public Life in Late Nineteenth Century America*. Cambridge, Mass.: Belknap Press of Harvard University.

Kelley, Robert (1979) *The Cultural Pattern in American History: the First Century*. New York: Oxford University Press.

Ketcham, Ralph (1984) *Presidents above Party: the First American Presidency, 1789–1829*. Chapel Hill, NC: University of North Carolina Press.

Kleppner, Paul (1979) *The Third Electoral System, 1853–1892: Parties, Voters, and Political Cultures*. Chapel Hill, NC: University of North Carolina Press.

Kohl, Lawrence Frederick (1989) *The Politics of Individualism: Parties and the American Character in the Jacksonian Era*. New York: Oxford University Press.

Lewis, Jan (1983) *The Pursuit of Happiness: Family and Values in Jefferson's Virginia*. New York: Cambridge University Press.

Link, Arthur S. and Patrick, Rembert W. (eds) (1965) *Writing Southern History: Essays in Historiography in Honor of Fletcher M. Green*. Baton Rouge: Louisiana State University Press.

Livermore, Shaw (1962) *The Twilight of Federalism: the Disintegration of the Federalist Party, 1815–1830*. Princeton, NJ: Princeton University Press.

McCormick, Richard L. (1981) *From Realignment to Reform: Political Change in New York State, 1893–1910*. Ithaca, NY: Cornell University Press.

McCormick, Richard L. (1986) *The Party Period and Public Policy: American Politics from the Age of Jackson to the Progressive Era*. New York: Oxford University Press.

McCormick, Richard P. (1966) *The Second American Party System: Party Formation in the Jacksonian Era*. Chapel Hill, NC: University of North Carolina Press.

McCoy, Drew R. (1980) *The Elusive Republic: Political Economy in Jeffersonian America*. Chapel Hill, NC: University of North Carolina Press.

McCoy, Drew R. (1989) *The Last of the Fathers: James Madison and the Republican Legacy*. New York: Cambridge University Press.

McCrary, Peyton (1978) *Abraham Lincoln and Reconstruction: the Louisiana Experiment*. Baton Rouge: Louisiana State University Press.

McCurry, Stephanie (1995) *Masters of Small Worlds: Yeoman Households, Gender Relations, and the Political Culture of the Antebellum South Carolina Low Country*. New York: Oxford University Press.

McDonald, Forest (1976) *The Presidency of Thomas Jefferson*. Lawrence: University Press of Kansas.

McFaul, John M. (1972) *The Politics of Jacksonian Finance*. Ithaca, NY: Cornell University Press.

McGerr, Michael E. (1986) *The Decline of Popular Politics: the American North, 1865–1928*. New York: Oxford University Press.

McMath, Robert C. (1993) *American Populism: a Social History, 1877–1898*. New York: Hill and Wang.

McMillan, Malcolm C. (1986) *The Disintegration of a Confederate State: Three Governors and Alabama's Wartime Home Front, 1861–1865*. Macon, Ga.: Mercer University Press.

McPherson, James M. (1988) *Battle Cry of Freedom: the Civil War Era*. New York: Oxford University Press.

McPherson, James M. (1990) *Abraham Lincoln and the Second American Revolution*. New York: Oxford University Press.

Maizlish, Stephen E. (1983) *The Triumph of Sectionalism: the Transformation of Ohio Politics, 1844–1856*. Kent, Ohio: Kent State University Press.

Marcus, Robert D. (1971) *Grand Old Party: Political Structure in the Gilded Age, 1880–1896*. New York: Oxford University Press.

Marszalek, John F. (1997) *The Petticoat Affair: Manners, Mutiny, and Sex in Andrew Jackson's White House*. New York: The Free Press.

Merk, Frederick (1972) *Slavery and the Annexation of Texas*. New York: Alfred A. Knopf.

Messer-Kruse, Timothy (1998) *The Yankee International: Marxism and the American Reform Tradition, 1848–1876*. Chapel Hill, NC: University of North Carolina Press.

Meyers, Marvin (1957) *The Jacksonian Persuasion: Politics and Belief*. Stanford: Stanford University Press.

Mitchell, Reid (1993) *The Vacant Chair: the Northern Soldier Leaves Home*. New York: Oxford University Press.

Mohr, Clarence L. (1986) *On the Threshold of Freedom: Masters and Slaves in Civil War Georgia*. Athens: University of Georgia Press.

Moore, Barrington (1966) *Social Origins of Dictatorship and Democracy*. Boston: Beacon Press.

Moore, Glover (1953) *The Missouri Controversy, 1819–1821*. Lexington: University Press of Kentucky.

Morgan, H. Wayne (1969) *From Hayes to McKinley: National Party Politics, 1877–1896*. Syracuse, NY: Syracuse University Press.

Morris, Thomas D. (1996) *Southern Slavery and the Law: 1619–1860*. Chapel Hill, NC: University of North Carolina Press.

Morrison, Chaplain W. (1967) *Democratic Politics and Sectionalism: the Wilmot Proviso Controversy*. Chapel Hill, NC: University of North Carolina Press.

Morrison, Michael A. (1997) *Slavery and the American West: the Eclipse of Manifest Destiny and the Coming of the Civil War*. Chapel Hill, NC: University of North Carolina Press.

Nedelsky, Jennifer (1990) *Private Property and the Limits of American Constitutionalism: the Madisonian Framework and its Legacy*. Chicago: University of Chicago Press.

Nevins, Allan (1950) *The Emergence of Lincoln*, 2 vols. New York: Charles Scribner's Sons.

Nichols, Roy F. (1948) *The Disruption of American Democracy*. New York: Macmillan.

Nichols, Roy F. (1966) *Blueprints for Leviathan: American Style*. New York: Harper and Row.

Nieman, Donald G. (ed.) (1992) *The Constitution, Law, and American Life: Critical Aspects of the Nineteenth-century Experience*. Athens: University of Georgia Press.

Novak, Wlliam J. (1996) *The People's Welfare: Law and Regulation in Nineteenth-century America*. Chapel Hill, NC: University of North Carolina Press.

Oestreicher, Richard Jules (1986) *Solidarity and Fragmentation: Working People and Class Consciousness in Detroit, 1875–1900*. Urbana: University of Illinois Press.

Ostler, Jeffrey (1993) *Prairie Populism: the Fate of Agrarian Radicalism in Kansas, Nebraska, and Iowa, 1880–1892*. Lawrence: University Press of Kansas.

Palmer, Bruce (1980) *"Man over Money": the Southern Populist Critique of American Capitalism*. Chapel Hill, NC: University of North Carolina Press.

Paludan, Phillip Shaw (1988) *"A People's Contest": the Union and Civil War, 1861–1865*. New York: Harper and Row (new edn 1996).

Paludan, Phillip Shaw (1994) *The Presidency of Abraham Lincoln*. Lawrence: University Press of Kansas.

Paul, James C. N. (1951) *Rift in the Democracy*. Philadelphia: University of Pennsylvania Press.

Perman, Michael (1984) *The Road to Redemption: Southern Politics, 1869–1879*. Chapel Hill, NC: University of North Carolina Press.

Pessen, Edward (1985) *Jacksonian America: Society, Personality, Politics*. Urbana: University of Illinois Press.

Peterson, Merrill (1987) *The Great Triumvirate: Webster, Clay, and Calhoun*. New York: Oxford University Press.

Pollack, Norman (1962) *The Populist Response to Industrial America: Midwestern Populist Thought*. Cambridge, Mass.: Harvard University Press.

Potter, David (1976) *The Impending Crisis, 1848–1861*. New York: Harper and Row.

Pound, Roscoe (1938) *The Formative Era of American Law*. Boston: Little, Brown and Co.

Rable, George C. (1994) *The Confederate Republic: a Revolution against Politics*. Chapel Hill, NC: University of North Carolina Press.

Randall, J. G. (1945) *Lincoln the President: Springfield to Gettysburg*, 2 vols. London: Eyre and Spottiswoode.

Reitano, Joanne (1994) *The Tariff Question in the Gilded Age: the Great Debate of 1888*. University Park: Pennsylvania State University Press.

Remini, Robert V. (1976) *The Revolutionary Age of Andrew Jackson*. New York: Harper and Row.

Remini, Robert V. (1991) *Henry Clay: Statesman for the Union*. New York: W. W. Norton.

Remini, Robert V. (1997) *Daniel Webster: the Man and his Time*. New York: W. W. Norton.

Richards, David A. J. (1993) *Conscience and the Constitution: History, Theory, and Law of the Reconstruction Amendments*. Princeton, NJ: Princeton University Press.

Risjord, Norman K. (1965) *The Old Republicans: Southern Conservatism in the Age of Jefferson*. New York: Columbia University Press.

Ritter, Gretchen (1997) *Goldbugs and Greenbacks: the Antimonopoly Tradition and the Politics of Finance in America*. Cambridge: Cambridge University Press.

Robinson, Donald L. (1970) *Slavery in the Structure of American Politics, 1765–1820*. New York: Harcourt Brace Jovanovich.

Rogin, Michael Paul (1975) *Fathers and Children: Andrew Jackson and the Subjugation of the American Indian*. New York: Alfred A. Knopf.

Rothman, David J. (1966) *Politics and Power: the United States Senate, 1869–1901*. Cambridge, Mass.: Harvard University Press.

Sanders, Elizabeth (1999) *Roots of Reform: Farmers, Workers, and the American State, 1877–1917*. Chicago: University of Chicago Press.

Schafer, Judith K. (1994) *Slavery, the Civil Law, and the Supreme Court of Louisiana*. Baton Rouge: Louisiana State University Press.

Schlesinger Jr, Arthur M. (1945) *The Age of Jackson*. Boston: Little, Brown and Co.

Schmidt, James P. (1998) *Free to Work: Labor Law, Emancipation, and Reconstruction, 1815–1880*. Athens: University of Georgia Press.

Schneirov, Richard (1998) *Labor and Urban Politics: Class Conflict and the Origins of Modern Liberalism in Chicago, 1864–1897*. Urbana: University of Illinois Press.

Schroeder, John H. (1973) *Mr Polk's War: American Opposition and Dissent, 1846–1848*. Madison: University of Wisconsin Press.

Schwarz, Philip J. (1996) *Slave Laws in Virginia*. Athens: University of Georgia Press.

Sellers, Charles G. (1966) *James K. Polk: Continentalist, 1843–1846*. Princeton, NJ: Princeton University Press.

Sellers, Charles G. (1991) *The Market Revolution: Jacksonian America, 1815–1846*. New York: Oxford University Press.

Semonche, John E. (1978) *Charting the Future: the Supreme Court Responds to a Changing Society, 1890–1920*. Westport, Conn.: Greenwood Press.

Semonche, John E. (1998) *Keeping the Faith: a Cultural History of the US Supreme Court*. Lanham, MD: Rowman and Littlefield.

Sewell, Richard H. (1976) *Ballots for Freedom: Antislavery Politics in the United States, 1837–1860*. New York: Oxford University Press.

Shade, William G. (1972) *Banks or No Banks: the Money Issue in Western Politics, 1832–1865*. Detroit: Wayne State University Press.

Sharp, James Roger (1970) *The Jacksonians versus the Banks: Politics in the States after the Panic of 1837*. New York: Columbia University Press.

Silbey, Joel (1985) *The Partisan Imperative: the Dynamics of American Politics before the Civil War*. New York: Oxford University Press.

Simpson, Brooks D. (1998) *The Reconstruction Presidents*. Lawrence: University Press of Kansas.

Sklar, Kathryn Kish (1995) *Florence Kelley and the Nation's Work: the Rise of Women's Political Culture, 1830–1900*. New Haven, Conn.: Yale University Press.

Sklar, Martin J. (1988) *The Corporate Reconstruction of American Capitalism, 1890–1916: the Market, the Law, and Politics*. Cambridge: Cambridge University Press.

Skocpol, Theda (1992) *Protecting Soldiers and Mothers: the Political Origins of Social Policy in the United States*. Cambridge, Mass.: Harvard University Press.

Skowronek, Stephen (1982) *Building a New American State: the Expansion of National Administrative Capacities, 1877–1920*. New York: Cambridge University Press.

Smith, Elbert B. (1975) *The Presidency of James Buchanan*. Lawrence: University Press of Kansas.

Smith, Elbert B. (1988) *The Presidencies of Zachary Taylor and Millard Fillmore*. Lawrence: University Press of Kansas.

Spetter, Allan B. (1987) *The Presidency of Benjamin Harrison*. Lawrence: University Press of Kansas.

Sproat, John G. (1968) *"The Best Men": Liberal Reformers in the Gilded Age*. New York: Oxford University Press.

Stanley, Robert (1993) *Dimensions of Law in the Service of Order: Origins of the Federal Income Tax, 1861–1913*. New York: Oxford University Press.

Stegmaier, Mark J. (1996) *Texas, New Mexico, and the Compromise of 1850: Boundary Dispute and Sectional Crisis*. Kent, Ohio: Kent State University Press.

Summers, Mark W. (1987) *The Plundering Generation: Corruption and the Crisis of the Union, 1849–1861*. New York: Oxford University Press.

Taylor, Alan (1995) *William Cooper's Town: Power and Persuasion on the Frontier of the Early American Republic*. New York: Alfred A. Knopf.

Thornton III, J. Mills (1978) *Politics and Power in a Slave Society: Alabama, 1800–1860*. Baton Rouge: Louisiana State University Press.

Tomlins, Christopher L. (1993) *Law, Labor, and Ideology in the Early American Republic*. Cambridge: Cambridge University Press.

Varon, Elizabeth (1998) *We Mean to be Counted: White Women and Politics in Antebellum Virginia*. Chapel Hill, NC: University of North Carolina Press.

Vinovskis, Maris (ed.) (1990) *Toward a Social History of the American Civil War: Exploratory Essays*. Cambridge: Cambridge University Press.

Wahl, Jenny Bourne (1998) *The Bondsmen Burden: an Economic Analysis of the Common Law of Southern Slavery*. Cambridge: Cambridge University Press.

Waldstreicher, David (1997) *In the Midst of Perpetual Fetes: the Making of American Nationalism, 1776–1820*. Chapel Hill, NC: University of North Carolina Press.

Wang, Xi (1997) *The Trial of Democracy: Black Suffrage and Northern Republicans, 1860–1910*. Athens: University of Georgia Press.

Ward, John W. (1962) *Andrew Jackson: Symbol for an Age*. New York: Oxford University Press.

Watson, Harry L. (1981) *Jacksonian Politics and Community Conflict: the Emergence of the Second Party System in Cumberland County, North Carolina*. Baton Rouge: Louisiana State University Press.

Watson, Harry L. (1990) *Liberty and Power: the Politics of Jacksonian America*. New York: Hill and Wang.

Watts, Steven (1987) *The Republic Reborn: War and the Making of Liberal America, 1790–1820*. Baltimore, MD: Johns Hopkins University Press.

Welch, Richard E. (1988) *The Presidencies of Grover Cleveland*. Lawrence: University Press of Kansas.

White, G. Edward (1991) *The Marshall Court and Cultural Change, 1815–1835*. New York: Oxford University Press.

Wiebe, Robert H. (1967) *The Search for Order, 1877–1920*. New York: Hill and Wang.

Wiebe, Robert H. (1984) *The Opening of American Society: From the Adoption of the Constitution to the Eve of Disunion*. New York: Alfred A. Knopf.

Wilentz, Sean (1984) *Chants Democratic: New York City and the Rise of the American Working Class, 1788–1850*. New York: Oxford University Press.

Williams, Lou Falkner (1996) *The Great South Carolina Ku Klux Trials, 1871–1872*. Athens: University of Georgia Press.

Williams, R. Hal (1973) *The Democratic Party and California Politics, 1880–1896*. Stanford: Stanford University Press.

Wood, Gordon S. (1970) *The Creation of the American Republic*. Chapel Hill, NC: University of North Carolina Press.

Wood, Gordon S. (1992) *The Radicalism of the American Revolution*. New York: Alfred A. Knopf.

Young, James Sterling (1966) *The Washington Community, 1800–1828*. New York: Columbia University Press.

Zagarri, Rosemarie (1998) "The rights of man and woman in post-revolutionary America," *William and Mary Quarterly*, 3rd ser., 55, pp. 203–30.

Zuczek, Richard M. (1996) *State of Rebellion: Reconstruction in South Carolina*. Columbia: University of South Carolina Press.

Foreign Relations

Anderson, David L. (1986) *Imperialism and Idealism: American Diplomats in China*. Bloomington, Ind.: Indiana University Press.

Bailey, Thomas A. (1948) *The Man in the Street: the Impact of American Public Opinion on Foreign Policy*. New York: Macmillan.

Beard, Charles A. and Beard, Mary R. (1927) *The Rise of American Civilization*, 2 vols. New York: Macmillan.

Beisner, Robert L. (1968) *Twelve Against Empire: the Anti-imperialists, 1898–1900*. New York: McGraw-Hill.

Beisner, Robert L. (1975) *From the Old Diplomacy to the New, 1865–1900*. New York: Thomas Y. Cowell.

Belohlavek, John M. (1985) *"Let the Eagle Soar!": the Foreign Policy of Andrew Jackson*. Lincoln: University of Nebraska Press.

Bemis, Samuel Flagg (1936) *A Diplomatic History of the United States.* New York: Henry Holt.

Bemis, Samuel Flagg (1949) *John Quincy Adams and the Foundations of American Foreign Policy.* New York: Alfred A. Knopf.

Benjamin, Jules R. (1990) *The United States and the Origins of the Cuban Revolution.* Princeton, NJ: Princeton University Press.

Campbell, Charles S. (1976) *The Transformation of American Foreign Relations, 1865–1900.* New York: Harper and Row.

de Conde, Alexander (1976) *This Affair of Louisiana.* New York: Scribner.

Cook, Adrian (1975) *The Alabama Claims.* Ithaca, NY: Cornell University Press.

Cooling, B. Franklin (1979) *Gray Steel and Blue Water Navy: the Formative Years of America's Military–industrial Complex, 1881–1917.* Hamden, Conn.: Archon Books.

Crook, D. P. (1974) *The North, the South, and the Powers.* New York: Wiley.

Darby, Philip (1987) *Three Faces of Imperialism: British and American Approaches to Asia and Africa, 1870–1970.* New Haven, Conn.: Yale University Press.

Duignan, Peter and Gann, L. H. (1984) *The United States and Africa.* Cambridge: Cambridge University Press.

Fairbank, John K. (1953) *Trade and Diplomacy on the China Coast: the Opening of the Treaty Ports, 1842–1854.* Cambridge, Mass.: Harvard University Press.

Frazier, Donald S. (ed.) (1998) *The United States and Mexico at War: Nineteenth-century Expansion and Conflict.* New York: Simon and Schuster.

Fredrickson, George M. (1971) *The Black Image in the White Mind: the Debate on Afro-American Character and Destiny, 1817–1914.* New York: Harper and Row.

Goetzmann, William H. (1966) *When the Eagle Screamed: the Romantic Horizon in American Diplomacy, 1800–1860.* New York: Alfred A. Knopf.

Gould, Lewis L. (1982) *The Spanish-American War and President McKinley.* Lawrence: University Press of Kansas.

Graebner, Norman (1955) *Empire on the Pacific.* New York: Ronald Press.

Hagan, Kenneth J. (1973) *American Gunboat Diplomacy and the Old Navy, 1877–1889.* Westport, Conn.: Greenwood Press.

Haynes, Sam W. (1997) *James K. Polk and the Expansionist Impulse.* New York: Longman.

Haynes, Sam W. and Morris, Christopher (eds) (1997) *Manifest Destiny and Empire: American Antebellum Expansionism.* College Station: Texas A and M University Press.

Healy, David (1963) *The US in Cuba, 1898–1902.* Madison: University of Wisconsin Press.

Hearden, Patrick J. (1982) *Independence and Empire: the New South's Cotton Mill Campaign, 1865–1901.* DeKalb, Ill.: Northern Illinois University Press.

Heidler, David S. and Heidler, Jeanne T. (1996) *Old Hickory's War: Andrew Jackson and the Quest for Empire.* Mechanicsburg, PA: Stackpole.

Hickey, Donald (1989) *The War of 1812: a Forgotten Conflict.* Urbana: University of Illinois Press.

Hietala, Thomas (1985) *Manifest Design: Anxious Aggrandizement in Late Jacksonian America.* Ithaca, NY: Cornell University Press.

Holbo, Paul (1983) *Tarnished Expansion: the Alaska Scandal, the Press, and Congress, 1867–1871.* Knoxville: University of Tennessee Press.

Horsman, Reginald (1981) *Race and Manifest Destiny.* Cambridge, Mass.: Harvard University Press.

Hubbard, Charles (1998) *The Burden of Confederate Diplomacy.* Knoxville: University of Tennessee Press.

Hunt, Michael H. (1983) *The Making of a Special Relationship: the US and China to 1914.* New York: Columbia University Press.

Hunt, Michael H. (1987) *Ideology and US Foreign Policy.* New Haven, Conn.: Yale University Press.

Iriye, Akira (1977) *From Nationalism to Internationalism: US Foreign Policy to 1914.* London: Routledge and Kegan Paul.

Johnson, John (1990) *A Hemisphere Apart: the Foundations of United States Foreign Policy towards Latin America.* Baltimore, MD: Johns Hopkins University Press.

Jones, Howard (1977) *To the Webster Ashburton Treaty: a Study in Anglo-American Relations, 1783–1843.* Chapel Hill, NC: University of North Carolina Press.

Jones, Howard (1992) *Union in Peril: the Crisis over British Intervention and the Civil War.* Chapel Hill, NC: University of North Carolina Press.

Kaplan, Amy and Pease, Donald E. (eds) (1993) *Cultures of United States Imperialism.* Durham, NC: Duke University Press.

LaFeber, Walter (1963) *The New Empire: an Interpretation of American Expansion, 1860–1898.* Ithaca, NY: Cornell University Press.

LaFeber, Walter (1993) *The American Search for Opportunity, 1865–1913.* Cambridge: Cambridge University Press.

LaFeber, Walter (1997) *The Clash: US–Japanese Relations Throughout History.* New York: Norton.

Langley, Lester D. (1976) *Struggle for the American Mediterranean: US–European Rivalries in the Gulf–Caribbean, 1776–1904.* Athens: University of Georgia Press.

Lewis Jr, James E. (1998) *The American Union and the Problem of Neighborhood: the United States and the Collapse of the Spanish Empire, 1783–1829.* Chapel Hill, NC: University of North Carolina Press.

Linn, Brian M. (1989) *The US Army and Counterinsurgency in the Philippine War, 1899–1902.* Chapel Hill, NC: University of North Carolina Press.

McCormick, Thomas J. (1967) *China Market: America's Quest for Informal Empire, 1893–1901.* Chicago: Quadrangle.

Mattox, Henry E. (1989) *The Twilight of Amateur Diplomacy.* Kent, Ohio: Kent State University Press.

May, Ernest R. (1968) *American Imperialism: a Speculative Essay.* New York: Atheneum.

May, Ernest R. (1975) *The Making of the Monroe Doctrine.* Cambridge, Mass.: Belknap Press of Harvard University.

May, Robert E. (1973) *The Southern Dream of a Caribbean Empire, 1854–1861.* Baton Rouge: Louisiana State University Press.

May, Robert E. (ed.) (1995) *The Union, the Confederacy, and the Atlantic Rim.* West Lafayette, Ind.: Purdue University Press.

Miller, Stuart Creighton (1982) *"Benevolent Assimilation": the American Conquest of the Philippines, 1899–1902.* New Haven, Conn.: Yale University Press.

Osborne, Thomas J. (1981) *Empire Can Wait: American Opposition to Hawaiian Annexation, 1893–1898.* Kent, Ohio: Kent State University Press.

Owsley Jr, Frank L. and Smith, Gene A. (1997) *Filibusters and Expansionists: Jeffersonian Manifest Destiny, 1800–1821.* Tuscaloosa: University of Alabama Press.

Paolino, Ernest N. (1973) *The Foundations of American Empire: William Henry Seward and US Foreign Policy.* Ithaca, NY: Cornell University Press.

Perkins, Bradford (1968) *The Great Rapprochement: England and the United States, 1895–1914.* New York: Atheneum.

Perkins, Bradford (1995) *Creation of a Republican Empire, 1776–1865.* Cambridge, Mass.: Harvard University Press.

Perkins, Dexter (1957) *Foreign Policy and the American Spirit.* Ithaca, NY: Cornell University Press.

Perkins, Dexter (1963) *A History of the Monroe Doctrine.* Boston: Little Brown.

Plesur, Milton (1971) *America's Outward Thrust: Approaches to Foreign Affairs, 1865–1890.* DeKalb, Ill.: Northern Illinois University Press.

Pletcher, David M. (1958) *Rails, Mines, and Progress: Seven American Promoters and Mexico, 1876–1910*. Ithaca, NY: Cornell University Press.

Pratt, Julius W. (1955) *A History of United States Foreign Policy.* Englewood Cliffs, NJ: Prentice-Hall.

Rakestraw, Donald and Jones, Howard (1977) *Prologue to Manifest Destiny: Anglo-American Relations in the 1840s*. New York: Scholarly Resources.

Rosenberg, Emily S. (1982) *Spreading the American Dream: American Economic and Cultural Expansion, 1890–1945*. New York: Hill and Wang.

Rydell, Robert W. (1984) *All the World's a Fair: Visions of Empire at American International Expositions, 1876–1916*. Chicago: University of Chicago Press.

Saul, Norman (1991) *Distant Friends: the United States and Russia, 1763–1867*. Lawrence: University Press of Kansas.

Schonberger, Howard B. (1971) *Transportation to the Seaboard: the Communication Revolution and American Foreign Policy, 1860–1900*. Westport, Conn.: Greenwood Press.

Schoonover, Thomas (1991) *The United States in Central America, 1860–1911*. Durham, NC: Duke University Press.

Schroeder, John (1995) *Shaping a Maritime Empire: the Commercial and Diplomatic Role of the American Navy, 1829–1861*. Westport, Conn.: Greenwood Press.

Shulman, Mark Russell (1995) *Navalism and the Emergence of American Sea Power, 1882–1893*. Annapolis, MD: Naval Institute Press.

Sofaer, Abraham D. (1976) *War, Foreign Affairs and Constitutional Power: the Origins*. Cambridge, Mass.: Harvard University Press.

Stagg, J. C. A. (1993) *Mr Madison's War: Politics, Diplomacy, and Warfare in the Early American Republic, 1783–1830*. Princeton, NJ: Princeton University Press.

Stephanson, Anders (1995) *Manifest Destiny: American Expansionism and the Empire of Right*. New York: Hill and Wang.

Stevens, Kenneth R. (1989) *Border Diplomacy: the Caroline and McLeod Affairs in Anglo-American–Canadian Relations, 1837–1842*. Tuscaloosa: University of Alabama Press.

Terrill, Tom E. (1973) *The Tariff, Politics, and American Foreign Policy, 1874–1901*. Westport, Conn.: Greenwood Press.

Thomson Jr, J. C., Stanley, P., and Perry, J. C. (1981) *Sentimental Imperialists: the American Experience in East Asia*. New York: Harper.

Trask, David F. (1981) *The War with Spain in 1898*. New York: Macmillan.

Tucker, Robert W. and Hendrickson, David C. (1990) *Empire of Liberty: the Statecraft of Thomas Jefferson*. New York: Oxford University Press.

Weeks, William (1992) *John Quincy Adams and American Global Empire*. Lexington: University Press of Kentucky.

Williams, Walter L. (1980) "United States Indian policy and the debate over Philippine annexation: implications for the origins of American imperialism," *Journal of American History*, 66, pp. 810–31.

Williams, William Appleman (1959) *The Tragedy of American Diplomacy.* Cleveland, Ohio: World Publishing.

Williams, William Appleman (1969) *The Roots of the Modern American Empire*. New York: Random House.

Young, Marilyn B. (1968) *The Rhetoric of Empire: American China Policy, 1895–1901*. Cambridge, Mass.: Harvard University Press.

The Economy and Class Formations

Abramovitz, Moses (1993) "The search for sources of economic growth: areas of ignorance, old and new," *Journal of Economic History*, 53, pp. 217–43.

American Social History Project (1989) *Who Built America? Working People and the Nation's Economy: Politics, Culture and Society*, 2 vols. New York: Pantheon.

Anderson, Ralph V. and Gallman, Robert E. (1977) "Slaves as fixed capital: slave labor and southern economic development," *Journal of American History*, 64, pp. 24–46.

Aron, Cindy Sondik (1987) *Ladies and Gentlemen of the Civil Service: Middle-class Workers in Victorian America*. New York: Oxford University Press.

Baron, Ava (ed.) (1991) *Work Engendered: Toward a New History of American Labor*. Ithaca, NY: Cornell University Press.

Beisel, Nicola (1997) *Imperiled Innocents: Anthony Comstock and Family Reproduction in Victorian America*. Princeton, NJ: Princeton University Press.

Bender, Thomas C. (1978) *Community and Social Change in America*. New Brunswick, NJ: Rutgers University Press.

Berk, Gerald (1994) *Alternative Tracks: the Constitution of American Industrial Order, 1865–1917*. Baltimore, MD: Johns Hopkins University Press.

Biggs, Lindy (1996) *The Rational Factory: Architecture, Technology, and Work in America's Age of Mass Production*. Baltimore, MD: Johns Hopkins University Press.

Blackmar, Elizabeth (1989) *Manhattan for Rent, 1785–1850*. Ithaca, NY: Cornell University Press.

Blatz, Perry K. (1994) *Democratic Miners: Work and Labor Relations in the Anthracite Coal Industry, 1875–1925*. Albany: State University of New York Press.

Bledstein, Burton J. (1976) *The Culture of Professionalism: the Middle Class and the Development of Higher Education in America*. New York: W. W. Norton.

Blumin, Stuart M. (1976) *The Urban Threshold: Growth and Change in a Nineteenth-century American Community*. Chicago: University of Chicago Press.

Blumin, Stuart M. (1989) *The Emergence of the Middle Class: Social Experience in the American City, 1769–1900*. Cambridge: Cambridge University Press.

Boydston, Jeanne (1990) *Home and Work: Housework, Wages, and the Ideology of Labor in the Early Republic*. New York: Oxford University Press.

Brady, Dorothy S. (1972) "Consumption and the style of life," in Lance Davis et al. (eds), *American Economic Growth: an Economist's History of the United States*. pp. 61–89. New York: Harper and Row.

Brody, David (1960) *Steelworkers in America: the Nonunion Era*. Cambridge, Mass: Harvard University Press.

Brown, John K. (1995) *The Baldwin Locomotive Works, 1831–1915: a Study in American Industrial Practice*. Baltimore, MD: Johns Hopkins University Press.

Brundage, David (1994) *The Making of Western Labor Radicalism: Denver's Organized Workers, 1878–1905*. Urbana: University of Illinois Press.

Bullock, Steven C. (1996) *Revolutionary Brotherhood: Freemasonry and the Transformation of the Social Order, 1730–1840*. Chapel Hill, NC: University of North Carolina Press.

Burrows, Edwin G. and Wallace, Mike (1999) *Gotham: a History of New York City to 1898*. New York: Oxford University Press.

Bushman, Richard L. (1992) *The Refinement of America: Persons, Houses, Cities*. New York: Vintage.

Carlson, W. Bernard (1991) *Innovation as a Social Process: Elisha Thomson and the Rise of General Electric, 1870–1900*. Cambridge: Cambridge University Press.

Carnes, Mark and Griffen, Clyde (eds) (1990) *Meanings for Manhood: Constructions of Masculinity in Victorian America*. Chicago: University or Chicago Press.

Carosso, Vincent P. (1987) *The Morgans: Private International Bankers, 1854–1913*. Cambridge, Mass.: Harvard University Press.

Chandler, Alfred D. (1977) *The Visible Hand: the Managerial Revolution in American Business*. Cambridge, Mass.: Harvard University Press.

Chandler, Alfred D. (1990) *Scale and Scope: the Dynamics of Industrial Capitalism*. Cambridge, Mass.: Harvard University Press.

Clark, Christopher (1990) *The Roots of Rural Capitalism: Western Massachusetts, 1780–1861*. Ithaca, NY: Cornell University Press.

Clark, Victor S. (1916) *History of Manufacturers in the United States*, vol. 1: *1607–1860*. Washington, DC: Carnegie Institution of Washington.

Clawson, Mary Ann (1989) *Constructing Brotherhood: Class, Gender and Fraternalism*. Princeton, NJ: Princeton University Press.

Clement, Priscilla Ferguson (1997) *Growing Pains: Children in the Industrial Age, 1850–1890*. New York: Twayne.

Cochran, Thomas C. (1981) *Frontiers of Change: Early Industrialism in America*. New York: Oxford University Press.

Cochran, Thomas C. and Miller, William (1942) *The Age of Enterprise: a Social History of Industrial America*. New York: Macmillan.

Commons, John et al. (1918–35) *A History of Labor in the United States*, 4 vols. New York: Augustus M. Kelley, 1966.

Craig, Lee A. (1993) *To Sow One Acre More: Childbearing and Farm Productivity in the Antebellum North*. Baltimore, MD: Johns Hopkins University Press.

Creighton, Margaret S. (1995) *Rites and Passages: the Experience of American Whaling, 1830–1870*. Cambridge: Cambridge University Press.

Cronon, William (1991) *Nature's Metropolis: Chicago and the Great West*. New York: W. W. Norton.

Curry, Leonard P. (1997) *The Corporate City: the American City as a Political Entity, 1800–1850*. Westport, Conn.: Greenwood Press.

Dalzell Jr, Robert F. (1987) *Enterprising Elite: the Boston Associates and the World They Made*. Cambridge, Mass.: Harvard University Press.

Danhof, Clarence H. (1969) *Change in Agriculture: the Northern United States, 1820–1870*. Cambridge, Mass.: Harvard University Press.

Davis, Lance E. and Cull, Robert J. (eds) (1994) *International Capital Markets and American Economic Growth, 1820–1914*. Cambridge: Cambridge University Press.

Dawley, Alan (1976) *Class and Community: the Industrial Revolution in Lynn*. Cambridge, Mass.: Harvard University Press.

D'Emilio, John and Freedman, Estelle B. (1988) *Intimate Matters: a History of Sexuality in America*. New York: Harper and Row.

Dobbin, Frank (1994) *Forging Industrial Policy: the United States, Britain, and France in the Railway Age*. Cambridge: Cambridge University Press.

Domosh, Mona (1996) *Invented Cities: the Creation of Landscape in Nineteenth-century New York and Boston*. New Haven, Conn.: Yale University Press.

Dublin, Thomas (1979) *Women at Work: the Transformation of Work and Community in Lowell, Massachusetts, 1826–1860*. New York: Columbia University Press.

Duis, Perry R. (1998) *Challenging Chicago: Coping with Everyday Life, 1837–1920*. Urbana: University of Illinois Press.

Dunlavy, Coleen A. (1994) *Politics and Industrialization: Early Railroads in the United States and Prussia*. Princeton, NJ: Princeton University Press.

Earle, Carville (1992) *Geographical Inquiry and American Historical Problems*. Stanford: Stanford University Press.

Edwards, Rebecca B. (1997) *Angels in the Machinery: Gender in American Party Politics from the Civil War to the Progressive Era*. New York: Oxford University Press.

Einhorn, Robin L. (1991) *Property Rules: Political Economy in Chicago, 1833–1872*. Chicago: University of Chicago Press.

Engerman, Stanley L. and Gallman, Robert E. (1983) "US economic growth, 1783–1860," *Research in Economic History,* 8, pp. 1–46.

Engerman, Stanley L. and Gallman, Robert E. (eds) (1986) *Long-term Factors in American Economic Growth.* Chicago: University of Chicago Press.

Engerman, Stanley L. and Gallman, Robert E. (eds) (1996–9) *Cambridge Economic History of the United States,* 2 vols. Cambridge: Cambridge University Press.

Ethington, Philip J. (1994) *The Public City: the Political Construction of Urban Life in San Francisco, 1850–1900.* Cambridge: Cambridge University Press.

Fink, Leon (1983) *Workingman's Democracy: the Knights of Labor and American Politics.* Urbana: University of Illinois Press.

Fishlow, Albert (1965) *American Railroads and the Transformation of the Antebellum Economy.* Cambridge, Mass.: Harvard University Press.

Fogel, Robert W. (1964) *Railroads and American Economic Growth: Essays in Econometric History.* Baltimore, MD: Johns Hopkins University Press.

Foner, Philip (1947–87) *History of the Labor Movement in the United States,* 8 vols. New York: International Publishers.

Formanek-Brunell, Miriam (1994) *Made to Play House: Dolls and the Commercialization of American Girlhood, 1830–1930.* New Haven, Conn.: Yale University Press.

Frank, Stephen M. (1998) *Life with Father: Parenthood and Masculinity in the Nineteenth-century American North.* Baltimore, MD: Johns Hopkins University Press.

Frisch, Michael H. (1972) *Town into City: Springfield, Massachusetts, and the Meaning of Community, 1840–1880.* Cambridge, Mass.: Harvard University Press.

Galenson, David W. (1981) *White Servitude in Colonial America: an Economic Analysis.* Cambridge: Cambridge University Press.

Gallman, Robert E. and Wallis, John Joseph (eds) (1992) *American Economic Growth and Standards of Living before the Civil War.* Chicago: University of Chicago Press.

Gates, Paul Wallace (1960) *The Farmer's Age: Agriculture, 1815–1860.* New York: Holt, Rinehart and Winston.

Gatewood, Willard B. (1990) *Aristocrats of Color: the Black Elite, 1880–1920.* Bloomington, Ind.: Indiana University Press.

Gerber, David A. (1989) *The Making of an American Pluralism: Buffalo, New York, 1825–1860.* Urbana: University of Illinois Press.

Gilbert, James B. (1972) *Designing the Industrial State: the Intellectual Pursuit of Collectivism in America, 1880–1940.* Chicago: Quadrangle.

Gilkeson Jr, John S. (1986) *Middle-class Providence, 1820–1940.* Princeton, NJ: Princeton University Press.

Gilmore, Glenda Elizabeth (1996) *Gender and Jim Crow: Women and the Politics of White Supremacy in North Carolina, 1896–1820.* Chapel Hill, NC: University of North Carolina Press.

Glaab, Charles N. and Brown, A. Theodore (1967) *A History of Urban America.* New York: Macmillan.

Glickstein, Jonathan A. (1991) *Concepts of Free Labor in Antebellum America.* New Haven, Conn.: Yale University Press.

Goldfield, David (1982) *Cottonfields and Skyscrapers: Southern City and Region, 1607–1980.* Baton Rouge: Louisiana State University Press.

Goldin, Claudia and Rockoff, Hugh (eds) (1992) *Strategic Factors in Nineteenth-century American Economic History: a Volume to Honor Robert W. Fogel.* Chicago: University of Chicago Press.

Goodrich, Carter (1960) *Government Promotion of American Canals and Railroads, 1800–1890.* New York: Columbia University Press.

Gordon, Sarah H. (1997) *Passage to Union: How the Railroads Transformed American Life, 1829–1929*. Chicago: University of Chicago Press.

Greenberg, Amy S. (1998) *Cause for Alarm: the Volunteer Fire Department in the Nineteenth-century City*. Princeton, NJ: Princeton University Press.

Greenwood, Janette Thomas (1994) *Bittersweet Legacy: the Black and White "Better Classes" in Charlotte, 1850–1910*. Chapel Hill, NC: University of North Carolina Press.

Gutman, Herbert (1977) *Work, Culture, and Society in Industrializing America: Essays in American Working-class History*. New York: Vintage.

Haber, Samuel (1991) *The Quest for Authority and Honor in the American Professions, 1750–1990*. Chicago: University of Chicago Press.

Hahn, Stephen and Prude, Jonathan (eds) (1985) *The Countryside in the Age of Capitalist Transformation*. Chapel Hill, NC: University of North Carolina Press.

Halpern, Rick and Morris, Jonathan (eds) (1997) *American Exceptionalism? US Working-class Formation in an International Context*. New York: St Martin's Press.

Halttunen, Karen (1982) *Confidence Men and Painted Women: a Study of Middle-class Culture in America, 1830–1870*. New Haven, Conn.: Yale University Press.

Hartz, Louis (1955) *The Liberal Tradition in America: an Interpretation of American Political Thought since the Revolution*. New York: Harcourt, Brace.

Hattam, Victoria C. (1993) *Labor Visions and State Power: the Origins of Business Unionism in the United States*. Princeton, NJ: Princeton University Press.

Henretta, James A. (1991) *The Origins of American Capitalism: Collected Essays*. Boston: Northeastern University Press.

Herbert, T. Walter (1993) *Dearest Beloved: the Hawthornes and the Making of the Middle-class Family*. Berkeley, CA: University of California Press.

Hewitt, Nancy (1984) *Women's Activism and Social Change: Rochester, New York, 1822–1872*. Ithaca, NY: Cornell University Press.

Higginbotham, Evelyn Brooks (1993) *Righteous Discontent: the Women's Movement in the Black Baptist Church, 1880–1920*. Cambridge, Mass.: Harvard University Press.

Hilkey, Judy (1997) *Character is Capital: Success Manuals and Manhood in Gilded Age America*. Chapel Hill, NC: University of North Carolina Press.

Hindle, Brooke and Lubar, Steven (eds) (1986) *Engines of Change: the American Industrial Revolution, 1790–1860*. Washington, DC: Smithsonian Institution Press.

Hofstadter, Richard (1955) *The Age of Reform: from Bryan to FDR*. New York: Alfred A. Knopf.

Hoke, Donald R. (1990) *Ingenious Yankees: the Rise of the American System of Manufactures in the Private Sector*. New York: Columbia University Press.

Holleran, Michael (1998) *Boston's "Changeful Times": Origins of Preservation and Planning in America*. Baltimore, MD: Johns Hopkins University Press.

Homberger, Eric (1994) *Scenes from the Life of a City: Corruption and Conscience in Old New York*. New Haven, Conn.: Yale University Press.

Hoy, Suellen (1995) *Chasing Dirt: the American Pursuit of Cleanliness*. New York: Oxford University Press.

Jackson, Kenneth T. (1985) *Crabgrass Frontier*. New York: Oxford University Press.

James, John A. (1978) *Money and Capital Markets in Postbellum America*. Princeton, NJ: Princeton University Press.

Jameson, Elizabeth (1998) *All that Glitters: Class, Conflict, and Community in Cripple Creek*. Urbana: University of Illinois Press.

John, Richard (1997) "Elaborations, revisions, dissents: Alfred D. Chandler Jr's *The Visible Hand* after twenty years," *Business History Review*, 71, pp. 151–200.

Johnson, Paul E. (1978) *A Shopkeeper's Millennium: Society and Revival in Rochester, New York, 1815–1837*. New York: Hill and Wang.

Judd, Richard W. (1997) *Common Lands, Common People: the Origins of Conservation in Northern New England*. Cambridge, Mass.: Harvard University Press.

Kasson, John F. (1990) *Rudeness and Civility: Manners in Nineteenth-century Urban America*. New York: Hill and Wang.

Kelly, Catherine E. (1999) " 'Well bred country people': sociability, social networks, and the creation of a provincial middle class, 1820–1860," *Journal of the Early Republic*, 19, pp. 451–79.

Kenny, Kevin (1998) *Making Sense of the Molly Maguires*. New York: Oxford University Press.

Kilbourne Jr, Richard Holcombe (1995) *Debt, Investment, Slaves: Credit Relations in East Feliciana Parish, Louisiana, 1825–1885*. Tuscaloosa: University of Alabama Press.

Kilmer, Paulette D. (1996) *The Fear of Sinking: the American Success Formula in the Gilded Age*. Knoxville: University of Tennessee Press.

Kirkland, Edward C. (1956) *Dream and Thought in the Business Community, 1860–1890*. Cambridge, Mass.: Harvard University Press.

Kirkland, Edward C. (1961) *Industry Comes of Age: Business, Labor and Public Policy, 1860–1897*. New York: Holt, Rinehart, and Winston.

Klein, Maury (1993) *The Flowering of the Third America: the Making of an Organizational Society, 1850–1920*. Chicago: Ivan Dee.

Krause, Paul (1984) *The Battle for Homestead, 1880–1892: Politics, Culture, and Steel*. Pittsburgh: University of Pittsburgh Press.

Kulikoff, Allan (1992) *The Agrarian Origins of American Capitalism*. Charlottesville: University Press of Virginia.

Kwolek-Folland, Angel (1994) *Engendering Business: Men and Women in the Corporate Office, 1870–1930*. Baltimore, MD: Johns Hopkins University Press.

Lamoreaux, Naomi (1985) *The Great Merger Movement in American Business, 1895–1904*. New York: Cambridge University Press.

Lamoreaux, Naomi (1994) *Insider Lending: Banks, Personal Connections and Economic Development in Industrial New England*. Cambridge: Cambridge University Press.

Lazerow, Jama (1995) *Religion and the Working Class in America*. Washington, DC: Smithsonian Institution Press.

Lazonick, William (1990) *Competitive Advantage on the Shop Floor*. Cambridge, Mass.: Harvard University Press.

Leach, William (1993) *Land of Desire: Merchants, Power, and the Rise of a New American Culture*. New York: Pantheon.

Lears, Jackson (1981) *No Place of Grace: Antimodernism and the Transformation of American Culture, 1880–1920*. New York: Pantheon.

Lessoff, Alan (1994) *The Nation and its City: "Corruption" and Progress in Washington, DC*. Baltimore, MD: Johns Hopkins University Press.

Levine, Bruce (1992) *The Spirit of 1848: German Immigrants, Labor Conflict, and the Coming of the Civil War*. Urbana: University of Illinois Press.

Lewis, Arnold (1997) *An Early Encounter with Tomorrow: Europeans, Chicago's Loop, and the World's Columbian Exposition*. Urbana: University of Illinois Press.

Lewis, W. David (1994) *Sloss Furnaces and the Rise of the Birmingham District: an Industrial Epic*. Tuscaloosa: University of Alabama Press.

Licht, Walter (1995) *Industrializing America: the Nineteenth Century*. Baltimore, MD: Johns Hopkins University Press.

Lichtenstein, Alex (1996) *Twice the Work of Free Labor: the Political Economy of Convict Labor in the New South*. New York: Verso.

Lipartito, K. (1995) "Culture and the practice of business history," *Business and Economic History*, 24, pp. 1–42.

Lott, Eric (1993) *Love and Theft: Blackface Minstrelsy and the American Working Class*. New York: Oxford University Press.

Lystra, Karen (1989) *Searching the Heart: Women, Men and Romantic Life in Nineteenth-century America*. New York: Oxford University Press.

McCaffery, Peter (1993) *When Bosses Ruled Philadelphia: the Emergence of the Republican Machine, 1867–1933*. University Park: Pennsylvania State University Press.

McClelland, Peter D. (1997) *Sowing Modernity: America's First Agricultural Revolution*. Ithaca, NY: Cornell University Press.

McCraw, T. K. (1984) *Prophets of Regulation: Charles Francis Adams, Louis D. Brandeis, James M. Landis, Alfred E. Kahn*. Cambridge, Mass.: Harvard University Press.

McCusker, John J. and Menard, Russel R. (1985) *The Economy of British America, 1607–1789*. Chapel Hill, NC: University of North Carolina Press.

McDonald, Terrence J. (1986) *The Parameters of Urban Fiscal Policy: Socioeconomic Change and Political Culture in San Francisco, 1860–1906*. Berkeley, CA: University of California Press.

McKiven, Jr, Henry M. (1995) *Iron and Steel: Class, Race, and Community in Birmingham, Alabama, 1875–1920*. Chapel Hill, NC: University of North Carolina Press.

McMurry, Sally (1995) *Transforming Rural Life: Dairying Families and Agricultural Change, 1820–1885*. Baltimore, MD: Johns Hopkins University Press.

Mills, C. Wright (1951) *White Collar: the American Middle Classes*. New York: Oxford University Press.

Misa, Thomas J. (1995) *A Nation of Steel: the Making of Modern America, 1865–1925*. Baltimore, MD: Johns Hopkins University Press.

Monkkonen, Eric H. (1988) *America Becomes Urban: the Development of US Cities and Towns*. Berkeley, CA: University of California Press.

Montgomery, David (1967) *Beyond Equality: Labor and the Radical Republicans, 1862–1872*. New York: Alfred A. Knopf.

Montgomery, David (1993) *Citizen Worker: the Experience of Workers in the United States with Democracy and the Free Market during the Nineteenth Century*. New York: Cambridge University Press.

Mumford, Lewis (1961) *The City in History*. New York: Harcourt, Brace.

Murphy, Teresa Ann (1992) *Ten Hours' Labor: Religion, Reform, and Gender in Early New England*. Ithaca, NY: Cornell University Press.

Neimi, Albert W. (1974) *State and Regional Patterns in American Manufacturing, 1850–1900*. Westport, Conn.: Greenwood Press.

North, Douglass C. (1961) *The Economic Growth of the United States, 1790–1860*. Englewood Cliffs, NJ: Prentice-Hall.

O'Connor, Carol A. (1994) "A region of cities," in Clyde A. Milner II, Carol A. O'Connor, and Martha Sandweiss (eds), *The Oxford History of the American West*, pp. 534–63. New York: Oxford University Press.

Ohmann, Richard (1996) *Selling Culture: Magazines, Markets, and Class at the Turn of the Century*. New York: Verso.

Park, Robert, Burgess, Ernest W., McKenzie, Roderick D., and Wirth, Louis (1925) *The City*. Chicago: University of Chicago Press.

Parker, Alison M. (1997) *Purifying America: Women, Cultural Reform, and Pro-censorship Activism, 1873–1933*. Urbana: University of Illinois Press.

Piore, Michael J. and Sabel, Charles F. (1984) *The Second Industrial Divide: Possibilities for Prosperity*. New York: Basic Books.

Porter, Glenn and Livesay, Harold C. (1971) *Merchants and Manufactures: Studies in the Changing Structure of Nineteenth Century Marketing*. Baltimore, MD: Johns Hopkins University Press.

Powers, Madelon (1998) *Faces along the Bar: Lore and Order in the Workingman's Saloon, 1870–1920*. Chicago: University of Chicago Press.

Prude, Jonathan (1983) *The Coming of Industrial Order: Town and Factory Life in Rural Massachusetts, 1810–1860*. New York: Cambridge University Press.

Rachleff, Peter (1984) *Black Labor in the South: Richmond, Virginia, 1865–1900*. Philadelphia: Temple University Press.

Ransom, Roger L. and Sutch, Richard (1977) *One Kind of Freedom: the Economic Consequences of Emancipation*. New York: Cambridge University Press.

Reps, John W. (1965) *The Making of Urban America: a History of City Planning in the United States*. Princeton, NJ: Princeton University Press.

Reps, John W. (1994) *Cities of the Mississippi: Nineteenth-century Images of Urban Development*. Columbia: University of Missouri Press.

Rodgers, Daniel T. (1992) "Republicanism: the career of a concept," *The Journal of American History*, 78, pp. 11–38.

Roediger, David (1991) *The Wages of Whiteness: Race and the Making of the American Working Class*. New York: Verso.

Rose, Anne C. (1992) *Victorian America and the Civil War*. Cambridge: Cambridge University Press.

Rosenzweig, Roy and Blackmar, Elizabeth (1992) *The Park and the People: a History of Central Park*. Ithaca, NY: Cornell University Press.

Rothenberg, Winifred Barr (1992) *From Market-places to a Market Economy: the Transformation of Rural Massachusetts, 1750–1850*. Chicago: University of Chicago Press.

Rotundo, E. Anthony (1993) *American Manhood: Transformations in Masculinity from the Revolution to the Modern Era*. New York: Basic Books.

Rousey, Dennis C. (1996) *Policing the Southern City: New Orleans, 1805–1889*. Baton Rouge: Louisiana State University Press.

Roy, William G. (1997) *Socializing Capital: the Rise of the Large Industrial Corporation in America*. Princeton, NJ: Princeton University Press.

Ryan, Mary P. (1981) *The Cradle of the Middle Class: the Family in Oneida County, New York, 1780–1865*. Cambridge: Cambridge University Press.

Ryan, Mary P. (1997) *Civic Wars: Democracy and Public Life in the American City during the Nineteenth Century*. Berkeley, CA: University of California Press.

Sawislak, Karen (1995) *Smoldering City: Chicagoans and the Great Fire, 1871–1874*. Chicago: University of Chicago Press.

Saxton, Alexander (1971) *The Indispensable Enemy: Labor and the Anti-Chinese Movement in California*. Berkeley, CA: University of California Press.

Schlesinger, Arthur M. (1933) *The Rise of the City, 1878–1898*. New York: Macmillan.

Schultz, Ronald (1993) *The Republic of Labor: Philadelphia Artisans and the Politics of Class, 1720–1830*. New York: Oxford University Press.

Schuyler, David (1996) *Apostle of Taste: Andrew Jackson Downing, 1815–1852*. Baltimore, MD: Johns Hopkins University Press.

Scott, Joan W. (1988) *Gender and the Politics of History*. New York: Columbia University Press.

Scranton, Philip (1997) *Endless Novelty: Specialty Production and American Industrialization, 1865–1925*. Princeton, NJ: Princeton University Press.

Sellers, Charles G. (1991) *The Market Revolution: Jacksonian America, 1815–1846*. New York: Oxford University Press.

Sheriff, Carol (1996) *The Artificial River: the Erie Canal and the Paradox of Progress*. New York: Hill and Wang.

Sicilia, David B. (1995) "Cochran's legacy: a cultural path not taken," *Business and Economic History*, 24, pp. 27–39.

Smith, Carl (1995) *Urban Disorder and the Shape of Belief: the Great Chicago Fire, the Haymarket Bomb, and the Model Town of Pullman.* Chicago: University of Chicago Press.

Steinberg, Theodore (1991) *Nature Incorporated: Industrialization and the Waters of New England.* Cambridge: Cambridge University Press.

Stevens Jr, Edward W. (1995) *The Grammar of the Machine: Technical Literacy and Early Industrial Expansion in the United States.* New Haven, Conn.: Yale University Press.

Stott, Richard B. (1990) *Workers in the Metropolis: Class, Ethnicity, and Youth in Antebellum New York City.* Ithaca, NY: Cornell University Press.

Stowell, David O. (1999) *Streets, Railroads, and the Great Strike of 1877.* Chicago: University of Chicago Press.

Strebnick, Amy Gilman (1995) *The Mysterious Death of Mary Rogers: Sex and Culture in Nineteenth-century New York.* New York: Oxford University Press.

Taylor, George Rogers (1951) *The Transportation Revolution, 1815–1860.* New York: Rinehart.

Taylor, George Rogers and Neu, Irene D. (1956) *The American Railroad Network, 1861–1890.* Cambridge, Mass.: Harvard University Press.

Teaford, Jon C. (1979) *The Unheralded Triumph: City Government in America, 1870–1900.* Baltimore, MD: Johns Hopkins University Press.

Thompson, E. P. (1963) *The Making of the English Working Class.* London: Gollancz.

Tonnies, Ferdinand (1963) *Community and Society,* trans. Charles P. Loomis. New York: Harper and Row.

Trachtenberg, Alan (1982) *The Incorporation of America: Culture and Society in the Gilded Age.* New York: Hill and Wang.

Turner, Frederick Jackson (1894) "The significance of the frontier in American history," *Annual Report of the American Historical Association for the Year 1893,* pp. 199–227. Washington: Government Printing Office.

Vickers, Daniel (1994) *Farmers and Fishermen: Two Centuries of Work in Essex County, Massachusetts, 1630–1850.* Chapel Hill, NC: University of North Carolina Press.

Von Hoffman, Alexander (1995) *Local Attachments: the Making of an American Urban Neighborhood.* Baltimore, MD: Johns Hopkins University Press.

Voss, Kim (1993) *The Making of American Exceptionalism: the Knights of Labor and Class Formation in the Nineteenth Century.* Ithaca, NY: Cornell University Press.

Wade, Richard C. (1959) *The Urban Frontier: Pioneer Life in Early Pittsburgh, Cincinnati, Lexington, Louisville, and St Louis.* Cambridge, Mass.: Harvard University Press.

Walker, J. E. K. (1998) *A History of Black Business in American Capitalism.* New York: Twayne.

Wall, Joseph Frazier (1989) *Andrew Carnegie.* Pittsburgh, PA: University of Pittsburgh Press.

Warner Jr, Sam Bass (1962) *Streetcar Suburbs: the Process of Growth in Boston, 1870–1900.* Cambridge, Mass.: Harvard University Press.

Warner Jr, Sam Bass (1968) *The Private City: Philadelphia in Three Periods of its Growth.* Philadelphia: University of Pennsylvania Press.

Way, Peter (1993) *Common Labour: Workers and the Digging of North American Canals, 1780–1860.* Cambridge: Cambridge University Press.

Weems, R. (1996) *Black Business in the Black Metropolis: the Chicago Metropolitan Assurance Company.* Bloomington, Ind.: Indiana University Press.

Weil, François (1998) "Capitalism and industrialization in New England, 1815–1845," *Journal of American History,* 84, pp. 1334–54.

Weir, Robert E. (1996) *Beyond Labor's Veil: the Culture of the Knights of Labor.* University Park: Pennsylvania State University Press.

Weiss, Thomas and Schaefer, Donald (eds) *American Economic Development in Historical Perspective.* Stanford: Stanford University Press.

Wilentz, Sean (1984a) "Against exceptionalism: class consciousness and the American labor movement, 1790–1920," *International Labor and Working Class History,* 26, pp. 1–24.

Wilentz, Sean (1984b) *Chants Democratic: New York City and the Rise of the American Working Class, 1788–1850.* New York: Oxford University Press.

Williamson, Harold Francis (ed.) (1953) *The Growth of the American Economy,* 2nd edn. New York: Prentice-Hall.

Wright, Gavin (1978) *The Political Economy of the Cotton South: Households, Markets, and Wealth in the Nineteenth Century.* New York: Norton.

Wright, Gavin, (1986) *Old South, New South: Revolutions in the Southern Economy since the Civil War.* New York: Basic Books.

Wright, Gavin (1990) "The origins of American industrial success, 1879–1940," *American Economic Review,* 80, pp. 651–68.

Zunz, Olivier (1982) *The Changing Face of Inequality: Urbanization, Industrial Development, and Immigrants in Detroit, 1880–1920.* Chicago: University of Chicago Press.

Zunz, Olivier (1990) *Making America Corporate, 1870–1920.* Chicago: University of Chicago Press.

Race, Gender, and Ethnicity

Adelike, Tunde (1998) *UnAfrican Americans: Nineteenth-century Black Nationalists and the Civilizing Mission.* Lexington: University Press of Kentucky.

Attie, Jeanie (1998) *Patriotic Toil: Northern Women and the American Civil War.* Ithaca, NY: Cornell University Press.

Ayers, Edward L. (1992) *The Promise of the New South: Life after Reconstruction.* New York: Oxford University Press.

Baker, Paula (1984) "The domestication of American politics: women and American political society, 1780–1920," *American Historical Review,* 89, pp. 620–47.

Barkari, Abraham (1994) *Branching Out: German-Jewish Immigration in the United States, 1820–1914.* New York: Holmes and Meier.

Baron, Ava (ed.) (1991) *Work Engendered: Toward a New History of American Labor.* Ithaca, NY: Cornell University Press.

Barton, Josef (1975) *Peasants and Strangers: Italians, Rumanians, and Slovaks in an American City, 1890–1950.* Cambridge, Mass.: Harvard University Press.

Bell, Caryn Cosse (1997) *Revolution, Romanticism, and the Afro-Creole Protest Tradition in Louisiana, 1718–1868.* Baton Rouge: Louisiana State University Press.

Berkofer Jr, Robert F. (1978) *The White Man's Indian: Images of the American Indian from Columbus to the Present.* New York: Alfred A. Knopf.

Berlin, Ira (1974) *Slaves without Masters: the Free Negro in the Antebellum South.* New York: Pantheon.

Berlin, Ira and Morgan, Philip D. (eds) (1993) *Cultivation and Culture: Labor and the Shaping of Slave Life in the Americas.* Charlottesville: University Press of Virginia.

Bieder, Robert E. (1986) *Science Encounters the Indian, 1820–1880: the Early Years of American Ethnology.* Norman: University of Oklahoma Press.

Blassingame, John W. (1972) *The Slave Community: Plantation Life in the American South.* New York: Oxford University Press.

Blewett, Mary H. (1988) *Men, Women, and Work: Class, Gender, and Protest in the New England Shoe Industry, 1780–1910.* Urbana: University of Illinois Press.

Bodnar, John (1985) *The Transplanted: a History of Immigrants in Urban America.* Bloomington, Ind.: Indiana University Press.

Bogger, Tommy L. (1997) *Free Blacks in Norfolk, Virginia, 1790–1860: the Darker Side of Freedom.* Charlottesville: University Press of Virginia.

Boydston, Jeanne (1990) *Home and Work: Housework, Wages, and the Ideology of Labor in the Early Republic.* New York: Oxford University Press.

Brodie, Janet Farrell (1994) *Contraception and Abortion in Nineteenth-century America.* Ithaca, NY: Cornell University Press.

Brown, Elsa Barkley (1989) "Womanist consciousness: Maggie Lena Walker and the Independent Order of Saint Luke," *Signs,* 14, pp. 610–33.

Brundage, W. Fitzhugh (1993) *Lynching in the New South: Georgia and Virginia, 1880–1930.* Urbana: University of Illinois Press.

Burton, Jeffrey (1995) *Indian Territory and the United States, 1866–1906: Courts, Government, and the Movement for Oklahoma Statehood.* Norman: University of Oklahoma Press.

Bynum, Victoria (1992) *Unruly Women: the Politics of Social and Sexual Control in the Old South.* Chapel Hill, NC: University of North Carolina Press.

Byron, Reginald (2000) *Irish America.* New York: Oxford University Press.

Capper, Charles (1992) *Margaret Fuller: an American Romantic Life,* vol. 1: *The Private Years.* New York: Oxford University Press.

Champagne, Duane (1992) *Social Order and Political Change: Constitutional Governments among the Cherokee, the Choctaw, the Chickasaw, and the Creek.* Stanford: Stanford University Press.

Cheng, Lucie and Bonacich, Edna (eds) (1984) *Labor Migration under Capitalism: Asian Workers in the United States before World War II.* Berkeley, CA: University of California Press.

Collison, Gary (1997) *Shadrack Minkins: From Fugitive Slave to Citizen.* Cambridge, Mass.: Harvard University Press.

Cott, Nancy F. (1977) *The Bonds of Womanhood: "Woman's Sphere" in New England, 1780–1835.* New Haven, Conn.: Yale University Press.

Debouzy, Marianne (ed.) (1992) *In the Shadow of the Statue of Liberty: Immigrants, Workers, and Citizens in the American Republic.* Urbana: University of Illinois Press.

Dew, Charles B. (1994) *Bond of Iron: Master and Slave at Buffalo Forge.* New York: Norton.

Diner, Hasia (1983) *Erin's Daughters in America: Irish Immigrant Women in the Nineteenth Century.* Baltimore, MD: Johns Hopkins University Press.

Dowd, Gregory Evans (1992) *A Spirited Resistance: the North American Indian Struggle for Unity, 1745–1815.* Baltimore, MD: Johns Hopkins University Press.

Dublin, Thomas (1979) *Women at Work: the Transformation of Work and Community in Lowell, Massachusetts, 1826–1860.* New York: Columbia University Press.

DuBois, Ellen, Buhle, Mari Jo, Kaplan, Temma, Lerner, Gerda, and Smith-Rosenberg, Carroll (1980) "Politics and culture in women's history: a symposium," *Feminist Studies,* 6, pp. 26–64.

DuBois, W. E. B. (1903) *The Souls of Black Folk: Essays and Sketches.* New York: Fawcett, 1961.

Dudden, Faye E. (1994) *Women in the American Theatre: Actresses and Audiences, 1790–1870.* New Haven, Conn.: Yale University Press.

Dusinberre, William (1996) *Them Dark Days: Slavery in the American Rice Swamps.* New York: Oxford University Press.

Edmunds, R. David (1983) *The Shawnee Prophet.* Lincoln: University of Nebraska Press.

Edmunds, R. David (1984) *Tecumseh and the Quest for Indian Leadership.* Boston: Little, Brown.

Elkins, Stanley (1959) *Slavery: a Problem in American Institutional and Intellectual Life.* Chicago: University of Chicago Press.

Engels, Friedrich (1884) *The Origin of the Family, Private Property, and the State,* ed. Eleanor Burke Leacock. New York: International Publishers, 1990.

Erickson, Charlotte (1994) *Leaving England: Essays on British Emigration in the Nineteenth Century.* Ithaca, NY: Cornell University Press.

Essah, Patience (1996) *A House Divided: Slavery and Emancipation in Delaware, 1638–1865.* Charlottesville: University Press of Virginia.

Farnham, Christie Anne (1994) *The Education of the Southern Belle: Higher Education and Student Socialization in the Antebellum South.* New York: New York University Press.

Ferrie, Joseph P. (1999) *Yankeys Now: Immigrants in the Antebellum United States, 1840–1860.* New York: Oxford University Press.

Fogel, Robert William (1989) *Without Consent or Contract: the Rise and Fall of American Slavery.* New York: Norton.

Foley, Neil (1997) *The White Scourge: Mexicans, Blacks and Poor Whites in Texas Cotton Culture.* Berkeley, CA: University of California Press.

Foner, Eric (1988) *Reconstruction: America's Unfinished Revolution, 1863–1877.* New York: Harper and Row.

Fox-Genovese, Elizabeth (1988) *Within the Plantation Household: Black and White Women of the Old South.* Chapel Hill, NC: University of North Carolina Press.

Franklin, John Hope (1961) *Reconstruction after the Civil War.* Chicago: University of Chicago Press.

Frantz, Klaus (1999) *Indian Reservations in the United States: Territories, Sovereignty, and Socioeconomic Change.* Chicago: University of Chicago Press.

Gabaccia, Donna (1994) *From the Other Side: Women, Gender, and Immigrant Life in the US, 1820–1900.* Bloomington, Ind.: Indiana University Press.

Gallman, J. Matthew (2000) *Receiving Erin's Children: Philadelphia, Liverpool, and the Irish Famine Migration, 1845–1855.* Chapel Hill, NC: University of North Carolina Press.

Gerber, David A. (1989) *The Making of an American Pluralism: Buffalo, New York, 1825–60.* Urbana: University of Illinois Press.

Ginzberg, Lori D. (1990) *Women and the World of Benevolence: Morality, Politics, and Class in the Nineteenth-century United States.* New Haven, Conn.: Yale University Press.

Green, Michael D. (1982) *The Politics of Indian Removal: Creek Government and Society in Crisis.* Lincoln: University of Nebraska Press.

Gribben, Arthur (ed.) (1999) *The Great Famine and the Irish Diaspora in America.* Amherst: University of Massachusetts Press.

Gutman, Herbert G. (1973) "Work, culture, and society in industrializing America, 1815–1919," in Herbert G. Gutman (ed.), *Work, Culture, and Society in Industrializing America: Essays in American Working-class and Social History,* pp. 3–78. New York: Vintage, 1977.

Handlin, Oscar (1951) *The Uprooted: the Epic Story of the Great Migrations that Made the American People.* Boston: Little, Brown, 1990.

Hansen, Debra Gold (1993) *Strained Sisterhood: Gender and Class in the Boston Female Anti-slavery Society.* Amherst: University of Massachusetts Press.

Hansen, Marcus (1940) *The Atlantic Migration, 1607–1860: a History of the Continuing Settlement of the United States.* New York: Harper, 1961.

Harring, Sidney L. (1994) *Crow Dog's Case: American Indian Sovereignty, Tribal Law, and United States Law in the Nineteenth Century.* Cambridge: Cambridge University Press.

Harrod, Howard L. (1995) *Becoming and Remaining a People: Native American Religions on the Northern Plains.* Tucson: University of Arizona Press.

Hartman, Saidya V. (1997) *Scenes of Subjection: Terror, Slavery, and Self-making in Nineteenth-century America.* New York: Oxford University Press.

Hatton, Timothy J. and Williamson, Jeffrey G. (1998) *The Age of Mass Migration: Causes and Economic Impact.* New York: Oxford University Press.

Hauptman, Laurence M. (1995) *Between Two Fires: American Indians in the Civil War.* New York: Free Press.

Hewitt, Nancy A. (1988) *Women's Activism and Social Change: Rochester, New York, 1822–1872.* Ithaca, NY: Cornell University Press.

Hodges, Graham Russell (1997) *Slavery and Freedom in the Rural North: African Americans in Monmouth County, New Jersey, 1665–1865.* Madison, Wisconsin: Madison House.

Hoerder, Dirk (1985) "An introduction to labor migration in the Atlantic economies, 1815–1914," in Dirk Hoerder (ed.), *Labor Migration in the Atlantic Economies: the European and*

North American Working Classes during the Period of Industrialization, pp. 3–31. Westport, Conn.: Greenwood Press.

Horton, James O. and Horton, Lois E. (1997) *In Hope of Liberty: Culture, Community, and Protest among Northern Free Blacks, 1700–1860*. New York: Oxford University Press.

Hoxie, Frederick E. (1984) *A Final Promise: the Campaign to Assimilate the Indians, 1880–1920*. Lincoln: University of Nebraska Press.

Hoxie, Frederick E. (1995) *Parading through History: the Making of the Crow Nation in America, 1805–1935*. Cambridge: Cambridge University Press.

Hurtado, Albert L. (1988) *Indian Survival on the California Frontier*. New Haven, Conn.: Yale University Press.

Ignatiev, Noel (1995) *How the Irish Became White*. New York: Routledge.

Isenberg, Nancy (1998) *Sex and Citizenship in Antebellum America*. Chapel Hill, NC: University of North Carolina Press.

Jacobson, Matthew Frye (1995) *Special Sorrows: the Diasporic Immigration of Irish, Polish, and Jewish Immigrants in the United States*. Cambridge: Cambridge University Press.

Jacobson, Matthew Frye (1998) *Whiteness of a Different Color: European Immigrants and the Alchemy of Race*. Cambridge, Mass.: Harvard University Press.

Jameson, Elizabeth and Armitage, Susan (eds) (1997) *Writing the Range: Race, Class, and Culture in the Women's West*. Norman: University of Oklahoma Press.

Jeffrey, Julie Roy (1998) *The Great Silent Army of Abolitionism: Ordinary Women in the Antislavery Movement*. Chapel Hill, NC: University of North Carolina Press.

Jensen, Joan (1986) *Loosening the Bonds: Mid-Atlantic Farm Women, 1750–1850*. New Haven, Conn.: Yale University Press.

Kamphoefner, Walter D. (1987) *The Westfalians: from Germany to Missouri*. Princeton, NJ: Princeton University Press.

Kazal, Russell A. (1995) "Assimilation revisited: the rise, fall, and reappraisal of a concept in ethnic history," *American Historical Review*, 100, pp. 437–91.

Kerber, Linda K. (1988) "Separate spheres, female worlds, women's place: the rhetoric of women's history," *Journal of American History*, 75, pp. 9–39.

Kerber, Linda K. (1998) *No Constitutional Right to be Ladies: Women and the Obligations of Citizenship*. New York: Hill and Wang.

Kessler-Harris, Alice (1982) *Out to Work: a History of Wage-earning Women in the United States*. New York: Oxford University Press.

Kidwell, Clara Sue (1995) *Choctaws and Missionaries in Mississippi, 1818–1918*. Norman: University of Oklahoma Press.

Klein, Kerwin Lee (1997) *Frontiers of Historical Imagination: Narrating the European Conquest of Native America, 1890–1990*. Berkeley, CA: University of California Press.

Kleinberg, Susan J. (1999) *Women in the United States, 1830–1945*. New Brunswick, NJ: Rutgers University Press.

Kolchin, Peter (1993) *American Slavery: 1619–1877*. New York: Hill and Wang.

Kraditor, Aileen (1968) *Up from the Pedestal: Selective Writings in the History of American Feminism*. Chicago: University of Chicago Press.

Kraut, Alan M. (1994) *Silent Travelers: Germs, Genes, and the "Immigrant Menace."* New York: Basic Books.

Kugel, Rebecca (1998) *To be the Main Leaders of our People: a History of Minnesota Ojibwe Politics, 1825–1898*. East Lansing: Michigan State University Press.

Lancaster, Jane (1994) *Removal Aftershock: the Seminoles' Struggles to Survive in the West, 1836–1866*. Knoxville: University of Tennessee Press.

Lane, Roger (1991) *William Dorsey's Philadelphia and Ours: On the Past and Future of the Black City in America*. New York: Oxford University Press.

Leonard, Elizabeth D. (1994) *Yankee Women: Gender Battles in the Civil War*. New York: Norton.

Lerner, Gerda (1969) "The lady and the mill girl: changes in the status of women in the age of Jackson," *Midcontinent American Studies Journal*, 10, pp. 5–15.

Lewis, David Rich (1994) *Neither Wolf nor Dog: American Indians, Environment, and Agrarian Change*. New York: Oxford University Press.

Lewis, Earl (1995) "To turn as on a pivot: writing African Americans into a history of overlapping diasporas," *American Historical Review*, 100, pp. 765–87.

Litwack, Leon F. (1961) *North of Slavery: the Negro in the Free States*. Chicago: University of Chicago Press.

Litwack, Leon F. (1979) *Been in the Storm so Long: the Aftermath of Slavery*. New York: Random House.

Litwack, Leon F. (1998) *Trouble in Mind: Black Southerners in the Age of Jim Crow*. New York: Alfred A. Knopf.

McCurry, Stephanie (1995) *Masters of Small Worlds: Yeoman Households, Gender Relations, and the Political Culture of the Antebellum South Carolina Low Country*. New York: Oxford University Press.

McDonald, Roderick A. (1993) *The Economy and Material Culture of Slaves: Goods and Chattels on the Sugar Plantations of Jamaica and Louisiana*. Baton Rouge: Louisiana State University Press.

McLoughlin, William G. (1986) *Cherokee Renascence in the New Republic*. Princeton, NJ: Princeton University Press.

McLoughlin, William G. (1990) *Champions of the Cherokees: Evan and John B. Jones*. Princeton, NJ: Princeton University Press.

McLoughlin, William G. (1993) *After the Trail of Tears: the Cherokees' Struggle for Sovereignty, 1839–1880*. Chapel Hill, NC: University of North Carolina Press.

Martin, Joel W. (1991) *Sacred Revolt: the Muscogees' Struggle for a New World*. Boston: Beacon Press.

Melish, Joanne Pope (1998) *Disowning Slavery: Gradual Emancipation and "Race" in New England, 1780–1860*. Ithaca, NY: Cornell University Press.

Meredith, Howard (1995) *Dancing on Common Ground: Tribal Cultures and Alliances on the Southern Plains*. Lawrence: University Press of Kansas.

Miller, Kerby A. (1985) *Emigrants and Exiles: Ireland and the Irish Exodus to North America*. New York: Oxford University Press.

Moore, William Haas (1994) *Chiefs, Agents, and Soldiers: Conflict on the Navajo Frontier, 1868–1882*. Albuquerque: University of New Mexico Press.

Moses, L. G. (1996) *Wild West Shows and the Images of American Indians, 1883–1933*. Albuquerque: University of New Mexico Press.

Nelli, Humbert S. (1983) *From Immigrants to Ethnics: the Italian Americans*. New York: Oxford University Press.

Nugent, Walter (1992) *Crossings: the Great Transatlantic Migrations, 1870–1914*. Bloomington, Ind.: Indiana University Press.

Okihiro, Gary Y. (1994) "Is yellow black or white?", in Gary Y. Okihiro (ed.), *Margins and Mainstreams: Asians in American History and Culture*, pp. 31–63. Seattle: University of Washington Press.

Osterud, Nancy Grey (1991) *Bonds of Community: the Lives of Farm Women in Nineteenth-century New York*. Ithaca, NY: Cornell University Press.

Owens, Leslie Howard (1976) *This Species of Property: Slave Life and Culture in the Old South*. New York: Oxford University Press.

Parker, Alison M. (1997) *Purifying America: Women, Cultural Reform, and Pro-censorship Activism, 1873–1933*. Urbana: University of Illinois Press.

Perdue, Theda (1979) *Slavery and the Evolution of Cherokee Society, 1540–1866*. Knoxville: University of Tennessee Press.

Perdue, Theda (1998) *Cherokee Women: Gender and Culture Change, 1700–1835*. Lincoln: University of Nebraska Press.

Phillips, Christopher (1997) *Freedom's Port: the African American Community of Baltimore, 1790–1860*. Urbana: University of Illinois Press.

Phillips, George Harwood (1993) *Indians and Intruders in Central California, 1769–1849*. Norman: University of Oklahoma Press.

Phillips, Ulrich B. (1918) *American Negro Slavery: a Survey of the Supply, Employment and Control of Negro Labor as Determined by the Plantation Regime*. New York: Appleton.

Piersen, William D. (1993) *Black Legacy: America's Hidden Heritage*. Amherst: University of Massachusetts Press.

Price, Catherine (1996) *The Oglala People, 1841–1899: a Political History*. Lincoln: University of Nebraska Press.

Prucha, Francis Paul (1994) *American Indian Treaties: the History of a Political Anomaly*. Berkeley, CA: University of California Press.

Radding, Cynthia (1997) *Wandering Peoples: Colonialism, Ethnic Spaces, and Ecological Frontiers in Northwest Mexico, 1700–1850*. Durham, NC: Duke University Press.

Riley, Glenda (1996) *Building and Breaking Families in the American West*. Albuquerque: University of New Mexico Press.

Ripley, C. Peter, Finkenbine, Roy E., Hembree, Michael F., and Yacovone, Donald (eds) (1993) *Witness for Freedom: African American Voices on Race, Slavery, and Emancipation*. Chapel Hill, NC: University of North Carolina Press.

Roediger, David R. (1991) *The Wages of Whiteness: Race and the Making of the American Working Class*. London: Verso.

Salvatore, Nick (1996) *We All Got History: the Memory Books of Amos Webber*. New York: Random House.

Salyer, Lucy E. (1995) *Laws Harsh as Tigers: Chinese Immigrants and the Shaping of Modern Immigration Law*. Chapel Hill, NC: University of North Carolina Press.

Sanchez, George J. (1999) "Race, nature, and culture in recent immigration studies," *Journal of American Ethnic History*, 18, pp. 66–84.

Scheckel, Susan (1998) *The Insistence of the Indian: Race and Nationalism in Nineteenth-century American Culture*. Princeton, NJ: Princeton University Press.

Schiller, Nina Glick, Basch, Linda, and Blanc-Szanton, Christina (eds) (1992) *Towards a Transnational Perspective in Migration: Race, Class, Ethnicity and Nationalism Reconsidered*. New York: New York Academy of Sciences.

Scott, Joan W. (1986) "Is gender a useful category of analysis?," *American Historical Review*, 91, pp. 1053–75.

Sidbury, James (1997) *Ploughshares into Swords: Race, Rebellion, and Identity in Gabriel's Virginia, 1730–1810*. New York: Cambridge University Press.

Sklar, Kathryn Kish (1973) *Catharine Beecher: a Study in American Domesticity*. New Haven, Conn.: Yale University Press.

Sklar, Kathryn Kish (1994) *Florence Kelley and the Nation's Work: the Rise of Women's Political Culture, 1830–1900*. New Haven, Conn.: Yale University Press.

Smith, Theophus H. (1994) *Conjuring Culture: Biblical Formations of Black America*. New York: Oxford University Press.

Smith-Rosenberg, Carroll (1975) "The female world of love and ritual: relations between women in nineteenth-century America," *Signs*, 1, pp. 1–29.

Stampp, Kenneth M. (1956) *The Peculiar Institution: Slavery in the Antebellum South*. New York: Vintage.

Stampp, Kenneth M. (1965) *The Era of Reconstruction, 1865–1877*. New York: Alfred A. Knopf.

Stansell, Christine (1987) *City of Women: Sex and Class in New York, 1789–1860*. Urbana: University of Illinois Press.

Stebner, Eleanor J. (1997) *The Women of Hull House: a Study of Spirituality, Vocation, and Friendship*. Albany: State University of New York Press.

Tadman, Michael (1989) *Speculators and Slaves: Masters, Traders, and Slaves in the Old South*. Madison: University of Wisconsin Press.

Thistlethwaite, Frank (1960) "Migration from Europe overseas in the nineteenth and twentieth centuries," in Rudolph J. Vecoli and Suzanne M. Sinke (eds), *A Century of European Migration, 1830–1930*, pp. 17–49. Urbana: University of Illinois Press, 1991.

Thornton, Russell (1987) *American Indian Holocaust and Survival: a Population History since 1492*. Norman: University of Oklahoma Press.

Turbin, Carole (1992) *Working Women of Collar City: Gender, Class, and Community in Troy, New York, 1864–86*. Urbana: University of Illinois Press.

Unrau, William E. (1996) *White Man's Wicked Water: the Alcohol Trade and Prohibition in Indian Country, 1802–1892*. Lawrence: University Press of Kansas.

Van Vught, William E. (1999) *Britain to America: Mid-nineteenth-century Immigrants to the United States*. Urbana: University of Illinois Press.

Varon, Elizabeth R. (1998) *We Mean to be Counted: White Women and Politics in Antebellum Virginia*. Chapel Hill, NC: University of North Carolina Press.

Vecoli, Rudolph J. (1964) "*Contadini* in Chicago: a critique of *The Uprooted*," *Journal of American Ethnic History*, 51, pp. 404–17.

Vecoli, Rudolph J. and Sinke, Suzanne M. (eds) (1991) *A Century of European Migration, 1830–1930*. Urbana: University of Illinois Press.

Vlach, John Michael (1993) *Back of the Big House: the Architecture of Plantation Slavery*. Chapel Hill, NC: University of North Carolina Press.

Wallace, Anthony F. C. (1970) *The Death and Rebirth of the Seneca*. New York: Alfred A. Knopf.

Wallace, Anthony F. C. (1999) *Jefferson and the Indians: the Tragic Fate of the First Americans*. Cambridge, Mass.: Belknap Press of Harvard University.

Welter, Barbara (1966) "The cult of true womanhood: 1820–1860," *American Quarterly*, 18, pp. 151–74.

West, Elliott (1998) *The Contested Plains: Indians, Goldseekers, and the Rush to Colorado*. Lawrence: University Press of Kansas.

White, Deborah Gray (1985) *Ar'n't I a Woman? Female Slaves in the Plantation South*. New York: Norton.

White, Richard (1983) *The Roots of Dependency: Subsistence, Environment, and Social Change among the Choctaws, Pawnees, and Navajos*. Lincoln: University of Nebraska Press.

Whites, Lee Ann (1995) *The Civil War as a Crisis in Gender: Augusta, Georgia, 1860–1890*. Athens: University of Georgia Press.

Whitman, T. Stephen (1997) *The Price of Freedom: Slavery and Manumission in Baltimore and Early National Maryland*. Lexington: University Press of Kentucky.

Williamson, Joel (1984) *The Crucible of Race: Black–White Relations in the American South since Emancipation*. New York: Oxford University Press.

Wilson, Carol (1994) *Freedom at Risk: the Kidnapping of Free Blacks in America, 1780–1865*. Lexington: University Press of Kentucky.

Wishart, David J. (1994) *An Unspeakable Sadness: the Dispossession of the Nebraska Indians*. Lincoln: University of Nebraska Press.

Wong, K. Scott and Chan, Sucheng (eds) (1998) *Claiming America: Constructing Chinese American Identities during the Exclusion Era*. Philadelphia, PA: Temple University Press.

Woodward, C. Vann (1955) *The Strange Career of Jim Crow*. New York: Oxford University Press, 3rd rev. edn, 1974.

Wyman, Mark (1993) *Round-trip to America: the Immigrants Return to Europe, 1880–1930*. Ithaca, NY: Cornell University Press.

Yans-McLaughlin, Virginia (1977) *Family and Community: Italian Immigrants in Buffalo, 1880–1930*. Ithaca, NY: Cornell University Press.

Young, Elizabeth (1999) *Disarming the Nation: Women's Writing and the American Civil War*. Chicago: University of Chicago Press.

Regional Perspectives

Adler, Jeffrey S. (1991) *Yankee Merchants and the Making of the Urban West: the Rise and Fall of Antebellum St Louis*. New York: Cambridge University Press.

Arrington, Leonard J. (1958) *Great Basin Kingdom: an Economic History of the Latter-day Saints, 1830–1900*. Cambridge, Mass.: Harvard University Press.

Ayers, Edward (1992) *The Promise of the New South: Life after Reconstruction*. New York: Oxford University Press.

Bond, Bradley G. (1995) *Political Culture in the Nineteenth-century South: Mississippi, 1830–1900*. Baton Rouge: Louisiana State University Press.

Brundage, W. Fitzhugh (ed.) (1997) *Under Sentence of Death: Lynching in the South*. Chapel Hill, NC: University of North Carolina Press.

Bunting, Robert (1997) *The Pacific Raincoast: Environment and Culture in an American Eden, 1778–1900*. Lawrence: University Press of Kansas.

Bynum, Victoria E. (1992) *Unruly Women: the Politics of Social and Sexual Control in the Old South*. Chapel Hill, NC: University of North Carolina Press.

Carter, Dan T. (1985) *When the War was Over: the Failure of Self-reconstruction in the South, 1865–1867*. Baton Rouge: Louisiana State University Press.

Cash, Wilbur (1941) *Mind of the South*. New York: Alfred A. Knopf.

Cayton, Andrew R. L. (1996) *Frontier Indiana*. Bloomington, Ind.: Indiana University Press.

Cayton, Andrew R. L. and Onuf, Peter S. (1998) *The Midwest and the Nation: Rethinking the History of an American Region*. Bloomington, Ind.: Indiana University Press.

Cobb, James C. (1988) "Beyond planters and industrialists: a new perspective on the New South," *Journal of Southern History*, 54, pp. 45–68.

Cobb, James C. (1992) *The Most Southern Place on Earth: the Mississippi Delta and the Roots of Regional Identity*. New York: Oxford University Press.

Conzen, Kathleen Neils (1976) *Immigrant Milwaukee, 1836–1860: Accommodation and Community in a Frontier City*. Cambridge, Mass.: Harvard University Press.

Cooper Jr, William J. (1978) *The South and the Politics of Slavery, 1828–1856*. Baton Rouge: Louisiana State University Press.

Cronon, William (1991) *Nature's Metropolis: Chicago and the Great West*. New York: W. W. Norton.

Cronon, William, Miles, George and Gitlin, Jay (1992) *Under an Open Sky: Rethinking America's Western Past*. New York: W. W. Norton.

Davis, James E. (1977) *Frontier America, 1800–1840: a Comparative Demographic Analysis of the Settlement Process*. Glendale, CA: A. H. Clark.

DeLeon, Arnoldo (1982) *The Tejano Community, 1836–1900*. Albuquerque: University of New Mexico Press.

Deutsch, Sarah (1987) *No Separate Refuge: Culture, Class, and Gender on an Anglo-Hispanic Frontier in the American Southwest, 1880–1940*. New York: Oxford University Press.

Ellis, David M. (ed.) (1969) *The Frontier in American Development: Essays in Honor of Paul Wallace Gates*. Ithaca, NY: Cornell University Press.

Emmons, David M. (1989) *The Butte Irish: Class and Ethnicity in an American Mining Town, 1875–1925*. Urbana: University of Illinois Press.

Etcheson, Nicole (1996) *The Emerging Midwest: Upland Southerners and the Political Culture of the Old Northwest, 1787–1861*. Bloomington, Ind.: Indiana University Press.

Etulain, Richard W. (ed.) (1991) *Writing Western History: Essays on Major Western Historians*. Albuquerque: University of New Mexico Press.

Faragher, John Mack (1986) *Sugar Creek: Life on the Illinois Prairie*. New Haven, Conn.: Yale University Press.

Faust, Drew Gilpin (1988) *The Creation of Confederate Nationalism: Ideology and Identity in the Civil War South*. Baton Rouge: Louisiana State University Press.

Fink, Deborah (1992) *Agrarian Women: Wives and Mothers in Rural Nebraska, 1880–1940*. Chapel Hill, NC: University of North Carolina Press.

Flores, Dan (1992) "Bison ecology and vision diplomacy: the southern Plains from 1800 to 1850," *Journal of American History*, 78, pp. 465–85.

Fox-Genovese, Elizabeth (1988) *Within the Plantation Household: Black and White Women of the Old South*. Chapel Hill, NC: University of North Carolina Press.

Freehling, William W. (1994) *The Reintegration of American History: Slavery and the Civil War*. New York: Oxford University Press.

Gates, Paul W. (1973) *Landlords and Tenants on the Prairie Frontier: Studies in American Land Policy*. Ithaca, NY: Cornell University Press.

Genovese, Eugene D. (1991) *The Southern Tradition: the Achievement and Limitations of an American Conservatism*. Cambridge, MA: Harvard University Press.

Gilmore, Glenda (1996) *Gender and Jim Crow: Women and the Politics of White Supremacy in North Carolina, 1896–1920*. Chapel Hill, NC: University of North Carolina Press.

Gjerde, Jon (1985) *From Peasants to Farmers: the Migration from Balestrand, Norway, to the Upper Middle West*. Cambridge: Cambridge University Press.

Gjerde, Jon (1997) *The Minds of the West: Ethnocultural Evolution in the Rural Middle West, 1830–1917*. Chapel Hill, NC: University of North Carolina Press.

Gray, Richard (2000) *Southern Aberrations: Writers of the American South and the Problems of Regionalism*. Baton Rouge: Louisiana State University Press.

Gray, Susan E. (1996) *The Yankee West: Community Life on the Michigan Frontier*. Chapel Hill, NC: University of North Carolina Press.

Gretlund, Jan Nordby (ed.) (1999) *The Southern State of Mind*. Columbia: University of South Carolina Press.

Gutman, Herbert (1976) *The Black Family in Slavery and Freedom, 1750–1925*. New York: Pantheon.

Hall, Jacquelyn Dowd and Scott, Anne Frior (1989) "Women in the South," in John B. Boles and Evelyn Thomas Nolen (eds), *Interpreting Southern History: Historiographical Essays in Honor of Sanford W. Higginbotham*, pp. 454–509. Baton Rouge: Louisiana State University Press.

Hall, Thomas D. (1989) *Social Change in the Southwest*. Lawrence: University Press of Kansas.

Heyrman, Christine Leigh (1997) *Southern Cross: the Beginnings of the Bible Belt*. New York: Alfred A. Knopf.

Hine, Robert V. and Faragher, John Mack (1999) *The American West: a New Interpretive Treatment*. New Haven, Conn.: Yale University Press.

Hobson, Fred C. (1983) *Tell about the South: the Southern Rage to Explain*. Baton Rouge: Louisiana State University Press.

Hudson, John C. (1994) *Making the Corn Belt: a Geographical History of Middle-Western Agriculture*. Bloomington, Ind.: Indiana University Press.

Hurtado, Albert L. (1988) *Indian Survival on the California Frontier*. New Haven, Conn.: Yale University Press.

Hyman, Michael R. (1990) *The Anti-redeemers: Hill-country Political Dissenters in the Lower South from Redemption to Populism*. Baton Rouge: Louisiana State University Press.

Jameson, Elizabeth and Armitage, Susan (eds) *Writing the Range: Race, Class, and Culture in the Women's West*. Norman: University of Oklahoma Press.

Jeffrey, Julie Roy (1979) *Frontier Women: the Trans-Mississippi West, 1840–1880*. New York: Hill and Wang.

Jensen, Richard (1971) *The Winning of the Midwest: Social and Political Conflict, 1888–1896*. Chicago: University of Chicago Press.

Johnson, David Alan (1992) *Founding the Far West: California, Oregon, and Nevada, 1840–1890*. Berkeley, CA: University of California Press.

Kantrowitz, Stephen (2000) *Ben Tillman and the Reconstruction of White Supremacy*. Chapel Hill, NC: University of North Carolina Press.

Kleppner, Paul (1970) *The Cross of Culture: a Social Analysis of Midwestern Politics, 1850–1900*. New York: The Free Press.

Klingaman, David C. and Vedder, Richard K. (eds) (1987) *Essays on the Economy of the Old Northwest*. Athens: University of Georgia Press.

Knobloch, Frieda (1996) *The Culture of Wilderness: Agriculture and Colonization in the American West*. Chapel Hill, NC: University of North Carolina Press.

Kousser, J. Morgan (1974) *The Shaping of Southern Politics: Suffrage Restriction and the Establishment of the One-party South, 1880–1910*. New Haven, Conn.: Yale University Press.

Lebsock, Suzanne (1984) *The Free Women of Petersburg: Status and Culture in a Southern Town, 1784–1860*. New York: W. W. Norton.

Levine, Lawrence (1977) *Black Culture and Black Consciousness: African American Folk Thought from Slavery to Freedom*. New York: Oxford University Press.

Limerick, Patricia Nelson (1987) *The Legacy of Conquest: the Unbroken Past of the American West*. New York: W. W. Norton.

Limerick, Patricia Nelson, Milner II, Clyde A., and Rankin, Charles E. (1991) *Trails: Toward a New Western History*. Lawrence: University Press of Kansas.

Lipin, Lawrence M. (1994) *Producers, Proletarians, and Politicians: Workers and Party Politics in Evansville and New Albany, Indiana, 1850–87*. Urbana: University of Illinois Press.

McKanna Jr, Clare V. (1997) *Homicide, Race, and Justice in the American West, 1880–1920*. Tucson: University of Arizona Press.

McKenzie, Robert Tracy (1994) *One South or Many? Plantation Belt and Upcountry in Civil War-era Tennessee*. New York: Cambridge University Press.

Maffly-Kipp, Laurie F. (1984) *Religion and Society in Frontier California*. New Haven, Conn.: Yale University Press.

Malone, Laurence J. (1998) *Opening the West: Federal Internal Improvements before 1860*. Westport, Conn.: Greenwood Press.

Marx, Anthony W. (1998) *Making Race and Nation: a Comparison of South Africa, the United States and Brazil*. Cambridge: Cambridge University Press.

Matsumoto, Valerie J. and Allmendinger, Blake (eds) (1999) *Over the Edge: Remapping the American West*. Berkeley, CA: University of California Press.

May, Dean L. (1994) *Three Frontiers: Family, Land, and Society in the American West, 1850–1900*. New York: Cambridge University Press.

Meining, D. W. (1993) *The Shaping of America: a Geographical Perspective on 500 Years of History*, vol. 2: *Continental America, 1800–1867*. New Haven, Conn.: Yale University Press.

Merrill, Horace Samuel (1953) *Bourbon Democracy of the Middle West, 1865–1896*. Madison: University of Wisconsin Press.

Miller, Donald L. (1996) *City of the Century: the Epic of Chicago and the Making of America*. New York: Simon and Schuster.

Miller, George H. (1971) *Railroads and the Granger Laws*. Madison: University of Wisconsin Press.

Milner II, Clyde A. (ed.) (1996) *A New Significance: Re-envisioning the History of the American West*. New York: Oxford University Press.

Milner II, Clyde A., O'Connor, Carol A., and Sandweiss, Martha A. (eds) (1994) *The Oxford History of the American West*. New York: Oxford University Press.

Morris, Christopher (1995) *Becoming Southern: the Evolution of a Way of Life, Warren County and Vicksburg, Mississippi, 1770–1860*. New York: Oxford University Press.

Morrissey, Katherine G. (1977) *Mental Territories: Mapping the Inland Empire*. Ithaca, NY: Cornell University Press.

Murphy, Lucy Eldersveld and Venet, Wendy Hamand (eds) (1997) *Midwestern Women: Work, Community, and Leadership at the Crossroads*. Bloomington, Ind.: Indiana University Press.

Nelson, Daniel (1995) *Farm and Factory: Workers in the Midwest, 1880–1990*. Bloomington, Ind.: Indiana University Press.

Neth, Mary (1995) *Preserving the Family Farm: Women, Community, and the Foundations of Agribusiness in the Midwest, 1900–1940*. Baltimore, MD: Johns Hopkins University Press.

Oakes, James (1982) *Ruling Race: a History of American Slaveholders*. New York: Random House.

Oakes, James (1990) *Slavery and Freedom: an Interpretation of the Old South*. New York: Random House.

Oestreicher, Richard Jules (1986) *Solidarity and Fragmentation: Working People and Class Consciousness in Detroit, 1875–1900*. Urbana: University of Illinois Press.

Ostergren, Robert C. (1988) *A Community Transplanted: the Trans-Atlantic Experience of a Swedish Immigrant Settlement in the Upper Middle West, 1835–1915*. Madison: University of Wisconsin Press.

Parker, William N. (1980) "The South in the national economy, 1865–1970," *Southern Economic Journal*, 46, pp. 1019–48.

Pascoe, Peggy (1990) *Relations of Rescue: the Search for Female Moral Authority in the American West, 1874–1939*. New York: Oxford University Press.

Patterson, Orlando (1982) *Slavery and Social Death*. Cambridge, Mass.: Harvard University Press.

Pederson, Jane Marie (1992) *Between Memory and Reality: Family and Community in Rural Wisconsin, 1870–1970*. Madison: University of Wisconsin Press.

Persky, Joseph J. (1992) *The Burden of Dependency: Colonial Themes in Southern Economic Thought*. Baltimore, MD: Johns Hopkins University Press.

Pickle, Linda Schelbitzke (1996) *Contented among Strangers: Rural German-speaking Women and their Families in the Nineteenth-century Midwest*. Urbana: University of Illinois Press.

Pisani, Donald J. (1996) *Water, Land, and Law in the West: the Limits of Public Policy, 1850–1920*. Lawrence: University Press of Kansas.

Price, Edward T. (1995) *Dividing the Land: Early American Beginnings of our Private Property Mosaic*. Chicago: University of Chicago Press.

Riley, Glenda (1996) *Building and Breaking Families in the American West*. Albuquerque: University of New Mexico Press.

Robbins, William G. (1994) *Colony and Empire: the Capitalist Transformation of the American West*. Lawrence: University Press of Kansas.

Robbins, William G. (1997) *Landscapes of Promise: the Oregon Story, 1800–1940*. Seattle: University of Washington Press.

Rohrbough, Malcolm J. (1978) *The Trans-Appalachian Frontier: People, Societies, and Institutions, 1775–1850*. New York: Oxford University Press.

Rohrbough, Malcolm J. (1997) *Days of Gold: the California Gold Rush and the American Nation*. Berkeley, CA: University of California Press.

Ronda, James P. (1984) *Lewis and Clark among the Indians*. Lincoln: University of Nebraska Press.

Ross, Steven J. (1985) *Workers on the Edge: Work, Leisure, and Politics in Industrializing Cincinnati, 1788–1890*. New York: Columbia University Press.

Sawislak, Karen (1995) *Smoldering City: Chicagoans and the Great Fire, 1871–1874*. Chicago: University of Chicago Press.

Scott, Anne Frior (1970) *The Southern Lady: from Pedestal to Politics, 1830–1930*. Chicago: University of Chicago Press.

Shortridge, James R. (1989) *The Middle West: its Meaning in American Culture*. Lawrence: University Press of Kansas.

Silber, Nina (1993) *The Romance of Reunion: Northerners and the South, 1865–1900*. Chapel Hill, NC: University of North Carolina Press.

Smith, Duane A. (1992) *Rocky Mountain West: Colorado, Wyoming, and Montana, 1895–1915*. Albuquerque: University of New Mexico Press.

Starrs, Paul F. (1998) *Let the Cowboy Ride: Ranching in the American West*. Baltimore, MD: Johns Hopkins University Press.

Stevenson, Brenda E. (1996) *Life in Black and White: Family and Community in the Slave South*. New York: Oxford University Press.

Stevenson, Elizabeth (1994) *Figures in a Western Landscape: Men and Women of the Northern Rockies*. Baltimore, MD: Johns Hopkins University Press.

Taylor, Quintard (1998) *In Search of the Racial Frontier: African Americans in the American West, 1528–1990*. New York: W. W. Norton.

Teaford, Jon (1993) *Cities of the Heartland: the Rise and Fall of the Industrial Midwest*. Bloomington, Ind.: Indiana University Press.

Thornton III, J. Mills (1978) *Politics and Power in a Slave Society: Alabama, 1820–1860*. Baton Rouge: Louisiana State University Press.

Van West, Carroll (1993) *Capitalism on the Frontier: Billings and the Yellowstone Valley in the Nineteenth Century*. Lincoln: University of Nebraska Press.

Varon, Elizabeth R. (1998) *We Mean to be Counted: White Women and Politics in Antebellum Virginia*. Chapel Hill, NC: University of North Carolina Press.

West, Elliott (1995) *The Way to the West: Essays on the Central Plains*. Albuquerque: University of New Mexico Press.

West, Elliott (1998) *The Contested Plains: Indians, Goldseekers, and the Rush to Colorado*. Lawrence: University Press of Kansas.

White, Richard (1995) *The Organic Machine: the Remaking of the Columbia River*. New York: Hill and Wang.

Williamson, Joel (1984) *The Crucible of Race: Black–White Relations in the American South since Emancipation*. New York: Oxford University Press.

Winkle, Kenneth J. (1988) *The Politics of Community: Migration and Politics in Antebellum Ohio*. Cambridge: Cambridge University Press.

Woodman, Harold D. (1995) *New South – New Law: the Legal Foundations of Credit and Labor Relations in the Postbellum Agricultural South*. Baton Rouge: Louisiana State University Press.

Woodward, C. Vann (1951) *Origins of the New South, 1877–1913*. Baton Rouge: Louisiana State University Press.

Woodward, C. Vann (1955) *The Strange Career of Jim Crow*. New York: Oxford University Press.

Worster, Donald (1992) *Under Western Skies: Nature and History in the American West*. New York: Oxford University Press.

Wrobel, David M. and Steiner, Michael C. (eds) (1997) *Many Wests: Place, Culture, and Regional Identity*. Lawrence: University Press of Kansas.

Wyatt-Brown, Bertram (1982) *Southern Honor: Ethics and Behavior in the Old South*. New York: Oxford University Press.

Wycoff, William (1999) *Creating Colorado: the Making of a Western American Landscape, 1860–1940.* New Haven, Conn.: Yale University Press.

Wyman, Mark (1979) *Hard-rock Epic: Western Miners and the Industrial Revolution, 1860–1900.* Berkeley, CA: University of California Press.

Wyman, Mark (1998) *The Wisconsin Frontier.* Bloomington, Ind.: Indiana University Press.

Cultures and Ideas

Abrams, Ann Uhry and Palumbo, Anne Cannon (1986) *Goddess, Guardian and Grand Old Gal.* Atlanta, GA: Emory University Press.

Adams, Bluford (1997) *E. Pluribus Barnum: the Great Showman and the Making of US Popular Culture.* Minneapolis: University of Minnesota Press.

Ahlstrom, Sydney (1972) *A Religious History of the American People.* New Haven, Conn.: Yale University Press.

Baird, Robert (1844) *Religion in the United States of America.* Glasgow: Blackie.

Banta, Martha (1987) *Imaging American Women: Idea and Ideals in Cultural History.* New York: Columbia University Press.

Biggs, Lindy (1996) *The Rational Factory: Architecture, Technology, and Work in America's Age of Mass Production.* Baltimore, MD: Johns Hopkins University Press.

Blake, N. M. (1956) *Water for the Cities: a History of the Urban Water Supply Problem in the United States.* Syracuse, NY: Syracuse University Press.

Blanchard, Mary Warner (1998) *Oscar Wilde's America: Counterculture in the Gilded Age.* New Haven, Conn.: Yale University Press.

Blondheim, Menahem (1994) *News over the Wires: the Telegraph and the Flow of Public Information in America, 1844–1897.* Cambridge, Mass.: Harvard University Press.

Boylan, Anne M. (1988) *Sunday School: the Formation of an American Institution, 1790–1880.* New Haven, Conn.: Yale University Press.

Bradbury, Malcolm (1995) *Dangerous Pilgrimages: Trans-Atlantic Mythologies and the Novel.* London: Secker and Warburg.

Braude, Ann (1989) *Radical Spirits: Spiritualism and Women's Rights in Nineteenth-century America.* Boston: Beacon Press.

Brekus, Catherine A. (1998) *Strangers and Pilgrims: Female Preaching in America, 1740–1845.* Chapel Hill, NC: University of North Carolina Press.

Brooke, John L. (1994) *The Refiner's Fire: the Making of Mormon Cosmology, 1644–1844.* New York: Cambridge University Press.

Brown, Richard D. (1989) *Knowledge is Power: the Diffusion of Information in Early America, 1700–1865.* New York: Oxford University Press.

Brown, Richard D. (1996) *The Strength of a People: the Idea of an Informed Citizenry in America, 1650–1870.* Chapel Hill, NC: University of North Carolina Press.

Burlingame, R. (1938) *March of the Iron Men: a Social History of Union through Invention.* New York: Scribner.

Burns, Sarah (1996) *Inventing the Modern Artist: Art and Culture in Gilded Age America.* New Haven, Conn.: Yale University Press.

Butler, Diana Hockstedt (1995) *Standing against the Whirlwind: Evangelical Episcopalians in Nineteenth-century America.* New York: Oxford University Press.

Butler, Jon (1990) *Awash in a Sea of Faith: Christianizing the American People.* Cambridge, Mass.: Harvard University Press.

Carey, James W. (1989) *Communication as Culture: Essays on Media and Society.* Boston: Unwin Hyman.

Carlson, W. Bernard (1991) *Innovation as a Social Process: Elihu Thomson and the Rise of General Electric, 1870–1900.* Cambridge: Cambridge University Press.

Carroll, Bret E. (1977) *Spiritualism in Antebellum America*. Bloomington, Ind.: Indiana University Press.

Ceaser, James W. (1997) *Reconstructing America: the Symbol of America in Modern Thought*. New Haven, Conn.: Yale University Press.

Chandler, Alfred D. (1977) *The Visible Hand: the Managerial Revolution in American Business*. Cambridge, Mass.: Belknap Press of Harvard University.

Cohen, Daniel A. (1993) *Pillars of Salt, Monuments of Grace: New England Crime Literature and the Origins of American Popular Culture, 1674–1860*. New York: Oxford University Press.

Conkin, Paul K. (1990) *Cane Ridge: America's Pentecost*. Madison: University of Wisconsin Press.

Conkin, Paul K. (1995) *The Uneasy Center: Reformed Christianity in Antebellum America*. Chapel Hill, NC: University of North Carolina Press.

Conn, Stephen (1998) *Museums and American Intellectual Life, 1876–1926*. Chicago: University of Chicago Press.

Conser Jr, Walter H. (1993) *God and the Natural World: Religion and Science in Antebellum America*. Columbia: University of South Carolina Press.

Corn, Charles (1998) *The Scents of Eden*. New York: Kodanshai International.

Cowan, R. S. (1983) *More Work for Mother: the Ironies of Household Technology from the Open Hearth to the Microwave*. New York: Basic Books.

Cutcliffe, Stephen H. and Reynolds, Terry S. (eds) (1997) *Technology and American History*. Chicago: University of Chicago Press.

Czitrom, Daniel J. (1982) *Media and the American Mind: from Morse to McLuhan*. Chapel Hill, NC: University of North Carolina Press.

Daniels, George H. (1968) *American Science in the Age of Jackson*. New York: Columbia University Press.

Daniels, George H. (1971) *Science in American History: a Social History*. New York: Alfred A. Knopf.

Davis, Lance E., Gallman, Robert E., and Gleiter, Karen (1997) *In Pursuit of Leviathan: Technology, Institutions, Productivity, and Profits in American Whaling, 1816–1906*. Chicago: University of Chicago Press.

Dilts, James D. (1993) *The Great Road: the Building of the Baltimore and Ohio, the Nation's First Railroad, 1828–1853*. Stanford: Stanford University Press.

Diner, Hasia R. (1992) *The Jewish People in America*, vol. 2: *A Time for Gathering: the Second Migration, 1820–1880*. Baltimore, MD: Johns Hopkins University Press.

Doan, Ruth Allen (1987) *The Miller Heresy, Millennialism, and American Culture*. Philadelphia, PA: Temple University Press.

Dobbin, Frank (1994) *Forging Industrial Policy: the United States, Britain and France in the Railway Age*. New York: Cambridge University Press.

Doezema, Marianne and Milroy, Elizabeth (eds) (1998) *Reading American Art*. New Haven, Conn.: Yale University Press.

Dolan, Jay P. (1985) *The American Catholic Experience: a History from Colonial Times to the Present*. Garden City, NY: Doubleday.

Dorchester, Daniel (1888) *Christianity in the United States from the First Settlement down to the Present Time*. New York: Phillips and Hunt.

Dunlavy, Colleen A. (1994) *Politics and Industrialization: Early Railroads in the United States and Prussia*. Princeton, NJ: Princeton University Press.

Dupree, A. H. (1959) *Asa Gray, 1810–1888*. Cambridge, Mass.: Belknap Press of Harvard University.

Farley, James L. (1994) *Making Arms in the Machine Age: Philadelphia's Frankford Arsenal, 1816–1870*. University Park: Pennsylvania State University Press.

Fleming, E. McClung (1967) "From Indian princess to Greek goddess: the American image, 1783–1815," *Winterthur Portfolio*, 3, pp. 37–66.

Fleming, James Rodger (1990) *Meteorology in America, 1800–1870.* Baltimore, MD: Johns Hopkins University Press.

Foley, Michael S. (1997) "A mission unfulfilled: the post office and the distribution of information in rural New England, 1821–1835," *Journal of the Early Republic*, 17, pp. 611–50.

Franehot, Jenny (1993) *Roads to Rome: the Antebellum Protestant Encounter with Catholicism.* Berkeley, CA: University of California Press.

Fryd, Vivien Green (1986) "Hiram Powers's *America*: 'Triumphant as liberty and in unity,'" *American Art Journal*, 18 (2), pp. 54–75.

Fryd, Vivien Green (1992) *Art and Empire: the Politics of Ethnicity in the United States Capitol, 1815–1860.* New Haven, Conn.: Yale University Press.

Fryd, Vivien Green (1995) "Rereading the Indian in Benjamin West's *Death of General Wolfe*," *American Art*, spring, pp. 73–85.

Garvey, Ellen Gruber (1996) *The Adman in the Parlor: Magazines and the Gendering of Consumer Culture, 1880s to 1910s.* New York: Oxford University Press.

Genovese, Eugene D. (1998) *A Consuming Fire: the Fall of the Confederacy in the Mind of the White Christian South.* Athens: University of Georgia Press.

Gilmore, William J. (1989) *Reading Becomes a Necessity of Life: Material and Cultural Life in Rural New England, 1780–1835.* Knoxville: University of Tennessee Press.

Glaude Jr, Eddie S. (2000) *Exodus!: Religion, Race, and Nation in Early Nineteenth-century Black America.* Chicago: University of Chicago Press.

Goodrich, Carter (1960) *Government Promotion of American Canals and Railroads, 1800–1890.* New York: Columbia University Press.

Gordon, Sarah H. (1997) *Passage to Union: How the Railroads Transformed American Life, 1829–1929.* Chicago: University of Chicago Press.

Gunn, L. Ray (1988) *The Decline of Authority: Public Economic Policy and Political Development in New York State, 1800–1860.* Ithaca, NY: Cornell University Press.

Gustefson, Thomas (1993) *Representative Words: Politics, Literature, and the American Language, 1776–1865.* New York: Cambridge University Press.

Hanley, Mark Y. (1994) *Beyond a Christian Commonwealth: the Protestant Quarrel with the American Republic, 1830–1860.* Chapel Hill, NC: University of North Carolina Press.

Harvey, Paul (1997) *Redeeming the South: Religious Cultures and Racial Identities among Southern Baptists, 1865–1925.* Chapel Hill, NC: University of North Carolina Press.

Hatch, Nathan O. (1989) *The Democratization of American Christianity.* New Haven, Conn.: Yale University Press.

Hildebrand, Reginald F. (1995) *The Times were Strange and Stirring: Methodist Preachers and the Crisis of Emancipation.* Durham, NC: Duke University Press.

Hill, Marvin S. (1989) *Quest for Refuge: the Mormon Flight from American Pluralism.* Salt Lake City, Utah: Signature Books.

Honour, Hugh (1976) *The European Vision of America.* Cleveland, Ohio: The Cleveland Museum of Art.

Hounshell, David A. (1984) *From the American System to Mass Production, 1800–1932: the Development of Manufacturing Technology in the United States.* Baltimore, MD: Johns Hopkins University Press.

Hughes, Thomas P. (1983) *Networks of Power: Electrification in Western Society, 1880–1930.* Baltimore, MD: Johns Hopkins University Press.

Hunter, Louis C. (1949) *Steamboats on the Western Rivers: an Economic and Technological History.* New York: Octagon Books, 1969.

Hutchison, William R. (1976) *The Modernist Impulse in American Protestantism.* Cambridge, Mass.: Harvard University Press.

Hutton, Frankie (1993) *The Early Black Press in America, 1827–1860.* Westport, Conn.: Greenwood Press.

Israel, Paul (1992) *From Machine Shop to Industrial Laboratory: Telegraphy and the Changing Contest of American Invention, 1830–1920.* Baltimore, MD: Johns Hopkins University Press.

Jaffe, David (1991) "Peddlers of progress and the transformation of the rural North, 1760–1860," *Journal of American History,* 78, pp. 511–35.

Johanningsmeier, Charles (1997) *Fiction and the American Literary Marketplace: the Role of Newspaper Syndicates, 1860–1900.* New York: Cambridge University Press.

John, Richard R. (1995) *Spreading the News: the American Postal System from Franklin to Morse.* Cambridge, Mass.: Harvard University Press.

John, Richard R. (1998) "The politics of innovation," *Daedalus: Journal of the American Academy of Arts and Sciences,* 127, pp. 187–214.

Johnson, Curtis D. (1993) *Redeeming America: Evangelicals and the Road to Civil War.* Chicago: Ivan Dee.

Kanigel, Robert (1997) *The One Best Way: Frederick Winslow Taylor and the Enigmas of Efficiency.* New York: Viking.

Kasson, John F. (1976) *Civilizing the Machine: Technology and Republican Values in America, 1776–1900.* New York: Penguin.

Keller, Evelyn Fox (1983) *A Feeling for the Organism: the Life and Work of Barbara McClintock.* San Francisco: W. H. Freeman.

Kelley, Mary (1996) "Reading women/women reading: the making of learned women in antebellum America," *Journal of American History,* 83, pp. 401–24.

Ketchum, Alton (1959) *Uncle Sam: the Man and the Legend.* New York: Hill and Wang.

Kielbowicz, Richard B. (1989) *News in the Mail: the Press, Post Office, and Public Information, 1700–1860s.* New York: Greenwood Press.

Klein, Rachel N. (1995) "Art and authority in antebellum New York City: the rise and fall of the American art-union," *Journal of American History,* 81, pp. 1534–61.

Kuhn, Thomas S. (1962) *Structure of Scientific Revolutions.* Chicago: University of Chicago Press.

Laderman, Gary (1997) *The Sacred Remains: American Attitudes toward Death, 1799–1883.* New Haven, Conn.: Yale University Press.

Lavid, Pamela Walker (1998) *Advertising Progress: American Business and the Rise of Consumer Marketing.* Baltimore, MD: Johns Hopkins University Press.

Layton, E. T. (1971) *The Revolt of the Engineers: Social Responsibility and the American Engineering Profession.* Cleveland, Ohio: Press of Case Western Reserve University.

Leach, William (1993) *Land of Desire: Merchants, Power, and the Rise of a New American Culture.* New York: Pantheon.

Lears, Jackson (1994) *Fables of Abundance: a Cultural History of Advertising in America.* New York: Basic Books.

Lehuu, Isabelle (2000) *Carnival on the Page: Popular Print Media in Antebellum America.* Chapel Hill, NC: University of North Carolina Press.

Lewis, W. David (1976) *Iron and Steel in America.* Greenville, Del.: Eleutherian Mills-Hagley Foundation.

Lindley, Lester (1975) *The Constitution Faces Technology: the Relationship of the National Government to the Telegraph, 1866–1884.* New York: Arno Press.

Lubin, David M. (1994) *Picturing a Nation: Art and Social Change in Nineteenth Century America.* New Haven, Conn.: Yale University Press.

Lurie, Edward (1960) *Louis Agassiz: a Life in Science.* Chicago: University of Chicago Press.

McLoughlin, William G. (1984) *Cherokees and Missionaries, 1789–1839.* New Haven, Conn.: Yale University Press.

Maffly-Kipp, Laurie F. (1994) *Religion and Society in Frontier California*. New Haven, Conn.: Yale University Press.

Magoc, Chris J. (1999) *Yellowstone: the Creation and Selling of an American Landscape, 1870–1903*. Albuquerque: University of New Mexico Press.

Maienschein, Jane (1991) *Transforming Traditions in American Biology, 1880–1915*. Baltimore, MD: Johns Hopkins University Press.

Marcus, Alan I. and Segal, Howard P. (1989) *Technology in America: a Brief History*. San Diego, CA: Harcourt Brace Jovanovich.

Marsden, George M. (1980) *Fundamentalism and American Culture: the Shaping of Twentieth-century Evangelicalism, 1870–1925*. New York: Oxford University Press.

Marty, Martin E. (1970) *Righteous Empire: the Protestant Experience in America*. New York: Dial Press.

Marx, Leo (1964) *The Machine in the Garden: Technology and the Pastoral Ideal in America*. New York: Oxford University Press.

Mathews, Donald G. (1977) *Religion in the Old South*. Chicago: University of Chicago Press.

Miller, Angela (1993) *Empire of the Eye: Landscape Representation and American Cultural Politics, 1825–1875*. Ithaca, NY: Cornell University Press.

Miller, H. S. (1970) *Dollars for Research: Science and its Patrons in Nineteenth-century America*. Seattle: University of Washington Press.

Miller, Randell M., Stout, Harry S., and Wilson, Charles Reagan (eds) (1998) *Religion and the American Civil War*. New York: Oxford University Press.

Montgomery, William E. (1993) *Under their own Vine and Fig Tree: the African-American Church in the South, 1865–1900*. Baton Rouge: Louisiana State University Press.

Moore, R. Laurence (1986) *Religious Outsiders and the Making of Americans*. New York: Oxford University Press.

Nora, Pierre (1989) "Between memory and history: *les lieux de memoire*," *Representations*, 26, pp. 7–25.

Nord, David (1984) *The Evangelical Origins of Mass Media in America, 1815–1835*. Columbia: University of South Carolina Press.

Novak, Barbara (1969) *American Painting of the Nineteenth Century*. New York: Praeger.

Novak, Barbara (1980) *Nature and Culture: American Landscape and Painting, 1825–1875*. New York: Oxford University Press.

Numbers, Ronald L. (1998) *Darwinism Comes to America*. Cambridge, Mass.: Harvard University Press.

Numbers, Ronald L. and Savitt, Todd L. (eds) (1989) *Science and Medicine in the Old South*. Baton Rouge: Louisiana State University Press.

Nye, David (1994) *American Technological Supreme*. Cambridge, Mass.: MIT Press.

Ohmann, Richard (1996) *Selling Culture: Magazines, Markets, and Class at the Turn of the Century*. New York: Verso.

O'Leary, Elizabeth L. (1996) *At Beck and Call: the Representation of Domestic Servants in Nineteenth-century American Painting*. Washington, DC: Smithsonian Institution Press.

Oleson, A. and Brown, S. C. (eds) (1976) *The Pursuit of Knowledge in the Early American Republic: American Scientific and Learned Societies from Colonial Times to the Civil War*. Baltimore, MD: Johns Hopkins University Press.

Oleson, A. and Voss, J. (eds) (1979) *The Organization of Knowledge in Modern America, 1860–1920*. Baltimore, MD: Johns Hopkins University Press.

Osthaus, Carl R. (1994) *Partisans of the Southern Press: Editorial Spokesmen of the Nineteenth Century*. Lexington: University Press of Kentucky.

Owen, Christopher H. (1998) *The Sacred Flame of Love: Methodism and Society in Nineteenth-century Georgia*. Athens: University of Georgia Press.

Perry, Lewis (1993) *Boats against the Current: American Culture between Revolution and Modernity, 1820–1860*. New York: Oxford University Press.

Pohl, Frances K. (1954) "Old world, new world: the encounter of cultures on the American frontier," in Stephen F. Eisenman (ed.), *Nineteenth Century Art: a Critical History*, pp. 144–62. London: Thames and Hudson.

Pravoyeur, Pierre and Hargrove, June (1986) *Liberty: the French–American Statue in Art and History*. Philadelphia, PA: Perennial Library.

Pred, Allan R. (1973) *Urban Growth and the Circulation of Information: the United States System of Cities, 1790–1840*. Cambridge, Mass.: Harvard University Press.

Promey, Sally M. (1993) *Spiritual Spectacles: Vision and Image in Mid-nineteenth Century Shakerism*. Bloomington, Ind.: Indiana University Press.

Raboteau, Albert J. (1978) *Slave Religion: the "Invisible Institution" in the Antebellum South*. Oxford: Oxford University Press.

Remer, Rosalind (1986) *Printers and Men of Capital: Philadelphia Book Publishers in the New Republic*. Philadelphia: University of Pennsylvania Press.

Reynolds, David (1995) *Walt Whitman's America: a Cultural Biography*. New York: Alfred A. Knopf.

Rosenberg, Nathan (1972) *Technology and American Economic Growth*. New York: Harpers Torchbook.

Rossiter, Margaret W. (1982) *Women Scientists in America: Struggles and Strategies to 1940*. Baltimore, MD: Johns Hopkins University Press.

Schmidt, Leigh Eric (1989) *Holy Fairs: Scottish Communions and American Revivals in the Early Modern Period*. Princeton, NJ: Princeton University Press.

Schneider, A. Gregory (1993) *The Way of the Cross Leads Home: the Domestication of American Methodism*. Bloomington, Ind.: Indiana University Press.

Schneirov, Matthew (1994) *The Dream of a New Social Order: Popular Magazines in America, 1893–1914*. New York: Columbia University Press.

Schwartzlose, Richard A. (1989/1990) *The Nation's Newsbrokers*, 2 vols. Evanston, Ill.: North-western University Press.

Scott, Donald M. (1980) "The popular lecture and the creation of a public in mid-nineteenth-century America," *Journal of American History*, 66, pp. 791–809.

Severa, Joan L. (1995) *Dressed for the Photographer: Ordinary Americans and Fashion, 1840–1909*. Kent, Ohio: Kent State University Press.

Shackel, Paul A. (1996) *Culture Change and the New Technology: an Archaeology of the Early American Industrial Era*. New York: Plenum Press.

Shaw, Ronald E. (1990) *Canals for a Nation: the Canal Era in the United States, 1790–1860*. Lexington: University Press of Kentucky.

Shi, David E. (1995) *Facing Facts: Realism in American Thought and Culture, 1850–1920*. New York: Oxford University Press.

Shipps, Jan (1985) *Mormonism: the Story of a New Religious Tradition*. Urbana: University of Illinois Press.

Silverburg, Helene (ed.) (1998) *Gender and American Social Science*. Princeton, NJ: Princeton University Press.

Snay, Mitchell (1993) *Gospel of Disunion: Religion and Separatism in the Antebellum South*. New York: Cambridge University Press.

Startup, Kenneth Moore (1997) *The Root of All Evil: the Protestant Clergy and the Economic Mind of the Old South*. Athens: University of Georgia Press.

Stein, Roger (1968) *View and the Vision: Landscape Painting in Nineteenth-century America*. Seattle: Henry Gallery.

Stephens, Lester D. (2000) *Science, Race, and Religion in the American South: John Bachman and the Charleston Circle of Naturalists, 1815–1895.* Chapel Hill, NC: University of North Carolina Press.

Summers, Mark Wahlgren (1994) *The Press Gang: Newspapers and Politics, 1865–1878.* Chapel Hill, NC: University of North Carolina Press.

Sund, Judy (1993) "Columbus and Columbia in Chicago, 1893: man of genius meets generic woman," *Art Bulletin*, 75 (3), pp. 443–66.

Sweet, William Warren (1930) *The Story of Religions in America.* New York: Harper and Brothers.

Taves, Ann (1999) *Fits, Trances, and Visions: Experiencing Religion and Explaining Experience.* Princeton, NJ: Princeton University Press.

Taylor, George Rogers (1951) *The Transportation Revolution, 1815–1860.* New York: Rinehart.

Taylor, Joshua C. (1976) "The American cousin," in *America as Art*, pp. 37–94. Washington, DC: Smithsonian Institution Press.

Thomas, George M. (1989) *Revivalism and Cultural Change: Christianity, Nation Building, and the Market in the Nineteenth-century United States.* Chicago: University of Chicago Press.

Thompson, Robert Luther (1947) *Wiring a Continent: the History of the Telegraph Industry in the United States, 1832–1866.* Princeton, NJ: Princeton University Press.

Trachtenberg, Marvin (1986) *The Statue of Liberty.* New York: Penguin.

Tucher, Andie (1994) *Froth and Scum: Truth, Beauty, Goodness, and the Ax Murder in America's First Mass Medium.* Chapel Hill, NC: University of North Carolina Press.

Turner, Elizabeth Hayes (1997) *Women, Culture, and Community: Religion and Reform in Galveston, 1880–1920.* New York: Oxford University Press.

Turner, Frederick Jackson (1893) *The Frontier in American History.* New York: Holt, Rinehart and Winston, 1962.

Underwood, Grant (1993) *The Millenarian World of Early Mormonism.* Urbana: University of Illinois Press.

Vance Jr, James E. (1995) *The North American Railroad: its Origin, Evolution, and Geography.* Baltimore, MD: Johns Hopkins University Press.

Wacker, Grant (2000) *Religion in 19th Century America.* New York: Oxford University Press.

Wallace, Anthony F. C. (1978) *Rockdale: the Growth of an American Village in the Early Industrial Revolution.* New York: Alfred A. Knopf.

Wigger, John H. (1998) *Taking Heaven by Storm: Methodism and the Rise of Popular Christianity in America.* New York: Oxford University Press.

Williams, Susan S. (1997) *Confounding Images: Photography and Portraiture in Antebellum American Fiction.* Philadelphia: University of Pennsylvania Press.

Wills, Gregory A. (1997) *Democratic Religion: Freedom, Authority, and Church Discipline in the Baptist South, 1785–1900.* New York: Oxford University Press.

Winter, Kari J. (1992) *Subjects of Slavery, Agents of Change: Women and Power in Gothic Novels and Slave Narratives, 1790–1865.* Athens: University of Georgia Press.

Wosh, Peter J. (1994) *Spreading the Word: the Bible Business in Nineteenth-century America.* Ithaca, NY: Cornell University Press.

Zafer, Rafia (1997) *We Wear the Mask: African-Americans Write American Literature, 1760–1870.* New York: Columbia University Press.

Zboray, Ronald J. (1993) *A Fictive People: Antebellum Economic Development and the American Reading Public.* New York: Oxford University Press.

Index